Acclaim for

MAURY KLEIN's

DAYS OF DEFIANCE

"How war came . . . is the subject that Klein addresses here. He does it so authoritatively, and with such an articulate flair, that his book belongs on the shelf of every serious student of the American heritage. Indeed, Klein is now the worthy successor of such highly esteemed causitive historians as Avery O. Craven and David M. Potter." —*Richmond Times-Dispatch*

"Maury Klein offers a well-written account of the critical months following Lincoln's election to the presidency, his stimulating narrative clearly tracking the downward spiral that culminated in South Carolina's April 1861 attack on Fort Sumter." —*The Seattle Times*

"A perceptive and balanced account, among the finest we have in our historical literature." —*The State* (Columbia, South Carolina)

"Drawing heavily on diaries and letters, Klein seeks to show what the people of both regions were like, how they felt, and insofar as possible what they were thinking . . . a highly readable account." —*The Philadelphia Inquirer*

"Clear . . . elegant . . . outstanding." —*The New Leader*

"A compelling account of the folly and brilliance displayed as the nation veered toward collapse . . . a dramatic narrative." —*Kirkus*

"A marvelously insightful and beautifully written account . . . [of] an incredible period that resonates through American life to this day." —*Booklist*

MAURY KLEIN

DAYS OF DEFIANCE

Sumter, Secession, and the Coming of the Civil War

Maury Klein is professor of history and director of the Honors Program at the University of Rhode Island. He is the author of nine books, as well as numerous articles and reviews on a wide range of subjects dealing with American history during the nineteenth and twentieth centuries. He lives in East Greenwich, Rhode Island, with his wife, Kathleen, and three stepchildren.

DAYS OF DEFIANCE

Sumter, Secession, and the Coming of the Civil War

MAURY KLEIN

Civil War Library

VINTAGE BOOKS

A DIVISION OF RANDOM HOUSE, INC.

NEW YORK

FIRST VINTAGE CIVIL WAR LIBRARY EDITION, MAY 1999

Copyright © 1997 by Maury Klein

All rights reserved under International and Pan-American
Copyright Conventions. Published in the United States by Vintage Books,
a division of Random House, Inc., New York, and simultaneously in
Canada by Random House of Canada Limited, Toronto. Originally
published in hardcover in the United States by Alfred A. Knopf, Inc.,
New York, in 1997.

Vintage Books, Vintage Civil War Library, and colophon are trademarks of
Random House, Inc.

The Library of Congress has cataloged the Knopf edition as follows:

Klein, Maury.
Days of defiance: Sumter, secession, and the coming of the Civil War /
by Maury Klein.
p. cm.
ISBN 0-679-44747-4
1. United States—History—Civil War, 1861–1865.
2. United States—Politics and government—1957–1861.
3. Secession—Southern States.
4. Fort Sumter (Charleston, S.C.)—Siege, 1861.
I. Title
E471.K48   1997
973.7—dc21   96-39156
CIP

Vintage ISBN: 0-679-76882-3

Author photograph © Susie Dittelman

www.vintagebooks.com

Printed in the United States of America
10   9   8   7   6   5   4   3   2   1

For Kathy
With love and thanks for showing me the way home

There are two things that a democratic people will always find very difficult, to begin a war and to end it.

—Alexis de Tocqueville

Contents

Preface   *xi*

Prologue: *Ship of Foils*   3

PART I: THE BATTLE FOR WASHINGTON

NOVEMBER

Chapter 1:   *Vox Populi*   19

Chapter 2:   *Something Old*   31

Chapter 3:   *Something New*   44

Chapter 4:   *The Senators from South Carolina*   64

Chapter 5:   *A Tale of Three Cities*   86

Chapter 6:   *A Change of Command*   105

DECEMBER

Chapter 7:   *The Politics of Bewilderment*   123

Chapter 8:   *Turning Points*   140

Chapter 9:   *At the Brink*   158

PART II: THE BATTLE OVER SECESSION

JANUARY

Chapter 10:   *War Beckons*   183

Chapter 11:   *War Recedes*   198

Chapter 12:   *The Peace Puzzle*   213

FEBRUARY

Chapter 13 : *Farewells and Forebodings*   233

Chapter 14 : *Two Journeys*   248

Chapter 15 : *Plums and Nuts*   268

Chapter 16 : *The Waiting Game*   281

PART III: THE BATTLE OVER FORT SUMTER

MARCH

Chapter 17 : *Last Gasps and First Breaths*   305

Chapter 18 : *Uneasy Arrangements*   321

Chapter 19 : *Decisions and Delusions*   338

Chapter 20 : *The Great Divide*   349

APRIL

Chapter 21 : *Ends Without Means*   369

Chapter 22 : *April Fools*   385

Chapter 23 : *The Good Fight*   403

Epilogue: *The Price of Pride*   421

Notes   431

Selected Bibliography   470

Index   483

A sixteen-page insert of photographs follows page 242

Preface

Later, much later, when the passions in this most passionate kind of war had finally cooled enough for sober and detached reflection, and when the generation that understood what those passions meant had passed on, the same stubborn question presented itself: How could the oldest, deadliest, most divisive conflict of a proud nation come down, after decades of bitter strife, to a dispute over an insignificant fort squatting on a hunk of rock in the harbor of the South's oldest and most defiant city? That a great tragedy had occurred all sides agreed, but they differed over what exactly had happened; as to why it had happened, they argued with a ferocity that approached the passions of the original dispute. Even mild-mannered professors, cloaking their differences in the guise of scholarship, took up cudgels of biting controversy against one another. But their debate was born of hindsight; they knew all too well the ghastly slaughter that followed the rending of a nation. What of the original disputants, who feared for the future but could not know that their actions or inactions would produce the bloodiest war in American history?

This book attempts to tell the story through their eyes, as they saw it at the time. It is not just about the Sumter crisis itself but about what it signified to that generation. It seeks to show what America was in 1860 and what it was becoming, and why certain forces drove her people into deadly and unavoidable conflict. I have centered the story around key characters, believing that history is at bottom the story of people, and that the stuff of people's lives is no less important than their public record.

The five months between the election of Abraham Lincoln and the firing on Fort Sumter was a time unlike any other in American history. The crisis that led up to the attack proved to be, in Matthew Arnold's magnificent phrase, "one world dying, another struggling to be born." In that fateful transition the world going under was not just that of the Old South but, more important, that of the old American Republic as conceived by the Founding

Fathers. In its place arose a new, more diverse, and far more complicated nation shaped by revolutions in transportation and communication. This transformed society, its nationality challenged anew by unexpected forces such as an enormous wave of immigration, changed and grew so rapidly as to shove past quarrels ever deeper into the dustbin of history. Yet the lessons of that forgotten past are worth retrieving; they remain both vivid and relevant to later generations.

It has long been the conventional wisdom that the great achievements of the Civil War were the preservation of the Union and the abolition of slavery. For most of American history the latter result has, for good reason, been the most heavily stressed and studied. Nevertheless, the case can be made that no result of the war was more important than the destruction, once and for all (except in the minds of occasional diehards), of the idea of secession. One nation, indivisible, with the hope of liberty and justice for all. Even the promise of those goals required the death of secession no less than that of slavery. Today, more than 135 years after the secession crisis, in a vastly different world and context, we seek to answer the same basic question that baffled the finest minds of that era as it does our own: What is an American? This book, in its way, is an inquiry into that question.

THE WRITING OF this book would not have been possible without the cooperation of many people at archives and libraries throughout the country. To those who answered my inquiries I tender sincere thanks. In particular I wish to express gratitude to Henry Fullmer and Laura Costello at the South Caroliniana Library, and to Alex Moore, Mark Wetherington, Kathleen Howard, Peter L. Wilkerson, Pat Hash, and Anne Rosebrock at the South Carolina Historical Society. In my own home library at the University of Rhode Island, special and continuing gratitude goes to the entire staff, particularly Marie Beaumont, Vicky Burnett, Kathe James, Marie Rudd, and Betty Sekator, for aid above and beyond the call of duty. No one performed more useful tasks more cheerfully than my secretary, Deborah Gardiner. My agent, Marian Young, was ever helpful with advice and encouragement. Special thanks go to Ash Green, my editor at Knopf, for his guiding hand in the shaping of the manuscript, and to his assistant, Jennifer Bernstein. Whatever errors remain are my responsibility alone. Finally, I wish to salute the memory of Bell I. Wiley, my mentor in graduate school, who did so much to nourish and cultivate my interest in the Civil War.

DAYS OF DEFIANCE

Ship of Foils

THE STEAMER *Arabia* was due to sail on the evening of March 3 from Queenstown on the southern coast of Ireland. Through the train ride from London to Liverpool and the boat trip to Dublin, William Howard Russell had managed to keep his luggage together, but he despaired of finding the proper train to Queenstown. Nor was his anxiety eased when, on the morning of his departure, the Dublin hotel clerk delayed him by refusing to accept his check. "Don't you know who I am?" he barked, his bearded, portly figure shaking in exasperation.[1]

"I don't know anything about Mr. Russell of *The Times*," replied the clerk.

Even fame had its limits, it seemed. And its price. There had been yet another difficult parting from his wife, Mary, still recovering from the birth of a fifth child and more than ever dependent on his presence. He ought to have stayed and he had tried, but it was hopeless. Instead he had taken the assignment and deposited Mary at Bath with the baby. The other four children were in boarding school—all the more reason for a steady paycheck. But that was not why he had left: He went because he desperately wanted to go, because he needed to go, and as always it hurt deeply. "Never can I forget the look in those dear eyes and the poor fretted face and the melting lips so tender and true," he told his diary after saying good-bye to Mary at Bath. "I went to the station in a storm of pain."[2]

He found the train to Queenstown and climbed aboard the *Arabia*, where he steeled himself for thirteen days of pitching and rolling in the rough March weather on the Atlantic. He had always been a good sailor, tucking away with gusto the bountiful Cunard meals in the fiercest of weather while his fellow passengers prayed for instant dispatch from their misery. But his feeling of indignation at the slight was slow to subside. It bothered him not to be known in his native land, where he had first been hailed as "Mr. Russell of *The Times*" and where his old college, Trinity, had bestowed an honorary doctorate on him for his accomplishments. But how could a mere Dublin hotel clerk know anything of such matters?

He was a large, convivial man with a pleasing baritone voice, a generous appetite for food, drink, and cigars, a fondness for the camaraderie of clubs, and a passion for travel. It was that passion that had elevated him to his place as the world's first war correspondent. He left Trinity early to work for the *Times* of London in 1841, doing odd assignments while studying law. In June 1850 he was called to the bar, poised at the brink of a career he did not want; that same month the *Times* sent him to cover a conflict that had erupted over Schleswig-Holstein, two small provinces lying at the base of the Danish peninsula. There he witnessed a battle and wrote his first account under fire. Apart from a minor flesh wound, little distinguished his effort. The business was too new to him, too large for him to grasp whole or divine his own special role in it.

But the experience changed him in more ways than he knew. John Thadeus Delane, the vigorous young editor of the *Times*, began to use Russell regularly as a descriptive reporter, feeding his love of travel in return for engaging accounts of events that revealed growing powers of observation and depth of insight. Then, in February 1854, Delane offered Russell the assignment that was to transform his life. Great Britain was about to go to war with Russia, and Delane wanted Russell on the ground in the Crimea to provide the *Times* with firsthand reports. With some reluctance Russell embarked on an assignment that, Delane promised, would have him home by Easter.

He was gone nearly two years, struggling in the field with an army whose officers mostly despised his presence as a witness to their staggering incompetence and callous disregard of their men's health and welfare. Russell took it all in and relayed the details home in a torrent of letters noted less for their elegance or artistry than for their hard-nosed, plainspoken recital of the facts regardless of whose reputation they bruised. One gloomy letter to Delane in January 1855 revealed this ability to convey the mood in the field unvarnished by tact or patriotic euphemisms:

This army has melted away almost to a drop of miserable, washed-out, spiritless wretches, who muster out of 55,000 just 11,000 now fit to shoulder a musket, but certainly not fit to do duty against the enemy. . . . My occupation is gone; there is nothing to record more of the British Expedition except its weakness and its misery—misery in every form and shape except that of defeat; and from that we are solely spared by the goodness of Heaven, which erects barriers of mud and snow between us and our enemies. While the people expect every day to hear of fresh victories they would be astonished to hear there is not an officer in command of the trenches at night who does not think of an attack by the Russians with dread and horror. I cannot tell the truth now—it is too terrible.[3]

When the government of Lord Aberdeen fell soon afterward, the retiring war secretary was not alone in blaming Russell for its collapse. Russell came home in December 1855 a national celebrity to everyone except hotel clerks in Dublin. His letters had provoked a debate on the role of the press in wartime in which the *Times* declared confidently that the people of Britain would "look for safety in publicity rather than in concealment."[4] Russell moved on to cover the coronation of Czar Alexander II in 1856 and then, in December 1857, set out for India, where Bengal soldiers of the East India Company had mutinied, massacred British civilians, and laid siege to the Residency at Lucknow. On the long voyage out he read everything he could find and talked for hours with fellow passengers—East India officials, army officers, missionaries—trying to sharpen his eye for the sights and contradictions that would soon assail him.

Russell stayed fifteen months in India, providing rich accounts of the fighting, the looting that accompanied it, and, increasingly, the folly of an imperial policy based on force, racial superiority, and brutality. He came home, in his own words, as "the only Englishman, I believe, who ever left India poorer than when he came into it."[5] After a summer sojourn in Switzerland with his family, he searched for a new direction to his career. He tried his hand as an editorial writer on foreign affairs but had no stomach for life behind a desk. He left the *Times*, became the editor of a new magazine, and reverted to free-lancing, but could not earn enough to pay his bills and all the while longed for more travel. After declining an offer to cover the 1860 election campaign in America, he finally agreed to report on the worsening crisis there for the *Times*. "You must go," urged his friend the novelist William Makepeace Thackeray. "It will be a great opportunity."[6]

And so he went to observe another foreign upheaval, this one with a twist that made it the most unusual and difficult assignment he had yet undertaken. Great Britain had been a participant in all the other conflicts he had covered, leaving no doubt where his sympathies lay. This time, however, he came as a neutral observer to a complex civil clash where any comment by him would antagonize those on whom it reflected. Although the *Times* maintained an official pose of neutrality, the men who controlled it leaned toward the South. "*Why* should we be so very anxious to see the Union preserved?" demanded John Walter, the chief proprietor. "What has it done to command our sympathy?"[7]

For himself, Russell professed to come to the struggle with an open mind and an unbiased eye. "No man ever set foot on the soil of the United States with a stronger and sincerer desire to ascertain and to tell the truth as it appeared to him," he insisted. "I had no theories to uphold, no prejudices to observe, no interests to advance, no instructions to fulfil; I was a free agent, bound to communicate . . . my own daily impressions of the men, scenes, and actions around me, without fear. . . . As to the questions which were distracting the States, my mind was a *tabula rasa*, or, rather, *tabula non scripta*."[8]

But of course he did not come entirely free of moral and intellectual baggage. He shared that sense of superiority held by so many Britons (and Europeans) toward the quaint Americans. He also possessed the strong dislike of slavery shared by his countrymen, and his stint in India had opened his eyes to the horrors resulting from attitudes of racial superiority. While Russell may have earned his fame in the Crimea, it was India that provided his frame of reference for the American experience. Nothing had prepared him for the rigid social code that prevailed among the British in India, the stifling snobbery and obsession with protocol, and, above all, the almost instinctive harshness toward the natives. He recalled dining with one "fierce-eyed, red-nosed, ferrety, bloodthirsty sort of man," the spitting image of one of his own uncles, who liked to boast of "the splendid style in which he hung up niggers." Gradually Russell had realized that all the British in India "in course of time become anti-nigger."[9]

One day, while making arrangements for his departure from India, Russell went to the railway office to have his baggage forwarded. He noticed several natives sitting idly in the shade of a wall when suddenly a large Brit burst into their midst. With eyes flashing he flailed about with a large stick, knocking them, maimed and bleeding, in every direction. Russell was appalled. "Good Heavens, stop!" he cried out. "Why, you'll kill those men!"

"What the —— business have you to interfere?" the man growled. "It's no affair of yours."

"Oh, yes, sir; but it is," Russell retorted. "I am not going to be accessory to murder. See how you have maimed that man! You know they dared not raise a finger against you."

"Well, but those lazy scoundrels are engaged to do our work, and they sneak off whenever they can, and how can I look after them?"[10]

Russell's disgust at the British treatment of Indians transferred easily to the plight of slaves in the South. No man who had seen India up close could be entirely perplexed by the extremes and contradictions, the contrasts and confusion, presented by the American scene. He understood why, during the uprising, it was the trusted household servants who had often turned most savagely on their British masters, and he wondered why the "sense of power, which nearly every Englishmen more or less enjoys, should need to be expressed so rudely. . . . I cannot believe the men who tell me it is essential to our rule that we should use brute force on all our dependents."[11]

He wondered, too, why the British had not only maintained the rigid Indian caste system but added to it an even more stultifying one of their own rooted in race. "The habit of speaking of all natives as niggers has recently become quiet [*sic*] common," he observed. "Every man of the mute, white-turbaned-file, who, with crossed arms, glistening eyes and quick ears, stands motionless along the mess room table, hears it every time a native is named, and knows it is an expression of contempt."[12]

Echoes of these attitudes resonated aboard the *Arabia*, where, as he had done on his voyage to India, Russell sought out those passengers who could educate him on the issues and scenes he would soon encounter. He found tutors in abundance. An army major named Robert S. Garnett was going home to Virginia to follow his state's fortunes. He had graduated from West Point in 1841, had earned two brevet citations for gallantry in the Mexican War, and was considered one of the best and brightest young officers in the United States Army. Well read, reserved, and somewhat dour, Garnett introduced Russell to the southern view of slavery and contempt for New England. He mocked the idea that all men were born equal or possessed equal rights. Men were born to a station, he assured Russell—some as slaves, others as laborers, a privileged few to rule those beneath them and to own those inferior to them.[13]

Similar views, delivered with more vehemence, came from a young South Carolinian returning home from his diplomatic post in Russia. Julian Mitchell staunchly defended the doctrines of John C. Calhoun on state rights and the Constitution. As for the new administration, Mitchell noted with a scowl that "no gentleman could tolerate such a Government" with men like Abraham Lincoln or William Seward. South Carolina could resist any force thrown at it by the North. "The North will attempt to blockade our coast," he predicted, "and in that case, the South must march to the attack by land, and will probably act in Virginia."

"But if the North attempts to do more than institute a blockade?" Russell asked. "For instance, if their fleet attack your seaport towns, and land men to occupy them?"

"Oh, in that case, we are quite certain of beating them."

Scratching his head in puzzlement, Russell turned next to a woman from Nashville, Tennessee, who was traveling with her son and daughter. To Russell they embodied the European notion of American speech and thought. They too believed in government by gentlemen and heaped ridicule on Yankee vulgarity, but they were not so eager to disrupt the Union or run the risks of war. This attitude, Russell learned, reflected the sentiments of the border states: less impulsive, more moderate, mindful of their place in the middle, and therefore hopeful of ultimate reconciliation.

Two Louisiana sugar planters gave Russell yet another slant. One owned thousands of acres of sugar land; the other had more than five hundred slaves. Both regarded secession as a violent and extreme response, but their state had followed that path because the secession of other states left them no choice. How, they asked, could Louisiana have stood alone, isolated from its sister southern states and the North alike? Russell came away from the conversation with the sense that at bottom politics mattered to the planters only insofar as it affected the price of sugar and the safety of their slave property.

Shifting to the other side, Russell encountered a bright, well-educated young merchant named Brown, who was returning from a stint as book-keeper at his uncle's firm in Liverpool. His father and uncle were English, the uncle a member of Parliament. In a moderate but firm voice, young Brown made clear his determination to prevent what he called the "glorious Union" from being wrecked. He believed passionately in America, but not in all its institutions. Universal suffrage was a grave error, he confided, as was complete freedom of the press, especially in New York City. The problem in both cases was immigrants, particularly the Irish. They were useful as laborers or servants, but to make them citizens and give them the vote was to corrupt the purity of government, and the dismal results could be seen throughout the municipal administration of New York.

Another young merchant, who had gone to college with Brown, echoed his sentiments. That his own father was the son of an Irish immigrant did not affect his beliefs in the slightest. He too vowed to uphold the Union at all costs and to defend that most curious (to Russell) of abstractions, the federal or general government. Southerners, it turned out, also despised the Irish for quite a different reason. They considered the Irish useful tools for labor too risky or dangerous for valuable slaves to perform, but the Irish also made up a large part of the United States Army and would be pitted against the best blood of the South if war should come. In that case, Mitchell assured him, there would be some "pretty tall fighting," and the idea of Paddy slaying the flower of southern manhood revolted him.

Another northern voice—the loudest and most vehement of all—belonged to the German immigrants below decks coming (or in some cases returning) to America, and it denounced the whole institution of chattel slavery. The southerners regarded these Germans with even more contempt than they did the Irish. "These are the swine who are swept out of German gutters as too foul for them," sneered Garnett, "and who come over to the States and presume to control the fate and the wishes of our people. In their own country they proved they were incapable of either earning a living, or exercising the duties of citizenship; and they seek in our country a licence denied them in their own, and the means of living which they could not acquire anywhere else."

Russell pondered the contradictions in what he had heard and came to a tentative conclusion: "Thus the agriculturalist and the trader—the grower of raw produce and the merchant who dealt in it—were at opposite sides of the question—wide apart as the Northern and Southern Poles. They sat apart, ate apart, talked apart—two distinct nations, with intense antipathies on the part of the South, which was active and aggressive in all its demonstrations."

But this did not satisfy him. Why had they grown so far apart? What made the southerners so defensive and belligerent? What indeed was this curious amalgam called America? It was nothing like India, he realized, but it was surely as elusive in nature. The Indians were inscrutable to him, suggesting behind whatever face they chose to present countless subtle layers of meaning that, like some ancient palimpsest, reached deep into the inchoate heart of their traditions. The Americans, by contrast, were all too scrutable; they just didn't make sense to him.

THE MORNING OF March 16 brought Russell his first glimpse of the snow-covered New York shore. By afternoon the sea had come alive with schooners and coasters, one of which approached the *Arabia* to serve as the pilot boat. Its deck swarmed with men in chimney-pot black hats and coats, the uniform of the port mariners. One of them climbed aboard the *Arabia* with a stack of newspapers, giving the passengers their first news in two weeks. Nothing in the view from the harbor impressed Russell: a thicket of masts behind which rose a low horizon of brick houses and blue roofs, and above them distant spires of churches and domes signaling the presence of a great city.

It was dark before the steamer carrying the passengers ashore reached the wharf on the New Jersey side of the river. Russell marveled at the traffic before his eyes. Huge ferryboats moved majestically up and down the river amid scurrying steamers and sailers and small craft. Tall factory chimneys belched columns of smoke above a shore littered with warehouses and other buildings. Armies of ragged workers and porters swarmed over the wharves, bellowing fragments of broken English. "These are all Irish and Germans," explained a New Yorker alongside Russell. "I'll bet fifty dollars there's not a native-born American among them."[14]

At the customhouse Russell was startled to find the officials dressed like their British cousins but without any insignia or buttons to identify them.

Once cleared through customs, he let an Irish porter stow his luggage aboard an ancient hackney and rode it aboard a ferry for the crossing to New York City. A short time later the hackney lurched up an incline and onto some wretched pavement before rattling through endless mudholes and banks of snow in narrow, dimly lit streets lined with cheap wooden buildings, most of them saloons, grogshops, oyster houses, and pool halls. The people Russell saw reminded him of the dregs in the slums of London or Antwerp or Hamburg.

Gradually the character of the streets improved until the hackney swung onto a wide street with tall houses and shops blazing with lights. Throngs of people jammed the muddy sidewalks, hurrying to and from omnibuses that jounced along the street. Here and there an entire block of brickwork with long rows of windows interrupted the shops. Russell smiled at the sight, the "barracklike glory of American civilisation—a Broadway monster hotel" towering above an endless sea of shops, saloons, restaurants, churches, and private homes. Just when Russell despaired of the procession's ever ceasing, the hackney pulled into a large square and deposited him at the Clarendon Hotel.

Russell settled wearily into his room and turned at last to the newspapers to catch up on events. During his crossing the new president had taken office. Lincoln's inaugural address had already reached Europe, where diplomats puzzled over its meaning no less than did Americans North and South. Like most Europeans, Russell was equally perplexed by the "declaration of causes" given by South Carolina to justify its secession and by the new "Confederacy" of seceded southern states. "The South Carolinian was nothing to us," he admitted; ". . . he was merely a citizen of the United States, and we knew no more of him in any other capacity than a French authority would know of a British subject as a Yorkshireman or a Munsterman."

But Russell understood that the force behind revolution was seldom reason or justice; it was rather passion or some special form of interest. What was at work here?

From the papers he gleaned that public attention centered on two forts named Sumter and Pickens. One lay in the harbor of Charleston, South Carolina; the other, off the coast of Florida. Both states had seceded, but the forts remained in the hands of United States troops with garrisons too small to defend themselves from attack. The southern states demanded their evacuation; the new administration had not yet made its policy clear, although Lincoln had stated in his inaugural a determination to maintain all property belonging to the federal government. "It is a strange situation," Russell thought. "The Federal Government, afraid to speak, and unable to act, is leaving its soldiers to do as they please."

He rose from breakfast the next morning to the sound of a procession headed by a small band trudging through the slush and cold. Dressed in their Sunday best, garnished with shamrocks and green sashes decorated with crownless harps, the men marched solemnly toward a church before a thin audience composed mostly of servants on their way to work. Some of the onlookers were black women made up with what Russell considered elaborate toilettes, holding their crinolines above the mud. "They're concayted poor craythures them niggirs, male and faymale," offered a waiter standing behind Russell.

"There seem to be no sparrows in the streets," Russell observed.

"Sparras!" exclaimed the waiter. "And then how did you think a little baste of a sparra could fly across the ochean?"

Gradually the street filled with well-dressed people released from the churches and braving the dismal weather for the Sunday ritual of parading up and down Fifth Avenue. Russell marveled at the Parisian costumes adapted ingeniously to the rigors of a northern winter by women whose beauty was to him rivaled only by that of the Hindus. There was about their delicate features that pallor so admired by the Russians that they sometimes took vinegar to produce it. Strolling the long avenue, engrossed in these pleasant sights, Russell was surprised to discover how abruptly the city around him turned into countryside. "Fifth Avenue might have been transported from some great workshop," he noted wryly, "where it had been built to order by a despot, and dropped among the Red men."

In the afternoon Russell called on George Bancroft, the former minister to Great Britain and a historian well into the writing of a sweeping multi-volume history of early America. Russell had hoped to get some insight into the crisis but came away disappointed. Bancroft seemed bewildered by the situation and distracted by the intricate philosophical debate over the right of secession—a cobweb of abstraction Russell found difficult to grasp. He dined with a New York banker who talked with surprising calm. The other guests, all men of prominence, also seemed little concerned about the raging storm. He returned in puzzlement to the hotel and dropped into what Americans called "the bar" to converse with its denizens. One man assured him that most New Yorkers were disgusted at the election "of such a fellow as Lincoln" and would surely back the South if a split came. Was there truth in this, or was it the whiskey talking?

The next morning Russell awoke to an explosion of drums, fifes, and bugles. Union Square was jammed with the Irish forming for the St. Patrick's Day parade, which had been put off until Monday morning. Flags rustled in the cold wind from windows and steeples as militia units formed and marched down Broadway amid cheering throngs. That the lancers looked to

Russell ill dressed and poorly mounted, and the troops ill fitted and tawdry, did not dampen the enthusiasm of the crowd. Every benevolent or provident society had its band leading the way with a cacophony of sound as the marchers snapped proudly along. Pickpockets worked the crowd undaunted by the police, who nabbed only a few in the act.

That evening Russell went by invitation to a celebration of St. Patrick's Day at the Astor House, a giant hotel whose facade reminded him of a railway station. He was startled by the hostile tone of the speeches toward England from Irishmen so far removed from their homes. Amid the prodigious eating and drinking he was prodded to make some remarks. Never comfortable at public speaking, he blurted out such gems as a quip that he had never seen so many good hats and coats in any gathering of Irishmen anywhere in the world. The next morning he awoke with a headache to read his remarks in the papers. The speech came out differently in every paper, and he could remember none of it, but every version he read made him cringe. "O Lord," he wrote in his diary, "why did I do it?" His friends in London shared his remorse when copies of the remarks reached them. Mowbray Morris, manager of the *Times*, said bluntly, "*I am very sorry* you attended that St. Patrick dinner and made that speech."[15]

It was not an auspicious debut.

Already it had become clear to Russell that he would not be traveling in obscurity. American reporters had pounced on his arrival and shadowed his every movement. The celebrated correspondent, noted one, "has short iron locks parted down the middle, a greyish moustache and a strong tendency to double chin, a very broad and very full but not lofty forehead: eyes of a clear, keen blue, sharply observant in their expression, rather prominently set and indicating abundant language."[16] It was an odd business being both an observer and an object of observation, and he wondered how much it tainted the effectiveness of what he did.

During the next day Russell talked to a steady stream of people and was amazed to find so little sympathy or respect for the new administration. Dining again with his banker friend, he met the former governor Horatio Seymour, a noted lawyer named Samuel Tilden, and other prominent Democrats. All spoke reverently of the Constitution and its lack of any provisions for preventing secession or compelling seceding states to remain in the Union. The federal government was in their eyes a mere instrument of the sovereign states. These abstractions utterly mystified Russell. That afternoon he had bought a copy of the Constitution for three cents in a Broadway store and read it closely, but he could find nothing in it that was self-expounding or even illuminating.

When talk turned to relieving Fort Sumter, one gentleman noted astutely: "If the British or any foreign power were threatening the fort, our Government would find means of relieving it fast enough." Instead the new administration found itself floundering in the dark, prodded on one side by zealots who demanded bold action and on the other by conservatives who prophesied disaster if any action was undertaken. The army and navy were not adequate to the crisis, and who knew how many within their ranks could be counted on? Every proposed solution bogged down in pieties about the Constitution and the inalienable rights won by their ancestors.

The new administration, in short, was embarrassed and groping for a policy, and the Democrats could not be more pleased at their discomfort. The men of wealth surrounding Russell, however, were Democrats in party only. To a man they deplored the mob empowered by universal suffrage, and the corruption, waste, and venality it spawned in City Hall. When pressed, they pointed to the core dilemma posed by the crisis. Most readily conceded that secession was at bottom nothing less than a form of treason which southern ultras had been plotting for years. Yet those plotters and their followers were fellow Democrats; how could loyal Democrats permit the vulgar new Republican party to invoke the authority of the federal government against them?

These distinctions clearly mattered, as did the finespun logic over constitutional principle, but all of it left Russell befuddled. The next day he strolled into Appleton's bookshop and found shelves of pirated European works and stacks of pamphlets denouncing or defending slavery, but not a single volume treating the present crisis. He dined that evening with a writer well known in England who had southern sympathies and was convinced that civil war loomed. The next day, braving a snowstorm he deemed worthy of Moscow, Russell called on Horace Greeley, whose eccentricities were as notorious as the radical antislavery sentiments of his New York *Tribune*, the most widely read newspaper in the United States. Greeley was delighted to hear that Russell planned to visit the South. "Be sure you examine the slave-pens," he exhorted. "*They* will be afraid to refuse you, and you can tell the truth."

On the morning of March 23 the papers announced with their usual confidence that Confederate authorities had definitely refused to allow any further supplies into Forts Sumter and Pickens. Emissaries from the new Confederate government were in Washington seeking negotiations, but Secretary of State William Seward would not receive them. Rumors continued to fly that secret expeditions were being prepared to relieve one or both of the forts, but no official statement had come from the White House. Russell shook his head in disbelief at the sensationalism of the papers, and their willingness, on the slightest pretext, to slander the most prominent people with the worst sort of abuse.

Two days later Russell accepted an invitation to meet the men who perpetrated this brand of journalism. He breakfasted with Henry Raymond and William Hurlbert of the *Times*, Bayard Taylor, Frederick Law Olmsted, Charles A. Dana of the *Tribune*, and other leading editors and writers. He had already met James Gordon Bennett of the *Herald* and privately dismissed him as "so palpably a rogue, it comes out strongly in the air around, in his eyes and words." The conversation at table was pleasant even when it turned to politics, though scarcely any two parties agreed with each other. Some thought a blockade of southern ports was imminent and wondered whether Britain would honor it. Foreign recognition would count for much in the outcome of secession, and few believed either England or France would rush to embrace the new southern government.

Russell could not find a pattern to the discussion and returned to the Clarendon to pack for his journey. His time in New York had been informative but not enlightening. He had little more sense of whether civil war actually threatened than he had upon his arrival, and precious little grasp of the American character—if such a thing existed. He would go to Washington to meet the leaders of the new administration and then south to observe the other side. Somewhere in their midst he hoped to find the insights that would illuminate this mystery called America. It was, he conceded, a country of contradictions—a whole that was somehow more than the sum of its parts and whose parts did not seem quite to make a whole.

PART ONE

The Battle for Washington

NOVEMBER

CHAPTER ONE

Vox Populi

*T*HE LONG LEGS crossed and uncrossed to keep from cramping, a lone sign of restlessness in the lanky frame folded onto the shabby sofa in the telegraph office. The sallow face, tempered by years of disappointment, gazed impassively at the operators bent over their clicking instruments. Their tale had yet to be told in full, but nearly every sign was favorable: The highest office in the land would soon belong to a man who had not won an election in fourteen years and whose entire record in national office consisted of a single term in the House of Representatives. The candidate of a party barely six years old, with virtually no organization or support in fifteen of the thirty-three states, was about to claim the strangest election in the history of the young Republic.[1]

The manager of the Illinois & Mississippi telegraph had invited Abraham Lincoln to await the "good news" at the office with his friends and had closed the doors at 9 p.m. to keep the noisy crowd outside.[2] Lincoln staked out his place on the sofa while his friends clustered about the room, talking, joking, glancing impatiently at the telegraph keys, which were slow to start before giving way to an incessant clatter through the night. The first returns, from towns and counties in Illinois, were solid for Lincoln and for Republican legislators whose votes would keep his friend Senator Lyman Trumbull in Washington for another term. Joyous shouts and cheers greeted every report; most were snatched up and rushed outside to be read to the throng milling about the street and the steps of the state capitol.

Lincoln listened attentively to every return but showed little reaction. Like all presidential candidates (except for Stephen A. Douglas this mad year), he had stayed at home during the campaign, receiving a steady stream of visitors while others did the speaking and exhorting. On election day itself he remained in the governor's room at the statehouse, amusing visitors with his endless flow of stories, until about 3 p.m., when he saw the voting lines at the Sangamon County Courthouse draw down enough to suit him. With his loose, unhurried gait he strolled to the courthouse in the company of three of his closest friends: William Herndon, his law partner; Ward Lamon, who served as bodyguard and confidant; and Colonel Elmer Ellsworth. A large crowd cheered as he marked his ballot, carefully clipping his name from it because he believed a candidate should not vote for his own electors.[3]

Now he sat quietly amid the din of excited voices and twitching telegraph keys, awaiting confirmation of results that everyone already conceded. October elections in Indiana and Pennsylvania had produced such decisive Republican majorities that even diehard Democrats realized their fragmented party was doomed. Lincoln himself took victory for granted—or as much for granted as he took anything in this uncertain world. As he sat or lay on the sofa, his features wore a haggard serenity that was one of his favorite masks. Whatever thoughts or emotions he harbored remained hidden from others, as they nearly always were. This most affable and accessible of candidates was also the most inscrutable of men, a master of showing others everything but his inner self while convincing them that he was as simple and right as rain itself.

The dispatches multiplied in number and portent. From Pennsylvania Simon Cameron reported a seventy thousand majority; Thurlow Weed, the longtime political boss in New York, declared: "All safe in this state." Every new announcement set off boisterous celebrations in the streets. Men raced about the city shouting, linking arms, and singing "Ain't I glad I joined the Republicans" until their voices cracked. But from Pensacola, Florida, came a very different message, informing Lincoln that he had been hanged in effigy there.[4]

Around midnight, returns from the Democratic states began to come in. Lincoln perked up to hear the news from Missouri, drawling, "We should now get a few licks back." The licks were bearable, and half an hour later he went over to a hall where the women of Springfield had laid out sandwiches and coffee to fuel the celebrants through the long night. There too was Mary Lincoln, the wife whose long-dashed hopes and expectations seemed on the verge of improbable resurrection. First Lady! There was a title capable of atoning for a thousand blasted ambitions and a strained if not fractured marriage.

Lincoln stood the adulation for half an hour before ambling back to the telegraph office. Henry Villard, who was in Springfield to cover events for the New York *Herald*, never ceased to marvel at Lincoln's "lean, lank, indescribably gawky figure" and his "odd-featured, wrinkled, inexpressive, and altogether uncomely face."[5] By 1 a.m. the returns were convincing enough to remove most doubt, yet Lincoln's expression changed little until a message arrived with returns from Springfield itself. Normally a Democratic bastion, the city had gone Republican by a narrow margin. At this news Lincoln brayed out something between a laugh and a cheer. With a contented wave he said good night to his friends and left for home.

In the streets the celebrations only gained momentum, growing louder and more raucous until about 4 a.m., when a large cannon was dragged out and fired to salute the first national victory of the Republican party.

> *We're the Lincoln boys!*
> *We're the Lincoln boys!*
> *Ain't you glad you joined the Republicans,*
> *Joined the Republicans.*
> *Ain't you glad you joined the Republicans.*[6]

ACROSS THE NATION telegraph operators bent wearily over their instruments through the night. Most of the thirty-three states except those on the Pacific coast were now connected by the wondrous device that sent messages through the "ether"; only that August the lines had reached remote Minnesota.[7] The ability to receive news from distant places within minutes instead of days or weeks was a marvel of the age that still astonished people in the interior. Reactions to the news of Lincoln's election were strong. "When eighteen millions of freemen speak as they spoke on Tuesday," said a Chicago paper, "they make a noise that even the most stupid secessionist cannot fail to hear. . . . The chivalry *will* eat dirt. They will back out. They never had any spunk anyhow. The best they could do was to bully, and brag and bluster."[8]

Carl Schurz of Wisconsin, who had campaigned hard to woo the large German vote in the North to Lincoln, rejoiced that "The election is over, the battle is fought, the victory is won. . . . I am happy in the thought of the future. We are to be one again, and unless I am greatly deceived we shall bring back a part of the old idyllic life." New England's Henry Wadsworth Longfellow agreed. "This is a great victory," he wrote. "One can hardly overrate its importance. It is the redemption of the country. Freedom is triumphant." His fellow poet, John Greenleaf Whittier, took a more sober view of the outcome. "Well God has laid the great responsibility upon us!" he observed. "We must take it up & bear it."[9]

Ohio's hotbed of abolitionism affirmed that the South's stranglehold on Washington had at last been broken. "The great object of my wishes & labors for nineteen years is accomplished in the overthrow of the Slave Power," Salmon P. Chase wrote Lincoln. "The space is now clear for the establishment of the policy of Freedom on safe & firm ground. The lead is yours. The responsibility is vast." A fellow Ohioan agreed that "A more complete vindication of the rights of the North was never witnessed. We can now safely say *'there is a North.'* "[10]

Reactions in New York, where politics was Byzantine in complexity and tempered always by business considerations, ran the gamut from braggadocio to prudence. Public reactions were measured, but George Templeton Strong, a blueblood conservative, vented his unexpurgated views in the privacy of his diary: "Lincoln elected. Hooray. . . . If they were not such a race of braggarts and ruffians, I should be sorry for our fire-eating brethren, weighed down, suffocated, and paralyzed by a nigger incubus 4,000,000 strong, of which no mortal can tell them how they are to get rid, and without a friend in the world except the cotton buyers who make money out of them, and the King of Dahomey. The sense of the civilized world is against them."[11]

In the city the largest and most effusive demonstration took place at Stuyvesant Hall, where an overflow crowd celebrated the victory with a "Jubilee" meeting. Amid the speeches two of the city's most popular and powerful editors, Horace Greeley of the *Tribune* and William Cullen Bryant of the *Evening Post*, electrified the faithful with stronger rhetoric than most of the merchants or Wall Street denizens could stomach. "The youngest of those who now listen to me," predicted Bryant,

> may live to the middle of the next century, and yet never witness an election so pregnant with great results. . . . We now stand upon the battlefield of the great contest, while around us and before us lie the carcasses of the slain. At our feet, conquered, lies that great oligarchy which has so long held the South through submission and fear, and has ruled the North through the treachery of Northern men. . . . A new era is now inaugurated, the old order of things has passed away, never, we hope, to return . . . and you, my friends, will now reap the harvest of liberty and peace.[12]

Nowhere was the response to Lincoln's election more mixed or anguished than in the border states, that twilight zone of slavery with roots planted firmly in both North and South.* Their people occupied the middle of the nation, were caught in the middle of the festering national crisis, and usually took the lead in proposing a middle ground for settlement. It did not help that most of these states were divided by geography and history into sec-

---

*The border states were Arkansas, Delaware, Kentucky, Maryland, Missouri, North Carolina, Tennessee, and Virginia.

tions that leaned North or South in sentiment or tried to embrace some elements of both.

One Kentuckian had no doubt what the outcome meant. "Lincoln's . . . election," insisted R. S. Holt, "is a declaration by Northern people . . . of a purpose to emancipate the slaves of the South, and to involve Southern States in all the horrors which that event would plainly entail." Holt voiced this prophecy to his brother Joseph, the postmaster general in President James Buchanan's cabinet. Others shared the belief of Iowa Senator James Harlan "that Mr. Lincoln will administer the government fairly and justly to all parts of the Union; and his inauguration will be a new era in the public affairs of this country."13

What would Lincoln do? A St. Louis paper believed he would "endeavor to make his Administration a just and conservative one," but admitted that he would "have more to contend with than any man who has ever been elected to the Presidency." A Memphis editor argued that "However much we deprecate the election of a sectional candidate, we ought at least to give his administration a trial." But a North Carolinian wrote his wife, "May God avert the dangers which threaten our country," and a newspaper in the same state warned that *"if we submit now to Lincoln's election, before his term of office expires, your home will be visited by one of the most fearful and horrible butcheries that has cursed the face of the globe."*14

Many in the border states looked to Virginia, the cradle of presidents, for cues, but opinion there was as hopelessly divided as elsewhere. "We fear no evil from his administration," declared a Petersburg paper. "We do not believe that he will trample our rights, but will pursue a vastly more conservative course than our politicians have endeavored to impress upon the Southern mind." Privately a Virginian admitted his belief that Lincoln "is conservative, and that the South has really nothing to fear from his administration." But a Richmond daily insisted that the "idea of submission to Black Republican rule, under any pretext, is as dangerous as it is degrading," and Edmund Ruffin predicted that "This . . . momentous election . . . will serve to show whether these southern states are to remain free, or to be politically enslaved—whether the institution of negro slavery on which the social and political existence of the south rests, is to be secured by our resistance, or . . . abolished in a short time, as the certain result of our present submission to northern domination."15

AFTER CASTING HIS VOTE for John C. Breckinridge, Ruffin rode to Petersburg and boarded the train for South Carolina, where the sentiments were more to his liking. The cotton states spoke with a voice that was by no means united but was loud enough to silence or drown out dissension. Lincoln received not a single vote there, and no one dared admit publicly to supporting him or his party. Nearly everyone shared the view of a Montgomery, Alabama, newspaper that "Henceforth, the Government . . . will be in the hands of the enemies of the Southern States."[16]

The election meant more than defeat; it was a call to arms. "The Cotton States are all on fire," reported a northerner then visiting Alabama. "They all agree . . . that the North has become so abolitionized that the South cannot remain any longer in the Union with them." In Georgia, Henry L. Benning argued that "the meaning of Mr. Lincoln's election . . . is the abolition of slavery as soon as the Republican party shall have acquired the strength to abolish it." Lincoln's conservatism, added an Atlantan, "will avail nothing. It is not *him* we resist—it is the growth of the sentiment he represents, which is simply hostility to us." That same view had been expressed bluntly by Senator Albert G. Brown of Mississippi months before the election. If the Republicans won, he warned, "The Negro will . . . insist on being treated as an equal—that he shall go to the white man's table, and the white man to his—that he shall share the white man's bed, and the white man his—that his son shall marry the white man's daughter, and the white man's daughter his son. In short, they shall live on terms of perfect social equality. . . . Then will commence a war of races."[17]

"Of course there were no votes for Lincoln," observed William Tecumseh Sherman, whose languishing military career had taken him to a military academy in Louisiana. An Ohioan whose brother John sat in Congress, Sherman had chosen not to vote at all in the election. "I would have preferred Bell," he said, "but I think he has no chance, and I do not wish to be subject to any political conditions." But Sherman could not have been pleased with the charge by a New Orleans editor that "The Northern people, in electing Mr. Lincoln, have perpetuated a deliberate, cold-blooded insult and outrage upon the people of the slaveholding States." Would the southern states be foolish enough to secede? He shuddered at what would follow if they did. "Secession," predicted Sherman, "must result in civil war, anarchy and ruin to our present form of government."[18]

If any state was the hothouse of secession, it was South Carolina. The movement had been born there in the nullification crisis of 1832 and nourished by extremists or ultras for nearly three decades until conditions grew ripe for it to flourish again in a new and more virulent strain. Extremists hailed the election. "There will have to be a separation from the North sooner or later—peaceably if we can, forcibly if we must," declared one planter ten days before the vote. This attitude, coupled with the dreary political outlook, left moderate men at a loss. "Every thing is so uncertain in the future of this State—of the South—and of the Union," grieved the former governor John L. Manning a few days before the election, "that I am bewildered as to the course of conservative men in the emergency."[19]

Ultras had no such qualms or doubts. "The issue before the country is the extinction of slavery," declared the Charleston *Mercury*, the personal organ of Robert Barnwell Rhett. "The Southern States are now in the crisis of their fate; and . . . nothing is needed for our deliverance but that the ball of revolution be set in motion." Writer-planter William Gilmore Simms agreed that Lincoln's election made separation inevitable; "by forcing us into independence," he noted, "the Black Republicans are doing us, undesignedly, a most essential service." Even Senator James Chesnut, normally the most cautious of men, unleashed a fiery speech the day before the election. "A line of enemies is closing around us which must be broken," he exhorted. ". . . For myself, I would unfurl the Palmetto flag . . . determined to live or die as became our ancestors. I would ring the clarion note of defiance in the insolent ears of our foe. . . . It is your duty . . . to withdraw. It is your only safety."[20]

On election night the *Mercury* office in Charleston stayed open for crowds eager to hear election returns. As dispatches were received from the telegraph operators, they were posted on the board outside. By 4 a.m. the outcome was clear, and the paper went to press with the news of Lincoln's election. At noon the *Mercury* unfurled a palmetto flag outside its office. Three of the city's federal officials took even stronger action. Judge A. G. Magrath, District Attorney James Conner, and Port Collector W. F. Colcock all resigned their offices and were hailed as heroes. "We are about to sever our relations with others, because they have broken their covenant with us," said Magrath, to which Colcock added, "I will not serve under the enemy of my country." The *Mercury* and its proprietors could not have been more pleased: "The tea has been thrown overboard—the revolution of 1860 has been initiated."[21]

THE CITY OF POLITICS ground to a halt on election day as clerks scurried out of their offices to the polling places in a drizzling rain and did not bother to return. So intense was the interest that a large audience at the theater that evening welcomed announcements of the returns from the stage during the performance. Secretary of the Interior Jacob Thompson was there with his family, as was Joseph Lane, the vice-presidential candidate on the Democratic ticket favored by secessionists. The audience cheered those returns favorable to the Democrats and hissed those boosting Lincoln.[22]

Later that evening Thompson and Lane were with Howell Cobb, secretary of the treasury, and Assistant Secretary of State William H. Trescot when Cobb received a telegram that New York had gone for Lincoln. A gloomy silence fell over the men. Finally Thompson, a Mississippian, said that if South Carolina dared secede before March 4, he would oppose it to the bitter end. Trescot, a native of Charleston, was shocked. While it was laudable to want to protect President Buchanan, he retorted, it was a very sad thing to hear such language applied to a state simply because it was advancing on a road Thompson declared himself willing to travel.

Lane agreed. How could the South hesitate for even a moment? The predominant mood in the North was hatred for the South, and it was growing. The time to resist was now, and he was ready to rally fifty thousand men to the cause if necessary. Trescot already knew how Cobb felt. A few days earlier, in a frank conversation, the Georgian admitted that after long, hard thought he had concluded that acquiescence to Lincoln's election would mean slow but certain ruin. Nor would it do to wait for concerted southern action or consultation; each state had to act for itself, and decisively. Such were the sentiments of two cabinet officers, a senator, and a high-ranking official.[23]

The election results posed a monstrous dilemma for everyone in the City of Politics. Washington might be a world unto itself, but it was also very much a southern city, complete with slaves. Except for brief interludes, the Democratic party had been in power for nearly thirty years, long enough to grow bloated with arrogance and corruption. For most of that time the southern wing had dominated the party and filled an undue proportion of the patronage posts in the departments. Buchanan, like his predecessor Franklin Pierce, was a "doughface," a name bestowed on northerners who gained office by wedding themselves to southern sympathies and support.

Now the tall, elderly Buchanan had a new nickname: "Lame Duck." Since Lincoln would not be inaugurated until March 4, Buchanan would preside over whatever happened during the next four months. Had the Democrats won, this interregnum would have been a mere inconvenience, a leisurely and pleasant ritual of leave-taking. But a Republican victory meant trouble of the worst sort, probably a secession effort by the cotton states. The lame-duck Congress would not meet until December, and Buchanan's cabinet was split down the middle: Three were northerners, two hailed from the border states, and two came from the cotton states.

The dilemma also had broad ramifications for American policy. A diplomat in Santo Domingo warned Attorney General Jeremiah S. Black of a report "current in Cuba and Porto Rico that Spain is to resume only so much control of her ancient colony of St. Domingo as will enable her to pass it over to France. . . . Cuba, St. Domingo and Porto Rico will keep step in the march of Africanization and coolie servitude. . . . No member of the Cabinet, from North or South, will be pleased to see these fine islands hopelessly Africanized. . . . There is a movement brewing on the Haytian frontier, and it is almost beyond doubt instigated by French agents. . . . The object is partly to intimidate the whites into accepting European masters. I am slow to believe that President Buchanan will abandon this island *and the white race* at this crisis."[24]

Those in Washington had more immediate concerns. "The die is cast, and Lincoln is elected," the Post Office official Horatio King wrote Black. ". . . What course should we, here, pursue? . . . Nearly all I possess is in real estate in this City. . . . With us, everything depends on the Union being preserved." The same letter went to the president but drew no reply. Buchanan had no response to the situation other than despair. For months he had writhed in agony over the fate that had turned his time in the White House into a nightmare. Even his friends gave him cold comfort. "I deeply regret the embarrassments which will surround you during the remainder of your term," wrote Senator John Slidell of Louisiana, long an intimate of the president. "I need scarcely say that I will do everything in my power to modify them . . . and to arrest any hostile action during your administration." But Slidell was quick to add, "I see no possibility of preserving the Union, nor indeed do I consider it desirable."[25]

That past spring Buchanan had told a party of newspapermen, "The duties of the presidency are severe and incessant. I shall soon retire from them; and if my successor shall be as happy in coming in as I will be in going out, he will be one of the happiest men in the world."[26] The remark had been made in jest, or so the newsmen thought, but Buchanan laughed no longer.

THE PEOPLE HAD SPOKEN, but what exactly had they said?

In this most bizarre of elections Lincoln had faced three other candidates, each representing a shard of the shattered Democratic party. His Illinois rival, Stephen A. Douglas, was the darling of the party in the North. In his zeal to gain the presidency, Douglas had challenged the long stranglehold of the South over the party; southern Democrats had responded by bolting the convention and running their own ticket, headed by John C. Breckinridge. Moderates who disliked both choices formed the Constitutional Union party with John Bell of Tennessee and Edward Everett of Massachusetts as their slate. Ironically, this smallest of the factions offered the only ticket that represented both sections of the nation.

In an age when nominees stayed home like coy maidens, most people saw a candidate in the flesh less often than they saw a perfect rainbow. From May to November Lincoln made no political speeches, leaving that work to a network of Republican committees at every level. Stump speakers entertained crowds at rallies, barbecues, processions, and other gatherings; the best of them toured the country like circuit riders. In cities and towns lodge brothers, volunteer firemen, and a new corps of young faithful called the Wide-Awakes held rallies, staged marches, and greeted farmers who came long distances by wagon to watch the fun. Delegations visited Lincoln at Springfield to stage mammoth celebrations at which food, drink, and rhetoric flowed freely.[27]

Stump speeches and rally rhetoric were neither polite nor accurate. They pandered unabashedly to local prejudices and spared no excess of language or image, misrepresentation or character assassination, to debase the enemy. The usual extremes of campaign emotion had been further inflamed this season by a strong undercurrent of violence in the form of threats, the most ominous of which was that of armed resistance to Lincoln's election. In this atmosphere the attempt by Bell and Everett to inject reason and moderation into the debate came across like polite parlor talk in the midst of a riot.[28]

Douglas alone broke the traditional mold. Desperate to capture the office that had so long eluded his grasp, aware that unprecedented times called for unprecedented acts, he became the Republic's first active candidate, touring twenty-three states at a killing pace. Campaigning as much for the Union as for himself, he threw his magnetic charm and bulldog personality into an orgy of handshaking, pleading, cajoling, joking, and haranguing those who baited him. He spoke two or three times a day, his indomitable energy defying a hoarse and failing voice. A popular joke said he possessed the constitution of the United States itself. This exhausting performance shocked the staid sensibilities of establishment politicians, as if one of their own had been found performing vulgar tasks normally left to menials. And it was in vain, partly because the electoral system itself was stacked against him. Four times in American history, most recently in 1828, presidential candidates had drawn their support primarily from one section of the country. Since then, the winners had gained support from both free and slave states and could consider themselves national candidates.[29]

No longer. The Whig party had perished because it could not find a basis on which to hold its northern and southern wings together. In its place came the defiantly sectional Republican party, rooted in the northern states and implacable in its opposition to slavery—or at least to the spread of slavery beyond its current borders. Its first candidate, John C. Frémont, captured eleven states and 114 electoral votes in 1856. Buchanan had won by holding the South along with three key northern states: his native Pennsylvania, Illinois, and Indiana. Ominously, all eleven of the states won by Frémont except Ohio lay north of the twenty captured by Buchanan.[30]

A dramatic restructuring of American politics was taking place. No presidential candidate would again come close to winning both the North and the South until Franklin D. Roosevelt in 1932. For Douglas and the Democrats this new order spelled doom. The steadily growing imbalance of population between the sections enabled a Republican candidate to win without a single vote from the South, and therefore allowed him to run on a platform appealing solely to voters in that section. Frémont had demonstrated this by becoming the first major party candidate ever to come out publicly against slavery. Democrats, by contrast, faced an insoluble dilemma. Even if their ranks had been united, the numbers looked bleak: No southern Democrat could win without forty-two northern electoral votes, and no northern Democrat could win without sixty-six from the South.[31]

But the ranks were far from united. With three Democratic candidates in the field, Douglas faced a hopeless task. The Deep South had revolted against his nomination and would deny him the support so crucial to past Democratic victories. Border state Democrats would divide their votes among all three candidates, with the moderate Bell most likely to triumph. In the North, Douglas had to fight an uphill battle against a vigorous new party eager to capitalize on widespread discontent with past Democratic administrations. Moreover, two new states, Minnesota and Oregon, had joined the Union since 1856 and were likely to add their votes to the Republican cause.

To gain election, Lincoln needed only to hold the states Frémont had won and take two of the three large northern states Frémont had lost: Pennsylvania, Indiana, and Illinois. So promising was this prospect that Republicans believed any solid candidate could win. "I am for the man who can carry Pennsylvania, New Jersey, and Indiana," declared Fitz-Henry Warren of Iowa months before the convention, "with this reservation, that I will not go into cemetery or catacomb; the candidate must be alive, and able to walk at least from parlor to dining room." But even Warren expected something more from the nominee. "Brain is nothing compared to the dorsal column," he added. "Let no man be eligible to the nomination who can take a kick behind with no change of countenance perceptible to the spectator in front."[32]

Douglas was a popular candidate and might do well despite all these obstacles, but unfortunately for him the electoral college was a winner-take-all game. He could run up impressive vote totals all across the nation only to finish second to some other candidate and have nothing to show for it. Lincoln, by contrast, would have few wasted votes as a sectional candidate. This fact turned the national election into a collection of state elections in which the four-way contest evolved into a pair of two-way struggles, one between Lincoln and Douglas in the North, the other between Bell and Breckinridge in the South.[33]

On election day Lincoln received only 40 percent of the popular vote, a mere 0.3 percent higher than Herbert Hoover managed in the Roosevelt landslide of 1932. But his 1,865,593 votes garnered him 180 electoral votes, while Douglas's 1,382,713 votes won him a paltry 12. However, even if the entire Democratic vote had gone to any one of the three candidates, Lincoln still would have won the electoral count by a majority of 35. A minority president he might be, but he was a legitimate one; no one questioned the legality or the constitutionality of the election.[34]

Amid the postmortems one striking fact went unnoticed. The American people recognized clearly and understood deeply the importance of this election. They flocked to the polls in record numbers. No less than 81.2 percent of eligible voters cast their ballots in 1860, the highest proportion of any presidential election in American history except that of 1876, another bitterly disputed contest that was to close the national crisis unfolding in the autumn of 1860.[35]

CHAPTER TWO

Something Old

No material change in the state of the nation. It's a sick nation, and I fear it must be worse before it's better. The growing, vigorous North must sooner or later assert its right to equality with the stagnant, semi-barbarous South, and that assertion must bring on a struggle and convulsion. It must come. Pity it could not be postponed some twenty years, when Northern preponderance would be overwhelming. If Northern Abolitionism precipitate the crisis and force battle on us now, it will be a fearful and doubtful contest.

—George Templeton Strong
December 22, 1859[1]

*W*HAT MAKES A NATION? What are the bonds that unite a people with one another and separate them from others? Those who have wrestled with these questions agree on a list of ingredients, if not on their weight: common descent, language, territory, political entity, customs, traditions, and religion.[2] By these standards Americans seemed a homogeneous people. The vast majority of white Americans were of British descent, spoke a common language, practiced some version of evangelical Protestantism, inhabited the same bountiful continent, believed in a republican form of government, shared a broad range of customs, values, and traditions, and subscribed to a common vision of national greatness.

Certainly Americans considered themselves a nation and a people, even if they did not know exactly what that meant. They had created a unique form of government and held it up to the world as a model of enlightened self-rule. Thanks to an abundance of land, the primary source of wealth in an agricultural society, the nation had mushroomed in size and wealth. Most Americans believed that ultimately their flag would wave over the entire continent, that they had been chosen by the Almighty to show the world what a free people could accomplish. In 1845 an editor named John L. O'Sullivan had coined a phrase for this credo embraced so fervently by so many people: Manifest Destiny.

That same year Florida and Texas joined the Union as the twenty-sixth and twenty-seventh states. Their arrival marked the first time newcomers to the Union outnumbered the original thirteen states which had fought the Revolution and banded together in a new government under the motto "E pluribus unum." In half a century the Union had grown far more diverse and sprawling; by 1860 six more states had been added, including two on the West Coast that were detached from the rest of the Union. The national motto had been given a new twist: Out of many had come many more. Were they still one nation in more than name?

The roots of American nationalism had always been fragile. Behind the similarities that seemed so obvious lay important differences. To say that most Americans were of British descent ignores the wide range of types and class found in Great Britain. How much did a Scot have in common with someone from Cornwall or Yorkshire? The language they shared was in fact a babble of regional dialects that took on an even greater variety in America. Evangelical Protestantism had many divisions in the Old World and even more in the New World.[3]

Although most Americans believed ardently in the democratic republic as a form of government, they disagreed widely over what they meant by "democratic" and "republic." In this model republic only a small minority of people—free white men above the age of twenty-one—could vote. Many states had once imposed property requirements as well, and South Carolina still had them for officeholding. Nowhere did voters elect United States senators; the state legislatures did that. In South Carolina the legislature also chose the governor, presidential electors, and many state officials. Everywhere could be found among the "better" people a profound distrust of "the mob" in politics.

"E pluribus unum" turned out to be as much riddle as motto. The Founding Fathers created a framework for growth only to have it evolve into a formula that was more cherished than understood. Although they had conceived of the Constitution as a work in progress, later generations embraced it as Holy Writ to be taken literally even though men disagreed vigorously over what exactly it meant. The Founding Fathers had left many issues ambiguous or untouched because no agreement could be reached and argument over them threatened to scuttle the Constitutional Convention. Two of the most explosive of these were slavery and the permanence of the federal compact.

The Founding Fathers had carefully omitted the word "slavery" from the Constitution but left references to its presence, the most obvious being the notorious "three-fifths compromise." On the question of permanence they left no clear trail at all, thereby allowing two sharply contrasting views of the Union to develop. Was the Republic a unified nation in which the individual states had merged their sovereign rights and identities forever, or was it a federation of sovereign states joined together for specific purposes from which they could withdraw at any time?[4]

The question of permanence was an abstraction of interest only to theorists until some concrete issue sent interested parties scrambling to it for relief. Conflicts arose early and often, and resolution of them was complicated by one ominous fact: The federal government, that marvelous creature of the Constitution, was itself an abstraction in many respects. Except in Washington, where it dwelled in its own peculiar vacuum, the federal government barely intruded at all on the lives of people. For the vast majority of Americans its only tangible presence was the post office, which was staffed by locals. Some places had a military post, an arsenal, a customhouse, or a mint to remind people of what most called the "General Government." Those living on the frontier, who relied on troops for protection, were the citizens most keenly aware of the federal presence.

What Americans lacked above all else was a history. Most regarded this as an advantage; after all, they or their forefathers had fled the Old World to escape the shackles of class, custom, and tradition and carve out new lives in a world where anything was possible. But the nation was still too new—and many of its people still too new to the nation—for its permanence to be taken for granted. Dogged efforts had been made to create a sense of American nationalism. There had been wars and national heroes; the Founding Fathers had been enshrined with indecent haste as mythic figures, and their deeds writ into folklore by the likes of Parson Weems. No day was more sacred to Americans than the one great national holiday, Independence Day.

More than anything else, political campaigns brought American nationalism to life on a regular schedule. But all politics in America were local long before House Speaker Tip O'Neill made the phrase famous in our own time. For that matter, all life in America was local, and so were loyalties. The nation was a collection of states, towns, villages, and farms with little contact or experience beyond their own pale. People considered themselves New Yorkers or Marylanders first and only then Americans, because New York or Maryland was the tangible world of their daily lives, the context in which their families and friends dwelled. Nobody lived in "America" or the "United States."

Nationalism, like all else in American life, was filtered through local experience. It became whatever people wanted it to be for themselves and their way of life. Every shared national concept—democracy, religion, freedom—differed from region to region, from village to village, even while they united diverse people as part of the abstract national myth. Americans in different parts of the country were a people "separated by a common nationalism."[5]

And the nation was changing. A new generation of leaders had come to power who knew neither the Founding Fathers nor the principles of the old politics. The Great Triumvirate of Clay, Calhoun, and Webster had been dead for a decade, and to many disgruntled Americans their successors were pygmies standing on the shoulders of giants. Two new technologies, the railroad and the telegraph, were altering the face of the nation, linking its far-flung corners, opening new opportunities, and transforming the way it did business. New peoples were pouring into the land, most of them from famine-riddled Ireland and politically embroiled Germany. Of the 26.9 million white Americans in 1860, 4.1 million were foreign-born; of that number, more than 1.6 million were Irish and nearly 1.3 million German.[6]

This was proportionally the largest influx of newcomers ever to land in America. New York boasted more Germans than any city in the world except Berlin and Vienna. While the Germans carried political radicalism in their baggage, the Irish brought with them a devotion to that institution most despised by evangelical Protestants, the Roman Catholic Church, which by 1855 had become the largest denomination in America. The large numbers of Irish in the cities also tilted political allegiances and gave rise to charges of political corruption and demagogy in local politics. These accusations came mainly from genteel citizens whose long-settled dominance over politics was being rudely displaced by new organizations using the immigrant vote as their base.[7]

In response there arose a nativist movement determined to halt the foreign invasion, reverse its corrupting influence, and convert the heathen "Papists" to American ways. During the 1840s and 1850s the protest was widespread enough to spawn riots, restrictive legislation, and a national political party in several incarnations, the last of which, the American party, had run former President Millard Fillmore in 1856 and captured one state, Maryland. Although the party fell into disarray soon afterward, it signaled the way in which rapid changes in society were breaking down the political system.

POLITICS WAS A mechanism to harmonize differences, but American politics had been out of joint for more than a decade. Parties tended to be unstable because their machinery was loose and disorganized, a mosaic of state organizations lacking any clear central direction. The national Democratic party, for example, was a coalition of its thirty-one state and some territorial organizations, each one reflecting local interests and prejudices and subject to local rivalries. Only the presidential election was held on the same date across the land, and a few states did not even honor that convention. Every state fixed its own times for elections; in practice this meant that somewhere in the United States an election took place during eight months out of every year.[8]

The two-party system had been around only since the 1820s, and already it had been shattered—some thought forever. Nothing illustrated its fragility better than the short, unhappy life of the Whig party. Born in 1834 as a refuge for those who opposed Andrew Jackson, it managed to elect two presidents—both of them generals with no political experience who died in office—before disintegrating in 1854 over the explosive Kansas-Nebraska Act. The Democratic party had older roots, claiming its heritage from both Thomas Jefferson and Andrew Jackson, but it too lacked a core of ideology or policy that bound its members together, and it did not even bother to adopt an official name until 1844.[9]

The American party began life as an aberration and died looking ominously like a harbinger of the new politics. The goal of any major party was to win elections by attracting the most voters, which meant taking positions that alienated as few constituencies as possible. Where the major parties waffled desperately to avoid taking strong stands on divisive issues, new parties like the American or the earlier Liberty took defiant stands on them. They could not hope to win national elections, but they could drain voters from one or the other of the major parties until it shifted position toward that embraced by the third party. In this way controversial issues entered the political mainstream in attenuated form, almost like a live vaccine seeking to slay its more lethal self. But some issues proved too potent even in diluted form.

Just as Americans lacked a history, so did their way of politics lack a binding core to provide party unity. Parties struggling to reconcile and minimize the differences among their members usually found it easier to unite around what they opposed than what they proposed. Victory went to the party with the most popular or innocuous candidate and the least internal disarray. Parties seldom tried to win elections; they sought rather not to lose them. As long as campaigns remained so strikingly local, it was possible to tell constituents what they most wanted to hear with little fear of offending others elsewhere. This was at bottom the fine art of the stump speaker.

Elections offered a doorway to power, and power was a highly sensitive issue to Americans. They had fought a revolution to seize it for themselves and had then devised a form of government to balance and separate it so ingeniously that too much power could never again concentrate in one pair of hands. With almost medieval precision and symbolism the federal system operated through three horizontal layers (executive, legislative, judicial) and three vertical levels (local, state, federal). It was an elaborate, labyrinthian system, capable of skilled and subtle manipulation, but it could not maintain the static goal of balance in a world where change was coming ever faster.

The Founding Fathers had sought this balance of power through the Constitution, but not even that marvelous instrument could reconcile major differences among the original thirteen states. Growth and expansion sharpened these conflicts as the northern states moved increasingly into commerce and manufacturing while the southern states expanded their agricultural economy into a plantation system based on slave labor. North and South divided sharply on the key issues of the nineteenth century: banking, tariffs, internal improvements, land policy, expansion, and slavery. Gradually their rival attitudes, values, and needs fused into broader identities of mutual interests that acquired a new and ominous label: sectionalism.

A dangerous new abstraction emerged; people regarded themselves not just as Ohioans or Georgians or Americans but also as northerners or southerners, an image that rivaled and even threatened the national identity. Gradually this package of mutual interests forged from differences hardened into stereotypes that allowed each section to trumpet its values as superior to those of all others. Lyon G. Tyler, son of the last Virginia president, John Tyler, drew the comparison this way: ". . . [W]hile the energy of the North was . . . one of speculation, or of adding figures in the easy retreat of a counting room, that of the South was mainly the energy that wrestles with nature in its strength—superintending the farm or holding the plow." This clash of stereotypes became potent ammunition in the sectional conflict. "Free society!" wrote an editor in Muscogee, Georgia. "[W]e sicken at the name. When it is but a conglomeration of greasy mechanics, filthy operatives, small farmers, and moon-struck theorists? All the northern, and especially the New England states, are devoid of society fitted for well-bred gentlemen. The prevailing class one meets is that of mechanics struggling to be genteel, and small farmers who do their own drudgery, and yet hardly fit for association with a southern gentleman's body servant."[10]

Northerners repaid such compliments in kind. "We know that Southern aristocracy is not synonymous with comfort, thrift, cleanliness, and usefulness, honesty, decency, or common humanity," wrote a New York editor; "we have learned to recognize it by the opposite of these traits." Edward Bates, a Missouri Republican, shook his head at the impractical ways of southerners. "They are an anomalous people," he observed, "the only agricultural people that I know of, who cannot live upon the products of their own labor, and have no means of their own to take those products to market."[11]

The sectional conflict was itself a struggle over balance of power, and it too changed rapidly as new states entered the Union. Geography dictated that there would never be another New England state, but there might be more southern states, and there would most certainly be more western states. For decades the quarrel between sections had revolved around what the North or South wanted. Since 1850, however, it had shifted increasingly to the West's desires. The child of expansion had grown large and ungainly, still raw of manner and unsure of its power, but loud and boisterous in its demands for recognition.

The West was literally a child of the other sections: Most of its people hailed from either New England or the South, and genteel inhabitants of both regions regarded westerners with the same condescension that the British reserved for Americans in general. The genteel complained that the country was being "westernized" by its newest elements and cringed at the results. Westerners were more coarse and vulgar, full of energy but with a certain brutality that rode roughshod over more refined sensibilities. Now, for the first time, one had been made president, and his lean, gawky frame and awkward manner seemed a perfect mirror of the West itself.

Whatever others thought of the West, they could not deny its growing economic clout. By 1860 Illinois led all other states in corn and wheat production, and Chicago had become the greatest primary wheat depot in the world as well as the capital of King Corn. The South had always had close trade ties to the West, thanks to a river system that drained traffic from north to south; the bulk of western grain flowed down the Mississippi to New Orleans. More recently, however, the fast-growing rail system had begun to erode that connection. More and more western grain now moved eastward by rail to the Atlantic seaboard for shipment overseas, enriching eastern merchants and bankers at the expense of southerners.[12]

"Southern policy . . . is rapidly forcing all the trade of the country through Northern cities and more and more North at every step," Jacob Thompson had complained that past June. "Southern policy is creating an entire monopoly of manufactures in the East, and the monopoly becomes more complete with every year." But most southerners were content to find consolation in the superiority of their culture and their way of life, some of which even infected Yankeeland. The Charleston *Mercury* took great pride in informing its readers that by one estimate, music publishers sold five hundred copies of "Dixie's Land" every day throughout the United States.[13]

FOR FORTY YEARS northerners and southerners had quarreled incessantly over the tariff, land policy, and other public issues. They fought over social matters from family values to education, and their spats over religion led many Protestant sects to separate into northern and southern branches. All these issues and more heightened feelings between the sections, but none of them could touch the passions aroused by the one question that divided them above all others, slavery.

No other issue has ever dominated American politics so completely for so long. "We have the wolf by the ears," mourned Thomas Jefferson, "and we can neither hold him, nor safely let him go." In 1848 an exasperated Senator Thomas Hart Benton likened the question to the biblical plague of frogs. "You could not look upon the table but there were frogs, you could not sit down at the banquet but there were frogs, you could not go to the bridal couch and lift the sheets but there were frogs!" So was it with slavery, "this black question, forever on the table, on the nuptial couch, everywhere!"[14]

No one had expected it to prove so enduring or so malignant. All the original states had once had some form of slavery. Between 1777 and 1804, however, every state north of Maryland passed laws to abolish it, and the Northwest Ordinance of 1787 barred it from that region. Even the southern states did not then cling to it rigorously except in regions like the coastal Southeast, where slave labor was deemed vital to rice-growing. But Yankee ingenuity then gave history a perversely ironic twist. The invention of the cotton gin in 1793 made possible the production of short-stem cotton on a grand scale. From this technological leap evolved the plantation system dependent upon slave labor.

As a public issue slavery lay dormant until 1819, when it stirred to life in a manner that was to become a prototype of controversy. The Union then had twenty-two states, eleven in each section, but the North's population had grown much more rapidly than the South's. Even with the help of the "three-fifths" compromise, the slave states had only 81 members in the House of Representatives, compared with 105 from the free states. They could never hope to close that gap, but they could find protection in the Senate, where every state had 2 members, so long as the number of free and slave states remained even. When Missouri and Maine applied for statehood in 1819, the balance looked to be preserved.

But Representative James Tallmadge of New York offered an amendment to the bill that would have barred new slaves from entering Missouri and gradually freed the children of those already there. The amendment triggered a fierce debate that, said the aged Thomas Jefferson, "like a fire-bell in the night, awakened and filled me with terror."[15] Slavery had made its debut in Congress as a national issue and quickly showed its potency in unleashing sectional feelings. The Tallmadge amendment passed the House but went down in the Senate, and a compromise settlement ended the dispute. But more territories were waiting in the wings for statehood, and Pandora's box had been opened in a way that could not be easily closed again.

At the heart of the dispute lay the question of what power Congress had over slavery. Southerners believed that the Constitution protected their right to own slaves even though it contained no explicit language on the subject.[16] Virtually all northerners agreed that Congress had no authority to interfere with slavery in the states where it already existed, but the territories were another matter. The Constitution declared that "New States may be admitted by the Congress into this Union."[17] What exactly did this mean? How much authority did Congress have in imposing conditions upon a territory applying for statehood? This was the question debated so ferociously in the Missouri case, and no satisfactory answer emerged.

For a time the issue damped down, only to flare up again in the 1830s with the rise of the antislavery movement in the North. Efforts to preach the gospel of abolition drew harsh responses from the South. Abolitionist missionaries were driven out of southern states, and their tracts burned. In Charleston a boatload of antislavery propaganda from New York was impounded by the postmaster, then seized by a mob and torched. A Georgia law of 1835 imposed the death penalty on anyone publishing material intended to incite slave insurrections. Gradually the southern states retreated into the prison of a closed society where public debate on slavery and related topics was not permitted and civil liberties were curbed or ignored in the name of public order.

Unable to get at the peculiar institution in the South, reformers turned their zeal to eliminating slavery and the slave trade from the District of Columbia, where Congress had clear authority. Petitions flooded into Congress, thrusting the unwanted issue back into national politics and provoking hot exchanges between northern and southern representatives. In 1836 a weary Congress imposed a gag rule on such petitions that lasted until 1844, but the truce was an uneasy one at best. Slavery showed itself to be the most polarizing issue ever known because of its completely sectional nature. There were then no slaves in the North and no abolitionists who admitted to being such in the South, and therefore no way to build some bridge of compromise or reconciliation between the two interests.

This polarization created a unique, bizarre kind of frustration. In a world where life was local, the adversaries were distant and could not easily get at each other directly. The issue of slavery in the District of Columbia drew its vehemence from the fact that it was the one venue where both sides could assail each other directly. The issue was concrete, and the authority of Congress in the matter undeniable. This was to a lesser extent true of the western lands waiting to be organized into states, but the Missouri Compromise of 1820 seemed to have disposed of that danger. It had not only resolved the immediate crisis but also provided a formula for all future territories carved out of the Louisiana Purchase: Any applicant lying north of latitude 36°30′ would come in as a free state, while those south of that line would enter as slave states.

Like the Constitution's "three-fifths" clause, the Missouri Compromise had less to do with logic than with expedience. It satisfied the majority of people in both sections, who wished only to avert conflict and took the compromise as an article of faith as well as a device for keeping the slavery issue out of Congress. But this view reckoned without two powerful forces in American life that were now on a fatal collision course. The first was the mounting bitterness of the clash over slavery; the second was the onrushing momentum of Manifest Destiny.

The antislavery movement was an outgrowth of the evangelical Protestant explosion of the 1820s and 1830s. In 1833 the American Anti-Slavery Society was born, with a program of immediate emancipation, racial equality, and nonviolence. The movement soon splintered into five factions that fought one another as vigorously as they fought the evil of slavery. Since the tactic of moral suasion had no effect in the South, where the evil existed, antislavery advocates devoted their efforts to winning converts in the North. In so doing, they fed growing suspicions in the South that a giant conspiracy against slavery was forming in the North. Over time the suspicion mushroomed into paranoia.[18]

Northern attitudes toward slavery would not have mattered much to southerners, who after all were not exposed to them, as long as no means existed to translate antislavery feelings into concrete policies. Therein lay the importance of keeping the issue out of national politics. But the expansionist urge brought Congress in 1845 to annex Texas as a state and thereby provoke war with Mexico. From this fight the United States emerged in possession of a huge territory embracing the present states of Arizona, California, Nevada, and Utah and much of Colorado, New Mexico, and Wyoming. Together with Texas, the acquisition added nearly 1.2 million square miles to the national domain.

The new real estate came at a dangerous price; once again decisions had to be made about the role of slavery there. While Texas already grew cotton using slave labor, most of the lands gained from Mexico had yet to prove their agricultural worth. Moreover, Mexican law banned slavery in all of them, creating a precedent displeasing to southerners eager to extend the domain of the Cotton Kingdom. The discovery of gold in California sent fortune hunters rushing westward, bringing that territory to the brink of statehood and giving the issue of sectional balance new urgency. If California came in as a free state, the South would become a minority in the Senate as well.

"The United States will conquer Mexico," predicted Ralph Waldo Emerson, who never could make up his mind about expansion, "but it will be as the man swallows the arsenic, which brings him down. Mexico will poison us."[19]

Already the issue had been joined in a manner eerily reminiscent of the Missouri crisis. In 1846, amid debate over an administration bill for $2 million to expedite negotiations with Mexico, Representative David Wilmot of Pennsylvania offered an amendment barring slavery from any territories acquired from Mexico. He might as well have thrown a bomb into the House. The Wilmot Proviso touched off a firefight of rhetoric between the sections. Although defeated, it kept reappearing on later bills. A new party, the Free Soil, made its debut in 1848 with the Wilmot Proviso as its central plank.

During the months after Wilmot's initiative, there emerged four basic positions that were to define the issue of slavery in the territories for the next decade. The first, advanced by Wilmot, insisted that Congress had the power to regulate slavery in the territories and should exclude it there. At the opposite extreme, Senator John C. Calhoun of South Carolina flatly denied that Congress had any such authority. A third position sidestepped the question of whether Congress had such power by arguing that it should continue to do what it had done in the past: recognize the claims of both sections by arranging de facto compromises that partitioned the nation into free and slave zones. In practice, this called for extending the Missouri Compromise line through the newly acquired territories. A variety of prominent politicians, including Henry Clay, James K. Polk, and James Buchanan, favored this position. It was pragmatic, it ducked the ideological shoot-out, and it had maintained relative peace since 1820.[20]

A fourth approach tried to take the slavery issue out of politics in a different way. Offered originally by Lewis Cass of Michigan and later taken up by Stephen A. Douglas, the new principle of popular sovereignty called for letting the voters of each territory decide their own destiny through their territorial governments. This doctrine had the virtue of being local and democratic, but it harbored a fatal ambiguity that few grasped: Neither Cass nor anyone else clarified at what point or stage of political evolution the people of a territory were to decide the fateful question of slavery.

In one form or another, these positions became the vocabulary of the debate over slavery in the territories between 1848 and 1860. The dispute over territory raised by the Mexican War and the application of California for statehood unleashed the most virulent sectional diatribes yet heard in the longest and most vitriolic session of Congress yet endured. For the first time since the Nullification Crisis of 1830, rumblings of secession cascaded from the mouths of southern ultras. "There is a bad state of things here," wrote an Illinois representative, "and, as little as it is thought about, I fear this Union is in danger. . . . It is appalling to hear gentlemen, Members of Congress, sworn to support the Constitution, talk and talk earnestly for a dissolution of the Union."[21]

The Great Triumvirate of Clay, Calhoun, and Webster all sang their swan songs in the search for a solution. Alone among them, Calhoun, so frail a colleague had to read his speech for him, sounded a sour note of warning about the depth of the South's discontent and desire for disunion. When Clay's efforts to arrange a new compromise faltered, he yielded to Stephen A. Douglas, the harbinger of a new generation of political leaders who had the bad fortune to inherit the worst crisis of the young Union. Through some deft maneuvering, Douglas managed to nudge through Congress a parade of bills known in their original package as the Omnibus bill and later as the Compromise of 1850.

Under its terms California entered the Union as a free state, New Mexico and Utah were organized as territories with no restrictions on slavery, and Texas received $10 million from the federal government for surrendering its claims to New Mexico territory. The slave trade (but not slavery) was finally abolished in the District of Columbia, and a new Fugitive Slave Act amended the 1793 law by giving the federal government exclusive jurisdiction over fugitive slave cases. Antislavists were outraged by one provision that allowed alleged runaways to be claimed with no more than an affidavit of ownership, and by another that set payment of a $10 fee when the claim was upheld and only $5 when it was denied. Nor were they mollified by the ban on slave-trading in the District, since the traders simply packed up and moved their business across the Potomac to Alexandria, Virginia.[22]

As the last measures slipped through an exhausted Congress, crowds thronged the streets of Washington to serenade members. The more exuberant of them, Douglas leading the way, celebrated by getting thoroughly drunk. "I do not believe any party could now be built up in relation to this question of slavery," predicted the more sedate Lewis Cass. "I think the question is settled in the public mind." Others, however, recognized that little more had been done than to stave off immediate disaster. "The question of slavery in the territories has been avoided," warned Salmon P. Chase. "It has not been settled."[23]

For all the cheers and cries of relief, the settlement won only grudging approval even from its friends. Within its provisions lay something to displease everyone. Chase was right: The crisis had been postponed, not eliminated. The Compromise of 1850 was in fact little more than an armistice, if not a stay of execution for the Union.

CHAPTER THREE

Something New

*We have the Executive with us, and the Senate & in all probability the H.R.
too. Besides we have repealed the Missouri line & the Supreme Court in a decision of great power, has declared it, & all kindred measures on the part of the
Federal Govt. unconstitutional null & void. So, that before our enemies can
reach us, they must first break down the Supreme Court—change the Senate &
seize the Executive & by an open appeal to Revolution, restore the Missouri
line, repeal the Fugitive slave law & change the whole governt. As long as the
Govt. is on our side I am for sustaining it, & using its power for our benefit, &
placing the screws upon the throats of our opponents.*

—Francis W. Pickens
June 27, 1857[1]

O N T H E F I R S T D A Y of what looked to be a most gloomy December
in 1860, the irascible George Templeton Strong pondered the enigma that
was the national crisis. "Why *do* the people so furiously rage together just
now?" he mused. ". . . What has created our present unquestionable irritation against the South? What has created the Republican party?"[2]

Its nucleus, in his view, was "the abolition handful that has been
vaporing for thirty years, and which, till about 1850, was among the more
insignificant of our *isms*. Our feeling at the North till that time was not hostility to slavery, but indifference to it, and reluctance to discuss it." The furor
over the gag rule in Congress had not roused northerners, but "the clamor of
the South about the admission of California ten years ago introduced the
question of slavery to the North as one in which it had an interest adverse to
the South. That controversy taught us that the two systems could not coexist in the same territory."

On one point at least, Strong agreed with a wide range of people caught
up in the crisis. The issues behind the sectional conflict, most notably
slavery, were older than the nation itself, but since 1850 they had taken on a
life of their own, a malign momentum that sent events spinning out of the
control of the reasonable men on whom the Union—and the politics of business as usual—depended so heavily.

The Fugitive Slave Act injected fresh animosity into the fray. Although the number of slaves fleeing north was small and most were caught, a few reached northern havens only to spark confrontations between their pursuers and local citizens. Sometimes the pursuing slaveholders and their minions weren't too particular about which black body they seized, putting free blacks in jeopardy as well. Nine northern states responded by passing "personal liberty" laws to prevent such outrages. These laws, along with the generally rude reception tendered southerners when they ventured north in pursuit of runaways, offended southern sensibilities just as the Fugitive Slave Act itself raised Yankee hackles. A more ingenious form of continuous irritation could hardly have been devised.3

Here was a classic American dilemma, the unavoidable clash between law and conscience. A storm of denunciation from the heirs of Puritanism in New England and their relatives in the Midwest rained down on the Fugitive Slave Act from press, podium, and pulpit, blowing the issue of runaway slaves out of proportion and feeding the growing southern conviction that northerners had no intention of allowing the rule of law to protect slavery. One dutiful Puritan wife of a seminary professor mulled over the whole issue of slavery as well as the potent image of the runaway, and drew from them a first novel that became a runaway best seller, if not the most influential book of the century.

The appearance in March 1852 of *Uncle Tom's Cabin* in book form after a ten-month run as a magazine serial gave northern readers a series of striking, deeply affecting concrete images to flesh out what had till then been an abstract issue for most of them. That these images were crude stereotypes mattered less than the fact that they imprinted readers with a vivid sense of the horrors inflicted by slavery on human dignity. They felt the lash biting into flesh, heard the bloodhounds snapping at Eliza's heels, gasped at the vicious sadism of Simon Legree, saw how even a benign slaveholder wielded absolute power over his charges, and perceived the many ways slavery worked its evil. Or thought they did. That Harriet Beecher Stowe sought to portray slavery as a national problem rather than a southern aberration escaped most readers entirely.

At first the book circulated freely across the nation, drawing early criticism from the North, where attacks on slavery pinched certain financial nerves. A debate over its merits arose; then, in June 1852, in an abrupt shift, the South moved to suppress its circulation while northerners rushed to its defense. The issue was no longer literature but a new chapter of the Great National Debate, provoked by an obscure Maine housewife.4

The book sold more than 300,000 copies the first year alone, and ultimately more than 3 million in the United States and 3.5 million abroad. A steady stream of knock-offs from North and South alike soon followed, but failed to capture even a fragment of the attention garnered by the original. Pirated editions of the original conquered Britain, where the venerated Charles Dickens pronounced it "noble but defective," and then the Continent. In August a staged version began playing at theaters across the North; it would not stop until 1931. No play in the world's history was ever performed more continuously in so many places for so many years as *Uncle Tom's Cabin*. Probably more Americans read this book or were exposed to this story than any other except the Bible. That autumn Americans could play, sing, and weep over eight Uncle Tom songs ranging from "Little Eva" to "Uncle Tom's Lament"; a Providence, Rhode Island, company brought out a card game entitled "Uncle Tom and Little Eva."[5]

Stowe had done what no amount of political rhetoric could do: given the slavery issue and particularly the Fugitive Slave Act a cast of characters to make them vividly real, and a working vocabulary of stereotypes to enrich the debate. Hate mail poured in from the South, some of it obscene (one parcel contained a severed black ear), some of it accusing Stowe of trying to foment a slave revolt that would drench the South in blood. She had also touched the national heart and inflamed sectional passions over slavery during an election year, when local appeals for votes pandered to whatever emotions aroused the electorate. The uproar especially hurt the already faltering Whig party. A Democratic doughface, Franklin Pierce, gained the presidency as both parties affirmed the Compromise of 1850. Southern extremists, who had hoped to keep discontent alive, conceded gloomily that their efforts were failing. The death of Calhoun created an enormous leadership void that had yet to be filled, and a prosperous economy helped buoy the national mood. Then came the legislation that erupted into the defining issue of the decade.[6]

The Kansas-Nebraska Act began as an attempt to organize the territory west of Missouri and Iowa for statehood; instead it promoted a disastrous escalation of the sectional conflict. The indefatigable Stephen A. Douglas hoped to open the way for white settlement of the West, provide a route for a railroad to the Pacific coast, and ride this triumph into the White House. But southern opposition was fierce. The South wanted the transcontinental railroad to take a southern route, for which land had been provided in the Gadsden Purchase of 1853. More important, the territory in question was part of the Louisiana Purchase, which put it under the terms of the Missouri Compromise. Since all the land lay north of 36°30′, there would be no slavery in any of the new states.[7]

Northern votes blocked federal aid to build a railroad along the southern route; southern votes kept a territorial bill from passage. Reluctantly Douglas concluded that the only way to gain southern support for the bill was to organize the territories on the principle of popular sovereignty, which meant repealing the Missouri Compromise. "I will incorporate it in my bill," Douglas told a Kentucky senator, "though I know it will raise a hell of a storm."[8] But even Douglas, the consummate political warrior, could not imagine just how much hell would be raised by this decision.

The final version, passed in May 1854 after three months of savage debate, created two territories whose people were to decide the slavery question for themselves. By that time slavery had long since bumped the railroad issue from center stage. Southerners already harbored a vision of the Great Northern Conspiracy to end slavery; from the Kansas-Nebraska Act some northerners gleaned their own Great Slave Conspiracy in which wily southern interests supported the bill to gain a foothold for slavery in free territory. The basic framework of sectional demonology was now in place. That both conspiracy theories were absurd did not stop many people from fervently believing in one or the other.

A disastrous chain of consequences flowed from passage of the bill. Whatever virtue popular sovereignty had as an approach to the slavery issue was destroyed by its use (in northern eyes) as a device for allowing slavery to go where it was not supposed to be. Northern Democrats who supported it were routed in the congressional elections of 1854 and 1855, losing sixty-six of ninety-one seats and giving real substance to the old charge that the party was a prisoner of its southern wing. The Whig party, unable to find a way to hold its northern and southern wings together, simply collapsed and limped off the stage of history. The party test had been brutally clear. Thirteen southern Whigs had joined the Democrats in voting for the Kansas-Nebraska bill; if they had remained loyal to their party instead of their section, the bill would have been defeated.[9]

From these ruins rose two new parties with disturbing pedigrees. Slavery had undercut the southern Whigs, forcing them to choose between voting Whig and voting southern. In the North, however, the Whigs also lost ground to a rising tide of intolerance against Catholic, mostly Irish immigrants. Nativist Whigs shifted increasingly to the new American or Know-Nothing party, while antislavery Whigs flowed into the new Republican party. Both new parties had narrow constituencies and positions that were unlikely to give them suitable appeal nationwide. Other small parties also sprang into being. Only the Democrats still boasted a national constituency, but they too teetered on the edge of splintering into sectional factions.[10]

The result was an election in 1856 filled with even more turmoil than usual. A coalition of former Whigs and other disgruntled political refugees gathered in convention, borrowed the name "Republican," from Jefferson's old party (which eventually became the Democrats), and nominated a

popular explorer and political innocent, John C. Frémont, on a platform bar-
ring slavery from any further expansion. The new American party could not
even unite around one candidate. Northern members bolted the convention
and rallied behind Frémont, while the southern wing nominated former
President Millard Fillmore. To these threats the battle-scarred Democrats
countered with an unexpected and, to some observers, inspired choice.[11]

A cabal of four senators—Jesse Bright of Indiana, James A. Bayard of
Delaware, and John Slidell and Judah P. Benjamin of Louisiana—joined
forces to send the inept Pierce back to New Hampshire. The phlegmatic
Bright, like his southern colleagues, wanted to deny Douglas the nomination
at all costs. Perilous times called for a candidate with little or no controversy
attached to his coattails. By every measure James Buchanan seemed the perfect man. He had spent forty-two of his sixty-five years in the public service,
most recently as Pierce's minister to Britain. This posting had kept him conveniently free of the ugly squabble over Kansas and the latest internecine
warfare within the party.

Buchanan was not only experienced but ambitious as well. He had earlier made three determined runs at the nomination, and had all but abandoned hope when this new opportunity was presented to him. Though a
strong Unionist, Buchanan was also a doughface with many friends among
southern Democrats. There was nothing fast or slick about Old Buck, as
some called him. He was a plodder, the tortoise that got to its goals slowly
but surely, utterly lacking the hare's speed or brilliance or quickness of quip
or step. In this sense it was altogether fitting that he came so late to the nomination that had so long eluded him. He was, said his good friend Howell
Cobb of Georgia, "the most suitable man for the times."[12]

Buchanan won the election by an ominously slim margin. Frémont swept
New England along with Michigan and Wisconsin, while Fillmore captured
22 percent of the popular vote even though he got only Maryland's eight electoral votes. The new president announced that he would not seek reelec-
tion—he was, after all, the oldest man elected to the office except for William
Henry Harrison, who had survived only a month—and that "the object of my
administration will be to destroy any sectional party, North or South, and
harmonize all sections of the Union under a national and conservative government, as it was fifty years ago." It was a noble and worthy goal; unfortunately, events carried him in the opposite direction.[13]

He got off to a rocky start by struggling through his own inauguration
after being stricken by the notorious "National Hotel disease," a kind of
dysentery that would not go away. No one was ever able to explain the affliction, which may have been caused by sewage backing up into the hotel
kitchen. Some claimed it was caused by dead rats tumbling into the vats that

collected rainwater for use; others thought poison gas from the sewers had penetrated the food. Inevitably rumors flew that the disease was part of a plot to assassinate the president, that poisoned rats had been deliberately dropped into the water tanks. Conspiracy theories still abounded for the sudden deaths of two previous presidents, Harrison and Zachary Taylor, and recently they had been embellished with the dark suspicions aroused by the sectional struggle.[14]

Buchanan survived the disease, but the ordeal confronting him proved even more wearing. An ugly incident shortly before his nomination had left feelings inflamed in the City of Politics. Charles Sumner, the tall, courtly senator from Massachusetts, whose erudition was matched only by his arrogance, had delivered a blistering indictment of the South in a speech, "The Crime Against Kansas," that included studied personal attacks on Senators Douglas, James M. Mason of Virginia, and the elderly Andrew P. Butler of South Carolina. This besmirching of personal honor was too much for Preston Brooks, who represented South Carolina in the House and was Butler's cousin.

Under the southern code of honor one did not challenge an inferior, because that would suggest he was a social equal and give him undeserved respectability. The proper punishment was a whipping. Accordingly, Brooks chose a gutta-percha cane given him recently by a friend, then waited until he could find Sumner alone in the Senate chamber. When his moment arrived, he strode up to Sumner, announced his intention, and began raining blows on Sumner's head. "Every lick went where I intended it," Brooks wrote his brother afterward. "For about the first five or six licks he offered to make a fight but I plied him so rapidly that he did not touch me. Towards the last he bellowed like a calf. I wore my cane out completely but saved the Head which is gold."[15]

The incident unleashed protest from the North and applause from the South. Public rallies gathered in cities throughout the North, leading one shrewd Michigan observer to console Sumner with the message that "Every blow from the ruffian Brooks gives ten thousand [votes] to liberty." Southerners repaid the insults in kind. "The feeling is pretty much sectional," declared the excitable Lawrence Keitt of South Carolina a week later. "If the northern men had stood up, the city would now float with blood. . . . Everybody here feels as if we are upon a volcano." But not all the feelings were sectional. Some conservatives in the North thought Sumner had got what he deserved; one member of a prominent family said coldly, "I wish they had killed him."[16]

Efforts to expel Brooks from the House failed, but he resigned his seat in defiance and was promptly reelected by an approving constituency. Except for a single one-day visit, the severely injured Sumner did not return to the Senate for thirty months. Republicans pointed to his empty seat as mute but eloquent testimony to southern barbarism; southerners scoffed that Sumner was feigning his long convalescence to make political capital of it. The mood in Congress grew darker, uglier, more edgy, and many members drew the proper moral from the affair: They armed themselves before venturing onto the House or Senate floor. Sectional feeling had turned Congress itself into an armed camp.

ON MAY 21, 1856, the day before Brooks pummeled Sumner, a band of Missouri ruffians and some local proslavery men, rode into Lawrence, Kansas, burned down the Free State Hotel, and sacked the town. Three nights later a fanatic named John Brown led four of his sons and two other men in a midnight raid on some proslavery families living on Pottawatomie Creek. Citing earlier proslavery outrages, Brown executed five settlers in cold blood. Guerrilla warfare had raged in the territory since November; now it turned into a miniature civil war. The sectional brawl over slavery spread its infection to a region where most of the settlers cared far more about land titles than about anything else.[17]

"Bleeding Kansas" became a battleground, a symbol, and an omen for what the slavery issue could do if left unsettled. The Kansas-Nebraska Act moved the conflict from Congress to the parched plains of Kansas, where strife and bloodshed soon shipped it back to a Congress that wanted nothing to do with it. Proslavery supporters from Missouri poured over the border in hopes of organizing Kansas as a slave state; antislavery men formed an Emigrant Aid Society to people the territory with their own kind. When the shooting started, eastern antislavery men bought Sharp rifles and sent them west, some in crates marked as containing Bibles. Three territorial governors tried in vain to stop the shooting; the last of them threw up his hands and quit the day Franklin Pierce left office.

Later estimates put the losses in Kansas at about two hundred killed and $2 million worth of property destroyed. What Kansas became above all else, however, was a propaganda mill used by zealots on both sides to manipulate public opinion. Northern antislavery reporters got much the better of the war of words. Their exaggerated accounts of events and atrocities on the prairie invariably put the proslavery action in the worst possible light. The New York *Times* and the *Tribune* twisted the Pottawatomie massacre story so grotesquely that by the end readers might conclude that Brown had had nothing to do with it, Indians may have been responsible, the killings were done in self-defense, and the victims were lowlife scum anyway.[18]

From the first day of his administration Bleeding Kansas haunted Buchanan as it had Pierce, driving him ever deeper into the sectional quagmire from which he had pledged to lead the nation. Before the new president had even unpacked, disaster struck from yet another quarter. Two days after the inauguration the Supreme Court handed down a decision that shook the nation with controversy as no other case would until *Brown v. Board of Education of Topeka*, a century later. Buchanan already knew of the decision because Justice John Catron had foolishly told him of it in February. Unfortunately the president compounded this breach of judicial propriety by alluding briefly to the case in his inaugural, thereby allowing critics to view it later as one more tile in the mosaic of the Great Slave Conspiracy.

The *Dred Scott* case had followed a tortuous road since 1846, when a black slave by that name first sued for his freedom. Scott had belonged to an army surgeon who had taken him to posts in Illinois and Wisconsin before returning to Missouri. When the surgeon died in 1843, Scott first tried to buy his freedom and then, with the help of a white family, sued for it on the ground that his period of residence in a free territory made him free under the Missouri Compromise. He won a verdict, then lost on appeal in the Missouri state courts. In 1854 he tried again in the federal Court.[19]

By that time the case had become unabashedly political because of the tantalizing questions it raised. The Court had to decide whether Scott was a citizen and therefore eligible to sue at all, as he could not do if he were a slave. Then it had to rule on the question of whether the time he spent in free territory made him free, which could involve a decision on the constitutionality of Wisconsin's strong antislavery law. Above these questions loomed an even larger one that had never been settled: Was the Missouri Compromise itself constitutional? The Supreme Court could tackle all these issues or avoid most of them through technicalities.

Here was a chance to confront the leitmotif that had run through the whole controversy: What power, if any, did Congress have to regulate slavery in the territories? Congress had shown repeatedly that it had no stomach for the hard questions raised by slavery, and the Supreme Court had done almost as well in ducking them. For a decade Congress had tried to wrest a ruling from the courts, and in their first session on the case the justices decided again to evade the issue with a narrow ruling that they had no jurisdiction in the case. But this time a new element entered deliberations. Two antislavery justices, John McLean and Benjamin Curtis, informed their brethren that they were preparing dissents that would discuss the status of slavery in the territories.

This declaration forced the other justices to follow suit. In the end each of the nine men, five of them southerners, wrote an opinion in the case, and no two opinions followed the same line of reasoning. This shift in position was what led Catron to notify Buchanan that a broad decision on the question was pending and prompted the president to assert in his inaugural that the Court would soon settle the matter. The lead opinion was delivered by Roger B. Taney, a Marylander who had been born the year after Lexington and Concord and had succeeded John Marshall as the chief justice in 1835.

Thirty years earlier, Taney had freed all his own slaves except two who were too old to provide for themselves. These he supported for the rest of their lives. "I am glad to say," he noted with pride, "that none of those whom I manumitted disappointed my expectations, but have shown by their conduct that they were worthy of freedom; and knew how to use it."[20] But his judicial opinion showed a different attitude toward slavery as an institution. In an elaborate argument he declared that Scott was not a citizen, and that no freed slave or his descendant could become a citizen. The temporary residence in free territory did not make him free, and therefore Scott was not eligible to sue in a state or federal court.[21]

Taney might have stopped there and dismissed the appeal on these grounds. Instead he plunged into the broader question. He concluded that the Missouri Compromise was unconstitutional on the grounds that slaves were a form of property and therefore the act violated due process by denying slaveowners the right to carry their property into certain states. No one could accuse Taney or the Court of timidity. For the first time ever it had overturned a major act of Congress, and it had done so by taking a clear stand on the most controversial issue of the age.

Unfortunately, this brush with the real world of politics proved disastrous. The Supreme Court came under attack as never before in its history. One New York paper asserted that "The Court, in trying this case, is itself on trial." Others denounced the decision as a "wicked and false judgment" and a "willful perversion," and warned that "If people obey this decision, they disobey God." Those who expected the populace to accept the decision got a rude awakening. As David Potter observed, the ruling "invalidated a measure passed by Congress, and ... sought to validate a position that Congress had repeatedly voted against."[22]

The *Dred Scott* decision stood politics on its head, forcing nearly everyone into an awkward reversal of position. It sent into limbo not only the Missouri Compromise but the Wilmot Proviso and popular sovereignty as well. Douglas had hoped to win southern support for his presidential bid through the loophole popular sovereignty offered for admitting slavery into territories where it could otherwise not go; Republicans had blasted the doctrine for the same reason. But *Dred Scott* opened every territory to slavery, at least in theory, leaving some recast version of popular sovereignty as the only potential tool for keeping it out. Suddenly the South viewed popular sovereignty as a threat rather than a helpmate, while Republicans became its friend, though never under the name that associated it with Douglas.

Dred Scott gave slavery in the territories the shield of law from the highest court in the land, thereby placing those who opposed it in the position of defying the law. When abolitionists contemptuously dismissed the decision and spoke of a "higher law," they fueled southern fears that no legal or political bulwark could protect slavery from northern aggression. Even when William Seward invoked the higher-law doctrine in a deprecating way, it clung to him for the rest of his career in a manner that made him seem far more radical than he was.[23]

While the people raged over Bleeding Kansas and *Dred Scott*, Buchanan was preoccupied by the business of politics. For the first several months of his administration his cabinet met daily for four or five hours to consider one overshadowing subject: appointments to office. One of the most critical of these was a new governor for Kansas. Buchanan consulted with Douglas before choosing a nationally prominent Democrat, Robert J. Walker, who took the job reluctantly but plunged into it vigorously. His task was to secure from the bona fide residents of Kansas an honest constitution through an honest vote. This would stop the bleeding in Kansas, just as obedience to *Dred Scott* would end the controversy over slavery in the territories. Or so Buchanan hoped.[24]

But Walker arrived in Kansas too late to persuade the free-state factions to take part in a June election for delegates to a constitutional convention. The ensuing proslavery victory put Walker in a hole from which he never extricated himself. In October he exerted a firm hand over elections for the territorial legislature. This time the free-staters participated with gusto and won a majority after Walker threw out some fraudulent returns that would have given proslavery elements control. But the proslavery constitutional convention, meeting in the town of Lecompton, produced a remarkable document offering voters a choice on the slavery question that was in fact no choice at all. This tainted constitution, created by a faction that no longer controlled the state legislature, then passed to Congress for its approval or rejection. Thus did the fatal issue of slavery in the territories return in yet another guise to haunt Congress.

To make matters worse, a panic seized Wall Street late in August 1857, fraying already edgy nerves and giving Buchanan one more crisis to watch. Antislavists in the North denounced the Lecompton Constitution as a swindle and demanded its rejection. Walker agreed, and urged Buchanan to reject it. The president found himself impaled on the horns of an ugly dilemma. Earlier he had strongly defended the legality of the Lecompton Convention; rejecting its work risked alienating the southern wing of the Democratic party, which had provided 112 of his 174 electoral votes, as well as half his cabinet and his close southern friends. But acceptance of the constitution put him in the position of betraying Walker and embracing a fraudulent document that antagonized every political interest in the North, thereby fanning belief in the Great Slave Conspiracy.

Aware that either choice promised disaster, Buchanan swallowed hard and chose to endorse the constitution. His decision brought loud protests from Walker and an angry visit to the White House from Douglas, who regarded Lecompton as a mockery of popular sovereignty. In a testy exchange Douglas threatened to oppose Buchanan when the constitution reached the Senate. "Mr. Douglas," countered Buchanan stiffly, "I desire you to remember that no Democrat ever yet differed from an administration of his own choice without being crushed." He reminded Douglas of the fate of two politicos who had foolishly tried to cross Andrew Jackson. "Mr. President," replied Douglas, "I wish you to remember that General Jackson is dead."[25]

In this exchange could be heard the deathknell of the Democratic party. On the day after Buchanan declared his support of Lecompton, Douglas blasted the policy in a long and impassioned speech. The president, who had vowed to unite the sections, now turned all his power and skill toward passing the Lecompton bill and punishing Douglas. In one of the bitterest fights ever witnessed in Congress, Buchanan drove deeper wedges into his party without getting what he wanted. Instead he had to settle for the English bill, a compromise that sent the Lecompton Constitution back to the voters of Kansas in a form that allowed both sides to save face.[26]

Ultimately the large antislavery majority prevailed in Kansas, but the English bill satisfied neither northern ultras nor southern fire-eaters. The former opposed it while most of the latter voted for it. Asked why the South Carolina delegates had supported the bill, William Porcher Miles said wearily, "We voted for it because the South did. Kansas was already lost. We were sick and tired of the whole matter and felt instinctively that we ought not to vote with Seward, Hale, Wilson, Giddings." He might have added Douglas to the list. The Little Giant's opposition to Lecompton had made him anathema to the South; indeed, his stand against the English bill helped give it much-needed southern support.[27]

Lecompton completed the bizarre spin given to Douglas and popular sovereignty begun by the *Dred Scott* decision. Where once the doctrine had been applauded by the South and condemned by the North as a device for slipping slavery into the territories, now it was clutched by the North and denounced by the South as a way of keeping slavery out of the territories. Douglas's heroic stand on Lecompton convinced many northerners that he stood right on slavery after all, even as it alienated the southern wing of the party which he needed so desperately for a run at the presidency. It had also made a mortal enemy of Buchanan, whose vindictive spirit sought revenge in the Illinois senate race of 1858. That his party was in tatters and the sectional split turning into a chasm did not deter him from using every means at hand to defeat Douglas. The fledgling Republican party saw a chance for victory and nominated Abraham Lincoln, a former Whig who had never been prominent nationally and had retired from politics, but was one of the state's most eminent lawyers.

The campaign was waged full-bore; Lincoln gave 63 speeches, while Douglas claimed to have made 130. Seven of them occurred in a series of debates that riveted national attention to Illinois and provided the most thoughtful and incisive analysis of the slavery question ever made in American politics. In seven small Illinois towns the two candidates waged their verbal war before large crowds of country folk in the torpor of late summer heat. Douglas used the debates to elaborate his notion of how popular sovereignty could prevent slavery from entering regions where the Court had said it could go. To survive, slavery required the protection of sympathetic local legislation; to exclude it, people needed only to withhold that legislation. "Slavery cannot exist a day," he argued, "in the midst of an unfriendly people with unfriendly laws."[28]

Often maligned wrongly as a man of overweening ambition with no principles, Douglas believed ardently in the Union above all else and in popular sovereignty as the best way of getting slavery out of national politics. Slavery was to him a practical rather than a moral issue, and it was on this point that Lincoln hit hard. "The real issue in this controversy," he said in the final debate, ". . . is the sentiment on the part of one class that looks upon the institution of slavery *as a wrong*, and of another class that *does not* look upon it as a wrong . . . and one of the methods of treating it as a wrong is to *make provision that it shall grow no larger*. . . . It is the eternal struggle between these two principles—right and wrong—throughout the world."[29]

Like the vast majority of white Americans, Douglas believed that blacks were inferior to whites as a race. The government "was made by white men, for the benefit of white men and their posterity, to be executed and managed by white men. . . . The Negro is not a citizen, cannot be a citizen, and ought not to be a citizen." But that did not mean he had to be a slave, Douglas added. "The Negro, as . . . an inferior race, ought to possess every right, every privilege, every immunity, which he can safely exercise, consistent with the safety of the society in which he lives."[30]

Four years earlier, Lincoln had described Douglas as a man who "has no very vivid impression that the negro is a human; and consequently has no idea that there can be any moral question in legislating about him." Now Lincoln found himself retreating before his adversary's barbs that he considered black men equal to white men. "I am not, nor ever have been in favor of bringing about in any way the social and political equality of the white and black races," he countered. There was "a physical difference between the white and black races which I believe will for ever forbid the two races living together on terms of social and political equality. And inasmuch as they cannot so live . . . there must be the position of superior and inferior, and I as much as any other man am in favor of having the superior position assigned to the white race."[31]

Here the two men had reached the heart of the dilemma. The immediate issue was slavery, but the ultimate question was race, and for that neither man had an answer. Douglas asked it in his blunt manner: If slavery ceased, what should be done with the freed slaves? "The Republicans say that he ought to become a citizen," Douglas said, "and when he becomes a citizen he becomes your equal, with all your rights and privileges." To this some in the audience shouted, "He never shall," and Lincoln only repeated the lame reply he had given in an 1854 speech: "If all earthly power were given me, I should not know what to do, as to the existing institution. My first impulse would be to free all the slaves, and send them to Liberia—to their own native land."[32]

For all their insight and intelligence, Lincoln and Douglas could not undo the same Gordian knot noted a quarter century earlier by that shrewd Frenchman Alexis de Tocqueville, who had toured the United States and gone home to write a study brimming with profound insights about what he had seen. On this point he could not have been more chillingly prescient:

> I do not regard the abolition of slavery as a means of warding off the struggle of the two races in the Southern states. The Negroes may long remain slaves without complaining; but if they are once raised to the level of freemen, they will soon revolt at being deprived of almost all their civil rights; and as they cannot become the equals of the whites, they will speedily show themselves as enemies. . . . I can discover only two modes of action for the white inhabitants of these states; namely, either to emancipate the Negroes and to intermingle with them, or, remaining isolated from them, to keep them in slavery

as long as possible. All intermediate measures seem to me likely to terminate, and that shortly, in the most horrible of civil wars.[33]

Douglas won the election, besting not only Lincoln but Buchanan as well and leaving the Democratic party in shambles. More than ever before, clashes over policy involved sectional positions split along sectional lines that caught up even moderates in the growing rhetoric of extremism. Lincoln himself had resorted uncharacteristically to the language of apocalypse in a speech at Springfield the previous June when he declared, " 'A house divided against itself cannot stand.' I believe this government cannot endure, permanently half *slave* and half *free*. I do not expect the Union to be *dissolved*—I do not expect the house to *fall*—but I *do* expect it will cease to be divided. It will become *all* one thing, or *all* the other."[34]

Lincoln never meant these words as a call to arms or prophecy of doom, but southerners were quick to pounce on them as such, just as they did with an unfortunate phrase uttered four months later by William H. Seward. "Shall I tell you what this collision means?" he asked in a Rochester speech. ". . . It is an irrepressible conflict between opposing and enduring forces; it means that the United States must and will, sooner or later, become entirely a slaveholding nation, or entirely a free labor nation." The notion of an "irrepressible conflict" was not original with Seward, but it soon became the war cry of northern abolitionists and southern ultras. Coupled with his "higher law" speech, it marked Seward in many eyes as far more radical than he really was.[35]

Southerners also heaped scorn on one of their own, an obscure North Carolinian named Hinton R. Helper, for daring to publish a book arguing that slavery was the prime cause of the South's economic miasma. *The Impending Crisis of the South* had no kind words for the slaves themselves— Helper was a violent racist who wanted all blacks deported—but it amassed a parade of statistics to show how the institution of slavery had reduced a growing number of nonslaveholding whites to poverty. In so doing, Helper violated the sacred tenet of the chivalry that race transcended class. For urging nonslaveholders to throw off the domination of the slaveowning class, he was denounced as a traitor, an apostate, a "dishonest, degraded, and disgraced man," and his book was banned from circulation in the South.[36]

Republicans embraced Helper's book and distributed an abridged edition throughout the North. Sixty Republican congressmen signed a letter endorsing Helper's work, which made southern members furious. In December 1857 Senator James Henry Hammond of South Carolina confided to a friend that "it *may* be, that the *final & decisive* Crisis is close at hand which is to settle the destiny of the Slaveholders of the South forever." The following March he took the floor of the Senate to warn the North: "No! you dare not make war upon cotton; no power on earth dares to make war upon it. Cotton is king; until lately the Bank of England was king; but she tried to put her screws, as usual . . . on the cotton crop, and was utterly vanquished."[37]

In this hypercharged atmosphere, in which conservative men despaired of restoring reason or healing wounds that seemed to cut ever deeper, a lightning bolt struck with a force as devastating as it was unexpected. On October 16, 1859, John Brown of Kansas infamy led another motley band of followers in a raid on the federal arsenal at Harpers Ferry, Virginia. There he remained for two days until a detachment of U.S. Marines, led by Colonel Robert E. Lee, stormed the building and captured Brown and seven of his followers. Altogether fourteen people died in this strange affair, but their deaths were only the beginning of the repercussions that flowed from the event.[38]

It soon became clear that Brown's goal had been to secure arms for a major slave uprising in Virginia and elsewhere in the South. Even worse, most of his funds had come from a small group of radical abolitionists in New England, one of whom had told Brown that he was "always ready to invest in treason."[39] Although the raid turned into a debacle, Brown aroused in southerners a horrifying image of their worst nightmare, the bloodbath of a slave insurrection, and tied it to the very abolitionists who southerners had long insisted were trying to foment a race war. Blood had been spilled in the cause of abolition; paranoia had shifted yet another notch closer to reality.

The timing of Brown's raid could not have been worse. It took place a few weeks before elections, enabling candidates to add it to their already overheated rhetoric, and less than two months before Congress was to convene. During that time Governor Henry A. Wise of Virginia chose to try Brown on charges of treason, murder, and conspiracy. Brown was convicted and hanged on December 2. His calm, even heroic demeanor through this ordeal belied the image of a mad fanatic, giving abolitionists a martyr to their cause of equal force to his role as bogeyman in the South. The ghost of John Brown haunted the nation as the man could not have imagined in his wildest dreams. The reaction to his raid and execution inflamed the sectional crisis far more than the events themselves.

In the North Brown's death inspired an outpouring of mourning, memorial services, the tolling of bells, prayer meetings, and a flood of verse bemoaning his loss, like this lament from the young Louisa May Alcott:

> *No breath of shame can touch his shield*
> *Nor ages dim its shine.*

Living, he made life beautiful
Dying, made death divine.

Ralph Waldo Emerson, who gave two memorial addresses on Brown, observed solemnly that the fallen martyr would "make the gallows as glorious as the cross." For abolitionist Wendell Phillips, the lesson of the hour was insurrection. "Virginia . . . is a pirate ship," he charged, "and John Brown sails the sea, a Lord High Admiral of the Almighty, with his commission to sink every pirate he meets in God's ocean of the nineteenth century." Brown, said the Reverend Fales H. Newhall, had made the word "treason" "holy in the American language."[40]

Leading Republicans like Lincoln and Seward, along with a host of moderates and conservatives in the North, dismissed Brown as a lunatic who deserved his fate, but their pronouncements did not satisfy most southerners. Mere words could not explain away the springing to life of a nightmare. "The pikes brought to Harper's Ferry by John Brown," wrote Edmund Ruffin, were "devised and directed by Northern Conspirators, made in Northern Factories, paid for by Northern funds, and designed to slaughter sleeping Southern men and their awakened wives and children."[41]

Congress convened early in December under the shadow of John Brown and never escaped it. The president signed off early from the sectional struggle. Having exhausted his political capital on the Lecompton fight, Buchanan did little more than admonish Congress to solve the nation's problems. His annual message warned that Harpers Ferry was a symptom of "an incurable disease in the public mind, which may . . . terminate, at last, in an open war by the North to abolish slavery in the South," but no one paid any attention. The House responded by opening an investigation into whether Buchanan had used improper influence to get the English bill passed. The findings of the Covode Committee blended familiar charges of corruption with the new taint of sectional paranoia as Republicans read into them a portrait of the puppet president manipulated by the Great Slave Conspiracy.[42]

So prickly and contentious was Congress that the House wasted two months fighting over the selection of a Speaker. The Republicans could not elect John Sherman of Ohio because he had been among those who had endorsed Helper's infamous book, and the Democrats could not elect anyone at all. It had become painfully clear that the Democratic party consisted of two sectional wings whose leaders, Douglas and Buchanan, despised each other. Finally Sherman withdrew, and the weary members settled on an inept New Jerseyan, William Pennington. The hostility among members ran so deep that little business got done, and many came to the chamber armed. "The only persons who do not have a revolver and a knife," observed Hammond tersely, "are those who have two revolvers."[43]

In the House, members hurled denunciations and charges at one another to a chorus of raucous whistling, clapping, laughter, hisses, and foot-stomping from the galleries. Outside the chamber the representatives had to wade through a motley medley of lobbyists, loafers, and sycophants milling about. No one could remember anything like it in Congress; there had often been excitement or even anger, but never so ugly or palpable an air of con-frontation veering so near the edge of violence. Not only the members but their friends in the galleries bore arms, and one rash shot might have plunged the chamber into bloodshed and even dissolved the Congress.

Through all the rhetoric of insult flew the name and image of John Brown like an angel of doom. Southerners resented the widespread mourning in the North for Brown, who was hanged only three days before Congress convened. "Every village bell which tolled its solemn note at the execution of Brown," protested C. G. Memminger of South Carolina, "pro-claims to the South the approbation of that village of insurrection and servile war." Senator Jefferson Davis of Mississippi repeated the familiar theme that Brown had intended to "incite slaves to murder helpless women and chil-dren." In the House Reuben Davis wanted to hang Seward and others of like sentiments. Senator Robert Toombs of Georgia demanded, "Who is respon-sible for the treason, murder, and arson of John Brown? I have never known of his acts being approved, defended, or palliated by any other person than a Republican."[44]

Amid the escalating rhetoric and threats of violence came an old threat with a new twist. "The Capitol resounds with the cry of dissolution," wrote Senator James Grimes of Iowa, "and the cry is echoed throughout the city." Talk of secession had been around for decades; southern ultras had raised it to an art form since the nullification crisis. During the uproar before the Compromise of 1850 it burst forth with renewed vigor. When the clash over the Kansas-Nebraska Act brought it out again, Senator William P. Fessenden of Maine, a staunch Republican, said in disgust that "we have talked here of a dissolution of the Union. We have heard that threat until we are fatigued with the sound. We consider it now . . . noise, and nothing else. It produces not the slightest impression upon the thinking portion of the public."[45]

Now the noise had come again, louder and more insistent than ever, but to many northern ears it was only more crying wolf. Long and tedious famil-iarity with the politics of crisis had bred a contempt for it and an insensitivity to any real threat posed by it. But some saw a fearful new element that gave the threat of separation a painful edge of reality. Southerners who had long declared themselves staunch Unionists wavered, confessed doubts over the

possibility of preserving a united nation, and defected to the cause of secession. "The Harpers Ferry invasion," observed a Richmond paper with satisfaction, "has advanced the cause of disunion more than any other event . . .
since the formation of its [*sic*] government." A rival paper in the same city
agreed:

> Recent events have wrought almost a complete revolution in the sen-
> timents, the thoughts, the hopes, of the oldest and steadiest conser-
> vatives in all the Southern states. In Virginia, particularly, this
> revolution has been really wonderful. There are . . . thousands of
> men in our midst who, a month ago, scoffed at the idea of a dissolu-
> tion of the Union as a madman's dream, but who now hold the
> opinion that its days are numbered, its glory perished.[46]

Editors and politicians were not alone in sensing this revolution of sentiment. "The whole country is in a state of fearful agitation—disunion! Disunion! is the cry with our Southern friends," wrote the mother of Army
Major Edmund Kirby Smith from her home in St. Augustine, Florida; "it is
boldly spoken of by the fireside, in public, in all places it is the absorbing
subject. . . . If our rights as guaranteed by the Constitution are trampled
under foot defiantly—disunion must follow. Southern men and Southern
women will not sit down with folded hands if the masses elect a Black Republican President." On New Year's Day 1860 the Massachusetts Democrat
Caleb Cushing issued this gloomy warning to former President Pierce:

> We seem to be drifting into destruction before our eyes, in utter
> hopelessness. The Administration is utterly depopularized; the
> President is embarrassed with insoluble questions; Congress is para-
> lyzed by party spirit; and everybody seems to despair of any help
> from man, though many are looking vaguely for they know not what
> interposition from Providence.[47]

Was this some perverse form of the new politics? Nearly everyone
sensed that some radical change had taken place in American politics since
1850, but few agreed on what it was. Buchanan thought he knew. "In the last
age," he observed late in 1858, "although our fathers, like ourselves, were
divided into political parties which often had severe conflicts with each
other, yet we never heard, until within a recent period, of the employment of
money to carry elections." Marylander John Pendleton Kennedy had long
since come to a similar conclusion. "Nothing can be more contemptible than
the state politics and management of Maryland," he said in 1850. "We have

not a man in public service above mediocrity, and the whole machinery of our politics is moved by the smaller, narrowest, and most ignorant and corrupt men in the State."[48]

Corruption and the expansion of the electorate had weakened the political process even without a sectional conflict. Many people also believed that the new generation of leaders were not even pale imitations of the Founding Fathers or their successors like Jackson, Clay, Calhoun, and Webster. The latter had been men for whom politics was a serious business and to which they had brought shining talents if not genius. Since 1850, however, politics had become more a profession as well as a predatory culture in which thousands of officeholders and placemen thrived with little regard for any larger principle than self-interest. And there was another element not yet fully appreciated. As the historian William J. Evitts observes, "Politics became a mass entertainment as much as it was a means of carrying on the public business."[49]

Another new element in American political life, new at least in the form it was assuming, had surfaced amid the imbroglio over slavery in the territories. Sumner had dismissed popular sovereignty as "altogether a modern invention, unknown to our fathers," and in a sense he was right. What he failed to see was its role in arresting the gradual erosion of state authority by the federal government. Douglas, with his keen eye for political realities, had grasped this early and invoked it in his debates with Lincoln. "I would never consent to confer the right of voting and citizenship upon a negro," he argued, "but still I am not going to quarrel with Maine for differing from me in opinion. Let Maine take care of her own negroes . . . without interfering with Illinois, and Illinois will not interfere with Maine." Popular sovereignty guaranteed every territory the right to do as it pleased in local and domestic matters without interference from Congress. "Our fathers intended that our institutions should differ," Douglas insisted. "They knew that the North and the South having different climates, productions, and interests, required different institutions. This doctrine of Mr. Lincoln's of uniformity among the institutions of the different States is a new doctrine, never dreamed of by Washington, Madison, or the framers of this Government."[50]

Lincoln denied the charge, but the point raised an old conundrum that the new politics had yet to address: How could a nation endure as a nation without some elements of uniformity? Could national unity coexist with local differences when those differences involved fundamental principles? Other issues had evoked these questions, but none pierced their heart so directly as slavery. They harbored a deadly dilemma: How could slavery be treated as a local issue when to many Americans its existence contradicted the very essence of the principles on which the nation was founded? And how could the nation itself survive if slavery were treated as a national rather than a local issue?

Events of the 1850s had spawned a malignant growth on the body politic that separated its parts by drawing them together. Just as John Brown pushed the South into a unity unimagined even by ultras only a short time earlier, so did southern intransigence drive a divided North in the same direction toward the One Grand Unity of Politics: that of common opposition to a common foe. The election of 1860 revealed how far this malignancy had spread. The Democratic party gathered in, of all places, Charleston, the hotbed of secession sentiment, where sympathetic crowds cheered those standing fast against the expected nomination of Douglas. When the Douglas forces gained control of the convention, the delegations of eight states walked out. The Democrats reassembled in Baltimore and nominated Douglas; the southern Democrats met first in Richmond, then in Baltimore, where they nominated Vice President John C. Breckinridge. Remnants of the Whig and American parties joined the parade to Baltimore, created the Constitutional Union party, and chose John Bell of Tennessee as their candidate.

As the Republicans swept gleefully to victory, they left in their wake the old order of American politics. Certain hard facts marked the new order that could not be denied or ignored. The crude balance between the sections in 1850 had vanished. Data from the census of 1860 soon confirmed what the South already knew: It had become a permanent minority at a time when it believed its way of life, along with the institution that sustained it, was under savage attack. The national Democratic party had crumbled into ruins and could no longer serve as a power base for its protection. The South's hold on the federal government had been broken, never to be revived, and the party assuming power could only be viewed as its mortal enemy. Unity had come to the political order but in the lethal form of opposing sectional blocs.

The politics of compromise was yielding to the politics of confrontation, and knowledgeable observers shrank from the implications of this change. No one dreaded the prospect more than the tired, stooped old man who still had four more months to serve in the office that had become for him a prison. His friends and associates, whose ranks thinned almost daily, noticed anxiously how careworn and haggard he had grown in recent months despite his insistence that he never felt better or slept more soundly. But the wife of Virginia Representative Roger Pryor, standing quietly in the corner of the White House veranda where Buchanan sometimes sat in the afternoon, overheard him muttering to himself like an incantation, "Not in my time—not in my time."[51]

The Senators from South Carolina

We are an agricultural people; we are a primitive but a civilised people. We have no cities—we don't want them. We have no literature—we don't need any yet. We have no press—we are glad of it. We do not require a press, because we go out and discuss all public questions from the stump with our people. We have no commercial marine—no navy—we don't want them. We are better without them. Your ships carry our produce, and you can protect your own vessels. We want no manufactures: we desire no trading, no mechanical or manufacturing classes. As long as we have our rice, our sugar, our tobacco, and our cotton, we can command wealth to purchase all we want from those nations with which we are in amity, and to lay up money besides.

—Louis T. Wigfall[1]

NORTHERNERS CALLED THEM the "chivalry," a term southerners embraced with pride as fierce as the scorn with which it was usually delivered. The chivalry ruled the South, had always ruled it even before they fell prisoner to a self-invented mythology about who and what they were. Slavery lay at the bottom of it, as it did of so many things. Soon after 1830, when the South began to defend its peculiar institution from northern attacks, it started to concoct idyllic visions of slavery and plantation life. From these images arose an ideal of the planter himself and a full-blown fantasy of the South as a chivalric society grounded partly in the romantic fables of Sir Walter Scott and partly in the necessity of masking certain harsh realities about life in a slave society.[2]

The ideal of the planter as aristocrat reached back into the Virginia of the 1700s, to a wealthy gentry that presided over huge tobacco plantations with large numbers of slaves. From their way of life evolved the code of the gentleman, who commanded certain rights and privileges and in turn had obligations to his inferiors and to society as a whole. The gentleman was courteous, a man of truth and honor (if sometimes backsliding in matters of the flesh), learned in the classics, and proficient in the rituals of outdoor sport. Out of this tradition sprang the great line of Virginia presidents and statesmen, men of imposing intellect with a talent for leadership.[3]

The golden age of Virginia faded early in the nineteenth century as tobacco gave way to the "white gold" of cotton, the flow of great leaders slowed to a trickle, and the land petered out from overfarming. But the ideal lingered and was overlayered by a mania for the novels of Scott, five million copies of which rolled off American presses between 1813 and 1823. While the romantic age put the broader sentiments into the air, it was Scott's fables (especially *Ivanhoe*) that imprinted on the South an indelible image of medieval chivalry with all its pageantries and the convenient resemblance of a baronial manor surrounded by serfs to a plantation served by slaves.[4]

The cult of chivalry that flowed from these influences assumed many forms: cults of manners, of women, of the military, of oratory, of medieval pageantry, and of the code duello. Southern women were elevated to the highest of pedestals. "Our women are all conservative, moral, religious, and sensitively modest," proclaimed James De Bow, an indefatigable editor who started life trying to make southerners better farmers and businessmen and wound up exhorting them to be better southerners. "She lives only to make her home happy," added Daniel R. Hundley. "She literally knows nothing of 'woman's rights,' or 'free love,' or 'free thinking'; but faithfully labors on in the humble sphere allotted her of heaven."[5]

As sectional animosities deepened, the ranks of believers swelled until by the 1850s it seemed to many southerners as if chivalry had always been the polestar for their way of life. The civilization north of Mason and Dixon's line was crass and commercial, the lair of the "respectable citizen"; that below it boasted the flower of southern knighthood. "We are the most aristocratic people in the world," claimed De Bow. Even a rugged, cantankerous backwoodsman like Parson Brownlow of Tennessee, who differed with his brethren on most things, subscribed to the myth. "Ours is the land of chivalry," he rhapsodized, "the land of the muse, the abode of statesmen, the home of oratory, the dwelling-place of the historian, and of the hero."[6]

The South proved an ideal receptacle for the wave of romanticism that swept over the Western world early in the nineteenth century. Some attributed it to the climate, which one southerner called "a sort of cosmic conspiracy against reality in favor of romance." The sultry heat, blazing sunlight, extravagant colors, and intoxicating flowers produced a dreamy temperament, a wistful imagination that floated like the haze settling on the land at twilight. John A. Quitman, a Yankee who married into a large Natchez plantation, surrendered happily to this subversive influence. "It is an indolent, yet charming life," he told friends, "and one quits thinking and takes to dreaming."[7]

Like all agricultural people, southerners placed great emphasis on ties of kin and custom. The cult of chivalry elevated these to fantastic heights.

Hundley, a product of the Alabama planter class, was the first to codify the social structure of the South. He portrayed the southern gentleman as a man of aristocratic lineage, tall and with a graceful carriage born of an outdoor life spent largely on horseback. He lived in a grand style (often beyond his means), entertained lavishly, looked after his own, was "always hospitable, gentlemanly, courteous, and more anxious to please than to be pleased." He displayed the tastes and prejudices of his caste and had a natural dignity of manner that flowed from "his habitual use of authority from his earliest years."[8]

Above all, the southern gentleman wore his sense of honor like a badge and was quick to notice any stain upon it for himself, his womenfolk, and his kin. From this raw nerve of honor stemmed the notorious southern predilection for dueling. "The duel guarded personal honor, where the law was powerless to defend," explained Mrs. St. Julien Ravenel. A young South Carolinian agreed. "The matter of dueling is at first a fearful affair," he shrugged in December 1860. "But really it is not much moment. It is seldom fatal to either party." And if fight he must, "it were ten thousand times better that I die and be honorably buried, than that through me, cowardice and infamy should be ascribed to the family. If I die the reputation and honor of the family is sustained, yea! elevated."[9]

A sense of honor lay upon the southern gentleman, making him at once the most congenial and the most prickly of companions. Chivalry exaggerated the already heightened sense of self-importance born of aristocratic leanings. The habit of command came easily to planters, too easily in the opinions of those who saw in it the habit of dismissing others as inferiors. True believers insisted it was in the blood. "The Cavaliers, Jacobites, and Huguenots, who settled the South," said De Bow, "naturally hate, contemn, and despise the Puritans who settled the North. The former are a master-race—the latter a slave race, the descendants of Saxon serfs."[10]

De Bow conveniently overlooked how many descendants of those same Puritans had come south, but he understood one salient point that lay at the foundation of the cult of chivalry: Somehow it always came back to race. "Pride of caste and color, and privilege, makes every white man an aristocrat in feeling," he declared. On that point white southerners were unanimous. "No white man, in a slave-holding community is the menial servant of any one," observed Jefferson Davis. ". . . The distinction between classes . . . is a distinction of color." Journalist Frederick Law Olmsted, traveling through the South, saw this attitude everywhere. "It is this habit of considering themselves of a privileged class," he wrote, "and of disdaining something which they think beneath them, that is deemed to be the chief blessing of slavery."[11]

Long before Olmsted made his odyssey through the South—a journey not duplicated by any southerner venturing north who cared to leave a record of it—Tocqueville had grasped the tension underlying this air of superiority. Southerners, he noted, had "two powerful passions which will always keep them aloof: the first is the fear of being assimilated to the Negroes, their former slaves; and the second, the dread of sinking below the whites, their neighbors."[12]

NO MAN WAS MORE southern or more a gentleman than James Chesnut, Jr. The junior senator from South Carolina was the thirteenth child of parents with illustrious bloodlines. James Senior was one of the wealthiest planters at Camden, thanks to a father who had come there around 1756 and flourished as a merchant before becoming a planter. The grandfather had fought in the Revolution and bore proudly all his life the scars of shackles worn when the British took him prisoner; the grandmother had been a childhood friend of Nellie Custis and so a familiar sight in George Washington's household. Both generations had held a variety of public offices, leaving deep footsteps for James and his older brother John to follow.[13]

From earliest childhood his parents impressed on James what was expected of him. "Your position in life," wrote his father, "*demands* of you to be able to meet your contemporaries, on the great Theatre of Life, well prepared to sustain yourself, & the reputation of your Father & grandfather . . . it is the most sacred trust." An exalted position would be his "unless, by your own follies, you do something to forfeit the stand you will enjoy by inheritance & other circumstances." Young James was not in the least given to follies. Serious and earnest to a fault, he graduated from Princeton as his father had done and went in 1837 to study law with James L. Petigru in Charleston.[14]

During this stay in Charleston James renewed his interest in a pert dark-eyed girl named Mary Boykin Miller, whom he had met the previous summer. He was twenty-three, a tall, handsome, reserved gentleman of great wealth and promise; she was fourteen, the daughter of a former governor and a student at Madame Talvande's French School for Young Ladies. Her personality brimmed with charm and energy and a saucy intelligence that confounded and delighted him. James found her irresistible. Two years later they became secretly engaged before James left on a tour of Europe. In March 1840, three weeks after Mary turned seventeen, they were married and went to live with James's parents at Mulberry, the Chesnut plantation three miles south of Camden.

At Mulberry, Mary joined not only the senior Chesnuts, then in their sixties, but also James's two unmarried sisters in their late twenties. All of them regarded her as little more than a child. Growing up, Mary had always been the center of attention; now she found herself buried in the shadow of her formidable mother-in-law, Mary Cox Chesnut, who ran Mulberry with a brisk efficiency born of long years of practice. Strong-willed and partially invalided, she had borne fourteen children and buried ten of them. She regulated her life as carefully as she did her servants, deferring to her husband out of duty while matching his strength of will in her own way. No amount of suffering could unseat her mask of cheerfulness. She rarely criticized, and to those who breached decorum she was content to murmur, "Ah—you were not brought up at Bloomsbury," her father's estate on the Delaware River.[15]

Old Colonel Chesnut was an amiable man of courtly manners so long as he was not crossed. His elaborate courtesy and lavish hospitality masked a despotic temper fortified by a set of convictions never to be violated. He believed, among other things, that no woman in the family should wear a red dress, no horse should be driven beyond a slow trot, and no onion should ever defile his table. His wife had seized upon this last eccentricity to strike a bargain that long endured: She never served onions, and he never smoked in the house.

Amid these formidable personalities young Mary struggled to find her own place. She had been well trained in the complex duties of running a plantation, but in the presence of her mother-in-law she was little more than an appendage. Increasingly she retreated to her lovely front room on the third floor, where, from the deep window seats, she could gaze across the immaculate grounds surrounding the house. She had little to do and, in her own mind, never did anything well enough to suit her mother-in-law. "A pleasant, empty, easy going life," she wrote. "If ones heart is at ease. But people are not pigs; they cannot be put up and fattened. So here I pine and fret."[16]

Mary never learned how to cope with the older woman's way of killing her with kindness. To the latter's polite, solicitous ways Mary responded in kind or, losing her temper, with sarcasm or rudeness that required later apology. The old lady had a gift for making Mary feel inadequate, and on one sensitive point she could never satisfy her mother-in-law or herself. The prime directive of every southern wife was to provide children to carry on the family name; Mary did not have even one. Nothing gnawed at her more than this failure in a society where a married woman without children was seen as a rudderless ship. For comfort she read voraciously (as did her husband), went for long drives on which she could indulge herself by running the horses contrary to the colonel's decree, and sought outlets for her gregarious nature in local projects. For five years she endured this world of stifling order while James climbed the first rungs of a career in public service. She never forgot its petty humiliations.

They were an odd couple in many respects. James was tall and slim with a wide brow, dark eyes, high cheekbones, and a narrow jaw. He possessed his father's flawless manners and his mother's self-control, but lacked any hint of dash or spirit or warmth. He stood stiff as a rail and rarely dropped his formal manner. By contrast, Mary was short with a soft, plump figure. A broad nose convinced her that she was not beautiful, but high cheekbones, a full mouth, and soulful dark eyes that burst suddenly from introspection to vivacity, coupled with her wit and energy, made her attractive to men. She loved beautiful clothes but not the tedious ritual of dressing, and so bought elegant dresses and left the details of her toilette to her maid.

The couple delighted in exchanging books and views. Mary liked history and the great poets and essayists, but she loved the romantic writers. She had absorbed Chaucer, Shakespeare, Donne, Spenser, Swift, and Pope and doted on Wordsworth, Keats, Byron, Shelley, Coleridge, Burns, and, of course, Scott. Constant rereading enabled her to memorize and recite long passages from her favorites. Madame Talvande's school had given her fluency in French; she read Rabelais, Voltaire, Fontaine in their own language. She also read Schiller and Goethe in German, comparing the originals with translations in English and French. The library at Mulberry was extensive, though old Mrs. Chesnut kept novels she considered immoral under lock and key. Mary devoured novels, not only Dickens and Scott but also Austen, Fielding, Sand, Balzac, and Brontë.

At Mulberry Mary took up reading religious works as well. She loved the ritual of church and went regularly, while James avoided it whenever possible. He disliked most social gatherings, a curious flaw for a budding politician, and felt most comfortable in the company of family or horses. He seemed to need quiet as much as his wife craved excitement, and these opposing traits never ceased to puzzle them. His politics were as reserved and conservative as his temperament. He had principles and adhered to them, and he spoke well if without the fire that ignited crowds. James Hammond, who first got to know Chesnut at the Nashville Convention in 1850, found him "a very quiet and apparently unpretending man, but . . . quick and keen, with a strong turn for *management*. Being wealthy, of good family, and sound sense with a tolerably cultivated mind, . . . he would yet play an important part in public affairs."17

In 1848 James and Mary finally moved into their own house. Six years later they built another, more elegant house in a fashionable part of Camden so remote they named the place Kamchatka after the Siberian peninsula. The coming of the railroad to Camden in 1848 allowed Mary to flee the town's stifling provinciality for the pleasures of Columbia and Charleston. As James's career advanced, it dawned on Mary that politics offered an escape to that larger stage for which she had always yearned. But the bitterness born of those early years never left her. Late in life she admitted that "My experience does not coincide with the general idea of public life. . . . Peace, comfort, quiet, happiness I have found away from home. Only your own family, those nearest and dearest, can hurt you. Wrangling, rows, heart burnings, bitterness, envy, hatred, and malice, unbrotherly love, family snarls, neighborhood strife, and ill blood."[18]

The Nashville Convention marked the beginning of James's rise in politics. Delegates had been called to consider the compromise proposals, but only nine of the fifteen slave states sent representatives. James attended as one of what Mary called "the conservative and moderate wing of the southern rights party." At the convention Langdon Cheves of South Carolina issued a fervent call for southern unity that utterly ignored the existence of a black population. "Unite, and you shall form one of the most splendid empires in which the sun ever shone," he said, "one of the most homogeneous populations, all of the same blood and lineage."[19]

Cheves's plea went unheeded, but immediately after the convention Robert Barnwell Rhett issued the sort of secessionist pronunciamento that reminded everyone how deep the divisions ran in South Carolina politics. The death of Calhoun that same year widened the split into a chasm by removing his influence from the ambitions of an entire generation of restless politicians. James moved with greater ease than most within this vacuum because he seemed less hungry for advancement. Elected to the state senate in 1852, he became its president four years later. Mary rejoiced at his rising popularity. The Nashville Convention had stirred her own interest in politics, which she began to discuss with James as intensely as she did literature. A proud but not compliant mate, she disagreed with him freely on many subjects, including slavery. Having grown up with slavery as an inseparable part of their world, they believed it a duty to treat their slaves humanely and shrank from its worst excesses. James had bought a slave only once, and that at the slave's own request to avoid breaking up a family.[20]

But Mary harbored more doubts about the institution than James ever did, and confessed to being "not the *hearty* lover of slavery this latitude requires." Black people were to her "dirty—slatternly—idle—ill smelling by nature," but they *were* people, and it baffled her how men who boasted of personal honor could own them. Mary had taught slaves and been taught by them as a child. She had grown fond of servants and certainly enjoyed being waited on. At Mulberry and elsewhere she had seen the best of slavery, but a deeper, more personal resentment toward the worst of it tugged at her. "I wonder if it be a sin to think slavery a curse to any land," she wrote in her journal. "Sumner said not one word of this hated institution which is not true. Men & women are punished when their master & mistresses are brutes & not when they do wrong. . . . God forgive *us*, but ours is a *monstrous* system & wrong & iniquity." In her sorrow Mary saw the most monstrous wrong of all:

> We live surrounded by prostitutes. An abandoned woman is sent out of any decent house elsewhere. Who thinks worse of a Negro or Mulatto woman for being a thing we can't name. . . . This *only* I see: like the patriarchs of old our men live all in one house with their wives & their concubines, & the Mulattoes one sees in every family exactly resemble the white children—& every lady tells you who is the father of all the Mulatto children in everybody's household, but those in her own, she seems to think drop from the clouds or pretends so to think. . . . My disgust sometimes is boiling over.[21]

It enraged Mary because she had seen it first hand—not with her beloved James, who apparently did not consort with slave girls, but with his father, the proud old colonel. Mary's mother-in-law had warned her soon after the wedding not to send female servants into the streets on errands because they were easily led astray. "So they told *me* when I came here," she added placidly. ". . . I was very particular, *but you see with what result.*" The irony of that remark galled Mary. Did the old woman not know the obvious source of some of the mulatto children in her own yard, or did she simply refuse to know?

In Mary's mind the hideousness of it all got thoroughly mixed with her own predicament. One day she awoke nervous and miserable from having had a tooth pulled the day before and from the news that her second cousin had become engaged to a man twice widowed with ten children. She had argued long into the night with a sister-in-law and gone to bed exhausted and embittered. On this day when she already felt so wretched, Mrs. Chesnut chose to boast proudly of her twenty-seven grandchildren. Mary winced in pain as the old colonel replied to his wife, "*You* have not been a *useless* woman in this world."[22]

Mary bore the slight in silence but wrote afterward in her diary, "God help me—no good have I done—to myself or any one else—with the [power] I boast so of—the power to make myself loved. Where am I now. Where are my friends. I am allowed to have none." In her misery she seized not only on what the colonel had said but on the ultimate hypocrisy he represented and scrawled fiercely, *"He did not count his children!!!"*

The escape Mary had long sought came in 1858, when the legislature elected James to the U.S. Senate. Here at last was the larger stage she craved for herself as well as her husband—but it came at a price. They needed money to live six years in Washington; the Chesnuts were wealthy, but the old colonel kept everything in his own hands and allowed James to live on his law practice and an allowance from him. Reluctantly James and Mary decided to sell Kamchatka and disperse the servants to Chesnut plantations except for a few who were hired out to the Camden Hotel. Mary fortified her wardrobe, and the Chesnuts departed for the City of Politics, where they joined the "southern mess" at Brown's Hotel on Pennsylvania Avenue.

As James scaled the political ladder, Mary had come to identify her own worth with his success. In Washington, however, she soon earned a reputation of her own as a sparkling conversationalist and "literary" lady. Her fluency in French and German led many to believe she had been educated abroad and brought invitations to affairs for foreign dignitaries. At one dinner she sat between a Spanish visitor and President Buchanan in order to speak French with the Spaniard and translate for the president. When she fell into extended conversation with the visitor, Buchanan protested that he was being shut out. She took charge of James's social obligations, to his great relief, and grappled with his dislike of parties and other functions. Sometimes she won and he attended; other times he balked and embarrassed her with his absence. In a town where gossip and scandal were mother's milk, James's need for privacy had at least one advantage: His morals were deemed as impeccable as his manner was dull. Socialite Rose O'Neal Greenhow once joked that scandal never attached to James's name because he never spoke to a woman.

In Washington, Mary spun a wide web of new friendships. For years she had known Harriet Lane, the president's niece who served as White House hostess. Now she grew close to Charlotte Wigfall, the wife of the Texas senator; the bright, clever Virginia Clay, whose husband, Clement, was a senator from Alabama; and the young wife of Mississippi Senator Jefferson Davis, Varina Howell Davis. She renewed the Chesnuts' ties with the Custis and Washington families by growing close to the invalided Mary Custis Lee, whose husband Robert was a colonel in the army, and to her sons, Custis and Rooney. That nearly all her new friends were southerners did not strike her as odd; her social connections merely followed the fault lines laid down by the sectional conflict.

Weary of hotel life, the Chesnuts moved in January 1860 to a house at Tenth and H streets. James welcomed a refuge from the social rituals of the southern mess at Brown's; Mary relished the new setting because it allowed her to entertain. She promptly hired a Frenchwoman as cook. John Manning, the former governor of South Carolina and friendly political rival of James's, dined with the Chesnuts one evening and reported to his wife that he had received "a very plain but nice dinner, Julien soup fish tenderloin of beef and mushrooms & veal larded with vegetables & green peas & salad. Ice cream & champaign & Madeira as concomitants."[23]

The handsome, dashing Manning, one of South Carolina's richest men, was fascinated by Mary even if he didn't know what to make of her. To his wife he described her as a talkative name-dropper, "full of gossip on the inside and of unneatness on the outside," whose quick tongue gave "her husband sharp hits in a quite unprovoked way." Whatever names Mary dropped were genuine, for she had grown intimate with the upper strata of Washington society in a remarkably short time. On vacations or trips to meet relatives she collected other prominent acquaintances. Once in New Jersey she met the imposing general of the army Winfield Scott and stoutly argued with him the South's right to secede. "I know your little South Carolina," answered Scott when she had finished. "I lived there once. It is about as big as Long Island—and two thirds of the population are negroes—Are you mad?"[24]

During the summer of 1860 the Chesnuts traveled, enabling James to avoid the worsening political turmoil in South Carolina. While the fall election campaign raged, Mary went south to visit her family. After two weeks with her sister Kate in remote Florida, she returned to Charleston, aware that events were pushing her life toward great and ominous changes. On the train she had learned of Lincoln's election, which would force James to make an agonizing decision about his future. But she too had decisions to make. For all her recent triumphs, twenty years of marriage—and no children—still had not provided enough outlets for her passionate, dynamic nature. She was thirty-seven years old; what else did life hold for her?

WEALTH AND STATUS could be inherited, or they could be acquired. What James Chesnut received at birth, his Senate colleague James Henry Hammond had to pursue by his own wits. A shrewd, calculating man forever at war with his own overpowering desires, he chose the route most favored by ambitious southerners: He married a rich wife.

It was for him a natural, even logical choice. Hammond began life not so much poor as hungry for advancement. Born in 1807 in the uplands of South Carolina, he was the son of a farmer and merchant with roots in Massachusetts who had married a South Carolina woman of good family. The elder Hammond struggled all his life, waiting in vain for his wife to receive a gift from her wealthy uncle. So desperate was he for the inheritance that he overlooked the uncle's repeated attempts to seduce his daughters, a fact the father later confided ruefully to young James. It was a lesson James never forgot.[25]

At South Carolina College, James rubbed elbows with the chivalry and spent more time on "women, wine, and cigars" than on studies. His brush with aristocracy ended abruptly upon his graduation in 1825, when he felt obliged to take a teaching job. He soon turned to the law and supported his studies by writing for a newspaper. After being admitted to the bar in 1828, he moved to Columbia and built up a lucrative practice just as the nullification crisis was unfolding. Hammond jumped onto the nullification bandwagon and founded a newspaper to support the cause. These efforts drew the attention of prominent politicians in the state rights party, but he still lacked the social credentials requisite to real political advancement. For that he needed the coin of the realm, land and slaves, and to get them he needed a rich wife.[26]

Hammond heeded well the admonition of his close college friend Thomas Jefferson Withers that "we cannot be independent without money." Like Chesnut, Hammond was a tall, handsome man, somewhat cold of manner but capable of great charm and with a flicker of licentiousness in his smile utterly lacking in Chesnut. The daughter of a close friend said he looked like "a reincarnation of some Greek demigod. His cold and chiseled classic beauty; his statuesque form and stately poise were antique in impressiveness." In 1829 the demigod began courting a shy young woman of fifteen named Catherine FitzSimons, who was so plain that some Charleston wags claimed they wouldn't marry her "if every pimple on her face was worth a million dollars." Hammond determined to give them no chance to change their minds. It was not love but lust for status that moved him. Four years earlier, Catherine's father had died and left her one of his plantations with more than ten thousand acres and a hundred slaves. The crown jewels of South Carolina society for any man were politics and planting. Hammond had already insinuated his way into the one; Catherine offered him access to the other.[27]

Catherine's mother and older brother Paul considered Hammond a fortune hunter and opposed his suit, but they were helpless against his charm and persistence. During the spring of 1831 Hammond realized his two fondest ambitions. The great John C. Calhoun sought his counsel on political matters, thereby conferring on him tangible evidence of his status as a rising star, and Catherine FitzSimons became his wife. Paul FitzSimons refused to attend the wedding and, as his sister's trustee, fought Hammond for control of her property. He lost after a bitter struggle. Hammond had won his toehold in society, if not the love of his new in-laws.

"But what occupation more noble than Agriculture," Hammond later observed. He left the newspaper, closed his law practice, and moved to his new plantation in the Barnwell District. Silver Bluff sat above a bend in the Savannah River in a remote corner of South Carolina thirty miles via the meandering river from Augusta, Georgia. Hammond was distressed to find the property so run-down; Catherine's brothers had left it in the hands of an indolent overseer who had cleared only 967 of its 10,800 acres for crops. The tracts near the river were malarial bogs; those on the plateau, woods of red clay soil through which the livestock ran untended. The house was dreary and filled with crude furniture, much of it broken, but there was a sawmill, a gristmill, a gin house, a blacksmith's shop, a carpenter's shop, and quarters for the 147 slaves.

Above all, there was promise. Eager to earn his niche as a planter, Hammond threw himself into the work of making Silver Bluff not only profitable but a model plantation. The slaves posed the first problem. Grown accustomed to life without a resident master, they were wary of any intrusion into their own intricate social order. Hammond realized that to replace that order with one of his own design, he had to break their will and then bond them into a large family with himself at the head. What he could never reconcile in all his plans was an inherent contradiction: He desperately wanted the slaves not only to accept his domination but also to love him.

The slaves tested him early. Hammond responded by flogging those who violated rules, neglected their work, or challenged his authority. He was careful to deliver the whippings in the presence of other slaves to impress his authority upon them. When eight slaves, who had been punished by the overseer for resuming work too slowly after Christmas, pleaded for mercy to Hammond, he ordered them flogged again. There could be no mercy until everyone accepted his power fully; that required claiming their souls as well as their bodies. "Intend to break up negro preaching & negro churches," he vowed in his diary. He wished the slaves to be good Christians, but under white supervision and following a Gospel that did not include resistance or rebellion.[28]

The slaves preferred the task system, which gave them free time once their assigned work was completed. Hammond replaced it with the gang system under the watchful eye of an overseer. He regulated the slaves' diet and tried to improve their hygiene and health habits to ward off sickness and the appalling infant mortality rate that claimed 72 percent of slave children before the age of five during Hammond's first decade at Silver Bluff. Plantation medicine became an obsession that led him through a labyrinth of fads and superstitions in his dogged quest to improve conditions. Gradually the birthrate, helped in part by Hammond's continual purchase of new slaves, overtook the death rate.

Part of the master plan involved building strong, stable family ties among the slaves. The law might not recognize marriage between slaves, but Hammond did. He officiated at weddings, made it a point never to separate families by sales, and willingly accepted old or disabled slaves as part of a family package when buying new workers. He gave permission for marriages, presided over divorces or infidelity cases, and whipped those convicted of adultery or other disruptive behavior. On one occasion he reluctantly whipped a slave named Tom Kollock, who had never before been flogged. "Gave him 30 with my own hand," he noted tersely, "[for] interfering with Maggy Campbell, Sullivan's wife."[29]

But who punished the judge or his people? Hammond's meticulous records listed 22 percent of newborn slave children as having no father. Some were categorized simply as "mulatto," and one was fathered by a white stable hand who had been fired for drunkenness. The name that never appeared was Hammond's own; his rage for order did not extend that far. In 1838 he paid $900 for a seamstress named Sally Johnson and her daughter, Louisa. Both became household servants, and in time both became Hammond's mistresses. Children were born to Louisa that she claimed were his, but Hammond was not so sure. Catherine knew nothing of these affairs for a long time, just as she remained ignorant of the "situation" with the Hampton girls.

Gradually Hammond realized that force alone could not break the slaves' resistance or mold them into an efficient work force. He shifted to more subtle methods, introduced rewards to complement punishments, and even compromised on the task versus gang labor system. He struggled to control theft, then reconciled himself to certain losses, such as the potato crop, which vanished every year before it was harvested. He found some solace in the fact that none of the fifty-three escape attempts between 1831 and 1855 succeeded, largely because the isolation of Silver Bluff made flight difficult.

The rise of abolitionism filled Hammond with dismay because it seemed impossible to prevent word of the doctrine from spreading among the slaves. "I fancy . . . there is a growing spirit of insubordination among the slaves in this section," he complained in 1844. "In the lower part of this district they have fired several houses recently. This is fearful—horrible." Yet he made no effort to prevent his slaves from learning how to read. "These people may or may not read the Tribune &c.," he told a friend, "I have never enquired." Gradually Hammond accepted the inevitable truth that he was as much a prisoner of his slaves as they were of him. The more he refined his methods of domination and control, the more elaborately they bound him as well as the slaves. In the end he could control neither them nor his own voracious emotional needs. When he sought consolation in the belief that "my negroes . . . love & *appreciate* me," he was taking refuge behind a wall of self-deception.[30]

Hammond was a man perpetually in conflict with himself as well as others. He was difficult and argumentative, always on the attack, and critical in a cold, clinical way. Yet he whined privately that the "world judging by appearances my bearing & conversation have been wholly deceived in my character." In his own eyes he was a "shy & sensitive person. . . . The very excess of my sensitiveness has led me to assume . . . the reverse in order to conceal it." He longed for personal contact yet could not bear to reveal his emotions, hungered for an intimacy of feeling with others that he was himself utterly incapable of giving. He could not harmonize these two sides of himself any more than he could bring together his personal and public lives. Of one thing he was certain: His wife never understood these deeper cravings in him and could not satisfy them.[31]

His public career underwent the same perambulations as his emotions. While struggling to transform Silver Bluff, Hammond was elected to Congress in 1834. There he reiterated his defense of slavery, but after two years in office his health failed, and he fled for relief to Europe. He traveled for more than a year, then came home to Silver Bluff and spurned all lures to reenter public life until 1839, when the old restlessness and emotional cravings seized him again. Unable to bear the isolation, he took Catherine to Columbia in 1841, built an expensive house for entertaining, and renewed contact with his network of political friends.

Ironically, Hammond found the soul mate he sought not in Columbia but on a plantation only fifty miles from Silver Bluff. The tall, portly William Gilmore Simms, with a gruff manner and an imposing head crowned with curls, was in the opinion of some the South's finest writer. Hammond found him an ideal companion, a raconteur full of talk and ideas and joviality enough to lift the most drooping spirit from its doldrums. Simms shared beliefs with Hammond as well as a darker, introspective side that bitterly resented how little the South appreciated or even noticed his particular genius. Hammond regarded his corner of South Carolina as an intellectual dead zone; Simms extended that view to the entire South.

There were other similarities. Simms too had had an unsettled and

unsettling childhood, losing his mother to childbirth and his father to bankruptcy. He had studied law and gained admission to the bar before abandoning it for a literary career. In 1836 he married his second wife and took
over her father's Barnwell plantation, Woodlands, where he spent the rest
of his life. Unlike Hammond, however, he fared poorly as a planter and
struggled constantly to make ends meet. Nothing galled him more than his
inability to earn a living as a writer, and no one shared his sense of disappointment more fully than Hammond. Late in life Simms called Hammond
"my most confidential friend for near twenty-five years. Never were thoughts
more intimate than his and mine."[32]

Simms also had political aspirations. His broader experience opened
Hammond's eyes to a larger intellectual and political realm and with it a more
exalted vision of his own stature. Hammond soon dismissed most of his new
Columbia neighbors as bores whose minds seldom strayed from drinking,
smoking, and playing backgammon. But his presence in the capital boosted
his political prospects. Although he lost a bid for the governorship in 1840,
he cemented his place in the first rank of leaders. In 1841 he was appointed
general of the militia and the director of a state bank branch and was invited
to become a trustee of South Carolina College. Nevertheless, politics left him
as unsettled as did the rest of life; he loved its enticements but loathed its
fickle character. The loss in 1840 wounded and embittered him deeply.
"Political honors," he told Simms, "are the most ephemeral of all earthly distinctions." Then his friends and even his enemies, the faction led by Robert
Barnwell Rhett, let it be known that they would not oppose him in 1842. Victory was his at last.[33]

Ensconced in the governor's chair, resplendent in the gaudy uniform of
office, Hammond basked in what was largely a ceremonial post even as he
tried to surmount its limitations. His efforts at agricultural reform drew him
close to Edmund Ruffin, the eccentric Virginian who had accepted a post as
surveyor in South Carolina. Ruffin too felt unappreciated in his native state
and welcomed the friendship of one who shared his views that southern agriculture was in urgent need of reform. Hammond hoped to use his office to
spur change there and in other areas. He expected opposition to arise, and it
did; what he did not anticipate was the devastating blow dealt his ambitions
by the darker side of his own conflicted nature. The most shameful secret
of that nature, his relationship with the Hampton girls, was seeping to the
surface.

Wade Hampton II, one of South Carolina's richest and most powerful
planters, had married a sister of Catherine FitzSimons. He had opposed the
latter's marriage to Hammond and also Hammond's election to Congress.
Diligent efforts by Hammond gradually eased the strain between them.

Hampton accepted business advice from Hammond but maintained an air of superiority that Hammond viewed as mere jealousy. After Hammond had moved to Columbia, he noted gleefully that Hampton "threw away $30,000 to make his house [Millwood] finer than mine. And he was galled . . . that . . . I beat them in *their own line*, furniture, balls, dinner parties."[34]

The children did not share these tensions. Young Wade Hampton III loved to visit his cousins at Silver Bluff, as did his sisters. In Columbia the four older girls became frequent visitors to their uncle's house. Harriet was nineteen, Catherine seventeen, Ann fifteen, and Caroline fourteen. Hammond was thirty-three when his relationship with the sisters took a bizarre and erotic turn. Their loose ways and lack of restraint in showing affection startled him; they lavished kisses and embraces in a way that went beyond family. Harriet was the first to seek out and encourage his attentions, and the others soon followed. Hammond described what happened:

> Here were four lovely creatures . . . each contending for my love, claiming the greater share of it as due to her superior devotion to me, all of them rushing on every occasion into my arms and covering me with kisses, lolling on my lap, pressing their bodies almost into mine, wreathing their limbs into mine, encountering warmly every portion of my frame, and permitting my hands to stray unchecked over every part of them and to rest without the slightest shrinking from it, in the most secret and sacred regions, and all this for a period of more than two years continuously.[35]

Overwhelmed with shame and delight, Hammond found himself acting out an erotic fantasy that tapped the deepest wellsprings of his repressed feelings. One or more of the girls came to his house every week seeking these newfound pleasures. Hammond could neither curb his kissing and groping nor carry it to the final act of intercourse. He condemned his behavior but found some solace in making this stand. "Is it in flesh and blood to withstand this?" he moaned. "Is there a man, with manhood in him . . . who could tear himself from such a cluster of lovely, loving, such amorous and devoted beings? Nay are there many who would have the self-control to stop where I did? Am I not after all entitled to some, the smallest portion of, credit for not going further?"

For two years, even after becoming governor, Hammond indulged these appetites that had been so long starved—not only sexual but those of a lonely man craving attention and affection. Then, in April 1843, Catherine Hampton abruptly rebuffed him in one of the acts that had become so commonplace between them. Alarmed by her change in attitude, he stopped his intimacies with all the girls. For eight weeks relations between them remained as cordial and frequent as if nothing had occurred. Hammond, persuaded that nothing more would come of his past indiscretions, took his family to Silver Bluff for the summer. Certainly the girls would say nothing, lest they ruin their own reputations and chances for a good marriage.

What happened next is unclear. Someone, possibly Catherine herself, told her father about the episode of April 1843. On November 1, Hampton wrote Hammond denouncing his behavior and severing relations between the families. Hammond asked a mutual friend, John Preston, to intervene, but Preston refused, remarking tersely that "atonement and oblivion were impossible." Hammond thought Hampton might challenge him and made himself available, but no challenge came. Instead, rumors of their split seeped insidiously through Columbia society, poisoning minds against Hammond without revealing the cause, hinting that he had fled Columbia that summer to avoid the repercussions of some heinous act.

A peculiar standoff ensued. Hampton could do nothing overt without revealing details (if he even knew them) that would disgrace his own family, nor was it wise to threaten a governor. Hammond could not counter the rumors of a gross indiscretion without revealing the awful truth to his wife, who remained so oblivious to the situation that she dispatched invitations for the governor's ball to the usual members of the family and was mystified when the Hamptons and their set did not attend. In desperation, Hammond wrote Hampton a frank account of his dalliances with all the daughters, hoping this would prompt Hampton to probe the matter more deeply. Hampton did not respond.

What kind of man was this? Hammond wondered. He agonized through the legislative session, then took his family back to Silver Bluff the day after Christmas. By then it was clear to him that Hampton posed no immediate threat but rather intended some slow, tortuous revenge, a "low and cowardly malignity . . . to black ball me and to mortify me and mine by keeping us out of Society and all respectable persons from coming to our House."

And politically as well. Hammond's incisive, logical mind was helpless against Hampton's waiting game. He closed out his gubernatorial term with a succession of minor blunders and disappointments and returned to Silver Bluff for what turned into a thirteen-year exile from public life. In December 1846, when the legislature seemed on the verge of electing Hammond to the U.S. Senate, Hampton made his move. Privately he offered to show Hammond's friends and foes alike certain documents he said would ruin him forever. Hammond was thunderstruck that Hampton would destroy the reputations of his own daughters to thwart him politically, but he could do nothing. Only a few legislators deigned to examine the documents, but Hampton swayed enough votes to block Hammond's election. Convinced that his public career had ended, a disconsolate Hammond retired from politics.[36]

Who had undermined him? In the byzantine maze of South Carolina politics with its ever-shifting alliances, Hammond pointed the finger less at Hampton than at the latter's brothers-in-law John Manning and John Preston. Hampton, he suspected, was "the dupe and victim of Manning and Preston, who would destroy him and his to prostrate me." Whether true or not, everyone lost in the end. The four Hampton girls were stigmatized for life and never married. As one young bachelor observed, "after all the fuss made no man who valued his standing could marry one of the Hampton girls." Hammond mourned their ostracism. "I feel no joy but the sincerest remorse to have had any hand in blasting these girls whom I still love," he said, but he too had been blasted. His public career was in ruins, and his private life in tatters.

"The public is still burning with curiosity to know all about the Hampton affair, and is disposed to taunt us both in order to get it," Hammond noted in November 1850. He maintained his pose of official retirement and in rare moments even believed it himself. A month later, confronted by a fresh disaster, he admitted to being "utterly broken down and prostrated forever. The Hamptons and all my enemies triumph over me." Despite his efforts, Catherine had found out about the episode and had since watched him closely. Then, having barely absorbed the horror of the Hampton girls, Catherine uncovered his relationship with Sally and Louisa Johnson. It was for her a crushing blow. She demanded that the women be sold, and when Hammond refused, she left for Charleston with their two young daughters to stay with relatives. Her absence stretched into weeks, then months, and finally years.[37]

"*Fate* so willed it that I was caught at last—as I always am," Hammond whined. His mood fleeted from self-pity to self-flagellation to shrewd insight into himself and the fickle, feckless world about him. "The great craving of my nature is for the beautiful—both the ideal and the real," he mused. ". . . My love has been either lustful or purely platonic." His wife loved him, he was certain of that, and she had "unbounded admiration of my intellect, though unable to appreciate and comprehend its range. A purer, more high minded and devoted woman never lived." He loved her no less even though she (and others) never fathomed the sacrifices he had made for her. "I have surrendered my heart if not to her—*for* her, again and again. I have extinguished its emotions and cauterized their sources."[38]

His heart ached with sorrow, and his blood boiled at the humiliating exile forced upon him by Catherine and his enemies. It was as if they had schemed together, though in his innermost heart he knew the real blame lay with himself. To these woes was added the sudden death of his son Willie from typhoid in the winter of 1851–52. Not even this tragedy brought Catherine back. Friends asked for explanations of the separation that he could not provide. He found himself shunned at resorts and realized that the FitzSimons family, whose animosity he had labored so hard to overcome, was spreading the news of his domestic crisis. Catherine rebuffed his overtures of reconciliation because he would not accept her terms, which included selling the Johnson women. "Nothing will satisfy," he wrote his brother, "but that I shall surrender captive & be a *pardoned convict.* . . . This is too much."[39]

From afar he followed the twisting vagaries of state politics. Appointed one of four delegates to the Nashville Convention in June 1850, he worked hard behind the scenes only to have Rhett and Langdon Cheves upstage him by coming out vociferously for disunion. Disgruntled, Hammond refused even to attend a second session in November. "I have, for near or quite twenty years, been in favour of disunion and believed it inevitable," he noted privately. "But no state save our own is ready to go to such lengths." The death that year of Calhoun and Franklin Elmore, who had replaced him in the Senate, raised in Hammond a faint hope that he might get the seat, but Rhett defeated him. "My career as a public man is over," he wailed, "I am crushed—*annihilated forever.*"[40]

In the solitude of Silver Bluff his life seemed utterly in shambles. He had quarreled with his dearest brother, Marcellus, who had married a wealthy Georgian and, after a failed military career, planted cotton on his wife's plantation, where he distinguished himself chiefly as a prodigious if amiable drunk. Hammond did not like his youngest brother John, an army surgeon whom he once called the "most disagreeable man" in the service. When his sister Caroline married an itinerant Bible salesman, Hammond indignantly severed relations with her, and he did not bother attending her funeral when she died suddenly two years later. There had been continual trouble with his third son, Edward Spann, that peaked in 1855 when Spann became engaged to a second cousin. Hammond learned that the young lady's dowry was encumbered and peremptorily broke off the engagement.[41]

Since his father's death in 1829 Hammond had ruled his family like a tyrant. He had an obsessive need to control not only his slaves but everyone around him. His mother, who lived with him until her death in 1864, submitted meekly to his rule, as did Catherine except for her rebellion during these years. His brothers and sister, and his children, groaned beneath the yoke of demands they could never satisfy. Brother John called it a "dreadful burden" and protested being treated like "a son disowned." Half a century after the event Spann mourned his broken engagement as "the blow that . . . left an anguish in which a life-time is comprised."⁴²

What Hammond called the crisis in his fate loomed much larger than politics. The man with an overpowering need to control had lost control of nearly everything in his life. "It is a coarse and vulgar era," he complained, "in which exposures of all kinds are the rage. . . . So much for democracy and so much also for bringing men's private or rather *secret* lives into public affairs." He had lost all social as well as political standing. "All the women, and the nice men shun me. . . . Can a man do anything more on earth, who is driven from the field of politics and black-balled by Society?"⁴³

Still, Hammond persisted. He roamed the state giving talks on agricultural or political topics, keeping alive in the thoughts of others a reminder that whatever else they thought of him, he had the mind and manner of a statesman. At a hotel in Aiken he endured the snub of old friends who never called on him and the polite diffidence of those on whom he called. "God is Love," he scribbled bleakly early in 1854. "Ah—if you are wise never *love* anything or any body in this world." The penalty for his sins seemed to him almost biblical in its crushing totality. He gained fifty pounds between 1850 and 1853. Yet even in his despair he felt pride when his eldest sons, Harry and Spann, graduated from the medical school at the University of Pennsylvania (though he probably did not reveal these feelings to them), and he never ceased trying to repair the breach in his family life.⁴⁴

Slowly, painfully, he mended his relationship with Catherine. She rented a house in Aiken, then moved to one in Augusta. There were visits back and forth until at last she relented in the spring of 1855. A relieved Hammond bought a house named Redcliffe on nearby Beech Island and moved there with Catherine while erecting a larger, more elegant mansion. The terms of their reconciliation remained as secret as the cause of their separation, but they did not include selling Sally and Louisa Johnson, who stayed at Silver Bluff in the field quarters far from the main house. Hammond looked after them and made careful provision for the boy Louisa said was his son, binding him as an apprentice to a German grape grower.⁴⁵

Hammond took care of his own even when they were black, but always within the bounds of the slave system in which he believed ardently. It was, after all, one more system of control, worth the unceasing struggle it entailed. But he had failed to control himself or his children, who resembled the spoiled offspring of other planters in taking for granted their access to money and power over others. "Boys fit for nothing but to spend money," Hammond lamented in 1858, and strife always marred his relationship with them.

His younger sons he dismissed as "dead weights" who "growl, grumble, sulk and do nothing. . . . All the negroes see they are mere dilettanti—theatrical planters."[46]

With his wife returned and a new house going up, Hammond seemed to have been reborn. Reconciled to her fate, Catherine never again revolted against the role of dutiful wife. But the deeper wounds within the family did not heal. On this matter Catherine for once had the last word. "With every thing to make us happy," she murmured, "there are few families that are less so."[47]

To Hammond's surprise and delight, his political career rose unexpectedly from the dead as well. Since Calhoun's death factionalism had devoured South Carolina politics, causing alliances to shift abruptly and leaving deep scars between former friends. Hammond's enforced absence proved a blessing because his reputation as a statesman lingered and he had offended no one recently. As one observer noted wryly, "Hammond is a big gun in this country from not having been fired off at any time since the Revolution." Wade Hampton never forgave him, but he moved to Mississippi, and slowly the stain of scandal faded. "I have never been disposed to believe," said the former congressman Waddy Thompson, "that anything really bad could be concealed under that beautiful face."[48]

When Senator A. P. Butler died in 1857, Hammond's friends in Columbia got him elected to the seat. It was, he admitted, "the strangest and most unexpected chapter of my history." The following January he took Catherine, his son Paul, and daughters Cattie and Bettie to Washington. They moved into Brown's Hotel and were quickly showered with invitations from all sides, having had the good fortune to arrive in a season of what one hostess called "reckless gaiety." While Catherine struggled to master the social amenities, Hammond reveled in striding that grander social stage that had so long eluded him. Not to be undone in the race of entertaining, he sent home for Carolina wine and delicacies from Redcliffe to adorn his table.[49]

The political scene was more distasteful. In society Hammond mixed easily with the men he fought in the political arena, but he held a low opinion of them. To his imperious eyes the majority were "mere sharp shooters, County Court lawyers, and newspaper politicians." He said not a word in the Senate until March 4, 1858, when in reply to a speech by William Seward on Kansas statehood he delivered his ringing "Cotton *is* King" declamation. He came home in June and, in a speech at a dinner tendered him by Beech Island neighbors, unveiled a new conservatism. The Union, he declared, "will not be dissolved by the *first* election of a Black Republican President." This remark caused such an uproar that he later repudiated the sentiment.[50]

Ultras protested with some justice that Hammond was abandoning the

gospel of state rights. "For 15 or 20 of the best years of my life I was a dis-
unionist," he observed privately. ". . . But latterly I have changed my
opinion." He had chosen to assume the long-discarded mantle of Calhoun
and mediate the gap between the state and Washington. The irony was delicious. After decades of trying vainly to move the South toward secession, he
now sought to slow the process just as it seemed finally to be gaining
momentum. But events worked against him, as they had before. John
Brown's raid cut the ground out from any moderate stance.[51]

Overwhelmed by the savage debate that ensued in Congress, Hammond
could find no middle way. Ultras at home pounced on his "soft" position and
demanded that he state what he would do in the event of a Republican victory. His efforts to extricate himself only made matters worse. So confused
did things become that in October 1860 Hammond felt obliged to draft a
position statement to bolster his chances for winning election to a full term.
He dispatched it to the state capital two days after Lincoln's election, which
posed a much more immediate threat to his remaining in Washington.[52]

Suddenly the question that had for so long seemed theoretical became a
hard choice for both Hammond and Chesnut. With that finely honed intelligence that harbored such contempt for lesser minds and meaner motives,
and was capable of exerting such powerful influence over so many things
except his own hungers, Hammond saw that fate had played yet another
trick. Once again the prospect of redemption and triumph was to be
snatched from him.

"It is a very great misfortune to be too keen and clear sighted," he had
observed in the depths of his exile. "All Happiness in this world is a delusion. The greatest source of it is self-delusion."[53]

CHAPTER FIVE

A Tale of Three Cities

There exists a great mistake . . . in supposing that the people of the United States are, or ever have been, one people. On the contrary, never did the sun shine on two peoples as thoroughly distinct as the people of the North and . . . South. . . . Like all great nations of antiquity we are slaveholders and understand free governments. The North does not. They are a people wrapped up in selfishness. They have no idea of free government. Their idea of free government is this, that when three men get together, the two are to rule the one; when five men get together, the three are to rule the other two . . .

—Robert Barnwell Rhett
November 10, 1860[1]

CHARLESTON WAS A CITY of intoxicating contrasts. The scent of its omnipresent flowers vied for attention with the stench from sewers that lay below water level because the city was built so low. A harsh, brilliant sun splashed the city with a shifting geometry of light and shadow, accented by day with an occasional gauze of cloud and by night with an inklike stain of blue-black. Sunshine gleamed on the surface of brightly painted plaster softened by salt air, and on brick colored and weathered by time. Strong winds choked the air with dust from its sandy streets, and clouds imposed a melancholy mood. Young James Chesnut once called it a "City of arrogance and gloom."[2]

Its buildings were a jumble of all the ages it admired. St. Michael's Church, the best-known and most imposing structure, was a model of classical simplicity. In 1764 it received from London bells that still tolled over the city and a four-sided clock for the steeple that lacked a minute hand until 1849. Imitation Greek temples like the Huguenot Church mingled with Georgian structures such as the City Hall, a smattering of Adam grandeur, the pleasantly nondescript courthouse, and the sturdy Fireproof Building panned by one visitor as "about as eccentric a freak of architecture as you will see or hear of anywhere between this and the Middle Ages."[3]

It was a city of seasons, socially dormant from the spring rains in June until the first frost in the fall ended the fever season. In the summer families fled to the shore or upcountry springs or summer places on Sullivans Island to escape the heat and fever. All the city's charms could not conceal what Olmsted labeled "the worst climate for unacclimated whites of any town in the United States." When an epidemic of yellow fever claimed seven hundred lives in 1858, the local papers remained discreetly silent on its presence. At Christmas the planters returned to the country for the holidays. Their families began trickling back to Charleston in January for the social season and the rituals of courtship that forged the chains among them.[4]

It was an old city by American standards. History dripped like the humidity from its pastel walls and fetid streets. No colony except Pennsylvania had a more diversified people than South Carolina. To the first English settlers of 1670 had been added French Huguenots, Scots high and low, Dutch, Swiss, Germans, a smattering of Jews, northerners numerous enough to found their own New England Society, and black slaves, who as early as 1724 outnumbered whites in the low country three to one. The rice plantations of the low country gave birth to the great families that became the rulers of the most oligarchical colony in America and turned a growing settlement on the peninsula between the Ashley and Cooper rivers into their own city-state during the social season.[5]

Visitors saw in Charleston an air of decayed elegance, what Fanny Kemble in 1838 called the "genteel infirmity . . . of a distressed elderly gentlewoman." Sir Charles Lyell was more blunt; the city, he complained in 1841, "stinks so intolerably." A dozen years later Olmsted found it "much more metropolitan and convenient than any other Southern town; and yet it seems to have adopted the requirements of modern luxury with an ill grace. I saw as much close packing, filth and squalor in certain blocks inhabited by laboring whites in Charleston as I have witnessed in any Northern town of its size, and greater evidence of brutality and ruffianly character."[6]

Like Boston, at once its polar opposite and its nearest kin, Charleston was an odd blend of ancestor worship, stifling custom, and practicality. The difference, said one wag, was that a Boston gentleman looked as if he knew everything while a Charlestonian looked as if he knew everything worthwhile for a gentleman to know. The great families of both cities cherished the Revolution as the defining moment in their history, the morality play that produced the heroes and lessons they treasured most. They revered its iconography even as they tightened their own hold over the city and the state. In 1860 a mere 155 of its 40,500 people owned half of Charleston's wealth.[7]

The city's elite huddled together at the bottom of the peninsula between Broad Street and the Battery, a graceful promenade along the seawall that overlooked the harbor. At White Point, where the Battery turned into East

Battery, the city planted gardens set off by pagodas and broad pathways. Along the narrow streets behind the gardens lay an exclusive enclave of charming pastel residences with tiled roofs, high-walled gardens, and gateways of delicate ironwork. Long piazzas and balconies caught the summer breeze from the harbor. A small park near the post office grew popular as a site for satisfying wounded honor. Two residents of Legare Street once managed to settle a dispute without leaving home; they simply stood in the upstairs windows of their facing houses and fired at each other across the street.[8]

Like the aristocracy they so admired, the Charleston elite were as oblivious to the rest of the city as they were sensitive to their own sense of self. Behind doors that faced the curb in the European style and opened into courtyards instead of dwellings, society indulged itself in a ritual of glittering dinners, balls, and parties. The chivalry doted on people of good looks, refined manners, bright chatter, and well-rounded, if shallow, tastes. In their company the dilettante thrived at the expense of the solitary thinker or earnest intellectual. This mixture of social gaiety and intellectual vacuity moved an exasperated William Gilmore Simms to complain, "The South don't care a damn for literature or art." Poet Paul Hamilton Hayne, born to Charleston's inner circle of wealth and status, dismissed its natives as "intensely provincial." Its society, added William P. Trent more delicately, offered "few opportunities to talents that did not lie in certain beaten grooves." Charles Fraser scandalized society by abandoning the law for painting. It was one thing to accept a fee for legal advice, quite another to sell a picture like a tradesman offering a bolt of linen.[9]

The chivalry were too inbred, too interlocked by blood and shared values to tolerate or even grasp any deviation from norms they deemed proper to a superior class. Yet their aspirations had a practical side. They liked nothing more than to scorn Yankees as worshippers of the Almighty Dollar, but they valued wealth no less and were no less materialistic. The chivalry measured it less in dollars than in land and slaves and were far more addicted to the amenities and pleasures wealth brought and more dependent on it for their way of life. The problem was that they tended to be careless with a dollar. Still, like their Boston alter egos, they found marriage the surest way to attain or perpetuate wealth.

Above Broad Street lay the city's commercial heart with its nine banks, commission merchants, brokers, lawyers, import houses, and auctioneers. There were also fourteen gristmills, six rice mills, six iron foundries, six turpentine distilleries, six factories for making blinds, sashes, and doors, a railroad machine shop, sawmills, and factories for making umbrellas, cordage, and hats. During the 1840s some local investors had started a large cotton-manufacturing firm with machinery brought down from Rhode Island, but it soon failed, and the city took over the three-story building for a poorhouse.[10]

Enterprise found Charleston a shallow, arid soil in which to take root because the chivalry clutched power so tightly. Nowhere else in America did so few people exert so much social, political, and economic control. The chivalry controlled the legislature, which controlled nearly everything else. They appointed judges, the governor, most other state officials, even presidential electors. The governor was little more than a ceremonial figurehead without the power to appoint officials or veto bills. No other state still had a property requirement for holding office. To serve in the legislature, a man had to own property worth at least 150 pounds sterling for the house or 300 pounds for the senate. And the chivalry controlled the Bank of Charleston, the dominant financial institution.[11]

Viewing this as the natural order of things, the chivalry ignored the way it sacrificed creativity for order and diversity for exclusiveness or how it triggered a mad scramble for office among so select an elite. Obsessed by their desire for place, ambitious men shifted alliances and ruptured old friendships as easily as they changed their linen while professing the desire to serve only from a sense of duty. "The object of a southern man's life is politics," observed William C. Preston, an old ally of the Hamptons', "and subsidiary to this end we all practice law." Calhoun had taken pride in the fact that "Our State is organized on the far broader, and more solid and durable foundation of the concurrent majority, to the entire exclusion of the numerical."[12]

A small circle of dissenters saw how politics warped relationships and personal ambition alike. "I regard politics as a sorry trade," declared the jurist John Belton O'Neall in 1860. "I have never found the man whom it warmed, fed or clothed. But I know many . . . whom it has made naked, cold and hungry." Simms agreed. "The attractions of what is called public life," he insisted, "have perverted many a fine intellect in our Southern country, from its true design."[13]

Calhoun's death in 1850 left an enormous vacuum into which ambitious men rushed with indecent haste. Benjamin F. Perry, a strong Unionist, thought it "relieved South Carolina of political despotism. Every man may now breathe more freely as England did after the death of Henry the Eight. There will be divisions amongst us [and] I am glad of it." Alfred Huger, the postmaster of Charleston, cautioned that "While Mr. Calhoun lived, the only lesson either taught or comprehended . . . was to obey orders!" Hammond saw the great man's death as "the greatest calamity to SoCa. He kept her in check. He held up her high pretensions. He put his foot upon her evil passions and restrained her degenerate tendencies. He has gone and already the flood of passion, pretension, folly, and corruption has broke lo[o]se from its barriers." This frenzy for place locked arrogant, strong-willed men in constant battle with former friends, creating enmities that outlasted older ties. They found more comfort in thwarting rivals than in serving the public interest and, like other aristocracies, never forgot a slight.[14]

While they battled for prominence, Charleston was changing in ways few of them noticed. Disgruntled planters were taking or selling large numbers of slaves to plantations opening in the Southwest. In their place came a motley assortment of sailors, vagrants, and immigrants seeking work. During the 1850s the black population shrank from 53 percent to 42 percent. By 1860 the working class of the city was 40 percent white, of whom 60 percent was foreign born. Some people were shocked to find whites, most of them Irish or German, acting as servants. The city's population had shrunk 6 percent since 1850 and developed a mix where class divisions glared as boldly as racial ones. Crime was on the upswing, and the poorhouse population doubled between 1850 and 1856. In the summer of 1860 the city compounded its woes by turning savagely on its 3,237 free blacks, many of whom earned decent livings and 122 of whom themselves owned slaves. The police launched a door-to-door inventory, demanding proof of freedom. Those unable to provide it were resold into slavery; many fled the city.[15]

A decade earlier Simms, searching his own tormented soul, had warned that there were two Charlestons in "deadly conflict." One was the world of the practical and industrious people, "coerced by the necessities of life, devoted to toil and business, and bringing to their work the capital of fresh energies, eager hopes and sleepless enterprise." The other was an entrenched chivalry that "had acquired a certain permanence of position." The first had no place in society; the second dominated society. "Its people could boast of a *past*. They could look back with pride to their ancestry." One looked forward and aspired to progress; the other was content to feed upon its past and behave as if time stood still for its convenience. Although Simms did not say as much, the first represented growth, and the second decay. In 1860 decay still reigned in the city-state the chivalry cherished as their Rome, their Athens, their Abbotsford. During its illustrious history the city had survived war, fire, floods, and hurricanes. The question now was whether it could survive its own pretensions and the grand illusions that sustained them.[16]

The most potent of those illusions concerned the viability of independence. For thirty years South Carolina had steered a maverick course in national politics, resisting efforts to bind it to parties or programs not its own. Charleston had always been both leader and symbol of this attitude. Early in the century, before such matters were even thought of, citizens had changed the name of Union Street to State Street. The Georgian splendor that was now City Hall had once been the Bank of the United States. Yet the seat of the state government lay upstate in Columbia, and the federal government was a more visible presence in Charleston than in most places. Along with the ubiquitous post office there was a customhouse, an arsenal, and no less than four forts, all of them named after revered state heroes of the Revolution.[17]

Lincoln's election had thrown an ancient tension into bald conflict, forcing the confrontation that ultras had dreamed of and conservatives had dreaded for thirty years. Judge Magrath and the other federal officials threw down the gauntlet by resigning their offices with great ceremony. Governor William H. Gist summoned the legislature into special session on November 5, ostensibly to choose electors but also to arrange for measures should Lincoln triumph. Once the election results were known, discussion turned quickly to calling a convention to consider secession. "The election to the Presidency of a sectional candidate," declared Gist, "by a party committed to the support of measures which, if carried out, will inevitably destroy our equality in the Union . . . [and] the only alternative left, in my judgment, is the secession of South Carolina from the Federal Union."[18]

Not since nullification had such excitement gripped Charleston. Minutemen drilled; fire companies formed into military companies; crowds roamed the streets eager for the latest rumor, then gathered in the evening in front of the hotels to serenade whichever dignitary was on hand to pump them up with a fiery speech. Everywhere there were meetings, more speeches, patriotic music, bold slogans cast upon the crowd, and loud cheers for those who demanded secession. Against this clamor the Unionists in the legislature had no chance. On November 9 the debate shifted dramatically toward the calling of a convention, and the bill steamrollered through both houses.[19]

Delegates were to be elected on December 6 for a convention to meet on December 17. At meetings across the state ultras pushed hard to get secession candidates elected. Attention turned to the congressional delegation. Suddenly Chesnut and Hammond found themselves caught in the same dilemma for different reasons. The Chesnut family had always been strong Unionists, a fact that annoyed Mary because her father had been a nullifier. Hammond had long been an apostle of secession, yet had spent the past summer working against hasty withdrawal, fearing that South Carolina would again commit the folly of going out alone. He managed to stir up so much confusion over his position that a group of legislators formally requested his views on the crisis.[20]

Two days after Lincoln's election Hammond answered the request with a letter to his friend Alfred P. Aldrich, who thought its views too conservative and pocketed it. Before Hammond learned this, he found himself upstaged by Chesnut, whose own views had been waffling for the past month. "My mind is daily inclining to the necessity of trying the issue of secession . . . even by the solitary movement of the state," he wrote Hammond on October 27. "But I wish to consult with you and other friends before I fully decide." On the evening of November 5, responding to a crowd gathered outside Janney's Hotel in Columbia, Chesnut sounded like the most ardent of ultras. "A line of enemies is closing around us which must be broken," he warned. ". . . For myself, I would unfurl the Palmetto . . . determined to live or die as became our ancestors. I would ring the clarion note of defiance in the insolent ears of our foe. . . . It is your duty . . . to withdraw. It is your only safety."[21]

The applause was deafening.

Five days later, while Hammond pondered his decision, Chesnut resigned his Senate seat. Hammond got the news next morning and within twenty minutes wrote his own resignation. It looked bold and resolute, but like so much in Hammond's life it was subterfuge. "I thought Magrath and all those fellows were great asses for resigning and have done it myself," he admitted to his brother. "It is an epidemic and very foolish." To Simms he reported wryly, "it is all over with me. No more of Uncle Sam's pass, no more documents, no more stationary. . . . I resigned because Chesnut resigned. . . . What Chesnut & the others resigned for I don't know. In a short note . . . Chesnut gives no other reason than that he thought he could do more good at home."[22]

The representatives followed suit. A wave of excitement swept over Charleston. "The momentum is irresistible," wrote an exultant Simms to a New York friend. "The event is inevitable. . . . Disabuse your mind of the notion that there is any party, or body of men, in S.C. not willing for secession . . . it is a complete landsturm, a general rising of the people, and the politicians are far behind them." But there were dissenting voices. The strongest and most articulate of them belonged to the old lawyer James L. Petigru. "My own countrymen here in South Carolina are distempered to a degree that makes them to a calm and impartial observer real objects of pity," he told Edward Everett of Massachusetts. "They believe anything that flatters their delusion or their vanity; and at the same time they are credulous to every whisper of suspicion about insurgents or incendiaries."[23]

"The City . . . is clamorous for secession," observed William D. Porter, the president of the state senate. ". . . [I]n the State I think no one can resist the current. We are too far committed." The spectacle of Charleston's succumbing to the secession frenzy saddened Petrigu beyond hope. "We shall be envied by posterity for the privilege that we have enjoyed of living under the benign rule of the United States," he told his daughter Sue. "The constitution is only two months older than I. My life will probably be prolonged till I am older than it is."[24]

LITERARY MEN SELDOM liked what they saw in Washington. One who ventured there that troubled winter called it a "paradise of paradoxes,—a city of magnificent distances . . . the Elysium of oddities, the Limbo of absurdities, an imbroglio of ludicrous anomalies." Its architecture, like its statesmen, was Brobdingnagian of design and Lilliputian in execution. The city was a mudhole in winter, when even army mules stalled in its muck, and a dust cloud in summer, when everyone with a place to go fled its unspeakable heat. On its unpaved streets the carcasses of animals often rotted for weeks.[25]

The city of monuments had little about it that was monumental. The Capitol, White House, Treasury, and Interior buildings were the most imposing federal structures along with the strange-looking red imitation castle that was the Smithsonian Institution. Like the Republic itself, the Capitol and Treasury were works in progress surrounded by the litter of construction. So was the truncated shaft of white marble along the road leading to the Long Bridge over the Potomac. Half a century of good intentions had not completed the monument to the Founding Father who had given the city his name and done so much to create the country now being torn apart. For Republic and monument alike, the question loomed large whether the work would ever be finished.[26]

The Capitol still awaited its dome and its statue of Freedom, which sat forlornly in the East Park. Wags thought a Capitol with an empty top perfectly suited to Congress. Cradled atop a hill, it struck one unimpressed visitor as "formed of heaps of rubbish." Its passageways were dark and stained with tobacco juice. In December the Supreme Court was to be freed at last from its basement quarters and moved to the old Senate chamber. The State Department resided in a drab, antiquated two-story building at the corner of Fifteenth Street and Pennsylvania Avenue. Within its dingy interior the venerable chief clerk, William Hunter, whose service had begun under John Quincy Adams, presided over a staff of twenty-three clerks, two messengers, and four watchmen.[27]

Most of the city's sixty thousand inhabitants lived in plain houses of wood or brick and drew their water from wells or nearby springs. Poor, squalid neighborhoods huddled amid empty lots, swampland, and cypress groves. In the fall and spring the west end of town turned into an impassable sea of mud. No street was immune; even Pennsylvania Avenue was deeply rutted and in urgent need of repair. At many corners large wooden pumps with long iron handles greeted travelers and horses. Shabby carriages driven by black men in shabbier garb served as public hacks. The whole place reminded Henry Villard of an overgrown village with "a distinctly Southern air of indolence and sloth."[28]

Like resorts and spas, Washington was a city of two populations, the regular and the seasonal. The nomads, led by lobbyists, adventurers, job seekers, and their camp followers, flocked there in the late fall for the opening of Congress and stayed until the late spring or early summer, when season and session had played themselves out. Most ensconced themselves at one of the giant hotels, around which much of the city's political life revolved, or at an endless string of boardinghouses. Northerners favored Willard's, a massive six-story fortress on Pennsylvania Avenue, while southerners preferred Brown's. The National also attracted a large crowd, and that winter Texas Senator Louis Wigfall moved his family to an emerging favorite, Wormley's.[29]

The native upper crust lived in elegant town houses along the more fashionable avenues or in Georgetown, already an exclusive enclave of culture and refinement. "Passing from the reek of a hotel ball, or the stewing soiree of a Cabinet secretary into the quiet *salon* of a West End home, the very atmosphere was different," noted one insider. The ranks of privilege included old money long in residence, the Supreme Court justices, some lawyers and bankers, military officers from good families who disdained politics, the foreign legations, whose standard of living remained constant even when the personnel changed, and politicos with social credentials that outshone their office.[30]

Rarely did the social mix stray far from politics, and nowhere was the blend more subtly woven than in the exquisitely appointed parlors of the lady lobbyists. They were a breed unto themselves: widows of officers, daughters of congressmen, or refugees from scandals in distant small towns. With practiced graciousness they lured congressmen from the bad cooking and drab confines of their hotels to pleasant games of euchre around a table near a cheerful fire, followed by midnight suppers of cold duck, venison pie, broiled oysters, salads, and cheese washed down with champagne or burgundy. In such settings it took no siren to sing a persuasive song. Hostesses in Washington relied heavily on the bounty of Chesapeake Bay and the Potomac River for the largess of their tables. Even the most frugal could afford brant, ruddy duck, canvasback, sora, oysters, and terrapin. Nothing was consumed in greater quantity than oysters. Housekeepers planted them on their dank cellar floors and fed them with salt water, a bath appreciated also by the huge, ungainly terrapins that roamed the cellar floors like watchmen until their time for the pot had come.[31]

During the social season, which began after New Year's Day, hostesses aspired to brilliance but achieved mostly gloss. Since enormous hoops were still in vogue, making their heads look like "small handles to huge bells," women widened their coiffure into broad braids and bandeaux, adorned with garlands of flowers and headdresses of tulle, lace, and feathers. Furniture was massive and thick-legged enough to withstand the tidal sweep of onrushing hooped gowns, and no ball costume went without its garnish of flowers. Southern ladies had long controlled Washington society just as their men had its politics. The large functions over which they presided with charm and finesse were affairs at which every couple was "Somebody" and "Somebody's wife." The women were bright and witty, the men reticent or pensive. Talk turned to art and artists, Paris fashions, anything but the political miasma in which they all felt trapped. Military officers were popular because no one expected them to talk politics and their positions detached them from the usual struggles for place.[32]

The White House had long ago forfeited all pretense of social leadership. John Tyler had been restrained by the deaths of his predecessor and his own wife. The wife of James Polk had clamped a stern Presbyterian morality on social affairs, banning liquor and dancing from the White House and frowning on cards, horse racing, and gambling. Mrs. Zachary Taylor had regarded contact with politicians as degrading and refused even to appear publicly with her husband, whose early death cast a pall over society. Mrs. Millard Fillmore was a shy former schoolteacher socially ill at ease. The more convivial Mrs. Franklin Pierce was devastated by the sudden death of her son and avoided public appearances, and Buchanan was a bachelor who relied on his niece Harriet Lane for social direction. Reporters starved for signs of social life at the White House gushed over the charming, icily correct Harriet, calling her "Our Democratic Queen."[33]

As the new season approached under the cloud of Republican victory, the mood ran more to dread than to anticipation. Disruption of the political order had plunged society into confusion, forced painful choices upon every southern family, and replaced social ambition with political intrigue. Nowhere was this strain felt more keenly than within the administration. The official family, haggard from four years of strife, found no relief in the growing postelection crisis that magnified attacks from without and bickering from within. The cabinet was in turmoil. Its members had always treated Buchanan with obsequious deference in public, while ridiculing him in private. Most of them still respected or feared him but had grown weary of his sanctimonious air, just as they had with one another's foibles and eccentricities. Petty dislikes might be endured for a few months more, but the sectional split forced them into unwilling conflict among themselves and ultimately into a struggle to capture the president's soul.³⁴

Howell Cobb, the acknowledged leader of the cabinet, was utterly baffled about what course to take. The amiable, heavyset Georgian, who had always been Buchanan's favorite, was skilled at conciliating opposite wings of the official family. He came from a long tradition of public service and had increased his stature by marrying the daughter of a wealthy planter. Since his first election to Congress in 1842 he had been a strong Unionist even when it cost him politically, as it had in recent years, when the southern rights Democrats in Georgia gained power and marked him for destruction. Cobb disliked slavery and hoped it would gradually expire. Once he calculated that he could make more money by selling his plantation and investing the funds, but he could not bear to sell his slaves or leave them to an uncertain fate as freemen. He was adept at the politics of compromise, but all his skills could not ward off the awful choice marching toward him. "The days of the union are numbered," he had admitted a year earlier. "I write this as my unwilling conviction."³⁵

His fellow southerners shared this sentiment. Secretary of the Interior Jacob Thompson, a warmhearted man with a cool head and persuasive tongue in times of crisis, was a Mississippian who knew well the influence of secessionist sentiment at home. He had gone there from North Carolina as a young lawyer, settled in Oxford, and improved his fortunes by wedding the daughter of a planter. He spent six terms in Congress before losing his seat in the Unionist reaction of 1851. After being named to the cabinet, he reorganized the Interior Department with impressive vigor. His colleague Jeremiah Black called Thompson "as upright, true and honest a man as ever lived; one of the most efficient executive officers this Government ever had."³⁶

Secretary of War John B. Floyd was from the critical border state of Virginia, where he had once been governor, as his father had before him. As the man in charge of the Army, the affable Floyd occupied what would be a key position should a crisis arise. He was not personally as close to Buchanan as were the others, and had never even met him at the time he was offered a cabinet post. Floyd had a generous, careless nature, noble of intention but inept of detail. He too found himself caught in the fatal southern contradiction of believing in the right of secession while regarding it as unnecessary at the present time.³⁷

The northern members were less impressive. Judge Black, the attorney general, was the most capable of them. An awkward, ungainly man with the rumpled air of one whose clothes and wig never quite fitted, he held strong principles and rarely ducked a fight on their behalf. His incisive, legalistic mind had no use for intrigue or prevarication; it was a narrow shaft of conviction, however true its aim. He had a flair for the dramatic, loved to flirt with the ladies and bombard them with snatches of Shakespeare or Milton, but with a touch so heavy that one likened him to "an elephant trying to dance a hornpipe."[38]

Secretary of State Lewis Cass was a relic from a bygone era. Once a Democratic presidential candidate, he was at seventy-eight a feeble, lethargic old man whose daughter wrapped him in flannels and put him to bed every night at nine. He wreathed his massive bald head with an antique brown wig, and at cabinet meetings said little but constantly sucked air between his teeth as if tasting something unpleasant. Never a sharp thinker, Cass had grown timid and confused with age.

Secretary of the Navy Isaac Toucey also belonged to Buchanan's generation. A renowned constitutional lawyer from Connecticut, he had been governor, held seats in both houses of Congress, and served briefly as attorney general for James Polk. He was a quiet, thoughtful man dismissed by many as timid and indecisive.[39]

Postmaster General Joseph Holt was a man apart from the others. He had earned his reputation as a lawyer in Kentucky, then moved to Mississippi and made a fortune. Despite these roots, he was a staunch Unionist with no sympathy for southern ultras. Weakened by tuberculosis, which killed his wife, he had retired at thirty-five and returned to Kentucky. There he entered politics as a protégé of Amos Kendall. Holt's stern countenance seemed always tinged with sorrow or a scowl, yet in discussion he had a mild, serene manner free of gesture or effect. "The tones of his voice," recalled a friend, "had something in them inexpressibly soft and touching." Holt also had a sharp wit and sense of humor. Although he had remarried, Mary Chesnut knew of his affair with a Mrs. Phillips, whom she called "a mad, bad woman."[40]

The southern members—always excepting Holt—were much closer as a group than the northerners and had more influence with the president. This was true even of their wives. Mary Ann Cobb was a domestic, unpretentious woman who liked to dip her toe into society but had no desire to swim in it. She was frank and witty, full of good sense, and once endeared herself to Buchanan by introducing him to a Georgia widow who quite entranced him. The charming, impetuous Kate Thompson was Buchanan's favorite. A bubbly, scatterbrained creature, she loved to flirt and could wheedle favors from the president when others could not. Mary Ann Cobb called her "an easy and free-hearted woman." Mary Chesnut was less kind. "I fancy Mrs. T was so astonished at her position in the cabinet she could never be sufficiently grateful for it," she sniped. "What a coarse couple they were." Floyd's wife had been invalided by a fall shortly after he took office and stayed at home.[41]

This closeness to Buchanan, for which they had worked so hard, put the southerners in an untenable position. A week before the election Cobb confided to William H. Trescot, the South Carolinian who was the assistant secretary of state, that he could see no other course than resistance; acquiescing to Lincoln's election would mean slow but certain ruin. But how to square their loyalty to their states with their loyalty to the president? None of them wanted Buchanan to bear the burden of the crisis, and all hoped earnestly that it could be deferred until after the inauguration of his successor on March 4. But events did not give them the luxury of time. On election day a distressed Buchanan summoned Floyd to inform him of a rumor that the federal forts in Charleston had been assaulted and seized. If the forts should be taken because of our neglect, he said, "it were better for you and me both to be thrown into the Potomac with millstones tied about our necks." Floyd scoffed at the rumor but agreed to dispatch Major Fitz-John Porter to investigate the situation at Charleston.[42]

The president had begun work on his annual message but didn't know what to say about the crisis. He and Floyd had discussed the probability of secession and concluded that it looked inevitable. Buchanan had also been startled by an unexpected position paper from the commander of the army, Lieutenant General Winfield Scott, in which the aged and infirm Virginian blithely conceded the right of secession and said the president had no power to prevent it by force. The general's political views Buchanan dismissed as absurd; what shocked him more was a warning that all the federal forts on the southern coast were undermanned and could easily be taken. These facilities, Scott concluded, "should be immediately so garrisoned as to make any attempt to take any one of them by surprise . . . ridiculous."[43]

But where to get the troops? The army was small, spread out, and preoccupied with protecting the Indian frontier. Buchanan feared that Scott's "Views" would only spur southern ultras to some rash move; thus his alarm at the rumor of an attack on the Charleston forts. At a cabinet meeting on November 9, he raised the question of how to deal with the situation in South Carolina, calling it "the most important ever before the Cabinet since his induction into office." He also asked for opinions on holding a convention of the states, as provided in the Constitution, to thrash out a compromise. Black denounced secession and urged the sending of troops to the forts to deter any thought of disunion. Cass roused himself to condemn secession and approve the use of force. Cobb, Thompson, and Toucey opposed any form of coercion and supported the idea of a convention. Holt was skeptical of the latter, while Floyd spoke against both secession and coercion. As the meeting broke up, Trescot arrived with news of an incident in Charleston that was more than mere rumor.44

The commandant of the forts, Colonel J. L. Gardner, reluctant to leave large quantities of arms stored at the arsenal in the city, where they might be seized, sent a squad of soldiers to move them to Fort Moultrie. The men were dressed in civilian clothes so as not to alarm the citizenry. But the owner of the wharf spotted them loading their boat and threatened to raise an alarm unless the supplies were returned to the arsenal. Not wishing to inflame feelings in the city, the soldiers carted them back. Later the mayor gave Gardner permission to load the supplies, but the colonel refused to acknowledge that the mayor had any authority in the matter.45

The next day the cabinet met again to discuss Gardner's situation. Buchanan read a passage from the draft of his annual message affirming that he would not recognize any right of secession and would protect federal property. Cass, Black, Holt, and Toucey approved; Cobb, Floyd, and Thompson disagreed strongly. "I do not see what good can come," Floyd wrote privately, ". . . and I do see how much mischief may flow from it." Turning to the Charleston matter, Buchanan summarized the report of Major Porter, who had just returned. Given the delicacy of the situation, Porter suggested replacing both the aged Gardner and the keeper of the arsenal. It was agreed to send Colonel Benjamin Huger to take charge of the arsenal and Major Robert Anderson to succeed Gardner. Huger was a native Carolinian, Anderson a Kentuckian with a wife from Georgia.46

"Not in my time," Buchanan had intoned to himself like a mantra, but here it was. The election was barely over, and already trouble had started in the South. Even worse, a schism had opened in the cabinet that would inexorably widen over the coming days. Buchanan went to Black and asked for an opinion on the precise powers of the president to deal with secession and the resistance of states to federal law. He did not know that the southern members of the cabinet were already meeting with Trescot and others to determine what course they should pursue.

SPRINGFIELD LOOKED AS nondescript as the prairie beneath its weathered face. As in so many western towns, its center was the square. In this case it housed a state capitol built of native stone in the Greek Revival style in a park too new for trees and shrubs to relieve its bleak appearance. An iron fence separated the fragile grass from a street that was unpaved, like all the others in town. To the east of the square sat two other imitation Greek structures, the Sangamon County Courthouse and an insurance company. A host of firms in drab quarters occupied the rest of the square, and residences filled the streets running at right angles from it.[47]

The town had fewer than ten thousand people, a college that boasted of being the state university, two railroads, one hotel aspiring to first class, nine other hostelries, and sixteen boardinghouses. The election results proved a bonanza for local hotelkeepers and rum sellers. By sweeping out the "ins," it had opened up the cornucopia of federal jobs for the Republican faithful. It was, said Lincoln's friend Ward Lamon, "a party that had never fed; and it was voraciously hungry." Early in November the would-be feeders began flocking to Springfield, jostling for quarters with politicos come to consult with and measure the new president, reporters, and the inevitable tourists.[48]

Those eager to see Lincoln's house at Eighth and Jackson streets found it as humble as his origins. The plain two-story frame dwelling and stable occupied a cheerless yard barren of fruit or shade trees, shrubbery, and flowers. "I never cared for flowers," he admitted. "I seem to have no taste, natural or acquired, for such things." The cow and horse in the stable were fed and milked by his own hands, which also chopped and sawed the wood burned. Those who wished to see him in person went to his temporary office on the second floor of the statehouse. Officially the governor's room, it was normally frequented by legislators and lobbyists. The small room had high ceilings and long windows looking out over the south and east sides of the square. A few chairs, a sofa, a table, a worktable, and a stove served as furniture with some party mementos as ornaments. Barely twenty people could squeeze into it.[49]

In this room Lincoln stood every day from ten to noon and again from three to half past five to receive a swelling flow of visitors. Some were strangers come merely to gawk and press the flesh; others were old friends or neighbors, crusty farmers who offered blunt advice on what to do about the South or whom to put into the cabinet. A large number were what Lamon called "gentlemen . . . with light baggage and heavy schemes," party bush-beaters and Wide-Awakes turned overnight into seekers of place. More important visitors, men of standing in the party, saw Lincoln at home or in their hotel rooms, or in a room of the state central committee on a side street that he used for consultations.[50]

Lincoln had tried longer hours at first, but the human tidal wave forced restrictions. Overwhelmed by his new role as celebrity on top of his emerging responsibilities and the incessant demands on his time, he turned his law practice over to his partner, William Herndon, and became a full-time president in waiting. Every morning before eight he walked to the statehouse to meet his secretary, John G. Nicolay, who slept in the building. They tackled the flood of mail from all over the nation until the doors opened. In the evening they went at it again unless Lincoln had visitors to see or consultations.[51]

To the governor's office came the prominent and the obscure, delegates of a nation eager to know this stranger who had been elected president. The surface of the man was so striking as to handicap efforts to get beyond it. Donn Piatt, an Ohio politician who visited shortly after the election, called him "the homeliest man I ever saw . . . a huge skeleton in clothes" with a "dull, heavy, and repellent" face that "brightened like a lantern when animated. His dull eyes would fairly sparkle with fun, or express as kindly a look as I ever saw."[52]

Lincoln described himself as six feet four inches tall, weighing 180 pounds, with a dark complexion, coarse black hair, and gray eyes. But none of the parts were attractive, and all were put together in an odd way. Henry Villard, the young *Herald* reporter who had grudgingly consented to submit his Bavarian refinement to the barbarities of the prairie, saw an "indescribably gawky figure, an odd-featured, wrinkled, inexpressive, and altogether uncomely face. He used singularly awkward, almost absurd, up-and-down and sidewise movements of his body to give emphasis to his arguments." His chest was thin, and his shoulders were rounded. Too much of his height was in the legs; when he sat down, his knees rose so high that a marble placed on one of them would roll down a steep incline. Usually he threw one scrawny leg over the other when seated.[53]

Villard grew fascinated watching Lincoln work the crowd, whose members thought they were working him. He handled the visitors with amazing tact, never ducking a question worth answering, always ready for a good-natured argument with some original line of reasoning and an inexhaustible supply of stories. No one told a story better or used it more deftly to make a point. He was his own best audience, capping his punch line with high-pitched laughter while his body shook with glee. The story could be (and often was) coarse or even nasty so long as the point was made. He was good, Villard concluded, very good, with a knack for handling people that seemed natural and effortless. A New York *Times* reporter agreed that he "never knew a public man who knew so well how to hold his tongue, and yet not offend his best friends. And yet Mr. Lincoln is so honest, that it seems to me a miracle that he does not commit himself in some way by telling too much truth." One visitor marveled at how Lincoln "chatted, told stories, laughed at his own wit . . . and in one way or another made a couple of hours pass merrily and never once lost his dignity or committed himself to an opinion."[54]

The glare of publicity had banished his privacy forever, exposing every detail of his life to intense scrutiny and speculation. He had ceased to be a private citizen and become a public property. The number of reporters increased, the volume of mail swelled. Some of it offered congratulations and advice, some appealed or begged, some flattered or cajoled, and some threatened or warned against threats. Two presidents, Harrison and Taylor, had died in office, both abruptly and therefore mysteriously. In these tense times well-wishers wanted no such fate for their new leader. "I believe Harrison was poisened [sic]," wrote an old Vermonter, who urged Lincoln to replace the White House servants with "good Northern Servants who will be true & cant be bribed." A New York doctor offered the same advice to "know your household at Washington. You must not die the death of a rat." Others thought Buchanan had been poisoned when he fell ill before his inauguration, and implored Lincoln to take every caution. One man sent a detailed report on Washington doctors.[55]

The two most pressing issues in the mail were the crisis in the South and choosing the cabinet. On the first question, opinions divided sharply. Many influential people urged Lincoln to speak out and reassure the South that it had nothing to fear from him; others exhorted him to keep silent until his inaugural address. A slump on Wall Street, triggered by fears of secession, made the demands for Lincoln to say something even more insistent. "The main thing," urged Henry Raymond of the *Times*, ". . . is to have you say the South misunderstands the Republican party, and that a Republican Administration can alone correct the error." Others agreed with the New Yorker who argued that "any explanation as to your public policy would be mistaken for weakness & satisfy neither side."[56]

Lincoln shared this latter view. As early as October 29 he drafted a reply to George Prentice of the Louisville *Journal*, who had asked him to reassure the South. "If I were to labor a month," Lincoln wrote, "I could not express my conservative views and intentions more clearly and strongly than they are expressed in our platform, and in many speeches already in print and before the public"; anything new would merely be seized on by ultras and misrepresented. Lincoln never sent this letter, but on November 9 he said much the same thing to Truman Smith of New York. "I am not insensible to any commercial or financial depression that may exist," he added pointedly, "but nothing is to be gained by fawning around the *'respectable scoundrels'* who got it up. Let them go to work and repair the mischief of their own making; and then perhaps they will be less greedy to do the like again."[57] This view of Wall Street's wicked ways did little to cheer its influential constituency.

As for the cabinet, Lincoln found himself beset by all sides pleading the case for this man or that. Every state expected a representative; in the larger ones, such as New York, Ohio, and Pennsylvania, the infighting had already begun among warring factions. Editors also pressed advice on the new president. "A swarm of quidnunc correspondents of Eastern newspapers," said Joseph Medill's Chicago *Tribune*, "have dropped down upon Springfield to make up Mr. Lincoln's cabinet, and to mark out the lines of policy for the administration."[58]

As Indian summer turned blustery and cold, Lincoln left town for a brief trip to Chicago with the Lyman Trumbulls and Donn Piatts. Presidents-elect might be celebrities, but they were not yet men of privilege. At the depot Lincoln bought his own tickets, and on the crowded train he sat uncomplaining when the conductor unceremoniously plunked four convicts in irons (one a murderer) traveling with a sheriff between his family and the Trumbulls. In Chicago, Lincoln met for the first time his vice president-to-be, Hannibal Hamlin, whose dark complexion had led some southerners to spread rumors before the election that he was a mulatto. Lincoln put Hamlin at ease with his usual barrage of stories, and together they saw the local sights, including the new Post Office and the Wigwam, where the convention nominating them had been held. That evening they endured a large reception at which they shook hands until their bones ached, and then a dinner at which they talked politics and the cabinet. Recognizing that it must include a New Englander, Lincoln offered Hamlin a short list and invited him to make the choice.[59]

The local politicos swarmed over them, forcing Lincoln to stay an extra night to get everything done. When he returned to Springfield on the 26th, a mountain of correspondence awaited him. "I firmly believe," wrote one supporter, "there are men base & reckless enough in some of the Southern States to assassinate both you & Mr. Hamlin & that they intend to do it." Three men from Spartanburg, South Carolina, offered to buy from Lincoln "a very likely & intelligent mulatto boy . . . known as Hannibal Hamlin." A resident of Pensacola, Florida, informed him that he had been hanged in effigy there.[60]

This kind of mail Lincoln could brush aside. What annoyed him was the way some papers reported a speech given by Trumbull on the 20th, which was widely (and correctly) viewed as representing Lincoln's views. It was intended as a gesture to soothe public fears, but some northern papers denounced it as proof that Lincoln planned to abandon Republican principles, while southern editors held it up as a declaration of war on the South. In response to Raymond's request for a direct statement, Lincoln pointed to how Trumbull's speech had been mangled. "This is just what I expected . . . would happen with any declaration I could make," he retorted. "These political fiends are not half sick enough yet. 'Party malice' and not 'public good' possesses them entirely."[61]

From Springfield, both North and South seemed so far away, remote worlds sending forth a steady stream of messengers with news of unfathomable events. The ferment in the South mystified him, made him doubtful that there was anything real or enduring in it. His old friend Leonard Swett agreed. "This flurry at the South it seems to me can be got along with," he advised, "but I dont think it ought to be trifled with. The Country wants firmness & justice." The mail pouring into the offices of Senator Trumbull and Congressman Elihu Washburne took an even harder line. *"The day of compromise has past,"* wrote one man. ". . . *Slavery* MUST be put in the way of ultimate extinction, or the Nation WILL BE." Another warned that "The thing we most dread is *Compromise*. . . . This whole matter must be met & decided sometime & now is the accepted time."[62]

The pressure to win the election paled before that of having won. The first rule of victory, forgotten by so many, was to remain calm. Whatever happened, he must not succumb to the epidemic of excitement raging about him. Lincoln had no trouble doing that; it had always been one of his strengths as well as stratagems. It was not so much grace under fire—he was too crude for that—as wit under fire, the coolness of one emotionally detached from everyone around him. The second rule, also forgotten too often, was learning whom to trust and how far to trust them, and how far to trust his own instincts.

What helped most in this effort was his ability to draw an impenetrable mask over his inner feelings. He was, Lamon thought, "a man apart from the rest of his kind, unsocial, cold, impassive." Another friend, David Davis, called him "the most reticent, secretive man I ever saw or expect to see." Others saw a face perpetually wreathed in sorrow until galvanized to life, but none knew the sources of that sorrow or its depths. Not even the alert Villard realized how much lay beneath that ungainly surface, though he did notice something new about the surface itself. An unsightly stubble had emerged. Was the president-elect growing a beard? That would at least be distinctive; the country had never had a president with a beard.[63]

A Change of Command

The difficulties of Mr. Buchanan's position will be very great. . . . If he suffers the revenue collections of this port to cease, he virtually annuls the tariff laws of the country, and cuts off the only certain source of income to the Government. . . . In such a case all foreign goods would naturally seek this port, to escape taxation. . . . Whether under the circumstances the President would be justified in employing the Federal Army & Navy in supporting the revenue department, or not is a question which I cannot determine. Upon its determination rests . . . the probability of a collision between So. Ca. & the U.S.

—William L. Trenholm
November 15, 1860[1]

SINCE HE WAS in New York on furlough when the summons came to report at once to Washington, Major Robert Anderson did the logical thing: He called on his friend and mentor Winfield Scott, who had for years maintained his office in New York. The old general himself had not been summoned to the City of Politics, a fact over which he brooded. Secretary Floyd was running the military, Scott told Anderson, and with little regard for the views of the general of the army. For that reason Scott hesitated to give orders or even advice, but he went over the ground carefully with Anderson.

Colonel Gardner had warned that the federal forts around Charleston could not be held without reinforcements. Scott had already urged Floyd to instruct the commander at Fort Moultrie to be alert for surprise assaults, but he had few reinforcements to send. Only five companies of regulars were even remotely within reach of the forts. Given this fact, Scott observed that it might become necessary to concentrate all the troops at Charleston Harbor in one facility, preferably Fort Sumter.[2]

Anderson nodded. Already he sensed the blighting influence of politics, a presence that never pleased him. Southern he might be, but not in his politics; that was why he had been chosen for this post. Duty and loyalty had always been in his illustrious bloodline. Eight of his relations had been officers in the Continental Army; his father had been wounded at Trenton and

Savannah and taken prisoner at Fort Moultrie, where he languished nine months in prison. His older brother had been a classmate of Scott's at William and Mary, and Robert had served on Scott's staff during the Mexican War. His mother was the cousin of John Marshall, the nation's first chief justice.[3]

Born in 1805 near Louisville, where his father had settled after the Revolution, Anderson went to West Point and became a close friend of Jefferson Davis's. He showed more grit than brilliance, graduating fifteenth in the 1825 class of thirty-seven. He fought in the Black Hawk War, where he mustered into the service a recruit named Abraham Lincoln, fought against the Seminole, Cherokee, and Florida Indians, served as an instructor at West Point, wrote an instruction manual for the artillery, and spent a year at Fort Moultrie. During the Mexican War he led a regiment until severely wounded at Molino del Rey. After the war he had performed the usual routine duties, gained a promotion to major of artillery in 1857, and helped found the Soldiers' Home.[4]

Anderson married the daughter of a general, Duncan Clinch, who lived in Georgia. Although Anderson had owned a plantation with slaves, he had sold it earlier that year. His proslavery sentiments never intruded on his professional conduct. He knew little and cared less about politics, had never even voted because he thought professional soldiers should show no political bias. He liked to say that he lived by his father's religion and General Washington's politics, and that he needed only three documents to guide his path: the Ten Commandments, the Constitution, and the book of army regulations. Of the three, the latter, with its 1,676 paragraphs, was by far the longest and the least enlightening.[5]

Nothing about the man attracted attention. He stood five feet eight inches and had a solid body, sloping shoulders, and a face so narrow that the hazel eyes could always be seen. He was so temperate in every aspect of his life that Erasmus D. Keyes, Scott's military secretary, doubted whether Anderson "had any quality which the world *ordinarily* denominates *a vice*. . . . He was a pattern of order and method, and worked out his plans slowly." To Keyes this mania for method *was* Anderson's vice. "His minute punctuality in all the duties, habits, and relations of life sometimes annoyed me," he admitted, "but did not diminish my respect for him."[6]

This most careful of men went about his new assignment with all deliberation. He called next on George W. Cullum, an engineer at Fort Hamilton who had spent nearly five years working on Fort Sumter and Charleston Harbor. Cullum told him bluntly that South Carolina would secede. When that happened, Charleston would become the hotbed of action and Sumter the only safe haven for troops. Anderson pondered these views as he said good-bye to his ailing wife, Eliza, and their four children and took the train to Washington. There Floyd confirmed that he was being sent to relieve Gardner in a delicate situation. He had nowhere near enough troops to defend the forts; the object was to avoid any confrontation that might lead to fighting.[7]

Anderson reached Fort Moultrie on November 21, a day after Benjamin Huger took charge of the Charleston arsenal. He set out at once to inspect the forts with the engineer in charge and quickly saw what Fitz-John Porter meant when he warned that "The unguarded state of the fort invites attack, if such design exists." Like all coastal fortifications, those at Charleston Harbor had been designed to repel attacks from the sea. No one had given any thought to defending them from sites they were supposed to protect; they were completely exposed to attack from inland.[8]

The ocean entrance to Charleston Harbor lay between the pincerlike extensions of Sullivans Island to the north and Morris Island to the south. Fort Moultrie overlooked the entrance from Sullivans Island. Fort Sumter sat squarely in the middle of the entrance on an artificial island of granite rubble brought from northern quarries. Next to Morris Island lay James Island, on which sat Fort Johnson. Deeper into the harbor, near the mouth of the Cooper River, lay a long, low strip of land like a sandbar with vegetation. Castle Pinckney, the fourth federal facility, occupied the southern corner of this strip.

Moultrie, the main fort, housed the small garrison of two companies from the First Artillery and nine band members. Castle Pinckney and Fort Johnson were occupied only by ordnance sergeants; Sumter was an unfinished work tended by an engineer overseeing 110 civilian workers. Sumter had been designed for a garrison of 650 men and Moultrie for 300, but only skeleton forces had ever occupied them. To Anderson's experienced eye Moultrie looked dishearteningly vulnerable. The twelve-foot walls were old and full of cracks that soldiers could use as footholds to climb. In front and east of the fort wind and waves had heaped sand dunes high enough for sharpshooters to command the parapet and render an assault by land difficult to repulse.[9]

Castle Pinckney was in better shape but lay in the shadow of the city. It would likely be the first target of any move against the forts since the powder for the arms at the arsenal was stored there. Johnson had little strategic value and was vulnerable to assault by land. Sumter, the most formidable and isolated of the forts, commanded the entrance to the harbor. With brick and concrete walls sixty feet high and eight to twelve feet thick, the fort loomed above its tiny island. A year earlier it had housed some Africans rescued from an illegal slave ship until they could be sent home. Since then it had been occupied only by an ordnance sergeant and his family.[10]

The officers looked reliable. Captain Abner Doubleday commanded one company; Brevet Captain Truman Seymour, the other. Doubleday had the distinction of being the only officer who had voted for Lincoln and was outspoken in his antislavery views. Captain John G. Foster was a gritty, experienced engineer. The lieutenants included the high-spirited Jeff Davis of Indiana and Theodore Talbot, whose energy and devotion to duty struggled constantly against delicate health. The noncoms and enlisted men were less impressive; their sluggish efforts suggested a lack of rigorous discipline.[11]

Anderson saw what should be done. Foster was strengthening Moultrie but could do only so much with its weaknesses. At Sumter he was mounting guns in the lower tier of casements. Four magazines were ready and filled with forty thousand pounds of powder and enough ammunition for one tier of guns. Pinckney was in decent shape and a crucial facility because it commanded the city. What the forts needed above all else were troops. On November 23, two days after his arrival, Anderson submitted his first report to Washington. "Fort Sumter and Castle Pinckney *must* be garrisoned immediately if the Government determines to keep command of this harbor," he warned. ". . . Castle Pinckney, being so near the city . . . they regard as already in their possession. The clouds are threatening, and the storm may break upon us at any moment."[12]

Five days later, Anderson renewed his request in more strident terms. He had noticed "a romantic desire urging the South Carolinians to *have possession* of his work [Moultrie], which was so nobly defended by their ancestors in 1776." Huger reported that Charleston was full of rumors that a steamer was en route with four companies of troops. Anderson knew of no such thing, but he was beginning to sense the contours of the trap into which he had been placed. "I am inclined to think that if I had been here before the commencement of expenditures on this work," he said in closing his report, "and supposed that this garrison would not be increased, I should have advised its . . . removal to Fort Sumter, which so perfectly commands the harbor and this fort."[13]

A CHANGE IN COMMAND was coming to the White House, but not fast enough. As fervently as its current prisoner prayed for deliverance, he could not escape the storm blowing up in the South. How ironic it all was, he thought sullenly. Four years earlier he had been the president-elect, hopeful and confident, ready to put things right in the strife-torn nation, smiling with contempt at the lame duck Franklin Pierce, fleeing homeward discredited and disillusioned. Now *he* was the victim of events, seeking relief at the earliest possible moment.

Nothing had gone right for him. He had barely got through his inauguration alive, thanks to the National Hotel disease that claimed the life of a nephew on whom Buchanan had relied heavily. Then had come the *Dred Scott* and Bleeding Kansas fiascoes, which had worsened beyond calculation the problems they were supposed to solve. Within two years his administration was in shambles, his confidence shattered, and his vitality so sapped that early in 1858 Alexander H. Stephens of Georgia described him as "quite feeble and wan."[14]

Young Jimmy Buchanan had been a tall, handsome, broad-shouldered man with wavy blond hair and an engaging twinkle in his blue eyes. A defect in one eye caused him to tilt his head forward and sideways, creating the illusion that he was an attentive listener. Now he was stooped and portly, the blond hair gone white and the fine features ruddy, but the twinkle in his eye lingered. It was, said one political adversary, a twinkle "which seemed to say that although he might occasionally not appear to be of your opinion, yet there was a secret understanding between him and you, and that you might trust him for it."[15]

This was the conceit of the diplomat, which Buchanan had been all his life. That had always been his strength and his weakness. He was a man not of vision but of realism, ready to accept the facts, however harsh or unpleasant they might be. His father had admonished him early that "The more you know of mankind, the more you will distrust them." James had tempered this cynicism with a strong religious faith. All his life he attended church and closed his long days by reading the Bible. From religion he drew an acceptance of things as they were as a reflection of divine will in all its mystery. The guide to his life became the phrase, often repeated, "Sufficient unto this day is the evil thereof." Deal with today's ills, and let God take care of tomorrow.[16]

It was the perfect adage for a man of great ambition but little imagination. He had marched through his long and impressive career with none of the politician's flair for self-dramatization. His mind was that of the lawyer, cold and precise, attuned more to inner logic than to larger ramifications. His gift for clear, analytical thinking and for detachment gave him perspectives others lacked. It also made him a better prophet than most politicos. He saw early the nation's weak point. "Touch this question of slavery seriously," he had warned in 1836, ". . . and the Union is from that moment dissolved." Two years later he lamented that "The Union is now in danger, and I wish to proclaim that fact."[17]

He continued to proclaim it, yet even his legalistic mind could not reconcile the contradictions that underlay the crisis. He had always been an ardent supporter of expansionism even though it turned the clash over slavery into a lethal struggle. He insisted, "Disunion is a word that ought not to be breathed amongst us even in a whisper," but he also argued that for the South, slavery was a matter not of expediency but of self-preservation. What he sought above all else was balance and restraint. The federal government was for him "nothing but a system of restraints from beginning to end," and the essence of those restraints was embodied in the separation of powers.[18]

Buchanan was, said an admirer, "the last of a race of eminent public men who had been bred in a profound reverence for the Constitution and intimate knowledge of it." No man since John Quincy Adams had come better prepared to the presidency. He had served well in both houses of Congress, as secretary of state for James K. Polk, and as minister to both Russia and Great Britain, and he had declined a seat on the Supreme Court. He possessed great stamina, an enormous appetite for work, and the diplomat's formidable tolerance for drink. Of an evening he might go through two or three bottles of Madeira, a generous helping of cognac, and a nightcap or two of rye with no discernible effect. "I can take my glass of Old Monongahela, indulge in Madeira, and sleep soundly," he boasted in 1858, "and yet my Cabinet is always dilapidated."[19]

Despite being the only bachelor elected president, he was a strong family man. When tuberculosis ravaged his family, Buchanan assumed direct responsibility for seven of his orphaned nieces and nephews. Harriet Lane had become his ward at fourteen, James Buchanan Henry at seven. Harriet had been a gay, flirtatious creature until the death of her brother Elliott. Devastated by the loss, she became a solemn woman devoted to the needs of the man she called Nunc. She presided over an orderly household, relieving her uncle of burdensome details, much as young James did with the mail. For the weekly state dinners she worked out the protocol of seating while young James figured out which gentleman should escort what lady into dinner.[20]

Buchanan found solace in the company of his family but little closeness. He treated them much as he did the cabinet, in a manner that led even Cobb to protest, "We were like a lot of boys." As president he had grown more fussy and dictatorial, irritable in a fashion that forced Harriet to stifle feelings of annoyance. He had also taken to prying into their affairs, sometimes even reading Harriet's mail while claiming that he had opened it by mistake. In 1859 his nephew finally quit and went to New York, grew an enormous mustache in defiance, and married without his uncle's blessing. Buchanan neither attended the wedding nor sent a present.[21]

Young Jimmy Buchanan had loved to dance and flirt with the ladies.

"Old Buck" had not lost his eye for feminine charms, but his zest for a good time lost ground steadily to his rigid, prudish side. His ban on dancing and cardplaying in the White House put a damper on social events. Only once, during the visit of the Prince of Wales that autumn, did he allow cards, but to Harriet's chagrin he vetoed her idea of a gala ball for the royal visitor. Buchanan felt his niece slipping away from him. She had always run her own social life, going alone to social functions or out riding sidesaddle on her beautiful white horse. He had never been close to her emotionally, yet he saw the gulf between them widening inexorably, leaving him more isolated than ever.[22]

Young Jimmy had become Old Buck and was just as surely becoming the Old Public Functionary, a label he had given himself in a rare pose of modesty only to see his detractors turn it against him with undisguised glee. He rose early, waded through his morning stream of visitors and afternoon cabinet meetings except on Sundays and reception days, and permitted himself an hour's stroll after lunch through Lafayette Square and the residential area north of the White House. In the evening after dinner he retreated to his study to read his correspondence or do other paperwork, pausing at the end to browse in the Bible before retiring around midnight.[23]

The energy for work was still there, but not the heart. He watched in dismay as the good things in his life emptied out: his family, his friends as they took sides in growing dispute, the cabinet as its fissures widened, and his crumbling reputation as a statesman. Much of it was his own fault; he had always known better how to keep people from him than how to draw them to him. Now that ability had turned on him, left him alone and consumed with self-pity.

Every crisis poses challenges that either feed on a president's weaknesses or nourish his strengths. For Buchanan this process had begun in earnest. The deluge would not come after him but in his time, and it would begin with his annual message on December 3. All sides waited impatiently to learn what position he would take on the secessionist mood in the South. Buchanan had always been, in Henry S. Foote's words, "morbidly sensitive to public reproach, and solicitous . . . to please everybody." These qualities were a gift to a diplomat but a curse to a president. He could not please or even mollify everyone on this issue. He desperately needed sound advice, but he had never been adept at knowing who his true friends were. His vanity had always been an easy target for flattery, and his favor too often bestowed on shallow, devious men gifted only at the art of fawning.[24]

In this dark hour, well might he cling to the hope that had seemed to beckon at the time of his election. Yet even that glimmer was deceptive. At his inauguration ball, a crush so great that one lady complained that "The members of Congress got so over-excited with wine that they had to be locked up in the upper rooms lest they should reappear in the ballroom," Buchanan and Harriet had left too early to catch the remark of Baron Edouard de Stoeckl, the Russian minister. While dancing with the wife of the French minister, Stoeckl observed that the scene in Washington reminded him of Paris in 1830, on the eve of the Revolution. There, at a ball given by Louis Philippe, the astute Talleyrand had whispered to his monarch, "Sire, we are dancing on a volcano."[25]

A CHANGE WAS COMING, not merely of command but of allegiance, and the outcome hinged on three critical questions. What would South Carolina do? How would the president and Congress respond? Would the rest of the South follow South Carolina's lead? William Henry Trescot thought South Carolina must surely secede. If it did, the southern contingent in Washington must do all it could to lead the president and Congress in the right direction. As for the rest of the South, he believed with Cobb that if South Carolina led, others would follow. In that process Cobb's own Georgia was the key. It wielded more influence and commanded more resources than any other cotton state.

In the unfolding of these events, Trescot was eager to play some large part. A small, voluble man with impeccable manners and a subtle intellect, Trescot had all the proper social credentials: a good Charleston family, a law degree, and a well-to-do wife with an estate on Barnwell Island. He had written elegant studies of American diplomacy during the Revolution and the administrations of Washington and Adams. What he craved now was to move beyond the role of scholar to that of participant. Sitting at the edge of the volcano, keenly attuned to its rumblings, he began even before the election spinning out elaborate scenarios of what was to come if Lincoln were elected.[26]

Circumstances made Trescot the intermediary between South Carolina authorities and the president, the southern cabinet members, and key southern congressmen. It was a role he savored, though he adopted the obligatory pose of finding it wearisome. Information flowed to him from long talks with Cobb, Thompson, and Floyd, as well as with the president himself. In their meetings Trescot exchanged what he learned with the southern cabinet members as they struggled to chart a course of action for themselves and to hold the president to an honorable course, by which they meant one that would not interfere with southern plans.

In houses throughout Washington the chivalry gathered to debate its future. To Virginian Roger Pryor's home, after evening supper or entertainment, came R. M. T. Hunter and Muscoe Garnett of Virginia, Lawrence

Keitt, William Porcher Miles, and William Boyce of South Carolina, Lucius Q. C. Lamar and William Barksdale of Mississippi, and others, to hold council. Sometimes the discussion lasted until dawn, and always the refrain was the same: Whatever happened, they must stand together.[27]

Northerners viewed such gatherings as cabals of conspiracy, but to Trescot and his peers the issue was one of conflicted loyalties that were forcing them to choose between their government and their way of life. If other, less noble motives lay beneath the surface, their presence went unacknowledged. For Trescot the immediate concern was to contain the crisis, both in Charleston and in Washington. Anderson was a good man to keep things calm in the harbor; Floyd was sympathetic to the cause but could not abide any attack on the federal forts. Buchanan too, Trescot thought, would not counsel the use of force unless an attack were made. The key to peaceful secession therefore lay in preventing any attacks on the forts.[28]

That secession would come few of them doubted. On the evening of November 10, the day Chesnut resigned from the Senate, Thompson and Cobb dined at Floyd's house. After dinner Trescot joined them along with Francis W. Pickens of South Carolina, a longtime Buchanan supporter just returned from his post as minister to Russia. Trescot assured them that South Carolina would secede. The next evening Floyd spent an hour with Buchanan and Thompson during which the conversation around the tea table never left the disunion movement in the South. On the 12th Floyd, Pickens, and Trescot dined with other friends, and talk turned again to secession. To Floyd's surprise the usually calm Pickens grew heated on the subject. "My own conservatism," noted Floyd wryly, "seems in these discussions to be unusual and almost misplaced."[29]

The situation in Washington was growing complicated. On November 5 Governor Gist of South Carolina had dispatched Thomas F. Drayton to Washington to buy ten thousand rifles from the War Department. For obvious reasons the mission had to be kept secret. Floyd agreed to the transaction, then told Drayton that rifled muskets could not be produced for three months and offered smoothbores instead. "Better do this," a disappointed Drayton told Gist," . . . than be without arms at a crisis like the present." Floyd then sent him to New York to persuade a sympathetic banker to buy the muskets as an intermediary so that South Carolina would not be directly involved.[30]

While in Washington, Drayton also spent time with Trescot, gleaning intelligence from the White House. "As long as Cobb and Thompson retain seats in the Cabinet," Trescot assured him, "you may feel confident that no action has been taken which seriously affects the position of any Southern State." But the row in the cabinet was growing worse; Trescot wondered how long the southerners could remain, torn between their desire to return home, where their influence was wanted, and their need to sway Buchanan from using force in Charleston Harbor.[31]

Nor was Charleston the only flash point. Tensions were also rising at three Florida installations: Fort Pickens at the Pensacola Navy Yard, Fort Jefferson in the Tortugas, and Fort Taylor at Key West. Jefferson had no guns at all, and the engineer in charge, Captain Montgomery C. Meigs, sought protection from the naval commander at Key West. The commander, T. A. Craven, asked Washington for permission to guard Jefferson, but Secretary Toucey refused. Still Craven determined to keep watch over Jefferson and Taylor. "The importance of the posts . . . can not be overestimated," he told a subordinate, "commanding as they do the commerce of the Gulf of Mexico."[32]

A rash act by extremists at any of these places could trigger a shooting confrontation. This had to be avoided at all costs, and it had energized Trescot in reacting to the incident at the Charleston arsenal. He got little help from Robert Barnwell Rhett, who wrote Buchanan on the 24th that "South Carolina, I have not a doubt, will go out of the Union—and it is in your power to make this event peaceful or bloody. *If you send any more troops into Charleston Bay, it will be bloody.*" But Anderson had urgently requested reinforcements, and Buchanan, after consulting with Black and Cass, had decided they should be sent. He told Floyd to prepare the necessary orders.[33]

The alarmed Floyd urged him to reconsider, saying he would pledge his honor that South Carolina would not attack the forts. "That is all very well," retorted Buchanan, "but . . . does that secure the forts?" At length Floyd persuaded Buchanan to do nothing until he had consulted General Scott, then hurried off to see Trescot. He would "cut off his right hand" before signing any order sending reinforcements, Floyd insisted to Trescot, yet at the same time duty obliged him to resist any move to seize the forts. If his hand was forced, he would resign from the cabinet, as would Cobb and Thompson. That would be the end of their influence.[34]

Trescot saw at once what must be done. He explained to the president that South Carolina considered it a matter of honor to conduct its movement according to principles of law. No attack would be made on the forts as long as the people were not aroused by the appearance of reinforcements. But if troops were sent, a bloody collision was inevitable. Buchanan made it clear that he wished to avoid a collision, but what if South Carolina acted without warning? It won't, Trescot assured him. If it secedes, it will send commissioners to negotiate all differences. "I would have to submit the question to congress," replied Buchanan. "God knows I have no power to decide it or power to force a state back if she goes."[35]

Let the status quo prevail, Trescot urged. Send no reinforcements, and no attack will be forthcoming. Having impressed this message on the president, Trescot relayed the news to Governor Gist. The whole tempest could blow over if Gist would assure Buchanan that "the State intended to move regularly in the exercise of her sovereign rights and while she remained in the Union and the Federal Government made no change in the present condition of things, no attempt would be made on the Forts." Once pledged, Trescot added, Gist must then prevent any open demonstrations or even preparations that gave the impression of violating this pledge.[36]

Gist responded with two letters. One asked Trescot to serve as a confidential agent for South Carolina while he remained in Washington. The other declared that "Although South Carolina is determined to secede . . . very soon after her Convention meets, yet the desire . . . is not to do anything that will bring on a collision before the ordinance of secession is passed and notice has been given to the President of the fact." But he and the legislature would be powerless to avoid a collision "if a single soldier or another gun or ammunition is sent." Gist authorized Trescot to show the letter to Buchanan.[37]

The letter eased Buchanan's anxiety over the immediate crisis, but he knew the stay was temporary. So much depended upon his message to Congress, and he was as divided as his cabinet over its contents. The question was not what he wanted to do but what he had the power to do. On that point Black delivered an opinion that left Buchanan no closer to a clear line of policy. Replying on November 20 to five questions posed by the president, Black declared that no legal basis existed for secession. "I do not say what might be effected by mere revolutionary force," he added. "I am speaking of legal and constitutional right." The president was obligated by law to collect import duties at specified points, and he was also bound to protect the public property from attack.[38]

However, the means to perform these duties were limited strictly by law, and existing law offered little leeway. Sometimes Congress gave the president broad discretion in carrying out legislation; other times it provided only narrow means. "Where the mode of performing a duty is pointed out by statute, that is the exclusive mode, and no other can be followed. The United States have no common law to fall back upon when the written law is defective." The president could not resort to illegal or extralegal means to carry out legal tasks. Duties, for example, had to be collected by an appointed collector in a specified port. The collector could do his job anywhere within that port, however, even on a boat offshore, so long as he remained within the confines of the port.

Only two statutes gave the president power to use force. The Act of 1795 authorized him to call out the militia "whenever the laws of the United States shall be opposed . . . in any State by combinations too powerful to be suppressed by the ordinary course of judicial proceedings, or by the power vested in the marshals." An act of 1807 merely empowered him to use military forces for any lawful purpose. But all such operations must be purely defensive, and the military had to be kept strictly subordinate to civil authority. No federal officers remained in South Carolina, and without them "troops would certainly be out of place, and their use wholly illegal." Nothing in the Constitution authorized the president to compel a state to remain in the Union; indeed, in Black's view, its framers seemed convinced "that military force would not only be useless, but pernicious, as a means of holding the States together."

What, then, could the president do? "I see no course for you," concluded Black, "but to go straight onward in the path you have hitherto trodden—that is, execute the laws to the extent of the defensive means placed in your hands, and act generally upon the assumption that the present constitutional relations between the States and the Federal Government continue to exist, until a new code of things shall be established either by law or force." The president could suppress a rebellion but could not make war on a state. Any use of force beyond this limited sphere required new legislation from Congress. Ultimately, then, a solution to the crisis had to come from Congress.

These views deeply influenced Buchanan's shaping of his message as well as the cabinet debate over it. Trescot thought the cabinet might break up over "the general doctrine of the message that the right of secession does not exist." On November 28 Buchanan put the message in final form, and two days later the cabinet spent nearly three hours debating it. Afterward Buchanan allowed a synopsis of its main points to be given to Trescot for delivery to Governor Gist. Trescot did not read the message itself but saw in the synopsis and reports from Cobb and Thompson enough to convince him that it would "not be acceptable North or South and indeed its points will scarcely be appreciated." On that point he was dead right.39

ANDERSON'S VISIT disturbed Winfield Scott far more than he let on, not because of what transpired but because it reminded him how little influence he wielded in the growing crisis. He was the commander in chief of the army, yet the president and the secretary of war were ignoring him. Clearly his "Views" had fallen on deaf ears. "I have no acknowledgment from either the President or Secretary," he reported gloomily to his good friend Senator John J. Crittenden of Kentucky, "nor has a single step been taken." He had also sent a copy of the "Views" to Lincoln, who at least thanked him in polite, if noncommittal, language. As matters stood, Scott did not expect to be in Washington before March 15.[40]

The general had long been Washington's most imposing monument, but he was now more like some ancient ruin, a magnificent mountain of a man eroded and crumbling with age but still impressive in appearance. Standing a quarter inch above Lincoln's six-four, he walked even a short distance with great difficulty. Age, infirmity, and an epicurean palate had ballooned his massive frame to somewhere around three hundred pounds. At seventy-four he could no longer sit on a horse, was afflicted with dropsy, and had lost the fire that once energized his blue eyes. Only his vanity, swollen with age like his girth, was equal to his reputation as the nation's foremost military hero since the sainted Washington.[41]

The general had devoted his life to the federal government. He had been a boy of three when Washington was inaugurated and been present at the trial of Aaron Burr. He distinguished himself in the War of 1812 and lost partial use of his left arm from a wound at the Battle of Lundy's Lane. Shortly after Napoleon's defeat at Waterloo he went to Paris, where he mastered both the French literature on war and its culinary art. Andrew Jackson's reliance on him during the nullification crisis of 1832 removed any doubts that Scott's Unionist sentiments overshadowed his Virginia heritage. He became the commanding officer of the army in 1841 and enhanced his already sterling reputation with his brilliant direction of the Mexican War.[42]

At thirty Scott wed Maria Mayo, a Virginia woman known for her bright wit as well as her beauty. Already a major general and a military hero, he admitted cheerfully that his new wife was "more admired in her circle than her soldier husband." She bore him seven children, but over the years their lives moved increasingly in separate spheres. Maria began spending more and more time in Europe and eventually stayed, ostensibly to ease a bronchial ailment but also because life there suited her tastes far more than that of wife to a military legend. In his later years Scott liked to quote Dr. Johnson's pearl of wisdom on "connubial infelicity," but he was never known to seek solace in another woman. He enjoyed the company of women, treated them with elaborate courtesy, and always called a young woman "fair lady," but the army was his only mistress apart from his flirtation with politics.[43]

What had broken his heart was not the distance of his wife but the fate of his daughter Virginia. A beautiful if delicate girl with a gift for language and music, she had during her long sojourns in Europe fallen under the spell of Catholicism and converted. A few months after returning home with her mother and sisters in 1844, she quietly made arrangements to enter a convent in Georgetown without telling either of her parents. At twenty-two, unmoved by the distress of her parents, she became a novitiate; a few months later, her frail constitution broken by the austerity of convent life, she was dead.44

Scott never forgave his wife for exposing Virginia to what he deemed Catholic proselytizers in France and Italy. In a curious way her death was a portent of another loss for him. As was soon clear, his long service to the nation and his long absences from home cost him not only his wife and daughter but his state as well. Never again would he have either of his beloved Virginias to console him or offer refuge from the sorrows of old age. In a world where local loyalty was the strongest tie of all, Scott had become a man with a country but without a state.

Not all his extravagance of wit and irony could ease the pain of being old and ignored. He craved nothing more than attention and sought it as avidly as his next meal. "At my time of life," he often sighed, "a man requires compliments." It was for him a hunger born of need and a cultivated taste. He liked to compare his own inventory of qualities with those of great men past and present, especially military commanders, and seldom did his account come up short. He filled his quarters with portraits of himself at different ages as well as a marble bust befitting the noblest of Romans. During a foot bath he called attention, childlike, to his bare limbs, saying "Most men at my age are covered all over with bunches, but you see my flesh is fair."45

Dwelling more and more in that peculiar twilight world where present distress merged imperceptibly into memories of past glories, he was often bored and irritable, obsessed alternately with his bodily ailments and the crisis of the Union. Ambition, long the fuel of his career, had been snuffed out by his failure to win the presidency. He found some pleasure in gardening and in animals, and he still played a mean game of chess and hand of whist. Food and drink brought him pleasure, but once satisfied, he would ask his servant David to wheel his large armchair about and put his feet up. Left again to the solitude of his thoughts, he would say, "A dull man would be the death of me now."46

There was to be no dullness that season, but irony enough to sate even the general's enormous appetite for it. On December 2, the day before Congress convened, a telegram summoned him to Washington. He did not yet know of the tug-of-war being waged in the cabinet over what policy Buchanan should pursue toward the forts at Charleston or that his being called was a ploy by Floyd to delay Buchanan from sending reinforcements at

once to Anderson. What he did know was an overwhelming sense of exhila-
ration and mortification. He was needed at last at the seat of action, but he
was sick in bed, unable to move, let alone travel. It would be another ten days
before he forced his protesting body to endure the trip. By that time he
would find the City of Politics a place of indescribable confusion.[47]

DECEMBER

CHAPTER SEVEN

The Politics of Bewilderment

Our greatest danger at this moment arises from the mutual ignorance of the South and the North of each other's real feelings and purposes. . . . The North is not really hostile to the South whatever party presses and party leaders have induced the South to think . . . great mistakes have been made, and great mischiefs have been done by both parties. . . . [T]he country is on the brink of disunion, and of disaster and misery of which no man can measure the magnitude or foretell the end.

—C. B. Haddock of New Hampshire
December 18, 1860[1]

THE CITY OF POLITICS belonged to the politicians again. From every corner of the nation they descended on the capital like a migratory herd returning to its ancient feeding ground. The water holes and boardinghouses sprang eagerly to life, along with the restaurants, the inevitable oyster houses, and the elegant lairs of the lady lobbyists. For that most endangered of species the lame duck, it was a final visit to the oasis of privilege, a last lapping up of franks, stationery, and other perks. In the smoke-palled parlors, the cavernous dining halls, and the corridors of the hotels the herds and their parasites gathered to trade rumors and predictions, their ears alert for the faintest hint of opportunity or danger.

Some, like young Robert Hatton of Tennessee, came in obscurity with only a few dollars in his pocket to reclaim his old room at Brown's. Others, like William H. Seward, the most powerful Republican except for Lincoln and the man who had expected to be president, arrived in expectation. Sniffing the political winds, Seward caught the scent of fear in the air everywhere around him. "The President, and all Union men here, are alarmed and despondent," he reported after only one day in town. "The Republicans who come here are ignorant of the real design or danger."[2]

Back too came Stephen A. Douglas, now as much a sectional leader as the southern ultras who had destroyed their party to defeat him. At forty-seven the Little Giant had already been the towering figure in American politics for a decade. Worn and ravaged by the campaign, he still stood ready to challenge any slight or allusion or idea that affronted him. With his beautiful young wife, Adele, a grandniece of Dolley Madison's and one of Washington's reigning beauties when Douglas married her in 1856, he reopened the house he had built for them on I Street west of New Jersey Avenue. The area had been neglected until Douglas moved there; now he was flanked by Vice President John C. Breckinridge and Senator Henry M. Rice of Minnesota on what had come to be called Minnesota Row.3

To the well-wishers who serenaded him on his return, Douglas offered a simple and pointed message. "Let all asperities drop," he said, "all ill feeling be buried, and let all real patriots strive to save the Union."4

No patriot embraced that sentiment more heartily than the senior senator from Kentucky. At seventy-four, John J. Crittenden was older than the Constitution he loved so ardently and was determined to preserve. For him politics had become a nightmare of painful choices. In 1858 he had supported Douglas in Illinois, even though Mary Lincoln's father was one of his dearest friends. A former Whig, he had grown disillusioned with both parties for their endless agitation over slavery and drifted reluctantly into the American party. "I am tired of the public life," Crittenden admitted in April 1860, "disgusted with the low party politics of the day, and the miserable scramble for place & plunder."5

But the crisis compelled him to shove such sentiments aside and embrace the role of the great compromiser long played by his old friend and mentor Henry Clay. No man was better suited to the task. Crittenden's politics were as moderate as his appetites, and his style was pleasingly understated. He had once owned nine slaves but had voted in the legislature as early as 1833 to restrict the importation of slaves into Kentucky. It took him only a few days to grasp how serious the crisis was. "Political affairs here look most gloomy," he wrote a friend in Kentucky. ". . . [T]hey are *mixed* up with darkness."6

As Congress convened on December 3, the chairs of South Carolina's senators, Chesnut and Hammond, were ominously vacant. The Carolina representatives were also expected to leave. Everyone had heard about the clash in the cabinet over the annual message, but no one knew who had prevailed or what the outcome would be.7

The message reached both houses of Congress at noon and promptly went over the telegraph wires to the nation. Buchanan reminded everyone that he had "long foreseen and often forewarned my countrymen of the now impending danger." He laid the blame for the crisis wholly on "the incessant and violent agitation of the slavery question throughout the North, for the last quarter of a century," which had "produced its malign influence on the slaves, and inspired them with vague notions of freedom. Hence a sense of security no longer exists around the family altar. This feeling of peace at home has given place to apprehensions of servile insurrections."[8]

With these words Buchanan articulated an issue many southerners preferred not to voice, their deep-rooted fear of a slave revolt. All that was needed to ease the crisis, the president asserted, was to assure southerners that their right to slavery was forever secure. To do this, he urged the calling of a constitutional convention to devise an amendment that would recognize the right to hold slaves as property, protect this right in all territories, and guarantee the right of a master to have a runaway slave returned to him. Pending that outcome, he insisted that the Republican victory posed no real threat to the South and that Lincoln's election offered no ground for secession.[9]

Buchanan flatly denied that any right of secession existed but admitted that resistance to oppression was legitimate. "This is revolution against an established Government," he declared, "and not a voluntary secession from it by virtue of an inherent constitutional right. . . . [S]ecession is neither more nor less than revolution." But the president could meet any such attempt only through lawful means, and the law provided no means for making war upon a state or coercing it in any way beyond protecting the public property. Moreover, the machinery of the federal government for enforcing the law had ceased to exist in South Carolina. It was up to Congress to pass new legislation or take whatever action it deemed appropriate to meet the crisis.[10]

As Trescot had predicted, the message pleased no one and had something to outrage everyone. Seward expressed in his wry way the reaction of disgruntled northerners. "The Message . . . shows conclusively that it is the duty of the President to execute the laws—unless somebody opposes him," he said, "and that no State has a right to go out of the Union—unless it wants to." An annoyed Crittenden agreed that "To say that no State has a right to secede . . . and yet that the Union has no right to interpose any obstacles to secession, seems to me altogether contradictory." Charles Francis Adams dismissed it as "in all respects like the author, timid and vacillating. . . . It satisfied no one and did no service in smoothing the waters."[11]

Moderate men despaired because the message offered no clear line of policy beyond the proposal for a convention that would take far too long to implement. Southerners were too angered by Buchanan's denial of the right of secession to see much else. "If the President thought to frighten our people by opposing secession," said one South Carolinian, "he is wofully [*sic*] mistaken." Even Charleston's most diehard Unionist was disgusted by the message. "Like himself, it is a shuffling, insincere and shabby performance," declared James Petigru. "He has receded from one point to another until he has given up all pretension to the respect of anybody."[12]

The message was vintage Buchanan. Couched in the well-reasoned logic of the lawyer, much of it was correct and perceptive. It summarized the dilemma as a string of knots and conundrums, showing what could not be done but not what could be done. Buchanan tried to go by the book at a time when the book no longer applied and was in the process of being discarded. Indeed, that was his point: Now, more than ever, it was crucial to go by the book. But he viewed its chapters through too narrow and legalistic an eye. However right his approach, it was utterly inadequate to the gravity of the crisis. What was needed was not a brief or a sermon but a course of action and a position around which reasonable men could rally. Buchanan provided neither one and thereby forfeited what little influence remained in his waning presidency.

Yet what could he have possibly said or done that would satisfy more than a minority of those clamoring for him to do something? What viable options did he have? He was, after all, a lame duck preparing to hand over the government to a president he had never met from a party he despised because it advocated principles he thought wrong and harmful. His policy, the only one that made any sense to him, was to avoid starting a war, act within the bounds of law, keep the door open for compromise, and wait for Congress to give him such authority as it saw fit. What other course was possible?[13]

He was caught in the fundamental dilemma of any democracy. How could he save the Republic by resorting to unrepublican means? How could he suppress one illegal act by the use of another? Like most men of his generation, Buchanan believed passionately in the separation of powers. "It is the true mission of the Democracy," he had said a decade earlier, "to resist centralism and the absorption of unconstitutional powers by the President and Congress." Now he was being urged to avoid a constitutional crisis by using unconstitutional means, to save what he most believed in by going directly against what he most believed. He might reappoint federal officers for Charleston and reinstall them by force, but on what grounds? The sending of citizens from one state to occupy the territory or offices of another amounted, in his view, to a flagrant violation of the Constitution and long-established custom.[14]

Custom, tradition, every tenet of his beliefs told Buchanan that he must refer the problem to Congress and look to it for direction. Yet what was Congress if not a mirror of the very forces that had torn the country apart for the past decade? Buchanan knew this firsthand from his own dismal term in office, when he had watched Congress fall prostrate from interminable wrangling over sectional issues that every year grew increasingly bitter and farther removed from any solution. Congress was the only forum to which a dutiful and desperate executive could look for help. Unfortunately it had become more a part of the problem than a solution to it.

CONGRESS RESPONDED by doing what it had always done best: It talked, created committees, and talked some more. The House formed a committee of thirty-three with one representative from every state, a vehicle so unwieldy that it did not begin meeting until December 11 amid refusals by some southern members to serve. No one expected much from the committee; Henry Winter Davis of Maryland dismissed it as "a humbug . . . but as it will amuse men's minds it *may* do no harm." The chairman, genial, witty Thomas Corwin of Ohio, took his job seriously. At sixty-seven the tall, heavyset Corwin was regarded as the peacemaker of the House. He was forceful and eloquent, bristling with nervous intensity yet capable of reducing the most churlish listener to helpless laughter with jokes.[15]

"One of the dangerous things to a public man," Corwin once lamented, "is to become known as a jester. People will go to hear such a man, and then they will be disappointed if he talks to them seriously." He was never more serious than he was in this post. He knew the fight was all uphill and against long odds. One of the first things he did was open a private correspondence with Lincoln, and one of the first things he told him was "I have never, in my life, seen my country in such a dangerous position . . . but I am resolved not to be paralyzed by dismay."[16]

The Senate showed its temper at the opening bell, when Thomas L. Clingman of North Carolina used the routine motion to print the president's message as a springboard to denounce the Republican party and warn of multiple secessions within sixty days. John Crittenden jumped in with a plea for the Senate not to get embroiled in an angry debate. It was a futile request. The next day John P. Hale of New Hampshire warmly defended the Republicans and was promptly rebuked by Alfred Iverson of Georgia, who reminded everyone that "there is an enmity between the northern and southern people that is deep and enduring, and you never can eradicate it—never!"[17]

Not until December 10 did Lazarus W. Powell of Kentucky, dodging the rhetorical salvos, manage to get onto the floor his resolution to create a select committee of thirteen. He was following in the footsteps of the venerated Henry Clay, who had secured a similar committee to put together the Compromise of 1850. The task had been fiendishly difficult a decade earlier, and many believed that statesmen had been of a much higher caliber then. Jefferson Davis of Mississippi, a key southern spokesman, dismissed Powell's motion as a "quack nostrum," a view shared less candidly by others. "The people, under God, must save this Union, if it is to be saved," offered James Dixon of Connecticut helpfully. "Politicians cannot do it."[18]

No one seemed clear about what exactly the politicians *could* do. Nothing even remotely resembling a consensus could be found on any policy or course of action. On the evening of December 3, after the opening session, the Republican members held a caucus and decided on a plan of action—or rather nonaction. "What we most want," reported Elihu Washburne of Illinois to his friend Lincoln, "is a 'masterly inactivity.' " The Republicans would push the regular public business, avoid discussing the crisis as much as possible, reject all overtures of compromise, and await the inauguration. "For Republicans to take steps towards getting up committees or proposing new compromises," Trumbull explained to Lincoln, "is an admission that to conduct the government on the principles on which we carried the election would be wrong. Inactivity & a kind spirit is [*sic*] . . . all that is left for us to do, till the 4th of March."[19]

But this was more easily said than done at a time when parties were made of eggshells. So much attention had been given to the shattering of the Democratic party that fault lines within the Republican party were often ignored. It was easy to forget how new and fragile the party was and how uneasily its factions sat with one another. The campaign had buried these differences beneath the struggle against its adversaries, but they emerged with force once victory was achieved and the crisis loomed.

The Republican party was a patchwork of former Whigs, abolitionist refugees from third parties, and a smattering of old Democrats, all searching for a clear political identity. Lincoln was a onetime Whig whose views on slavery were slippery enough to convince abolitionists that he was too soft on the issue, and southerners that he was an abolitionist. Seward qualified as a political gypsy, having been a National Republican, an Anti-Mason, and a Whig before becoming a Republican. Scarcely had the members of Congress warmed their seats when the differences among them began surfacing, especially on the sensitive issue of compromise. It emerged as the defining issue of the triumphant Republican party.

The pressure from all sides was immense. Even before Congress convened, Seward was put in an awkward position when his political mentor, Thurlow Weed, floated a compromise proposal in his Albany newspaper late in November. Taking the farsighted view that the victorious Republicans could afford some conciliatory gesture, he offered proposals that startled moderates and outraged ultras. Some New York Republican congressmen stopped at the *Tribune* office to complain and were told by Charles Dana that the articles had come from Seward, who hoped to fashion a great compromise in the tradition of Clay and Webster. An exasperated Seward noted that "Mr. Weed's articles have brought perplexities about me which he, with all his astuteness, did not foresee."[20]

Senator Preston King of New York told Weed bluntly: "It cannot be done. You must abandon your position. It will prove distasteful to the majority of those whom you have hitherto led. You and Seward should be among the foremost to brandish the lance and shout for war." Weed had no taste for either lances or war. "I want to occupy practical and efficient, instead of absurd and useless ground," he replied. "Some of the Slave States can be saved." The sagacious Weed saw a broader canvas that eluded men like King, and he tried at least to suggest its presence. "The fight is over," he added. "Practically, the issues of the late campaign are obsolete." But the effort was futile. Seward was already putting out political fires in Washington ignited by the intemperate remarks of Hale and others. He offered Weed a glimmer of his own views: "The Republican party to-day is as uncompromising as the Secessionists in South Carolina. A month hence each may come to think that moderation is wiser."[21]

Weed's proposal resembled one being readied by Crittenden, who hoped to undo the disastrous legacy of the Kansas-Nebraska Act by restoring some version of the Missouri Compromise line. In the House members offered resolutions advocating compromise or peaceful secession. On one busy day a motion for repeal of personal liberty laws sailed through, 153–14. Its preamble, calling for obedience to the Constitution, passed, 156–0, and a more radical version by abolitionist Owen Lovejoy of Illinois was approved, 136–0. The House even accepted a long-delayed resolution by Isaac N. Morris of Illinois upholding the Union. But everyone knew this was window dressing. All compromise proposals of substance were referred to the new committees, and little could be done until they spit something back or confessed bankruptcy. Meanwhile, the Republicans scrambled to hold their faltering ranks together. "All the mean material we've got is coming out now," wrote young Henry Adams to his brother Charles. ". . . Prepare yourself for a complete disorganization of our party."[22]

Henry's father, Charles Francis, held the seat in the House once occupied by his father, John Quincy Adams, the only man to enter Congress after having been president. Like his old friend Seward, Charles Francis Adams viewed the crisis as a surge of madness, a fever that needed time to abate, as well as a thinly disguised grab for power by southern politicians who had lost their hold on the federal government. "Nothing short of a surrender of everything gained by the election will avail," he observed. "They want to continue to rule." To keep the fever in check and maintain the status quo until Lincoln took office, some concessions might be possible that did not violate Republican principles.[23]

But what should those concessions be, and how to frame them for party members either riddled with fear or zealous in their righteousness? A sense of impending calamity hung in the air. "A fanaticism, an infatuation has seized the minds of many," observed John McClernand, an Illinois Democrat. James W. Grimes, the hardbitten senator from Iowa, was convinced that "Secession of one or more States is inevitable." Louisiana Senator Judah P. Benjamin saw "a revolution . . . of the most intense character. . . . I see not how bloodshed is to be avoided." Robert Hatton of Kentucky agreed that "we are on the eve of a revolution. . . . The folly of mankind has never been greater than is now being exhibited by the politicians of the South, and the North. Disunion is ruin to both sections."[24]

Ultra Republicans saw this same disaster unfolding, but most shared the view of Justin S. Morrill of Vermont that "There can be no compromise short of an entire surrender of our convictions of right and wrong, and I do not propose to make that surrender. . . . [W]e must accept the truth that there is an 'irrepressible conflict'—between our systems of civilization. I look for much suffering in all parts of the Union for the year to come."[25]

THE REPUBLICANS were not alone in trying to close ranks. Southern Democrats too groped for a stance that would unify them. Cotton state men argued with border state men and with one another on what to do and when to do it. The absence of the South Carolina senators prevented them from exerting leadership, leaving the task to the state's congressmen. One of them, Milledge L. Bonham, believed many southern members would walk once South Carolina passed its ordinance of secession. Learning of a concerted effort by Cobb, Floyd, Thompson, Jefferson Davis, and others to delay any action until Buchanan's term ended, Bonham let Cobb know in plain language that the idea was absurd, that most southerners favored immediate action, and that "The State will be eternally & forever disgraced now if she hesitates."[26]

Cobb needed no reminders, having already agonized over the address he had written for the people of his own state. On the evening of December 6 the ultras held a caucus to plot strategy. The next morning Cobb handed a copy of his address to Black to give Buchanan, knowing that it sealed his fate in the cabinet. "I hope to part from the old gentleman pleasantly," he wrote a friend. On the 8th, as bright weather turned to pouring rain, Cobb resigned his post. Sorrowfully his family packed up to leave Washington, their hearts aching with apprehension about the future. Politics, Mary Ann Cobb once observed, was "like a filthy pool—now and then throwing up mud and slime from its bottom."[27]

For the beleaguered Buchanan the slime was coming up all around him. Republicans ridiculed the annual message, and the president's southern friends dropped away in protest over its stand against secession. The few moderates who approved his approach were drowned out by voices demanding that he do something. But what was he to do? The options available were limited and unappetizing, given his objective, which was in Joseph Holt's words, "to preserve the peace if possible and hand over the Government intact to his successor." He might have tried to rouse the people with an impassioned speech, but that was not his style. What the country needed was reason, not rhetoric, of which it already had surplus. Reason demanded a tone and policy of conciliation and compromise, both of which happened to suit his temperament. As a veteran diplomat and politician he spoke the language of compromise. In this grave crisis what more logical and reasonable course to pursue than every possible avenue to accommodation?[28]

Even if Buchanan wished to pursue a more vigorous policy, what would it be? He had called for a constitutional convention, but Congress had to authorize any such body. He could appoint a new collector for Charleston and try to reestablish the federal presence there, but Congress had to confirm the appointment. He could send reinforcements to Anderson, and had taken steps to do so, but prudence dictated that he go slowly because no single step was more likely to trigger a war. What if he took these steps and a clash ensued? The army was ill prepared to respond, and he had no legal authority to use troops unless Congress passed a new force bill, as it was not likely to do.

Critics and carpers kept harking back to Andrew Jackson's tough stand against the nullifiers in 1832–33. "Oh for an hour of Old Hickory!" rang the cry across the North, but the image was as misleading as it was compelling. Those enchanted by Jackson's tough talk conveniently forgot that he had asked for and received a force bill from Congress to enforce the revenue laws, and that in the end he arranged a compromise to defuse the crisis before it came to blows. The issue of secession had not been tested, and the confrontation had taken place on a much smaller stage than existed thirty years later. Enough had happened in those three decades to overwhelm even a Jackson.[29]

Hannibal Hamlin was hardly alone in damning the administration as "criminaly [*sic*] negligent in its clear and unmistakable duty," and he was no less wrong in thinking that duty clear or unmistakable. For Buchanan to move aggressively under the circumstances would have been to go against not only his temperament and training but also every fiber of his belief in government. Any strong act would not only stretch the power of the executive but also undercut the work of the two congressional committees that had just been formed and had yet to try their hand at working out a compromise.[30]

And what would be gained by such a move? Ultras liked to proclaim the view that "A single armed ship and five hundred recruits, backed by a Presidential will, would manifestly have seriously crippled and might perhaps have effectually crushed this local insurrection." But reinforcements could not have secured all the forts. Those familiar with the southern temper realized that the arrival of more troops would have inflamed rather than cowed the locals, who could produce far more men in a hurry than could the government. Even if the forts could have been secured, what would have been gained other than time for more negotiation, precisely what Buchanan was already trying to do?[31]

About the only thing the sending of reinforcements would accomplish was to provoke a shooting war on Buchanan's watch. For reasons of both policy and prejudice, Old Buck wanted desperately to avoid that outcome. In his mind it was Lincoln's problem in every sense. Who had created the crisis but the Republicans, not merely by winning the election (and Buchanan's own state) but through years of agitation over the slavery issue? Why should he bear the burden of their follies? He had no liking for them or their beliefs, and no desire to aid them in any way.

The true policy, then, was to maintain the status quo, however precarious, and resist efforts by extremists on both sides to force his hand. This was not easy with a divided cabinet tugging relentlessly at him over the question of sending reinforcements. That issue took on a poignant hue when Eliza Anderson arrived from New York to pour out her distress over her husband's dangerous position and plead that help be sent him. The interview pained Buchanan deeply. Scarcely had she left the White House when the South Carolina congressmen arrived to argue their case. Buchanan stepped out of a cabinet meeting to greet them in the anteroom, where he told them pointedly of Eliza Anderson's visit and her fear that a mob might attack her husband's command at any moment. He had a responsibility to protect Anderson and his men; surely the congressmen could understand that.[32]

The way to put him at risk, countered William Porcher Miles and Lawrence Keitt, was to send troops; that would surely provoke an attack. They assured Buchanan that Anderson was in no danger and that no attack on the forts would even be contemplated until the state convention met on December 17 to consider secession. Maintain the status quo, they urged, and let the matter be resolved by negotiation. Buchanan hesitated. The conversation was useful, he said, but he preferred something in writing. The South Carolinians withdrew and delivered to the president a memorandum on Monday, the 10th.

> In compliance with our statement to you yesterday, we now express to you our strong convictions that neither the constituted authorities, nor any body of the people of the State of South Carolina, will either attack or molest the United States forts in the harbor of Charleston, previously to the action of the Convention, and we hope and believe not until an offer has been made, through an accredited representative, to negotiate for an amicable arrangement of all matters between the State and the Federal Government, provided that no reinforcements shall be sent into those forts, and their relative military status shall remain as at present.

Beneath this extraordinary paragraph lurked a huge iceberg of supposition and misunderstanding. Buchanan's shrewd eye scanned the language and quibbled over a word or two. Later Miles and Keitt insisted that they had explained exactly what was meant by "relative military status" and mentioned that any shift of troops by Anderson from Fort Moultrie to Fort Sumter would violate this provision. Buchanan demurred that his policy was to maintain the status quo but that he could pledge nothing. It was, after all, "a matter of honor among gentlemen," he added cryptically as they rose to leave. "I do not know that any paper or writing is necessary. We understand each other."[33]

What if you change your mind? they asked. Any shift would put them in an embarrassing position. "Then," replied the president, "I would first return you this paper." But what exactly was this paper? Certainly it was nothing official—merely a statement given the president by five congressmen who had no authority to speak for anyone except themselves, who could not and would not have been recognized as representatives of anyone or anything else. As a gentleman's agreement, whom could it commit to what? All parties went away believing a bargain had been struck, without knowing exactly what the bargain was, who the parties to it were, and what its precise terms were.

On December 9 Trescot returned to Washington. His trip south had not been altogether pleasant. He and Drayton had tried to persuade Governor Gist to get the secession ordinance postponed, but Gist had been forewarned by Bonham and told them flatly that if the convention tried to delay secession, he would give a speech in Charleston exhorting the immediate seizure of the forts. Gist was way ahead of Trescot. He intended to "pass the ordinance of secession[,] send a commissioner or commissioners to the President to inform him of the fact—direct the Legislature to take the necessary steps to carry out the movement & adjourn sine die, without providing for any other meeting of the convention. The door will then be locked & the key lost and it will take two thirds of both branches of the Legislature to find it, if they want to go in again."34

A disappointed Trescot canvassed enough leaders in Columbia to realize that postponement was impossible. He called on Buchanan on Monday and found him with the Carolina congressmen. After they had gone, Buchanan showed him the memorandum. Trescot remarked that it did not go any farther than the letter from Gist. "What letter?" asked Buchanan, puzzled. Trescot got the letter and read it to Buchanan, adding that his visit to Columbia confirmed the views he had offered earlier. What if Congress refuses to negotiate? asked Buchanan. "Then sir," Trescot replied, ". . . the State will take the Forts—what else can she do if she is in earnest? But I hope the negotiation will not fail."35

In one wobbly stroke Buchanan had veered from his determination to reinforce Anderson to a policy of standing pat, partly because his cabinet was crumbling about him. Cobb had departed, taking with him the potential support of Georgia, the key state in the Deep South whose alliance to South Carolina could assure a unified secession movement. Lewis Cass told Buchanan on the 11th that he was resigning. The next day he wrote indignantly that "additional troops should be sent to reinforce the forts" and "an armed vessel should likewise be ordered there . . . these measures should be adopted without the least delay."36

A few hours after Cass left the White House, two of Buchanan's oldest senatorial friends, John Slidell of Louisiana and William M. Gwin of California, called to chastise him for refusing to pledge that no reinforcements would be sent to Anderson. Buchanan's frayed temper snapped. Both of them were disunionists, he said curtly, and he was sorry ever to have heeded their advice. They stormed from the room, never again to speak a friendly word to him. Trescot handed his resignation to Cass and was preparing to leave Washington. Joseph Holt lay seriously ill with pneumonia and could exert no influence.37

Before Buchanan could absorb these events, seven senators and twenty-three representatives from southern states caucused on the 13th and issued a manifesto urging secession and the formation of a southern confederacy. "The argument is exhausted," they proclaimed. "All hope of relief in the Union, through the agencies of committees, Congressional legislation, or constitutional amendments, is extinguished . . . the Republicans are resolute in the purpose to grant nothing that will or ought to satisfy the South." To make matters worse, William M. Browne, the prosouthern editor of the Washington *Constitution*, considered the administration's organ, was brazenly advocating secession. Outraged Unionists assumed that Browne spoke for Buchanan and denounced the president's complicity in the southern conspiracy. "For God's sake," cried Horatio King to Judge Black, "let us see the government placed squarely and unequivocally on the side of the Union!"[38]

The sheer momentum of events threatened to steamroller Buchanan into oblivion or disgrace. Wearily he set about patching up his broken cabinet. He gave Cobb's Treasury post to the patents commissioner Philip F. Thomas, moved Black to the State Department, and replaced him with the assistant attorney general Edwin M. Stanton despite warnings that Stanton could not be trusted. Cass let it be known that he wanted his old post back, but Buchanan ignored the plea and declared himself well rid of the old man. In the midst of these events a rumor swept through the city on Sunday the 16th that Holt was dead. It did not abate until Holt appeared at his office on Monday gaunt but very much alive.[39]

Saturday the 15th was a snowy day in Washington. Three days earlier Scott had tried vainly to persuade Floyd to send reinforcements to Charleston; that snowy Saturday he went with Floyd to see the president and repeated his argument. Buchanan told them what he wrote Cass that same day: "[B]elieving as I do, that no present necessity exists for a resort to force for the protection of the public property, it was impossible for me to have risked a collision of arms in the harbor of Charleston." Later that day a discouraged Scott jotted a note to Buchanan reminding him that in 1833 Jackson had, *prior* to passage of the force bill, used an act of 1807 "authorizing the employment of the land & naval forces" to send a sloop of war, two revenue cutters, and reinforcements to Fort Moultrie to defend the fort and enforce the revenue laws. Scott knew this well because he had arrived in Charleston to oversee the troops the day after the nullification ordinance had been passed. But Buchanan was no Jackson; the most he could do was issue a proclamation declaring January 4 a day of national prayer and fasting.[40]

In South Carolina the tenure of William Gist came to an end. On that same Saturday the legislature surprised many Carolinians by choosing Francis W. Pickens as the new governor. Buchanan promptly sent Caleb Cushing, a Massachusetts Democrat sympathetic to the South, to Columbia with a letter asking Pickens to delay passing a secession ordinance. He did not know that Pickens had already dispatched a letter to him demanding surrender of the forts. If that were not enough, Floyd fell ill amid rumors of a scandal in his department. Never had Buchanan felt more like the Old Public Functionary. In his misery, March 4 looked as far away as the century's end.

.   .   .

THE DAY BEFORE SCOTT SAW BUCHANAN, he described to Lyman Trumbull Fort Moultrie's pathetic defense and asserted that eight hundred men could hold it for months. On the 17th, in a long visit with his old friend Elihu Washburne of Illinois, Scott repeated his views along with his conviction that Fort Sumter held the key to the whole harbor. "I wish to God that Mr. Lincoln was in office," he said. "I do not know him, but I believe him a true, honest and *conservative* man." He paused, then asked, "Mr. Washburne, is he a firm man?" Washburne replied that he had known Lincoln a long time and that he would do his duty. Then, said a gratified Scott, "all is not lost."41

The problem was figuring out what duty required right now. Ultra Republicans blasted Buchanan as a coward and a traitor. "I cannot see," asserted Hannibal Hamlin, "why the President is not just as guilty as the men in South Carolina." Trumbull feared that Buchanan was in league with the "traitors to his country." So did Washburne, Preston King, the elder Frank Blair, Joseph Medill, and scores of others. "But for the imbecility of President & the treachery of his subordinates," one observer wrote Lincoln, "even South Carolina would not venture upon secession." The implacable Charles Sumner hoped that four or five cotton states would stay out of the Union long enough "to be completely humbled and chastened and to leave us in the control of the Government."42

Those who had harsh words for the president were no less adamant about resisting any form of compromise. They bridled at the willingness of moderates to consider proposals, even to offer some of their own, and to play an active role in the select committees trying to hammer out a settlement. George G. Fogg of the Republican National Committee was aghast at what he saw. "On reaching Washington," he reported to Lincoln, "I found great numbers of our friends afflicted with the secession panic and almost ready to concede away the entire Republican platform to pacify the secessionists." Others showered Lincoln with similar views and pleaded with him not to say or do anything public, and to encourage no compromise.43

Those close to Lincoln knew their man. On the essential issue Lincoln never wavered. As early as December 10 he wrote Trumbull, "Let there be no compromise on the question of *extending* slavery. If there be, all our labor is lost, and, ere long, must be done again. The dangerous ground—that into which some of our friends have a hankering to run—is Pop. Sov. Have none of it. Stand firm. The tug has to come, & better now, than any time hereafter." Similar messages went out to Washburne, William Kellogg, an Illinois congressman flirting with compromise, Thurlow Weed, and others.44

To Weed he added his views on secession. "No state can, in any way lawfully," he said, "get out of the Union, without the consent of the others ... it is the duty of the President, and other government functionaries to run the machine as it is." On the forts, Lincoln was no less clear. "If the forts shall be given up before the inauguration [*sic*]," he wrote Frank Blair, an elder statesman who had once been a part of Andrew Jackson's "kitchen cabinet," "the General must retake them afterwards." He asked Washburne to assure Scott "to be as well prepared as he can to either *hold*, or *retake*, the forts, as the case may require, at, and after the inauguration."[45]

That such assurances went to the elder Blair was no accident; he had gone to Springfield on the 11th and urged Lincoln to reject all overtures of compromise. While these views of Lincoln were not circulated publicly, gratified Republican hard-liners used them to stiffen the backbones of wavering colleagues and to guide their own approach to efforts at compromise. They also got help from Ben Wade of Ohio, as crude and rough a piece of western lumber as could be found in Congress. On December 17, while moderates cringed, Wade stood up in the Senate before packed galleries and jammed cloakrooms and made a scathing speech denouncing secession and rejecting all compromise.[46]

What more could the South want? Wade asked scornfully. "You have had the legislative power of the country. . . . You own the Cabinet, you own the Senate, and I may add, you own the President . . . as much as you own the servant upon your own plantation." He pronounced the day of compromise to be over. "The most solemn compromises we have ever made have been violated without a whereas. What have we to compromise? . . . [W]e went to the people . . . and we beat you upon the plainest and most palpable issue that ever was presented to the American people." As for South Carolina, it was but "a small State; and probably, if she were sunk by an earthquake to-day, we would hardly ever find it out, except by the unwonted harmony that might prevail in this Chamber."[47]

"Wade's speech was just what was wanted," said Washburne, as was a strong speech against secession by the maverick Andrew Johnson of Tennessee. Moderates took a dimmer view. Robert Hatton approved Johnson's position but recoiled from Wade's extreme views as "calculated to do great harm, and render the prospect of any adjustment remote." The search for middle ground grew ever bleaker as positions hardened. Even Democrats of moderate views like Supreme Court Justice John A. Campbell of Alabama, who had staunchly supported Jackson against the nullifiers, despaired of averting disaster. Campbell had tried in vain to get Lincoln to issue some reassuring statement to help southern moderates in their struggle against ultras. "I believe that a final settlement of this slavery question should be made, or that disunion will follow," he confided to former President Pierce. "Agitation can not be carried on further, without a civil war."[48]

James Grimes of Iowa took an even grimmer view. "South Carolina will leave the Union, so far as she has the power, this week," he predicted on the 16th. ". . . Five or six States *may* follow her. . . . There will be an effort to go peacefully, but war of a most bitter and sanguinary character will be sure to follow in a short time. . . . No reasonable concession will satisfy the rebels. . . . They want to debauch the moral sentiment of the people of the North, by making them agree . . . that slavery is a benign, constitutional system, and that it shall be extended in the end all over this continent." Nowhere did Grimes see the faintest sign of leadership. "The whole cabinet is tumbling to pieces," he reported, "and what remains is without influence. Mr. Buchanan, it is said, about equally divides his time between praying and crying. Such a perfect imbecile never held office before."[49]

"THE SAME GLOOM AND DEPRESSION is still over this city," wrote a dejected Kate Thompson to Mary Ann Cobb, now back in Georgia, "no parties, no dinners, every body looks sad." Although the social whirl did not start in earnest until New Year's Eve, Kate already sensed it was aborted. With the usual rituals upset and her husband's future uncertain, time hung heavily on her hands. She refused to give in to it, ventured only twice to the Capitol galleries, and made a point of not calling on any Black Republicans or even the Douglases. She continued to see the president and Harriet Lane, if only because so many other friends were deserting them, but not a word of politics passed between her and Harriet. It was not only the uncertainty that bothered Kate but also the strange air of unreality that hovered over the city. The men who came home with her husband to dine, whether friends or strangers, talked calmly, even eagerly, of secession at the price of war if necessary. A Dr. Maynard called one evening and spent two hours trying to sell Thompson three thousand guns. "My head is nearly crazy," Kate admitted, "and my heart goes *pit-a-pat*, at any sound I hear. What are we all coming to? Where is the end of all this trouble?"[50]

The stillborn social season allowed at least one event, the wedding of John E. Bouligny of Louisiana to the daughter of a wealthy Washington grocer named Parker. Bouligny was a "South American," as southern members of the American party were called, and one of the few Deep South representatives opposed to secession. It was a magnificent if unusual ceremony. Parker transformed his large house into a conservatory splashed with roses and lilies and fountains illuminated by special lighting. The president and his niece were among the guests settled into the drawing room, where a crimson velvet curtain had been stretched across the area in front of the seats. When everyone was in place, the curtain drew back, revealing the bridal tableau with the bride at its center in her gorgeously elaborate wedding dress.[51]

After the ceremony, the guests remained in place until Buchanan had gone forward to wish the couple happiness and returned to his seat. Standing behind his chair, Sarah Pryor was shocked at how much he had aged since summer. As the crowd dispersed to admire the lavish display of gifts, Buchanan kept his seat and chatted with those who came to greet him. Suddenly he heard a commotion in an adjoining room. He glanced over his shoulder with a frown and asked, "Madam, do you suppose the house is on fire?"

Sarah went out to investigate and found Lawrence Keitt of South Carolina in the entrance hall. The flamboyant Keitt was regarded by many as a vain, clever political peacock whose bombastic and extravagant style undercut whatever he had to say. Only a few people knew of the corrosive sorrow that gnawed deep within him. That past February his brother had been lying sick in bed at his Florida plantation when one of the field hands crept into the room and slit his throat. On this day Keitt exhibited more than his usual state of frenzy, jumping in the air like a child and waving a piece of paper over his head. "Thank God!" he cried over and over. "Oh, thank God!"[52]

"Mr. Keitt, are you crazy?" murmured Sarah, grabbing hold of him. "The President hears you, and wants to know what is the matter."

"Oh! South Carolina has seceded! Here's the telegram. I feel like a boy let out of school."

Sarah looked at him in bewilderment, then hurried back to Buchanan. Bending low over the chair, she whispered the news to him. He looked at her with stricken eyes, then slumped back in the chair. "Madam," he croaked in a hoarse voice, "might I beg you to have my carriage called?" She did so, and the president departed without a word to anyone. Sarah found her husband, who was talking with Keitt, and they left at once to go to the house of Stephen A. Douglas. All thoughts of the bride and groom, wedding cake, and wedding breakfast had vanished.

CHAPTER EIGHT

Turning Points

I for one don't dare to look into the abyss of horror which opens before me. I am sure no country ever before contained the elements for more utter anarchy—three months back, so safe, so calm, so boastfully thriving, so proudly prosperous—& now with no foot of ground undisputed, no fireside safe, no interests protected, no law, no legislation. . . . North arrayed against South & South defending itself against the North is brother & sister attempting each other's life. . . . I am not Southern heaven knows & at heart if not abolition at least anti-slavery but I must concede that the tone of the South has been most firm, calm, manly & decided. . . . Carolina women say they are proud to give their sons & husbands to defend this country. Alas! I have no country to defend for the nation is dead.

—Sallie Baxter Hampton
Mid-December 1860[1]

AT SIXTY-SIX Caroline Gilman felt in her bones the chill of approaching winter more than she once had. The season could not be made to look anything but bleak to her, nor Christmas seem more unmerry. The world seemed so strange, turned upside down as never before in the forty-one years since she had come to Charleston from Massachusetts as the bride of the Reverend Samuel Gilman. During that time she had gained a modest reputation as a writer of verse, children's books, and other works. After twenty-six years her first book, *Recollections of a Housekeeper*, still delighted readers with its vignettes from the early years of her marriage. She had come a long way since the time when, at age sixteen, a newspaper printed one of her poems and reduced her to tears of embarrassment. The world, it seemed, had not come nearly as far.[2]

Literature and religion had always been the core of her life along with family, and now both seemed helpless to avert impending disaster. A few nights earlier, on the eve of the secession convention, Willie had been ordered to go with his unit, the Washington Light Infantry, aboard a steamer to block any aid being sent to Fort Sumter from Fort Moultrie. Caroline trembled in fear through the night, aware that a single cannon shot from either fort could sink the little steamer, but just after morning prayers Willie's boots were heard on the piazza, and everyone rushed to smother him in kisses.[3]

It was all a misunderstanding, he said. A captain at Moultrie had taken from the arsenal two boxes of ammunition ordered months earlier. Governor Gist learned of the move and, suspecting it might be intended for Sumter, sent troops to prevent the delivery. The boxes were returned under the agreement that no kinds of reinforcements should be taken into the forts. However, the next night Willie was sent to guard the arsenal and then was selected as part of a force put on the steamer to reconnoiter the coast and watch the forts. Caroline could not stop worrying about him. "What a volcano we stand over!" she mused.

On Christmas Eve day she mulled this over on her way to the cemetery. Mrs. Barrows had died the day before, and Caroline stood watching an elderly black man dig her grave, his wizened face impassive and his broad shoeless foot unflinching as it pushed hard against the cold metal spade. After a few minutes the man fetched up a piece of yellow-brown bone. He studied it, then said to her, "Dis ere is a piece of skull missis. My lor, how shallow dey dig before the revolution! Dis ere must be hundred year old."

"What do you do with the bones?" she asked.

"Why missis, I puts em all togedder . . . down at the bottom. You see, Missis, dis ere head was uncommon large, a powerful man, missis."

He surveyed the bit of bone, then set to digging again. "Missis," he ventured after a while, "you blieve dese bone goin to jine togedder at the resurrection?"

"No, Daddy, I do not. I hope to have some fresh new covering for my spirit in the great day."

"Well missis, I don know. I tink about de bones dat de fishes pick down in the ocean. He hard for come togedder again."

"It does not make much difference Daddy. If you and I do our work right the Lord will clothe us in his own good time."

"Just so missis." He paused, then smiled. "You know dis is de trute. De pure in heart shall see God."

She nodded and left. A week later she came again to the grave. The bit of skull was gone, and in its place lay a wreath of a dozen exquisite camellias.[4]

IT WAS THE ULTIMATE FRUSTRATION of Governor Gist that having longed so fervently and schemed so hard for secession, he had to leave office only days before it came. Events had elevated his office beyond a ceremonial seat, and no clear favorite loomed. Robert Barnwell Rhett coveted the place as a fitting reward for his long service to the secessionist cause, but too many men shared the sentiments of D. L. Wardlaw, who cried, "For God's sake and the sake of our beloved state don't let Rhett be elected governor." The legislature took up the question on December 11 and labored through seven ballots before rejecting a chagrined Rhett in favor of a compromise candidate, Francis W. Pickens.[5]

For Pickens the new office was an improbable climax to an erratic career. Living up to the reputation of his ancestors had always been for him a challenge in which his ambitions seemed to outstrip his achievements. Three generations of prominence had endowed him with the obligatory social polish, classical education, and gift for oratory. Through inheritance and shrewd investments he had acquired several plantations in the Edgefield District and in Mississippi and Alabama. By 1847, at forty-two, he owned 417 slaves and was one of the South's largest slaveholders. Pickens relished his role among the elite. He exuded that peculiar planter's brew of generosity, charm, and culture mixed with arrogance, pride, imperiousness, and a moody disposition. His keen, well-trained mind had always to fight its way through the romantic fantasy that enshrouded the chivalric code. In a world of aloof, egocentric men he stood out for his cold, overbearing manner. His gift for rhetoric could fire a crowd, but his personality lacked the warmth to draw men to him. "I believe it my destiny," he admitted that winter, "to be disliked by all who know me well."[6]

These qualities skewed his political career. A college chum of Hammond's, he had followed the usual path into law, the legislature, and the shadow of his cousin the mighty Calhoun, who was so close to Pickens's father that he named his first son Francis Pickens Calhoun. As a young man Pickens had been present at the creation: the nullification fight of 1832–33. "If we have not the right of secession," he said then, "we have that of glorious rebellion, and I am prepared to go into it." He joined Hammond and Rhett in support of Calhoun, prompting John Quincy Adams to dismiss him as "a coarse sample of the South Carolina school of orator statesman—pompous, flashy, and shallow."[7]

Like Hammond and Rhett, Pickens came gradually to see Calhoun as less a mentor than an obstacle to his own ambitions. After he had served in Congress from 1834 to 1843, his political career stalled, then sank with the death of Calhoun in 1850. He suffered a disastrous defeat for the Senate in 1851, tried in vain for a House seat in 1853, and four years later lost a contest for the Senate to Hammond. In the most savage irony of all, Pickens learned from Bonham that Hammond had discredited him by saying he had fathered an illegitimate son in New Orleans in 1842. Whether true or not, the charge outraged Pickens. "If a man's character depends upon maids or low women," he said loftily, "he would indeed be damned to this world as well as the next."[8]

His personal life had undergone similar frustrations. At twenty-two he had married his childhood sweetheart only to lose her and a son to fever in 1842. Three years later he took a second wife, the daughter of a rich Charleston merchant, calling it "a *Duty* I owed myself and my children." But she died in 1853, and Pickens sought solace in politics. He joined moderates Benjamin Perry and James L. Orr in supporting the National Democrat party and became a Buchanan loyalist in 1856. Buchanan rewarded him with the Russian embassy, which Pickens accepted only after he had lost the Senate race to Hammond. When he went to Russia in 1858, he took with him a new wife.[9]

Since the death of his second wife in 1853, Pickens had traveled with his children to northern resorts and southern spas. At White Sulphur Springs in the summer of 1857 he met Lucy Petaway Holcombe, a slender, beautiful woman with large, limpid eyes, full lips, and an independent spirit. Pickens was then fifty-two, a stout man with flabby features on an oversized, bewigged head and watery eyes that showed little fire. He had daughters older than Lucy, whose combination of beauty and intelligence seemed to put her out of his reach. But the one true love of Lucy's life, a young lieutenant named Crittenden, had been executed by the Cubans after an aborted filibuster expedition in 1851.[10]

For all her beauty, Lucy was at twenty-six crossing from the magical world of charming belle to the shadowland of spinster. Her search for a suitable husband had taken on a subtle air of urgency, and Pickens offered two choice assets: wealth and social status. She hesitated, then accepted his proposal, and went off to Russia with her new husband. There Czar Alexander II was struck by her beauty and developed a passion for her. But Lucy despised Russia and grew homesick. Pickens withstood her complaints until April 1860, when he resigned the post. He did not reach New York until two days before the election. A stop in Washington to see Buchanan helped rekindle his political ambitions. He came home to South Carolina as an elder statesman free of controversy, the ghost of Calhoun lifted at last from his shoulders.[11]

His selection as governor climaxed a series of clever political moves, including speeches in Edgefield and to the legislature that convinced many of his zeal for secession. "I would be willing to appeal to the god of battles," he declared, "if need be, to cover the state with ruin, conflagration and blood rather than submit." This rhetoric was a shift from his tone in Washington, where he had appeared to oppose secession, and helped get him elected.

With his wife and office, Pickens was born anew as his state was being born anew. His inauguration took place at 2 p.m. on December 17, two hours after the secession convention had assembled for the first time. These prizes inflated his already generous sense of self-importance. His joy would soon be tempered by reminders that the scars from old political battles still ached among many prominent families that had long disliked him, and the presence of a beautiful, intelligent young wife provided women with a convenient object of envy as well.[12]

Within hours of assuming office Pickens undertook a little private diplomacy in the form of a letter to his old friend Buchanan. Speaking grandly as one executive to another, Pickens warned that he had been "authentically informed that the forts in Charleston harbor are now being thoroughly prepared to turn, with effect, their guns upon the interior and the city." He wanted all work on the forts stopped, no reinforcements sent to them, and approval for a token force of state troops to occupy Fort Sumter as a way of keeping the peace. "If something of the kind be not done," he added, "I cannot answer for the consequences."[13]

Pickens was not content merely to write a letter. Hearing of another attempt to obtain muskets at the arsenal for the forts, he went to Charleston the next day and personally took charge of military affairs. Captain Charles H. Simonton of the Washington Light Infantry was ordered to prevent any transfer of arms from the arsenal and to intercept any shift of men or arms from Moultrie to Sumter. If any boat bearing troops resisted his demand to turn back, he was to sink the boat and seize Sumter at once. The captain put a detachment of men aboard a small steamer and began regular patrol of the waters between the forts that night.[14]

Rain dampened both the inauguration and the opening of the secession convention in the Baptist Church. The delegates included the state's leading families and political leaders. Gist was there, fresh from his governor's chair, as were Chesnut, Orr, Miles, Rhett, Manning, Keitt, Magrath, Robert W. Barnwell, Christopher Memminger, Gabriel Manigault, Robert N. Gourdin, and Isaac W. Hayne. Gist hoped to be elected chairman, but the convention chose D. F. Jamison, who declared, "[W]e have two great dangers to fear—overtures from without, and precipitation within. I trust that the door is now forever closed to all further connection with our Northern confederates."[15]

It was evident that even moderates like Orr had come over to the secession cause, but the ardor for action was diluted that first day by news of an outbreak of smallpox in Columbia. Amid rumors that a box of contaminated rags had been sent from New York to infect the delegates, patriotism gave way to panic as the convention voted to adjourn to Charleston. The ultras who objected were mollified at an evening session that passed resolutions approving secession and the drafting of an ordinance. The vote was 159-0.[16]

Rain still fell the next morning when the delegates climbed aboard the rickety train to Charleston. As they approached the city, the Marine Artillery fired a salute of fifteen guns. Troops marched forward to escort the delegates from the depot, but their maneuvers got so tangled up that many guests got lost in the crowd. Jamison was conveyed to the Mills House; the others scattered like tourists to find their own lodgings. At four o'clock they convened in Institute Hall. Amid the carnival atmosphere one spectator took in events with particular relish. He was a reporter for Greeley's *Tribune*, operating under cover and sending dispatches north. His work enraged local authorities, but efforts to unmask him had failed, and the reporter missed no chance to twit them for their ineptness.[17]

The next day the members moved to the smaller, more intimate St. Andrew's Hall, where secret sessions could be held without prying spectators, and busied themselves with procedural matters while a committee drew up the secession ordinance. Inside the hall, business moved along with a quiet drone. Outside in the streets people poured into the city from all directions to be present at the creation. Representatives from Alabama and Mississippi were already on hand; Howell Cobb was invited from Georgia. From Governor A. B. Moore of Alabama came a blunt dispatch: "Tell the Convention to listen to no propositions of compromise or delay." Edmund Ruffin arrived in town early on the 19th, checked into the Charleston Hotel, and hurried to witness the event he hoped would nudge his own Virginia down the same path.[18]

On December 20, after some preliminary business, the ordinance to dissolve the Union was brought forth at 1:07 p.m., and the litany of the roll call began. By 1:30 all 169 voices had chanted "yea," and the deed was done. Outside the chimes of St. Michael's pealed, and an artillery salute rumbled from The Citadel and from "Old Secession," the cannon by the post office on which a copy of the ordinance had been pasted. Businesses closed for the day. Mindful of history, mimicking the solemnity of the signing of the Declaration of Independence, the delegates decided to recess until 6:30, when the formal signing of the ordinance would occur.[19]

Men rushed joyously about, whooping and shouting, rending the air with cheers, waving palmetto flags and the blue cockades that were the secessionist badge. "The greatest enthusiasm pervades our entire community," said one staid celebrant. "We feel we have done right, and are prepared to defend our act." A morose James Petigru, who with C. S. Bryan were the only outspoken Unionists left in Charleston, encountered a friend near city hall on Broad Street just as the bells began to peal. "Where's the fire?" Petigru growled.[20]

"Mr. Petigru, there is no fire; those are the joy bells ringing in honor of the passage of the Ordinance of Secession."

Petigru turned on him. "I tell you there is a fire," he said fiercely; "they have this day set a blazing torch to the temple of constitutional liberty and, please God, we shall have no more peace forever."

The signing ceremony was moved back to Institute Hall, which could hold more people than St. Andrew's. Governor Pickens and the legislature were invited to attend, as was Caleb Cushing, the emissary from Buchanan who had arrived in time to see how utterly futile his mission was. Cushing wisely declined to witness what most northerners considered treason in the making. Shortly after six the delegates made their way, through streets thronged with celebrants, to St. Andrew's. Once assembled, they formed in files of two and marched arm in arm to Institute Hall beneath the glow of bonfires. At the stairs they were joined by the legislators. The hall was packed with spectators buzzing with expectation.[21]

Jamison, leaning on his clerk's arm, entered through a rear door and took his place at the podium. Behind him came the leaders of the state senate and house clad in their robes of office. An ancient clergyman intoned a prayer, after which Jamison unfolded the parchment containing the ordinance and began to read in a solemn, deliberate voice: "We, the People of the State of South Carolina, in Convention assembled, do declare and ordain . . . that the union now subsisting under the name of 'The United States of America,' is hereby dissolved." When he finished, the delegates stepped forward in alphabetical order to affix their signatures to history. The ceremony took two hours, but the enthusiasm of the crowd only grew stronger. When all had signed, Jamison said, "I proclaim the State of South Carolina an Independent Commonwealth."[22]

Military bands struck up martial airs, and militia companies marched proudly along the streets. Shots rang out from pistols and cannon. More bonfires sprang to life; one lit the liberty pole at the head of Hayne Street. "The most impressive feature in the action of South Carolina," noted the *Mercury*, "is the concentrated unanimity of her people." Who could doubt their purpose or resolve after seeing the euphoria everywhere in the streets? Even Alfred Huger, the old postmaster who had always been torn by mixed feelings, came to accept the need. "I was born before the Constitution and . . . have revered the Union from the breast of my mother to the verge of my grave," he said with deep emotion. "The signers of the Declaration were the friends of my father. I have seen them at his table frequently." But times had changed. "The South has been sorely aggrieved and cruelly menaced. I meet the calamity which is approaching & I make her sorrows mine."[23]

What exactly did secession mean? South Carolina's people rejoiced that it was no longer part of the United States, but what was it? Was it a nation-state, a sort of Sparta by the sea, or the cornerstone of a new republic in the making, the long-awaited slave nation? A government had to be created, and a military, and what about foreign policy now that everywhere else was foreign? Anomalies, like the post office, had to be resolved. The convention made a start by creating four standing committees on relations with other slaveholding states, foreign relations, commercial relations and postal arrangements, and the constitution. But much had to be done in very little time.[24]

One problem had to be dealt with at once. Except for the post office, which was in local hands, the forts, the arsenal, and the customhouse were now the last vestiges of U.S. government presence in Charleston. If South Carolina was to show the world it took independence seriously, it could not long permit this "foreign" power to occupy its soil. With the ordinance approved, the South Carolina representatives had no choice but to quit Congress, and that left no one to represent the state in Washington. On the 21st the convention decided to send three commissioners to negotiate for the forts, and elected James L. Orr, Robert W. Barnwell, and James H. Adams.[25]

Few of these concerns reached the streets outside, where men, black and white, jumped and clapped their hands over secession without quite knowing what they celebrated. Caroline Gilman went out that fateful afternoon and saw the bonfires and fireworks and soldiers marching, heard the bells ringing and bands playing. "What's the matter?" she asked one black daddy who was shouting and laughing. "I dono miss, I dono miss," he said, then went back to shouting. At home, while the servants were lighting Chinese lanterns in the windows, Daddy Albert asked Aunt Lou, "what time will the *Secession* pass by, mama." It was a far deeper question than anyone yet realized.[26]

IN WASHINGTON on the morning of that same fateful December 20 Pickens aide D. H. Hamilton handed Trescot the governor's letter to Buchanan. Trescot already knew its tenor from another source, knew that it was exactly what was *not* needed under the circumstances. The two men took the letter to the White House and watched uneasily while Buchanan read it. At the president's request, Hamilton agreed to wait for a reply until the next evening. As Trescot followed him out of the library, he was summoned back by Buchanan, who handed him the letter and asked him to return later to discuss it.[27]

Reading it confirmed Trescot's worst fears. The demand to put state troops into Sumter, and to respond in twenty-four hours, not only was impossible but made a mockery of the agreement to maintain the status quo. The tone was too belligerent and would only back Buchanan, already under fire for being too soft, into a corner. Trescot's resignation had been accepted that morning, but he saw there was still work to do. He hunted up Jefferson Davis and John Slidell, who agreed that the demands were embarrassing. Bonham and John McQueen said the same thing at dinner that evening. They agreed to ask Pickens for authority to withdraw the letter. Afterward Trescot returned to the White House and told Buchanan what had been done.

Buchanan had already drafted a response to Pickens that would have pleased his critics and confirmed Trescot's worst fears. He reiterated his duty to preserve the peace and his belief that only Congress could deal with commissioners or make any change in relations with a state. For himself, he would surrender none of the public property in South Carolina. "If South Carolina should attack any of these forts," he warned, "she will then become the assailant in a war against the United States." But the letter was never sent. The next morning at ten Trescot brought to the White House a telegram from Pickens authorizing him to withdraw the letter. The plea from the Carolina congressmen and a conversation with Cushing had convinced the governor not to press the issue.[28]

On hearing this news, Old Buck's tough talk melted into warm thanks to Trescot. He was committed to avoiding a clash and awaiting negotiations, he assured Trescot; South Carolina could rely on that. But fires were springing up faster than he could put them out. News of the arsenal incident and the armed steamer patrolling the waters off Fort Sumter reminded Buchanan how tenuous the status quo really was. Shortly after Trescot left, the cabinet met to review Anderson's situation at Moultrie. The discussion staggered Buchanan with another revelation, this one from the physically ill and distracted Floyd.

Buchanan asked what exact orders Anderson had at Moultrie. Floyd wasn't sure and had to send for his files to refresh his memory. He told the president that he had sent Major Don Carlos Buell to see Anderson and assess matters. From this visit had come a memorandum, dated December 11, summarizing instructions given verbally. Anderson was to avoid any act that might provoke aggression and make no hostile move, but he was also to "hold possession of the forts," and if attacked, he should defend himself "to the last extremity." Almost as an afterthought Buell acknowledged that

Anderson had too few men to hold all the forts. An attack on any one of them would be regarded as an act of hostility, and he was authorized to concentrate his men into any one of the forts.[29]

After hearing the instructions, Buchanan objected to the sentence calling for defense to the last extremity. Black insisted that a memorandum was not good enough; formal instructions were needed. He drafted a new version telling Anderson to exercise "sound military discretion on this subject. It is neither expected nor desired that you should expose your own life or that of your men in a hopeless conflict in defense of these forts." A compliant Floyd signed the message, and it was sent by courier to Anderson. Things grew worse on December 22, when Trescot informed Buchanan that the South Carolina commissioners were on their way to Washington. That night the president also learned to his horror just why Floyd was coming unraveled. More than illness and the crisis in South Carolina had plagued him for weeks. A scandal, long brewing in his department, was about to burst into the open.[30]

It was a messy affair in which a relative of Floyd's who worked in Thompson's office had "borrowed" $870,000 in bonds held in trust by the Interior Department for several Indian tribes and used them to pay army contractors hurting for funds. Floyd evidently knew nothing of it and was guilty of nothing more than sloppy management, hardly an original sin in Washington, but the transactions could be made to look far more juicy than they were. Moreover, they violated explicit orders given by Buchanan. Reluctant to fire Floyd outright, the president asked Black to persuade him to resign, but Floyd refused. Instead his behavior grew more erratic and more befitting the dark view held by Republicans that he was an outright traitor.[31]

Rumors of the scandal spread through the city on the 23rd. That same day Trescot received a telegram from Pickens inquiring into a report that 150 men were en route to Moultrie. "I desire to know immediately if it is intended to reinforce the forts or to transfer any force from Fort Moultrie to Fort Sumter," he wrote. "I want a clear answer on this immediately. Until the Commissioners shall negotiate at Washington there can be no change here." Trescot went to Floyd and saw at once his personal distress. Nevertheless, Floyd dismissed the story as pure fabrication. As for the shifting of troops, he saw no need to give Anderson special orders on that subject. Trescot relayed the news to Pickens. Another fire had been doused; how many more before the commissioners arrived?[32]

"I have never enjoyed better health or a more tranquil spirit than during the past year," Buchanan wrote James Gordon Bennett of the New York *Herald*. "All our troubles have not cost me an hour's sleep or a meal's victuals." Not a soul believed him. Those who knew him personally saw the ravages of stress in his aging face and slumping limbs. Those who did not know him were inclined to agree with the embittered Lewis Cass. "The people in the South are mad," he said; "the people in the North are asleep. The President is pale with fear, for his official household is full of traitors, and conspirators control the government." So widespread was the belief that Buchanan was consorting with traitors that the administration's credibility had all but vanished, and hope was the scarcest commodity in town.[33]

Half the trouble was the reporters, the damned reporters with their dispatches and fabrications. The role of the press was changing in ways that Buchanan had just begun to comprehend and that still puzzled him. Part of it was the impact of the telegraph, which had sped up the spread of news and rumors. "The public mind throughout the interior is kept in a constant state of excitement by what are called 'telegrams,' " he complained to Bennett. "They are short and spicy, and can easily be inserted in the country newspapers." The city papers could contradict false rumors the next day, but country journals had no such luxury. All of them thrived on sensational stories, however true or false. What mattered increasingly was not accuracy but sensation.[34]

Partisans on both sides seized on any scrap of rumor and sent inflated versions over the wires to advance their own cause. "They occupy their mind in inflaming the Southern mind," observed a Republican observer of the ultras in Washington. "Every little thing, however trifling in itself, they send off to the South, with the view of urging the people there to disunion." But there was something more that was as ominous as it was new. The reporters were becoming not just spectators but players in the larger drama. "I know of no more reckless body of men than the correspondents," said the same critic, "who hang around the hotels and public places of this city, & *manufacture* sensation articles. They overhear conversations & catch up what all sorts of men say, and send it all over the country for the purpose of magnifying their own importance & making their papers sell."[35]

Buchanan had been battered enough by this process to know something of it, and he moved to douse at least one fire it caused. On Christmas morning the Washington *Constitution* blasted him for his stand on the right of secession. An irate president promptly informed the editor, W. M. Browne, (and the city) that the paper was not to be considered the administration's organ. But nothing could stay the avalanche of criticism cascading down on him. On Monday the 24th Cushing returned from Charleston with a gloomy report that the convention seemed to control affairs and no one yet knew what it intended. That same day the South Carolina commissioners started for Washington, forcing Buchanan to decide what to do about them.[36]

It was a ticklish situation. He could not recognize them in any official way without legitimizing the state's act of secession. The cabinet debated the matter and agreed that the president could meet them as "private gentlemen" and forward to Congress any proposition they cared to make. Trescot, nursing his disappointment at not being chosen as a commissioner, set up a meeting for the morning of December 27. His longing to be a player made the role of intermediary repugnant to him, and he was ready to leave Washington as soon as the first meeting occurred.[37]

No one found much joy in the Christmas season this year. A howling storm covered the ground with snow and ice. "Even the childrens delight in the preparation of Xmas here," observed Trescot, "cannot overcome the complete oppression of spirit under which I am labouring." A lonely Robert Hatton, clutching the slippers and watch holder sent by his wife, celebrated the "gloomiest Christmas Eve of my life—infinitely so," and spent Christmas Day reading and writing in his cramped room. The next evening Mine Host Brown of Brown's Hotel hauled out the George Washington punch bowl, as he had done for twenty years, for the first hop of the season, but there was little gaiety among the guests.[38]

At the White House the Old Public Functionary felt older and more weary than ever. If there remained an epithet his critics had not yet flung at him, no one knew what it was. Two of their favorites, after "imbecile," were "timid" and "coward." But his timidity these days came more from fatigue and distress than old age. Worn down from the constant bickering and tension that had disrupted his entire presidency and was now reaching its explosive climax, he was fast coming to the end of his wits. All his life he had been less a statesman than a lawyer; now he found himself in a world ruled by madmen where the lawyer's logic was scorned. All that was needed at this desperate hour to tip the scales was one more crisis. It came with a suddenness that astonished him.

ON THE DAY SOUTH CAROLINA passed the ordinance of secession, Major Anderson completed his first month of duty at the harbor forts. It was far from the happiest month of his career. For nearly his entire stay he had implored the War Department to send reinforcements or clarify its policy. "The question for the Government to decide—and the sooner it is done the better," he had said as early as December 1, "is, whether, when South Carolina secedes, these forts are to be surrendered or not." If the first, he wanted to know what exactly he should do; if the second, he needed more troops and supplies at once.[39]

To his eyes the choice seemed as clear as the issues behind it were cloudy, yet he could get no clear response from his superiors. If attacked, he was to defend himself, but no reinforcements would be sent because they might increase already inflamed feelings and trigger the attack no one wanted. Meanwhile, all around him the locals were arming, organizing, drilling, boasting loudly about how the forts would be theirs once the state had seceded. Relations between the officers and the citizens had not yet grown hostile, but no one knew how long that civility would last. Rumors exploded like firecrackers and sent people flying in every direction. On the 5th Anderson and Huger went into the city to see the mayor and some other prominent citizens and received the same message from all of them: They would do everything to prevent any assault by a mob, but one way or another the forts would be theirs after secession.[40]

Buell's visit did little to ease Anderson's anxiety. Floyd had ordered him to look the situation over and give Anderson instructions that were neither explicit nor to be construed as orders. Buell spent the night in Anderson's quarters, and the two officers discussed matters at length. Afterward Buell decided on his own to give Anderson the written memorandum of the 11th as a guideline for what he knew to be a vague and unsatisfactory position. "This is all I am authorized to say to you," he told Anderson privately, "but my personal advice is, that you do not allow the opportunity to escape you."[41]

What did this mean? The ambiguities nagged at Anderson, who liked things clear and by the book. That same day, December 11, he wrote a curious letter to a Charleston friend, Robert N. Gourdin, who happened to be a delegate to the forthcoming secession convention. Anderson said he would be ready for whatever came, but his goal was to avoid bloodshed. "You may be somewhat surprised at the sentiment I express, being a soldier," he said, "that I think an appeal to arms and to brute force is unbecoming to the age in which we live. Would to God that the time had come when there should be no war, and that religion and peace should reign throughout the world."[42]

But he was getting precious little help. On the 13th the *Mercury* published a lengthy article on the forts and their defenses, while the *Courier*'s Washington correspondent warned of Buell's visit, "See that they make no change in the distribution of soldiers, so as to put them all in Fort Sumter; that would be dangerous to us." The absurdity would have amused a man with a sense of humor. Anderson's garrison of sixty men occupied a fort (Moultrie) with low walls commanded by sandhills a hundred yards away to shelter enemy sharpshooters and guns and numerous houses offering cover within pistol shot. The houses were private property and could not be leveled without cause, but by the time there was due cause, Anderson would have neither the time nor the ammunition to level them and enemy troops would already be there. "You will see at once," he wrote a minister friend, "that if attacked in force by any one not a simpleton, there is scarcely a probability of our being able to hold out."[43]

He could not be certain of the loyalty of the workmen toiling on the fortifications, and he could not even procure arms and ammunition from the arsenal. Captain Foster had tried on December 2 to obtain a hundred muskets for training the workmen in Sumter and Castle Pinckney. Floyd deferred the request, and Foster soon concluded that the loyalty of the workers was too unreliable to entrust them with arms. On the 17th Foster revived an order of November 1 for forty muskets that had been suspended by Colonel Gardner, got them from the arsenal, and put them in Sumter and Castle Pinckney. The next day he was told that the transfer had caused an uproar in the city and that the guns must be returned at once because Major Huger had pledged that no arms would be removed from the arsenal.[44]

Foster was furious and refused to budge until he received orders directly from Washington. He did not know that a telegram had already gone to Trescot, who took it at once to Floyd. From his sickbed Floyd ordered the muskets returned to the arsenal. The whole situation at the arsenal was strange. State troops had been posted there since November 9, ostensibly to prevent any mob attack but also to certify any movement of arms from the stores. Mindful of the absurdity that the garrison could not even obtain arms to defend itself from the government's own storehouse, Foster complied sullenly with Floyd's order. On the day he agreed to return the muskets, South Carolina passed its secession ordinance, and the game took on a new twist.[45]

The more Anderson brooded over the impossibility of his situation, the more he found to brood over. The men under Foster had done yeoman work strengthening the forts, but to what end? If South Carolina seized them, all the work would go to their benefit, and no amount of work could make Moultrie defensible with so few troops. Then came another unsettling piece of news: Foster and other men reported that steamers had begun patrolling the waters between Moultrie and Sumter on the night of the 20th. The night watch had hailed one of them from Pinckney and asked what it wanted. "You will know in a week" came the reply across the dark water.[46]

What did it mean? Anderson wondered. Were they going to move on Sumter? Or Pinckney? Or even Moultrie? He knew the Carolinians wanted to keep any federal troops from going to Sumter. "I think that I could, however, were I to receive instructions so to do," he wrote Washington, "throw my garrison into that work, but I should have to sacrifice the greater part of my stores." What bothered him most was that he didn't have enough troops even to man his guns. But no orders came from Washington. Floyd responded only with an aside to an engineer that he hoped these troubles could be got over without bloodshed.[47]

No orders. No clear policy other than to avoid a collision that might bring on war. No one willing to take a stand or make a tough decision in Washington while the tide of events swept South Carolina ever closer to securing the forts by force. Anderson knew of the departure of the commissioners on the 24th and concluded that his fate rested in their hands. But he had no feel for what was going on in Washington, no sense even of what options were being explored. All he knew was that he had issued repeated urgent requests and received no response or even a signal that one would be forthcoming. Someone had to make a decision, had to deal with the reality confronting him. If no one else would, he concluded grudgingly, then he must.

If the object was to avoid a confrontation, only one plan made sense to him. It had been there all along, talked about repeatedly. But every time his officers had urged him to move the command to Sumter, Anderson reminded them that he had been assigned to Moultrie and could not vacate it without orders. Now he realized that no orders would be forthcoming and that Moultrie would be even more helpless if state troops seized Sumter and turned its guns on him. With an energy and decisiveness that surprised perhaps even himself, Anderson perfected his plan. He hoped to make his move on Christmas, while the city was preoccupied, but rain forced him to wait until the next day.[48]

He had sent Lieutenant Norman C. Hall to charter three schooners and some barges ostensibly to move the women and children in Moultrie across the harbor to Fort Johnson. No one objected to this move, and the boats were brought to Sullivans Island. Anderson then had two of the schooners loaded with provisions for four months as well as with the women and children. By noon of the 26th the boats were filled; Anderson ordered Hall to move toward Fort Johnson but not to land. He was to await the firing of two signal guns from Moultrie. When he heard them, he was to sail instead for Sumter.[49]

Two local citizens turned up to watch the loading and departure. They trailed Hall everywhere and finally asked about the large store of provisions. Hall put them off with an evasive answer, and the observers left on a steamer after the schooners had headed out toward Fort Johnson. Another citizen spotted a box of ball cartridges being put on board and was appeased only when it was removed from the boat. None of the officers acted suspiciously because Anderson had not yet told them of his plan. Surgeon Samuel Crawford had gone over to Sumter looking for a boat to take him into the city. "Crawford," said the officer in charge there, "go back to Fort Moultrie, and don't take your eyes off Anderson." The puzzled Crawford returned to

Moultrie and found Anderson on the parapet, scanning the harbor. A large steamer paused at the mouth of the harbor as if to enter. Anderson watched the ship closely. "I hope she will not attempt to come in," he said. "It would greatly embarrass me. I intend to move to Fort Sumter tonight." Startled, Crawford had no chance to pack up the hospital or its supplies in time for the move. Elsewhere in the fort preparations went on even though the officers did not know the reason.

That same day Anderson broke up his mess without explanation. Around sunset Captain Abner Doubleday went to invite Anderson to tea. He found the major on the parapet with a circle of other officers, all of them strangely quiet. Before Doubleday could figure out what was wrong, Anderson told him he had decided to evacuate Moultrie immediately. "I can only allow you twenty minutes to form your company and be in readiness to start," he added. Doubleday nodded and raced off to organize his men and tell his wife, one of the last women left on the post. He was grateful that he had at least anticipated trouble enough to have sent his valuable things on to New York. Other officers were not so lucky; they had no time to collect their personal belongings. Foster lived with his family in a house outside the fort and stood to lose almost everything.

Doubleday needed only ten minutes to get his company formed, equipped, and inspected. Meanwhile, his wife hastily packed some belongings and waited outside the gate for a ride to the sutler's house. They embraced in a hasty good-bye, not knowing when they would be together again. Jeff Davis, assigned to command the rear guard along with Foster, Crawford, and eleven soldiers, readied five heavy columbiads to protect the move. Anderson ordered them to fire on any Carolina ship that tried to intercept the crossing. Shortly after dusk the men began marching through the gates to the landing. A bright moon shimmered on the still water, but by good fortune no one was around to observe their movements. At the landing several large rowboats waited under the command of Lieutenants George Snyder and Dick Meade, who crouched in the rocks with their crews to avoid detection. Anderson knew they had to set off by six o'clock or so to avoid the patrol boats, which usually appeared around nine.

The men hurried aboard the boats and pushed out into the harbor. About halfway across, the lookouts spotted one of the patrol steamers directly ahead. Two of the boats veered toward shore to swing an arc around it; the third, under Doubleday, decided to maintain course. Knowing that his rowers were unskilled, Doubleday ordered them to remove their hats and coats and conceal all arms and insignia. As the steamer passed within a hundred yards, they saw that it was towing a vessel to the bar. The other steamer, supposed to be on patrol that night, was still sitting at her dock awaiting orders. No one suspected them of being anything more than laborers en route to Sumter.

This ruse enabled Doubleday to reach Sumter before the others. Quickly his men gathered their gear and ran ashore. A crowd of workmen from the fort, some of them wearing blue secession cockades, rushed out to meet them. "What are these soldiers doing here?" shouted the more belligerent of them. Doubleday formed his men to advance with fixed bayonets, drove them back into the fort, and seized the guardroom that commanded the entrance. All cheers and other noise were silenced at once. Sentinels fanned out across the main gate and the ramparts as the boat returned to fetch Truman Seymour's company. In all the boat completed three trips between the forts.

After the boats had unloaded their cargoes, they were filled with those workmen considered disloyal and sent back to the mainland. Only laborers with solid Union credentials were allowed to remain. Anderson surveyed the situation at Sumter, then ordered the two signal guns fired, bringing Hall to Sumter with the women, children, and supplies. By eight o'clock that evening the transfer had been completed. No one in Charleston was yet aware of their movement. While the rear guard under Foster's eye spiked the guns at Moultrie and set fire to the carriages of the thirty-two-pounders, Crawford crossed to Sumter and Davis returned to Moultrie to gather some personal gear.

Everything had proceeded with calm efficiency and a curious lack of urgency. The overdue patrol steamer *Emma* made her belated appearance and, unaware that she no longer had anything to guard, settled in for the night. The city slept in ignorance of the fact that a turning point in the crisis had just been reached. Early the next morning Crawford went back to Moultrie to pack up the hospital. Near the shore he spotted a column of smoke rising above the parapet from the burning gun carriages. Hall's boats also returned to Moultrie to load the hospital equipment, a large supply of ammunition, everything but ninety days' worth of provisions, the fuel supply, a small amount of ammunition, and the men's personal effects.

It was done. Major Anderson had made the most important decision of his career and executed it with precision and efficiency. His entire command, except for the small band still at Moultrie and Dick Meade, who had been sent to Castle Pinckney, was now safely ensconced at Sumter. Some volunteers rowed back to Moultrie to fetch Mrs. Rippit, the housekeeper of the officers' mess, who had been left behind with the tea service she had laid out for that afternoon. The evening meal she had prepared at Moultrie was eaten cold at Sumter.

There would be hell to pay when Charleston awoke to the news, Anderson was sure of that. But he was even more certain that he had done the right thing, the only thing, to avert disaster. On that first night in Sumter, Anderson composed a report to the adjutant general, Samuel Cooper. "I have the honor to report," he began, "that I have just completed, by the blessing of God, the removal to this fort of all of my garrison. . . . The step which I have taken was, in my opinion, necessary to prevent the effusion of blood." The message did not reach Washington until December 29.[50]

Sumter was nearly impossible to take by assault without heavy casualties, and virtually impervious to bombardment. The fools in the city could not get at him here, could not precipitate a war he hoped desperately to avoid. He had at least four months' provisions and plenty of water from the fort's own well. The only thing lacking was an ample supply of fuel. Sumter was a fortress impregnable.

But it was also something more that Anderson had yet to realize. It was an island prison to which no one could gain entrance and from which no one could escape. Anderson had cut himself off from the mainland and from all direct communication with the government on which he depended for orders and succor.

For the moment he paid little heed to these concerns. Instead he went in his orderly fashion about the business of cleaning up the loose ends left by his move. He could not pretend to know how long he and his men would be holed up on their granite island. What he did know, and took considerable pride in, was that he had bought time for the politicians. The question was what, if anything, they would do with it.

CHAPTER NINE

At the Brink

I would save this Union if I could; but it is my deliberate conviction that it cannot now be done. . . . [T]he cold sweat of death is upon it. Your Union is now dead; your Government is now dead. . . . The spirit has departed, and it has gone back to those who gave it—the sovereign States.

—Senator Louis T. Wigfall
December 12, 1860[1]

IT WAS ONLY NATURAL that for relief from the crisis the nation should look first to the Senate, the site of so many past compromises. There, as usual, the bombast flowed freely. Not until December 18 did John J. Crittenden get his plan onto the floor. In a speech that commanded rapt attention, the old statesman set forth his compromise package of six constitutional amendments and four congressional resolutions. He spoke, said a young congressman who had squeezed into the chamber to listen, "as if the muse of history were listening to him." The amendments extended the old Missouri Compromise line to include all territory then part of the United States or "hereafter acquired," prohibited Congress from abolishing slavery or interfering with the interstate movement of slaves, provided compensation for fugitive slaves rescued by mobs, and forbade future amendments to undo these amendments. The resolutions sought to improve the fugitive slave law, eliminate personal liberty laws, and strengthen the statutes against the slave trade.[2]

No single aspect of the plan was original. Crittenden was groping for the boundary between the most the North would give and the least the South would accept, if such even existed. But his proposals leaned too far southward for Republicans; only one resembled a concession to the antislavery position. The main provision repudiated the basic plank of the Republican party and implanted the term "slavery" into the Constitution for the first time. The "hereafter acquired" clause horrified antislavists by raising the specter of a new slave empire built on expansion into the Caribbean. There were also grave doubts about the idea, let alone the legality, of constitutional amendments that could never be amended.[3]

On the same day Crittenden introduced his package, Senator Hale observed scornfully, "I do not know that this Congress can do anything; but this controversy will not be settled here." The Committee of 13 was not appointed until the 20th and did not meet until the next day. Despite all the hope vested in it, the committee had a short, unhappy life of only one week. The first day it sat without Seward, who had gone back to New York, and Jefferson Davis, who refused at first to serve. It considered proposals by Douglas, Davis, and Robert Toombs of Georgia, as well as Crittenden's, and accepted a motion by Davis that nothing be reported to the Senate without the support of both Democratic and Republican members. This made sense; how could the Senate be expected to agree on something if the committee could not?[4]

Although all three proposals were more radical than Crittenden's, both Toombs and Davis hinted that they would accept any one of them if the Republicans did so. The Republicans would not act without Seward, who was still in New York. Weed had gone to Springfield to get Lincoln's views on the compromise plans, and Seward wanted to bring them before the committee. He had been at his home in Auburn only three days when a letter arrived from Preston King saying he was needed for Senate business. Seward managed to connect with Weed in time to share the train ride from Syracuse to Albany, during which Weed told him the substance of Lincoln's views. On the 23rd, he caught the evening train to Washington and reached the Capitol in time for the third meeting of the Committee of 13 the next day.[5]

Seward offered three propositions framed after Lincoln's suggestions. The committee accepted only one of them, which barred any amendment to the Constitution that allowed Congress to abolish slavery in the states where it already existed. "We came to no compromise; and we shall not," Seward wrote his wife Frances afterward. "We shall, therefore, see the fuller development of the secession movement." At the next meeting, on the 26th, Seward trotted out a fourth proposition, which the Democrats amended and the Republicans promptly killed. A proposal by Douglas was brushed aside. That evening the Republican members assembled at Seward's house with Trumbull and Fessenden to consider the written version of Lincoln's suggestions and concluded that the ground had already been covered.[6]

On the morning of the 28th, amid wild excitement in the city over seizure of the Charleston forts, the committee met one last time. Crittenden brought in an abridged version of his plan; William Bigler and Henry Rice presented variations on it in a dogged effort to find some middle ground. All three efforts were voted down. In the end the committee could agree only to report that it could agree on no plan. Everybody blamed everybody else. Seward concluded that nothing would satisfy the Deep South. Some version of the

Crittenden plan *might* satisfy the border states, but no Republican would countenance it. Time would heal the rift, he assured Lincoln; "sedition will be growing weaker, and loyalty stronger, every day, from the acts of secession as they occur."[7]

The disheartened Crittenden took a gloomier view. It was clear, he wrote a close friend, that the Republicans meant "to do nothing, to yield nothing . . . They are disposed to believe that the threatening appearances in the South will pass away. . . . I firmly believe that a great majority of the people would accept my plan of settlement but its fate must be decided here, & by a *party* vote." He would not give up but rather seek other avenues of gaining acceptance for the plan. *"Washington is in black!"* he exclaimed. "God help us!! I mean still to struggle on for *peace* & *union*."[8]

Abruptly all hope of compromise passed from the Senate, where it had long dwelled, to the House, where it had usually been an unwanted guest. Speaker William Pennington appointed a committee that was as ill advised as it was unwieldy. The Committee of 33 had a majority of Republicans, four of whom had voted against creating the group and did little more than obstruct its work. Not a single northern Douglas Democrat was included, even though the Douglas Democrats had strongly supported formation of the committee. Instead the Douglas men came from the southern states, where they represented a minority opinion. The men from South Carolina and Florida refused to serve at all.[9]

The committee began meeting daily on December 11 and soon bogged down over several resolutions. Few members expected any results; many shared the view of Isaac Morris of Illinois, who pressed a proposal on the House, saying, "I have not the slightest idea . . . of ever letting this resolution be buried in the coffin of the committee." On the 17th, Albert Rust of Arkansas galvanized the meeting by offering what he called a southern "ultimatum," which, if not discussed at once, would compel the southern delegates to bolt the committee. Called the Rust-Nelson proposal after Thomas Nelson of Tennessee had presented it to the committee, it was very similar to the Crittenden plan.[10]

For three days the committee floundered in search of direction. Then, on the same day South Carolina seceded and the committee took up Rust-Nelson in earnest, Henry Winter Davis of Maryland stunned the members with a proposal to admit New Mexico Territory, which included all the remaining land south of the Missouri Compromise line, as a state and let its citizens decide the issue of slavery. This would in effect dispose of the territorial issue until the nation expanded again. It was, said Charles Francis Adams, "a cannon shot clear through the line," and the southern members scattered in confusion.[11]

The differences were subtle but crucial: The Davis plan opened existing territory south of 36°30′ to a vote on slavery, while Rust-Nelson (like the Crittenden plan) guaranteed all present and future territory to slavery. Davis let New Mexicans determine the status of slavery; Rust-Nelson designated it a slave state. The southerners rejected Davis and demanded an immediate vote on Rust-Nelson but did not get it. The next day Henry Winter Davis explained to Adams that the point of his plan was to drive a wedge between the Deep South and the border states. Adams saw enough value in this idea to wonder if it might not be useful to his fellow Republicans. That day Davis fleshed out his proposal to the committee, which agreed to postpone a vote on Rust-Nelson until the 27th.[12]

Adams sounded out the Republican members and found more agreement on the Davis plan than on any other scheme. Corwin assured Lincoln that "we cannot make slavery the normal condition of all territory *'to be conquered.'* I can myself yield much if the application of the principle is confined to territory we already possess." On Christmas Day a judge who had lived in New Mexico for nine years assured Republican members that slavery could not survive there. His views convinced Adams that the Davis plan offered the Republicans an alternative that was positive yet conceded little. A provision for a constitutional amendment to protect slavery where it already existed was added, and the Republican members agreed that Adams should present it to the committee.[13]

Seward got wind of this plan and told Adams on the morning of the 27th that the Republicans on the Committee of 13 opposed the Davis proposal. Senators Jacob Collamer of Vermont and Fessenden also let Adams know their objections. Adams agreed not to press the matter without full Republican support. At his own committee meeting Adams did not bring up the Davis plan but helped the other Republicans defeat Rust-Nelson, 16–13. Nelson then tried to bring up the resolutions used by Crittenden in the Senate committee but got nowhere with them. Another stalemate loomed.

A frustrated Adams saw that he lacked enough Republican support to spring the Davis plan. On the 28th he offered instead the less controversial amendment protecting slavery in the existing states. Although the Alabama member scorned it as useless and other southerners tried to graft the Crittenden proposals onto it, the committee approved the measure, 21–3, with only Republican ultras voting no. The same day a plan similar to Davis's was introduced into the Committee of 13, almost as an act of desperation. Adams smirked privately at how "our Senatorial friends who objected so much to our measure should have so soon slipped into it themselves."[14]

But the Committee of 13 died that day. On the 29th, Republicans from both committees held a caucus. Ben Wade declared himself "against everything," but other senators softened their stand against the Davis plan. It was, everyone realized, about the only thing left. Later that day, when the Committee of 33 rebuffed another Nelson attempt to pass the Crittenden resolutions, Miles Taylor of Louisiana withdrew, as five southerners had already done. Aware that there would soon be no representative southerners to vote on anything, Adams introduced the Davis plan. The southerners saw that it ignored their demand for slavery in future territories and, except for Davis and the Kentucky member, opposed it. Six Republicans insisted it undermined the party's stand on the nonextension of slavery and voted against it, yet the measure carried, 13–9. Andrew Hamilton of Texas, the lone Deep South man remaining, changed his vote when he saw it was not needed, making the tally 12–10.

This shard of a plan was all the politicians had been able to produce by December's end, and Adams paid a dear price for it. On one side Crittenden labeled him the major obstacle to conciliation; on the other, many of his friends in Massachusetts and elsewhere blasted his support of the Davis plan as a betrayal of the party's principles. "Is it possible," cried one, "that Adams agrees to the admission of New Mexico as a Slave State? God help us, if *he* deserts us." Sumner and other ultras snorted fire and indignation, but in fact nothing had happened yet. Compromise had crashed in ruins in the Senate and had gone nowhere in the House. Although Tom Corwin remained sanguine, the Davis bill was a long way from passage.[15]

The Washington correspondent of the New York *Tribune* saw vast promise in this deadlock. "Every hour," wrote an exuberant James S. Pike, "more and more clearly discloses . . . that no party . . . had such a triumphant and glorious future before it as the Republican party of this hour, if it have the grace and wisdom to seize and pursue the advantages that offer themselves. . . . The curtain of the future slowly lifts, and . . . behind it the eye of faith beholds a nobler, a loftier, a more glorious career than this nation has yet enjoyed. The transition to that more blessed state, we believe, will be both brief and bloodless."[16]

IT HAD BEEN a good first week of independence, Pickens thought. On Monday the 24th he had issued the formal proclamation of independence. The same evening the three commissioners left for Washington. The convention, meeting every day, including Christmas, was busily sorting out how much federal legislation had been abrogated by secession and had resolved that the forts should be returned to the state. A Declaration of the Immediate Causes of Secession had been approved along with an address to the people of other slave states. Committees were grappling with the problems of commerce, postal service, and foreign relations. Robert Barnwell Rhett offered a motion calling for the southern states to meet in Montgomery, Alabama, in February to form a new Confederacy. The state legislature reconvened on Wednesday the 26th.[17]

On Wednesday morning Robert Barnwell Rhett, Jr., who ran the *Mercury* for his father, dropped by to warn Pickens that a well-informed Washington friend had learned that Anderson was about to take Sumter. He implored the governor to move first. The forts were an obsession with the Rhetts. Earlier Junior had suggested chartering a large steamer, manning it with five hundred riflemen, and stationing it to command the harbor entrance. Rhett senior and three legislators had visited Pickens soon after his arrival in Charleston to urge that all measures be taken to keep federal soldiers out of Sumter. Rhett had also tried to get the convention to approve seizure of the forts. But Pickens was adamant; he would not move so long as the "understanding" remained in place and until the commissioners had a chance to fulfill their mission.[18]

The very next morning Pickens awoke to confusion in the city. On Sullivans Island the residents noticed a plume of smoke above the fort, then discovered the entrance to be barred, the parapet empty, the flagstaff missing, and no work going on. Reports that the fort was on fire sent boats filled with onlookers and reporters hurrying to the island. Crowds milled in the streets of Charleston along with hastily gathered military units. The newspaper offices swarmed with people seeking information and finding only more sensational rumors.[19]

Early that same morning Sam Crawford returned to Moultrie to pack up his hospital with its year's supply of stores. So effective had the move been that no one yet knew what had happened. Crawford paused to help Foster and Davis burn the last gun carriages, then watched as his stores and a large supply of ammunition were loaded onto two schooners. They were away by noon and made it to Sumter unchallenged. Inside the fort the men were settling into their new quarters and exploring its dark interior. So many of them crowded onto the parapet to watch Moultrie that the patrol steamer *Nina* noticed them and steamed back to the city with a report that Sumter had somehow been reinforced. No one appreciated the irony of this message even later.[20]

Pickens was aghast when the news finally reached him. He dispatched Colonel Johnston Pettigrew to visit Anderson and demand his return to Moultrie. At Sumter the colonel found Anderson and his officers in a small room on the second floor of the officers' quarters. The mood was formal and reserved; Pettigrew declined the seat offered him. He conveyed the governor's surprise that Anderson had reinforced Sumter. Not at all, countered

Anderson; he had merely shifted his command from one facility to another, as he had a right to do. Pettigrew reminded him stiffly of the agreement between former Governor Gist and the president to maintain the status quo in the harbor. Anderson looked at him in surprise and said he knew of no such agreement. No one had told him anything; he could not get clear orders from Washington, and he faced nightly threats from local troops at Moultrie. "I removed on my own responsibility," he declared, "my sole object being to prevent bloodshed." In this controversy his sympathies were entirely with the South. But he had a duty to perform, and that duty came first. Nevertheless, replied Pettigrew, Governor Pickens insisted that his command return to Moultrie. "I cannot and will not go back," replied Anderson. Pettigrew and his aide left as abruptly as they had come.[21]

Anderson realized that his men needed some tangible display to certify their new position. Shortly before noon he ordered them to form on the parade and sent the band onto the ramparts. The men and guard formed one part of a square near the flagstaff, with the 150 workmen filling in the other sides. Anderson stood at the staff, halyard in hand, with the chaplain in the center. The chaplain thanked God for their safe arrival and prayed that the flag would never be dishonored, that it would soon float over a prosperous and united nation. Anderson rose from his knees, the men presented arms, and the band swung into "The Star-Spangled Banner" as the major sent the flag to the top of the staff amid loud cheers. It was a very large flag, easily seen from the Battery at Charleston on a clear day, and it flapped defiantly in the crisp winter air.

A FURIOUS PICKENS wasted little time once the news of Anderson's refusal was conveyed to him. That same day, the 27th, without bothering to consult the legislature or the convention, he ordered Pettigrew to take Castle Pinckney and sent Lieutenant Colonel W. G. DeSaussure to take charge of Moultrie once Pinckney had been seized. At four o'clock that afternoon Pettigrew's troops disembarked from the *Nina* and marched to Pinckney's gate, which was barred. While some men covered the parapet with their rifles, others hoisted scaling ladders and, led by Pettigrew, scrambled up the wall. At the top Pettigrew met Dick Meade, the officer in charge and the only soldier on the premises except for Ordnance Sergeant Skillen, who lived there with his family.[22]

The gate was opened, and Pettigrew's men assembled on the parade. The colonel informed Meade of his orders but did not know what to do with him; he could not be declared a prisoner without implying a state of war. Meade extracted a promise that the old ordnance sergeant and his family would be treated well, then was allowed to go to Sumter. Pettigrew's men confiscated all government property and hoisted the palmetto flag. When Kate Skillen, the sergeant's fifteen-year-old daughter, began to cry, an officer assured her that she would not be harmed. "I am not crying because I am afraid!" she replied. ". . . I am crying because you have put that miserable rag up there."

From the parapet of Sumter, Anderson and Doubleday watched the occupation through spyglasses. As Anderson's indignation mounted, he talked of shooting out the light in the lighthouse, but his temper soon cooled. There was no useful retaliation for what Doubleday called "the first overt act of the Secessionists against the Sovereignty of the United States." Later they had to endure another outrage. A federal revenue cutter anchored in the harbor was turned over to state authorities by its captain and put into the state's service.[23]

That evening, under a brilliant moon, DeSaussure led two hundred handpicked men toward Moultrie from the land side. They moved gingerly, mindful of rumors that the approach had been mined and booby-trapped, but managed to get inside with little difficulty. The fort passed into state hands without incident, as did dilapidated old Fort Johnson and the arsenal in Charleston. On the 28th the governor informed the convention that he had seized the forts because he "considered the evacuation of Fort Moultrie . . . a direct violation of the distinct understanding between . . . the Government at Washington, and . . . this State, and bringing on a state of war." He had acted to protect the state and hoped there was "no immediate danger of further aggression for the present."[24]

Pickens was responding to a request for information sent him by the convention on the 27th. In secret session the members were debating a motion to seize the forts he had just taken as well as Sumter. Gourdin read them the letter he had received from Anderson, which was then forwarded to Pickens. That same day W. F. Colcock reported that he had reopened the federal customhouse as a state agency with all former employees now sworn into the service of the state. The post office remained in a state of limbo because Washington had taken no action in regard to its status. It was the last vestige of federal presence in Charleston except for the island fortress in the harbor, and it flew a palmetto instead of an American flag.[25]

Two days of bold, dramatic moves had transformed the situation, given it a clarity as decisive as it was deceptive. Convinced that an attack was imminent, Anderson had hoped to defuse tensions by removing the target. Pickens responded in an aggressive manner intended to stabilize the situation and assert the state's sovereignty. Without realizing it, they had done much more than rearrange the pieces on the playing board. Their actions galvanized attitudes throughout the North and South, replaced doubt and indecision with a unity of purpose and the determination to take a stand where one was needed. In two days they had brought the nation to the brink of civil war.

" 'ALMIGHTY DOLLAR' is beginning to raise its voice higher than public sentiment," observed Baron Rothschild in New York. "The factories are closing down from lack of work, trade has ceased and thousands of laborers are without employment." Appraising the American scene with his practiced eye, the baron sensed the weakening pulse of the city's commercial and financial interests. He was not alone. "I have never witnessed as much anxiety & apprehension as prevail at the present time," Hamilton Fish told Senator Fessenden. "The derangement of business, the depreciation of values have their inevitable effect." New York businessman W. S. Gilman estimated the depreciation of values at $300 million and warned Trumbull: "The condition of the United States . . . has become in a little over thirty days depressed in all industrial conditions beyond almost any precedent in time of peace."[26]

Unsettled conditions had staggered the stock market and stagnated business, especially among firms in the Northeast and mid-Atlantic states that did a large business with the South. Shipowners, dry goods dealers, cotton exporters, and others saw their southern trade shrivel away and feared a complete loss of their investments, estimated at between $150 million and $300 million. Businessmen in the great commercial centers of New York, Boston, and Philadelphia especially felt the pinch. "It is an awful time for merchants," said a Boston businessman, "—worse than in 1857; and if there is not some speedy relief, more than half the best concerns in the country will be ruined." The New York *Herald* harped on the plight of dismissed hatters, Philadelphia papers painted grim portraits of twenty thousand unemployed in the city, and the Boston *Courier* portrayed the city's streets as "full of discharged workmen."[27]

Relief seemed nowhere in sight. The secession movement, long dismissed as an idle threat, had spread well beyond South Carolina. During November Alabama, Florida, Georgia, and Mississippi had moved to hold elections for conventions to take up the issue. By December 12 Texas and Louisiana had joined the parade marching toward disunion conventions. This was a far cry from 1830, when South Carolina had ventured out on the limb and no other state had joined it. Already talk had gone beyond secession to the forming of a new southern confederacy.[28]

The growing sense of panic in business and financial circles spurred demands for conciliation and compromise in both parties. While ultra

Republicans struggled to keep wavering moderates in line, prominent
Democrats sought to assure their southern brethren that some reasonable
accommodation could be reached within the Union. On December 15,
Richard Lathers, a native of South Carolina who had settled in New York as
a commission merchant dealing in southern products, assembled a group of
prominent Democratic businessmen at his Pine Street office to register sympathy for the South. Three days later, a bipartisan group of thirty leading
New York capitalists gathered to urge conciliation and voice support of Crittenden's plan.[29]

The Pine Street meeting reaffirmed the right to hold slaves as property
and take them anywhere. Charles O'Conor, an influential lawyer, denied that
the South had anything to apologize for, and struck a chord that resonated
among many northerners. "The Declaration of Independence and the Constitution of the United States," he declared, "were made by and for the free
white Caucasian race. . . . We but follow the judgment of Almighty God
when we say, 'America for the white Caucasian, Africa for the negro who was
born in it.' " Horace Greeley's *Tribune* denounced Lathers as "a traitor to
the government" and O'Conor's speech as "the strongest and ablest defense
of Disunion that we have seen," but it could not ignore the growing current
of fear among commercial and financial interests. Even George Templeton
Strong conceded "a growing disposition here to offer liberal concessions to
the South."[30]

A peculiar fog of confusion enveloped the North, blinding efforts to
grasp the real issues and formulate policy. Some pleaded for reason and compromise; others argued vehemently against any form of concession. More
members of both camps voiced their fear that war was inevitable. Democrat
John A. McClernand insisted, "Peaceable secession . . . is a fatal, a deadly
illusion," and warned that if the party became "entangled with disunionism
we will be lost as a party. . . . We must train the public mind to look upon disunion with horror." Many Republicans shared John Sherman's blunt pro-
nouncement that "Disunion is war!"[31]

Another fear was taking hold among some Republicans. Rumors spread
of plots to kidnap or assassinate Lincoln, to seize Washington by a surprise
raid and prevent the inauguration. Enough people put stock in them to worry
about how to meet such threats. "The more the chances of the original secession movement decrease," warned an alarmed Carl Schurz, "the more will a
plan like that come into prominence as their last resort." Some southerners
suggested that Washington would make a fine capital for the new confederacy. Were they joking? Was the United States going the way of the unstable
republics to the south?[32]

A few people saw something more, felt the ground shifting under their feet. Thurlow Weed had been right: The issues of the campaign were already obsolete. All the compromise efforts concentrated on slavery, but the real issue was the Union itself: not merely preserving but sustaining the model, however flawed, of a workable free republic. "If we admit secession in one case," observed Illinois Republican Gustave Koerner, "we destroy all stability in the Government. . . . A civil war to preserve the union is a more sacred one than the war with Mexico was." Trumbull put it more succinctly. "The question," he told Lincoln, "is no longer about African Slavery, but whether we have a government capable of maintaining itself."33

Anderson's move and Pickens's seizure of the forts dispersed the fog with startling speed. After nearly two months of apprehension and fear, talk and posturing, stall and stalemate, someone had *acted*. Two quick, bold moves had pushed the crisis past the politicians and presented soul-searchers with the new dilemma of reacting to them. In the North the fissures of division began to close with a rapidity that surprised even skeptics. Anderson had shown the stuff of leadership so glaringly absent in Washington, while Pickens had cast himself as a handy villain by seizing federal property and hauling down the venerated national flag flying over national forts. To northerners this amounted to a sacrilegious act.

New England rejoiced at the news of Anderson's move. *"We could not but feel once more that we had a country,"* said a Boston paper. "These are times to develope [*sic*] manhood," businessman Joseph Sargent told Charles Sumner. "We have had none finer since 1776." The textile magnate Amos Lawrence, working to secure a compromise, conceded sadly, "The first blow struck by any State or local authority at the U.S. Govt will arouse & unite the whole Northern people." James Russell Lowell sensed better than most what Anderson had done. "What we want," he declared, "is an hour of Old Hickory, or . . . some man who would take command and crystallize this chaos into order. . . . God bless Major Anderson for setting us a good example!"34

Just as Anderson put fire in northern bellies, so Pickens stoked their fears of how far southerners would go in their mad schemes. The specter of plots to seize Washington or kill Lincoln no longer seemed so far-fetched. The capital was, after all, a southern city filled with southerners, many of them officeholders on their way out. They offered a potent support base for any coup and an obstacle to organizing the militia for defense of the city. And how loyal was the military, with its large coterie of southern officers? How was the administration, let alone the incoming Republicans, to know who could be trusted to stand by the government, especially when a growing number of Republicans and others believed firmly that Buchanan himself was in league with the traitors?

"The revolutionists will attempt to take possession of Washington city either on or before the 4th of March," Carl Schurz predicted flatly. A northerner with relatives in New Orleans warned Lincoln of "a perfect organization, fearful in numbers . . . whose object is to prevent the inauguration." Militia companies began forming in Illinois and elsewhere to protect Lincoln. A few reveled in the challenge. "We live in revolutionary times," said Horace White to his friend Trumbull, "& I say God bless the revolution!"[35]

THE MOST FATEFUL WEEK in the presidency of James Buchanan opened with two bizarre incidents. On snowy, stormy Christmas Day the president learned to his horror that John Floyd had ordered some heavy cannon to be shipped from the armory at Pittsburgh to forts in Texas that were in no condition to use them. News of the order aroused protest in Pittsburgh and excitement throughout Washington. Ultra Republicans pounced on the move as proof positive that Floyd was a traitor. "Our advice . . . to every Northern man," said a Pittsburgh paper, "is, Arm yourself at once." A shocked Buchanan quickly countermanded the order, and that night Black urged him to dismiss Floyd at the cabinet meeting the next day.[36]

The second incident never reached the president's ears. That same Christmas Day Louis Wigfall visited the overwrought Floyd on behalf of unnamed parties to enlist him in a scheme to kidnap Buchanan and replace him with the younger, more forceful vice president, John C. Breckinridge. Floyd dismissed the idea indignantly, but the episode did little to calm his emotions. At the cabinet meeting the next day Buchanan confronted him with an array of issues that asked how he could remain in office faced with possible indictment for malfeasance and charges of treason for sending arms to the South. Black and Stanton were absent at the Supreme Court, but to Floyd's astonishment Thompson pitched into him for miring the Interior Department in scandal. The distraught Floyd took refuge behind bluster. He accused his colleagues of trying to oust him before he could vindicate himself, flatly refused to quit, and bellowed rudely at Buchanan. His outburst bought him some time to seek a more graceful exit but did nothing to dispel doubts about his behavior.[37]

On that same Wednesday the 26th Trescot settled the newly arrived South Carolina commissioners into quarters on K Street next door to Floyd's chief clerk and near Black's residence on Franklin Square. Anxious to leave the city, he declined to serve as their secretary but agreed to act with them unofficially. That night he called at the White House to tell Buchanan of their arrival; the president agreed to meet the "private gentlemen" at one the following afternoon. The next morning, while Trescot was readying their credentials, Louis Wigfall burst in with a telegram that Anderson had spiked Moultrie's guns and moved to Sumter. The commissioners and Trescot were stunned. "True or not," said Trescot amid an animated discussion, "I will pledge my life that if it has been done it has been without orders from Washington."[38]

Just then Floyd arrived. He blanched at the news and confirmed what Trescot had said, that such a move "would be not only against orders but in the face of orders." Hurrying to the War Department, Floyd telegraphed Anderson to confirm or deny the report. "It is not believed," Floyd said, "because there is no order for any such movement." Trescot carried the news to Jefferson Davis and Robert M. T. Hunter at the Senate and went with them to the White House to demand an explanation. Buchanan seemed nervous when he received them but knew nothing of the report. As Davis told the story, Buchanan stood at the mantel crumpling a cigar in his hand, as he often did under duress. "Now Mr President," Davis concluded stiffly, "you are surrounded with blood and dishonour on all sides."[39]

Buchanan slumped into a chair. "My God!" he cried wearily. "Are calamities . . . never to come singly! I call God to witness—you gentlemen better than anybody else know that this is not only without but against my orders. It is against my policy." Perhaps it was all rumor; he sent for Floyd, who told them that he had telegraphed Anderson but had received no reply as yet. Davis and Hunter pressed Buchanan to recall Anderson and restore the status quo immediately before South Carolina seized the remaining forts. They argued long and hard, bending the nervous, pacing president but not quite breaking him. He could not condemn Anderson without hearing his side, Buchanan insisted stubbornly, and so could not promise to send him back to Moultrie.[40]

As Davis, Hunter, and Trescot left, they met Senators Jo Lane, William Bigler, David Yulee, and Stephen Mallory on their way to register protests. The news was racing across the city. Later in the day even Slidell overcame his grudge and visited the White House to pressure Buchanan. If Anderson did not return to Moultrie, they all warned, the sure result was secession and war. Still, Buchanan did not budge. He paced anxiously, begged them to remain calm, said they could state publicly that the move was without the president's orders, even against them, but nothing more. He would not tell them what he planned to do. He could not. He did not know.

The issue was clear. The southerners accused him of violating the December 10 agreement to maintain the status quo. He denied having made any such pledge or that he had done anything on his own to violate it. Nothing could be decided without consultation; he summoned the cabinet into session at once. As the members gathered at the White House, Floyd spotted Major Don Carlos Buell. "This is a very unfortunate move of Major Anderson," Floyd said to him. "It has made war inevitable."

"I do not think so, sir," answered Buell. ". . . I think that it will tend to avert war, if war can be averted."[41]

Floyd was not convinced. As the meeting dragged on into evening, he blasted Anderson. "It is evident," he read from a paper in a quavering voice, ". . . that the solemn pledges of this Government have been violated by Major Anderson. . . . One remedy only is left, and that is to withdraw the garrison from the harbor of Charleston altogether. I hope the President will allow me to make that order at once. This order . . . can alone prevent bloodshed and civil war." When he finished, Thompson and Thomas supported him, while Black, Holt, and Stanton staunchly defended Anderson. Toucey as usual said little. The suggestion astonished Buchanan; even in his weakest moments the idea of withdrawal had not entered his mind.[42]

Black was livid. He sent for the recent order he had drafted for Floyd, read it aloud, and insisted that Anderson had acted "in precise accordance with his orders." He shook the order in Floyd's face and shouted, "There never was a moment in the history of England when a minister of the Crown could have proposed to surrender a military post which might be defended, *without bringing his head to the block!*" Floyd's indignation pulled him up out of his chair, forcing Buchanan to restore order. Amid an uneasy calm the president conceded that the order seemed to give Anderson leeway to exercise his own discretion against any tangible evidence of a proposed attack on him. Nothing he had heard justified ordering Anderson back to Moultrie.

A critical corner had been turned without anyone's realizing it. Buchanan had decided nothing, nor had he conceded anything. The cautious, timid lame duck had not moved to support Anderson, but neither had he been bullied into recalling him. Outside the White House, where rumors owned the city, no one knew which way events were tending. Republicans saw the parade of southerners into the White House, knew of the commissioners' presence, and feared the worst. Trumbull surmised that Anderson's move would "probably bring matters to a crisis sooner than Mr. Buchanan expected." But even border state moderate Robert Hatton conceded that Anderson had done "what any prudent, discreet man would have done, under the circumstances."[43]

Buchanan had agreed to meet the commissioners the next afternoon, Friday, December 28, at two o'clock. That morning disaster struck again. While the cabinet was meeting, news arrived that Governor Pickens had seized Fort Moultrie and Castle Pinckney. Buchanan recognized at once the gravity of these moves. However Anderson might have disturbed the "gentleman's agreement," Pickens had shattered it with what could be construed as acts of direct aggression against U.S. property. Whether he recalled Anderson or let him stay at Sumter, the stakes had gone up.

The South Carolina commissioners were fully aware of this when they met with Buchanan in a two-hour session. Pickens's move meant that returning Anderson to Moultrie was no longer an option. They declared loftily that nothing could be negotiated until all federal troops were ordered out of Charleston; Buchanan must issue such an order if peace was to be preserved. The president listened intently, said little, paced nervously, and pleaded for time. Robert W. Barnwell pressed him hard, saying three times, "Mr. President, your personal honor is involved in this matter; the faith you pledged has been violated, and your personal honor requires you to issue the order."[44]

"Mr. Barnwell, you are pressing me too importunately," protested an exasperated Buchanan. "You don't give me time to consider; you don't give me time to say my prayers. I always say my prayers when required to act upon any great State affair."

Having found refuge in prayer, Buchanan terminated the interview without indicating what he would do. That night the cabinet thrashed over the question for six hours. Floyd lay on a sofa, both exhausted and agitated. That morning he had received a letter from General Scott (himself prostrate with diarrhea) urging him to reinforce Sumter with men, munitions, and ships, along with other key facilities on the southern coast. Floyd did not reply, but neither did he argue vehemently in the cabinet. Instead he lay torpid while Thompson spun out an insinuating argument that a great government could afford to be generous with a small state and should withdraw with grace from Charleston Harbor.[45]

When Thompson finished, Stanton reminded Buchanan of the acute embarrassment caused by Floyd's scandal. "Now it is proposed to give up Sumter," he said caustically. "All I have to say is, that no administration . . . can afford to lose a million of money and a fort in the same week." To all this Floyd said not a word in response.

The meeting broke up with nothing decided. Earlier the commissioners had prepared a letter for Buchanan but did not deliver it to him until Saturday, the 29th. Its tone oozed the formal majesty of a newborn republic as yet recognized by no one, cloaked in the imperiousness typical of the chivalry. Behind the hurt and anger lay a threat. South Carolina might have taken the forts at any time but had chosen instead to honor the agreement of December 10. That pledge—the president's own word—had been violated, making any negotiations impossible until a satisfactory explanation was forthcoming. Again the commissioners urged withdrawal of all troops from the harbor to show good faith and avoid possible bloodshed.[46]

Buchanan called in the cabinet that morning to discuss the letter, then withdrew to draft a reply. Floyd was not present. Having found at last a suitable exit cue, he resigned on the grounds that his advice of the 27th had been rejected and he could not, as an honorable man, be party to "a violation of solemn pledges and plighted faith." That evening Buchanan met again with the cabinet to go over the draft of his reply to the commissioners. Here at last was the moment he had hoped to avoid. Events had pushed him into a corner where he had to take a stand.47

While these events unfolded, Washington reacted to the rumors spilling all over town. No one knew what was actually going on, and the willingness to believe the worst fed a growing appetite for hysteria. The nonstop cabinet meetings since Anderson's move, and the news that South Carolina had seized the other forts, convinced many that a struggle was raging in the cabinet for Buchanan's soul. "I feel as though we were on the verge of civil war," said Horatio King, "and I should not be surprised if this city is under the military control of the disunionists in less than one month!" Fessenden thought Buchanan was "frightened out of his wits, and in the hands of traitors. It is rumored that Mr. Lincoln's inauguration is to be prevented by force, though I can hardly believe the secessionists are so mad as to attempt it."48

Supreme Court Justice Robert C. Grier, a fellow Pennsylvanian, dined with Buchanan on the 28th and cringed at what he saw. "He is getting very *old*—very *faint*," he told a friend. ". . . I should not be astonished . . . if Floyd was arrested and Buchanan impeached before 60 days." Young Henry Adams found amusement in the panic around him. "The terror here among the inhabitants is something wonderful to witness," he wrote his brother Charles. "At least the half of them believe that Washington is to be destroyed by fire and sword."49

Even Seward, normally a bulwark of reason and cynicism, fell prey to the prevailing mood. "Treason is all around and amongst us; and plots to seize the capital, and usurp the Government," he wrote his wife. "The White House is abandoned to the seceders. They eat, drink, and sleep with him." On the 29th he reported to Lincoln, "The Cabinet is again in danger of explosion. . . . The plot is forming to seize the capital and usurp the Government, and it has abettors near the President. I am writing you not from rumors, but knowledge." So unrelenting was the criticism that a political ally observed privately that Buchanan was "execrated now by four-fifths of the people of all parties."50

Even without the abuse heaped on him from all quarters, Buchanan was anxious and fearful. In his search for a solution he clung to the idea of a constitutional convention and sent the venerable Jacksonian advisor Duff Green to Springfield to sound out Lincoln on the idea. No word had come back by the 29th as the president drafted his reply to the commissioners. Late that evening he showed the statement to the cabinet. Black, Stanton, and Holt thought it conceded too much and demanded too little; Thompson and Thomas found the tone too hostile and feared it might provoke South Carolina into war. Toucey alone, ever loyal, accepted it. No one argued loudly or bluntly, knowing full well Buchanan's obstinacy under fire. They adjourned without deciding anything, acutely aware of the deep rifts that threatened to shatter the cabinet.[51]

Black went home to a wretched night of worry over the president's apparent determination to take a stand the judge considered disastrous. His mood was darkened by a disturbing note from Holt, who had heard from a supposedly reliable source that Buchanan had decided to restore the status quo, that the commissioners had accepted his pledge, and that Floyd was to return to the cabinet. "This rumor is certainly credited in the city," Holt added, "& I feel that I cannot sleep upon it, without endeavoring to ascertain whether it is well founded." Black knew nothing about the story, but it reinforced his belief that Buchanan's reply was unacceptable.[52]

On Sunday morning Black sought out not the president but his most loyal cabinet supporter, Toucey, and told him what he also told Holt and Stanton: If the President stood by his reply, Black saw no alternative but to leave the cabinet. As expected, Toucey took the news to Buchanan, who promptly sent for Black. While Toucey was there, Trescot arrived and tried again to persuade Buchanan to return Anderson to Moultrie. He got nowhere but came away with a sense that the obstacle was Pickens's seizure of the other forts. Trescot urged Senator Hunter to offer Buchanan a proposal giving back the other forts if Anderson would return to Moultrie. The commissioners could then declare the status quo restored and guarantee Anderson's safety. Hunter agreed and left for the White House.[53]

Well might Buchanan feel like a shuttlecock. That same morning a letter had arrived from General Scott, who, having been ignored by Floyd, asked the president directly to let him bypass the War Department and send a secret force of 250 men to Sumter along with munitions and provisions. Earlier, Supreme Court Justice John McLean and his wife had dined at the White House. At one point the judge took Buchanan aside and inquired about Major Anderson. He had evidently exceeded his orders, replied the president, and must be recalled. McLean grew agitated and, thrusting his hand almost in Buchanan's face, said, "You dare not do it, sir, you dare not do it."[54]

Whatever doubts still troubled Buchanan's mind were snuffed out by Black's visit. "Do you, too, talk of leaving me?" he asked the downcast judge. Given leave to speak freely, Black poured out his objections in his usual brew of logic, earnestness, and wrath. The reply conceded too much and would drive both the northern and southern elements from the cabinet. Anderson had to be not only maintained but reinforced as well. Buchanan argued with his old friend, but he saw the necessity. The seizure of the forts had aroused protest throughout the North among people of every political stripe. Even the Democratic New York *Herald* admitted that "South Carolina has placed herself in open and armed hostility to the government of the United States. . . . This is war."55

The president, so notorious for his inflexibility, now did an astonishing thing. "Here," he said, handing the reply to Black, "take this paper and modify it to suit yourself, but do it before the sun goes down." The surprised Black went to Stanton's office and drafted a new version, of which Stanton scribbled a copy as fast as the sheets were shoved at him.

The final product contained more than one indirect rebuke of Buchanan's course and parted company with Black's own November memorandum. He was adamant that there must not be even a hint of recognition of the commissioners or their right to negotiate anything, let alone the disposition of a federal military post. Nor could there be even an "implied assent" to the view that the president had entered into any pledge or agreement with South Carolina. The forts had to be held and Anderson spared even a wisp of criticism. "He is not only a gallant and meritorious officer," said Black, ". . . he has saved the country . . . when its day was darkest and its peril most extreme. He has done everything that mortal man could do to repair the fatal error which the administration have committed in not sending down troops enough to hold *all* the forts." Black conceded that his views were radical but warned that if the reply did not take this shape, "I can see nothing before us but disaster, and ruin to the country."56

In his own rewrite Buchanan discarded some of Black's suggestions and softened others with the slippery syntax of the lawyer-diplomat. He stood by the position taken in his annual message that Congress alone could determine the relations between the federal government and South Carolina, and that it was his duty to maintain all federal property and collect the revenues in Charleston. The December 10 agreement was never anything more than "the promise of highly honorable gentlemen to exert their influence for the purpose expressed." Neither side had the authority to make any pledge, yet the so-called promise had been kept on both sides. He had "acted in the same manner as I would have done had I entered into a positive and formal agreement with parties capable of contracting, although such an agreement would have been, on my part, from the nature of my official duties, impossible."57

In short, there had been no agreement, and it had never been violated anyway. Buchanan quoted in full Anderson's orders from Buell to show that the major had acted on his own responsibility but insisted that he deserved a fair hearing on his reasons. Once the president learned of the shift to Sumter, his first impulse had been to order Anderson back to Moultrie. Before he could act, however, the other forts had been seized, every customs officer had resigned, and the state flag had been run up over the customhouse and post office. Under these circumstances he was asked not merely to send Anderson back but to withdraw all federal troops from Charleston. "This I cannot do," he said in a rare burst of plain, tough language; "this I will not do. Such an idea was never thought of by me in any possible contingency."

Whatever else the reply said, and it said much to disappoint and infuriate the commissioners, these two short sentences alone gave Black, Stanton, Holt, and a vast majority of northerners what they wanted to hear. There would be no retreat, no backdown. Most likely Buchanan spoke the truth when he said he had never even considered a withdrawal from the harbor, and now Pickens had made it impossible for him to send Anderson back to Moultrie. "If I withdraw Anderson from Sumter," he confided to a friend at one point, "I can travel home to Wheatland by the light of my own burning effigies." Senator Hunter got the message when his attempt to persuade Buchanan to restore the status quo proved futile. Tell the commissioners it is hopeless, he informed Trescot after returning from the White House.[58]

The president had taken his stand and would not be moved. The southern cabinet members would not like it, and would probably quit if they could not sway him. But what then? If Anderson remained at Sumter, should he be reinforced? Scott was not alone in urging Buchanan to do so, but would such a move escalate the conflict? Then there was the vacuum at the War Department, for that same day Buchanan had ignored an apology from Floyd and accepted his resignation. Scott pressed him to name a successor quickly, and Buchanan obliged. Some thought it might be Scott himself; instead the president asked Holt to take charge.[59]

This appointment also sent a message to those who feared Buchanan might still sell out to the South. Trescot saw it at once. "Holt is Sec War," he telegraphed his uncle. "That means civil war." Thompson and Thomas would also be alarmed, Buchanan realized, and might quit the cabinet. The situation was still dangerous. Rumors of an attack on Washington continued to roam the streets, and Scott reminded the president of a new problem. With Anderson at Sumter, no mail or telegrams could go in or out of the fort without the permission of the Charleston authorities. "It is just possible," Scott warned, "in his state of isolation, a system of forged telegrams, from this place, may . . . betray him into some false movement."[60]

The situation had clarified, but what next? While informing Scott of

Holt's appointment, Buchanan invited him to call at the White House. The question of sending reinforcements had to be decided, and no one knew what the hotheads in Charleston might do. To make matters worse, Duff Green reported that Lincoln, after first indicating he would provide a written statement supporting the calling of a constitutional convention, backed away the next morning and gave the statement instead to Trumbull with instructions to let Green have it if he approved. Other conditions set by Lincoln made it clear to Buchanan that the Illinois enigma had a shrewd grasp of practical politics. In effect he had signaled that he would do nothing before March 4. Until then the issue of war and peace belonged to the president.[61]

Buchanan breathed a deep sigh of something other than relief. "At this gloomy period of our history," he had told the commissioners sorrowfully, "startling events succeed each other rapidly."[62]

PART TWO

The Battle over Secession

JANUARY

CHAPTER TEN

War Beckons

I have been for 30 days in a Com of 33. If the States are no more harmonious in their feelings & opinions than these 33 representative men then appaling [sic] as the idea is, we must dissolve & a long & bloody civil war must follow. I cannot comprehend the madness of the times. Southern men are theoretically crazy. Extreme northern men are practical fools, the latter are really quite as bad as the former. Treason is in the air around us every where & goes by the name of Patriotism. Men in Congress boldly avow it, & the public offices are full of acknowledged secessionists. God alone I fear can help us. Four or five States are gone others are driving before the gale. I have looked on this horrid picture till I have been able to gaze on it with perfect calmness.

—Thomas Corwin
January 16, 1861[1]

Long before the new year opened, the hyenas were out in force. Scarcely had the sun gone down on election day when they began gathering in packs for the prowl, sniffing the air for opportunity, eager to pick the patronage bones clean. Cautious at first, they circled warily about the post offices, marshalships, and other prizes of their districts through soliciting letters to friends and strangers of influence. Gradually they slunk closer, importuning those who might help, the boldest among them trotting into Springfield itself to stalk the president-elect during his open hours or even at home. As Herndon said, they belonged to a party that had never fed, and their hunger was voracious.

Lincoln bore their onslaught in his customary way, evading response and salving hurt feelings with patience and humor, cushioning disappointment with his endless supply of stories. But the ordeal wore him down, and his pain was aggravated by his wife's interference in the business of appointments from the cabinet down to the pettiest local office. The shock of a woman's meddling in such matters was worsened by Mary Lincoln's poor judgment and weakness for flattery. In one case she accepted jewelry from a New Yorker seeking a customhouse job, then badgered Lincoln unmercifully until he gave in to quiet her nagging. The man got the post and was later indicted for fraud.[2]

Wearisome as this process was, Lincoln endured it because he believed as strongly as did the party faithful in the spoils system. As the first Republican president he bore even more pressure. The party had come to power sweeping every northern governorship and controlling every northern legislature except New Jersey and Rhode Island. The new state administrations had their own feeding frenzies to satisfy, and also expected to be rewarded at the national level. This desire turned the creation of a cabinet into a balancing act requiring the utmost delicacy and diplomacy.[3]

Having ousted long-entrenched southerners, the Republicans vowed to stay in office even longer. This hope spurred every state leader to jostle for position. The elite coveted cabinet seats, which placed them at the president's elbow, rather than diplomatic postings, which sent them into exile abroad. Most of the predators in Springfield therefore consisted of cabinet hopefuls and their shills, who hoped to ride their favorites to lesser favors of their own. The factional infighting within most state parties complicated Lincoln's task. Seward and his éminence grise Thurlow Weed dominated New York but had to fend off reformers like Horace Greeley and William Cullen Bryant. In Pennsylvania the wily Simon Cameron loomed like a malign presence above a bewildering array of bickering factions. Ohio's Republican party pitted Salmon P. Chase against Ben Wade; in Indiana Caleb B. Smith's supporters opposed those of Schuyler Colfax. In Maryland Henry Winter Davis vied for supremacy against Montgomery Blair.[4]

Lincoln's home state had his friends on opposing sides. Jesse Dubois, an old crony, complained to Lyman Trumbull that in the state legislature "[Norman] Judd and [William] Butler on the one side and [David] Davis & Co on the other both undertake to run the machine and whilst poor me and my class of men . . . are left out in the Cold . . . I will not take part in the Squabbles of either wing but I am very fearful we will be Damaged on the whole in the State." Judd was even closer to Lincoln and desired a cabinet post that Davis, among others, hoped to deny him.[5]

Lincoln recognized early the forces circumscribing his choices. No state could receive more than one cabinet member without incurring the wrath of those left out. Custom dictated that Illinois get none, having already the honor of the president, yet this meant ignoring his close friends who had claim on a post. As a party leader Lincoln had to cement the loyalty of rivals, like Seward, who had run against him for the nomination. And much as Lincoln indicated otherwise, bargains had been made at the convention and would have to be settled. Men from both major elements of the party, former

Whigs and Democrats, should be included to avoid splitting the ranks. And what about southerners? In the crisis at hand the right southern appointment might do much to preserve the loyalty of the border states and create the illusion of a genuinely national cabinet.[6]

The fact that so few politicos, particularly in the East, knew Lincoln well added another intriguing dimension. Ward Lamon exaggerated when he wrote later, "Few men believed that Mr. Lincoln possessed a single qualification for his great office," but many shared Charles Francis Adams's view of him as "an absolutely unknown quantity." A strong cabinet was expected to dominate him; a weak one would provide little help in confronting the national crisis. Playing the selection game by the usual rules might produce a plateful of mush, yet ignoring them might embroil the party in vicious internecine fighting at a time when unity was most urgently needed.[7]

Lincoln's dilemma was how to make the cabinet his own while juggling all these considerations. He worked through these perambulations in his usual style, listening hard while saying little, and arrived at a policy that was as remarkable as it was logical. The best way to unite the party behind him, he concluded, was to bring its strongest leaders into the cabinet. They might not be the men he preferred, but they were the ones he had to have even though he knew their impulse would be to seek a dominant role. Without hesitation he prepared to draw the lions into the cage with him and make them perform under his persuasion.

The wiliest lion was Seward, and on December 8 Lincoln secretly tendered him the State Department. Weed had hinted that such an offer was due Seward as a courtesy but that he would refuse it and remain in the Senate. Lincoln assured him that "it has been my purpose from the day of the nomination at Chicago, to assign you, by your leave, this place in the administration . . . and I now offer you the place, in the hope that you will accept it." Seward responded with thanks and a plea for time to consider. An elaborate game opened between two masters of disingenuous sincerity to sound out each other's motives. Already Lincoln had extended it by inviting Weed to Springfield for consultation.[8]

A week later he welcomed to town Judge Edward Bates of Missouri, who had been endorsed by Orville Browning and Frank Blair, an influential political figure. Bates suited Lincoln's needs in several ways. He was an able lawyer, conservative, a strong Union man in a slave state, a former slave-owner turned against the institution, and a contender for the Republican nomination even though he had not actually joined the party. In their talks Lincoln portrayed Seward as a problem because there were as strong reasons not to appoint as there were to appoint him. Until he decided how to handle

Seward, therefore, he wished to offer Bates a cabinet position without naming it. If Seward declined State, Bates would get that post; if Seward accepted, Bates would be attorney general.[9]

Lincoln impressed Bates with his candor and flattered him into taking whatever post was offered, but he also said that he had neither spoken nor written to anyone else about a cabinet appointment when in fact he had tendered Seward the offer a week earlier. Either he was dissembling with Bates or he did not regard the offer to Seward as genuine. Whatever the case, he revealed here the gift for cold calculation and manipulation artfully masked behind what those who underestimated him liked to call his frank (read "simple") western manner and guileless country humor.

Bates was an easy choice quickly made public because he had many political assets and few enemies. Cameron and Chase were explosive selections for very different reasons. The soft-spoken Cameron wielded immense power in Pennsylvania. His political machine rewarded friends and punished enemies with ruthless efficiency, and its gears were notorious for being greased with graft and corruption. Cameron could afford to remain coy about the post he coveted while his minions pressed Lincoln hard. The president-elect knew that naming Cameron to a cabinet position would arouse outrage in and out of Pennsylvania. Moreover, to put both Seward and Cameron in the cabinet would convince reformers that Lincoln was a tool of the two most conspicuous political machines in the nation. But not to put them there would make him powerful enemies.

Chase too was a coy candidate. Like Seward and Cameron, he held a Senate seat and claimed that he could be more useful there. Like them too, he let Lincoln know through intermediaries that he had no desire to join the cabinet. Unlike them, however, Chase was a man of impeccable, even overweening personal and political virtue, a darling of the reformers who neither liked nor mixed well with Cameron or Seward. To invite all of them into the same cabinet was to create a volatile, perhaps uncontrollable mix if all accepted the offers—and it was by no means certain that they would do so.[10]

The other positions were no less complicated, and the partisans of every aspirant no less vigorous in courting Lincoln's favor. Lincoln had offered Hannibal Hamlin the courtesy of naming the New England member but had carefully narrowed the choice to a list of suitable candidates for the Navy Department. Two contenders emerged early: Charles Francis Adams of Massachusetts and Gideon Welles of Connecticut. The claim of Caleb Smith rested on promises made at the Chicago convention to gain the support of his state. Montgomery Blair had several valuable assets: strong Unionist sentiments, roots in the strategic state of Maryland, a West Point education, and a political sage of a father, who had been one of Andrew Jackson's intimates.[11]

Weed arrived in Springfield on the 20th along with the two Lincoln friends who had been his contacts, David Davis and Leonard Swett. The tall, somewhat shabby Weed, his lean profile accentuated by an outsize nose, spent two days in conversation with the man he had already come to respect and was careful not to underestimate. Amid their banter over the craft of cabinet making Weed urged Lincoln to appoint two Unionist southerners. "Well," drawled Lincoln, "let us have the names of your white crows." Weed listed John A. Gilmer of North Carolina, John Minor Botts of Virginia, Balie Peyton of Tennessee, and Henry Winter Davis of Maryland.[12]

When Lincoln mentioned Blair, Weed objected vigorously that "he represents nobody, he has no following, and . . . his appointment would be obnoxious to the Union men of Maryland." Going down the list for other posts, he approved of Bates, opposed Welles, and warned that Cameron would provoke bitter protests even though he personally liked the general. "Who is stronger or better than General Cameron?" Lincoln asked, reminding Weed that there had to be someone from Pennsylvania. Weed had no one to suggest. Instead he renewed his argument for a southerner and got Lincoln to write a letter sounding out Gilmer, which Weed personally carried to him in Washington.

On the heels of Weed's departure came David Wilmot—he of Wilmot Proviso fame—to boost Cameron, as had former Governor Andrew Reeder early in December. Wilmot admitted that Cameron had many enemies in the state but stressed that "It would hardly do to make an appointment very obnoxious to him." Letters opposing Cameron were already pouring in on Lincoln from influential Republicans. "I do not believe *one man* can be found amongst all our friends in the Senate who will not say it will be ruinous to apt Cameron," warned Hamlin. "There is an odor about Mr. C.," added Trumbull, "that would be very detrimental to your administration."[13]

Reeder tried to arrange a meeting between Lincoln and Cameron. At first the general played coy, pleading his unwillingness "to incur the misconception of motive," but on December 30 he turned up in Springfield on the noon train and sent a note to Lincoln. Whatever powers Cameron possessed lay masked behind a bland facade. He was a man of slight build with gray hair, deep-set gray eyes in a nondescript face, a thin mouth, and a gentle, soft-spoken manner. Nothing about him commanded attention, yet he had amassed a fortune in industry and long thrived in the twilight zone between business and politics.[14]

Lincoln greeted Cameron with his usual open, hearty style, but he had also summoned Bates, who arrived that evening and cut into Cameron's time. The judge found Cameron "pleasant enough in conversation, but rather reticent about politics and parties." He left the next evening without knowing why Cameron was there or that Lincoln had handed Cameron a letter offering him either the Treasury or War portfolio. Nor did he know that Lincoln had also that same day invited Salmon Chase to visit Springfield. What Bates did know was that Lincoln had just received a note from Seward accepting the State Department. Bates thought this unfortunate because many southerners considered Seward "the embodiment of all they deem odious in the Republican party," while in the North there was "a powerful fraction of the Repn. Party that fears and almost hates him—especially in N.Y."15

None of this information had yet gone public, a good thing for Lincoln. On New Year's Day, in Cameron's wake, came Alexander McClure, and Governor-elect Andrew G. Curtin, two of the general's bitterest foes in Pennsylvania. They had opposed both Cameron and Seward at the Chicago convention, and McClure protested the rumor that Cameron was to get a cabinet post for having thrown his support to Lincoln at Chicago. Letters from Cameron's men were already arriving in Springfield, but McClure's earnest pleadings, along with a heavy mail opposing the general, evidently shook Lincoln. McClure waited patiently while Lincoln hosted the traditional New Year's Day open house, then spent four hours with him the next evening before catching his train. He promised to furnish Lincoln "indubitable proof of Cameron's villany [sic]" and urged that William Dayton of New Jersey be named instead of a Pennsylvanian. "The only objection Cameron can have to him," claimed McClure, "is that he is an honest man."16

The next day Lincoln wrote Cameron an odd letter withdrawing the offer of a cabinet post. "You will say this comes of an interview with McClure; and this is partly but not wholly true," he said. "The more potent matter is wholly outside of Pennsylvania; and yet I am not at liberty to specify it. Enough that it appears to me to be sufficient." Cameron was free to make the offer public so long as he declined it publicly, but he had to act quickly, before Lincoln was forced to recall the offer openly. "Telegraph me . . . on receipt of this," said Lincoln in closing, "saying 'All right.' " The telegram never came. Cameron was far too practiced to ease Lincoln's task. Instead, projecting the silence of wounded feelings, he left the situation fluid enough for maneuver.17

The procession of men and mail toward Springfield increased. Chase arrived on January 4 along with Amos Tuck of New Hampshire, an entry in the Navy Department sweepstakes. Behind them in rapid succession came Gustave Koerner, Norman Judd, David Davis, an Iowa delegation boosting the prospects of Fitz-Henry Warren, George Julian of Indiana pushing Caleb Smith, and two Cameron stalwarts, Senator Edgar Cowan and John P. Sanderson of Pennsylvania, who entrenched themselves for the better part of three days until supplanted by three prominent New Yorkers who opposed Cameron.

By mid-January the procession had become a carousel, depositing new cadres of dignitaries with every spin. The reporters dutifully fleshed out their daily box score of arrivals and departures with rumors and speculations on who had the inside track for what position. Seward's acceptance had gone public, but little else was known for certain. "These volunteer counsellors appear to think that their patriotic motives give them a perfect title to the attention of Mr. Lincoln," observed a sympathetic Henry Villard. ". . . They will first endeavor to hunt him up and besiege him in his down town office. If unsuccessful there, they will call at his private residence. . . . Nor are they hardly ever satisfied with . . . one interview."[18]

Drained and distracted by the ordeal, Lincoln stopped his public receptions on January 12 and thereafter saw only select visitors at home or the small rented office downtown. Two days later he watched Governor Yates stumble through his inaugural message because he had fortified himself with a few stiff drinks. It seemed the perfect emblem for a gloomy winter. The inauguration was but two months away, Lincoln had his own message to write, the party was in disarray, and the cabinet situation was ever more out of control. The trip to Washington had to be arranged, and some kind of policy formulated to deal with the crisis.[19]

As Lincoln well knew, one question tormented minds throughout the North: Was the new president up to the challenge that faced him? A member of Buchanan's official family had pronounced views on that point. "Mr. Lincoln himself is very small potatoes and few in a hill," said Judge Black. "He had no reputation even in the region where he belongs except what arose out of . . . making comical faces and telling smutty anecdotes."[20]

THE TRADITIONAL NEW YEAR'S DAY reception at the White House struggled vainly to rise above the pall of foreboding that hung over the city. The weather was pleasant, the mansion bright with flowers and music, and in the morning the reception glittered with foreign envoys calling in their court uniforms. Behind them came the army and navy officers to pay their respects before the doors were thrown open to the public at noon, a practice patrician southerners still found amusing. "Here I am, Mr. President," cried one arriving matron, "and my cook will be here in a few minutes! I left her dressing to come."[21]

Some cabinet members stopped by briefly, but few members of Congress bothered to attend. Everyone knew the real hospitality of the day lay not in the social dungeon of the White House but in the well-appointed parlors of cabinet members, congressmen, foreign ministers, and social-climbing hostesses, their tables filled with delicacies and bowls of potent holiday punch from a special recipe. Southerners found the occasion especially poignant. Many were saying good-bye not only to the year past but to their offices, old friends, and the nation they had always known. For them the New Year promised nothing but uncertainty.

For young Henry Adams the ritual was already familiar: going with a friend to four or five receptions between noon and five, submitting himself "to more people than I ever saw before," landing finally at the crush hosted by the Stephen Douglases, where he sat for a time with Albert Rust of Arkansas. Robert Hatton of Tennessee turned up at the Douglases' by a very different route. He had spent all morning and New Year's Eve in his drab cell at Brown's Hotel franking documents for his constituents and writing letters until his colleague Horace Maynard insisted that they call on Senator Crittenden. The grateful Hatton splashed some water on his face, put on a clean collar, and embarked on what was a new social adventure for him.[22]

The senator was not at home, but his wife greeted them pleasantly. They went next to see fellow Tennesseean Thomas A. R. Nelson, who herded them to the Douglas reception. Hatton was amazed at the size of the crowd and smitten with the charm and beauty of Adele Douglas. She talked to him without a trace of condescension and was one of the few who did not look astonished at his refusing alcohol. Afterward they dropped in on the Georgian Joshua Hill, whose wife Hatton found "full of talk . . . ugly enough to justify any amount of gab; ugly people, you know, have a right to talk their faces *out of sight*, if they can."

For this grand social outing Hatton squandered a dollar in hack fare, only the second time he had indulged in such extravagance. Normally he walked everywhere because he could not afford to ride; indeed for two weeks he had done without a daily paper because he had no money. At every stop he found the company pleasant, if overexcited from drink, but little gaiety. Everyone seemed constrained, unsure of what to say, and talk seldom strayed from the crisis. The day was bright and sunny, the mood, dark and gloomy. Some saw what was coming. "I have despaired of the Union," wrote the wife of Georgia Senator Robert Toombs, "and will begin to pack up my own things today."[23]

For Buchanan the day's festivities offered the briefest of interludes. While he greeted visitors at the White House, the commissioners prepared their reply. It was an indignant letter full of recrimination and condemnation. "Major Anderson waged war," they charged. "No other words will describe his action. . . . You have resolved to hold by force what you have obtained through our misplaced confidence, and by refusing to disavow the action of Major Anderson, have converted his violation of orders into a legitimate act of your executive authority. . . . By your course you have probably rendered civil war inevitable." The letter reached him during a cabinet meeting the next afternoon, and he read it aloud. The tone so outraged the members that they urged him not to accept it. Buchanan jotted a note saying, "This paper, just presented to the President, is of such a character that he declines to receive it." His secretary carried it to the commissioners' quarters but found they had already departed for Charleston. Trescot was there but refused to take it. The secretary left it on a table. Thus ended the negotiations that never were.[24]

Shortly after his secretary left, Buchanan capped the discussion on Sumter by saying, "It is now all over, and reinforcements must be sent." Later Thompson and Thomas claimed not to have heard this remark. Black too was unsure, but Holt, Stanton, and Toucey agreed a decision had been reached, and Holt moved at once to implement it. He went to see Scott, in whom he found a kindred spirit. Now that he had the president's ear at last, Scott was eager to push the expedition to relieve Anderson and to reinforce federal outposts on the Gulf. Some of the latter were so lightly defended, the general warned Buchanan, they could be seized by "a rowboat of pirates."[25]

Scott had already ordered the sloop *Brooklyn* prepared to receive two hundred men and ninety days' provisions at Fort Monroe. No sooner had Buchanan agreed to the plan, however, than Scott decided it would be better to employ a merchant side-wheeler, which was faster and, with its lighter draft, could cross the channel bar more easily. Buchanan was dubious but deferred to superior military judgment. A ship named the *Star of the West* was hired. Amid elaborate efforts to keep the preparations secret, she left New York Harbor on the night of January 5. A letter was dispatched telling Anderson of the ship's departure and giving him leave to return any hostile fire against her. It reached him too late.[26]

Buchanan had at last taken his stand, yet within days events caused him to regret it. During the first week in January the governors of Alabama, Georgia, and Florida authorized the seizure of federal arsenals and forts in their states. Fort Pulaski in Savannah, two forts and an arsenal in Alabama, and the Apalachicola arsenal in Florida were occupied by state militias. While the shocked president absorbed this news, a report from Anderson reached the War Department on January 5, the day the *Star* sailed. Writing on the last day of December, Anderson declared his command secure enough that "the Government may send us additional troops at its leisure. . . . [W]e are safe. . . . [W]e can command this harbor as long as our Government wishes to keep it."27

That same day Buchanan also learned that South Carolina troops had put a new battery on Morris Island overlooking the harbor entrance. If Anderson felt secure, he asked Scott uneasily, why send an unarmed ship into a potentially dangerous confrontation? They decided to recall the ship, but the *Star of the West* had already departed. Two days later the *Brooklyn* was ordered to pursue and aid the *Star*. Would nothing in these wretched weeks go right? Buchanan wondered. For more than a month Anderson had pleaded for reinforcements, and now that they had finally been sent he suddenly stopped asking for them.

This irony was exceeded only by the abrupt reversal of Buchanan's own standing. Overnight the Republicans who had attacked him grudgingly sang his praises, while his longtime southern friends excoriated him as a turncoat. "The denunciation of him is fearful," sympathized the wife of California Senator William M. Gwin. ". . . He looks badly [*sic*]. His face indicates much unhappiness & when I see him I feel like comforting him, but . . . no one could approach him in that way." Fewer people saw Buchanan at all; his social calendar dwindled, and he reluctantly gave up the evening walk he had always cherished.28

While the *Star of the West* steamed southward and the president fretted over the consequences of what he had done, a reinvigorated Scott looked to the problem of defending the capital itself. He had only a limited number of troops and could not get more quickly. The local militia was in shambles, and much of it favored the South. With more southern states threatening to secede, the city's fate hinged on the tinderbox situations in Virginia and Maryland. If these states tilted southward, they could isolate Washington and open the way for its capture by a strike force of southern troops. Nothing would be more demoralizing to the Union cause than to lose the national capital. On New Year's Eve, Scott was visited by Charles P. Stone, who had served under him in the Mexican War. Scott sounded him out on the feeling in the District of Columbia and asked how many of the people would defend the government by force. Two-thirds, replied Stone. "But they are uncertain as to what can be done and what the Government desires to have done, and they have no rallying-point."29

"Make yourself that rallying-point!" exhorted Scott.

The next day Stone was made inspector general for the District and charged with organizing and inspecting volunteer units. He found the Potomac Light Infantry of Georgetown well armed and drilled, and appar-

ently loyal. The National Rifles of Washington was another matter. Most of
its men were Marylanders intent on defending that state; the captain confided
to Stone that he expected to be ordered soon to "guard the frontier of Maryland and help to keep the Yankees from coming down to coerce the South."
Stone learned that the captain had obtained his commission and the company its arms through orders from former Secretary Floyd. He complained
to Holt, who decreed that any future orders or commissions be routed
through Stone.

While Stone struggled to create a volunteer force, Scott put a garrison of
regulars into Fort Washington just below the city, sent for two artillery units,
and wrote Lincoln assuring him of his loyalty to the Union. The general's
actions moved students at the University of Virginia to hang their native son
in effigy, but Republicans applauded his efforts. Elihu Washburne still feared
"a formidable conspiracy to seize the Capitol," but shared Cameron's view
that "The old warrior is roused, and he will be equal to the occasion."
Leonard Swett also reported to Lincoln that Scott had complete control and
the danger seemed past. But James Pike, the *Tribune*'s man in Washington,
reminded readers that "this country is in full revolution, and this capital is in
undoubted peril," and another correspondent insisted that "The consumma-
tion of their [the secessionists'] grand scheme will be the seizure of the
National Capitol."³⁰

Whether or not there actually was any such conspiracy, many prominent people believed the danger to be real. Even the normally skeptical
Seward thought there might be an attempt to seize the city or disrupt the
counting of the Electoral College votes in February. Southern leaders scoffed
at this hysteria, insisting that men of honor would not stoop to such cowardly
tactics. Their way to revolution was not one of stealth but of proper procedure; the image of the Founding Fathers was fixed firmly in their minds. On
January 5, senators from six Gulf states and Arkansas held a caucus and
concluded that further attempts at reconciliation were a waste of time. They
urged the slave states to secede and form their own confederacy as soon as
possible.³¹

That same day a committee of border state congressmen agreed on a
compromise plan. But the committee was split, and its efforts were disrupted
by a rumor that South Carolina had begun firing on Fort Sumter. Everyone
realized how vital it was to keep the border slave states loyal, but no one
agreed on how to do it. Charles Sumner predicted gloomily that "Virginia
will go, and will carry with her Maryland and Kentucky.... *They will all go.*"
Even Charles Francis Adams found his earlier optimism wilting into a belief
that everything depended on what Virginia did, and that Virginia would
secede. When news leaked out that a ship was on her way to reinforce

Sumter, apprehensions jelled into the fear that a shooting war was but days, perhaps hours, ahead.[32]

On the 8th, Buchanan sent a special message to Congress stressing the gravity of the crisis and urging it to pass the Crittenden compromise or any similar measure. The seizure of federal forts, arsenals, and magazines by states that had not seceded had heightened the threat of war. These acts he labeled "by far the most serious step which has been taken since the commencement of the troubles." While pleading for peace, he reiterated his belief that *"the right and the duty to use military force defensively against those who resist the federal officers in the execution of their legal functions . . . is clear and undeniable."* But he had done all he could; it was up to Congress now to act.[33]

On this point Buchanan was more in the right than his critics were willing to admit. He had asked Congress for a force bill and been ignored. Only days earlier he had appointed a new collector for the port of Charleston, who was to perform his duties on a ship offshore, but Congress did not confirm him. No compromise plan had been forthcoming; Crittenden's measures had died in the Senate and the Committee of 33 was wrapping up its sessions. "Let the question be transferred from political assemblies to the ballot-box," Buchanan pleaded, ". . . before we plunge into armed conflict upon the mere assumption that there is no other alternative." But Congress had already shown its unwillingness or inability to act, and he had no reason to think it would deviate from that pattern.[34]

That same day the city rang eerily with the thunder of cannon celebrating Andrew Jackson's victory at New Orleans. Many wondered if the same echo was not already ringing in Charleston. Jacob Thompson was not one of them. He had left the cabinet meeting unaware that any decision had been made, and on the 4th he telegraphed a friend in Mississippi, "No troops have been sent to Charleston nor will be while I am a member of the cabinet." A similar message went to Judge A. B. Longstreet in South Carolina, but early on the 8th Thompson read in a Washington paper that a ship with troops was en route to Charleston.[35]

Furious at what he considered a betrayal, Thompson wrote an angry letter of resignation in Black's presence. Then, another inquiry arrived from Judge Longstreet. Despite Black's protests, Thompson insisted on replying that a ship was headed for Charleston. His clerk refused to take the message to the telegrapher and it was never sent, but later in the day Thompson passed the information on his own. For this act he was denounced as a traitor, but Wigfall and two other southerners also telegraphed the news to Charleston, where it arrived about 5 p.m. on the 8th. The ship was expected late that night or early the next morning.[36]

. . .

THE *STAR OF THE WEST* made good time in weather so fine that she paused awhile to fish off the coast of North Carolina. A skilled pilot was aboard to guide her into the harbor, but no lights greeted her arrival off the Charleston bar at 1:30 a.m. on January 9. Governor Pickens had ordered the lighthouses darkened, called in the warning lightship from Rattlesnake Shoal, and had the buoys marking the main ship channel taken up. Exasperated, the *Star*'s captain, John McGowan, doused his own lights and hove to until crewmen identified a lone light as coming from Fort Sumter. Taking careful soundings, the *Star* made her way slowly to the main ship channel and stopped again to await daylight before crossing the bar.[37]

A crescent moon hung in the clear sky as the spires of distant Charleston emerged toward dawn. At 6:20 a.m. McGowan ran up the Stars and Stripes, crossed the bar at high water, and headed up the channel on the side nearest Morris Island and farthest from Fort Moultrie. The need for constant soundings slowed her progress. A short distance away another steamer spotted the *Star* and began signaling with rockets and colored lights. To the left a red palmetto flag waved near a cluster of houses at the extreme end of Morris Island, called Cummings Point. "Is it possible that those fellows have got a battery off here?" asked one of the soldiers.

"No," answered another, "there is no battery there."

Suddenly the *Star*'s crew heard a dull thud and saw a cannonball skip across the water in front of the ship. A battery unmasked behind some sandhills and, when the *Star* ignored the warning shot, opened fire. One spent shot clanged into the ship near the rudder; another bounced off the fore chains just above the waterline. McGowan had been given a large garrison flag and told to hoist it as a signal to Major Anderson if the *Star* was fired upon. The flag was quickly hauled out and twice raised and lowered; no response came from Sumter. Although the *Star* had nearly passed the shore battery, she was running against a strong ebb tide on a course that would soon bring her in range of Moultrie's guns. Her draft was too heavy to alter course, and Moultrie greeted her with a wild round of fire from six guns just out of range. Still, Sumter stood silent. McGowan saw that he could not reach the inner harbor without exposing the *Star*'s broadside to direct fire from Moultrie. Reluctantly he slowed, hauled down the flag, came around, and headed back down the channel.

The Morris Island battery opened anew on her but hit nothing. The officers and men aboard the *Star* seethed with rage and frustration. No warning had been given, no communication attempted. Worst of all, no covering fire had come from Sumter. What was wrong there? Even as they grappled with this question, a more terrifying one loomed in their minds. Shots had been fired in anger; had war actually begun?

THE ONLY OFFICER on the parapet that morning was Abner Double-day, who was there with his spyglass because the night before he thought he had seen a signal from a distant pilot boat that something was coming. The previous day Doubleday had read, in a northern newspaper brought over from the city by one of the laborers, that a steamer called the *Star of the West* was en route to Charleston with reinforcements for Sumter. No one believed the story. Why would the government allow details of so delicate and secret a mission to leak? And why would it send a merchant vessel instead of a ship of war that could defend itself from attack? It made no sense to Doubleday.[38]

It had been a strange week even without the rumor. On the 3rd he was astonished to see his wife emerge from a boat filled with laborers come to get their back pay. She had simply put herself in a stern seat and told them to take her along, and the sentry neither asked for a pass nor questioned her. Foster's wife and sister were already there, having obtained permission from Governor Pickens. Seymour's wife had been denied passage by the comman-dant at Moultrie, but the two sons of sutler Dan Sinclair had rowed her to Sumter from a house on the beach where there was no guard.

The ladies hoped to stay, but there was no way to make them comfort-able or keep them out of danger. The weather had turned cold and fuel was scant; to keep his wife warm, Doubleday was obliged to chop up and burn a mahogany table. Reluctantly, Mrs. Doubleday and Mrs. Seymour returned to the mainland with the Sinclair boys at midnight. On the 6th Pickens allowed Eliza Anderson to visit the major, but only in the presence of wit-nesses since she had come down from the North. Her visit was brief, but she brought with her Peter Hart, who had been Anderson's orderly sergeant during the Mexican War. Pickens allowed him to remain at Sumter as a civilian. By such arrangements were the curious convolutions of protocol worked out in this bizarre situation.

Mulling over these matters on the parapet that clear, bright morning, Doubleday turned his spyglass seaward. To his surprise it found a vessel crossing the bar into the channel. Since she was flying the Stars and Stripes and was clearly not a naval ship, Doubleday concluded she must be the *Star*. He knew there was a battery at Cummings Point; on the 6th he had written a friend that "The Charlestonians are surrounding us with batteries on every point of land in the vicinity, and arming them with guns from Forts they have seized. This is done with the hope of preventing any vessel from coming to our assistance, and also . . . to force us ultimately to surrender from a lack of supplies."[39]

Through his glass he saw the battery open fire and watched as the ship hoisted her huge garrison flag. At once Doubleday raced down the back stairs to waken Anderson. The major ordered the long roll beaten to rouse the men and had them posted at the guns on the parapet. Within minutes the garrison was scurrying to their stations. Davis, Meade, and Crawford followed Anderson to the parapet and stood awaiting action. Only four guns had yet been mounted toward Morris Island, all of them too light to reach the battery or provide effective cover. Nevertheless, Anderson had them loaded and the gunners ready with lanyards in hand for the order to fire.[40]

But Anderson hesitated. Following the steamer with his glass, reporting her movements back to the other officers, he struggled to control his excitement. What leeway did his orders allow? Then Crawford noticed that the steamer had hoisted a large flag. What did it mean? Anderson wondered. He ordered a reply from his own flag, but the halyard snarled and could not be untangled in time. Jeff Davis shouted that Moultrie's guns had opened fire on the steamer and urged Anderson to punish the fort, which was well within range of two 42-pound cannon mounted on Sumter's lower tier. Anderson ordered Davis to take command of the two guns and await orders.

As Davis hurried off, Dick Meade pleaded earnestly with Anderson not to open fire lest it initiate the war they all hoped to avoid. Again the major hesitated, anxious to do his duty but unable to reconcile the conflict within himself over what that duty required. Should he protect the ship at all costs? This was, after all, defensive action even though, as Meade argued, Governor Pickens could easily repudiate the attack on the ship. For these few minutes, as never before, he felt the weight of the nation's destiny on his frail shoulders. If only he had specific orders!

Then he noticed the steamer turn and head back out of the channel. "Hold on," he said sharply, "do not fire. I will wait. Let the men go to their quarters, leaving two at each gun. I wish to see the officers at my quarters."

CHAPTER ELEVEN

War Recedes

We catch at straws now. If Anderson would only give up, all would be well. I do not think that there would be any war. How strange how romantic life is now in Charleston! Almost every man is dressed in some uniform—all are so anxious and solemn, no balls or parties. The only people who as yet really suffer, are the dress makers, who usually have their hands full of ball dresses at this time. . . . The more I think of it, the more I feel the need of separate confederacies, and the north ought to let the south part in peace. . . . I wish the struggle was over!

—Caroline Howard Gilman
January 11, 1861[1]

*I*T WAS EASY ENOUGH to start a war, Anderson knew. The difficult thing was to prevent one when passions roused by ambitious men spurred hotheads to rash acts. In searching for his ultimate duty through this maze of bewildering events, he kept coming back to his loyalty to the Union and his desire to avoid bloodshed that might precipitate a civil war. So fixed was he on these goals that he could not face or even admit the possibility of their being incompatible: that the Union could not be preserved short of war. What haunted him was the realization that some perverse trick of fate had made him the flash point for the crisis that had consumed an entire generation. One wrong move, one hasty act or ill-considered calculation, could bring disaster to the nation.

He had not sought this responsibility, and he felt its weight wearing him down. Whatever happened, he must not violate his duty or provoke a clash. He would fight if attacked, but he must not precipitate or provoke hostilities. That was why he had not fired, why he would not fire until he was certain that he must. To refrain was not to shirk responsibility but rather to accept its full and complex weight. The irony of the situation stalked him. On the 6th his brother Larz had visited the fort and, with permission from Pickens, carried a letter from the major back to Washington. In it Anderson mentioned that "it would be dangerous and difficult for a vessel from without to enter the harbor, in consequence of the batteries which are already erected and being erected." He also said frankly, "I shall not ask for any increase of my command, because I do not know what the ulterior views of the Government are." In his isolation he could not know that a policy had been decided on, or that orders governing the protection of a ship had been sent but had not reached him in time.[2]

But the national flag had been fired on. The country's most venerated emblem had been violated before him, and he had done nothing. The flag mattered passionately to Americans because it was the most tangible symbol of their elusive nationalism, and to suffer an insult to it was intolerable. Anderson knew how strongly some of his officers felt about his refusal to return fire. Foster had smashed his hat and stalked off the parapet. But while the major shared their feelings, he could not afford to give in to them. When the officers assembled in his quarters, he saw the indignation in their faces. He asked each one for his views. Hall and Snyder urged that the guns be used to close the harbor; Doubleday agreed. Meade dissented, saying it would trigger a civil war. Davis and Crawford suggested that before they took any action, an explanation be demanded from Pickens and notice served that the harbor would be closed if the reply was unsuitable.[3]

Anderson liked the latter suggestion and drafted a strong note, which the officers approved. Calling the act "without a parallel in the history of our country or of any other civilized government," he declared his intention of allowing no ship to pass his guns unchallenged unless the governor disavowed it. In full-dress uniform Hall carried the message ashore under a white flag. A crowd swarmed to his boat at the dock, and word of his arrival sped through the city along with a rumor that Charleston would soon be bombarded. With difficulty Hall made his way through the crowd to Pickens, who read the letter and summoned his executive council to discuss it. A short time later Pickens returned and handed Hall his reply. To avoid the crowds milling in the streets, he sent an aide with his own carriage to take the lieutenant back to his boat.

In his reply Pickens gave as good as he got. Reminding Anderson that South Carolina considered itself independent, he defined the move to Sumter as the "first act of positive hostility" that had terminated negotiations in Washington. Since then the state had moved to defend itself and its harbor from any aggressive incursion like that by the *Star of the West*. Firing on that ship, he insisted, was "perfectly justified by me." Anderson read the letter to his officers, who called it outrageous. The tone left them convinced that hostilities could not be avoided, that they had no choice but to close the harbor with their guns.[4]

After the meeting Anderson pondered his dilemma. He was walking the line of civil war in complete isolation, ignorant of the government's position.

With clear orders he would dare much; without any he hesitated to risk any step that imperiled peace. The obvious move, then, was to send a messenger to Washington for orders. This would buy time to ease tensions at the harbor. Anderson called the officers together again and posed the idea to them. Most agreed it was the proper course, though some wanted to close the harbor anyway. Satisfied, the major composed another letter to Pickens and chose Lieutenant Theodore Talbot to deliver it. The frail Talbot, weakened by consumption, needed desperately to get out of the dank fort. If Pickens agreed, he would go on to Washington. The lieutenant donned civilian dress and left in a small boat with Sam Crawford, who was in uniform. If the governor would only see reason and let Talbot go north, Anderson thought, the way was clear to step back from the brink. They might yet find a way out.

A CROWD FOLLOWED THEM from the boat to the Charleston Hotel and then to the governor's office, where they found Pickens in session with his council. He received Talbot at once and read the letter eagerly. Anderson's message was simple: He deemed it proper to refer the whole issue to Washington, and he asked Pickens to place no obstacles in the way. Pickens pronounced himself "very glad indeed" to assist Talbot. He introduced the officers to his cabinet and provided his own carriage and an escort for them. Talbot retrieved his luggage and went to the train station. Crawford was permitted to pick up the fort's mail before returning to the boat.[5]

None of the officers isolated in Sumter could have guessed how great a weight the offer lifted from Pickens's shoulders. On New Year's Day he had received from General James Simons a report on military operations that floored him. In blunt language Simons observed that Sumter commanded the line of communications for every other fort. Moultrie was "wholly untenable," lacking a single man who had ever loaded a siege gun or handled a heavy-caliber cannon. The same was true of Fort Johnson, whose force could be routed by a few shells from Sumter. The Morris Island battery was manned by cadets from The Citadel and a rifle corps, none of whom had artillery experience. No fort was equipped to repel incoming vessels. "Why, then, all this preparation and expense," asked Simons, "if the work cannot but terminate in disastrous failure?"[6]

Stung by these observations, which were endorsed by the other two members of the ordnance board, Pickens retorted defensively but could not deny the weaknesses of South Carolina's military. D. F. Jamison admitted that the artillery units had precious little powder or shot and few serviceable guns. Pickens found himself caught between belligerent cries for an immediate attack on Sumter and a military force pitifully inadequate to execute any such assault. Hawks like Rhett of the *Mercury* demanded war, and C. S. Bryan warned his friend Crittenden that "Our people will not bear a menace—and if a vessel is sent to re-enforce Fort Sumter, they will strike . . . if it cost a thousand lives."7

Others were less bloodthirsty. "It seems determined upon to let the best blood of Carolina run like water . . . to gratify the desire of the mob in Charleston to be doing something," complained J. S. Ervin. "There is no true chivalry in anything that is mad or unreasonable. . . . I regret to say the noisiest men . . . are the least ready to . . . bare their bosoms on the battle-field." Grumbling over the cost of military preparations grew louder, and the human toll had also begun. On January 7 a sentry at Castle Pinckney shot dead a soldier named Robert Little Holmes by mistake. "He was the first victim of the war," noted James Petigru, "and the war itself is a mistake." Before the month's end the *Tribune*'s secret correspondent declared that "Fatal accidents among the volunteers have been lately so much increasing that I have ceased to record the individual cases."8

Without realizing it, Anderson had bought Pickens time he urgently needed. On the same day the *Star* was fired on, the governor asked the state ordnance officer and three engineers for a plan to take Sumter. They replied that any direct assault on the fort would be too bloody until it had been reduced by a bombardment "of many hours' duration." The best approach was to install a powerful ring of heavy cannon and mortars on every side of Sumter, and prevent reinforcements from reaching it—in effect, isolate Sumter from the outside world until the state was ready to shell it into submission.9

Pickens embraced this plan because he had no other options. To accept Simons's conclusions, he noted irascibly, was to "yield, without a struggle, every point, and thus break down the spirit of our people, and cover our cause with imbecility and probable ruin." On the 11th he had four ship hulks loaded with stone towed out and sunk to block the main channel at the harbor entrance. That same day he sent Magrath and Jamison to demand the surrender of the fort. Anderson met the two emissaries at the wharf and took them to the guardroom. Magrath presented a letter from Pickens and made a long-winded speech on the theme that the Union was doomed, the fort was a mere pawn that could be seized at any time, and the only refuge from tragedy lay in surrender.10

Anderson was moved by the tragedy but not the refuge. He consulted his officers, who were unanimous that the demand should be rejected and nothing done until word arrived from Washington. Jamison warned that twenty thousand men from all over the state could hardly be restrained from rushing to Charleston to rip the fort to pieces, and that the harbor would flow with blood. When Anderson stood firm, Magrath urged him to reconsider. "I cannot do what belongs to the Government to do," replied Anderson. "The demand must be made upon them, and I appeal to you as a Christian, as a man, and as a fellow-countryman, to do all that you can to prevent an appeal to arms. I do not say as a soldier, for my duty is plain in that respect." Why not try diplomacy first? he suggested. "I will send an officer with a messenger from the Governor to Washington. I will do anything that is possible and honorable to do to prevent an appeal to arms." A prolonged silence followed. As the emissaries left, Anderson gave them a letter for Pickens proposing that both sides refer the matter to Washington.[11]

Pickens rejoiced. A mission to Washington would buy still more time for a military buildup around the fort at no cost to his credibility. Early the next morning he dispatched an aide to the fort with a message agreeing to the major's proposal. Anderson selected Lieutenant Hall for the task; Pickens chose his attorney general, Isaac W. Hayne. The two men left for Washington that same day. Both had written instructions, and Hayne carried a letter from Pickens to Buchanan demanding that the federal government abandon Sumter and turn it over to the state. "That possession," Hayne was told, "cannot become now a matter of discussion or negotiation." He was to tell the president that any attempt to hold the fort would surely lead to war.[12]

It was a curious paradox, buying time with a mission that amounted to an ultimatum. The demand would likely force Buchanan to take a hard line, yet so great was the pressure on Pickens to act that he dared not temporize too much. The governor knew that his military was in wretched shape and that any assault on Sumter would be bloody. The question was how quickly he could improve his forces and how long it would take to bring Sumter to its knees. This shift to a strategy of siege did not go unnoticed; the *Tribune* correspondent alertly caught the change in tactics before most people did. "Unless Fort Sumter be relieved very soon," he wrote on the 13th, "the Revolutionists rely confidently on having possession of it—if not by surrender from starvation, then from capture."[13]

"THE EXPULSION OF THE STEAMER *Star of the West* from the Charleston harbor yesterday morning was the opening of the ball of the Revolution," wrote the *Mercury*. . . . "We would not exchange or recall that blow for millions! It has wiped out a half century of scorn and outrage. . . . The first gun of the new struggle for independence (if struggle there is to be,) has been fired, and Federal power has received its first repulse."[14]

Charleston was giddy with excitement. In weather that seemed more like May, ladies flocked to the Battery to watch expectantly for other ships, oblivious to the danger that Anderson might turn his guns on the city itself. People streamed along Broad and Meeting streets late into the evening, laughing and chattering, uncertain of what the *Star* incident meant beyond a vindication of southern pride. The black children frolicking in the streets knew as much about what the future held as did the cream of Charleston society that graced the promenades talking grandly of the powerful southern confederacy that must surely come once other cotton states began to follow South Carolina's lead.[15]

On January 9, the day of the *Star* incident, Mississippi's convention voted, 84–15, to secede. Florida followed suit the next day by a 62–7 majority, and Alabama on the 11th by a 61–39 vote that revealed a deep split between its northern and southern counties. In all three states the ultras had their way. "If the relation of master and slave be dissolved," said one Alabaman, "and our slaves turned loose amongst us without restraint, they would either be destroyed by our own hands . . . or we ourselves would become demoralized and degraded."[16]

In Florida, thirteen-year-old Susan Bradford thrilled at being taken to the convention by her father, Dr. Edward Bradford. When her mother protested that she would miss school, the doctor replied, "[T]his is history in the making, she will learn more than she can get out of books, and what she hears in this way she will never forget." Susan heard plenty in Tallahassee and saw the fiery figure of Edmund Ruffin, whose age showed only in his flowing locks of white hair. She beamed with pride when a blue cockade was pinned on her, and she listened attentively to the speeches. She saw the final vote on the 11th and the signing of the ordinance the next day on the east portico of the capitol.[17]

Susan watched enthralled as a diehard Unionist, Colonel George T. Ward, held his pen aloft and said sorrowfully, "When I die, I want it inscribed upon my tombstone that I was the last man to give up the ship." Later a lame Baptist minister named Ownes said loudly, "Unlike my friend, Colonel Ward, I want it inscribed on MY tombstone that I was the FIRST man to quit the rotten old hulk." As cheers rent the air, Susan was moved by the tears rolling down the face of old General Richard K. Call, another strong Unionist. She tried earnestly to make sense of it all but could not. "Our world," she sighed, "seems to have gone wild."

In the North the mood was no less wild. "Our blood boils to hear that the flag of our Country has been insulted," said an Illinois physician. "That our Government is so ineffective in repelling and punishing the offenders, is sufficient to arouse all the latent *fight* there is in any man." A New Haven editor asserted that "This is not secession; it is not dissolution; *it is rebellion and aggressive war*!" A Pennsylvanian warned Buchanan that the *Star* "*must return to Charleston and land her troops at Fort Sumter*, or your administration will be disgraced through all coming time." Thurlow Weed, in his quiet, shrewd manner, hailed the firing on the *Star* as a "favorable omen" because it would, "while arousing the whole North, bring some Southerners to their senses."[18]

Weed was half right. Across the North, editors and legislators put aside old divisions to condemn the assault on Old Glory. The Republicans controlled all but two state legislatures, and the last two Democratic governors left office during January. The first new governor to take office, Austin Blair of Michigan, declared that "The Union must be preserved and the laws enforced. . . . It is a question of war that the seceded States have to look in the face." Andrew Curtin of Pennsylvania, in his inaugural on the 15th, rejected the legality of secession and warned that his state could "never acquiesce in such a conspiracy, nor assent to a doctrine which involves the destruction of the Government." Alexander Randall of Wisconsin insisted that "Secession is revolution; revolution is war; War against the government . . . is treason."[19]

Those who pleaded for compromise saw the ground cut out from under them. Indignant letters, some with offers of troops, poured in to congressmen. Even Democratic diehards like James Gordon Bennett of the *Herald* urged Congress to give the president power to call out sixty thousand militia. Speakers denounced southern treason in martial rhetoric that pleased Governor John Andrew of Massachusetts, who wanted the people "to get accustomed to the smell of gunpowder." Henry Adams took an even more calloused view. "If Major Anderson and his whole command were all murdered in cold blood," he surmised, "it would be an excellent thing for the country, much as I should regret it on the part of those individuals."[20]

Southern pride paid a dear price for the few feeble shots fired at the *Star*. As James Watson Webb wrote Lincoln, "It has left them without a sympathizer, even in the Democratic ranks; and the north as a unit, demands the enforcement of the Laws, the vindication of the Constitution and the punishment of the Traitors." But the attack did more than accelerate the healing of rifts within the North; it also made Fort Sumter more than ever the symbol of federal presence and the focus of the clash over war or peace. A few misaimed cannonballs had escalated the stakes and made it nearly impossible for either side to back away without losing face.[21]

One prominent southerner sensed the danger inherent in the changed status of Sumter. On the 13th Jefferson Davis advised Pickens that shutting the garrison up "with a view to starve them into submission would create a sympathetic action much greater than any which could be obtained on the present issue." Davis conceded that "We are probably soon to be involved in that fiercest of human strifes, a civil war." Time was needed to form a southern confederacy, and Pickens had to buy the South that time. "The little garrison in its present position presses on nothing but a point of pride," Davis added later, "and to you I need not say that war is made up of real elements. It is a physical problem from the solution of which we must need exclude all sentiment."[22]

WITH ALL EYES ON SUMTER, trouble was also brewing at the Pensacola Navy Yard and its nearby forts. There a young lieutenant named Adam J. Slemmer found himself playing a more modest version of the dilemma that had confronted Anderson two weeks earlier.

The navy yard lay seven miles south of the town, at the edge of Pensacola Bay, adjacent to the village of Warrington. Fort Barrancas stood a mile and a half west of the village, Fort McRee across the bay on the west shore. In the middle of the bay, nearly parallel to the yard, lay a forty-mile-long strip of land called Santa Rosa Island. Fort Pickens stood on its western tip but, like Sumter, had no garrison. The only federal troops were a contingent of marines at the navy yard and Company G, First Artillery, at the Barrancas barracks.[23]

In January both the captain and the senior first lieutenant of Company G were away. Two officers remained on duty: the scholarly-looking Slemmer, who had never expected to have such responsibility thrust upon him, and Second Lieutenant Jeremiah H. Gilman. Alarmed by the seizure of federal forts in Charleston Harbor and by Florida's march toward secession, Slemmer worked out contingency plans with Gilman while awaiting orders from Washington. On the 7th a disturbing rumor reached them that troops from Florida and Alabama were preparing to seize the navy yard and forts. The next day Slemmer had a store of powder moved from its usual location to Fort Barrancas and put under guard. This proved a wise precaution; at midnight a party of twenty men entered the fort, expecting it to be empty, and fled quickly when challenged and fired on.[24]

The rumor of approaching troops moved Slemmer to enlist the support of Commodore James Armstrong, the commander of the navy yard. A veteran of long service, Armstrong had woes of his own at the yard. His storekeeper was a secessionist, and some of his officers were openly southern sympathizers. The marines were loyal, but many of the laborers held southern views and all were surly because the navy had not paid them since November despite Armstrong's repeated pleas for funds. The yard with its two-foot brick wall could hardly be defended by a handful of marines and a few small cannon with rotten carriages. Despite the mounting excitement in Warrington, Armstrong refused to act without specific orders from his superiors.[25]

On the 9th, orders arrived for Slemmer and Armstrong to cooperate in defending the public property. They agreed that the only defendable fort was Pickens. Armstrong promised to provide what men and supplies he could, and to send the *Wyandotte* to move Slemmer's command to Pickens at one o'clock. When the ship did not come, Slemmer and Gilman hurried to the yard and learned that some of Armstrong's officers had persuaded him not to act lest he precipitate a war. Sensing that the commodore was losing his nerve, Slemmer argued hard. The steamer was promised again for five o'clock, but fog delayed it until the next morning. Hastily Slemmer and Gilman loaded a scow and several small boats with men, provisions, cannon, tools, ammunition, and whatever else they could carry, including an old mule and cart that later proved invaluable.

By 10 a.m. they were safely ashore at Pickens, having left behind families and personal effects. An old Spaniard named Francisco Gómez, who lived in a cottage in front of the Barrancas barracks, paced back and forth as he watched their preparations. Long a friend of the officers and a great admirer of Andrew Jackson, Gómez told Gilman with upturned eyes, "My God! My God! it is awful; nothing can be saved; we shall all be killed—everything destroyed. I am afraid to say anything. How I wish General Jackson was here."[26]

That same day Florida seceded from the Union.

Fort Pickens was in dilapidated condition, but, unlike Sumter, it sat on an island where supplies could reach it without interference. Slemmer had enough supplies for five months, but the assistance promised by Armstrong melted away in the heat of protest from his prosouthern officers. Gilman pleaded for the marines to be sent to Pickens along with more supplies; Armstrong provided only thirty ordinary seamen, who arrived without arms or even a change of clothes. "Great God," exclaimed the commodore, "what can I do with the means that I have?" The *Wyandotte* and the storeship *Supply* were ordered to assist the fort, but the former was not to fire any guns except in her own defense. On the morning of the 12th nearly four hundred troops from Alabama and Florida marched from Pensacola to the navy yard and demanded its surrender. Seeing that resistance was futile, Armstrong complied. The thirty-eight marines and other personnel were taken prisoner and paroled. Armstrong's attempts to explain his surrender convinced no one; he was later court-martialed and convicted of "neglect of duty."[27]

From Pickens, Slemmer and his men saw the flag lowered and knew that the navy yard with its dry dock, workshops, materials, and supplies had been seized. Only the *Wyandotte* and *Supply* escaped. Just before sundown four men landed at Santa Rosa and demanded surrender of the fort to the governors of Alabama and Florida. One was a civil engineer from the yard; the other three were officers unknown to Slemmer and Gilman. "I am here by authority of the President of the United States," replied Slemmer curtly, "and I do not recognize the authority of any governor to demand the surrender of United States property,—a governor is nobody here."[28]

"Do you say the governor of Florida is nobody, the governor of Alabama nobody?" snapped one of the officers.

"I know neither of them," retorted Slemmer, "and I mean to say that they are nothing to me."

The visitors left, and Slemmer looked to his defenses. The following night a patrol discovered some men lurking near the fort. A few shots were fired, and Slemmer's men redoubled their guard efforts. On the 15th Colonel W. H. Chase, commanding the state troops at the navy yard, came to the island with Captain Ebenezer Ferrand, the most ardent of Armstrong's prosouthern officers. Chase had built Fort Pickens and knew its every feature, but Slemmer and Gilman met them at the wharf and would not let them near the fort. "I have come to ask of you young officers," said Chase with deep emotion, "officers of the same army in which I have spent the best and happiest years of my life, the surrender of this fort."[29]

Chase tried to read a prepared statement, but after a few lines his voice choked and his eyes brimmed with tears. Stamping the ground in anger at his weakness, he handed the paper to Ferrand to read. Ferrand, whose eyes were also watering, protested that he didn't have his glasses and passed it to Gilman. It was another demand for surrender. Slemmer and Gilman conferred privately and promised an answer the next day. But they were merely buying time to rest their weary men. On the 16th Slemmer sent his refusal to the yard and braced for a possible attack. A new flash point had been created along with Sumter.

TIME COULD NOT MOVE QUICKLY nor events slowly enough for Buchanan. The lack of a response to the firing on the *Star* had burst his brief balloon of popularity. "The Old Pennsylvania Fossil is rumored to have relapsed into vacillation and imbecility," wrote George Templeton Strong. "It seemed a week ago as if he were developing germs of a backbone." Robert Toombs, the bright, bellicose senator from Georgia, noted gleefully that "The administration is dead broken down. . . . The old gentleman is alternately wreaking, wracking, cursing and railing. At one moment he exacts pity and anon contempt."[30]

Buchanan had endured enough in one week to try the hardiest soul. On the 11th, three days after Thompson had quit the cabinet, Philip Thomas resigned his Treasury post. Thomas had never felt comfortable in the office, and northern bankers were hostile to him. In his place Buchanan appointed General John A. Dix, who was already in Washington expecting to be made secretary of war. To succeed Thompson, Buchanan approached two southerners; when both declined, he left the duties of Interior to the chief clerk. The last southerner had quit the cabinet, leaving Buchanan in the company of conservative northern Democrats and Holt, the implacably Unionist Kentuckian.[31]

This new unity was little comfort to Buchanan. His southern friends had fled and now denounced him as savagely as did his northern adversaries. He had no party in Congress, no voice in the circles of power outside the White House, few friends anywhere, contempt from his opponents, and little sympathy even from those who had once supported him. The ordeal had worn him down like a rag doll caving in as each blow knocked out more of its stuffing. And the blows came quickly that fateful week: The *Star* was fired on, two cabinet members resigned, and three southern states seceded on successive days. The Pensacola Navy Yard had been seized, and a new crisis point created at Fort Pickens. Before all this could be digested, Talbot arrived with Anderson's urgent request for orders.

On the 10th Holt had assured Anderson of the government's support, praising his move to Sumter as "in every way admirable" and ordering him to "continue, as heretofore, to act strictly on the defensive." Two days later Talbot told Buchanan that Anderson had not fired in defense of the *Star* because the order to do so had not reached him in time, and he briefed the president on the negotiations with Pickens. On Sunday night the 13th, Lieutenant Hall and Isaac Hayne reached Washington. The next morning Buchanan saw Hayne unofficially and decreed that all communication between them be in writing. Hayne promised to return the next day with Pickens's letter. Hall then delivered his reports from Sumter, including Anderson's account of the *Star* episode and the temporary truce he had arranged with Pickens.[32]

The truce that bought Pickens breathing room also brought Buchanan relief. Distressed that the plan to relieve Sumter had miscarried and resulted in fresh criticism, anxious to defuse the crisis, and fearful that the slightest misstep might provoke war, the president gave warm approval to Anderson's caution. If this truce not of his making could be maintained, it would not be necessary to send another expedition to Sumter and he might yet escape office before the deluge. But the truce would hold only until Anderson received clear orders, and it might not even survive the letter Hayne carried from Pickens. Buchanan did not know the letter's contents, but he could guess that it included a demand to surrender the fort that must be rejected outright. Once that transaction occurred, how could a clash be avoided?

While Buchanan and his cabinet pondered this dilemma, Senator Clement Clay of Alabama urged Hayne to withhold the letter. He spoke for senators from the seceding states who thought that any clash between the federal government and South Carolina would be premature until the South had organized its own government and prepared for war. When Hayne hesitated, Clay returned the next day with a formal request signed by ten senators from states that had seceded or were about to secede. They asked South Carolina to make no move against Sumter as long as Buchanan sent no reinforcements there and to maintain this status quo at least until February 15. "Our people feel that they have a common destiny with your people," they stressed, "and expect to form with them . . . a new Confederation and Provisional Government."[33]

Hayne acceded to the request and referred it to Pickens for approval. Senators John Slidell of Louisiana, Stephen Mallory of Florida, and Benjamin Fitzpatrick of Alabama then dispatched copies of their proposal and Hayne's reply to Buchanan, seeking a pledge that no reinforcements would be sent if Anderson were allowed free access to mail and supplies. On the afternoon of the 16th Clay pressed Buchanan to ease the crisis by withdrawing Anderson from Sumter. Buchanan reiterated that he "could not under any circumstances withdraw the troops." Clay then mentioned the plan devised by the seceding senators to avoid bloodshed. Put it in writing, replied Buchanan. Clay alluded to the existing truce and hinted that it might be extended even to March 4. While the notion appealed to Buchanan, he said that it would hold only until Hayne left town in a few days. Nothing could be discussed, he repeated, unless it was in writing. Clay assured him that Sumter was safe until these options had been explored.[34]

Buchanan did not mention that he did not have to send another expedition because Anderson had assured him that none was needed. After lengthy cabinet discussion Holt wrote Anderson that the president fully approved his restraint in returning fire without clear orders. No further efforts to provide reinforcements would be made, Holt emphasized, unless Anderson himself requested them, in which case "a prompt and vigorous effort" would be made to furnish them. Meanwhile, Anderson was to watch enemy preparations closely, report frequently, and prepare his defenses for any contingency.[35]

This approach did not sit well with Black, who saw a dilemma that others missed or ignored. That night he laid out his views in a letter to General Scott asking him to correct his "errors, if errors they be." Black understood the irony of Anderson's ceasing to ask for reinforcements just when Buchanan had worked himself up to send them. The present "truce," while giving both sides breathing room, made a bad situation worse. If Anderson was not to be withdrawn from Sumter, as now seemed certain, then time worked against him. Every passing day allowed South Carolina's forces to grow stronger while Anderson's men became weaker as the siege exhausted their strength and supplies.[36]

"If the troops remain in Fort Sumter without any change in their condition," concluded Black, "and the hostile attitude of South Carolina remains as it is now, the question of Major Anderson's surrender is one of time only." If he was not to be relieved, then he had to be reinforced, and the time to do that was now, before the enemy grew strong enough to prevent it. Black thought the difficulty of reinforcing "very much magnified to the minds of some persons." Any good vessel could run the Morris Island battery—the *Star* had done so—and cross the bar if Anderson provided covering fire against Fort Moultrie. It could be done by any pirate or slaver or smuggler eager to make five hundred dollars, let alone a daring naval officer. But the attempt had to come soon.

Scott's reply to this inquiry is not known. What is clear is that Black had touched the heart of the matter. The status quo of a siege worked in favor of South Carolina and against the government. In personal terms it worked in favor of Buchanan and against the man who would inherit the crisis from him. Black averred that the fact that "other persons are to have charge of the Government before the worst comes to the worst has no influence upon my mind," but the same could not be said for Buchanan. Partisan politics aside, Black could not escape a feeling of failure. "If the skirts of the administration were altogether clear in this business," he confided to the American minister in Ecuador a week later, "I should feel more comfortably than I do. We might have throttled this revolution by taking the right steps to put it down where it first broke out at Charleston." But they had not. Was it too late now?[37]

While Black deliberated, Hayne tried to persuade Pickens that he had bought him needed time. During the next week he sent the governor three letters and five telegrams urging him to withhold action as long as Buchanan sent no reinforcements. Jefferson Davis wrote three letters to Pickens; Wigfall, William Porcher Miles, Maxcy Gregg, and others also counseled delay. Pickens made no response. His silence gave the anxious southern senators little comfort as the crisis at Fort Pickens unfolded. "We think no assault should be made," they wired Florida Governor Marshall S. Perry on the

18th. "The possession of the fort is not worth one drop of blood to us. Measures pending unite us in this opinion. Bloodshed now may be fatal to our cause."[38]

Ephemeral as it was, the truce cast a brief aura of calm over Washington. Pleasure continued to mix with business in the most improbable of ways as northerners and southerners met at dinners or soirees. Erasmus Keyes, the aide to General Scott, complained that the rigors of his social calendar fatigued him with "overwork, feasting, and gayety." No one fascinated him more than the southern belles he met at parties. All of them were to his eyes beautiful, elegant, and incorrigibly partisan. During one visit to Judge Campbell's the charming daughters of the host and John Slidell assured Keyes that if he were wounded or captured in war, they would bring him comforts and, after the South's victory, welcome him again to their homes.[39]

George Templeton Strong, on a visit to Washington, was amused to see a friend huddled in one corner of his small parlor with Charles Sumner, whom Strong called the "Martyr," and another friend in the opposite corner with Florida Congressman George Hawkins (an "unhanged traitor"), chatting sotto voce. Buchanan began his annual levees promptly on the 15th, and the usual dinner parties continued despite the crisis and a growing rancor that sometimes spilled across the dinner table or ballroom. Scott and Robert Toombs clashed at one party, Sumner and Charles Francis Adams at another. "Sumner, you don't know what you're talking about," Adams told his old friend. "Your's [sic] is the very kind of stiff-necked obstinacy that will break you down if you persevere."[40]

Beneath the veneer of civility, feelings ran hard. The departing Kate Thompson condemned Judge Black as "the meanest man living," and Edwin Stanton as "a mean, low-life Scamp." Erasmus Keyes floated home from one dinner party charmed by the beauty and grace of Mrs. John Slidell. But even in his reverie he realized that "no blandishments could moderate my desire for war." Robert Hatton, whose name adorned no list of prominent guests for a dinner party, saw absurdity in the "gay and showy men and women—all gadding to be seen" on the streets in the evening. The mood of the city was mercurial, shifting like the weather that had lately turned Washington into what one southerner called a "Siberian bog—all mud, sleet and icicles."[41]

The Washington correspondent for the Charleston *Mercury* found profound insight in the city's fickle weather. Had not Buckle and other historians argued that men were in large measure the creatures of the climate in which they lived? If so, then surely Buchanan's vacillation and treachery (in southern eyes) could be explained by "the peculiar instability of Washington weather. Last night the stars shone softly in the sky; to-day is cold, rainy, wretched. If we want an administration to have a fixed policy, the seat of government must be in a locality where at least two consecutive days have the same temperature."[42]

William Henry Trescot had a more cynical explanation for the procession of "folly in high places." Just arrived on Barnwell Island off Beaufort, South Carolina, no longer a major player in the greatest game of his age, he viewed events with the disdain of a professional watching amateurs at play. "It really does seem," he observed dryly, "that a revolution works its way through the blunders of those who attempt to direct it."[43]

CHAPTER TWELVE

The Peace Puzzle

*The question before the country . . . has become something more than an issue
on the slavery question growing out of the construction of the Constitution. The
issue now before us is, whether we have a country, whether or not this is a
nation. . . . Who does not see that by adopting these compromise propositions
we tacitly recognize the right of these States to secede? Their adoption at this
time would completely demoralize the Government, and leave it in the power
of any State to destroy. . . . I could agree to no compromise until the right to
secede was fully renounced, because it would be a recognition of the right of
one or more States to break up the Government at their will.*

—Senator James W. Grimes
January 28, 1861[1]

*T*HE PRESS CENTER OF AMERICA occupied a modest area near
City Hall Park in New York. There could be found the unassuming offices of
the nation's only eight-page daily newspapers, the *Tribune*, the *Herald*, and
the *Times*. A few blocks away, at the corner of Broad and Wall streets, a small
dingy building housed the only formal news-gathering network in the nation.
Owned by the seven leading papers of New York, the Associated Press had
bureaus in Washington and Albany, a handful of full-time reporters, and fifty
agents around the country culling local papers for news. It also had a special
contract with the two leading telegraph companies providing it and the
papers that owned it special rates in return for all their telegraph business.[2]

Little in the place hinted at the dawn of a media revolution or the seeds of
a media conglomerate. Amid the staccato chorus of telegraph instruments,
clerks at one row of worn oak desks copied dispatches in longhand for the
member papers while their comrades in a second row combed the incoming
wires and local papers for news to put into the releases that were furnished
twice a day to papers throughout the country. But observers already felt the
power wrought by these overworked clerks. "The reports of the associated
press find their way into every newspaper from Maine to Texas and California," noted an upstate paper. "It is the most potent engine for affecting
public opinion, the world ever saw."[3]

Already New York had emerged as the center of the news business, as it had of commerce and finance. None of the nation's 372 daily and 2,971 weekly papers in 1860 even approached the influence of the New York dailies. The rapid proliferation of telegraph wires not only spread and speeded up the flow of information but also allowed it to be centralized and dispersed like other commodities. "The telegraphic reporter has, in modern newspaper business, almost entirely taken the place of ordinary general reporters," added the same New York editor. To the extent that this was true, it made the nation more dependent on New York for news because the Associated Press dominated the telegraph dispatches and the New York press controlled the Associated Press.[4]

The *Herald*, *Times*, and *Tribune* also delivered to homes across the nation. The Philadelphia *Inquirer* complained that the big three's distribution "literally carries New York over every railway, sets it down at every station, and extends it everywhere." *Harper's Weekly* observed smugly, if accurately, that the citizens of Washington "actually look to the New York papers for news of their own city." Even Rhett's *Mercury* in distant Charleston grumbled that "we have to go to the New York papers for news of our own affairs." Another Philadelphia journal labeled the telegraph "a curse to the country" and warned people to "beware of this new power in our midst, more potent than an 'army with banners.' Its whole stock in trade consists in the perpetual excitement of the community—in a morbid appetite for startling news and a monomania for extravagant and almost incredible rumors."[5]

Although few people realized it, the big three papers were already shifting in their character from organs of personal journalism to institutions. Horace Greeley, easily the best-known journalist in America, had turned the running of the *Tribune* over to Charles A. Dana, the first man on any paper to hold the title of managing editor. James Gordon Bennett, at sixty-five nearly as famous as Greeley, had done much the same thing by leaving the *Herald* in the capable hands of Frederic Hudson. Even Henry J. Raymond, whose *Times* was only a decade old, allowed his interest in Republican party politics to distract him from the paper.[6]

Greeley remained the soul of the *Tribune*, but its moving spirit was Dana, who once defined a managing editor as "a being to whom the sentiment of remorse is unknown." Bennett was a public icon, Hudson as drab and efficient as the *Herald* was spicy and insouciant. "To manage a paper properly," Hudson observed, "one must work steadily and perseveringly. There is no let-up, no rest, no play that is not mixed up with business." For many reporters, however, work remained a peculiar form of play. They dwelled at the edge of a society that did not yet grasp their function or the influence they wielded over people's lives. Nor did the reporters understand this power. In hangouts like Pfaff's Cave on Broadway, where Walt Whitman claimed "there was as good talk around that table as took place anywhere in the world," they downed sausages and lager and caroused like the free-spirited outcasts they were.7

While news was a deadly serious business to editors, it was to most reporters still a grand adventure, a game of varying stakes. Nothing had ever offered them a grander adventure or higher stakes than the national crisis. A few months earlier, John Bigelow of the *Evening Post* had asked Rhett about sending a reporter to cover events in Charleston, only to be told that he "would probably be hung." Even the prosouthern *Herald*, which had sent a man on a southern tour, recalled him after he was nearly lynched. Most southern towns forbade delivery of the *Tribune* and returned copies stamped "Undeliverable."8

Through these dreary weeks editors and reporters in every part of the country labored mightily to influence their readers' mood and turn it in their own direction. To disgusted observers they seemed to be everywhere, pursuing rumors or inventing them, aiding partisans who worked to arouse feelings at home. Like their peers of a later generation, many took themselves more seriously than they took much of what they saw, relished cynicism as a savory, and could laugh at anything but themselves. They gloried in lavishing and embellishing detail on a scene to swell its importance, saw too often what they wanted to see, and so misled readers as well as themselves.

Above all, editors and reporters alike sensed that they had gone from being merely spectators to becoming players in the great national crisis. Their efforts had transformed an obscure army major into a national hero known familiarly as "Our Bob." In their quest for readers they did not hesitate to flog one another for the sin of pride. "It is a pitiful dodge on the part of leading papers—this modern system of manufacturing news," said a small Pennsylvania paper, "and it has done and is now doing more to destroy public confidence in the veracity or reliability of the American press than any or all other causes combined." The Providence *Journal* agreed that "some of the 'sensation special dispatches,' which have so amazed the public, have been manufactured to order."9

The very speed of transmission heightened the crisis by giving people more news faster, much of it slanted in the language and images of sectional stereotypes. It had become easier to boil up a crisis on a national scale than ever before. The result was confusion and deception, sometimes random, often harnessed to a cause, and never were causes more desperate than during the winter of 1860–61. In this war of words each side tried to infiltrate the citadels of the other. The public learned about the *Star*'s saga in detail because a reporter from the New York *Evening Post* stowed away on the vessel and other papers reprinted much of his account. The *Tribune* had the redoubtable James S. Pike in Washington and a clever, cheeky rascal named Charles D. Brigham under cover in Charleston. Brigham had been there since November, sending back accounts in coded letters and infuriating local authorities, who itched to catch him.[10]

The *Mercury* had a man in Washington to counter the reports of *Tribune* reporters, but Rhett also needed someone under cover to send back dispatches for use on the home front. Two such operatives in Washington and New York had already been exposed; that January he recruited a new Washington man named G. W. Bagby, whose letters to the Richmond *Dispatch* had impressed him. For three dollars each (his top fee), Rhett wanted a daily letter from the capital sent to a cover man to avoid having it stopped as earlier dispatches had been. No one, even in the *Mercury* office, was to know Bagby's identity. "The wisdom and consequent usefulness of your letters will depend entirely on this," Rhett stressed. "If you are known, it is impossible to criticise and use names as you otherwise can do, to the great benefit of the southern cause."[11]

It was the latter that interested Rhett most. He was not after news so much as propaganda. "I shall sometimes strike out of your letters what I do not like," he told Bagby, "and add *arguments* such as I desire to come out in the shape of correspondence instead of editorially." He urged Bagby to "Criticise Keitt & Co., and don't be squeamish about using names." In particular he wanted an earlier Richmond dispatch in which Bagby claimed to have seen a letter from a reputable New England gentlemen giving Hannibal Hamlin's pedigree as a mulatto. Bagby furnished a copy of the letter, and Rhett eagerly published it on January 22 as evidence that "HAMLIN had negro blood in his veins, and that one of his children had kinky hair." If that was not enough, Rhett reminded his readers that "Hannibal and Scipio are both favorite names on the plantation."[12]

Shrewd observers saw that the war of words had the power to warp men's minds. "The great men of the country," said an Iowa editor, "are greater slaves than the negroes of the South; they are slaves to every newspaper, telegraph operator or correspondent in the country. . . . The newspaper press rules everything from a quack doctor to the President." Frederic Hudson conceded that thanks to the telegraph, "Village gossips are magnified into world gossips." A Pennsylvania colleague warned: "Unless it is shorn of its strength, by unbelief in all it says and does, it [the telegraph] can bring upon us a war at pleasure; it can cry down the good and elevate the bad; it can achieve the success of any party; it can elect any man, almost,

President of the United States; and it can . . . play, as with a foot-ball, with the great interests of labor and industry."[13]

NOWHERE DID THE WAR OF WORDS resound with more noise or less effect than in its most traditional arena. Congress had always been a chamber in which sound and fury served as a substitute for action, and the gravity of the national crisis raised it to new heights of paralysis thanks in part to a gridlock that had emerged. Few members could even grasp what the main issue was, let alone find ways of dealing with it. Those who cringed from the threat of civil war could not get at the source of that threat. Not only was the choice between peace and war unclear, but it was also unclear exactly what those alternatives meant in practical terms or what policies were needed to secure them.

One dilemma above all others compounded confusion. While the sparring over compromise revolved mostly around slavery, the immediate problem was secession. "Slavery is no longer the matter in debate," said James Russell Lowell, whose contempt for the administration knew no bounds, "and we must beware of being led off upon that side issue. The matter now in hand is the reestablishment of order, the reaffirmation of national unity, and the settling once and for all whether there can be such a thing as a government without the right to use its power in self-defence." But even those like Senator Grimes, who understood this crucial issue, groped vainly for a way to translate it into policy.[14]

The gridlock was as obvious as it was unbreakable. Some believed secession was legal, others thought it legal but wrong, and still others considered it illegal. Some argued that the use of force to prevent secession was illegal, others thought it legal but impractical or impolitic, while still others considered it legal and absolutely necessary to maintain national unity. In dealing with the question, one branch of government (the executive) had deferred to another (the legislative), which had so far refused to act or to give the executive any power to act through new legislation. The third branch (the Supreme Court) was powerless to act and remained a spectator to events.

Another paradox underlay the confusion. The United States had been founded on the sanctity of written law, yet had also been born in the womb of revolution. How could these contrary birthrights be reconciled? The long, tortuous debates over the right of secession, in which advocates on both sides cited the sacred (often the same) texts of the Founding Fathers, never got past this fatal contradiction. Nor could they reconcile their desire for a unified national government with their fear and distrust of federal power.

To some extent this fear arose from generational differences in outlook. For men like Buchanan, Scott, Crittenden, and Senator James F. Simmons of Rhode Island, who boasted of having lived under every president the American people had elected, the prospect of civil war threatened a bloody close not only to the Union but to the history of what they regarded as a glorious era. Yet experience was also a snare. The older generation had learned its lessons (different for each section) from the crisis of 1830 and determined to act on them in 1860 even though conditions had changed greatly.[15]

The same older generation that cherished the Union also tended to view it as a confederation of sovereign states, while younger men, who had known only the Union, saw it more as an inviolate national entity to which the individual states were subordinate. The torment for many elder statesmen stemmed from a conviction that the Union was vital but at its core voluntary, and could not or should not be maintained by force. This belief was what lay behind their reluctance to endorse a military response and their ambivalence toward Buchanan's policy, which had succeeded in avoiding a clash but had failed to uphold the integrity of the national government. Few cared to admit that these objectives were irreconcilable, that a choice must be made between them.

For some idealistic northerners who had not grown up with the nation or fought the battles to create it, any union infested with slavery was not worth having. Others who opposed compromise believed that much more was at stake. "What we feared most," recalled Carl Schurz, "was . . . that, under the influence of a momentary panic, a step might be taken that would—to use a term current at the time—'Mexicanize' our government—that is, destroy in it that element of stability which consists in the absolute assurance that when the officers of the government are legally elected, their election is unconditionally accepted and submitted to by the minority. When that rule is broken . . . the republic will be in a state of intermittent revolution."[16]

For these men secession posed the graver threat because it destabilized the republican form of government. Slavery was an issue that had somehow to be resolved, but secession undermined the foundation of free government. It contravened the whole basis of the American political system, which relied on compromise and majority rule. As Schurz noted, it struck at the heart of the system, the acceptance by all sides of the results of a free election. Nothing was more fatal to the future of free government than the lack of such acceptance. Secession also invoked the deeper clash between federal and state power at a time when most members of Congress feared the growth of federal power.

For decades southern extremists had used the threat of secession to wring concessions from the North. So often had it been brandished that many northerners dismissed it as crying wolf. "We are still just where we started six months ago," joked Schuyler Colfax of Indiana in 1859, "except that our Southern friends have dissolved the Union forty or fifty times since then." The idea of secession surfaced only when some concrete grievance led someone to seek refuge in it. Yet the unfinished nature of the Union ensured that someone, somewhere, at some time would actually attempt it, and that the issue would have to be settled once and for all, most likely by force of arms.[17]

As a threat secession was not some fine old brandy kept in the cellar for special occasions but rather a house wine always on hand to be passed around whenever the occasion arose. Being common, it was cheap, intoxicating, spilled as often as drunk, and befuddling of the senses. "Nothing less than secession by the South will ever bring the North to its senses," argued William Gilmore Simms. "Were we not to secede, they & you & every brave man would despise us." Whether some other issue might have grown desperate enough to provoke such a crisis is academic; the fact is that slavery proved to be the issue.[18]

Here, then, was the Gordian knot wrought by South Carolina's secession and made worse as other states seceded. For decades the contest had been over slavery; now it shifted inexorably from the reasons for secession to the act of secession itself. The latter had lurked near center stage since the nullification crisis, but never until this unhappy winter had the nation been forced to confront it directly. Once it upstaged slavery, prospects for a compromise grew even more bleak. Even if a settlement could be found for slavery, it would not touch the problem of secession. As long as one of these issues remained unresolved, the other could never be settled, and no compromise could get at both of them.

Helpless to find a solution, the members of Congress talked and talked and appealed to God for guidance, if not relief. But blast after blast of the most formidable rhetorical batteries failed even to dent the stronghold of deadlock. As for the Almighty, the members learned anew that while the Lord might provide, He did not offer advice. Men felt the need for divine help because so many of them looked anxiously into the future and saw only a dark void. Where ultras on both sides envisioned brave new worlds unfolding, moderates saw nothing—not even hope that the Union could be saved and war averted. Most men stepped back from the awful chasm of war that loomed before them. They looked backward wistfully or forward with apprehension; only a few dared think about the horrors that awaited them.

Through this ritual the border state men writhed in personal and political agony. They did not know whom to blame more: the Republicans for their intransigence or the southern ultras for their foolhardy ambition that hoped to drag the border states after them. The firing on the *Star of the West* had dealt their hopes for adjustment a lethal blow. That northern opinion had hardened since the incident was obvious. Among hundreds of letters from his constituents Elihu Washburne found only two favoring compromise. A Pittsburgh editor alerted Simon Cameron to a "fierceness of sentiment here in opposition to anything that looks like a Compromise" that "amounts almost to a fury."[19]

Secessionists urged slave states to withdraw at once and northern states to recognize them. Virginia proposed the calling of a border state convention, Kentucky the seating of a constitutional convention. Buchanan's advisers favored the idea of a national convention, as did former President John Tyler, who wanted a peace conference to which every state sent delegates. Douglas and others pushed compromise plans as a basis for conciliation. Senator John Mason of Virginia offered the idea of two presidents; old General Scott made the more cumbersome proposal of four separate unions. Some even suggested that Lincoln electors defuse the crisis by voting instead for Breckinridge.[20]

A compromise required some basis for agreement, but what was it to be? The Committee of 13 had flamed out, and the Committee of 33 closed its labors on January 8, leaving a weary and frustrated Tom Corwin to write its final report as three more southern states seceded. At its last meeting on the 14th, the committee approved a mélange of measures sponsored mostly by Republicans and voted for by Democrats. None of them offered anything that could be labeled conciliatory.[21]

Three versions of a compromise plan still tantalized the House. Crittenden's proposal had the federal government guarantee slavery everywhere south of the Missouri Compromise line and in territory hereafter acquired. The border state plan, devised by fourteen congressmen chaired by Crittenden himself, dropped the "hereafter" clause that so offended northerners and forbade either Congress or a territorial legislature from restricting slavery south of the Missouri Compromise line. Charles Francis Adams's plan protected slavery in existing states with a constitutional amendment and proposed an act of Congress admitting all territory south of $36°30'$ as New Mexico, which could choose for itself whether or not to have slavery.[22]

One clear difference involved the role of the federal government. Crittenden invoked federal authority to protect slavery; the other plans removed it from the slavery issue. The latter suited northern sensibilities, offended by any government endorsement of slavery, but outraged southerners, who demanded positive guarantees. Removing the federal government from the fight eliminated one major irritant but left the issue undecided. Benjamin Stanton of Ohio cast the difference in party terms. "The Republican party," he declared, "holds that African slavery is a local institution, created and sustained by State laws and usages that cannot exist beyond the limits of the State. . . . The Democratic party holds that African slavery is a national institution, recognized and sustained by the Constitution . . . throughout our entire territorial limits."[23]

The Committee of 33 buried the Crittenden resolutions on January 3 before limping to a close in which no majority vote could be secured either for any report or for making no report to the House. A narrow vote directed Corwin to write a report, and even then seven minority versions accompanied it. Corwin responded on the 14th with some general resolutions and five proposals: Repeal all personal liberty laws, uphold the Fugitive Slave Act, guarantee slavery where it existed by constitutional amendment, admit New Mexico as a state at once, and grant fugitives a trial in the state from which they had fled. The House opened debate on the 21st and thrashed away for nearly six weeks.[24]

Every member felt obliged to address the "national crisis" for the benefit of his constituents. William H. English of Indiana, whose name adorned the bill that had laid the Lecompton dispute to rest, tried vainly to revive the Crittenden resolutions. Adams despaired of making any progress and did not take the floor until the 31st to speak in favor of his plan. By that time the rhetoric had flowed freely on every side of the question, and events pressed relentlessly onward. On January 19 Georgia seceded despite dogged efforts by Unionists to delay action. Louisiana followed suit a week later, and Texas on February 1.

"State after State secedes," admonished Samuel S. Cox of Ohio, "and yet . . . we still stand, like mere spectators on the shore, in helpless bewilderment." A fellow Ohioan denounced secession as "the very wildest, phantasy of the nineteenth century," and others denied the right, but no one agreed on what to do about it. Despite protests, the debate slithered around consideration of other bills and private bills. Slowly the southern members of seceded states vacated their seats with little ceremony, leaving the debate in the hands of their opponents. Robert Hatton applauded their departure from his hotel, if not from the House. He had become "thoroughly . . . sick of hearing them blow and gas," but the "regular buncombe speaking" that now filled the chamber also sickened him.[25]

On the 21st English tried again to get the Crittenden resolutions on the floor and was voted down, 92–60. John A. Bingham of Ohio introduced a "force" bill that went nowhere, leading him to comment on talk of any peaceable remedy that "You might as well talk about a peaceable earthquake." A Pennsylvania member suggested that every representative resign his place as of February 21 and new members be elected to take their seats the next day;

no one paid any attention. "The great evil of the times," observed Tennessee's Emerson Etheridge dolefully, "is, that the people of all the different sections have listened so much to persistent misrepresentation, that they actually know less of each other's true purpose and feelings to-day than they did thirty years ago."[26]

John A. Gilmer of North Carolina vented the frustration of border state moderates. On one side the cotton states were trying to push the other slave states into secession; on the other, the North offered no staying hand, no refuge for them to embrace. "If you will not give us the Crittenden proposition," he pleaded, "give us the border state proposition." To this ultra Charles H. Van Wyck of New York replied, "What have we to concede? . . . You have suggested no compromise that . . . concedes anything to the North."[27]

Amid the torrent of words an obscure congressman from New York delivered a chilling prophecy. "In this material age, war is a very humdrum thing," warned Roscoe Conkling. "The battles known to the crusaders, and sung by the Troubadours, have all been fought. War is no longer a question of personal valor or individual prowess; but a mere question of money—a question of who can throw the most projectiles, who can indulge in the most iron and lead. It is no longer regulated by the laws of honor and chivalry, but entirely by the laws of trade." These words might have chilled the chivalry had they been heard or heeded. But most of the Deep South members had left the House, and no self-respecting southern gentleman would admit that any number of northern rabble could stand against him in a fight. To southern ears Conkling's words were simply more bluster, part of a verbal cannonade with unlimited ammunition. To ensure that every member had time to deliver his hour's salvo, the House agreed on the 31st to hold evening sessions as well.[28]

Against this riptide Adams swam with little hope when he spoke that same day. He reiterated his support for the plan to admit New Mexico as a slave state, even though many of his colleagues and old friends, Sumner foremost among them, censured him for betraying the cause. One by one he addressed the South's three grievances—the personal liberty laws, the denial of equal rights in the territories, and the fear that growing northern political supremacy would lead to interference with slavery in existing states—and tried to show how they were unfounded or how concessions had already been made. The New Mexico proposal, he stressed, ought to "extinguish every future complaint about the exclusion of slaveholders from the Territories."[29]

But conciliation had its limits. Adams warned that the North had gone as far as it could go. "For the sake of these three causes of complaint, all of them utterly without practical result," he said tartly, "the slaveholding States, unquestionably the weakest section of this great Confederacy, are voluntarily and precipitately surrendering the realities of solid power." Adams thought some southerners did not want *any* form of settlement. "You *want* the Union dissolved," he charged. "You *want* to make it impossible for honorable men to become reconciled." But any new confederacy would "scarcely be other than a secondary power. . . . THE EXPERIMENT WILL IGNOMINI- OUSLY FAIL."[30]

Friends and moderates applauded Adams. "I've never seen papa more affected than by the reception he met," observed son Henry. Ultras on both sides were not so kind, and the breach with Sumner widened. Shrewder heads understood what Adams himself well knew: that the offer had to be made, if only so the South could reject it. "The disunionists will of course refuse everything," noted Samuel Curtis of Iowa, "but we want [to] deprive them of every ground of complaint and then let them stand clearly on persis- tent wrong." Sharing the common belief that compromise was impossible, he added: "The sooner the appeal to arms be made, the less extended will be the conflict and the sooner we may hope to see peace."[31]

The drone in the Senate exceeded that of the House in quality and inti- macy, if not in results. On February 3 the dogged Crittenden offered a new version of his plan and asked for a national referendum on it. This took even ultra Republicans off the hook, for Crittenden asked them to vote not for his plan but for one to let the people decide. Bigler of Pennsylvania put forth a bill to that effect, but it languished. Horace Greeley later conceded that such a national referendum, if held, would have overwhelmingly approved the plan, but the idea was too novel or radical for many, unconstitutional to some, and just plain dangerous to others.[32]

Crittenden shrewdly linked his plan to two proposals offered by Stephen A. Douglas, one banning black suffrage in the territories and the other providing for the colonization of free blacks. Douglas's support, in a long, rambling speech, was dubbed by Elihu Washburne "the crowning atrocity of his life." After denouncing secession as "unlawful, unconstitu- tional, criminal," Douglas asserted: "South Carolina had no right to secede; *but she has done it. . . . Are we prepared for war? . . .* I confess I am not. . . . [W]ar is disunion, certain, inevitable, irrevocable. I am for peace to save the Union." Washburne and other Republican ultras feared the influence this coalition for compromise might wield in Congress and out.[33]

Despite the efforts of Crittenden and his allies, the proposal died. Ultras on both sides talked about everything but compromise; John Slidell of Louisiana used the occasion to blast the "mendacity of the reporters of the associated press." The Pacific railroad bill kept bobbing to the surface.

George Templeton Strong listened to that debate until he could stand it no longer. He stalked out of the gallery and went to the Smithsonian, preferring "stuffed penguins and pickled lizards to the dishonest gabble of the Senate." But Crittenden's plan could not be ignored; petitions supporting it flooded the Senate in growing numbers.[34]

Much depended on what stance Seward took in the debate. Once his appointment as secretary of state was known, many presumed him to be Lincoln's eyes and ears, if not his voice, in Washington. Seward embraced the role with private relish covered by a mask of weary necessity. No man in the City of Politics divided opinion more sharply. Those who loved him hesitated to trust him; those who trusted him found him difficult to love. He coupled the sly, subtle mind of the diplomat with a coarse, almost slovenly manner that mocked convention. "At table, among friends," recalled Henry Adams, "Mr. Seward threw off restraint, or seemed to throw it off, in reality, while in the world he threw it off, like a politician, for effect. In both cases he chose to appear as a free talker, who loathed pomposity and enjoyed a joke; but how much was nature and how much was mask, he was himself too simple a nature to know."[35]

Everything about Seward contradicted. His appearance was at once striking and unassuming. His thin, stooped body shuffled awkwardly about in clothes innocent of style. Beneath silvery hair that was always disheveled lay shaggy brows, a beaked nose, protruding ears, secretive eyes that often seemed to be relishing a private joke, and a sallow complexion creased with lines. His look reminded Henry Adams of "a wise macaw," and his whiskey voice, made hoarse from a longtime addiction to cigars, tossed out words with seeming carelessness yet was also capable of rolling out rhetoric that, in Adams's choice phrase, "would inspire a cow with statesmanship."[36]

His sense of humor could be as raw as Lincoln's, and his manner in company even more outrageous to proper folk. He did not sit so much as sprawl, and did not hesitate to remove wet shoes to warm his feet before a fire. He belched and snorted and swore without apology, and he tested the dignity of proper ladies by patting them absently on the head or bare shoulders. Guests arriving for dinner once found him garbed in a faded silk robe and worn slippers and working with two clerks. When dinner was announced, Seward went in and presided over the meal without changing.[37]

The dinner party was Seward's favorite arena. Some regarded these four-hour marathons with their eleven courses as a trial of endurance; Seward welcomed them as a venue for hearing the views of others and for displaying his repertory of moods and roles. Sometimes the mimic or the comic, often the cynic, ever the raconteur, he loved conversation over wine or brandy, his thick voice rolling and his keen eyes scrutinizing through the haze of cigar smoke. His choice of company extended equally to friend or foe. Like Lincoln, he loved telling a good story, including some that dripped acid, and did not hesitate to laugh at his own wit. In public debate or private talk alike he was tolerant and good-natured.[38]

His glib, easy manner led many men to believe that neither he nor his words could be trusted. Charles Francis Adams, Jr., voiced a common perception when he described Seward as "more of a politician than a statesman." Henry Clay had once dismissed him as "a man of no convictions." His long association with Weed reinforced this image of a man whose political interests orchestrated his every move. But no hint of personal scandal or corruption ever stained his career, and he took care to have it so. In that respect Weed had always been his alter ego, handling in his deft way the sordid details of machine politics while Seward remained conveniently ignorant of them. Yet even Adams was quick to concede that Seward was "a great believer in his countrymen and their institutions."[39]

Nearly sixty years of age, Seward had long aspired to the role of statesman. Few public men had traveled abroad more extensively; as recently as the spring of 1859 he had toured the capitals of Europe and made the acquaintance of leading rulers and statesmen. It was easy for him to view himself as the magnetic pole of the new administration, and to play the dominant role in its creation as well as its policy. He knew everyone, knew the game as well as or better than anyone, and even had a mole in Buchanan's official family in the person of Edwin Stanton, the new attorney general, who deemed it his duty to keep the Republican leadership informed of developments.[40]

It was a curious path that brought Stanton to Seward. A well-known lawyer close to Judge Black, Stanton had taken office the same day Anderson moved to Sumter. The heated debates over this issue were his first cabinet meetings, and he was anything but a shy newcomer. When Floyd demanded that the troops be withdrawn from Charleston Harbor, Stanton retorted that surrendering Sumter was a crime equal to Benedict Arnold's. "We had high words," he recalled of that evening's session, "and had almost come to blows." Buchanan's handling of the crisis reduced the high-strung Stanton to despair. "Something must be done," he told his friend Dan Sickles of New York.[41]

Never one to let legal or ethical niceties stand in the way of larger issues, Stanton made himself a conduit to the only obvious source of power capable of protecting the Union: the opposition party in Congress. In offering himself to Seward and Thomas Ewing, he betrayed his official trust as a cabinet member in the name of patriotism. Stanton met with Ewing on ten or twelve nights to pass along information, but kept his contact with Seward more secret. Only twice did they meet personally, but every day an associate of Stanton's slipped a verbal or written message to Seward. No one, not even Buchanan and Black, suspected what was going on. The arrangement began early; two days after Stanton took office, Seward informed Lincoln that "At last I have gotten a position in which I can see what is going on in the councils of the President."[42]

The graver the crisis grew, the more importance Seward attached to his own role. As early as January 3 he wrote his wife, "The revolution gathers apace. It has its abettors in the White House, the Treasury, the Interior . . . I have assumed a sort of dictatorship for defense; and am laboring night and day, with the cities and States." Once, while walking through the city, he was struck by the absence of national flags even on hotels and places of amusement. He urged friends to display flags at their residences and places of business, and sent men to key cities like Baltimore and Philadelphia to do likewise. By the 8th he was satisfied that Washington itself was safe, but he implored Lincoln to arrive earlier than expected.[43]

When Seward delivered his speech on the 12th, the galleries had been packed for more than two hours. Even southerners who usually made a point of ignoring Republican speeches listened intently to hear what might be offered them. Seward told his audience first what would *not* save the Union: eulogia, mutual criminations, more debate on the power of Congress over slavery, or further discussion of the rights of secession and federal coercion of seceded states. Nor were congressional compromises the answer. To make any progress, two notions had to be discarded: "that the Union is to be saved by someone in particular; and . . . that it is to be saved by some cunning and insincere compact of pacification."[44]

Instead Congress should redress any real grievances while giving the president whatever means were needed to keep the nation whole. Secession was not only wrong but impractical, and the formation of a new government out of the Gulf states "obviously impossible." Dissolution, he warned, was "for the people of this country, perpetual civil war" and would "not only arrest, but extinguish the greatness of this country." To avoid it, he would accept repeal of all personal-liberty laws, a constitutional amendment protecting slavery where it already existed, and the creation of two states out of all remaining territory. He urged the building of two Pacific railroads, one north and one south, to bind the nation together, and closed with a plea for conciliation and calm.

The speech moved many senators, Crittenden among them, but what did it say? "I have listened to every word, and by the living God I have heard nothing!" said an exasperated Thaddeus Stevens of Pennsylvania. "A more Delphic utterance was never given to mankind," wrote a *Mercury* correspondent, who labeled its author MACHIAVEL SEWARD. Erasmus Keyes thought Seward had argued that "the Union was not worth preserving at the expense of civil war!" Charles Sumner agreed and was appalled. Edward Everett claimed that it said nothing and disappointed everyone. The Associated Press thought it conciliatory without yielding "a single Abolitionist principle"; so did Edouard de Stoeckl, the Russian minister in Washington. Senator John Hemphill of Texas said grimly that it was "a fine address for the Fourth of July, but we are going to secede."45

The split between those who thought the speech vague and those who protested that it surrendered Republican principles extended even to Frances Seward, who admonished her husband that he was "in danger of taking the path which led Daniel Webster to an unhonored grave ten years ago. . . . I fear to hear your name execrated . . . as I hear that of your chief counsellor [Weed] now." Seward admitted, "The city is bewildered by the speech," but he assured Frances that his "concessions" were "not compromises, but explanations, to disarm the enemies of Truth, Freedom, and Union, of their most effective weapons." The plots against the city had ended, and the speech had helped by restoring public feeling for the Union.46

But the peril remained, and Seward thought he grasped its nature more clearly than anyone else. The southern states, led by reckless politicians, were bent on extorting from the free states a recognition of slavery at the risk of civil war and disunion. Most Republican senators were just as reckless in assuming the government would conquer the South while they did little more than sit and watch. "Mad men North, and mad men South," he explained to Frances, "are working together to produce a dissolution of the Union, by civil war." Both the outgoing and incoming administrations looked to Seward to avert this disaster. "It seems to me," he said soberly, "that if I am absent only three days, this Administration, the Congress, and the District would fall into consternation and despair. I am the only *hopeful, calm, conciliatory* person here."47

His task was to "gain time for the new Administration to organize and for the frenzy of passion to subside." At present that passion cowed the strong Unionist sentiment in the South, especially in the border states. Once it eased, that sentiment would reassert itself and oppose the demagogues who were leading the South to its doom. The trick was to gain enough time for reason to return without conceding anything substantial. One possibility occurred to him. "If the Lord would only give the United States an excuse for a war with England, France, or Spain," he confided to the stunned minister from the Bremen Republic, "that would be the best means of reestablishing peace."48

On the 24th Seward attended a dinner party hosted by Senator Douglas. The guests included Crittenden, Senator James Dixon of Connecticut, Supreme Court Justice John Campbell, and several foreign ministers. Asked to make a toast, Seward responded with "Away with all parties, platforms, and previous commitals [sic] and whatever else will stand in the way of restoration of the American Union." The next evening he dined with the Adamses, where Henry studied him like a specimen and confessed, "He puzzles me more and more. I can't see how he works at all." Was he really a compromiser? Henry wondered. Had all of Weed's efforts in that direction actually come from Seward? Whatever his game, Henry thought it a deep one. "Scott and he rule the country," he concluded, "and Scott's share in the rule is but small."[49]

On the 21st Seward had introduced a bill to admit Kansas as a state and steered it to a 36–16 majority, thereby launching the long-suffering territory on its final journey to statehood. But that day he was upstaged as the Senate began its version of the Farewell Symphony. Senators Benjamin Fitzpatrick and Clement Clay of Alabama, Stephen Mallory and David Yulee of Florida, and Jefferson Davis of Mississippi bade their colleagues good-bye with brief speeches. An air of sorrow mixed with apprehension hung over the chamber. These were men who loved power, had long clung to it, and relinquished it with obvious reluctance. All were solemn; Clay alone was bumptious, while Davis moved even Republican senators and their ladies in the gallery to tears.[50]

Their departure marked the beginning of a momentous shift of power. The old blood that had dominated Congress for so long was gone, never to return in its present form. The Republicans owned the House and did not yet control the Senate, but the committees lost their entrenched southern rulers. A sign of things to come emerged with the passage of the Kansas statehood bill and the organization of the Colorado, Dakota, and Nevada territories with no mention of slavery. Attempts to get the Crittenden measures onto the Senate floor were beaten back once in favor of the Pacific railroad bill and again to enable the Pennsylvania senators to get their pet tariff bill enacted. When his plan was dumped in favor of tariff discussion, Crittenden snapped, "Well, sir, it is a melancholy question to ask, but we are compelled to ask it: to what part of the United States would this tariff apply; what ports and harbors?"[51]

Undaunted, the compromise forces redoubled their efforts, some in the belief that Seward had joined their ranks. That same week Dan Sickles of New York and Sherrard Clemens of Virginia fought to get the Crittenden resolutions on the House floor in place of the Committee of 33 report.

J. Morrison Harris of Maryland pushed the border state plan, and John Cochrane of New York brought in Senator Bigler's bill for a popular referendum on Crittenden's plan. Determined to avoid a record vote on any of them, Republicans resisted these efforts. No plan could hope to succeed without Republican support, and no member of that party had yet cast a vote for any version of Crittenden's plan.[52]

They received a welcome diversion on the 28th, when Senator Alfred Iverson of Georgia took his leave with a belligerent parting shot. "In whatever shape you attack us, we will fight you," he said. ". . . You may whip us, but *we will not stay whipped*." Three days later Seward presented a petition signed by thirty-eight thousand New Yorkers favoring compromise and offered, or seemed to offer, concessions. His words drew a waspish response from Mason of Virginia and triggered another fight on the old themes, in which Wigfall of Texas said pointedly that he would support no compromise resolution "which does not receive the support of the Republican party."[53]

While Congress wrangled, a new front opened on the 23rd when former President John Tyler arrived in town as an emissary for Virginia's version of a peace plan. Four days earlier the general assembly had called for every state to send delegates to a peace conference in Washington on February 4. Tyler presented the resolutions to Buchanan on the morning of the 24th and asked him to maintain the status quo on Forts Sumter and Pickens. Buchanan repeated his familiar position: He could make no pledge on the truce and had the power only to submit the resolutions to Congress.[54]

The next day Tyler listened to the draft of Buchanan's message to Congress. He was alarmed by rumors that the *Brooklyn* had sailed south carrying troops. Buchanan assured him that the ship was on "an errand of mercy & relief" that was "in no way connected with South Carolina" and that the order had been given before Tyler's arrival. Tyler accepted this explanation and on the 28th watched as the Senate received Buchanan's message containing the Virginia plan. The next day he headed home satisfied but undeceived. Buchanan's policy, he saw, was obviously "to throw all responsibility off of his shoulders." As for Washington, it was, to Tyler's disgust, an "atmosphere where lunacy . . . prevails."[55]

The Virginia plan threw all sides into a quandary. Even the seceded states, which ignored the plea to send delegates, hesitated to offend Virginia and undermine its secessionists. Northern ultras despised the idea but feared that a convention sitting without them might advance the cause of compromise. Congress simply ignored the request, but it could not ignore the rising pressure for action any more than the beleaguered Buchanan could. Trouble was also brewing in Maryland, where Governor Thomas Hicks had so far resisted demands to call a convention to consider secession. Even a *Mercury* correspondent in Washington agreed that "BUCHANAN ought either to reinforce ANDERSON or to recall him. . . . Were the South in possession of these fortifications, there would long since have been an end to all the war talk at the North. By delay you keep up the irritation and excitement, and may end by *getting up* a civil war."[56]

For all his fears Buchanan was fast coming to the same conclusion. Holt had on the 29th sent Slemmer in Pensacola orders similar to those given Anderson to avoid conflict and stay on the defensive but to fight if attacked. Hayne, who saw Buchanan the same day, could not be fended off much longer. "It is time," the president wrote Holt on the 30th, "we should have decided whether it is practicable . . . to reinforce Major Anderson at Fort Sumter, should the action of the authorities at South Carolina or his request render this necessary." Later that day he met with Holt, Scott, and Toucey to consider options.[57]

This discussion was urgently needed. On the next day Hayne, having received at last his reply from Charleston, formally delivered Pickens's letter with one of his own demanding the surrender of Sumter and offering to buy the fort from the United States. The truce had ended.

FEBRUARY

CHAPTER THIRTEEN

Farewells and Forebodings

Will the generations that are to succeed us believe that at such a time we sat out a whole winter with these guns still pointed at us, trying how far we might go to comply with the demands of traitors, and what new securities we might devise for the protection and spread of human bondage?

—Representative Samuel S. Blair, Pennsylvania

January 23, 1861[1]

*F*ROM THE DISTANT OUTPOST OF FORT MASON on the Texas frontier a veteran lieutenant colonel of cavalry pondered the crisis with growing dismay. At fifty-three Robert E. Lee had already served thirty-one years in the U.S. Army and still stood behind twenty-two officers awaiting command of a brigade. As the husband of an invalid wife and the father of four unmarried daughters he could not regard his prospects for promotion with optimism. To make matters worse, politics, which had always disgusted him, seemed to have enveloped the nation he loved so deeply.[2]

"I am so remote from the scene of events," he wrote a friend, "and receive such excited and exaggerated accounts of the opinions and acts of our statesmen, that I am at a loss what to think." But his troubled mind had reached some conclusions. He could imagine no greater calamity for the country than a dissolution of the Union and believed that "Secession is nothing but revolution." Still, he could not embrace a Union held together by force. "If the Union is dissolved, and the Government disrupted," he concluded, "I shall return to my native State and share the miseries of my people, and save in defence will draw my sword on none."

The crisis that had seemed so distant drew inexorably closer to Lee. Since the November election Governor Sam Houston of Texas had worked tirelessly to stave off secession by refusing to call a convention or the legislature. In January, however, he was obliged to bring the legislature into session, and secessionists organized their own convention despite his protests. Reluctantly the old warrior agreed to abide by the convention's decision subject to a popular referendum. The ad hoc convention assembled on January 28 and three days later took Texas out of the Union by a 166–8 vote.

When the galleries hissed James Throckmorton, one of the diehard Unionists, he replied defiantly, "When the rabble hiss, well may patriots tremble."[3]

Lee counted himself a trembling patriot. "May God rescue us from the folly of our own acts," he wrote his son Custis. None of the officers in Texas knew which way to turn. Pay had ceased, and allowances were slashed. The commanding officer, seventy-year-old General David Twiggs of Georgia, had asked to be relieved of duty and fretted over receiving no instructions of any kind. While Lee mulled over his own future, unexpected orders arrived summoning him to report in person to General Scott. On February 13 he caught a ride aboard an ambulance to San Antonio. Three days later he drew up in front of the Read House in San Antonio, only to find the ambulance surrounded by men wearing crude red insignia.[4]

Lee spotted the wife of a friend and asked who the men were. "General Twiggs surrendered everything to the state this morning," she answered, "and we are all prisoners." A stunned Lee went inside the hotel, changed to civilian clothes, and reported to headquarters. There too he found the secessionists in control, but after some hesitation they let him go his way. The world had turned upside down. "When I get to Virginia," he told a fellow officer before leaving, "I think the world will have one soldier less. I shall resign and go to planting corn."

TO DEPARTING SOUTHERN MEMBERS of the official family, it seemed clear that Buchanan had gone over to the other side. A friend of Kate Thompson's called at the White House to find Harriet Lane and the president chatting amicably with, of all people, Lyman Trumbull and his wife. "What a change!" cried Kate. ". . . *All their* old friends are thrown off and new ones in their place." And a new attitude. A southern observer reported glumly that Buchanan "allowed Holt & Scott to exercise the powers they have, from a *knowledge* that their acts will conform to Lincoln's policy." The president tried to retain cordial ties with old friends. Early in February he hosted a farewell dinner for the Thompsons, who accepted reluctantly. It went off agreeably, but Kate Thompson still blushed with embarrassment, especially when Buchanan asked her who was to be *"our President."* She answered, "Howell Cobb."[5]

Farewells were in the air. On the 4th the once-powerful Louisiana senators took their leave in language lacking its accustomed grace. John Slidell still smarted from a final rupture with his old friend Buchanan a week earlier. Slidell had helped get his brother-in-law Major Pierre G. T. Beauregard appointed superintendent at West Point. But scarcely had Beauregard taken his post when Holt noticed the major's southern sympathies and learned that the choice had been made without regard to the claims of several older offi-cers. The secretary relieved Beauregard of command, prompting Slidell to ask Buchanan whether he had approved this action.[6]

Buchanan showed the note to Holt, who said, "We have heard the crack of the overseer's whip over our heads long enough." The president agreed. He sent Slidell a polite note saying he had full confidence in Holt and approved all his actions. The two men never spoke again. In leaving the Senate, Slidell said, "We all consider the election of Mr. Lincoln . . . conclu-sive evidence of the determined hostility of the northern masses to our insti-tutions." But his tone was moderate, even sorrowful. Quoting the count d'Anterroches at the Battle of Fontenoy, he pledged: "Gentlemen, we will not fire first."[7]

Judah Benjamin was more belligerent. A small, round man with a full face, olive complexion, and dark, glittering eyes, he was once described by an acquaintance as "Hebrew in blood, English in tenacity of grasp and pur-pose . . . [and] French in taste." A less charitable Ben Wade characterized him as "an Israelite with Egyptian principles." Benjamin had a silvery tongue, a soft, insinuating voice, and a manner seldom ruffled by stress. On this day he astonished his listeners by denying that Louisiana had ever been "conveyed to the United States for a price as property that could be bought or sold at will," then spun a web of rhetoric that brought tears to the eyes of southern ladies, one of whom called it "perfectly *thrilling*," and sneers from detractors like James Pike, who dismissed both speeches as "two more trai-torous harangues."[8]

One senator from a seceded state clung conspicuously to his seat. Louis Wigfall of Texas manned his post like a rear guard, claiming blandly that he had received no official notice of his state's withdrawal from the Union. Amid the wrangling and recriminations he treated the brethren to a sermon on southern mythology. "Slaveholders are men of enlarged ideas, of education, and of property," he claimed. ". . . Not only are our non-slaveholders loyal, but even our negroes are. We have no apprehension whatever of insurrec-tion—not the slightest. We can arm our negroes, and leave them at home when we are temporarily absent. . . . Every time that a negro touches a cotton pod . . . he pulls a piece of silver out of it. . . . Exhaust the supply of cotton in Europe for one week and all Europe is in revolution."[9]

At the White House another sermon was under debate. Hayne's letter reasserted South Carolina's right to "take into her own possession everything within her limits essential to maintain her honor and her safety." He could discuss compensation for the fort but not the right itself, which was indis-putable. Any attempt to reinforce the fort would be deemed an act of war. None of these demands was acceptable to Buchanan and his cabinet; talk

turned not only to the response but also to a new expedition for relieving
Anderson. The peace conference opened its sessions in Washington, and
delegates from the seceded states converged on Montgomery, Alabama, to
begin forming a new government.[10]

On the 6th, Holt replied to an impatient Hayne by dismissing his proposal as "simply an offer . . . to buy Fort Sumter," buttressed by the threat of
seizing it if the offer was refused. The president had no more right to sell the
fort "than he can sell and convey the Capitol of the United States" to Maryland. He reaffirmed the right to reinforce the fort and wondered how "the
presence of a small garrison" could so "compromise the dignity or honor of
South Carolina." Buchanan had repeatedly stated his policy to be defensive
and peaceful; any effort to seize the fort would throw on the attackers full
responsibility for what followed.[11]

Stung by this language, Hayne followed in the futile footsteps of the
commissioners: He dispatched an insolent reply to Buchanan and left town.
The president rejected it as "one of the most outrageous & insulting letters
. . . which had ever been addressed to the head of any Government."
Learning that Hayne had gone, he returned the letter to him by mail. John
Tyler called at the White House on the 8th to report how upset Hayne had
been at Holt's letter. When Buchanan insisted that the letter contained
nothing offensive, Tyler offered to see Hayne and get him to withdraw his
reply. Told that Hayne had left town, Tyler pleaded with Buchanan to
pledge that he would send no reinforcements or, better yet, to withdraw the
garrison. Buchanan rejected both pleas.[12]

The mood in Washington veered back toward alarm. "It will not surprise me," said Horatio King, "if we are engaged in a civil war before the end
of this month unless all the forts in the seceding States are peaceably given to
the revolutionists." Erasmus Keyes, still making the rounds of the dinner
parties, discovered that "The rumors of perils to the capital thicken." One
tale had squads of rebels sneaking into different neighborhoods ready to
assemble in large numbers on signal. Many feared their objective was to disrupt the counting of the Electoral College votes on February 13. Keyes
passed along to Elihu Washburne his belief in the evidence for *a wide
spread and powerful conspiracy to seize the capitol.*" Washburne in turn
sounded the alarm to Lincoln. "I have been slow to believe, as you know," he
added, "but I am satisfied that we must soon begin *to prepare for the worst.*"[13]

News that Louisiana had seized the federal mint and customhouse in
New Orleans on February 1 provoked more outrage. Aware that federal
revenue cutters were also in jeopardy, Secretary of the Treasury John A. Dix
sent one of his clerks south to help keep the vessels out of secessionist hands.
When the clerk wired that the commander of one cutter refused to obey

orders, Dix fired back a telegram saying, "If anyone attempts to haul down the American flag, shoot him on the spot." Northern papers pounced on these bold words and made Dix an instant hero, but the reply did not save the cutter from falling into southern hands.[14]

"More than the loss of forts, arsenals, or the national capital," proclaimed Charles Sumner, *"I fear the loss of our principles."* This fear had become an obsession in recent weeks. Seward's speech had nearly unhinged Sumner with its seeming gesture toward compromise. The two men despised each other anyway; Henry Adams quipped that "Each was created only for exasperating the other." Sumner had tried in vain to talk Seward out of delivering the speech. Now he collared anyone who would listen to denounce Seward for his betrayal of cause and principle. The wily Edwin Stanton fed Sumner's anxiety by making him another of his secret confidants. Virginia's peace effort was a ruse, Stanton confided. Its real design was to "constitute a Provisional Govt. which was to take possession of the Capital & declare itself a nation."[15]

On February 2, prodded by Massachusetts Governor John Andrew, Sumner went to the White House. He was not a willing visitor, having already blasted the president as "a traitor, who lets the vessel drift to destruction." Earlier he had rebuked Edward Everett, Amos Lawrence, and Robert Winthrop of his own state, who had come to town with a petition favoring Crittenden's compromise, dismissing their pleas as "mere *wind* . . . a penny-whistle in a tempest." Even an appeal to Sumner's notorious vanity provoked only a response Everett described as "approaching to insanity." Buchanan fared no better. When Sumner asked, "What else can we do in Massachusetts for the good of the country?" the president urged support of Crittenden's plan.

"Is that necessary?" Sumner asked. Told that it was, he replied loftily, "Massachusetts has not yet spoken directly on these propositions, but . . . such are the unalterable convictions of her people, they would see their state sink below the sea and become a sandbank before they would adopt propositions acknowledging property in man."[16]

Sumner's wrath extended to Charles Francis Adams after the latter's January 31 speech betrayed a willingness to compromise. Compromise was to Sumner a disease, and now it had infected an old friend whose distinguished family had long been immune to it. He could not reason with Adams. As Henry Adams observed, Sumner could "no more argue than a cat"; he could only orate and sermonize. He had been close to Charles Francis Adams for fifteen years and for much of that time had taken Sunday dinner with the family. In recent weeks the ritual had been marred by ugly political wrangling. Sumner had conspicuously absented himself from the

House when Adams made his speech, and the following Sunday he did not come to dinner. No entreaties for reconciliation moved him. "To bring him round is impossible," observed Henry Adams. "God Almighty couldn't do it. . . . As usual I suppose he will stand on his damned dignity."[17]

Although Sumner came twice again at the urging of Mrs. Adams, who did not want the breach made public, the friendship was dead. Those near Sumner feared that he was losing his balance. "His manner and language amazed me," recalled Charles Francis Adams, Jr. "He talked like a crazy man, orating, gesticulating, rolling out deep periods in theatrical, whispered tones,—repeating himself, and doing everything but reason. . . . Even now I can see Sumner's eyes gleaming with something distinctly suggestive of insanity." For his part, Sumner was not content to leave the matter as a private parting. Quietly he turned to undermining Adams's political position in Congress and in Massachusetts. Adams and Seward alike, he intoned, had become "Ishmaelites."[18]

To Sumner's alarm, the ranks of the infidels seemed to be swelling. On Monday the 4th, the peace conference summoned by Virginia held its opening session at the hall in Willard's Hotel. Only 60 delegates were present for the first meeting; eventually their ranks swelled to 132 representatives from twenty-one states. The absentees were glaring. No one was there from any seceded state or from the Northwest, where radical Republicans denounced the whole proceeding, or from the Pacific coast. The invitation to send delegates had thrown Republicans throughout the North into a quandary over how to respond. Many wanted to ignore the conference; others argued that it was best to send "reliable" men as delegates to control the outcome.[19]

Sumner took the first position, then switched to the second when assured the Massachusetts men could be relied on to scuttle any compromise. Indiana Governor Oliver P. Morton favored sending delegates not because he "expected any positive good to come from it, but to prevent positive evil." Illinois did so, explained a Lincoln ally, because "if we had not done so, some of our knock kneed brethren, would have united with the democracy." Thurlow Weed advised Lincoln that "Virginia can be held awhile if the Free States send commissioners." A suspicious Ohio legislature authorized the governor to appoint delegates but resolved not to agree to the terms of settlement proposed by Virginia. Their retinue included Salmon P. Chase, who was astonished to find himself the only one not favoring the border state compromise plan.[20]

Moderates in every state endorsed the convention as staunchly as ultras denounced it. "Nobody," claimed the *Mercury*, "has the slightest hope of any satisfactory adjustment being arrived at." James Pike conceded that there was "great pressure here from the business and high social circles of all our great cities for a compromise," but he did not expect the conference to produce it. Washington opened its arms to the conference. Willard donated the hall, which was a converted church. Mayor James E. Berret provided policemen to guard the entrances along with a portrait of George Washington to dignify the chamber and remind the delegates of their lofty purpose.[21]

The roster of representatives included six former cabinet members, nineteen ex-governors, fourteen former senators, fifty former representatives, ten circuit judges, twelve state supreme court justices, and one former president. Nowhere on the planet had more political scar tissue assembled in one place. From Ohio came the patrician John C. Wright, now feeble and nearly blind, who had once advised William Henry Harrison, and Thomas Ewing, who had sat in the cabinets of both Tyler and Zachary Taylor. The venerable Reverdy Johnson of Maryland and William C. Rives of Virginia were present, along with Charles A. Wickliffe of Kentucky, who had been Tyler's postmaster general.[22]

These ancient political warriors had come to plead for peace, but others were there to ward off compromise. The latter's ranks included Chase, David Wilmot, Senator Fessenden of Maine, George S. Boutwell of Massachusetts (a close friend of Sumner's), and David Dudley Field of New York. James B. Clay, son of Henry, was not so eager to be a great compromiser. Stephen T. Logan, Lincoln's former law partner, came, as did Thomas Ruffin of North Carolina, cousin of Edmund. General John E. Wool, who commanded the Department of the East, had the distinction of being older than even Winfield Scott.

The congregation resembled nothing more than the ghosts of politics past. Twelve of the delegates were seventy or older, seventy-four had passed the age of fifty, and only seven were not yet forty. The *Tribune* scorned it as the "Old Gentlemen's Convention"; others labeled it the "Old Fossils' Convention," better suited for an exhibit at the Smithsonian. No one personified this image more strikingly than the conference chairman, John Tyler. Nearly seventy-one years old, the former president had come out of retirement from Sherwood Forest, his James River plantation, to save the Republic. Admirers spoke of his graceful figure and "animal vigor"; detractors described a "tottering ashen ruin" who had been "more cordially despised" than any other occupant of the White House.

In one respect, at least, Tyler had been the father of his country. No other president has ever produced more children than his fifteen offspring. Seven of them had come with his second wife, Julia, a New Yorker thirty years his junior; the youngest was still a toddler when the convention sat.

Julia Tyler was forty years old, but to the dazzled eyes of Robert Hatton, who sat with the Tylers at breakfast one morning, she seemed about twenty-eight, elaborately dressed, and "well contented with herself, and her position in the world." Julia had no doubt of her husband's place or role. "The President is the great centre of attention," she wrote happily. "Everybody says he is looked to to save the Union."[23]

But Tyler seemed an unlikely savior. A Democrat turned Whig, he had been the first man to gain the office through the death of a sitting president, which had earned him the derisive title of "His Accidency." His presidency had been a political disaster that blighted the Whig party's first term in office. Tyler managed to alienate just about everyone, was denied the nomination in 1844, and went home to retirement. Now the man who had driven his entire cabinet to resign stepped forward as peacemaker, though one with a decidedly southern slant to his views. It did not bode well that on the same day Tyler took the chair of the peace conference, his own granddaughter proudly hoisted the flag at the state capitol in Montgomery, Alabama, over the opening session of a southern government struggling to be born.[24]

WHY GO TO MONTGOMERY to set up a new government? Because, said some, otherwise no one would go there.

The idea originated with Robert B. Rhett, who on the day Anderson moved to Sumter introduced what became known as the South Carolina Program, calling for a convention to meet at Montgomery and form a southern confederacy. The Charleston convention approved it on the last day of 1860 and selected nine "commissioners" to preach the program in ten of the slave states. Rhett favored Montgomery because it was centrally located and, as the home of William Yancey, a hotbed of secession in a badly divided state.[25]

Like Rome, the city sprawled across seven hills, but the resemblance ended there. Perched on high bluffs above the Alabama River, Montgomery boasted some iron foundries, mills, warehouses, two hotels, a theater, and a few stores deemed "elegant." Its eight thousand citizens took special pride in the new state capitol, a neoclassical pile of gleaming white marble set on a hilly site that struck one unimpressed viewer as "worthy of a better fate and edifice." Main Street, broad and sandy, ran from the capitol down the slope to a square that five streets entered. A rickety line strung together by four separate railroads linked the city to Atlanta and to Pensacola on the Gulf.[26]

On the streets leading away from Main Street could be found pleasant houses with bright gardens and neatly kept grounds, some wooded areas and public gardens, and a large neighborhood of blacks and mulattos. The two hotels sat on the square equidistant from Main Street and from each other.

The smaller Montgomery Hall, likened sourly by one visitor to the " 'Raven of Zurich,' noted for uncleanliness of nest and length of bill," was favored by cattlemen and country merchants. The Exchange House, run by a northern firm, was more comfortable and pretentious, but no one could forget that cotton planters dominated the local economy. Just outside its doors, the steps of a public fountain served as the site for slave auctions.[27]

Even one who thought the city delightful admitted that "there was very much lacking of what the worldling expects of a metropolis." Those short-comings, and its strengths as well, were no match for the horde of visitors that in February nearly doubled the population. Days of heavy rain had turned the unpaved streets into a sea of mud. A train carrying Robert Toombs, Thomas R. R. Cobb (Howell's brother), Alexander Stephens, and the Chesnuts derailed outside Montgomery when a rail laid that very morning snapped. No one was hurt, but their arrival was delayed two hours. "This comes," smirked Mary Chesnut, "from Sunday traveling."[28]

Mary was a rare wife in accompanying her husband to Montgomery, though others came later, and she thought the event worthy of starting a journal to record it. This account was to be "entirely *objective*. My subjective days are over. No more *silent* eating into my own heart." But she could never escape her own feelings, which had been sorely tested that season. She had been away when James resigned from the Senate. On hearing the news, she wrote glumly, " 'burnt the ships behind him.' The first resignation—& I am not at all resigned." A nervous dread gnawed at her, a fear not only of war but of losing that larger stage on which she had finally mounted her life. "Going back to Mulberry to live," she wrote, "was indeed offering up my life on the altar of country."[29]

They spent Christmas at a cousin's rice plantation on the Combahee River before going on to Charleston. But this season was unlike any other, dominated by the brick eminence in the harbor with the huge flag flying above it. Mary surveyed the leaders of South Carolina's government and winced in dismay. "Invariably some sleeping dead head long forgotten or passed over," she complained. "Young & active spirits ignored. . . . When-ever there is an election they hunt up some old fossil ages ago laid on the shelf. There never was such a resurrection of the dead & forgotten." Was it to be nothing more than the same old political game played by the same tired players? Even in Montgomery?[30]

The faces filling up the Exchange Hotel lobby seemed drearily familiar. As a group they were overwhelmingly middle-aged, prosperous, educated lawyers or planters—hardly the stuff of revolution. They had come not to overturn but to preserve a way of life. The fire-eaters who had set the stage for secession were in scant supply; Yancey, the hometown favorite, was not even a delegate. "There is more conservativism . . . than I expected to see," observed Stephens, "and this increases my hopes." The scrawny, under-sized Stephens, whose emaciated body was never a match for his mind, epitomized the general character of the delegates—moderate, experienced, and politically savvy.[31]

Although they relished the image of themselves as the South's "Found-ing Fathers," many if not most of them belonged to a generation that viewed politics as more a job than a duty, a personal opportunity rather than service to the nation. For Republicans, opportunity beckoned in the form of victory at the polls; for these southerners, it loomed in the act of secession. The for-mation of a new government offered the tantalizing prospect of filling *all* the offices themselves. Rarely did duty fit so snugly with self-service. Principle dictated that they oppose the threat posed to their way of life by the Repub-lican triumph while spurring them toward a vision that had long enticed them: the creation of a government of the right people by the right people for the right people.

On Monday the 4th thirty-seven representatives from six states (the Texans had not yet arrived) gathered at noon in the senate chamber of the state capitol, which had been set aside for their deliberations. Portraits of Calhoun, Jackson, Clay, Francis Marion, Yancey, and no fewer than three of Washington adorned the wall behind the rostrum. As the ritual of organiza-tion proceeded, Tom Cobb was pleased to see his brother Howell elected chairman of the convention, but he feared trouble from South Carolina, already "making technical points on powers and privileges," and from Alabama, which had a strong Unionist cadre in its delegation. The next day serious deliberations began behind closed doors, to the consternation of the visitors who jammed the balcony overlooking the chamber. Unruffled, the *Mercury* correspondent reminded his readers that "The lobby of the Exchange is a pretty respectable conversational Parliament." Tom Cobb marveled at the harmony that prevailed, and managed to find time to shop for a dress for his wife. "The day is beautiful, the air is as balmy as a morning in May, the sun shines brightly," he wrote home, "and I cannot help feeling that the Giver of Light smiles kindly on our efforts."[32]

As expected, the delegates turned to the men who had always led them. The results astonished even those who hoped for prompt and decisive action. On that second day the body approved rules drawn up by Stephens, the key provision being that all votes should be by states rather than by indi-viduals. A committee was named to bring in a plan for a provisional govern-ment. Tom Cobb and Stephen F. Hale of Alabama helped shape a bold stroke to define the convention's mission. This temporary body of delegates,

POINTS OF CONFLICT *Views of Washington,* above *(USAMHI) and,* below, *Charleston (LC),*
the latter from the steeple of St. Michael's Church

MEN UNDER SIEGE I *President James Buchanan and his divided cabinet (LC).*
From left: *Jacob Thompson, John B. Floyd, Lewis Cass, Buchanan, Howell Cobb, Isaac Toucey, Joseph Holt, Jeremiah S. Black.*

MEN UNDER SIEGE II *The officers at Fort Sumter (USAMHI).*
Seated from left: *Capt. Abner Doubleday, Maj. Robert Anderson, Surg. Samuel Crawford, Capt. John G. Foster.* Standing from left: *Capt. Truman Seymour, Lt. George Snyder, Lt. Jeff Davis, Lt. Dick Meade, Capt. Theodore Talbot.*

TWO INAUGURATIONS
Above, *the crowd gathers for Lincoln's inauguration beneath the domeless Capitol (LC). Below, the only known photograph of the inaugural ceremony at Montgomery (NA).*

WASHINGTON ADVERSARIES
Clockwise from top left:
Stephen A. Douglas (LC),
Charles Sumner (USAMHI),
Jeremiah S. Black (NA),
John C. Breckinridge (LC)

SOUTHERN ADVERSARIES
Clockwise from top left:
*Robert Hatton (LC), Edmund Ruffin
(LC), Robert Barnwell Rhett (LC),
Louis T. Wigfall (LC)*

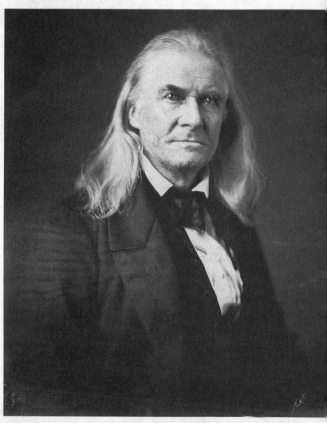

**THE CHIVALRY'S
CONFLICTING VOICES**
*The "outrageously handsome"
John L. Manning, above (SCHS)
and*, below, *the staunch Unionist
James L. Petigru (SCL). Opposite:
A rare daguerreotype of James and
Mary Chesnut, apparently taken
shortly after their marriage
in 1840 (MF).*

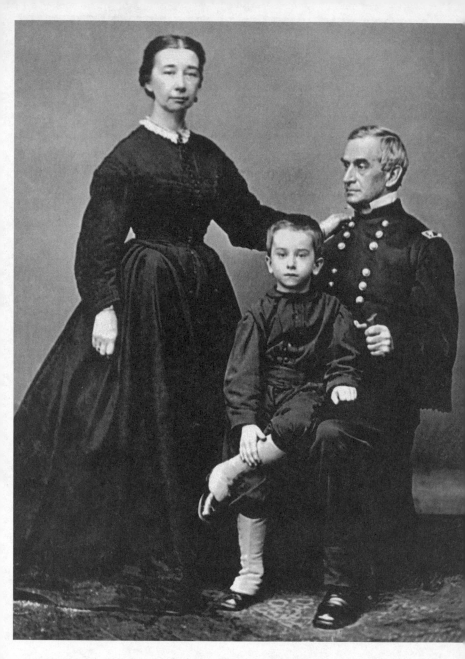

"OUR BOB" *The North's newest celebrity, Maj. Robert Anderson, poses with his wife, Eliza, and son, Tad (NA).*

SOLDIERS AND POLITICIANS Above, *the obscure hero of Fort Pickens, Lt. Adam J. Slemmer (USAMHI) and the celebrated hero of Charleston, Gen. Pierre G. T. Beauregard (NA).* Below, *the wily Simon Cameron (USAMHI) and the indefatigable William H. Seward (NA).*

ENGINES OF WAR Above, *the well-worn entrance to Castle Pinckney (VM).*
Below, *the notorious Floating Battery at anchor off Sullivan's Island (VM).*

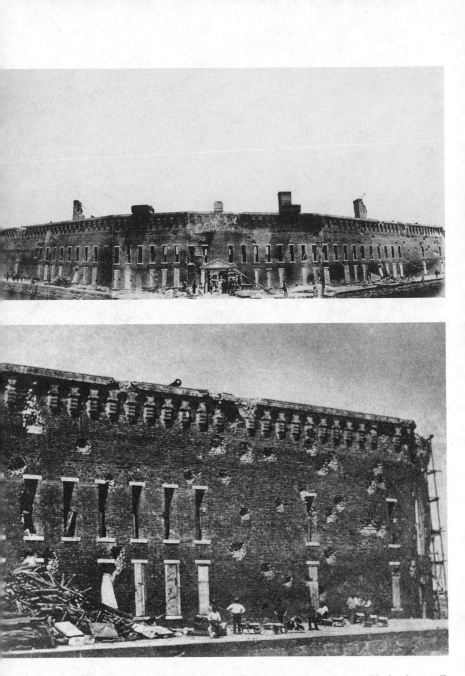

SCARS OF BATTLE Above, *a panoramic view of the face of Fort Sumter scarred by battle as well as by Foster's handiwork in closing the lower embrasures (LC). Below, a closer view of part of the wall shown above (USAMHI).*

VICTORS AND SPOILS *After the surrender, Charleston photographers rushed to capture the triumph for posterity. These two images, when juxtaposed, show the spacious interior of the fort as well as the occupying troops. Sumter's beacon lantern, removed from its place on the parapet, sits on the parade ground near the columbiads that had been rigged as mortars (VM).*

THE DAMAGE DONE Above, *the flag of the new Confederacy flaps above soldiers posed in front of the shot furnace (USAMHI). Below, a view of the interior showing the blasted barracks and walls (VM).*

Photographic sources will be found on page 497.

its members chosen in different ways by different states, would not only create a new government but assume legislative duties as well. It would draw up a constitution, elect a president and vice president, enact laws, and act as a congress until the permanent government got under way. And it would simply assume these extraordinary powers without asking the states or the voters for approval.[33]

Robert Barnwell Rhett gagged on this radical scheme, as did the Mississippi delegates, but the other states overrode their objections. "We are now in the midst of a revolution," said Stephens, who had opposed secession until the last hour. "It is bootless to argue the causes that produced it or whether it be a good or a bad thing in itself." While an impatient Tom Cobb fumed at the delays and threatened to go home if the work was not speeded up, others wondered how it could possibly go any faster. Bombast and posturing were kept to a minimum. Even the usually flamboyant Lawrence Keitt was subdued, saying that his wife had told him when he left home to keep his mouth shut and his hair brushed.[34]

On Thursday, February 7, the committee chaired by Christopher Memminger of South Carolina submitted its plan for a provisional government. The thoughtful Memminger had come to town with a draft for a provisional constitution based on the federal model cherished by all. Debate began the next afternoon and concluded that evening near midnight, when the convention unanimously adopted the provisional constitution with only a few changes from the federal version. After all, stressed Jabez Curry of Alabama, "The states withdrew not from the Constitution, but from the wicked and injurious perversion of the Compact." The next day work began on the permanent constitution.[35]

On Saturday, the 9th, the convention moved to the task that absorbed everyone's attention: choosing a president and vice president. From the start Jefferson Davis was the favorite; on the convention's first day a correspondent from the *Mercury* had predicted confidently that "Fort Sumter and Fort Pickens will elect him." Howell Cobb insisted that "There is no effort made to put forward any man," but he too thought that "Jeff. Davis will be the man." Tom Cobb, while conceding that there had been little "intriguing" for the office, noted wryly: "The crowd of presidents in embryo was very large, I believe the government could be stocked with officers from among them."[36]

As the largest and most influential state, Georgia hoped to provide the first president, but its ranks were divided. Two of its leading lights, Howell Cobb and Stephens, cordially disliked each other; the third contender, Robert Toombs, alienated delegates by turning up drunk nearly every night. Those two longtime ultra leaders, Rhett and Yancey, waited for a call that never came. With only seven of the fifteen slave states bound to the new government, the delegates decided to woo the border states by choosing conservative—and familiar—leaders. Howell Cobb ended the suspense by endorsing Jefferson Davis, and Georgia was appeased when the second place went to Stephens.37

Toombs found consolation in the fact that "Fatty" Cobb came away empty-handed, and that his support had helped get his old friend Stephens chosen. "The latter is a bitter pill to some of us," grumbled Tom Cobb, "but we have swallowed it with as good grace as we could." He was also disappointed in the name chosen for the new government. The "Confederate States of America" seemed uninspired to him, and he hoped to get it changed to "The Republic of Washington" in the final constitution. Desperately lonely for his family, he implored his wife, Marion, to join him with their newest child. "The truth is Marion," he wrote, "I want to show that baby here, do bring her."38

While the committees toiled at creating a permanent constitution, the provisional government began to take shape. Davis was at his plantation in Mississippi and had to be notified to come down for the inaugural. In his absence Stephens was sworn in on Monday, the 11th, his forty-ninth birthday. The next day the convention–turned–provisional congress named a peace commission to negotiate with the United States and assumed authority over the question of the forts. These steps marked the beginning of a fateful shift in the political equation. No longer was the quarrel over Sumter merely between the federal government and South Carolina or that over Pickens between Washington and Florida. A new player had emerged, one with inflated pretensions and aspirations that posed a far graver threat to the peace process.

FOR THE SOLDIERS, Sumter had become the most familiar activity of all, the waiting game. It was the isolation that was different. They were an island unto themselves, their view of the world winnowed down to the keyhole of what they could see from the ramparts, supplemented by occasional scraps of information picked up by chance. Of larger events and smaller sensations they knew nothing. What they saw through the keyhole only made them more uneasy: colonies of ants, black and white, moving methodically to transform the surrounding forts into fortifications capable of resisting fire from Sumter.

Captain Foster, ever the diligent engineer, followed every detail of the work through his spyglass and recorded its progress in letters to his superior officer, General Joseph G. Totten, who at seventy-two had been the army's chief engineer since before the Mexican War. Day after day Foster watched teams of black men and white soldiers toiling to strengthen the forts. At Moultrie the parapet was lined with merlons, and four traverses were erected on the sea side facing Sumter and protected by merlons formed of solid timber, sandbags, and earth. The guns left there were refitted in new carriages, and more guns were put in. By late January the fort was no longer vulnerable to fire from Sumter and had become a formidable threat.[39]

Foster knew of two other batteries set up on Sullivans Island to protect the channel, but could not see them directly. At Castle Pinckney little had been done beyond some sandbags to protect sharpshooters. Three guns had been installed beyond earthworks at Fort Johnson, and a second battery was going in, this one of mortars. The battery on Morris Island that had fired on the *Star* was enlarged from two to four guns. But it was the work at Cummings Point that most disturbed Foster. Boatloads of timber and other materials arrived along with large numbers of blacks, who worked steadily at what appeared to be extensive bombproof works for some batteries. The guns were housed in enclosures framed with heavy timber reinforced by iron rails and covered with earth.[40]

The strength of this battery posed a serious problem. Anderson agreed that this was not amateur work but good engineering which would make it difficult for reinforcements to enter the harbor except at a "great sacrifice of life." Cummings Point lay only about 1,350 yards from Sumter, close enough that on a clear day it seemed as if you could stand on the parapet of Sumter and shake hands with someone on the point. By contrast, the distance to Moultrie was 1,800 yards, to Fort Johnson 2,300 yards, to Castle Pinckney 4,500 yards, and to the Charleston wharfs 5,800 yards. Work had also begun on a "floating battery" that could be maneuvered to fire at any vulnerable point of Sumter.[41]

Anderson and Foster had worked hard to strengthen Sumter against attack by artillery or storming parties. Most of the heavy guns lying unmounted about the parade were laboriously hoisted onto the parapet or the lower tier with makeshift rigging and placed on refitted carriages or mounted *en barbette*. For three 10-inch columbiads too heavy to lift with improvised tackle, platforms were devised to utilize them as mortars. In all, Anderson managed to get fifty-one guns into position. The shutters for the embrasures and all loopholes were secured. A solid wall of masonry five feet high and three feet thick was built behind the main gate, leaving only a narrow doorway twenty inches wide.[42]

Foster placed an eight-inch howitzer to protect the entrance and the wharf below. Two more guns swept the landing, and the lanyards of all three were extended back through the second gate. A large number of shells were

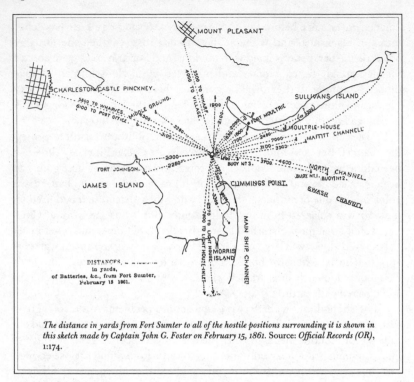

The distance in yards from Fort Sumter to all of the hostile positions surrounding it is shown in this sketch made by Captain John G. Foster on February 15, 1861. Source: *Official Records (OR),* 1:174.

fixed with friction tubes to be used with these long lanyards. Other shells were converted into crude hand grenades. To make cartridges for the columbiads, Foster had to use flannel shirts for the bags because material was so short. Everything was running low; the wall behind the main gate consumed the last of the cement and brick, but Foster scrounged tirelessly for what he needed.[43]

Communication posed a delicate problem. The truce provided for a resumption of mail service in a roundabout way. Mail was carried to Fort Johnson, where someone from Sumter could pick it up and hand over mail for delivery. But Anderson suspected his outgoing mail might be read, and he had no way of knowing if it was even being delivered. To test his situation, he informed the War Department that he would send some missive every day. If it was received, he would know that access was still open; if not, he would know that South Carolina had cut off communication. He realized too that false information or messages might be foisted on him to lower the men's morale or lead him to some misstep.[44]

Food posed another obvious yet subtle problem. The truce allowed the garrison to procure supplies in the Charleston markets as they had always done. In January Pickens had sent to Sumter a supply of fresh meat and vegetables, telling Anderson that he would provide more every day on order from the major. The excited troops carried the food directly to the kitchen only to be told by Anderson to return everything to the boat. In a polite note he told Pickens that he could accept nothing that was not purchased by his own men in the usual way. The men mourned their loss but made no complaint.[45]

A few days later Anderson wrote the contractor who had always supplied him with beef to renew his shipments, but no meat came. Anderson suspected that the contractor feared reprisals if he sold to the Yankees, but the explanation proved simpler. The contractor had not been paid for seven months and hesitated to ship more meat. Once money reached his hands, the shipments of beef resumed. Still, supplies remained tight. An inventory on January 27 listed thirty-eight barrels of salt pork, thirty-seven barrels of flour, thirteen barrels of hard bread, two barrels of beans, one barrel of coffee, half a barrel of sugar, three barrels of vinegar, ten pounds of candles, forty pounds of soap, and three-fourths of a barrel of salt.[46]

The dwindling larder surprised Anderson. Instead of a six-month supply of staples he had barely enough for four. The need for belt tightening forced him to another painful decision: The women and children had to be evacuated. Reluctantly he asked Pickens to permit one of the New York steamers to take the civilian dependents back to that city lest the shortage of supplies "produce sickness among them." Pickens granted the request readily, and on February 1 a lighter arrived to take the forty-two women and children to Charleston, where they were to board the steamer. At noon on the 3rd the men crowded the parapet to watch the steamer cruise past the fort on her way out of the harbor. Loud cheers filled the air, and a gun was fired in salute. They watched sorrowfully until the steamer had vanished over the horizon, aware more painfully than ever before that they were now truly alone.[47]

CHAPTER FOURTEEN

Two Journeys

The President of the Southern Confederation is a gentleman, a scholar, a soldier, and a statesman. . . . The President Elect of the United States is neither a scholar, a soldier, nor a statesman. . . . Without the polished elegance of the well bred man he has all the rough manners and coarse sayings of the clown.
—Philadelphia *Pennsylvanian*
February 18, 1861[1]

*H*E WAS STANDING in the garden of Brierfield helping his wife with some rose cuttings when the messenger arrived. Even before the man dismounted, telegram in hand, Jefferson Davis knew it was the summons to duty he had long awaited. In his usual manner, disclaiming all desire for place in the new government, he had been content to leave his fate in the hands of others. The presidency, he wrote one delegate, was a difficult post, and he had "no confidence in my capacity to meet its requirements." He thought he could serve as the commander of the southern army but said frankly he preferred not to have either position. Yet duty was a handy vehicle for driving the reluctant spirit to higher ground than mere ambition could reach. Not that Davis had ever lacked ambition. Sam Houston called him "as ambitious as Lucifer and as cold as a lizard." To James Hammond he was "the most irascible man I ever knew . . . as vain as a peacock as ambitious as the Devil." His old enemy Winfield Scott, himself no stranger to vanity or ambition, denounced him as "a false man—false by nature, habit, and choice. . . . There is contamination in his touch."[2]

This was not the man Varina Howell Davis knew so well, whose fragile health she had guarded so fiercely over the years. The constitution that mattered most to her had been strained severely by the tension of the past months in Washington. Worn and emaciated, unable to sleep, obsessed with the looming catastrophe that he believed could not be averted short of war, Davis had endured the long journey home to what Varina hoped would be a haven of rest in the setting he loved among the people and things he cherished most. But he had not been there two weeks when the messenger arrived to lure him away. Varina watched him read the telegram, saw his features register a profound grief that suggested bad news about some member of the family.³

After a painful silence Davis said he had been elected president and must go at once to Montgomery. His face was wreathed in gloom. He longed to lead the army, not the government; that was the role he saw for himself, the one befitting his West Point background. His native state recognized this talent. Scarcely had he stepped from the train in Jackson on his homeward journey than he learned that he had been made major general of the Army of Mississippi. Varina knew his preference and thought him more suited to the army. "As a party manager, he would not succeed," she admitted bluntly. "He did not know the arts of the politician, and would not practice them if understood." In his exhausted state the strain could kill him, but duty called and he must obey.⁴

He had no illusions about what awaited him in Montgomery. It was a journey to which he had come by a strange and winding road. His life had begun in Kentucky on June 3, 1808, barely a hundred miles from where Abraham Lincoln was born eight months later. Lincoln moved north to Indiana and Illinois; Davis went south to Louisiana and Mississippi but, unlike Lincoln, was sent back to school in Kentucky. At sixteen he left Transylvania University to enter West Point, where his hot-blooded, fun-loving nature nearly got him expelled and doomed him to twenty-third place in a class of thirty-three. So low a standing consigned him upon graduation in 1828 to the infantry and a post on the Wisconsin frontier.⁵

No one predicted greatness for him. He was a mediocre newcomer to a dead-end profession in which promotion was so glacial he might wait well over half a century to reach the pinnacle of colonel. "I cannot say that I like the army," he confessed, "but I know of nothing else that . . . I would like better." At least it beat being a politician, "whose struggles begun in folly are closed in disgrace." Then Zachary Taylor arrived to command the First Infantry at Fort Crawford, and with him came Sarah Knox, or "Knoxie," Taylor. Davis fell hopelessly in love with her, but Taylor did not want his daughter to marry a soldier, and an unfortunate incident alienated him from Davis. After two turbulent years in the army culminating in a court-martial for what amounted to insubordination, Davis resigned his commission and married Knoxie over her parents' objections, if not opposition.

They were wed in June 1835 and went to live at Davis Bend, the family plantation, while Davis sorted out his future. His brother Joseph, twenty-three years older and more like a father to Jefferson, offered him eight hundred of the five thousand acres at Davis Bend if he wished to clear and plant it. Jefferson accepted and named it Brierfield because of the dense briers there. But three months after their marriage Knoxie lay dead of malaria or yellow fever, and Jefferson plunged into an abyss of gloom and introspection from which he did not emerge for eight years. During that time he developed Brierfield from wilderness into a plantation prison that housed a grieving recluse who did little but work and read. He saw no one but his slaves, to whom he became a kindly and generous master, and Joseph, who fed him books and ideas during long hours of conversation.

Gradually his interest in the larger world reawakened. He took some trips, developed a network of correspondents, and acquired the Democratic politics of his brother. In 1843 he let himself become a candidate for the legislature and lost, but the experience kindled his ambition. That same year Joseph introduced him to a vivacious seventeen-year-old Natchez brunette named Varina Howell, who read his character with astonishing clarity. "I do not know whether this Mr. Jefferson Davis is young or old," she mused after their meeting. "He looks both at times . . . he is the kind of person I should expect to rescue one from a mad dog at any risk, but to insist upon a stoical indifference to the fright afterward."[6]

The meeting aroused in Davis emotions he had thought long dead. Their courtship was turbulent, exacerbated by a difference in age similar to that between Joseph and his second wife. In 1845 past, present, and future came unexpectedly together for Davis. On his way to see Varina at Natchez in February, he encountered Zachary Taylor, who buried all past differences with him. That same month he wed Varina and took her to Brierfield. In the summer, Davis agreed to run for Congress and left to stump the district. "Then I began to know the bitterness of being a politician's wife," Varina observed later, "and that it meant long absences, pecuniary depletion from ruinous absenteeism, illness from exposure, misconceptions, defamation of character; everything which darkens the sunlight and contracts the happy sphere of home."[7]

For Davis, the transformation of his life was far more sunshine than shadow. He won the election and took Varina to Washington, where she met and dismissed President James K. Polk as "an insignificant looking little man." Six months later, over Varina's protests, Davis left Congress to become the colonel of a Mississippi regiment in Mr. Polk's war against Mexico. At Monterrey he gained both distinction and controversy under Zachary Taylor; at Buena Vista he performed heroically and sustained a serious foot wound that sent him home to Varina and appointment to a vacant Senate seat. Davis then won the seat for himself and seemed to have found the career that had so long eluded him.[8]

But even his new reputation as a military hero did not smooth life's path for him. There was trouble with Varina, who resented not only his long absences but also Joseph's influence over their lives, and with his health. The foot wound plagued him for life with pain and periodic infections. Bouts of inflammation in his eyes made reading or writing impossible at times. Politics too turned ugly. Davis clashed with both his former friend Jacob Thompson and his Whig rival Henry S. Foote. Normally a man of seething emotions kept carefully pent up beneath a placid surface, he lost control in an argument with Foote and started pummeling him. After this brawl they remained implacable enemies for life.

Davis emerged as a thoughtful apologist for the South in the clash over slavery. That his former father-in-law had become president made his position no easier. "I came to this session of Congress with melancholy forebodings," he said in 1850, "with apprehension that it might be the last of our Government." He opposed the compromise measures vigorously, and defeat convinced him that the South could no longer hope for an equal voice in the expanding Union. The events of that fateful year pushed him toward the separation that ultras had already embraced.

Unable to deter the compromise that put sectional strife at bay for a time, stunned by the sudden death of Taylor that summer, Davis let himself be persuaded to run for governor in 1851 against his old nemesis Henry Foote. He lost by a slender margin and for a time enjoyed a respite from public life in the new house and garden at Brierfield. In 1852 Varina gave birth to their first child, and his domestic bliss seemed complete except for the recurring bouts of fever and inflammation of the eyes. That same year his old friend Franklin Pierce was elected president and made Davis his secretary of war.

Varina objected vehemently but in vain, painfully aware of how Davis threw himself into any commitment whatever the toll on himself. In the War Department he toiled mightily to bring efficiency to an archaic system. Spoilsmen and sluggards alike drew his wrath, as did blighting traditions like the seniority system. He modernized forts, arsenals, equipment, and attitudes where possible, tried to acquire the latest information on principles of warfare, and experimented with new techniques, including the importation of fifty-four camels for use on the southwestern desert. The idea was ridiculed and later abandoned, but in fact the camels proved their effectiveness.

No one worked harder or provoked more controversy. Well-publicized rows with Winfield Scott and John E. Wool revealed weaknesses he struggled vainly to conceal: a childish petulance when he believed he had been wronged (which was often), self-righteousness that made him high-handed, pettiness, and the vanity of one who thinks himself right and others wrong because he acts only from the noblest of motives while they are merely self-serving. "If anyone differs with Mr. Davis he resents it," noted Varina astutely, "and ascribes the difference to the perversity of his opponent." Obsessed with being right and doing everything the right way, he could not delegate or excuse weakness in others. Because he drove himself to the limits of his strength, it was easy for him to believe that others gave less than their full devotion to duty.

His sense of duty exacted a high toll. Overwork worsened his eye affliction until by 1855 a cloudy film had begun covering his left eye and eventually rendered it useless. His darling little boy Sam had died a year earlier, and the arrival of five more children never slaked his grief over this loss. Through the Kansas-Nebraska struggle he chafed in the silence required of a cabinet member. As the political climate heated up, he longed for his old place in the Senate, where he could speak out and influence events. In March 1857, with Buchanan inaugurated, he left office gratefully and stepped back into the Senate chamber.

Despite his gift for making enemies, Davis was good at separating issues from personalities and got on well with many men he opposed in politics. One of them, surprisingly, was Seward, who ingratiated himself with the Davises. When Varina lay desperately ill after childbirth and deep snow prevented a neighbor who was nursing her from reaching her, Seward had his horses hitched to a sleigh and delivered the woman despite a broken harness. He had not even met Varina before that incident, and neither Davis ever forgot his kindness. Shortly afterward Jefferson fell ill with eye trouble and laryngitis. For weeks he lay blind and speechless, able to communicate only by slate. Seward called every day to cheer him with reports from the Senate and to relieve Varina's anxiety with banter. Told that Davis might lose an eye, he exclaimed, "I could not bear to see him maimed or disfigured." No amount of political animosity clouded the feelings the Davises felt toward Seward in later years.9

The contrast between Seward's ability to depersonalize his politics and Davis's tendency to take everything personally could not have been more striking. The pragmatism of the northern politico stood in glaring relief against the proud, unbending chivalric spirit. After Bleeding Kansas and John Brown's raid, the political atmosphere deteriorated rapidly. Unlike most southerners, Davis viewed Brown's act as the gesture of a ragtag band of fanatics rather than as part of some monstrous conspiracy, but he also saw that southern resentment could no longer be curbed. In February 1860 he offered the Senate six resolutions defining the southern position on the relations of the states within the Union and under the Constitution. They passed after months of delay but did little other than speed the split between northern and southern Democrats.

His loathing of Stephen Douglas did not blind him to the catastrophe of a divided party. Ever the defender of southern rights, Davis found himself a southern leader in a Senate growing ever more northern and western, and a voice of moderation in a South growing ever more ultra. To avert disaster, he tried to persuade Douglas, Bell, and Breckinridge to withdraw in favor of some other candidate around whom Democrats could unite. Douglas alone refused, thereby scuttling the plan. After Lincoln's election, Davis backed away from his insistence that the South should secede if the Republicans won. He advised restraint when a South Carolina committee headed by Rhett asked his views on secession and resistance. But events in Mississippi and Washington raced past his caution, leaving Davis in search of his duty. On December 14 he signed the statement of a caucus of southern congressmen that the argument was exhausted and all hope of relief in the Union vanished. Six days later, when South Carolina seceded, he checked two books out of the Library of Congress: a history of South Carolina and a history of the national flag.

The failure of the Committee of 13 convinced Davis that secession was the only recourse. When Mississippi seceded, he telegraphed, "Judge what Mississippi requires of me and place me accordingly." Wracked by facial neuralgia, distressed by the crisis and the standoff at Sumter, he rose from a sickbed to deliver his farewell speech and returned home to Brierfield to await the next call to duty. Now it had come, and he prepared to honor it. The long and often strange journey of his life had in the most improbable of ways brought him to Montgomery, but how well had it prepared for him?

He was in many respects the reflection of the chivalry that had chosen him. His tall, thin, lean figure exuded the dignity and pride of aristocracy. The habit of command came easily to him, as did gallantry and courtesy to those who did not oppose his will. A polished veneer of intellect and manners concealed the passions raging within him. An unwavering sense of righteousness made him imperious and intolerant of those who disagreed with him. He was earnest and sincere, devoted to duty and principle in a high-minded, humorless manner that equated seriousness with solemnity. Nowhere in his character was there evidence of flexibility or growth; he was what he had been since Knoxie's death.

But there were also ways in which Davis differed from the chivalry. He was an austere, even ascetic man who ate and drank little, did not chew tobacco, and was indifferent to sport. His gaunt face with its high forehead, deep-set eyes, high cheekbones, firm jaw, and thin lips might have been the model for an icon of a saint. The right eye glowed with a fire that contrasted oddly with its dead, film-covered mate. His face was a canvas of long years of suffering with its deeply etched lines and perpetual twitching from neuralgia. Suffering had become for him an inseparable companion, an enduring test of will and character. He viewed life in most of its guises, good and bad, as an ordeal to be borne.[10]

There was time only to pack a few things and say good-bye to Varina, the children, and the slaves, some of whom rowed him downriver to the landing where the packet boat docked. While waiting in the rowboat for the *Natchez*, he talked quietly with Ben Montgomery and the other rowers, revealing little of himself except his obvious affection for them. "Jeff Davis," said Montgomery later, "was a man you couldn't tell what was in his mind." None of them dreamed that it was the last time they would see each other. The *Natchez* took him to Vicksburg, where bands and soldiers greeted him. To them he spoke fondly of the old Union and uttered the fervent hope that the new nation would not be born in blood.[11]

A special train took him to Jackson. There he resigned his post in the state militia and spoke to an eager audience that included his brother Joseph. Again he talked of the conflict to come, expressing his hope that it would be averted while promising that if it came, "There will be no war in our territory. It will be carried into the enemy's territory." Some men of the First Mississippi went with Davis when he left Jackson on the 14th. Crowds gathered at every town and junction, greeting him with bonfires, cannon salutes, and wild enthusiasm. He spoke twenty-five times in two days, denouncing the "hell born fanaticism" of the North and promising recognition of the new government by Britain and France. "We have separated from them," he exclaimed, "and separated *forever*."

The train rolled into Atlanta two days later, and Davis gave a half hour speech reiterating what he had said along the way. A reception committee joined him on the trip across Georgia before surrendering him to a committee from Montgomery for the final leg of the journey. In all Davis traveled nearly seven hundred roundabout miles to reach a city that lay only two hundred miles east of Jackson. Exhausted by the steady parade of bands, artillery, and raucous enthusiasm, he still found energy to talk warmly with those sharing his private car. Everyone wanted to know whether war was imminent. Davis admitted freely that he thought it was, even though he hoped to avoid it.

Not until 10 p.m. on the 16th did the train reach Montgomery. Davis said a few words to the crowd and went to the Exchange Hotel for the official reception. Yancey was there to greet him and escort him to a balcony for yet another speech. There had been rumors that Davis was softening on secession and looking to reconciliation; if so, Tom Cobb feared, "we shall have an explosion here." But Davis had no such ideas. Despite his fatigue and hoarse voice, he rattled the sword again, promising no concessions and victory at the end of whatever strife lay ahead. When he had finished and gone back inside, Yancey spoke briefly in praise of the new president. "The man and the hour have met," he cried. "Prosperity, honor and victory await his administration."[12]

The next day being Sunday, the inaugural was put off until Monday, the 18th. People flocked into the city from every direction; at the west end of the capitol a crowd estimated at between three and ten thousand waited. Ladies who had come early filled the balconies and front windows, clutching flowers to shower on their heroes. At noon the self-appointed congress met to await the arrival of the procession, which was assembling at the Exchange Hotel. The Columbus Guards, in bright red coats and sky-blue trousers, formed at the head of the column. Behind them rode Davis and Alexander Stephens in an open carriage drawn by six white horses. A train of vehicles and dignitaries, including the governors of the seceded states, followed. Slowly they wound their way through the cheering crowds that lined Commerce Street.[13]

The sun shone brightly in a clear sky as the procession reached the capitol. As Davis stepped out of his carriage, some ladies draped a gorgeous wreath of flowers over his arm. Lacking a national anthem to play, the band struck up a rousing "Marseillaise." Bouquets rained from the windows as Davis walked into the chamber, where Rhett formally introduced him to the congress. Aurelia Fitzpatrick, wife of the former Alabama senator and the only woman brazen enough to sit among the members, poked Davis in the back with her parasol until he spoke to her. The members formed a line and followed Rhett, Davis, and Stephens to the portico for the ceremony. After the chaplain offered a prayer, Howell Cobb announced the election results. Davis stepped forward to give his inaugural address and claim his place in history. There had been many southern presidents, but he was to be the first president of the South.[14]

He spoke in a firm, clear voice that reached everyone. Defending the southern cause to the world and to humanity, he reminded Europe of its need for southern cotton and assured his listeners that "a reunion with the states from which we have separated is neither practical nor desirable." They had a nation to build; other slave states would soon join, and all must work to make it grow. Five times he alluded to the possibility of war with the North, which the Confederacy did not wish but would not shirk. He dedicated himself to the task of building a new nation and asked patience for the mistakes he would surely make. On this great work the countenance of the Almighty would surely shine.[15]

It was for Davis a remarkable speech—brief, on target, uncluttered by bloated rhetoric or strained literary allusions, and well suited to the ears of the South, the North, and Europe alike. Even those who disliked him conceded its grace and taste. The journey that had borne Davis in such unexpected ways to this unexpected place in history had ended, and a new one was about to begin. He had no illusions about its difficulties. "Upon my weary heart was showered smiles, plaudits, and flowers," he wrote Varina, "but beyond them, I saw troubles and thorns innumerable. We are without machinery, without means, and threatened by a powerful opposition; but I do not despond and will not shrink from the task imposed upon me."[16]

How well would he fare? Would he be the George Washington of the new republic? Tom Cobb, who never cared for Davis, conceded the grace of his inaugural but took his measure early. "He is not great in any sense of the term," he confided to his wife. "The power of will has made him all that he is."[17]

LINCOLN VISITS CHARLESTON!!!

What mileage an enterprising newsmonger might have got from such a headline. It even had the virtue of being true, if grossly misleading.

He had to get away, if only for a day or two. The men hungry for jobs stalked Springfield in ever-growing numbers, overwhelming the hotels and boardinghouses until many were forced to take refuge in sleeping cars. The cabinet game bogged down as Cameron continued to play coy. Pleas for help came from moderates North and South, seeking from Lincoln some word of conciliation to wield in the fight for a compromise. Mary did not help by going to New York in search of a wardrobe suitable for a First Lady and taking her sweet time to return. On three successive cold, snowy nights in late January Lincoln dutifully trudged to the depot to meet the evening train, only to find her not on it. She finally appeared on the fourth night.[18]

To escape the supplicants, he resorted to an office at the Illinois *State Journal* and the studio of sculptor Thomas D. Jones, for whom he was sitting, to read his mail or work. With both home and office besieged, he contrived to meet important visitors in their hotel rooms. The mail went to his office, where Nicolay fed most petitions for jobs and other mundane items directly to the stove. Still, Lincoln found no peace, no respite from the responsibilities settling on his shoulders. He sensed the force of change drawing him inexorably away from the people and places that had been the texture of his adult life. In his moody, fatalistic way he doubted that he would ever see again this world which had made him what he was and was so indelible a part of him.[19]

Memory had always been a strength to him, and so it was again. On the morning of January 30 he slipped aboard a train to visit his stepmother near the village of Charleston, Illinois. For once the reporters honored his plea for privacy and did not follow him, preferring to amuse themselves with the chagrin of the arrivees in Springfield who found their prey absent. An old friend, Henry Whitney, rode with him partway. Another old friend, the superintendent, could not keep the train from arriving late at Mattoon, where Lincoln missed his connection. Undaunted, he climbed aboard the caboose of a freight train and rode unceremoniously to Charleston. When the train reached there at dusk, Lincoln slogged through slush and mud to the buggy waiting to take him to spend the night at a friend's house.[20]

He passed a pleasant evening doing what he liked best: reminiscing with old friends and telling stories. The next morning he jounced eight miles in a buckboard to Farmington, the tiny settlement where his father had settled thirty years earlier. There, in the log cabin for which he had helped cut logs, he embraced the woman who had most been his mother. He had something new to show her: the scruffy start of a beard as well as a display of affection he rarely showed anyone. He visited the unmarked, neglected grave of his father and ordered a tombstone for it, though he later forgot the matter. He traded reminiscences with relatives and old friends who came to see him, and that evening he took Sally Lincoln to Charleston for a public reception at the town hall. When the time came for him to leave, the aged Sally clutched him tightly and said she was certain she would never see him again because his enemies would kill him.

"No, no, mamma: they will not do that," he assured her. "Trust in the Lord, and all will be well: we will see each other again."

But she would not be consoled, and he left her embrace feeling more gloomy than ever. Many of his friends in Springfield shared this fear, as did strangers who warned him by letter. One urged him to "Reflect a moment upon the Death of Harrison & Taylor . . . they both came to there [*sic*] Death by poison." But he could not worry about these things; he had too much else to do. The cabinet wrangles had to be resolved, and the endless flow of visitors curbed. His house had to be rented, and his personal effects disposed of or stored. And he had an inaugural speech to write. He had already begun work on it with no other sources than Andrew Jackson's proclamation against nullification, Henry Clay's compromise speech of 1850, and Daniel Webster's immortal reply to Hayne.[21]

When he returned to Springfield on February 1, a Californian ambushed several hours of his time seeking a cabinet post for John C. Frémont. Already Norman Judd, sensing his cause lost to the legions behind Caleb Smith, had expressed his disappointment. "I came down here oppressed with a sense of injustice," he wrote glumly. "I cannot shake it off. . . . I can hide my head and close my small political life in a foreign land. . . . Good bye and may you meet as true friends in the future as in the past." Salmon Chase, like Cameron, had as many enemies as friends importuning Lincoln. Less shy candidates let their friends besiege Lincoln, but their efforts paled before the Cameron conundrum.[22]

"It is now nearly a month since the opening act of the Cameron melodrama was performed by the old stager himself in this village," wrote Henry Villard late in January. ". . . It has been your correspondent's devout prayer . . . that the curtain be dropped in this all but farcical piece of political chicanery. Yet it seems that there is to be no end of it." Cameron, whom one adversary called "as corrupt as a dung hill," had struck a clever pose, telling all who asked that he would not join the cabinet while he maneuvered deftly behind the scenes to undermine any Pennsylvania rivals for a post. The deluge of letters on his behalf included one from his pastor attesting to Cameron's "unexceptional moral character in all his domestic, and social relations."[23]

Cameron's enemies were no less busy. Reformers, horrified at the idea of a cabinet with both Seward and Cameron, pressed the cause of Chase with renewed vigor. A minister not his own denounced the general as "a political trickster, fattening on unrighteous 'jobs' in our public works & using those whom he employs & enriches to promote his personal objects." Senator Fessenden labeled him "utterly incompetent to discharge the duties of a Cabinet officer." Grimes of Iowa agreed, as did Lyman Trumbull, who advised Lincoln that "Members of the Senate who know him intimately . . . assure me he is wholly unfit for the Treasury. . . . you had better put Chase into the cabinet & leave Cameron out even at the risk of a rupture with the latter."[24]

Desperate for some breathing room, Lincoln decided to suspend work on cabinet appointments and concentrate on his speech. The cabinet could be dealt with after he reached Washington, where he planned to submit Cameron's fate to a caucus of Republican senators. "All our people here say Amen!" wrote a Washington friend after hearing the news. Seward too applauded the decision. "The temper of your administration," he added, "whether generous and hopeful of Union, or taut and reckless will probably determine the fate of our country."[25]

As if Lincoln could forget that fact. It permeated every paragraph of the inaugural address he was drafting, and the opening of the peace conference in Washington swelled the pleas for him to speak out or offer some concession. To the delight of ultras like Horace Greeley, who visited in February, Lincoln stood firm. "On the territorial question . . . I am inflexible," he wrote Seward. "I am for no compromise which *assists* or *permits* the extension of the institution on soil owned by the nation." On other issues he was less adamant. "As to fugitive slaves, District of Columbia, slave trade among the slave states . . . I care but little, so that what is done be comely, and not altogether outrageous. Nor do I care much about New Mexico, if further extension were hedged against."²⁶

"Mr Lincoln yet remains firm as a rock," reported William Herndon. "He has told me . . . often that . . . rather than concede to traitors, his soul might go back to God from the wings of the Capitol." Old friend Orville Browning met Lincoln in the basement of the statehouse and was pleased to find him "firmer than I expected." Lincoln realized the time was near when he must finally speak out—not at the inaugural but earlier, at the many stops planned on his journey to Washington. He had to decide what to say and what not to say or imply.²⁷

While pondering these great issues, he also had some housekeeping to do. The house on Eighth Street was rented, and an ad put in the paper offering its contents for sale. The local druggist picked up six chairs for $12, a spring mattress for $26, a wardrobe for $20, a stand for $1.50, some stair carpet for $4.75, four comforters for $8, and a "whatnot" for $10, receiving an itemized receipt carefully made out and signed by the owner. On February 6, the Lincolns hosted a farewell reception. A small announcement in the morning paper drew hundreds of people to the house, where they waited patiently in the cold to shake Lincoln's hand at the door and be greeted inside by Mary, their sons, and her sisters. Mary was radiant in a white silk gown with a French lace collar, one fruit of her shopping trip to New York.²⁸

The next day W. S. Wood gave the press an itinerary of the journey that would carry Lincoln over the tracks of eleven separate railroads. An expert at arranging such trips, Wood had been sent by Seward. By the 9th Lincoln had finished the draft of the speech; that night he gingerly tried on his inaugural suit, which had been on display in town for the previous two days. At every step he heard the doors of his past closing with a finality that depressed him. He grew more solemn and subdued, less ready with a joke or story. "Parting with this scene of joys and sorrows during the last thirty years and the large circle of old and faithful friends," concluded Henry Villard, "apparently saddens him and directs his thoughts to his cherished past rather than the uncertain future."²⁹

Sunday the 10th was unseasonably warm and rainy. Carl Schurz was in town to lecture; Lincoln visited him at his hotel and got an earful about standing firm against any compromise. To reassure Schurz, he read through the draft of the inaugural and discussed it point by point with him. Later he went to see Herndon at the law office. After going over the books and taking care of some last unfinished business, Lincoln sprawled on the worn office sofa and stared silently at the ceiling. "Billy," he said finally, "how long have we been together?"[30]

"Over sixteen years."

"We've never had a cross word during all that time, have we?"

"No, indeed we have not," answered Herndon.

His eyes still fixed on the ceiling, Lincoln reminisced on the early days of his practice, then told Herndon how many times some lawyer had tried to replace him as Lincoln's partner. Herndon was surprised at how cheerful he seemed. Lincoln got up and gathered a bundle of books and papers to take with him. As he headed out, the sign swinging on its rusty hinges at the foot of the stairs caught his eye. "Let it hang there undisturbed," he said. "Give our clients to understand that the election of a President makes no change in the firm of Lincoln and Herndon. If I live I'm coming back some time, and then we'll go right on practising law as if nothing had ever happened."

He took a last look around, then ambled into the hallway and down the stairs. Herndon followed. "I am sick of office-holding already," Lincoln said abruptly, "and I shudder when I think of the tasks that are still ahead." The good cheer had vanished entirely, replaced by the familiar mask of gloom. It hurt deeply to leave old friends and familiar sights, he admitted, and for a special reason: He could not shake the feeling that he would never return to Springfield alive. Herndon tried to downplay the notion, but Lincoln would not be moved. They shook hands, and Herndon watched him stroll down the street.

He could not explain the feeling and no one understood it, any more than anyone could fathom why, after all those years with a clean-shaven face, he had decided to grow whiskers. Maybe it was the dream or image or whatever it was he had had after going home on election night. Lying on a sofa, tired to the bone, he glanced at a bureau mirror across the room and saw himself full length but with two faces. Startled, he got up and the image vanished, but when he lay down again it came back: two faces, one more pale than the other. A few days later he tried the experiment again, and the image returned, but only once. He told Mary about it and tried to show her, but could not make it happen again.[31]

What did it mean? A worried Mary thought it was a sign: He would be elected to a second term, and the pallor of the second face meant he would not live through the second term.

A cold rain fell on Monday morning, the 11th. Lincoln rose early, roped his trunks, and affixed labels reading, "A. Lincoln, Executive Mansion, Washington." Parts of his life were scattered across town. The house was leased, its contents sold off along with the horse, buggy, and cow, the dog handed over to a neighbor, and the law office left in Herndon's faithful hands. He had to be at the Great Western depot early to say a few words to the crowd gathered to bid him good-bye. All was ready except for Mary, who chose this moment to demand that Lincoln promise an office to one of her friends. When he refused, she threw herself on the floor, screaming that she would not budge until he agreed.[32]

A friend appeared to learn the reason for the delay. He entered to find Lincoln seated in a chair, his head bowed in disgust and shame. At last he yielded. Mary composed herself, and they went to the station. He paused in the waiting room to shake hands with as many well-wishers as he could, then followed Wood onto the platform of the rear coach. He removed his hat and let the rain trickle down a face that for once did not wear one of its accustomed masks but was pale and quivering with emotion. The crowd waited in respectful silence for words that came hard even to a master of language.[33]

"My friends," he began at last,

no one, not in my situation, can appreciate my feeling of sadness at this parting. To this place, and the kindness of these people, I owe every thing. Here I have lived a quarter of a century, and have passed from a young to an old man. Here my children have been born, and one is buried. I now leave, not knowing when, or whether ever, I may return, with a task before me greater than that which rested upon Washington. Without the assistance of that Divine Being, who ever attended him, I cannot succeed. With that assistance I cannot fail. Trusting in Him, who can go with me, and remain with you and be every where for good, let us confidently hope that all will yet be well. To His care commending you, as I hope in your prayers you will commend me, I bid you an affectionate farewell.[34]

With these words he stepped inside the coach and left his world behind. Never would the town's citizens forget his presence among them, yet what had he really built there beyond his own reputation? He had never been civic-minded, had done nothing to promote local schools, churches, asylums, or railroads. Politics was his entire world, and even there he had paid little heed to local elections or the aspirations of friends. "He did nothing out of mere gratitude," recalled one who came to know him, "and forgot the devotion of his warmest partisans as soon as the occasion for their services had passed."[35]

He left Springfield behind as he had so many other things in his life, good and bad. In this case he also left behind Mary and all the children except Robert; they were going first to St. Louis and would join him later in the trip. The special train of two coaches and a baggage car held a mixed lot of friends and officials, some of whom rode only a short distance. The politicos included Norman Judd, Governor Richard Yates, Ebenezer Peck, Jesse Dubois, and O. M. Hatch. Lincoln's secretary, John G. Nicolay, was joined by his new assistant, John Hay, Lincoln's brother-in-law physician, Dr. W. S. Wallace, and two bodyguards, Ward Lamon and Elmer E. Ellsworth. A dozen young Republicans, one of them a Harvard classmate, joined Robert Lincoln. Villard was there along with E. L. Baker of the Illinois *State Journal.* Three of the four officers assigned by Scott—Major David Hunter, Captain George W. Hazzard, and Captain John Pope—were aboard; Colonel E. V. Sumner joined the party at Indianapolis.[36]

The weather cleared as the Rogers locomotive chugged along at thirty miles an hour over tracks lined with people for most of the route. A section of one coach had been set up as a refreshment saloon, and most of the riders crowded around early. Lincoln wrote out a draft of his farewell remarks for Villard, then worked on the speech he would give at Indianapolis. At every hamlet the train slowed or paused while he stepped to the rear platform to wave and say a few words. "I am leaving you on an errand of national importance, attended as you are aware with considerable difficulties," he told the crowd at Tolono, the last stop in Illinois. "Let us believe, as some poet has expressed it, 'Behind the cloud the sun is still shining.' "[37]

A thirty-four-gun salute greeted the train at the Indiana state line. After a stop for lunch the politicians began scrambling aboard, led by cabinet hopefuls Caleb Smith and Schuyler Colfax. From Lafayette to Indianapolis the track was enclosed by people eager to get their first and probably only glimpse of the president to-be. The clamor at every depot brought him out to say hello and tell a story. He understood their enthusiasm as few men did; they were the source of his own strength, the core of the only religion he practiced. "His 'master' was the 'plain people,' " Ward Lamon said later. "To be popular was to him the greatest good in life. . . . To gain or keep it, he considered no labor too great, no artifice misused or misapplied."[38]

Shortly before 5 p.m. the train rolled into Indianapolis. Lincoln responded to Governor Oliver P. Morton's official welcome with a brief speech, then endured a carriage ride to the Bates House as part of a parade. The hotel was so jammed with people that a wedge had to be formed to get Lincoln inside. He made his way to a balcony overlooking the street and delivered the speech he had expected to make later to the legislature. He was acutely aware of the significance of the moment: After months of rigorous silence he was finally speaking out, and the crowd listened intently to what he had to say.[39]

"The words 'coercion' and 'invasion' are in great use about these days," he said. Would marching an army into South Carolina without the consent of its people be coercion or invasion? He thought it would be both "if the people of that country were forced to submit." But what if the government simply held or recaptured its own forts, or enforced the laws by collecting duties or even stopping mail delivery in "those portions of the country where the mails themselves are habitually violated; would any or all of these things be coercion? Do the lovers of the Union contend that they will resist coercion or invasion of any State, understanding that any or all of these would be coercing or invading a State?" If so, he stressed, "the means for the preservation of the Union they so greatly love . . . is of a very thin and airy character. If sick, they would consider the little pills of the homeopathist as already too large for them to swallow. In their view, the Union, as a family relation, would not be anything like a regular marriage at all, but only as a sort of free-love arrangement . . . to be maintained on what that sect calls passionate attraction."⁴⁰

The crowd roared its approval, and reporters eagerly passed his words on to waiting readers North and South. For the first time they read his determination to hold or even retake the captured forts and uphold federal authority. Ultras cheered, moderates sagged in despair. Many were disgusted by what they deemed the vulgarity of the reference to free love.

At the hotel, Lincoln had to wait half an hour for a meager meal, and his party had to sleep four and five to a room. That evening he endured a reception in the parlor at which, Villard estimated, "No less than three thousand ladies and gentlemen filed past their Presidential victim." The next day, Lincoln's fifty-second birthday, crowds gathered early outside the Bates House and rocked the street with cries of "Old Abe" until he came out on the balcony to greet them. Already Morton had taken him to breakfast at the governor's mansion and to greet the legislature at the capitol. At the hotel his old Illinois friends Jesse Dubois and Ebenezer Peck said emotional farewells and left bearing locks of his hair.⁴¹

At 10:30 a.m. the presidential party, now reinforced by Mary and the children, finally fled Indianapolis. At every stop people flocked to see Lincoln with an enthusiasm that awed even jaded reporters. There was another crush in Cincinnati, where the pageantry was exceeded only by the enormous size of the crowd. Lincoln stood erect in an open carriage with his head uncovered, acknowledging the cheers with bows and waves. One spectator applauded the "homely character" of this arrangement. "The times are unsuited to show," noted the city solicitor, Rutherford B. Hayes. "The people did not wish to be entertained . . . they did wish to see the man in whose hands is the destiny of our country."⁴²

The next morning the train headed for Columbus. Lincoln had developed a cold and was growing hoarse, but he managed a few words at every stop. Every community was eager to show the president its best, but the real object of display was Lincoln himself. That afternoon a dispatch from Washington told him that the electoral vote count had proceeded without incident and that he was now officially president-elect.[43]

That evening in Columbus he endured another reception and left early the next morning. Between stops Lamon enlivened things in the car by strumming some slave songs on his banjo that all joined in singing. A derailed freight train delayed their arrival at Allegheny City until 8 p.m., two hours late. They took carriages through the rain to the Monongahela House in Pittsburgh, where Lincoln stood on a balcony and croaked out a few words to the umbrellas below.

The rain poured down all night, but Lincoln had promised the crowd a speech the next morning and, true to his word, he appeared on the balcony at 8:30 a.m. Mindful that he was in Pennsylvania, where the tariff occupied most minds, he devoted much of his text to that subject. But he also had some words about the broader issue that caught people's attention. "There is really no crisis, springing from anything in the government itself," he assured the crowd. "In plain words, there is really no crisis except an *artificial one* . . . as may be gotten up at any time by designing politicians." Shrewd heads perked up at these words, as did others across the nation who read them in their newspapers. Some took the statement as a discouraging sign that Lincoln did not understand the crisis or underestimated its gravity.[44]

At 10 a.m. the train left Pittsburgh and backtracked toward Cleveland. It made six stops before reaching that city in a driving snowstorm. Still, the crowds turned out along the way, and the most lavish welcome yet greeted the train that afternoon. At the Wedell House, Lincoln reiterated that "The crisis, as it is called, is altogether an artificial crisis. . . . It has no foundation in facts. It was not argued up, as the saying is, and cannot, therefore, be argued down. Let it alone and it will go down of itself."[45]

That evening he decided to reject all the offers of a house in Washington and wrote Elihu Washburne asking him to reserve rooms in a hotel, adding, "Mrs. L. objects to the National on account of the sickness four years ago." The president-elect was coming to town and needed quarters until the inauguration. By choosing a hotel, he exposed himself to a rush of visitors, which is doubtless what he intended.

On the way to Buffalo the stops grew more frequent and Lincoln's replies shorter to accommodate his hoarseness. At Girard he received several baskets of fruit and a surprise visit from Horace Greeley, who rode along about twenty miles.[46]

A large gathering greeted the train at Westfield, just across the New York border. "I am glad to see you," Lincoln told the ladies in the crowd. "I suppose you are to see me; but I certainly think I have the best of the bargain." Three months earlier he had received a letter from a young girl in the town advising him to let his whiskers grow. Well, he said with a smile, he had done it, and he wanted to thank her in person if she was there. A pretty little girl with black eyes, blushing madly, was carried through the crowd to the platform. Lincoln gave her a hearty kiss and waved his good-byes.

At Dunkirk, before an audience of nearly fifteen thousand, Lincoln took a very different tone. He stepped onto a platform where a flag had been placed and took hold of the staff. *"Standing as I do,"* he rasped, *"with my hand upon this staff, and under the folds of the American flag,* I ASK YOU TO STAND BY ME SO LONG AS I STAND BY IT." The train moved on to Buffalo, where former president Millard Fillmore greeted Lincoln. The wildly enthusiastic crowd overwhelmed the inadequate guard of police and soldiers and surged forward with such a crush that Lincoln barely made it to his carriage unharmed. Major Hunter suffered a dislocated shoulder struggling to protect him. There was another tumultuous squeeze at the American House, another speech, and yet another reception that evening.[47]

It was clear that something magical was happening. The size of the crowds everywhere, their sincere outpouring of affection for Lincoln, their fervent support for the Union, had turned the journey into the train of democracy rolling across the country. "The whole trip from Indianapolis," marveled David Davis, who had come aboard at that city, ". . . has been an Ovation such as never before been witnessed in this Country. It is simply astonishing." Davis thought it was not Lincoln himself but the state of the country that evoked such enthusiasm.[48]

Yet Lincoln did leave a deep impression on many who saw him for the first time. "He is distressingly homely," admitted a young lawyer named James A. Garfield. "But through all his awkward homeliness, there is a look of transparent, genuine goodness which at once reaches your heart and makes you trust and love him." A *Tribune* reporter, who watched the people flock to Lincoln at every stop and studied his responses to them, agreed: "The power of Mr. Lincoln is not in his presence or in his speech, but in the honesty and gloriously revealing sincerity of the Man." Villard's close study of Lincoln brought him to the same conclusion. "No one can see Mr. Lincoln without recognizing in him a man of immense power and force of character and natural talent," he observed. "He seems so sincere, so conscientious, so earnest, so simple-hearted, that one cannot help liking him."[49]

Sunday, the 17th, offered Lincoln a blessed day of rest. Fillmore took him to church and then to dinner at his home. At 5:45 the next morning the train was off again, weaving its way through a snowstorm that did not faze crowds at Rochester, Clyde, Syracuse, Utica, Little Falls, Amsterdam, Fonda, and Schenectady. Everywhere the people could not get enough of Lincoln, or he of them, as if they fed on each other for strength and hope. The train entered Albany at 2:30 p.m., only to encounter another botched reception. Thousands of people had jammed the crossing where the reception was to take place. The mayor was there with a few policemen, but neither the city council nor the military escort had arrived. The mayor, jostled about by the crowd, finally reached the platform and asked Lincoln to wait for the military. Mindful of the Buffalo fiasco, he agreed to the delay.[50]

They lingered for half an hour while the crowd, frustrated that Lincoln did not appear, battled with the police. At last the troops arrived, the reception went forward, and Lincoln escaped to a carriage while the band played "Hail to the Chief." On both sides of the road cheering people jammed the sidewalks, porches, and roofs. The cortege wound its way to the capitol, where Governor E. D. Morgan and other officials performed the usual welcoming ceremony and Lincoln addressed the state assembly. The inevitable reception that night left him exhausted. The next morning he climbed gratefully back on the train for the trip to New York City. Along the way he summoned the strength for half a dozen stops.[51]

By three that afternoon he was in New York City, home to the worst financial jitters and most savage political infighting outside of Pennsylvania, and the place where his road to the presidency had begun a year earlier with a memorable speech at Cooper Union. The Lincolns stayed at the Astor House, where the reception that evening was limited to party dignitaries. The next morning Lincoln breakfasted at the home of Moses Grinnell with some thirty pro-Seward Republicans led by Weed. More politicians streamed in there and at the Astor House, their ranks broken only by the resourceful P. T. Barnum, who slipped in and invited Lincoln to visit his museum. At eleven Lincoln rode through large crowds to City Hall and a tepid welcome by Mayor Fernando Wood.[52]

Earlier in the crisis Wood had suggested that the city secede from New York State so as not to lose its southern business. Now he spoke pointedly of a "dismembered government" and expressed the fear that "if the Union dies the present supremacy of New York may perish with it." Lincoln let the remarks slide, saying that he would do his best to preserve the Union. Another reception followed, and more visitors saw Lincoln in his rooms that afternoon, including Hannibal Hamlin, who had just reached the city. That evening the Lincolns dined with Hamlin and his young wife, whom one reporter described as "about twenty-five years of age, smaller, and not so full in form as Mrs. Lincoln. She has a mild blue eye, rather sharp features, but a gentle expression."[53]

At dinner Lincoln encountered his first-ever plate of oysters. He eyed them warily, then drawled, "Well, I don't know that I can manage these things, but I guess I can learn." Afterward they went to the Academy of Music to see Verdi's *A Masked Ball*. They crept in silently during the first act, but at its end the audience erupted in cheers. A huge American flag was brought onstage, and the principals and chorus stepped forth to belt out "The Star-Spangled Banner." A few snobs relished seeing Lincoln's gangly hands clad in kid gloves rather than proper white evening gloves. After one more act he left to confer with more party leaders at the Astor House while the wives held a reception.[54]

Through these meetings Lincoln artfully dodged the cabinet question, listening to all and committing to no one. At midnight a band of Wide-Awakes gathered under his window to serenade him. For once Lincoln declined to appear, leaving Hamlin to appease them. The next morning he boarded a ferry and crossed to New Jersey, endured a brief ceremony at Newark, and said a few words to each house of the legislature at Trenton. By four o'clock he was in Philadelphia, braced for more cabinet fireworks. While in New Jersey, Lincoln had been escorted by William Dayton, the man most prominently mentioned as an alternative to Cameron. Now he rode through cheering crowds to the Continental Hotel, where office seekers and Cameron minions awaited him.[55]

From a balcony Lincoln responded to Mayor Alexander Henry's welcome with a few words repeating his belief that the crisis was an artificial one. He deftly fended off the cabinet sharks and suffered through yet another reception that evening. Outside the hotel Chestnut Street was festive with people cheering and singing. Lincoln was to raise a new flag over Independence Hall early the next morning, then head for Harrisburg to address the state legislature. But that night a new element entered the picture. A worried-looking Norman Judd managed to pull him away from the reception to his hotel room, where he introduced the president-elect to Allan Pinkerton, a detective who had a disturbing report to deliver.[56]

CHAPTER FIFTEEN

Plums and Nuts

I fear the more we concede the more will be demanded, till we will have either to give up the Union or to disband our party! . . . Seward is full of mystery— he either does not comprehend the depth of these events—or else he greatly overrates his power with the party. If he supposes these events are to pass without a storm, he is mistaken—if he supposes that he can bring our party to meet by compromise the demands of the slave powers he is not only mistaken but ruined*!! I rather think we must take at present a divided empire. . . . Let disunion fever run its course—and let us get Canada, by negotiation . . . guar- rantee [sic] the freedom of the Mississippi river—divide the public property & debts with the South—receive the seceding states . . . only as free states, acknowledge the independence of Hayti . . . we will be stronger than* now*! have a homogeneous people, and some "peace of our lives."*

—Cassius M. Clay
February 6, 1861[1]

STORIES OF A PLOT had been circulating for weeks, even months, but no one knew how seriously to take them. As the national crisis deepened, so did the anxiety levels among those directly involved. No one was more anxious than Samuel M. Felton, president of the Philadelphia, Wil- mington & Baltimore Railroad, a key link between Washington and New York. A staunch Unionist, Felton worried that conspirators or fanatics might seize the Susquehanna River steamboat or burn the two wooden bridges on his line. Dorothea Dix, the humanitarian who had worked extensively in the South, had given him details of a conspiracy to seize Washington and cut the city off from the North. Her warning moved Felton to hire Allan Pinkerton to investigate the threat.[2]

Pinkerton set up shop in Baltimore, planted operatives around the city, and uncovered plots not only of secession but of assassination. With Felton's consent he sent Kate Warne, the head of his "Female Detective Force," with a letter to Judd, who agreed that the threat should be taken seriously. On Thursday, the 21st, Pinkerton met Felton in Philadelphia. While they talked, Pinkerton heard music and realized that Lincoln's procession was moving down Walnut Street. Through an operative they got a note to Judd, who met them that evening in Pinkerton's room at the St. Louis Hotel. After Judd had heard Pinkerton's tale, Felton added that he had heard similar rumors from other sources and had no doubt that blood would be shed in Baltimore if Lincoln went there as planned. The danger, stressed Pinkerton, would not come on the train but during the ride from the Calvert Street station to the Camden Street depot to change trains. The president-elect had no armed guard or Secret Service men with him. Since there was no national police force, protection everywhere along the route depended on local arrangements. Baltimore, alone of Lincoln's stops, had issued him no invitation and arranged no public reception because the political situation there was so explosive. The police protection looked pitifully inadequate.[3]

What would happen, asked Pinkerton, if a small band of assassins, armed and ready to die in the attempt, attacked the presidential party, hemmed in by a crowd, unable to move? Convinced that the danger was real, Judd pondered Felton's suggestion that Lincoln leave the party and go directly to Washington by special train. He and Pinkerton waded through the milling crowd on Chestnut Street to the Continental Hotel and with difficulty made their way to Lincoln's room. Not until 10:30 p.m. did they manage to get Lincoln to Judd's room to hear Pinkerton's report. Lincoln listened intently, then fell silent. Could he be persuaded, Judd asked at last, to leave for Washington that night by train?[4]

"No, I cannot consent to this," Lincoln answered. The next day was Washington's Birthday. He had agreed to hoist a flag early that morning at Independence Hall and then go to Harrisburg to address the legislature. Once these things were done, he was free to change his itinerary. They discussed that option, and Lincoln returned to his room around eleven o'clock. There, to his surprise, another messenger waited for him. Frederick Seward had been sent to Philadelphia by his father, who had learned from General Scott of a plot to assassinate Lincoln at Baltimore. Lincoln questioned young Seward closely and saw that his story originated in entirely different sources from those of Pinkerton. This convinced him that the plot might be real.[5]

There was also a spate of letters from well-wishers like the woman who warned that she had heard in Baltimore of "a league of ten persons who have sworn that you should never pass through that city alive. That may be but one of the thousand threats." A Republican ally in Baltimore told him ruefully that "it has been deemed unadvisable, in the present state of things, to attempt any organized public display on our part, as Republicans." Baltimore was notorious for its "plug uglies" and mob violence, which had marred every recent election. Captain G. W. Hazzard, who had lived in the city, told Lincoln bluntly that the greatest risk he might encounter would be in Baltimore.[6]

Early Friday morning Lincoln went to Independence Hall and raised a flag with thirty-four stars, the extra one for newly admitted Kansas. In his brief remarks he dwelled on the meaning of the Declaration of Independence and its promise that "in due time the weights should be lifted from the shoulders of all men, and that *all* should have an equal chance." If the country could not be saved on the basis of that principle, he added with deep emotion, "it will be truly awful. . . . If this country cannot be saved without giving up that principle—I was about to say I would rather be assassinated on this spot than to surrender it."[7]

In Harrisburg, Governor Andrew Curtin greeted him with an imposing military display and a pledge to provide men and money when needed. "Allow me to express the hope," Lincoln replied, "that in the shedding of blood their services may never be needed, especially in the shedding of fraternal blood." At the capitol his obligatory remarks to the legislature were met with prolonged cheers and applause. While Lincoln completed his rounds, Pinkerton had been busy all night deploying his forces and arranging details to carry out the new plan. That afternoon Judd summoned David Davis, Lamon, Colonel Sumner, Major Hunter, and Captain Pope to see Lincoln in a private parlor at the Jones House. He revealed the plan to them and asked for opinions, fully expecting the shocked expressions that registered. The officers took it as a challenge to their competence; Sumner was the first to react, denouncing it as "a damned piece of cowardice." They talked some more, but Sumner would not be appeased. "I'll get a squad of cavalry, sir," he roared, "and *cut* our way to Washington sir!"[8]

"Probably before that day comes," said Judd wryly, "the inauguration day will have passed. It is important that Mr. Lincoln should be in Washington that day."

Asked his views, Lincoln said the plan should be carried out. On the question of who should accompany him, Judd said it should be only Lamon. An indignant Sumner complained that it was his duty to see the president safely to Washington. After the meeting Lincoln downed a hasty dinner before the carriage arrived around six o'clock. He hurried to his room, put on a brown Kossuth hat and a different cloak from his usual one to conceal his identity, and slipped through the halls to the carriage. Sumner was there, determined to go with Lincoln. Judd put his hand on Sumner's shoulder and said, "One moment, Colonel." As Sumner turned around, the carriage drove away with Lincoln and Lamon. The colonel stamped the ground in anger.

Pinkerton and Felton had arranged with telegraph officials to cut all wires out of Harrisburg at six o'clock, so that news of Lincoln's departure could not spread. A special train took Lincoln to the Philadelphia, Wilmington & Baltimore depot at West Philadelphia, where tickets on the regular sleeper to Washington had been procured. To ensure the connection at Philadelphia, Felton sent a note to the conductor instructing him not to give the signal for departure until he had received a package addressed to E. J. Allen (Pinkerton's alias). A trainmaster named H. F. Kenney was given the bogus package to deliver. Pinkerton posted agents along the route to display a prearranged signal visible from the car that all was well.

Pinkerton had a carriage waiting when Lincoln stepped out of the West Philadelphia depot. They drove about to kill some time, then went to the PW&B depot. Lamon offered to furnish Lincoln with a revolver and bowie knife, but Lincoln refused. He remained calm and self-possessed, assuring Pinkerton that he had complete trust in him and his plan. Kate Warne had already boarded the train and managed to save four adjacent double berths in the sleeping car. Pinkerton escorted Lincoln and Lamon inside through the rear, Kenney handed the package to the conductor, and the train started minutes later. "Mr. Lincoln is very homely," observed Warne, "and so very tall that he could not lay straight in his berth."[9]

No one was sleepy. They chatted or rode in silence until the train reached Baltimore at 3:30 a.m. Everyone stayed aboard while Warne visited a nearby hotel to gauge the mood of the locals; she found the city quiet. From the President Street station on the eastern edge of the harbor, Lincoln's car was drawn slowly by horse down Pratt Street to the Camden Street depot of the Baltimore & Ohio Railroad, enabling him to avoid exposure. At 4:15 the train departed without incident, and it arrived in Washington at 6 a.m. Everyone got quickly off the car and headed into the depot. Inside, a man eyed Lincoln closely and drawled, "Abe, you can't play that on me." Pinkerton feared they had been discovered and elbowed the man back, but he approached again. As Pinkerton raised his fist, Lincoln grabbed his arm. "Don't strike him, Allan, don't strike him—that is my friend Washburne—don't you know him?"[10]

"THE CRISIS IN MARYLAND is rapidly approaching," warned the *Tribune* correspondent in Baltimore on the 6th. No one knew that better than Governor Hicks, who presided over a state in which politics were even more fractured than elsewhere, and of which he was a living monument. At sixty-one, the oldest of thirteen children who had grown up on an Eastern Shore farm, Hicks had been both a Democrat and a Whig before joining the

American party. He got elected governor in 1857 by 8,460 votes, thanks to carrying Baltimore by a majority of 9,639. But in November 1859 the Democrats regained control of the legislature, leaving Hicks, like Buchanan, a lame duck without a party to support him.[11]

Maryland was itself a house hopelessly divided and fearful of becoming a battleground between the warring sections. Slaves, most of them in the farm-rich southern part of the state and the Eastern Shore, formed only 12.7 percent of its population. The northern and western regions had few slaves and numerous small farms, many of them worked by German immigrants adamantly opposed to slavery and state rights. Baltimore was a city of southern traditions with strong manufacturing and commercial ties to the North. Since the election a severe recession had blighted the city and the state, adding a further source of tension to the discontent already brewing.[12]

Breckinridge had carried the state in November, winning half of Baltimore's votes in a close race with Bell. Hicks had backed Bell but was a staunch supporter of slavery. "I have never lived . . . in a state where slavery does not exist," he declared, "and I never will do so if I can avoid it." Known to harbor secessionist sympathies, he flirted with the idea of a middle confederacy of border states, and he strongly opposed any policy of coercion. But he feared both immediate secession and union with the Deep South, arguing that "We of the border States cannot allow our interests to be compromised by the extremists of the South, whose interests, social and pecuniary, differ so widely from ours."[13]

With his own views as divided as those of his constituents, Hicks stumbled toward a position that made him a de facto Unionist. Marylanders, he vowed, "would never agree to disunion for *any* cause. . . . [T]hey demand their rights, *under* the Constitution *in* the Union." He surprised everyone by resisting appeals to call the legislature into session, which could then have ordained a secession convention. The *Tribune* correspondent regarded Baltimore as a "nest of conspirators" eager for that move. The praise pouring in on Hicks from the North seemed to strengthen his resolve. "My feelings and sympathies are naturally with the South," he told Governor Curtin, "but, above and beyond all these, I am for the Union."[14]

What Hicks wanted above all else was a compromise that would defuse the crisis. "That something should be done, *all must know!*" he told Crittenden, "& to my mind that something is the passage of your proposition." The pressure mounted late in January, when secessionists chose members to a state convention of their own, which was to meet on February 18 at Annapolis. When Virginia issued its call for the peace conference, Hicks responded by appointing seven delegates on his own. On February 13 he went reluctantly before a House committee to testify on the existence of secret organizations and possible plots against Lincoln. There he pleaded for a speedy compromise, warning that he could not hold out much longer. He also asked General Scott in vain for two thousand rifles "to meet an emergency if it shall arise."[15]

Unimpressed, the *Tribune* reporter scoffed that "Secession is becoming as scarce in this State as integrity in a den of thieves." Union sentiment had become a rising tide, and Mayor George W. Brown of Baltimore had announced his intention of meeting Lincoln on his arrival and riding with him in an open carriage between train depots. The self-appointed gathering of February 18 talked tough but merely resolved that a convention was desirable and adjourned until March 12, giving Hicks until after Lincoln's inauguration. Union sentiment seemed strong in Maryland, but Baltimore remained uncertain.[16]

At eleven-thirty on the morning of the 23rd, Mayor Brown stood waiting at the Calvert Street station amid a crowd estimated at ten or fifteen thousand, many of them hostile to the president-elect. Rumors asserted that Lincoln was already in Washington, but no one believed them. The train arrived, bearing Mary Lincoln and the children. Believing Lincoln to be aboard, onlookers cheered or shouted curses, stuck their faces against or into windows, and even boarded the car. Some got into Mary Lincoln's suite before John Hay shoved them out and locked the door. With the crowd milling about in confusion, the Lincolns took a carriage to the home of the railroad's president while the rest of the party boarded a large omnibus and rode through the crowd to the Eutaw House amid a stream of both cheers and obscenities. One spectator mistook W. S. Wood with his trim beard for Lincoln and began to shout hurrahs; others joined him and dashed after the bus.[17]

At the depot, Mary and the boys endured more foul language and pushing against the car before the train departed. "Oaths, obscenity, disgusting epithets and unpleasant gesticulations, were the order of the day," wrote Joseph Howard of the New York *Times*, who was with the party. A spectator friendly to Lincoln applauded his decision to avoid Baltimore, insisting that "By your course you have saved *bloodshed and a mob*." But the locals felt indignant and insulted. "Had we any respect for Mr. Lincoln," said the Baltimore *Sun*, ". . . [this] would have utterly destroyed it." In Washington a foreign minister had a similar reaction on hearing the news. "Like a thief in the night," he noted, "the future President arrived here on the early morning of the 23rd."[18]

. . .

THE HACK HAD ALREADY DEPOSITED LINCOLN at the side door
of Willard's Hotel by the time Seward arrived. He had planned to meet Lincoln at the depot but had overslept, and now had to mask his annoyance
while Washburne introduced him to the man who had ruined his own presidential hopes. They greeted each other cordially and discussed the dangers
just averted before Lincoln went up to his rooms for some rest. Hardly
anyone knew he was in town; these were the only quiet hours he would have
in Washington. The inauguration was nine days away, and much remained
to be done.[19]

Seward took Pinkerton and Lamon to his house and heard their account
of the night's events. Afterward a weary Pinkerton returned to Willard's,
enjoyed a bath and breakfast, and sent his contacts a telegram in code indicating that the scheme had come off successfully: "Plums arrived here with
Nuts this morning—all right." He then ran into Lamon, who was eager to
telegraph a Chicago reporter the story of the adventure. Pinkerton saw that
Lamon, although sworn to secrecy on the episode and Pinkerton's role in it,
could not wait to tell the world about his own part in saving Lincoln's life.
"He talked so foolishly that I lost patience with him," Pinkerton noted privately, "and set him down in my own mind as a brainless egotistical fool." An
hour later Pinkerton was infuriated to find Lamon drinking and talking with a
Herald reporter, and had some harsh words with him.[20]

While Pinkerton fumed, Seward returned to Willard's with a sense of
satisfaction. Despite having missed Lincoln at the depot, he had the new
chief in hand and planned to keep him there. It had been a rough course to
the counting of the electoral votes on February 13. All the fears of an attempt
to disrupt the count had proved unfounded, thanks in part to the conspicuous presence of what one southerner bitterly called Scott's "janizaries, with
their cannon cocked and primed, to belch death and destruction on the
people if they interfered." Robert Hatton regarded the spectacle as imposing;
Ben Wade thought it "The quietest joint Assembly of the two houses that I
have ever known."[21]

Encouraging news had come from key border states. On the 9th Tennessee had voted against calling a convention to consider secession; nine
days later Missouri and Arkansas did likewise. Compromise hopes soared at
the news, though some complained that the results would only make Republican ultras more arrogant and implacable. The peace conference droned on
despite a stroke suffered by the elderly Judge Wright. Things were proceeding just as Seward expected. "Each day brings the people apparently
nearer to the tone and temper, and even to the policy I have indicated," he

wrote Frances with satisfaction. With the vote official he was at last "out of direct responsibility. I have brought the ship off the sands, and am ready to resign the helm into the hands of the Captain whom the people have chosen."[22]

But not entirely ready. The captain clearly needed a first mate who knew the ropes better than he did, one who might steer a safer, surer course through rough seas. Seward considered himself the only man capable of assuming that role, although he well knew that others resented his influence. Some thought his conciliatory views too soft; others wanted him out of the cabinet in favor of an ultra like Chase. Much depended on how the cabinet fight fell out and who gained the inside track with the uncouth new president. Of him Charles Francis Adams had as yet formed no firm opinion. "His speeches have fallen like a wet blanket here," he complained. "They put to flight all notions of greatness."[23]

What Adams did see clearly was that "two distinct lines of policy advocated by opposing parties within our ranks are developed. The index of one of them is Mr. Seward. That of the other Mr. Chase. As yet there is not evidence . . . which will be adopted. Until it appears, there will be no firmness here." Hannibal Hamlin shared this view. Having arrived in town the night before Lincoln after a harrowing trip through Baltimore, he rushed to Willard's the next morning as soon as he learned of the chief's secret arrival. During their talk Hamlin, a strong Chase supporter, asked bluntly whether the new administration was to be a "Seward Administration for the benefit of Mr. Seward or a Lincoln Administration." The latter, Lincoln assured him, but Hamlin left unconvinced.[24]

On his heels came Seward to squire Lincoln about the official circuit. They paid a courtesy call on Buchanan, who introduced them to his cabinet, then in session. Harriet Lane, who had heard that Mary Lincoln was "awfully *western*, loud & unrefined," caught only a side view of Lincoln and thought he resembled "our tall, awkward Irishman who waits on the door." From the White House Lincoln and Seward went to see General Scott, who was not at home but who hastened to drag his huge, protesting body to Willard's once he learned of the call. For an hour Lincoln and Seward rode together, talking and taking each other's measure. Seward found him "very cordial and kind toward me—simple, natural, and agreeable."[25]

Lincoln returned to Willard's and settled into Parlor No. 6 for the rush of visitors that would descend on him nonstop until the inauguration. Scott lumbered in, wheezing graciousness and charm. The entire Illinois delegation paid their respects, with Douglas the most effusive of all. Behind them came the elder Frank Blair and his son Montgomery, the latter still aching for a cabinet post. Seward had gone to retrieve Lincoln's family from the depot and escorted Mary into the hotel on his arm. The peace conference dele-gates, sitting next door, asked to greet Lincoln and were told to come at nine that evening.

At six Seward hosted a dinner for Lincoln and Hamlin, at which they discussed policy and prospects. The thrust of the talk did not please Hamlin, who left with apprehensions about Lincoln's "honest simplicity and want of necessary knowledge of men." Lincoln returned to Parlor No. 6 for the eve-ning shift. The peace conference delegates filed in behind Salmon Chase and John Tyler. All of them, especially the southerners, were curious to meet the man who was more myth to most of them. What they saw was a huge, stooped figure on whose gangling body the clothes hung loosely. Kindly eyes peered out from beneath a cavernous brow with an unfathomable mixture of humor and sorrow.[26]

The tired, wrinkled face expanded into a smile as he greeted each man, usually with some bit of lore he knew about him. His voice was hearty and cheerful, his manner strikingly unstudied and informal. Where most veteran politicos would have been all caution and reserve, Lincoln seemed as natural as if he were welcoming neighbors into his own parlor. The southerners were fascinated in spite of themselves. They poked at him with questions to draw him out and were impressed by the ease and agility of his answers. Even when the cadaverous James Seddon of Virginia pushed hard at him, Lincoln replied in a manner that neither evaded nor offended.

William E. Dodge, a delegate and New York businessman who had sur-rendered his suite to the Lincolns, worried that the country would be plunged into bankruptcy and "grass shall grow in the streets of our commer-cial cities." Lincoln quipped that "If it depends upon me, the grass will not grow anywhere except in the fields and the meadows." When Dodge per-sisted, Lincoln stressed that he would defend the Constitution with all his ability. "The Constitution will not be preserved and defended," he added, "until it is enforced and obeyed in every part of every one of the United States. It must be so respected, obeyed, enforced, and defended, let the grass grow where it may."

The southern delegates listened to this exchange in sepulchral silence. Ultras left the room disturbed by these words, but the moderates stayed on to hear more. William C. Rives of Virginia went away convinced that Lincoln "has been both misjudged and misunderstood by the Southern people. They have looked upon him as an ignorant, self-willed man, incapable of indepen-dent judgment, full of prejudices, willing to be used as a tool by more able men. This is all wrong. He will be the head of his administration, and he will do his own thinking."[27]

John Sherman of Ohio came in; Lincoln took both his hands and said,

"Well I am taller than you; let's measure." Challenging tall men back to back was a favorite ritual of his, and he smiled at being told he was two inches taller. The members of Buchanan's cabinet arrived to return Lincoln's morning call, after which Lincoln was free to retire. The next morning, Sunday, Seward was there to convey Lincoln to services at St. John's Church, where the sexton handed him the thick prayer book inscribed "The President of the United States." Back at the hotel Lincoln gave Seward the draft of the inaugural address for his comments.[28]

By Sunday evening Seward had his response ready. He thought the argument "strong and conclusive" but urged that two early paragraphs on the Chicago platform be dropped because their effect would be to drive Virginia and Maryland from the Union. "I know the tenacity of party friends," he counseled, "and I honor and respect it. But I know also that they know nothing of the real peril of the crisis. It has not been their duty to study it, as it has been mine. Only the soothing words which I have spoken have saved us and carried us along this far." He suggested closing with some conciliatory words to curb passion and prejudice in the South and despondency in the East. "Some words of affection," he urged. "Some of calm and cheerful confidence."[29]

While Seward studied the draft, Lincoln welcomed more visitors, including Charles Francis Adams and three ultra Republican senators, Sumner and Wilson of Massachusetts and Hale of New Hampshire. Adams saw in his new leader a bundle of contradictions: a "tall, illfavored man, with little grace of manner or polish of appearance," yet with a "plain, good-natured, frank expression which rather attracts one to him." Sumner, his composure already ruffled by meeting Adams in the antechamber, was befuddled by Lincoln's offer to measure backs for height and managed the ponderous admonition that this was "the time for uniting our fronts against the enemy and not our backs." Appalled by Lincoln's lack of social poise and breadth of culture, he still noticed extraordinary "flashes of thought and bursts of illuminating expression." But he was helpless to deal with Lincoln's droll western wit.[30]

On Monday morning Lincoln received calls from Senators King, Doolittle, and Powell. John C. Breckinridge stopped by, as did Lewis Cass. Buchanan repaid Lincoln's formal visit to the White House. Seward was there as usual, and in the afternoon he took Lincoln to the Capitol to visit Congress. "SEWARD," grumbled a southern observer, "has had Old ABE under his thumb every moment since his arrival." In the Senate Republicans welcomed him cordially, as did some northern Democrats like Douglas and Bigler, but Andrew Johnson of Tennessee was the only southerner to greet him. Mason of Virginia made a point of snubbing him. More southerners stepped forward in the House, if slowly and tentatively. Afterward Seward took Lincoln to the Supreme Court, where he shook hands with the justices who had formulated the *Dred Scott* decision.[31]

That evening, while the Lincolns hosted a reception at Willard's, he slipped away at one point for a long chat with John Bell. For some, the absorbing topic was the national crisis; for others, the selection of the remaining cabinet members. On Tuesday morning congressmen called mostly to lobby for cabinet hopefuls. The omnipresent Seward came with his Senate successor, Ira Harris, as did Hamlin, Sumner, and Governor Hicks, who pressed Lincoln for some gesture of conciliation to hold the border states. In the afternoon Lincoln escaped to the Senate, where he fulfilled a promise of asking each Republican member to give his choice for treasury secretary. Chase won the straw vote over Cameron handily, but Lincoln offered no comment.[32]

That evening a number of prominent Virginians led by Rives visited Lincoln hoping to soften the position he had taken in his speeches en route to Washington. Lincoln overflowed a chair, feet on rungs, elbows on knees, chin cupped in hands, and warmed his visitors with some stories before telling them that slavery must not spread to the territories. The Virginians objected and went away unconvinced. Sherrard Clemens, a Unionist from western Virginia, denounced Lincoln as a "cross between a sandhill crane and an Andalusian jackass. . . . The weakest man who has ever been elected . . . vain, weak, puerile, hypocritical, without manners, without moral grace . . . surrounded by a set of toad eaters and bottle holders." But Clemens took grim satisfaction in the belief that "The Republican party is utterly demoralized, disrupted, and broken up. Cameron & Chase, Weed & Greeley, can never affiliate."[33]

Behind the Virginians came their prodigal son, General Scott. All day Lincoln had been besieged by pleaders for cabinet hopefuls, as he had in Springfield, but now he had also to deal with those pressing affairs of state on him. Wednesday the 27th brought Bell in the morning at Lincoln's request; he returned that afternoon along with Douglas, Hicks, and Greeley to discuss the border state situation. At an evening reception Mayor Berret formally welcomed Lincoln to the city. Speaking his first words in a place where slavery dwelled, Lincoln said graciously that "I think very much of the ill feeling . . . is owing to a misunderstanding . . . I hope . . . when we shall become better acquainted—and I say it with great confidence—we shall like each other the more."[34]

Cameron dropped by to test the cabinet waters and did not like what he found. Lincoln had decided against him for Treasury and tried to appease him with an offer of Interior. The general declined. Douglas managed to get

Lincoln alone for an intense talk. His appearance must have shocked Lincoln: the face furrowed with stress, the eyes deep caverns of pain. Some said he was drinking heavily again to slake his gloom and fatigue. In a raspy voice he begged Lincoln to encourage the floundering peace conference and endorse Seward's proposal for a national convention. He promised to eschew partisanship and stand by any policy intended to save the Union, and he pleaded with Lincoln, "in God's name, to act the patriot, and to save our children a country to live in."[35]

At nine some border state peace conference delegates arrived to promote compromise. Rives joined fellow Virginian George W. Summers, James Guthrie and Charles S. Morehead of Kentucky, and Alexander W. Doniphan of Missouri, For three hours they thrashed away at the dilemma of Union versus coercion. All were Unionists, the phalanx crucial to Seward's hope of averting war and gradually luring back the seceded states. Morehead argued that withdrawal from Fort Sumter and guarantees to the cotton states would achieve that goal. Slavery could be guaranteed where it presently existed, Lincoln replied, but little more could be offered that would satisfy the Deep South.[36]

Morehead spun an elaborate argument for limited federal action, moving Lincoln to recall an Aesop fable about a lion so eager to enter society that he appeased the other animals' fears by having his claws cut off and teeth pulled, whereupon the others cracked his skull with a club. Very interesting and apropos, retorted Morehead, but not satisfactory. We are staring fratricidal war in the face, he said. "I appeal to you, apart from these jests, to lend us your aid and countenance." Before Lincoln could reply, the elderly Rives rose and said in a trembling voice that for all his ancient love of the Union, if Lincoln resorted to force at Fort Sumter, Virginia must secede, and he himself would fight. Lincoln jumped up from his chair. "Mr. Rives, Mr. Rives," he said, walking to him, "if Virginia will stay in, I will withdraw the troops from Fort Sumter."[37]

In effect Lincoln was offering to evacuate Sumter if the Virginia convention, which was still sitting, adjourned. The delegates promised to use their influence and went away unsatisfied. The next morning Crittenden came to plead his case before making a last desperate drive in the Senate, but he left frustrated and despondent. That night businessman E. G. Spaulding hosted a gala dinner at the National Hotel for Lincoln and Hamlin. Seward and his friends held sway, but Chase was there along with Scott, David Davis, Caleb Smith, and a smattering of peace seekers from other factions.

A serenade that night from enthusiastic Republicans closed out the month of February and with it Lincoln's initiation into the insular world of the City of Politics. The inauguration was but four days away, and over it hung the crushing weight of responsibility for coping with the crisis that paralyzed the nation. The thought troubled but did not paralyze him. Whatever mask he revealed to others, he was inwardly confident that he knew as well as or better than anybody else what must be done. It was not that he knew yet what to do, but rather that he would find the right path to take when the time came.

CHAPTER SIXTEEN

The Waiting Game

We are here two races—white and black—now both equally American, holding each other in the closest embrace and utterly unable to extricate ourselves from it. A problem so difficult, so complicated, and so momentous never was placed in charge of any portion of Mankind.

—James H. Hammond
February 2, 1861[1]

WASHINGTON IN THE LAST DAYS OF FEBRUARY was a place of extremes. The weather veered from snow to sun to choking dust to unseasonable warmth with rain hanging in the air. Amid the pervasive gloom society offered up dollops of gaiety. Charlotte Cushman drew large crowds to the Eleventh Street Theater with what one reporter called her "superb *physique.*" Hostesses mustered up a few straggling balls and receptions to close out a regime that had begun with such high hopes. Its demoralized leader presided over his last reception and was upstaged by a ball at the Douglases', where Henry Adams found "the wildest collection of people I ever saw." He smirked as one crowd of admirers engulfed "the ancient buffer Tyler" and another "that other ancient buffer Crittenden."[2]

The crush was so great that Adams had to rush his partner from the suffocating room to apply ice. He admired the looks and grace of Adele Douglas but wondered how she endured life with a brute he considered "gross, vulgar, demagogic; a drunkard; ruined as a politician; ruined as a private man . . . in debt, with no mental or literary resources; without a future." On another day he and brother Charles dined with the family of the absent Colonel Robert E. Lee, whose son Rooney had been at Harvard with Henry. The volatile mood in Maryland did not prevent Henry Winter Davis from hosting dinners for political friends. Robert Hatton was privileged to attend one sumptuous meal limited to twelve men of all political stripes. Mrs. Davis, the only woman present, retired at nine, leaving the men to their wine and cigars. Hatton endured the usual gibes over his temperance principles but was grateful to escape for one night the drudgery of dispatching hundreds of copies of speeches to his constituents. "This is no place for fun," he wrote his wife, "at least, in the year 1861."[3]

Fun had long since departed the White House, where Buchanan rejoiced only at serving out the final days of his sentence. Weary and haggard, deflated of all ambition greater than the longing for rest, he looked anxiously for relief from other quarters. Congress had talked much and done nothing. Kentucky moderates struggled to bring about a national convention, but in the end it was Virginia's resolutions that convened a peace convention. Buchanan submitted the resolutions to Congress with a strong endorsement only to see them die of neglect without even the courtesy of referral to committee. The convention itself dawdled along in the congressional style of much rhetoric and little progress. Meanwhile, Virginia's state convention to consider secession opened on February 13 and remained a ticking bomb to advocates of compromise.[4]

The presence of an embryo government in Montgomery heightened the crisis and the threat to Washington itself. Buchanan had been deluged with criticism for allowing Scott to fill the city with troops. Both the Corps of Engineers and the regular garrison had been called away from West Point, something never before done in peacetime. Congress fired angry resolutions at him questioning the necessity of turning the capital into an armed camp. "Old Buck has so many soldiers there," said one southerner, "it looks more like a Camp Ground than a City." Troops and artillery galloped through the streets at all hours, and Kate Thompson reported guns and pistols stacked in every department ready for use. "Was there ever such *Tom foolery*," she lamented.[5]

Holt delivered a stout defense of the need for the 653 troops and urged Buchanan to do likewise. "The act of assembling troops at the capital, and providing for the inauguration under the shelter of their guns, is one of the gravest and most responsible of your administration," he argued. "For this step your administration has been, and still continues to be mercilessly denounced. . . . Congress is now engaged in spreading broadcast over the country . . . a report intended to show that the safety of the capital has never been menaced, and of course that all your preparations here have been prompted by cowardice, or the spirit of despotism. *Now* is the time to meet this calumny." But he could not rouse Buchanan from his lethargy on the matter.[6]

A similar mood infused Buchanan's attitude toward the Sumter crisis. The question of how best to sustain Anderson nagged constantly at him. With the truce ended and Anderson reporting steady progress in the strengthening of the forts around him, the threat of an attack loomed larger than ever. When Holt asked what Anderson should do if the fort was undermined, Buchanan replied that he should "crack away at them." But he balked at firing the first shot. While the cabinet again pondered how best to reinforce Anderson, Scott received a plan from former naval officer Gustavus V. Fox calling for a commercial steamer, escorted by two light tugboats and two warships, to carry the troops and supplies. Scott summoned Fox to Washington, liked what he heard, and took the plan to Holt, who agreed to show it to Buchanan that same evening, February 7.[7]

It did not help Fox's case with Buchanan that the plan had come to Scott through his brother-in-law Montgomery Blair, a renegade Democrat turned Republican. Nor did it appear that Buchanan had to move at once. John Tyler was hard at work urging Pickens not to act despite the lapsed truce, and he assured Buchanan that the governor would make no aggressive move before conferring with the new Montgomery government. But the dispatches from Anderson grew more ominous; one received on the 11th mentioned reports of South Carolina's getting new rifled cannon from Britain that would "make our position much less secure." Two days later Anderson asked for instructions on how to treat vessels bearing foreign flags should hostilities commence.[8]

Still, Buchanan hesitated. On the 19th the cabinet took up the question again, spurred this time by a report that Pickens planned to attack Fort Sumter before the new Montgomery government asserted its authority over the issue. An alarmed Buchanan relayed the news to Tyler, who scrambled to obtain a denial from Pickens. Meanwhile, Scott, Holt, and Toucey organized a fleet of four Treasury Department vessels under Commander James H. Ward to load and sail at once should the need arise. But even as Scott ordered the ships loaded with supplies and recruits readied for boarding, Louis Wigfall somehow got wind of the preparations and alerted Pickens by telegraph on the 20th. That same day Tyler received a flat denial from Pickens that any attack was planned. Scott pressed Buchanan to send the reinforcements anyway before the forces around Sumter grew too strong, but the president clung to Tyler's assurance and to the hope that the peace convention would accomplish something.[9]

Tyler also urged Buchanan not to arouse sensibilities in the city by permitting the usual military parade on Washington's Birthday. Like so many other well-intended acts, this turned into a fiasco. Buchanan agreed with the suggestion but did not know that Holt had already issued the order and put the usual notice in the *National Intelligencer*. On the morning of the 22nd, as citizens gathered along the route to watch the parade, Buchanan ordered Holt to countermand the order. Holt sent word to Scott, who was at breakfast and dispatched Erasmus Keyes to circulate the order dispersing the troops.[10]

Congressman Dan Sickles learned of the order and rushed to the War Department, where he found Buchanan with Holt. In his voluble, agitated way he persuaded Buchanan that canceling the parade would be more disastrous than holding it. Buchanan sighed agreement and sent Holt to tell Scott that the parade was on again. Impossible, grumbled Scott; most of the troops had been dispersed and could not be quickly reassembled. Meanwhile, the crowds grew restless and impatient at seeing only local militia pass in review. By strenuous efforts Scott's staff got enough troops mustered back into line for the parade to resume. While the men and artillery marched and maneuvered smartly through clouds of dust, Buchanan appeased Tyler with an apologetic note.[11]

What did it say about the prospects for peace when the government could not even manage a traditional display honoring the Father of the Country in his namesake city? The *Tribune* blamed the fiasco on Buchanan's "characteristic vacillation," and the mood remained tense. The next morning Lincoln slipped into the city. In the hall at Willard's, where he came to stay, the peace convention was unraveling from the same tug-of-war between advocates of compromise and ultras that plagued Congress. "Good nature & masterly inactivity," said a Massachusetts delegate, "is the policy till Lincoln is inaugurated." He got the inactivity, if not the good nature. On February 6 the convention formed a committee composed of one delegate from each state to review all proposals and report on those "right, necessary, and proper to restore harmony and preserve the Union." For nine days the convention marked time while the committee haggled over a report, which finally reached them on the 15th.[12]

The sudden death of temporary chairman John C. Wright on the 13th cast a pall over proceedings, though privately ultras welcomed any loss of conservative votes. "Among so many *very old gentlemen*," observed an Ohio cynic, "such an *actuary* as Mr. Wright would tell us, the chances are that every sixty days will improve the *quality* of the convention." Congress in general and Tom Corwin's committee in particular waited impatiently for the convention to produce something, as did the Virginia convention. The report that finally appeared on the 15th with two alternatives bore a striking resemblance to Crittenden's measures and bogged down at once in debate as extremists on both sides assailed its provisions.[13]

Driven by the rage of Virginia's James Seddon, with his "hatred of all forms of Northern life," and the implacable stance of the Massachusetts and other northern ultras, the sessions dragged on into the late hours most nights. In vain did moderates seek to draw extremists to some middle ground. "I *hate* that word secession, because it is a cheat!" shouted an exasperated James Guthrie of Kentucky. "Call things by their right names! The

Southern States have . . . originated a *revolution*." The rhetoric was as flowery as it was futile; even ultras despaired of the brethren faltering. "I am afraid of everybody," admitted one. "I would not trust *myself* in that damned Conference."[14]

For a week the delegates stalled out over the Guthrie report. Some agreed with Doniphan of Missouri that "The Convention cannot move a wheel until Lincoln gets here. If he is under Seward's guidance, we will compromise in a day—if he is under the Chase and Greely [*sic*] faction, then we may go home and tell Gabriel to blow for the nation will be dissolved in a few days or months at most." For that reason they went eagerly to see Lincoln after his arrival, but the interview gave little solace to moderates. On the 26th ultras from both sides, ignoring the pleas of border state delegates, voted down a crucial section restoring the Missouri Compromise line. Frantic efforts the next day produced a reversal of this vote and a confused, lame endorsement of what amounted to a cumbersome variation on the Crittenden proposals.[15]

When the convention adjourned on the 27th, Scott honored them with a hundred-gun salute. The proposals went to Congress, which studiously ignored them. Moderates went home glumly, ultras with pleased smirks. "We *did* one thing," said Massachusetts ultra John Murray Forbes: "Talked three weeks & amused the readers of the Tribune. Not such very bad eggs to hatch after all."

"THE PEACE CONFERENCE is like the Senate," observed Charles Sumner with grim satisfaction, "—powerless to mature any system of harmony."[16]

Harmony was hard to come by in either house as Congress, like so many others, waited hopefully for the peace convention to do what that body had failed so conspicuously to do: find a way out. Meanwhile, the members continued to talk at one another. In the gloom of that desolate winter clashing voices did not so much echo as ricochet about both chambers, aimless, futile missiles seeking targets they could never reach. The stalemate seemed as inexorable in February as it had in December, the prospects for compromise even more bleak. For all the ideas and proposals that had paraded through Washington, some version of the Crittenden plan remained the last best hope for compromise.

The problem was that the compromise remained far more popular with the country than with Congress. Sumner voiced the feelings of most ultras by dismissing the proposals as "wrong in every respect, in every line, in every word." Desperate moderates like William B. Stokes of Tennessee offered to "vote for any compromise . . . to meet the crisis." He was not the only border state man enraged that "a few conspiring madmen, ambitious, disappointed politicians, men who are seeking for power, can band themselves together and say this Union must be destroyed at their bidding." But even Stokes conceded that no known plan of compromise would appease South Carolina.[17]

News of the fledgling government at Montgomery only deepened fears that the secession virus had spread too far to be contained. Even those who agreed with William Kellogg of Illinois that "The introduction of . . . slavery into politics is the source of all our troubles," saw that another peril had become more immediate and lethal. "This heresy of secession was in full development before slavery . . . became a part of our national politics," warned John W. Killinger of Pennsylvania. ". . . Any compromise . . . must be accompanied with a distinct renunciation of secession; otherwise, the security which we thus provide for the present will guaranty us no indemnity for the future." James Humphrey of New York agreed that "We cannot avert secession by compromise, because that would be the most distinct recognition of secession as a right."[18]

More and more moderates sensed the fatal trap into which the crisis had led them. All the compromise proposals and most of the debate had centered on slavery, but once secession emerged there was no way to deal with both issues at the same time. Moreover, the people trying to arrange a compromise, moderates from the North and the border states, were not the source of the trouble. Any deal they cut had to be approved by ultras from both sides, but the Republicans refused to endorse *any* form of compromise, and border state moderates had no assurance that they could sell any plan to the cotton states. Where, then, was the common ground on which agreement could be reached?

Robert Hatton saw the trap looming before him and lashed out at both sides. "The leaders of the disunionists of the cotton States," he charged, "in their reckless selfishness . . . are *practically* our enemies, as truly as are the most unprincipled fanatics of the North." He shared with William Allen of Ohio the conviction that "The idea of peaceable secession, however desirable . . . is . . . utterly impossible" and warned his colleagues of the fate awaiting them. "If, on account of our wicked perverseness and want of patriotism . . . revolution and civil war ensue . . . we will be pointed at by our fellow-citizens, who will say, as in shame we avert our faces, 'He was a member of the Thirty-Sixth Congress!' "[19]

Shame was never in short supply in Congress, but John Carey of Ohio, one of the oldest House members, saw something more sinister abroad in the land. "There is a fast, young-America feeling which pushes us into all the evils under which we labor," he complained. "Too many persons . . . are trying to live at the expense of somebody else." In vain did Henry Burnett of

Kentucky remind the House that "the country wants action more than speech-making." The truth was that no one knew what action to take beyond familiar fare such as private bills and public appropriations. To the distress of men like Carey, these bills continued to slip quietly through Congress beneath the rhetoric of stalemate.[20]

So did bills of larger import unrelated to the national crisis, thanks to the absence of so many southern Democrats. Kansas entered the Union, and the Colorado, Nevada, and Dakota territories were created with no mention of slavery. The slumbering tariff bill sprang to life with a slew of amendments and was quickly signed by the president from Pennsylvania. Two ancient sources of corruption and intrigue were reformed when Congress revised the patent laws and created the Government Printing Office to eliminate the blatant jobbery of private partisan printers. But the force bill intended to strengthen the president's hand in the crisis was strangled along with the Pacific railroad bill.[21]

The force bill extended the Militia Act of 1795 to the federal government, allowing the president to put down an insurrection. Benjamin Stanton of Ohio, the chairman of the House military committee, introduced it on February 17 as "the most harmless thing in the world," but moderates and border state members objected that any such bill would drive the Virginia convention to secession. "This, sir, is a war measure, not only mad and desperate in its designs, but a measure in direct violation of the Constitution," protested William E. Simms of Kentucky. "This cry of coercion is the most baseless and absurd," countered William Howard of Michigan. ". . . If a Government has not the power of self-defense, it is no Government at all." After a long wrangle the House on the 26th voted 100–74 to postpone the bill.[22]

When the peace convention concluded with little to show for its efforts, despondent House moderates made one last drive at securing some version of the Crittenden compromise. In their path stood the savvy Tom Corwin, who had conferred with Lincoln and determined to offer as a pacifier a revised version of the constitutional amendment guaranteeing slavery where it already existed. By a deft parliamentary maneuver he managed to close debate on the report of his own committee, which Dan Sickles tried to keep alive as a vehicle for getting the Crittenden plan on the floor. But radical Republicans filibustered Corwin's move until all sides agreed to vote on everything the next day.[23]

On the 27th the House dissolved into pandemonium as bill after bill came up and was voted down. From the gallery Charles Francis Adams, Jr., raged at the "indecision and lack of force of the old owl of a Speaker. The fate of the country seemed hanging in the balance, and the dolt had not the force to drive business ahead." But stronger men than William Pennington might have faltered in the confusion. After defeating the proposal for a constitutional convention, 108–74, the House took its first vote on Crittenden's plan and routed it 113–80, thanks to a solid Republican vote. Corwin managed to get the declaratory resolutions in its first section passed, 136–53, but the constitutional amendment failed to secure a two-thirds vote and died 123–71. The peace convention report was not even dignified by a vote.[24]

The next day the hapless Pennington struggled again to clear the crowds off the floor so business could proceed. A vigorous effort by Republican David Kilgore of Indiana got the constitutional amendment back on the floor. After a motion to reconsider passed 128–65, four Republicans switched votes and three abstained, enabling the measure to get a two-thirds majority 133–65. There was little else to cheer. William A. Howard submitted a report for the special committee of five blasting secession and dismissing the rationales for it as "fallacious, deceitful, and false, if not traitorous." Secession would "not only destroy the noble fabric of our fathers, but plunge the world into barbarism and anarchy by rendering all government impossible. . . . We are not Mexicans. We are unaccustomed to violent disruptions and peaceful reconstructions of our Government. The Anglo-Saxon race do not throw away the greatest of all benefits in a mere fit of frenzy."[25]

Two members issued strong dissents, showing the committee as divided as the House itself. From this unpleasantness the members escaped gratefully to the civil appropriations bill and other matters, leaving the rest of the Corwin report for the following day, March 1. The Senate was at the same impassse with only a few days remaining in the session. Henry Wilson of Massachusetts railed against the southern conspiracy; Simon Cameron and John Hale found diversion in lambasting the appropriation for the Smithsonian Institution as folly and waste. While a procession of other bills received earnest attention, Lazarus Powell made another futile attempt to get the Crittenden plan on the floor. Crittenden himself tried to force a vote on the peace convention plan and had a testy exchange with Hale, who tried to sidetrack it.[26]

The deadlock could not have been worse, nor the sense of frustration greater, among those seeking conciliation. As February closed, neither the president nor Congress was any nearer a solution than in December. Never in the history of the Republic had the separation of powers been more separate or more powerless. To partisans on both sides, never had the chasm between them seemed greater or more ominous. Samuel Curtis of Iowa thought he saw what was coming. "The breach has grown too wide and too deep to be remedied by threats or denunciations," he said. "Settlement or civil war is now the dilemma. . . . Liberty must subscribe to law or anarchy follows and despotism after. Many are now beginning to favor a stronger government. If the republicans break up and democracy resume the ascendance, the danger is that they will supply anarchy with a powerful military government."[27]

CHARLESTON TRIED TO MAINTAIN at least a veneer of the normal social whirl. The Cecilia and Jockey societies scrapped their usual winter balls, but race week went on as usual, opening on Wednesday, the 6th, beneath sunny skies. Governor Pickens joined the crowds flocking to the track. An amateur troupe tried to fill the entertainment vacuum with a production of *Lady of Lyons*, but it was difficult to promote gaiety in a city that had come to resemble an armed camp. That same Wednesday Pickens ordered all posts and batteries readied for a forty-eight-hour bombardment. Three days later, on the last day of the races, he proclaimed martial law over Sullivans Island, thereby increasing expectations that Fort Sumter would be stormed any day.[28]

Business was as dull as society, the shops and hotels were lethargic, and the price of cotton was low. Mail trickled into Charleston only once a week, and no one knew how long the service would continue. On Washington's Birthday the city mustered a gala parade and cannon salutes, but the pageantry only reminded everyone of the threat looming in the harbor. Nerves remained prickly, ears tuned keenly to every rumor flying about the city. "We are here in such a disturbed condition," said James Petigru, "that the things that are going to happen in a week are as uncertain as if they belonged to the distant future." No one caught the darkest mood better than an upcountry farmer. "I fear that we will have a long Civil, Bloody war," he said, "—and perhaps an inserections [*sic*] among the slaves—The Lord save us from such a horrid war."[29]

"About the only amusement in Charleston at present is *The Mercury*," said Charles Brigham, the *Tribune* reporter who was himself a source of keen interest, if not pleasure, for the locals. Early in February his artful dodging came to an abrupt end, though his pursuers never realized it. Having already arrested half a dozen wrong suspects, the authorities seized Brigham and hauled him before Pickens and his advisers. Judge Magràth handled the interrogation but failed to crack Brigham's cool facade. Finally the authorities concluded that he was a spy for the federal government and put him on trial for one day lasting from 9 a.m. to 9 p.m.[30]

Brigham was turned over to a well-known criminal lawyer, Alexander H. Brown, for questioning. Brown grilled the prisoner relentlessly but could not break him. "Mr. Brigham," he said at last, "while I think you are all right, this is a peculiar emergency, and you must see that, under the circumstances, it will be necessary for you to leave the South at once." Brigham protested, then yielded gracefully to his fate. The conversation grew more convivial over a bottle of wine. "By the way," asked Brown, "do you know who is writing the letters from here to *The Tribune*?" Brigham shook his head and commented blandly that the local papers said the letters were pure fiction. No, they were real, countered Brown. The man had constantly eluded them, and he asked Brigham to find out for him when he returned to New York.

Brigham said he would not be a spy but would learn what he could. As he prepared to leave, a local detective named Shoubac growled, "You haven't fooled *me*, if you have Brown." But Brigham was allowed to leave, and Charles Dana, who already had two other *Tribune* men in Charleston, soon sent a third. None of them knew the others, and all wrote their letters in elaborate codes to commercial addresses in New York. There Brigham added his own touch to make the letters consistent. The reports continued, and Charleston's authorities never knew they had bagged the hated *Tribune* reporter.[31]

For Pickens too, the ordeal was nearly over. Since December he had danced gingerly between exhortations to assault Sumter and to avoid hostilities. As February closed, the Stars and Stripes still waved defiantly in the harbor, but he was about to hand the problem over to Confederate authorities. He masked his gratitude well, not only for the weight lifted from him but also for the freedom to resume the more congenial role of fire-eater. Sumter fever raged as virulently as ever in Charleston; all month long Pickens had been showered with advice on how and when to reduce the fort. Hayne's return from Washington with news of his rebuff increased the pressure on Pickens to act. Even Brigham urged Washington to send reinforcements and risk a fight now rather than wait until South Carolina was prepared and could launch an attack at will.[32]

The truce had served Pickens well. While work on the fortifications and the floating battery pressed steadily forward, complained Brigham, the garrison had "for upward of a month, every day and every hour in the day, been compelled to see transported within pistol shot of its battlements the huge engines that were to be used against them the moment South Carolina could say she was ready. . . . These things have been well known to the Federal Government, and yet it had done nothing." Ultras hounded Pickens to order the long-awaited attack, and resolutions to that effect, offered repeatedly in the convention, were beaten back until it finally adjourned on the 5th.[33]

At heart Pickens was more eager to load the gun than to pull the trigger. Fortunately for him, the demands for action were offset by pleas from Jefferson Davis, John Tyler, Robert Toombs, Joe Brown of Georgia, and others outside the state to maintain the status quo. At home the venerable Alfred

Huger denounced the madness of "lavishing Human life upon the unprofitable result" of storming Sumter. To escape this dilemma, Pickens hit on a shrewd tactic: He would huff and puff the threat of seizing the fort to appease the ultras and also goad Montgomery into relieving him of responsibility. Much as he longed to make history, he shrank from making a decision that might prove fatal.

On the 7th Pickens wrote William Porcher Miles in Montgomery, "There is danger ahead unless you give us immediately a strong organized government to take jurisdiction of all military defense." Two days later he told Tyler that South Carolina might yield to the new Confederate government if it assumed authority on the question. On Tuesday, the 12th, he telegraphed Toombs, "I hope to be ready by Friday night, and think I am prepared to take the fort or to silence it." An alarmed Howell Cobb wired Pickens the same evening that the provisional Congress had taken charge. In a lengthy reply the governor urged that the fort be seized before Lincoln assumed office and warned that he would not stand idle if the new government hesitated. He had thrust the burden neatly back on them.[34]

IN RICHMOND the Virginia convention waited impatiently for news from the opposing poles of the peace convention and the Montgomery government. The delegates believed, as did leaders North and South, that whichever way Virginia went, most of the border states would follow. But Virginia was divided and did not know which way to go. John S. Preston of South Carolina arrived to exhort the delegates toward secession and was surprised at what he found. "All are under the strange delusion that the Southern Confederacy is to be voluntarily dissolved & the former Union reconstructed," he reported. "It is this illusion . . . which prevents action by either party. . . . All believe it may come. I labour day and night to remove this idea."[35]

The state that had given the nation more presidents than any other chose what one delegate called "the ablest body of men that I ever saw assembled." John Echols saw them split into three broad factions: "Precipitators, Fair Union men & absolute unconditional submissionists." In one respect, however, Virginia's convention resembled every other assembly that had taken up the great national question: The members talked much and did little while waiting for someone else to act. They got small encouragement from their delegates at the peace conference. Only William Rives and George Summers held out any hope for results; the others reported only gloom.[36]

"The only good which the Convention had done thus far," wrote a *Tribune* reporter in Richmond, "is that it has done nothing, after sitting nearly two weeks." The rhetoric allowed old divisions between the northwest and the rest of the state to surface with renewed animosity. Unionists hoping for some sign from Lincoln on his pilgrimage to Washington were not only disappointed but offended. One moderate who had known Lincoln in Congress called his speeches en route "revolting" and asked how he could shake the hand of a man who, on the steps of Independence Hall, promised to extend the principles of the Declaration of Independence "not only to the white race, but to the slaves?"[37]

After the peace convention adjourned with little to show for its endeavors, John Tyler hurried back to take a seat in the convention. "I bring you," he said sourly of the peace convention bill, ". . . a poor, rickety, and disconnected affair, not worthy of your acceptance." James Seddon and Edmund Ruffin also came to town to add their voices to the ultras' cause. Ruffin could not stay long, vowing to "be out of Va before Lincoln's inauguration & so will avoid being . . . under his government even for an hour." On the last night of the month a band serenaded the three men at their hotel, and each responded with a speech.[38]

The failure of the peace convention staggered the moderates and emboldened the secessionists. Jeremiah Morton denounced Seward for using the crisis to advance his own political interests. "It is shrewdly suspected," he charged, ". . . that there is an organization progressing throughout this Union, that looks to the keeping of the Border States within this Confederacy, and that the High Priest of that new party is to be Wm. H. Seward."

ON THE EVENING AFTER HIS INAUGURAL Jefferson Davis hosted his first levee in Montgomery. The ladies transformed Estelle Hall into a garden of flowers and ferns for the crowd of elegantly dressed ladies and gentlemen who streamed in all night to shake Davis's hand before going to the theater to dance or listen to music. In the streets bands played while town people and country folk alike celebrated the birth of the new republic. Every house from Exchange Street to the capitol gleamed with lights, as did the theater. Hardly a soul of any importance missed the levee except Tom Cobb, who sat dutifully in his dreary room working on legislative bills past one in the morning.[39]

By the next morning the cheering had given way to cold reality. Robert Toombs had learned by telegram that his daughter was seriously ill and left town at once. Robert Barnwell Rhett, already despondent by having been denied high place in the new government, received word that his twelve-year-old daughter had contracted scarlet fever. Before he could act, another telegram informed him of her death. He was doomed to more disappointment as Davis revealed his cabinet choices. No state received more than one place, and Davis was known to favor Robert W. Barnwell for the state portfolio. Someone asked Lawrence Keitt if this did not make Rhett long to be in Abraham's bosom. "Rhett had rather be in Davis's bosom just now," quipped Keitt.[40]

Davis could not get Barnwell because the South Carolina delegation united in asking that Christopher Memminger be given treasury. The offer of state went instead to Toombs, who accepted reluctantly. For the war department Davis wanted his old friend Clement Clay of Alabama, but Clay's poor health forced him to decline and the post was tendered to Leroy P. Walker, whom Davis did not even know. The navy department went to Stephen Mallory of Florida, who had chaired the Senate's Naval Affairs Committee. For attorney general Davis chose Judah P. Benjamin of Louisiana, and for postmaster general John H. Reagan of Texas. Of this group, only Mallory had any experience in the area of his new position.

As consolation Rhett was made chairman of the committee drafting the permanent constitution, with Tom Cobb as his secretary. They completed the work in seventeen days and presented it to the provisional congress on the 26th. The new constitution paid homage to its illustrious ancestor while offering some improvements. The president and vice president received six-year terms but could not run again. The president was given unconditional power of removal over major and minor officers, and could veto separate items in appropriation bills. Congress could appropriate money only by a two-thirds vote of both houses unless the funds were requested by the president, and it could grant cabinet officers seats in either house to discuss departmental matters.[41]

Other changes reflected the sensitivities of the cotton states. The preamble acknowledged state rights with the phrase "We the people of the Confederate States, each state acting in its sovereign capacity. . . ." The right to own slaves in both states and territories was protected, but in a hotly debated move the foreign slave trade was explicitly prohibited. Congress could not pass any law impairing the right to own slaves as property. Neither could it impose a protective tariff or appropriate funds for internal improvements. Other provisions tightened restrictions on expenditures and required the post office to be self-supporting after two years. This was to be a frugal, downsize government that would not make its largess a trough for the feeding of politicians and parasites.

The new government set up shop on the second floor of a building at Commerce and Market streets. Handmade signs pinned to the doors identified the department offices. Davis occupied one of these, working at a worn desk in an office furnished with a sofa, chairs, and a table covered with an oil-cloth. Above him hung an odd gallery of portraits: Clay, Calhoun, Webster, and Napoleon. The president endured a constant stream of visitors as well as the first wave of applications for office. He longed for Varina, who did not reach Montgomery until the month's end. In her absence he tried to be agreeable by dining every day at the Exchange Hotel with his fellow statesmen, making a rare, if clumsy, effort at small talk and political palaver.[42]

As the new government assumed its first crude form, the mood shifted toward business as usual. A cranky Alexander Stephens admitted being "bored to death with company and calls" and with the debates in congress. Feeling overworked and convinced that Buchanan would never recognize the Confederacy or sign a treaty with it, he declined Davis's request that he head a new commission to negotiate with Washington. Instead Davis chose Georgian Martin J. Crawford along with John Forsyth of Alabama and A. B. Roman of Louisiana and sent them on a fishing expedition to Washington.[43]

Inside the government and out, the backbiting began in earnest. Toombs could not resist twitting Howell Cobb and on one occasion said gleefully that Cobb as treasury secretary had done more for secession than any man by leaving the Treasury so bare. "He did not," said Toombs, "even leave old 'Buck' two quarters to put on his eyes when he died." Cobb suffered these barbs in silence. More lethal hits took place behind the victim's back, a favorite target being Davis. No one was more unsparing than Mary Chesnut's uncle Judge Thomas Jefferson Withers, who was a South Carolina delegate. The cantankerous Withers railed against the corruption of congress, Cobb, Toombs, and others, but nothing roused his rancor more than an act leasing a house for Davis. When Withers dismissed the people who had sent him to Montgomery as fools and knaves, even James Chesnut lost patience and retorted, "Then you ought to go home—if I thought as you do of my con-stituents I would not keep office an hour." The judge's ranting and the carping of others did not fool Mary Chesnut. "Every body wants office," she noted, "& every body raises an outcry at the corruption of those who get the offices."[44]

Mary too felt restless and uneasy. Having endured what she called "some terrible matrimonial squalls," she took offense at a letter from William Trescot with some anecdotes she considered "too *frenchy*" and refused to reply. She hesitated even going into supper with Governor Andrew Moore because "the old sinner has been making himself ridiculous" with an actress then in town. She found some consolation in the company of John L. Man-ning, the wealthy former governor of South Carolina, and Stephen Mallory, despite his reputation as a dissolute, and in other admirers. Bored by the parade of human folly, she mused, "I never was handsome. I wonder what my *attraction* was for men did fall in love with me wherever I went."[45]

Tom Cobb combated his homesickness by burying himself in work. He could scarcely bring himself to eat, complaining that "the filth at the hotel is almost starving me." The weather grew oppressively warm, the temper of the congress shorter, and old frictions among the leading figures emerged anew. Cobb opposed Davis at every turn. When the president vetoed a law on the African slave trade, Cobb vowed to get it passed over his head, "It will do my very soul good," he said grimly, "to *rebuke* him at the outset of his *vetoing*."[46]

Above all the complaints loomed the shadow of Sumter. The leadership of the new government regarded Pickens as a loose cannon and were eager to get the crisis out of his hands. On February 15 the provisional congress authorized the president to take all necessary steps to acquire possession of Forts Sumter and Pickens through negotiation or force. Davis sent a copy of the resolution to Governor Pickens along with Major W. H. C. Whiting, an experienced engineer, who was ordered to examine the works at Charleston and inventory available armaments. Pickens welcomed his arrival as tangible evidence that the decision was no longer his.[47]

But not entirely. On the 27th, acknowledging Whiting's presence, Pickens could not resist giving Davis one last nudge. "In the mean time," he said, "I will go on with the same activity as ever in preparing our defenses and our men for any event that may arise. We would desire to be informed if when thoroughly prepared to take the fort shall we do so, or shall we await your order; and shall we demand the surrender, or will that demand be made by you?"[48]

Tom Cobb took heart at the government's move to take charge in Charleston. "The feeling gains strength here," he reported, "every day that there will be no war." But Pickens had not yet been heard from, and Mary Chesnut, for one, scoffed at reports saying Davis had told the governor to use his discretion. *"Pickens' discretion!"* she said, sneering at what she deemed an oxymoron.[49]

NEVER HAD ROBERT ANDERSON suffered such a winter of discontent. In his long career he had endured turmoil in the field, dissension in the ranks, and the coils of army bureaucracy, but Sumter was like nothing he had experienced. To be on the short end of a siege was bad enough, but to be surrounded by one's own countrymen and not know whether the future held war or peace made it bizarre, dreamlike. "God grant that these people may not make the attack which they have so long threatened," he wrote with deep emotion.[50]

The men were holding up surprisingly well, turning their tensions away from one another and toward a loathing of the Charleston authorities for the petty slights they imposed. Along with the shortage of food, the garrison had run out of whiskey and tobacco, forcing troops to chew spun cotton. Once they managed to buy some tobacco while getting the mail at Fort Johnson only to have local militia confiscate it. Mail had been opened, the personal belongings left behind at Moultrie unreturned, and now the women and children were gone, leaving them alone in the damp, dreary dungeon of the fort.[51]

On February 8 some photographers were permitted to come over and take group pictures of the officers. One of them proved later to be a spy, but no one cared much what was seen inside the fort. From some northern papers the men learned that plays dramatizing Sumter were on the boards in Boston and New York. The sight of their names on playbills and the image of actors spouting mock heroics gave them a few sardonic laughs. Lieutenant Jeff Davis had to suffer interminable ribbing about his name. Captain Edward McCready of Charleston, an old friend of Sumter's officers, wrote urging them to change sides and join the Confederacy. No one bothered to reply.[52]

Privately Anderson agonized over what to do if war should break out. He was neither clever nor sly enough to tease out a solution to the conflict between his sense of duty and his southern loyalties. His wife, Eliza, had made her choice. When Henry William Ravenel, a friendly Carolina planter, called on her in New York, she told him bluntly that she would "never be found in the same Confederacy with *South Carolina*," that "for the first time in my life, I was ashamed of being a *Southerner*." In reporting this to her husband, she added tartly, "I, for one, will *not* be satisfied if you are made to leave . . . Fort Sumter to the Carolinians. . . . *I* would make it a special request—to let you blow it up, sky high, on leaving it."[53]

Anderson admired his wife's spirit, as he did that of the Reverend S. W. Crawford, his surgeon's father, who assured the major that his son would "defend the Stars & Stripes to the last; or make them his winding sheet. If he would not he is no son of mine." Anderson was aware that some of his officers, notably young Crawford and Abner Doubleday, harbored doubts about the staunchness of his own loyalty because of his southern roots. They could not fathom the anguish in his heart over the tangle of loyalties that held him prisoner much as Sumter held them all captive. How could they know what it meant to be a Kentuckian in this ordeal, to believe in slavery but not in the course of those who defended it?

Whatever his own conflicts, Anderson could not perform his duty without clear direction, but he got little help from Washington. He had no way of knowing what debates, if any, were taking place in the government about his situation or even how much of what he wrote actually reached the War Department until a reply came. Lieutenant Hall returned from the capital on the 10th with no news of any import. Doggedly Anderson peppered Washington with questions for which no answers were forthcoming. The days passed, supplies kept dwindling (most of his own wool socks had gone to make cartridge bags), the Carolinians continued to improve their works, and still no word came. What was he to do? What in God's name was he to do?54

At the very least he could make Sumter as impregnable as possible. The front gate was secured, and most of the guns were mounted with improvised block and tackle. One ten-inch columbiad was mounted as a mortar on the parade and aimed at Charleston. Lacking mortars, Anderson rigged four eight-inch columbiads as substitutes by laying heavy timber at the bottom of a trench and setting the guns in notches cut at equal intervals. To repel an assault, Truman Seymour put a cannon cartridge in the center of a barrel filled with paving stones. When rolled off the parapet, his "flying fougasse" would explode just above the ground and spray stones in all directions. A successful demonstration, watched closely from afar, led a Charleston paper to speak ominously of a devastating "infernal machine." Charges were also put inside standing piles of stone to scatter them, and crude hand grenades were improvised.55

But day after day the ring of fortifications around Sumter grew stronger, and the Carolinians had all the labor and materials needed for their work. The iron bombproof shielding the batteries at Morris Island looked finished. A mortar arrived to reinforce the guns at Fort Johnson, the works at Cummings Point were being extended, and the floating battery neared completion. The Carolina guard boats ventured nearer the fort; when one got too close on the morning of the 12th, a sentinel warned it off with a shot, and Anderson sent Pickens a note of protest. This was precisely the kind of incident he feared most, an act of carelessness or defiance that could trigger hostilities.56

On the 22nd Castle Pinckney fired a salute of thirteen guns to honor Washington's Birthday. At noon Anderson returned the compliment with a salute from the guns on the barbette. Like everything else that winter, Washington's Birthday took on a bizarre character. Each side had something very different to celebrate, yet never had the day been observed in more funereal gloom. Everything Washington stood for was under attack; everything for which he was honored was coming unraveled. He was the father of a country splitting in two (or more) factions, like a family torn asunder by violent disagreements.

The next day Holt wrote at last, reaffirming that Anderson was to stand

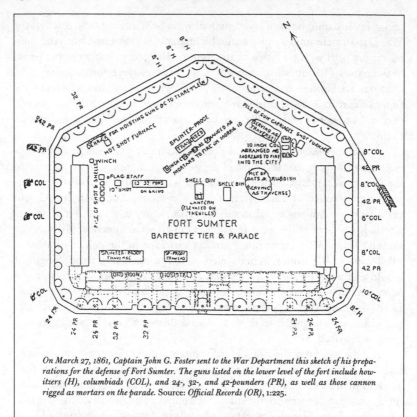

On March 27, 1861, Captain John G. Foster sent to the War Department this sketch of his preparations for the defense of Fort Sumter. The guns listed on the lower level of the fort include howitzers (H), columbiads (COL), and 24-, 32-, and 42-pounders (PR), as well as those cannon rigged as mortars on the parade. Source: Official Records (OR), 1:225.

strictly on the defensive and avoid a clash by all means "compatible with the safety of your command." He was to forbear the launch and the approach of the floating battery unless it posed a direct threat, just as he endured the growing fortifications around him. Holt told him of the new Confederate government, rumors of which had already reached Sumter, and reminded him that the peace convention still toiled. Everyone hoped for a peaceful resolution.[57]

The formation of the Confederate government disturbed Anderson. He had little fear of the South Carolina militia, which played at war in the earnest but inept way of amateurs, but any shift of responsibility to Confederate officers changed the whole situation. They would be professionals, many of them old friends whose abilities he knew and admired. He had taken the measure of Pickens and had some sense of whom and what he was dealing with, but if Pickens handed the problem over to a new government, that insight became useless. Gloomily Anderson realized that he was pawn in a game he did not know, and with a change in both southern command and administrations in Washington, he would no longer even know the players.

"My course has been," he wrote his friend Crittenden, "to pray daily to God, to give me a clear understanding of my duty and to give me strength of purpose & resolution fully to perform it." Circumstances were changing the major's mind on what that duty must be. The guns at Fort Moultrie had begun practicing to find their ranges on the main channel. On the 26th Captain Foster pulled down a third temporary building to use the wood for fuel. He had only two left, along with twelve unused gun carriages and a small store of new lumber set aside for emergencies. Holt's letter told Anderson little other than that the government was either still undecided on a course of action or simply marking time until its term of office expired.[58]

All along Anderson had believed he was a pawn in the game of political expediency. He accepted the role, like the good soldier he was, and the personal toll it had taken on him as the price demanded by duty. But the shadow of war loomed ever larger over him, and he did not know how well or poorly Washington grasped the actual situation. With the untested Lincoln administration coming to office and the local situation on the brink of radical change, the time had come to spell out the realities in graphic detail. The major summoned his officers and asked them to submit in writing an estimate of how large a force was required to relieve Sumter. On the last day of February he sent these to the War Department along with his own views.[59]

Crawford said that at least 2,000 men were needed against state troops and twice that number against a Confederate government force, plus naval support. Jeff Davis considered 3,000 regulars and six ships a bare minimum. Doubleday agreed that 3,000 could handle the locals but 10,000 were required to face reinforcements from the Confederacy. Foster figured 3,000 regulars or 10,000 militia; Hall 3,500 regulars with seven ships; Meade at least 5,000 men; Talbot 1,000 to 3,500; and Seymour at least 20,000. Snyder's estimate ranged from 4,000 to 9,000, depending on the plan of operation.

Anderson believed most of his officers were too optimistic. "I confess," he wrote, "that I would not be willing to risk my reputation in an attempt to throw reenforcements into this harbour, within the time for our relief rendered necessary by the limited supply of our provisions . . . with a force of less than twenty thousand good and well disciplined men." He knew full well that this information would come as an unpleasant surprise to the government, but he had to impress upon it the reality of the situation. That was his duty, and he would not shirk from performing it, come what may.

PART THREE

The Battle over Fort Sumter

MARCH

CHAPTER SEVENTEEN

Last Gasps and First Breaths

I begin to recognize the fact that the Union is at an end—that treason has triumphed, and that our once glorious and well beloved Union is overthrown; and I am trying slowly, reluctantly, sadly to reconcile myself to it. The attempt to break up this Union is the most atrocious piece of political wickedness the world ever saw, and it is very, very bitter to have to accept the fact that that attempt has succeeded. . . . The men who had the power and means to maintain it, and failed to use them, deserve death. History will consign them to everlasting obloquy. Thank God, the responsibility is not with you. Surely no man ever assumed the reins of government beset by such complicated and oppressive difficulties as have surrounded you.

—Orville H. Browning (to Lincoln)
March 26, 1861[1]

FOR THREE MONTHS the walls of both chambers of Congress resounded with rhetoric, and now only three days remained. Through these tortuous months torrents of words cascaded against the cold marble surfaces and ricocheted about the rooms, missing more ears than they caught. The flood flowed almost without interruption: the rhetoric of melting conciliation and stubborn defiance, passion and anxiety, gloom and doom, fear and prophecy, logic and abstraction, accusation and vindication, scripture and dogma. Far more wished to speak than cared to listen; few let the flood of words penetrate the fortress of their own beliefs. Congress knew not what else to do, so it did what it had always done best: It talked and talked and talked still more while the nation came apart and speaker after speaker complained that the nation was coming apart while they talked.

If rhetoric alone could have saved the Union, Congress and the peace convention could have more than done the job. Both forums overflowed with stirring eloquence and appeals that moved men deeply but changed not a single position. No middle ground could be found because there was none to be had. Negotiation could not succeed because there was nothing to negotiate, on either slavery or secession. On these intractable issues opponents remained as far apart in March as they had been in November.

"This Government cannot be permitted to fall to pieces," implored a shaken Benjamin Stanton. Both houses made a last frantic effort to avert that disaster. Tom Corwin watched the House scuttle the rest of his committee bill. The New Mexico part was tabled, 115–71; the fugitive slave component passed, 92–83, but a companion bill compelling governors to extradite fugitives triggered an angry debate over state rights and was buried, 125–48. An attempt to get the peace convention resolution on the floor failed, though bills organizing the Nevada and Dakota territories sailed through, along with one protecting the rights of citizens who discovered guano deposits. Little else got done beyond the postal act and some housekeeping duties. The House adjourned with nothing to show beyond Corwin's lone amendment protecting slavery where it already existed.[2]

The Senate lingered longer and louder. Crittenden labored to get either the peace convention proposal or his own plan on the floor for the required three readings before adjournment. When Douglas moved consideration of the Corwin amendment on the 1st, however, Crittenden supported him. "I go . . . not for this resolution or that resolution," he declared, "but any . . . proposition that will pacify the country." But he could not pacify the Senate itself. Although he won support from George Pugh of Ohio and Edward Baker of Oregon, a close friend of Lincoln's, the adversaries of compromise took refuge behind procedural dodges to squander most of the day despite efforts by Pennsylvania's Bigler to suspend the rules.[3]

On Saturday, the 2nd, the Senate sat from noon until midnight in what moderates hoped would be a last push for compromise. Instead they got the theater of the absurd. Sumner confounded everyone by arguing that the motion had not had its second reading because of his objection and moved successfully to correct the *Journal*. The rest of the afternoon was lost when Jo Lane of Oregon insisted on making a speech defending his southern views and Andrew Johnson roasted him in response. The galleries grew so unruly that they were cleared after a lengthy debate. It was six o'clock when Douglas called up the House resolution before a hungry, surly body.[4]

Without the second reading the amendment could not pass unless the Senate held a Sunday session. Crittenden moved to hold one, saying, "If we may help an ox out of the pit on Sunday, we shall be excused for trying to help a nation out of its difficulty." More wrangling followed on the sanctity of the Sabbath before the motion was defeated. Bigler and Douglas then managed to get the rules suspended so that the amendment did not require readings on three consecutive days. Realizing with Crittenden that nothing else had a chance of passing, Douglas led the charge to secure the Corwin amendment. More time was lost when Mason of Virginia objected and Lane spoke feelingly on the number of ladies waiting to enter the still-closed galleries.[5]

Douglas survived these obstacles only to confront a bizarre demand by Pugh to correct the sloppy grammar of the amendment. "If we cannot preserve the Constitution intact . . . or preserve the Union," said Pugh blandly, "shall we preserve at least the purity of the English language?" Aware that any such change would require House approval, for which there was no time, Douglas and Crittenden pleaded against it, the latter arguing, "I prefer bad English expressing a good thing, to good English expressing a bad thing." But the Pugh amendment carried, only to be reconsidered on a motion by Pugh himself, who wanted Crittenden's plan. On this question the hungry, irritable senators, some fortified with bourbon, unleashed more oratory.

Spectators rushed into the reopened galleries, adding their voices to the chaos on the floor. After quashing a motion to adjourn, the senators voted again on Pugh's amendment and this time rejected it, 20–17. With the Corwin amendment back on the floor, Pugh moved to substitute the Crittenden plan. Another flood of rhetoric washed through the chamber. "This is not a question of compromise," said Zachariah Chandler of Michigan, "this is a question whether we have or have not a Government. . . . If the right is conceded to any State to secede . . . I would rather join the Camanches [*sic*]."

"God forbid!" rejoined Louis Wigfall. "I hope not. They have already suffered much from their contact with the whites." The galleries roared their approval, and Wigfall pressed on. As always, he had the advantage over the solemn New Englanders. They knew only how to be righteous; he knew how to be outrageous. "I did think at one time, there was going to be war," he said. "I do not think so now. . . . The *Star of the West* swaggered into Charleston harbor, received a blow planted full in the face, and staggered out. Your flag has been insulted; redress it, if you dare. You have submitted to it for two months, and you will submit to it for ever."

Shortly before midnight the Senate recessed until seven o'clock Sunday evening. The galleries filled early in expectation of a final showdown and a valedictory speech from Crittenden. Lincoln himself slipped into the chamber to hear the man he had long admired. Senators could not get onto the floor until it was cleared, and more confusion followed when those evicted tried to elbow their way into the full galleries. "I trust the Senate is not to be broken up by a mob," said an exasperated Douglas. His motion to clear the men's galleries carried, and the last battle for compromise began.[6]

Crittenden opened with a moving call for action. "We have done nothing," he said. ". . . We see the danger, we acknowledge our duty; and yet, with all this before us, we are acknowledging before the world that we can do nothing." His plea for senators to rise above party and preserve the Union went unheeded; Lyman Trumbull urged that the government be given the power to defend itself. Baker gently rebuked Trumbull's hard line and asked fellow Republicans to face the fact of secession in a more conciliatory manner. The border states deserved compromise even if the cotton states did not. "I believe there is to-night danger that all the fifteen southern States will be gone," he warned. ". . . I do believe now it is necessary to preserve the Union by yielding, conceding, compromising, a little more than I believed a year ago."

It was near midnight when Baker finished. With inauguration day dawning, the senators settled in for a last haul, some fortifying themselves with bourbon, others catching naps on the sofas or at their desks. Douglas tried again to get a vote on the Corwin amendment but fell into a peevish exchange with Pugh and Mason. Morrill of Maine and Ben Wade denounced the Democratic party as "tainted with this doctrine of rebellion and secession." Wigfall surfaced through a haze of alcohol to sermonize on quack remedies for the body politic and the history of race relations, and taunted those demanding his ouster. "If the Senator and those who act with him will acknowledge my State to be out of the Union," he told James Doolittle of Wisconsin, "I will take my seat without a word further."

As the clock ticked toward four, the haggard senators edged sullenly toward voting. Pugh's motion to substitute the Crittenden plan for the Corwin amendment went down, 25–14, with even Crittenden opposing because it had no chance. An amendment by Bingham of Michigan that the Constitution needed no changes lost, 25–13. Johnson of Arkansas tried to substitute the peace convention plan for the Corwin amendment and was buried, 34–3. After a flurry of rhetoric the Corwin amendment finally came to a vote and squeaked through by the exact two-thirds majority, 24–12, thanks to support from eight Republicans.[7]

At last some small action had been taken, though few senators expected anything from it. Mason then astonished everyone by raising Crittenden's plan from the tomb. After some skirmishing over amendments, Crittenden moved to substitute the peace convention plan. His attempt was routed, 28–7, setting the stage for a vote on his own plan. In the last hours of the last day of the session, the Senate finally addressed the compromise that was best known to the country and had the most popular support. It went down to defeat, 20–19. Not a single Republican voted for it; Seward and four other Republicans did not vote at all. The message could not have been plainer. In these waning hours, when a lone vote would have changed the result, it was not forthcoming.

To the end the Republicans stood fast against compromise. Never during these tortuous months did the Crittenden plan gain a single Republican vote. Nor did a Republican majority support any piece of compromise legislation in either house, on the floor or in committee, and without Republican support there could be no compromise. Chase's motto of "Inauguration first, adjustment afterward" had come to pass. Some routine business got transacted, but the Republicans voted against going into executive session to confirm late Democratic appointments, and too few Democrats were present to resist. At seven the Senate adjourned until ten, when it waded through a last swamp of private bills and other business before Hannibal Hamlin arrived at noon to take his oath of office. After Breckinridge had administered it, the Thirty-sixth Congress passed into history with neither a bang nor a whimper.[8]

HE WAS AN ELEMENTAL MAN who had, through long struggle, mastered his elements or at least most of them. All his life he had read books, but even more, he had studied people, learned what drove them and sent them in wrong directions, what brought out the best and the worst in them, drew their loyalty or aroused their enmity. He was a professor of human nature, holding an advanced degree from two of life's most illuminating classrooms: the foibles of legal clients and the rituals and rivalries of local political partisans. His reticence and his rough, good-natured style made him easy to underestimate, and he liked this because it gave him the kind of advantage he always sought, one that remained closed tightly within himself. He let others become a window to him while he remained a wall to them.

Now, within hours, he was to become president, the first administrative office he had ever held in a career that had been marked by many more losses than wins.

His many friends knew but scarcely comprehended him. He was a remote, secretive man who loved being around people without quite being one of them. Possessions clung to him no better than affection. He loved life yet shunned most of its pleasures, moving instead in an abstract, untidy world of his own. Some thought him cold, and he was reticent and distant, the observer who played only on his own terms which he concealed from others. He understood the world of men but not that of women, based as it was more on feelings and affections he could not grasp, and he had never learned to deal with women as well as he did with men.[9]

No one knew his inner thoughts or grasped his strength of will and purpose. He viewed human nature for the lowlife thing it was, but with wry amusement rather than indignation. His good nature rubbed incessantly against his bleak melancholia and an unsparing eye that never sought refuge in the cant of religion or cosmic explanations. He invoked them freely, but they were neither crutch nor comfort to him personally. "I am sure I shall meet with some terrible end," he used to tell Billy Herndon, but he never let that fear deflect his ambition, which Herndon once described as an engine that knew no rest.

As his hour of triumph neared, the important thing was to take hold and maintain control. The days in Washington had shown him, as nothing else could, that the crisis was not artificial but real and that the forces of greed and ambition in the form of office seeking were ruthless in trampling over other business. The cabinet carousel spun as madly as ever during these last days. On the 1st Cameron came by invitation to Parlor no. 6 and resisted all overtures to accept the War Department, saying that only Treasury would do. One of his minions followed and was told that only War was available; that night the general came again and this time accepted.[10]

Cameron in War signaled that Treasury would go to Chase, whom Seward and Weed vigorously opposed. Seward feared a "compound Cabinet" with old Whigs and Democrats, who would divide sharply with Republicans over whether to offer concessions to the South. A mixed cabinet was not only unworkable but also a threat to his dominance. On the 2nd some of his friends visited Lincoln to argue that Seward and Chase could not sit in the same cabinet, and that Seward was needed most for the Union cause. Lincoln listened patiently, then took a sheet from a drawer with his proposed choices. His preference was for Seward in State and Chase in Treasury, he said blandly, but if they were not compatible, then he had in mind William L. Dayton for State. Stunned, the visitors left to tell Seward of the outcome.[11]

Later that day Seward wrote Lincoln asking with pointed politeness to withdraw his acceptance on the grounds that the differences between Chase and himself were too great. The story leaked to the papers, and a party of Virginians descended on Lincoln to warn that the presence of Chase or Montgomery Blair in the cabinet would be a death blow to Unionists in the state. Few doubted that their visit was inspired by Seward, who had labored hard to cultivate the Virginia Unionists. In this and other ways pressure mounted on Lincoln to reconsider his radical notion of a "compound" cabinet. Seward opposed not only Chase but also the implacable Blair and Gideon Welles, preferring his friend Charles Francis Adams and Henry Winter Davis or a suitable southern man.

Lincoln saw the game and at one point said to his secretary John Nicolay, "I can't afford to let Seward take the first trick." The next morning he scribbled a note to Seward asking him to "countermand the withdrawal." The public interest demanded it, Lincoln added, and his own personal feelings deeply wished it. He also added to his inaugural address a comment approving the Corwin amendment passed by Congress even though he had not yet read the actual text.[12]

By Sunday the city swarmed with strangers who had come to view the inauguration and lobby for jobs. They scrounged everywhere for shelter, some sleeping on hotel mattresses sprawled across whatever floor space they could find. Never had Washington seen so many outsiders for an inauguration, and never had so many of them come from the West, that raw, primitive region whose people were to local sensibilities scarcely civilized. A large number were big, rawboned young men, Wide-Awakes proud to salute their leader and defend him from those who threatened him or tried to prevent the inauguration.

General Scott had his own ideas on that subject. That afternoon he summoned his staff, Colonel E. V. Sumner, and Colonel Charles Stone to fix plans for Inauguration Day. Mindful of the threats against Lincoln, Stone had drilled his District of Columbia volunteers into a reliable support force for the regulars Scott had brought to the capital. Scott determined to take no chances. The regulars from West Point would march in front of the carriage holding Buchanan and Lincoln, with District volunteer infantry following behind it and double files of District cavalry flanking both sides. Riflemen would be stationed on the roofs of key houses along Pennsylvania Avenue with regular cavalry patrolling the cross streets. A battalion of District volunteers would guard the steps of the Capitol, and riflemen would be posted in every window of the building's wings.[13]

That night Stone received notice that an attempt would be made to blow up the temporary platform erected on the steps for Lincoln to deliver his address. He sent troops to guard the platform and the next morning dispatched more to ring the great stairway and prevent access to the structure. Policemen in plain clothes were detailed to mill through the crowd and watch for any suspicious behavior. On the brow of the hill across from the east portico Scott planted a battery of flying artillery. Still, the general did not feel easy. No fewer than forty-three army officers had resigned since South Carolina seceded; the very officer who took notes at the afternoon conference quit that same night and went south. It was more difficult than ever to know whom to trust.[14]

At the White House, Buchanan presided over a few last routine duties. The packing was complete, the long-awaited escape only hours away. Martin Crawford, a Confederate commissioner who arrived in town on Sunday morning, saw Buchanan and was shocked at his appearance. "His fears for his personal safety, the apprehension for the security of his property, together with the cares of state and his advanced age," he reported, "render

him wholly disqualified for his present position. He is as incapable now of
purpose as a child."15

THOSE WHO COVETED OMENS had no trouble finding them on Inauguration Day. The morning dawned raw and cloudy with enough rain to
damp down the merciless dust, then gave way to bright sunshine as a cool
northwest wind swept out the old weather system. A large crane loomed
above the domeless Capitol, reminding all that the temple of democracy
remained unfinished. On the grounds below the east entrance sat the bronze
statue of Liberty with sword in one hand and wreath of flowers in the other,
awaiting her place atop the dome. A half-naked marble George Washington
stared with classical dignity at the platform as if awaiting the inaugural
speech. As the crowd gathered to watch the sacred rite of democratic free
elections, the streets bristled with soldiers and cannon, a sight that dismayed
some observers as more worthy of a Latin American country than the greatest
free republic in the world.

Scott had his men in place well before the ceremonies. Too large and
infirm to mount a horse, the general rode in his coupe on a street parallel to
the presidential brougham down Pennsylvania Avenue. He paused at
Seward's house to brief him and hand him some new thoughts on the crisis
he had written the day before, then took up a post near the artillery battery
overlooking the east portico while his aide Erasmus Keyes rode about in
civilian clothes to gather information. The general was tense and alert, ready
for any hint of disturbance. As noon neared, a huge crowd packed the walks
of Pennsylvania Avenue from the Capitol to the Treasury. Above the avenue
every window, balcony, and housetop brimmed with spectators. At Willard's
some troops were busy clearing a path to the entrance on Fourteenth Street.16

Businesses, schools, and public buildings were closed for the day, as
were saloons by Scott's order. At 10 a.m. the cabinet except Holt joined
Buchanan in the president's room at the Capitol for the ritual of signing the
flurry of late bills from Congress. Old Buck rejoiced in the knowledge that he
was performing his last official duty. Suddenly Holt burst into the room with
news of an extraordinary dispatch just received from Anderson, stating that
without twenty thousand troops to subdue the batteries surrounding him he
could not maintain himself at Sumter. Holt was astonished because he had
offered reinforcements only to be told they were not needed.17

Buchanan frowned. Like Banquo's ghost, the issue would not down.
There was no time to discuss it before the ceremonies; the cabinet agreed to
meet with him that night. Meanwhile, Holt would compose a letter to Lincoln explaining the matter. Buchanan ordered his carriage and rode to pick

up Lincoln. The President's Mounted Guard and the Georgetown Mounted Guard presented arms. Lincoln climbed into the carriage along with Senators Baker and James Pearce of Maryland, who headed the arrangements committee. The band struck up "Hail to the Chief" as the procession moved forward with its protective ring of troops.

Behind the soldiers trailed an impressive parade of representatives from the judiciary, the clergy, the foreign ministers and the diplomatic corps, many in court dress, Congress, the peace convention, bureau heads, state governors, military men, veterans from the Revolutionary War and War of 1812 in carriages, and other organizations, including a Republican Association float drawn by four white horses with thirty-four young girls in snow-white frocks, one for each state, as well as bands. The crowd strained for views of the presidential carriage through the bouncing, shifting file of cavalry.[18]

The two leaders said little, having nothing to discuss beyond the crisis that had consumed the one and awaited the other, and of that they could hardly speak. Buchanan did not mention the dispatch from Anderson. At the Capitol they filed into the Senate chamber through a private entrance to watch Hamlin take the oath as vice president. The chamber was packed, with only Hunter and Mason of Virginia conspicuous by their absence. The diplomats and ministers were there in unusually large numbers, and the Supreme Court justices had arrived as well. A procession formed to escort the presidents down a corridor to the east portico and onto the platform. The crowd greeted their appearance with polite applause as the dignitaries found their seats.[19]

The platform became a sea of black silk hats and suits with Buchanan, the Lincoln family, Hamlin, Chief Justice Roger B. Taney and his clerk, and the arrangements committee in front. Surrounding them were congressmen, military officers, governors, department heads and officials on one side, and justices in their black robes, more senators, diplomats, officials, judges, and the mayors of Washington and Georgetown on the other. Lincoln stood awkwardly in his new black suit, searched for a place to set his ebony cane with its gold head, and finally shoved it into a corner of the railing. His hat too needed a home. Stephen Douglas quickly took it from him and held it during the ceremony.[20]

For this brief time the alert eye could catch on the platform a stunning tableau vivant of the men who had brought the slavery crisis crashing to this unlikely climax during the decade past. There stood Douglas, the man who had helped forge the Compromise of 1850 and then wrecked it with his advocacy of the Kansas-Nebraska Act four years later. Nearby was Buchanan, whose fight with Douglas over the Lecompton Constitution had fractured the Democratic party and plunged the nation into turmoil over "Bleeding Kansas." Opposite them stood Taney, who had written the infamous *Dred Scott* decision in 1857. Breckinridge, the last hope of southern extremists to retain power in 1860, was there too. So was Seward, the man who had done so much to bring the Republican party into existence and who still could scarcely believe he was not president.

Amid them all, at the center of the tableau, stood Lincoln, who had risen from political obscurity to become president after failing to get himself elected senator two years earlier, and whose election had propelled the Republic into the last full measure of crisis. Those on the platform were infused with a sense that the man about to take the oath of office was inadequate, as nearly any man must be, to the collapse of a republic that had rushed to its doom through some fatal mix of hubris and ambition.

Baker introduced him briefly, and Lincoln stepped forward, pulled a set of papers from his coat pocket, adjusted his spectacles, and began reading in a strong, calm, deliberate, high-pitched voice that carried well across the crowd below. Never had an inaugural speech been awaited more urgently, and seldom had one been received with such reserve. For half an hour he read on amid a smattering of cheers. A disturbance alarmed the crowd briefly, but it proved to be a man who had climbed a tree to deliver his own speech until the branch snapped and sent him tumbling to the ground.[21]

The wind chilled those standing on the platform. Gustave Koerner, the Illinois Republican, noticed Douglas shivering in the cold and threw his heavy shawl across his shoulders. Douglas scarcely noticed the gesture, so intent was he on following the speech. More than once he squeezed Koerner's arm and murmured, "Good, good." Louis Wigfall leaned with folded arms against a Capitol doorway, his face wreathed with contempt. Thurlow Weed, attending his first inauguration, did not listen to a speech he had already read but wandered about the grounds, pausing to speak first with General John Wool and then to tell Scott that all was going well. "God be praised!" cried Scott.[22]

The speech drew to a close with a moving appeal. Seward had urged some gesture of conciliation and offered two drafts for consideration. Lincoln took one of them and wove into it the peculiar poetic conciseness that was one of his supreme gifts: "I am lo[a]th to close. We are not enemies, but friends. We must not be enemies. Though passion may have strained, it must not break our bonds of affection. The mystic chords of memory, stretching from every battlefield, and patriot grave, to every living heart and hearthstone, all over this broad land, will yet swell the chorus of the Union, when again touched, as surely they will be, by the better angels of our nature."[23]

When he finished, Taney, whom the acerbic Mrs. Clement Clay of

Alabama once described as having "the face of a galvanized corpse," tottered forth to administer the oath. His hands trembled with emotion as he performed the ceremony. When it was done, cannon boomed in salute, and the platform began to empty. Buchanan breathed a sigh of relief. He rode with Lincoln back to the White House, which he formally turned over to the new resident. "My dear sir," he said, "if you are as happy in entering the White House as I shall feel on returning to Wheatland, you are a happy man indeed."[24]

A temporary building had been erected behind City Hall for what was dubbed the Union Ball. White muslin, flowers, evergreens, and flags sheathed its plain board interior beneath the light of five gas chandeliers. The crowd was thin and restrained, lacking the gaiety of former years. It struck Erasmus Keyes that this was the first inaugural ball he had known that was not dominated by leading southerners. Lincoln stood greeting guests for more than two hours, looking distracted but never impatient. At eleven the Marine Band swung into "Hail to the Chief" as Lincoln linked arms with Mayor Berret to lead the grand march, followed by Mary on the arm of her former suitor, Stephen A. Douglas. The new president ducked out of the waltzes and square dances, while Mary partnered Douglas in the quadrille. Dressed in a new blue gown, a large blue feather in her hair, Mary was in her element at last as First Lady. Lincoln stood talking to Lord Lyons and laughed so hard at one point that he braced himself with both hands on the British minister's shoulder. But the crowd was serious, not festive, and consumed with the question that teased people across the nation: What exactly had Lincoln said in his inaugural address?[25]

Across town at Wormley's Hotel the mood was even less festive. Wade Hampton, Jr., and other southerners enjoyed a final supper before departing for Montgomery, having delayed only long enough to bring with them a copy of Lincoln's inaugural. Wormley himself stepped in to tell them that Scott was dining in an adjoining room. "He looks worrit in his mind," Wormley added. "He don't talk as usual, but he eats, does 'the General'—he eats powerful!" As they headed out, an omnibus passed them with the Marine Band on its way to the inaugural ball, followed by a light artillery battery. The officer, a Virginian named John S. Saunders, trotted over to their hack.[26]

"So you fellows are off!" he sighed. "Wish I were with you. But today settled it, and my resignation goes in tonight. I shan't wait for Virginia. If I *have* to shoot at Americans, I'll do it from the other side of the Potomac."

BY TELEGRAPH, TRAIN, HORSE, AND HUMAN HAND the most anxiously awaited message of any president spread across the land. More than an inaugural speech, it was the first official word of a new president of a new party on a crisis that dangled the nation between peace and war. Everywhere it was read, scrutinized, dissected with anticipation, and everywhere it aroused strong feelings. Hardly anyone agreed on what it said or, more important, what it meant. The Illinois *State Journal* was right in saying that it "electrified the whole country," but half the people were left galvanized and the rest in a state of shock.

"Well, I hardly know what he means," admitted Douglas. "Every point in the address is susceptible of a double construction; but I think he does not mean coercion." Louis Wigfall disagreed. "Inaugural means war," he wired Pickens, and L. Q. Washington agreed it "undoubtedly means war, and that right off." Martin Crawford and three Virginia ultras concurred. They also concluded that Lincoln was "a man of will and firmness." Even Sumner found in the speech Napoleon's simile of "a hand of iron and a velvet glove."[27]

Northern opinion divided sharply. George Templeton Strong praised the speech's "strong individuality and the absence of conventionalism of thought or diction. It doesn't run in the ruts of Public Documents . . . but seems to introduce one to *a man* and to dispose one to like him." The *Tribune* liked its brevity and thought its "plainness and directness of speech will make its meaning clear to the lowest capacity." But a Philadelphia paper dismissed it as "a lame, unsatisfactory and discreditable production inferior in every respect to anything that has ever emanated from any former President." One Pittsburgh journal hailed its language as "so clear, so simple, so direct, so free from ambiguity, that it has but one meaning, and that meaning finds a responsive chord in every patriotic heart"; another pronounced it "a sad disappointment to the country." While a Detroit paper called it as "clear as a mountain brook," many more editors puzzled over the real meaning beneath the surface. Some thought they saw Seward's influence in its language.[28]

The same confusion tinted with partisanship reigned in the border states. In North Carolina one Raleigh editor insisted that it was *"not a war message,"* while another condemned it as "deceptive. It coats with the semblance of peace and friendship what smells of gore and hate." Where Parson Brownlow's Knoxville *Whig* lauded its "temperance and conservatism," a Nashville paper denounced it as *"a declaration of war against the seceded States."* Two ultra Richmond papers agreed that "Civil War must now come," while a Virginia moderate complained that the inaugural "has been greatly distorted, from its true intention, by our people" to influence opinion in the convention.[29]

Few people in the cotton states found anything hopeful in the speech. An Atlanta paper labeled it "a medly [*sic*] of ignorance, sanctimonious cant—and tenderfooted bullyism," while a perplexed Georgia planter thought it a "queer production" and asked, "What does it mean? It means this, and it means that; and then it may mean neither." A New Orleans editor sniffed at "a very inferior production, whether considered as a literary, logical, or statesmanlike production. The language is mean, involved and inconclusive, evidently such as only persons of very imperfect education would employ."[30]

In Montgomery, Tom Cobb insisted that "it will not affect one man here, it matters not what it contains." Mary Chesnut wondered, "Means he war or peace[?] An insidious villain. I fear he only means, if he can, to get away from us the border states." Although an undercover *Tribune* man claimed to have heard Alexander Stephens pronounce the speech "the most *adroit* State paper ever published on this Continent," the consensus was that the message meant war. In Charleston opinion lined up solidly against it. "Well! Mr. Lincoln has spoken!" exclaimed William Gilmore Simms. "And we are to have war." Emma Holmes agreed it was "just what was expected from him, stupid, ambiguous, vulgar and insolent, and is everywhere considered as a virtual declaration of war." Even James Petigru found it "significant of measures that will likely lead to the use of arms."[31]

What did Lincoln actually say to provoke such contrary interpretations? He assured southerners that he had no intention of meddling with slavery in the states where it already existed because he had "no lawful right to do so." But he was bound to defend and enforce the Constitution, and he believed the Union to be perpetual. "No government proper," he pointed out, "ever had a provision in its organic law for its own termination." Secession was illegal, and thus "acts of violence, within any State or States, against the authority of the United States, are insurrectionary or revolutionary, according to circumstances."[32]

Lincoln took this to mean that he must enforce the laws in all states, that he would "hold, occupy, and possess the property, and places belonging to the government" and "collect the duties and imposts; but beyond what may be necessary for these objects, there will be no invasion—no using of force against, or among the people anywhere." Mail service would continue, "unless repelled," and every step would be taken toward a "peaceful solution of the national troubles." To those who truly loved the Union, Lincoln addressed a moving yet rigorously argued plea to consider carefully the consequences before acting. "Plainly," he said, "the central idea of secession, is the essence of anarchy," and "the rule of a minority, as a permanent arrangement, is wholly inadmissable."

"One section of our country believes slavery is *right*, and ought to be extended," he reiterated, "while the other believes it is *wrong*, and ought not to be extended. This is the only substantial dispute." Was this difference worth destroying the union of a people who physically could not separate? Lincoln thought not. "Suppose you go to war, you cannot fight always," he observed trenchantly, "and when, after much loss on both sides, and no gain on either, you cease fighting, the identical old questions, as to terms of intercourse, are again upon you." He indicated willingness to abide by any popular desire for constitutional amendment and specifically endorsed the Corwin amendment.

Lincoln urged the people to think long and calmly before acting. "Nothing valuable can be lost by taking time," he said. No good reason existed for hasty or rash action, and every good reason existed to go slowly. "In *your* hands, my dissatisfied countrymen, and not in mine, is the momentous issue of civil war," he reminded them. "The government will not assail *you*. You can have no conflict, without being yourselves the aggressors. *You* have no oath registered in Heaven to destroy the government, while *I* shall have the most solemn one to 'preserve, protect and defend it.' " Directly following this passage, Lincoln added his poignant closing paragraph.

"A more lamentable display of feeble inability to grasp the circumstances of this momentous emergency could scarcely have been exhibited," exclaimed the *Mercury*. If, as seemed clear, Lincoln tried to collect import duties offshore, the Confederate government had but two options. "The one, immediate attack upon Fort Sumter; the other, to besiege and starve out the fortress. . . . [s]alt meat and warm weather may most effectually do our work for us. To reinforce Fort Sumter is now only to hasten the period of starvation."33

MANY EDITORS WERE CHURLISH about not knowing the membership of the cabinet until the 5th, unaware that Lincoln himself did not have the full lineup until that day. After the ceremony the new president slipped off for a long talk with Seward, during which he suggested the idea of Seward's serving as minister to Britain. The next morning Seward agreed to withdraw his letter of withdrawal, explaining to Frances that "I did not dare to go home, or to England, and leave the country to chance." The cabinet was finally set with Seward in State, Cameron in War, Chase in Treasury, Caleb Smith in Interior, Gideon Welles in Navy, Bates as attorney general, and Montgomery Blair as postmaster general. Chase demurred a day before accepting, and the news went public only when the list reached the Senate on the 5th.34

Lincoln had taken the first trick. He had his "composition cabinet," and he could not have chosen a more prickly group over which to preside. Aware that there had never been one like it in the nation's history, one reporter concluded that it contained "elements which may render smooth working difficult, and produce embarrassments from the start." Lincoln brought them together for the first time on the 6th around the green table in the president's room for a formal, introductory meeting that Bates privately dismissed as "uninteresting." He need not have worried; things were about to get much more lively.³⁵

On the evening of his liberation James Buchanan found himself not yet free. He sat down with the members of his cabinet at the home of his host, Robert Ould, to discuss Anderson's startling letter. The next morning they met again at the War Department and approved the letter Holt had composed for Lincoln explaining their shock at Anderson's missive. Holt sent the papers to Lincoln that afternoon. Buchanan learned this shortly before catching his train at two o'clock for the journey home to Wheatland, where the locals at least still admired him.³⁶

Holt's letter, with its enclosures, shocked Lincoln as much as Anderson's had Buchanan. The secretary reviewed and quoted past correspondence with the major. Since January 16, he noted, "Major Anderson has regularly & frequently reported the progress of the batteries being constructed around him . . . but he has not suggested that their works compromised his safety, nor has he made any request that additional supplies or reinforcements should be sent to him." Despite that silence, the administration had prepared an expedition that could sail from New York on a few hours' notice, but it was nowhere near the scale proposed by both Anderson and Captain Foster, "now offered for the first time, and for the disclosures of which the government was wholly unprepared."³⁷

Taken aback, Lincoln asked Holt privately whether he had any reason to doubt Anderson's loyalty. Absolutely none, replied Holt. Lincoln then sent the letters to Scott for his opinion. The general studied them and that night laboriously wrote out his views, which he gave not to Lincoln but to his close friend Seward. Normally the note would have gone through the War Department, but Cameron was not yet on duty and Scott did not want to give it to Holt, who was minding the store. Before passing the note to Lincoln, Seward showed it to Edwin Stanton, who let John Dix see a copy. Not until the 7th did Lincoln actually read Scott's response.³⁸

Seward, who was playing a deeper game as usual, had enlisted Scott as an ally behind his formula for handling the crisis. On the 3rd the general had written Seward, doubtless at the latter's request, his revised views giving the president four policy options. First, he could "throw off the *old*, and assume a *new* designation—the *Union party*,—adopt the conciliatory measures proposed by Mr. Crittenden, or the Peace Convention." Scott obviously favored this approach, believing it would end the rush to secession and bring most states back. The other options were to collect duties offshore and blockade southern ports, conquer the seceded states with an invading army, or "Say to the seceded States *wayward sisters, depart in peace!*"[39]

Seward sent this letter to Lincoln the next day. The president chose to ignore its views, but he could hardly ignore the advice of his top military man. In his note of the 5th Scott also offered advice that neatly fitted Seward's views. "When Major Anderson first threw himself into Fort Sumter," he said, "it would have been easy to reinforce him. . . . The difficulty of reinforcing has now been increased 10 or 15 fold." Given the buildup in the harbor, Buchanan's failure to send help, and the "imbecility" of the *Star of the West*'s captain in not completing his mission, Scott saw only one alternative: "Evacuation seems almost inevitable . . . if, indeed, the worn out garrison be not assaulted & carried in the present week." General Totten, he added, shared this view.[40]

This position reversed Scott's earlier stance. Lincoln ordered the general to study the matter more thoroughly and meanwhile to use all vigilance to protect Forts Sumter and Pickens. On the 6th Scott, Totten, and Holt briefed Welles on the Sumter crisis and Anderson's letter. Astounded at Holt's news that Anderson would be starved out in six weeks, Welles proposed that measures be taken at once to relieve the garrison. The army could do nothing, replied Scott; any solution had to come from the navy. He added that Commander James Ward stood ready to lead an expedition and urged Welles to consult with him. They adjourned to meet the next day with Lincoln at the White House.[41]

Here was a monstrous predicament. While the nation puzzled over the inaugural speech, Lincoln grappled with a very different message that undercut the whole line of policy he had advocated. That it should come so soon and so unexpectedly seemed a cruel blow, and he could not help wondering if his first breath of power would prove to be the last gasp of the Republic.

CHAPTER EIGHTEEN

Uneasy Arrangements

Taken altogether, this is a most singular state of war. . . . Fort Sumter is surrounded by batteries prepared to batter or shell it. . . . Nearly the like state of things exists as to Fort Pickens. . . . The officers of the fort & the besieging C.S. army even exchange friendly visits, & dine at each other's quarters. . . . Two different governments are now existing, & the new one completely organized & established . . . peaceful relations have continued between the two peoples, despite of [sic] the violent animosity of the communities, & still more of individuals of the two sections. While every participation & aid of secession in the South is denounced in the North as treason . . . & even so declared judicially, southern & northern men freely visit & travel any where in the other section, without being interfered with by any legal restraint or penalty. . . . The mails are uninterrupted, & the railway trains, express transportation & telegraph lines.

—Edmund Ruffin
March 17, 1861[1]

*T*HE FIRST FLAG OF the Confederate States of America was adopted on March 4 and run up at noon to the roar of saluting cannon. The time had been chosen to coincide with Lincoln's inaugural speech. Still lacking an anthem, the band played "Massa's in de Cold Ground." The Chesnuts watched from a balcony along with Stephen Mallory, ever attentive to Mary, and other friends. During the ceremony James Chesnut whispered to Mallory that he had been confirmed as secretary of the navy after a struggle. Mallory bowed to him and went on talking to Mary. Apart from her husband, Mary found Mallory the most refined man of her crowd, even though rumor had it that his mother was a washerwoman.[2]

Earlier that day Mary had seen something that depressed her deeply. On the fountain steps outside the hotel she encountered an auction of mulatto women in silk dresses. She watched in disgust as one girl, who looked remarkably like her own Nancy, eyed the winning bidder coyly. "This is not worse than the willing sale most women make of themselves in marriage," Mary reasoned without conviction. "The Bible authorizes marriage &

slavery—poor women, poor slaves! 'Still—slavery thou art a bitter draught disguise it as we will & then thousands have drunk.' " She fled in relief to the ceremony and to a dinner with witty repartee, but the image continued to haunt her.[3]

More and more Mary's loathing of slavery nagged at her, yet it was the bedrock for the brave new republic being launched at Montgomery. Two weeks later Alexander Stephens made this unmistakably clear in a speech at Savannah. The old Constitution, he asserted, "*rested upon the assumption of the equality of the races. . . . [I]t was a sandy foundation.*" The cornerstone of the new government "*rests upon the great truth that the negro is not equal to the white man; that Slavery, subordination to the superior race, is his natural and normal condition. This, our new Government, is the first in the history of the world, based upon this great physical, philosophical, and moral truth.*"[4]

Although Tom Cobb complained irritably that "We are traveling very slowly," the new government hastened to organize itself. By the 10th the provisional congress had adopted the constitution and set up an army for which Davis had to find men, money, and matériel. Already he had resorted to his old vice of overwork, handling the flood of office seekers, visitors, correspondence, paperwork, internal frictions, and ceremonial functions with the help of a lone secretary. After appointing Beauregard, he put Braxton Bragg in charge of the forces at Fort Pickens and gave his old friend Samuel Cooper the same post of adjutant general he had just left in the U.S. Army. Finding good men to staff the new army frustrated Davis; there were plenty of applicants eager to lead a division or a brigade, but few who knew what they were doing.[5]

His biggest concerns were Forts Sumter and Pickens. He could not escape the harsh truth that the Confederacy was nowhere near ready for action. Davis lacked reliable information on troops, supplies, powder, equipment, and ammunition. He needed time to get hold of things, to ensure that any first move made by the fledgling army did not turn into a disaster. The commissioners had to buy that time in Washington, as did Beauregard in Charleston. If the negotiations actually proved successful, so much the better.

This policy of delay aroused suspicions that it sought some form of reconciliation. "The game, now, is to reconstruct *under our Constitution*," complained Tom Cobb. ". . . Stephens and Toombs are both for leaving the door open. . . . *Confidentially*, and to be kept a secret *from the public, Mr. Davis* is opposed to us on this point also and wants to keep the door open." Little sympathy remained in Montgomery for reconstruction. "We look upon union," declared William M. "Constitution" Browne, former editor of that Washington paper, "as impossible as the annexation of the Confederate

States to Great Britain in their old colonial condition." John Slidell agreed that no hope of reconciliation existed, a view to which even Varina Howell Davis subscribed.[6]

The rejection of union, coupled with the lack of readiness for war, left the mood in Montgomery uneasy and anxiously attuned to every fresh rumor from Washington or Charleston. "The cry today is *war*," noted Mary Chesnut on the 6th. Then came reports from Martin Crawford and John Forsyth offering a very different slant. A talk with Seward convinced them that he was to rule the new administration. Both Seward and Cameron were on record as favoring a peace policy, and the former was "urgent for delay." Seward had spelled out a plan to hold the border states in the Union while bringing back the cotton states, and he needed time to accomplish this. Why shouldn't this fantasy be encouraged for a while? "Until we reach the point of pacific negotiations," they wrote, "it is unimportant what may be his subsequent hopes and plans. It is well that he should indulge in dreams which we know are not to be realized."[7]

Crawford also heard that Anderson had written a letter saying his fuel supply would run out by April 1. On the heels of this report came a rumor that Sumter was to be evacuated. The story turned up in the New York papers on the 10th and was confirmed the next day by a telegram from Louis Wigfall. "Too good to be true," murmured Mary Chesnut at the news, but a euphoric sense of relief surged through Montgomery. Mary was pleased because James had from the first insisted there would be no war.[8]

EVERYTHING IN SEWARD'S LIFE seemed as unsettled as the country itself. The new red-brick house facing Lafayette Square, which he had agreed to rent for $1,800 a year, would not be ready until April while the owner painted, papered, put in city water, and installed gas fixtures and a furnace. When it was ready, Frances would not be there to preside as hostess. She remained at Auburn, pleading the need to oversee repairs to their house, but Seward knew better. She would not come to Washington again, and he must grow accustomed to her absence. Gradually their lives had retreated to separate spheres that seldom overlapped. It was a painful loss at a most difficult time in his life.[9]

There had always been strains between them, a pattern of estrangement and reconciliation born of deep love tested repeatedly by their differences and by Seward's incorrigible mistress, politics. Frances was a passionate, idealistic, introspective woman who loathed the chummy, expedient style of practical politics. An ardent abolitionist, she feared that Seward had sold his soul to gain office and wield power. That she was also a devout prohibitionist made her a poor hostess in a city where wine and liquor flowed unceasingly. The struggle between love and principle had taken a fierce toll on her health over the years, had left her steeped in melancholy and hypochondria.[10]

Seward loved Frances deeply, but he knew himself. She could not live in Washington, and he would not go to Auburn. Nor would her principles or her health permit her to act as hostess; the social rituals of Washington bored her to madness. For years he had made do with a variety of substitutes, and now he had Anna, the wife of his son (now his secretary) Frederick. She was lovely and charming, loved the social whirl, and presided at the table with grace, dignity, and obvious pleasure. Seward could be himself around her, smoke his cigars and enjoy his wine, play the raconteur to his heart's content. He need not even trouble with the details of the new house; Anna saw to them. Although he missed Frances dreadfully, he did not miss the tensions that lay beneath their love.

He had a new role in a new administration facing an unprecedented crisis. His sense of self, nurtured assiduously by Weed over the years, lacked any awareness of limits. He did not know what he could or, more important, could not do in this role. Throughout his career Weed had sheltered him from the uglier side of political infighting, but Weed could not help him master the new president or his enemies in the cabinet, who were eager to challenge his influence. It was not self-confidence he lacked but rather a clear tactic. Seward was pontifical enough to offer Edwin Booth advice on improving his acting or a discourse on the art of dress to the fastidious Adamses. He believed he knew the formula for riding out the crisis and could make it work. It was a puzzle of many pieces forming a whole that he grasped and parceled out carefully to those whose help he needed without revealing the larger picture. He also understood that no one would be entirely satisfied with the results. "I learned early from Jefferson," he once said, "that in political affairs we cannot always do what seems to us absolutely best."[11]

The grand design embraced two major goals. First, the confrontation had to be defused long enough to keep the cotton states isolated and allow submerged Unionist sentiment in the South to resurface and reverse the trend toward secession. Then a new political coalition of Unionists North and South could be forged, and with it a new Union party strong enough to bridge the sectional chasm. Seward was a natural leader for such a party; so were Douglas and a host of former Whigs, conservative Republicans, border state Democrats, cotton state conservatives, and other political gypsies who had been forced into what they considered unnatural political allegiances.

Any hope for such a party depended on avoiding a collision. That was why Seward had persistently counseled delay and forbearance, supported the peace convention, urged Lincoln to put loyal southerners in the cabinet, and paid court to Unionists from the border states, especially Virginia. Talk of a Union party had been in the air for months, nowhere more hopefully than in Virginia. James Barbour urged Seward to "place yourself and the new administration at the head of a national conservative party which will domineer over all other party organizations North and South for many years to come." He also told Douglas that "a new party *can* and ought to be entrenched which will command the country for 25 years. . . . You and Mr. Seward have the capacity to see and know this." Seward saw the idea clearly enough to drop it into Martin Crawford's ear at their meeting. "In advancing his policy," Crawford reported, "the name Republican . . . is to be dropped and the word slavery is to be ignored, and every thing merged into the Union cause and Union party."[12]

The idea of a new national party was no secret. Southern politics had long been in tatters, and many observers doubted the Republican party could survive its internal strains. The Richmond *Whig* declared flatly that "the conservative Whigs and Democrats of the South and the conservative Republicans of the North must unite to form a new Union party." A New York *Times* writer speculated whether "Mr. Lincoln shall become the head of the great 'Union Party' of the country, or whether a party upon that issue shall be permitted to grow up in hostility to his Administration." Private appeals implored Seward to seize the issue. "All *old* party platforms are now either breaking down or being swallowed up in the universal desire of the people to save the republic from dissolution," wrote one admirer, "and a new one, constructed upon Union principles *per se* will inevitably spring up after the 4th of next March. *It is for you to take the lead or not in the movement.*"[13]

Seward was more than willing to take the lead, but first he had to get his footing in the new administration. On one side he had the Confederate commissioners, newly arrived and seeking recognition as delegates of a "foreign power." On the other side he had the ultras of his own party, inside the cabinet and out, who opposed all conciliatory efforts and distrusted any move he made. Somehow he had to fend them all off while exerting his influence over Lincoln and leading him to the proper policy. "The political troubles of the country . . . are enough to tax the wisdom of the wisest," he wrote Frances. "Fort Sumter in danger. Relief of it practically impossible. The Commissioners from the Southern Confederacy are here. These cares fall chiefly on me."[14]

With his usual deftness Seward made himself the liaison between Lincoln and the rest of the cabinet. He took it upon himself to ask the others for lists of vacancies in their departments and summoned them to cabinet meetings. When Chase suggested regular meeting days, Lincoln agreed to Tuesdays and Fridays at noon. Even then Seward told Lincoln that he would "notify the members specially." He made himself useful to Lincoln in numerous small ways and meddled in everyone else's business. "He was vigilantly attentive to every measure and movement in other Departments, however trivial, as much as his own," noted Gideon Welles acidly, "watched and scrutinized every appointment that was made or proposed to be made, but was not communicative in regard to the transactions of the State Department."[15]

Resentment slid easily off Seward as long as it did not interfere with his purpose. Twelve years earlier another new president, Zachary Taylor, had leaned heavily on Seward for guidance in critical times; why should this one not do likewise? Scott's views had apparently impressed Lincoln, who told the cabinet to make no office changes or removals in the South, especially Virginia, and to avoid any action that might give offense. But what could be done about Sumter? And the commissioners?[16]

On the 7th Seward was at Lincoln's side when he met with Welles, Captain Silas Stringham, a naval officer Welles trusted, Scott, and Totten. The generals repeated their belief that Anderson could not be reinforced. Seward offered questions and suggestions that convinced Welles of his opposition to any attempt at relief. That same day Adjutant General Samuel Cooper, the man with whom Anderson corresponded in the War Department, resigned and left to join the Confederate service. A New Yorker by birth, Cooper had married a sister of Virginia Senator James Mason and became a southern sympathizer. Already forty-three army officers had quit, and no one knew how many more stood at the crossroads of their personal and professional loyalties. Welles was told that only five of forty officers at the Naval Academy were loyal.[17]

The next evening Lincoln hosted his first public reception, "a motley crowd and terrible squeeze" to the jaundiced eye of Edward Bates. Seward was absent, having broken down and taken to his bed for a few days. While Lincoln shook the interminable line of hands, hurrying strangers along while bending down to whisper a few words to people he knew, Sumter occupied his mind. On the 9th he asked Scott for a written opinion on three questions: (1) How long could Anderson hold out; (2) could he be relieved with existing forces; and (3) if not, what additional forces were needed? That evening he told the cabinet of Anderson's letter. Most learned of the crisis for the first time and were flabbergasted to hear that Scott and Totten thought Sumter must be evacuated. The discussion was indignant but inconclusive.[18]

By Monday the nation knew of it too, as major papers carried stories of the meeting along with a rumor that Anderson's command would be withdrawn from Sumter. "If the fort cannot be reenforced by sea," observed the

Tribune's James Pike, "nor succored by a military force on land before its supplies are exhausted, then . . . it will be starved out." That same day Scott replied to Lincoln's questions. Anderson had supplies enough to hold out perhaps a month or more, the general thought, but the fort "ought to be taken by a single assault, & easily; if harassed perseveringly for several previous days & nights by threats & false attacks." The surrounding forces had grown strong enough to repel any relief expedition. To dislodge them would require a fleet of warships and transports, five thousand regular troops, and twenty thousand volunteers. To raise and organize such a force would require an act of Congress and at least six months.[19]

Scott saw no alternative but to evacuate Anderson. He prepared orders to that effect and enclosed a draft for Lincoln to consider. "As a practical military question," he added, "the time for succoring Fort Sumter with any means at hand had passed away nearly a month ago." Appalled, Lincoln groped desperately for options to the trap he sensed closing about him. For most of Monday afternoon the cabinet thrashed over the question with no resolution. Watchful reporters shared the view of the *Mercury*'s man that "The President has given orders for the evacuation." So rapidly did this rumor spread that already the reaction from ultra Republicans had begun. "The act is deprecated and denounced in every form of anathema," noted James Pike, who was quick to excuse it as one of military necessity forced on Lincoln by Buchanan's failure to act.[20]

At the same time Seward and Lincoln were sorting out the diplomatic appointments with more than usual care because of the need to prevent any recognition of the Confederacy by European powers. Strong men were needed in the major embassies, especially Britain and France. Lincoln suggested William Dayton for Britain and John C. Frémont for France; Seward preferred Dayton for France and Charles Francis Adams for Britain, arguing that the latter would be "infinitely more watchful capable—efficient, reliable every thing." He got his way. Mexico also mattered greatly because supplies could reach the new Confederacy from there if a blockade were imposed. Lincoln had Tom Corwin in mind, but Corwin didn't want the job.[21]

The key positions had to be settled quickly and tactfully, but it was hard to concentrate on affairs of state when every department was overrun by applicants. The swarm engulfed Bates as soon as he stepped from his train. Chase tried vainly to close his doors against them; Seward made his son Frederick sentinel against "the whole array of friends seeking offices—an hundred taking tickets where only one can draw the prize." Nor was the White House spared. There too, reported Seward, "the grounds, halls, stairways, closets, are filled with applicants." Every supplicant tried to enlist the support of his senator or representative as well. "My rooms are full from early morning till midnight with debaters about 'office,' " complained Charles Sumner, "and the larger part go away discontented."[22]

Lincoln could not escape the horde that followed him everywhere, taking full advantage of his affable manner. Two lines of callers, one coming and one going, streamed through the White House doors every day. Others waited to pounce when the president left the office for his meals. "He came here tall, strong, and vigorous, but has worked himself almost to death," said William Fessenden of Maine. "The good fellow thinks it is his duty to see to everything, and to do everything himself, and consequently does many things foolishly." But the good senator had his own agenda and disappointments. "Everything in the way of office goes West," he grumbled. "We shall hardly get the pairings [sic] of a toenail in New England."[23]

Every cabinet member had his own friends and favorites to advance for positions, none more than the virtuous Chase, thrusting the scramble for office into the highest circle of advisers. "The spoils belong to the victors," conceded the new Oregon senator James W. Nesmith. "The only question is as to the time when it is proper to scalp the dead and strip the wounded." But now was not the time. "If I were Mr. Lincoln," he said dryly, "considering the exigencies of the country, considering that the Union is dissolving and disintegrating beneath our feet, I would turn the Federal bayonets against the office-seekers. I would drive them from this city, and I would not leave a man to tell the tale."[24]

In the dispensing of offices Seward assumed as large a role as paymaster as he could, interfering freely in other departments while protecting his own. He also had the commissioners seeking recognition for their new government and settlement of the Sumter issue. Martin Crawford and John Forsyth realized that Seward offered the best doorway to a solution because he had long advocated a peace policy. Their needs met at a curious intersection: Where Seward hoped that delay might bring reconstruction of the Union, the commissioners viewed it as breathing space for the new government. Using Senator William Gwin as an intermediary, they told Seward they were prepared for war unless some agreement could be reached and assurances given of a peaceful resolution.[25]

Seward protested that the barely organized administration could not act quickly and asked for terms in writing for some brief delay. On the 8th a memorandum delivered to the State Department agreed to postpone action on the mission for twenty days, provided the present military status was preserved and no attempt was made to reinforce the forts. The commissioners believed the signing of any such agreement would amount to virtual recognition of the Confederacy. But Seward was not so easily caught. He lay ill in bed at home and unable to conduct any business, though he wrote Lincoln the next day that "I could muffle up and ride to your House if necessary at any time to day."[26]

Seward did not return to his desk until the 11th. By then Senator Hunter of Virginia had replaced Gwin as the intermediary for the commissioners. Hunter brought the memorandum to Seward and found him "perceptibly embarrassed and uneasy." Seward demurred that he could not see Hunter before clearing it with the president; the next day he left a note for Hunter saying he could not meet with him or the commissioners. With approval from Montgomery, the latter responded on the 13th with a note requesting an official interview. If Seward refused, they would leave Washington and close all peaceful communications between the two governments, thereby setting the stage for war.[27]

This action put Seward in a dilemma. He understood that the issue of secession had turned into one of recognition and that no hint of recognition could be given. If he refused and they left town, however, his only policy would be shattered. For two days he stalled, saying a reply was being prepared. Instead he created a memorandum for the files to clarify his position and protect himself from any appearance of granting recognition. Lincoln approved the document. The commissioners acquiesced because they did not wish formal rejection of their demands since other sources indicated that the administration wanted peace. Crittenden told Crawford that Scott favored Seward's policy and hoped Sumter would be evacuated. "We are sure," the commissioners reported to Montgomery, "that within five days Sumter will be evacuated."[28]

This view was widely shared in the city and across the nation. "Public opinion is fast settling down," noted the *Tribune*, "to the imperative necessity of a step which could not be avoided by any foresight, expedient or policy of the Administration." The *Herald*'s man first denied the rumor, then on the 13th assured readers that the administration had decided on withdrawal. Holt, Stanton, and Dix, still in Washington, were convinced of it. "I confidently believe Sumter will be evacuated," Forsyth wrote Montgomery, "and think a Government messenger left here yesterday with orders to that effect." The same day Lincoln held two cabinet meetings to discuss the question along with appointments.[29]

The Senate, convened in special session to approve appointments, joined the fray. Thomas Clingman of North Carolina used the motion to print the inaugural speech to launch an attack on its overtones of war. Douglas leaped to the defense and was goaded on by Wigfall, who denounced the Republicans and felt obliged to rebut the arguments in Daniel Webster's classic speech for Union in March 1850. Lafayette Foster of Connecticut moved to expel Wigfall, touching off another verbal firefight until the resolution was banished to committee limbo. On the 14th Douglas sought information on the forts from the administration, but the Republicans beat him back. Fessenden moved to strike from the roll the names of all southern senators who had vacated their seats.[30]

Everything bogged down the next day, when Douglas fell into an ugly wrangle with Fessenden, who felt insulted and repaid the compliment in kind. This bickering suited Republican aims nicely. They cared only about the executive sessions where appointments were considered and willingly let the Democrats have the rhetorical stage. Douglas alone seemed to be defending Lincoln. Steering a slippery course among his roles as friend of Lincoln, Union supporter, opposition Democrat, and potential leader of a new Union party, he tried to force the administration to reveal its intentions, disarm threats of war, and possibly separate Lincoln from the hawks in his party.[31]

Douglas desperately craved a role in making peace, and John Forsyth was an old friend and longtime supporter. But Douglas was also exhausted and drinking again to fortify his stamina. He had the courage but not the finesse to walk so fine a line. In trying to coax disclosures from Lincoln, he was by turns adept and incisive, resourceful at finding new ways to hammer home the theme that Sumter should be evacuated and a peace policy adopted. But under duress he could not restrain his temper or his tendency to bully. No one relished the debacle more than Wigfall. "The question now is not of saving the Union, but of saving the peace of the country," he said. ". . . If you want war, you will have it; if you want peace, we are anxious for it. . . . Preserve the Union you cannot; for it is dissolved. Conquer those States and hold them as conquered provinces, you may. . . . You must withdraw your troops; take your flag out of our country; allow us the right of self-government."[32]

While the Senate wrangled, Lincoln deliberated over what to do. His own sentiments balked at the arguments of his generals and advisers that evacuation was the only sound course. He could not deny their expertise, but neither could he accept their conclusions. The cabinet sessions left him frustrated, as did the rumors that withdrawal from Sumter was a done decision. In the cabinet it was Montgomery Blair who advocated reinforcing the fort and Seward who protested against any such policy. A tall, lean man with small, rodentlike eyes set deep in a head that one observer called "an anvil for ideas to be hammered on," Blair was a West Pointer and the only man in the cabinet with military experience.[33]

But Blair could make no headway against the opinions of Scott and

Totten backed by Seward. Even Commander James Ward, who had stood ready to lead a relief expedition since Buchanan had ordered it prepared, gave in to the general's belief that the mission was hopeless and returned to New York on the 11th. That same day some senators urged Frank Blair, who had heard rumors that the fort would be abandoned, to see Lincoln personally. Blair, once a stalwart Jacksonian and later a founder of the Republican party, left his Silver Spring home in a fury and burst in on the president demanding to know if the fort was to be given up. Such an act amounted to treason not only to the country but to the garrison. He pleaded with Lincoln to issue an appeal to the people like that of Jackson in 1832, setting forth the facts and affirming defense of the fort.34

The next day, when his temper had cooled, Blair asked his son to "contrive some apology for me." Montgomery had already taken more tangible action. Recalling the plan proposed earlier by Gustavus Fox, Blair wired his brother-in-law to come at once to Washington. Fox arrived the next morning and went at once with Blair to explain the plan to Lincoln and the military officers. At lengthy cabinet meetings on the 14th Blair used the plan as part of an appeal to reinforce rather than withdraw the garrison. Fox's plan intrigued Lincoln but lacked broad support. Dissatisfied by the inconclusive outcome of the debate, the president asked every cabinet member the next day to answer in writing one question: "Assuming it to be possible to now provision Fort-Sumpter [*sic*], under all the circumstances, is it wise to attempt it?"35

Seward used the occasion to present his peace policy in its fullest form. One telling statement revealed the key assumption behind his approach. "The people of the other slave States," he wrote, "divided and balancing between sympathy with the seceding slave States and loyalty to the Union, have been intensely excited, but at the present moment indicate a disposition to adhere to the Union if nothing extraordinary shall occur to renew excitement and produce popular exasperation." The sympathy of the border states for the seceding states could be eliminated in only one way, "by giving time for it to wear out, and for reason to resume its sway." Sumter had no practical value; even if reinforced, it could be little more than a flash point at which war might start. Why maintain it, then, especially if it could be resupplied only by armed force? "I would not initiate a war to regain a useless and unnecessary position on the soil of the seceding States," Seward argued. "I would not provoke war in any way *now*. I would resort to force to protect the collection of the revenue, because that is a necessary as well as legitimate public object." War could not save the Union. "Fraternity is the element of union—war is the very element of disunion."36

Bates agreed that the fort had no practical value and the attempt might well trigger civil war, "the terrible consequences of which would, I think, find no parallel in modern times. . . . To avoid these evils, I would make great sacrifices—and Fort Sumter is one; but if war be forced upon us by causeless & pertinacious rebellion, I am for resisting it with all the might of the nation." Cameron, finally on board, also advised against resupplying the fort on the ground that all the military men had said the effort was neither possible nor practical. Caleb Smith thought the attempt would be politically unwise, a view to which even Gideon Welles had reluctantly come. Welles shrank from provoking civil war. "It may be impossible to escape it under any course of policy," he said, "but I am not prepared to advise a course that would provoke hostilities."37

Blair alone gave an unqualified yes. Buchanan's weak policy, he argued, had legitimized a rebellion which was fast becoming accepted as "rightful Government." Moreover, Blair was convinced that southerners *believe that the northern men are deficient in the courage necessary to maintain the Government.* The surrender of Sumter would feed this belief and embolden the seceders to demand the rest of the forts, thereby ensuring a collision. Sumter had to be reinforced, and Fox's plan offered the best way to do it. Chase, widely regarded as the palace ultra, offered a surprisingly guarded response, saying that if the attempt would initiate a war, he was against it, but he did not think it would and so he was for it.38

On the 15th Lincoln met again with the cabinet, Scott, Totten, Stringham, and Fox. Totten reviewed several plans for reinforcing Sumter and concluded that all of them would result in a clash of arms. Scott added that even if Fox's plan succeeded, it would do little more than buy time before the attempt would have to be made again. With five of seven cabinet members and his generals against the attempt, Lincoln was in more of a quandary than ever. But he may have noticed, buried in the waffling language of Chase's response, a key assumption that later proved crucial to his thinking: "The attempt to provision is to include an attempt to reinforce, for it seems to be generally agreed that provisioning without reinforcements, notwithstanding hostile resistance, will accomplish no substantial beneficial purpose."39

No one had discussed the possibility of sending supplies without troops, and for a time the notion lay dormant. Hearing that Mrs. Abner Doubleday was in town, Lincoln paid a visit and read her husband's letters for the light they shed on conditions inside Sumter. He also directed Scott to send someone to Sumter to get information directly from Anderson. Scott chose Fox, who left on the 19th. "Our Uncle Abe Lincoln has taken a high esteem for me," Fox wrote his wife, "and wishes me to take dispatches to Major Anderson at Fort Sumpter [*sic*] with regard to its final evacuation and to obtain a clear statement of his condition which his letters, probably guarded, do not fully exhibit."[40]

No matter how Lincoln weighed the facts, the scales tipped heavily in favor of evacuation. Sumter could not be held without reinforcement and could be starved out in a month or two without firing a shot. It had no real military value, and its abandonment would remove a major source of friction. Moderates would be encouraged and praise the administration for pursuing a conservative policy; ultras who had long rallied support on the battle cry of "coercion" would be frustrated. If the fort fell by attack or siege, it would be a devastating blow to the administration and a triumph, even a rallying cry, for secessionists. On the other side of the ledger, withdrawal might demoralize the Republican party and embolden the secessionists, who could view it as a move of necessity rather than concession and therefore a sign of weakness.[41]

And what about Pickens? Ordered by Lincoln to protect the fort, Scott had dispatched the *Mohawk* on the 12th with instructions to land a company on board as reinforcements. The chance of a collision there was smaller, but it could happen if impatient local troops launched a rash attack. Did it make sense to yield Sumter and defend Pickens? Or the small forts in the Florida Keys? Would withdrawal from Sumter spur the new Confederacy to flex its muscles by taking Pickens? Could the new administration and the fragile mosaic that was the Republican party survive the loss of one, let alone both, of the forts? How was he to balance these concerns against the threat of civil war?[42]

While Lincoln wrestled with these questions, Seward groped for a way to keep the commissioners at bay. On the 15th, the day Lincoln solicited the views of his cabinet, an opportunity arose when Supreme Court Justice Samuel Nelson called to discuss what he viewed as serious constitutional issues in using coercive measures to enforce federal laws in the South. Seward assured him that he would spare no effort to maintain a peace policy but that he was embarrassed by the presence of the commissioners. After leaving Seward, Nelson ran into fellow Justice John A. Campbell of Alabama and had a long talk with him. They concluded that peace would best be served by having Seward see the commissioners in some unofficial capacity, and they returned to the secretary's office to impress these views on him.[43]

Out of the question, Seward replied. No one in the cabinet would agree to it. He pulled out a letter from Weed warning that the surrender of Sumter was a bitter pill and would damage the Republicans in the next election and that some better arrangement with the commissioners should have been made. Surprised to hear that Sumter was to be evacuated, Campbell offered to mollify the commissioners and write Jefferson Davis as well. "What shall I say on the subject of Fort Sumter?" he asked Seward.

"You may say to him," replied Seward, "that before that letter reaches him . . . the telegraph will have informed him that Sumter will have been evacuated."

Asked about the Gulf forts, Seward said no action would be taken on them. Campbell offered to convey this news to the commissioners and request that they delay action. Seward emphasized that he needed an answer that very day. Campbell hurried to see Crawford, who agreed to the delay but demanded to know the source of the justice's information about Sumter. Campbell refused to divulge his source but assured him in writing that Sumter would be evacuated in five days. Crawford said he would inform Davis, and Campbell wrote Seward an account of what had transpired.

In effect Campbell, a strong Unionist, had made himself a private intermediary between Seward and the commissioners in hopes of preserving the peace. If the proposed timetable held true, Sumter would be surrendered on the 20th. Of these conversations Lincoln evidently knew nothing. Seward saw him daily and involved himself in every matter that caught his eye, but the deal with Campbell remained his little secret.

THE HAPPY TIDINGS traveled southward fast, thanks to the indefatigable Louis Wigfall. On March 11 he wired both Jefferson Davis in Montgomery and General Beauregard in Charleston that Anderson would be ordered to evacuate Sumter in five days. The cabinet, he added, had reached this decision two days earlier, though he cautioned Beauregard that it "may have been done as ruse to throw you off your guard and enable them to reenforce." By the time Forsyth added his confirmation on the 14th, euphoria was already sweeping Charleston. "Sumter is to be ours without a fight," declared the *Mercury*. "To those who have troubled themselves with vague fears of war on a large scale . . . the relief will be as great as the apprehensions have been grievous."44

The fort had long since become an obsession to Charleston's citizens. Its presence in the harbor, the defiant Stars and Stripes waving above the walls, loomed as a constant reminder that the revolution of 1860 was far from complete and might yet have to be purchased with blood. "How my heart sinks with apprehension for the future," mourned Emma Holmes, "particularly after the last happy month when our boys have been with us." For staunch Unionist Benjamin Perry the threat symbolized by the fort was even more cruel. "That *my son* should ever fight against the Union is what I never expected," he wrote. "But I may have to do so myself."[45]

The mood of the city revealed itself quickly to Beauregard, who had arrived on the 3rd to take command of the Confederacy's Provisional Forces. Making his headquarters in a house at 37 Meeting Street with twin stone towers that gave it a fortresslike charm, the general moved briskly to have his military and social presence felt. On the night after his arrival he attended the theater with Governor Pickens to see *Lady of Lyons* staged by the ladies of Charleston, with the proceeds going to equip the Sumter Guard. It was a glaringly amateur production in which, Emma Holmes complained, the play was not so much acted as "murdered."[46]

Such was Beauregard's opinion of the harbor defenses he inspected with a careful eye on the 4th and 5th: earnest but inept, the work of amateurs. He knew harbor fortifications well, having spent most of the past twelve years on that duty along the Gulf and the Mississippi River. For seven years he had also served as the superintending engineer for the great white elephant of the South, the New Orleans customhouse. Like so many other soldiers who had distinguished themselves in the Mexican War, he nursed a lingering bitterness over the lack of recognition for his performance and slowness of promotion. His removal from the superintendency of West Point had only deepened his resentment.[47]

Secession opened the door to his ambitions. A strong southern sympathizer with roots deep in the Creole culture of New Orleans, he was quick to commend Jefferson Davis on his selection as president; in the next breath he asked for an appointment to the new army. Davis summoned him to Montgomery, offered him the Charleston command, and made him the first brigadier general in the Confederate Army. He seemed the ideal man for the job, having an enviable military record, a reputation as a fine engineer, and a demeanor that would impress the haughtiest of the chivalry. It was a position he could never have hoped to obtain in the U.S. Army at the age of forty-two.

Even Beauregard was surprised at the degree to which Charleston's finest lionized him. His long face with its olive complexion, high cheekbones, dark, brooding eyes, cropped mustache, and protruding chin maintained a grave but courteous reserve. So impassive was his expression that friends swore he went months without smiling. His pleasant voice with its trace of French accent added to his exotic appearance. He fitted the image he wanted for himself as much as others saw in him: that of the French marshal, the modern Napoleon. The ladies adored him and flooded his headquarters with flowers and other gifts. He accepted this shower of devotion as his due, telling War Secretary Leroy Walker he was "very well pleased with this place."

But not with its fortifications. Beauregard began making changes at once, shifting the work to defend the exposed coast better from attack by sea and positioning the guns at his disposal in a ring about Sumter. To give raw troops time to drill, he recruited a large corps of slaves from nearby planters to do the hard labor. He sympathized with complaints from professional officers like R. S. Ripley about the lack of equipment and trained men. "I find a great deal of zeal and energy around me," he told Montgomery, "but little professional knowledge and experience." Nevertheless, he pushed the work forward, telling Walker on the 8th that he hoped within ten days to have the harbor defenses strong enough to prevent any reinforcements from getting to Sumter.[48]

Walker approved the effort and reminded him that reinforcements "must be prevented at all hazards, and by the use of every conceivable agency. Fort Sumter is silent now only because of the weakness of the garrison. Should reinforcements get in, her guns would open fire upon you." Beauregard shared that belief. "If Sumter was properly garrisoned and armed," he observed, "it would be a perfect Gibraltar to anything but constant shelling, night and day, from the four points of the compass. As it is, the weakness of the garrison constitutes our greatest advantage." To exploit it, he built new works, strengthened fortifications, and relocated guns to new positions. Even the *Tribune*'s correspondent conceded that Beauregard had "thrown new life into operations in and about the harbor." Only a short time earlier, he added, "Morris Island and Fort Moultrie were so much exposed that they might easily have been overcome by a force of 1,000 men."[49]

But the general remained uneasy. He inspected the area around the Stono River, down which reinforcements might be carried to Sumter, and laid out works to protect against such a move. Who would oversee the work? His top engineer and ordnance officer, both Georgians, had been abruptly recalled by the governor of that state. "Their absence fills me with care and grief," he wrote Walker, "for other very important matters demand my attention." While Beauregard worked, the rumor mill churned furiously. On his arrival he found the city braced for war, its fears fed by Lincoln's inaugural speech. Then came reports that Sumter would be evacuated without a fight. Beauregard took the news with a grain of salt. On the 9th Walker informed him that the *Pawnee* had left Philadelphia fully provisioned and ready to go to sea. Five days later Walker telegraphed Beauregard and other southern commanders that five steamers had sailed from New York the previous night. "Said to carry arms, provisions, and men," he warned. "Destination not known."[50]

For many people the uncertainty had become as unbearable as the prospect of war. Even the *Tribune* men in Charleston felt this profound uneasiness and began to question Anderson's role in it. Three times he had assured Washington that he needed nothing at a time when he could have been easily resupplied. "During the next six or eight weeks he saw going on all around him the gigantic preparations to wall him in. His fate was as clear as the unclouded sun, if he was not relieved." Yet only twenty days earlier he had assured the government that he required nothing and could hold his position even though he depended on food from the city.[51]

How, asked the *Tribune*'s man, could Anderson not have foreseen that the fort "must be evacuated, or the garrison left to be starved out or relieved by employing thousands of men at the sacrifice of many lives and with the certainty of inaugurating civil war?" Helpless to answer that question, the *Tribune* reporters had to content themselves with playing the old game of cat and mouse with the local authorities close to their heels. "Be easy, gentlemen; I'm not going to stay much longer," said one. "Things are one way or another coming to a close before long."[52]

CHAPTER NINETEEN

Decisions and Delusions

*I can hardly realize that I am living in the age in which I was born and edu-
cated. In the . . . face of the humiliating spectacle of base intrigues to overthrow
the Government by those who are living upon its bounty, and of a pusillani-
mous or perfidious surrender of the trusts confided to them, the country turns
with a feeling of relief . . . to the noble example of fidelity and courage presented by you and your gallant associates.*

—John A. Dix (to Major Anderson)
March 4, 1861[1]

*T*HEY WERE CLOSING THE HARBOR, that much was obvious.
The work had intensified at Fort Johnson and Morris Island, especially at
Cummings Point, where Anderson knew of nine new guns that had been
landed. He figured that any vessel would draw fire from the time it crossed
the bar until it reached the fort. On March 4 the major learned that Beauregard had assumed command. Two days later the new flag of the Confederacy
was hoisted above the customhouse. Did all the activity have to do with Lincoln's inauguration? The men in Sumter did not yet know what Lincoln had
said, but they heard that Charleston's citizens were in an uproar over what
they considered to be its "coercive" character.[2]

The guns at Moultrie, Cummings Point, and Sullivans Island practiced
regularly, marking their ranges. Anderson did not allow his gunners this
luxury because powder and shot were in such short supply. On the 8th one
of the guns at Cummings Point was accidentally loaded with shot during
practice and sent the ball flying at Fort Sumter. As it splashed down near the
wharf, the aroused garrison wheeled out its guns eager to respond. Before the
perturbed Anderson could demand an explanation, an emissary from
Colonel Maxcy Gregg arrived with a letter of apology. The incident left
nerves frayed; some men, weary of confinement, hoped it would lead to a
fight and settle things once and for all.[3]

Instead the siege dragged on. Anderson, unaware of Samuel Cooper's
defection to the South, kept addressing his reports to that worthy. The
weather turned from warm to cold and back again. Captain Foster noticed

that the mouth of the Stono River had been fortified and that a guard ship had been anchored inside the main bar and two of the seized revenue cutters in the main channel near Cummings Point. He was busy filling the loopholes on every tier with solid stone. The back side of Sumter, known as the gorge, especially bothered Foster. Lined with windows and ventilators, it was the fort's Achilles' heel. His men covered the windows with iron shields and added two thirty-two-pounders along with a heavy ten-inch columbiad to defend it from Cummings Point. A third shack was pulled down to burn for fuel. With the blacksmith shop next in line, Foster moved the bellows and apparatus into a casement on the second tier.

On the 12th the guns at Fort Moultrie fired a hundred blank cartridges, and those at other batteries another fifty. The display enabled Anderson to verify that all of Moultrie's guns were in place, but the outburst puzzled him. Then came the news that was already galvanizing Charleston: The fort was to be evacuated. Apparently the city believed it; there was widespread rejoicing, and work on fortifications around the harbor abruptly halted. But no official word had come to Anderson, and until it did, his work would go forward.[4]

He prayed fervently that it was so. "My policy," he wrote three weeks later, "feeling—thanks be to God!—secure for the present in my stronghold, was to keep still, to preserve peace, to give time for the quieting of the excitement . . . in the hope of avoiding bloodshed. There is now a prospect that that hope will be realized, that the separation which has been inevitable for months, will be consummated without the shedding of one drop of blood." That was why he had never asked Holt for reinforcements; had he done so, they would have been sent and precipitated a war. It was not the old administration or the new that was at fault but the cruel circumstances. He did not require reinforcements at the time when they might have easily been sent, and now that he needed them, he could not get them without triggering the war everyone dreaded.[5]

"God has, I feel, been pleased to use me as an instrument in effecting a purpose which will, I trust, end in making us all a better and a wiser people. . . . Our errant sisters . . . may at some future time be won back by conciliation and justice."

ON THE 18TH, a cold, blustery Monday with the gray sky spitting snow, George Templeton Strong took time before visiting the Senate to walk alone to "that hideous unfinished Washington Monument." He found little inspiration there and even less at the Senate. Breckinridge deplored coercion as sure to drive the border states from the Union and condemned the North for refusing to make any concessions. Hale responded in his "slang-whanging stump-orator" style and drew return fire from Wigfall. That evening Strong dined with Senators Baker of Oregon and Anthony of Rhode Island, Simon Cameron, and Truman Smith at the home of Henry S. Sanford, the new minister to Belgium. Nobody seemed to know where matters stood. Even Cameron professed ignorance of Lincoln's policy, a conceit Strong took to be "an official white lie."[6]

There was much talk at table about the growing Union party in Kentucky and Virginia, which Strong dismissed as a delusion. The reports that Sumter would be evacuated made him uneasy, as they did most ultras. From his study at Wheatland, however, the man who had so often made Strong choleric took a more sanguine view. "The people are now becoming gradually reconciled to it," Buchanan said of the withdrawal. "There is a general desire for peace." Joseph Holt agreed that evacuation would "do much to allay popular excitement in South Carolina, & thus take away the ailment on which the revolution is feeding."[7]

At the White House the man who had been president only two weeks felt the strain and a sense of helplessness. Already he was being denounced for drifting and waffling. Montgomery Blair touched off a row by urging that the Chicago postmaster be dismissed at once. Chase wanted his own man for the Columbus post office, Seward wished to review appointments for the territories, and Bates had advice for the Russian post. A supporter suggested helpfully that now was the perfect time for taking steps to annex Canada. That week Tad and Willie Lincoln came down with measles.[8]

The papers assured readers that withdrawal was imminent. Somehow they knew that the entire cabinet except one favored evacuation, as did Scott. Seward was suspected of leaking the news. Rumors also persisted that a collision might occur any day at Fort Pickens. In Texas the outlaw secession convention deposed Sam Houston for refusing to recognize the new Confederate government. The old governor blasted his enemies for yet another high-handed act but would not accept a quiet offer of troops from Lincoln to hold his position. The public mood in the North seemed harder to read than ever. "It cannot be denied," observed the New York *Times*, "that there is a growing sentiment throughout the North in favor of *letting the Gulf States go*."[9]

But Lincoln didn't want to let anything go even though the cabinet and the generals agreed it was the only thing to do. Was he deluding himself in searching for an alternative? Was Seward right in believing that time would heal the breach? Could he afford to hesitate for very long?

Desperate for options, Lincoln wrote Bates on the 18th for an opinion on whether he had power to collect duties offshore, and he sent notes to Chase and Welles asking about the practical difficulties of such an attempt. Three days later he summoned Stephen A. Hurlbut, a lawyer friend from Illinois, who happened to be in Washington that week. Knowing that Hurlbut was a native of Charleston, Lincoln asked him to go there and find out how much, if any, Unionist sentiment remained. Hurlbut left on the Friday evening train in the company of Ward Lamon, who had his own mission to perform in Charleston.[10]

IN CHARLESTON the euphoria subsided and the waiting began again, this time for the official order to come from Washington. "For several days each one successively has been named as 'Evacuation Day,' " noted Emma Holmes peevishly, "& today a telegraph was received appointing tomorrow, but scarcely anyone credits it." Her uncle Edward, who was in Washington, had asked Scott himself whether Sumter really would be given up and had been told it would. Later Scott assured him that there would be no fight but did not mention the fort. Some smelled a rat. "The report of the delivery of Fort Sumter," said William Gilmore Simms, "seems to me a mere *ruse de guerre*, meant to disarm our vigilance."[11]

Was the whole thing a ruse to slip reinforcements into the harbor? The governor, looking gouty and somewhat shabby without his Lucy, who had gone to visit her family in Texas, displayed himself at St. Michael's on Sunday, the 17th, to bask in the reaffirming gospels of salvation and secession from ministers who, quipped the *Tribune*'s man, breathed fire but did not intend to get near the powder. Two days later, on the heels of a winter more like spring, the skies dumped half a foot of snow on the city, killing fruit that had bloomed early. On the 20th George W. Lay, one of Scott's staff, checked into the Charleston Hotel, announced that he had resigned, and went into conference with Pickens and Beauregard.[12]

The next day Pickens was astonished to see at his door Gustavus Fox in the company of Captain H. J. Hartstene, an old friend. Showing his order from Scott, Fox asked permission to visit the fort to ascertain the precise state of Anderson's command and provisions. Pickens must have thought it odd to send as emissary a man who, according to the papers, had devised the most impressive plan to reinforce Sumter. Still, he consented after being assured that the mission was a peaceful one, and he ordered Hartstene to accompany Fox.[13]

They reached Sumter shortly after dark and were met by Anderson and some other officers. Fox handed the major some letters, then walked with him while Hartstene talked with the others. As they reached the parapet, Anderson earnestly condemned Fox's plan for sending relief. It was too late, and he agreed with Scott that nothing could get in from the sea. The only result would be a fight and the onset of civil war, a horror not only in itself but for the political consequences that must follow. While Anderson talked, Fox heard oars nearby but could not see any boat. He mentioned this, adding that the shore guns could not fire with any accuracy on a boat coming in under cover of night, and pointed to a spot where such a landing might be attempted.

Anderson showed little interest, and Fox said no more. The major handed him an inventory of provisions that made painfully clear his inability to hold out beyond April 15. He wanted an engineering officer to brief Fox but ignored Foster, with whom his relations were strained, and took Fox to George Snyder. While they conversed, an indignant Foster rushed up and blurted out a full account of his work on the fort. All of it was being done without instructions or encouragement from Anderson, he said. The visit lasted little more than an hour. Fox returned to Charleston, talked briefly with Beauregard, and left for Washington that same night. The general did not like what he heard. "Were you with Captain Fox all the time of his visit?" he asked Hartstene after Fox had left.

"All but a short period, when he was with Major Anderson."

Beauregard sighed. "I fear that we shall have occasion to regret that short period."[14]

Anderson thought otherwise. The next day he looked closely at the landing spot Fox had pointed out and came away even more convinced that any attempt would be folly. "A vessel lying there will be under the fire of thirteen guns from Fort Moultrie," he told the War Department. In the same letter Anderson enclosed his list of dwindling provisions. Surely at this late stage even the Republican administration must see that it was time to go.[15]

But he did not go, and Charleston and Montgomery grew more uneasy at the delay. "Has Sumter been evacuated?" the puzzled Confederate commissioners wired Beauregard on the 20th. They were fidgety because Secretary Toombs wanted to know why he had received no news. "You have not heard from us because there is no change," they informed Montgomery. Still, they counseled delay, reminding him that "in the present posture of affairs precipitation is war. We are all agreed." An anxious Pickens persuaded Montgomery to extend Beauregard's command to include the South Carolina coast from Beaufort to Georgetown.[16]

On Sunday, the 24th, Lamon and Hurlbut alighted from the 8 a.m. train and went their separate ways to avoid suspicion. Lamon registered at the Charleston Hotel as a Virginian and drew mild curiosity. Hurlbut made himself conspicuous as a native son. On Sunday afternoon he attended church and chatted with old friends; in the evening more came to visit him at his sister's home. That morning he had ridden through the city, lingering along the Battery and the wharves to examine the harbor. To his surprise, not a single ship flew the Stars and Stripes. Foreign vessels had their own flags, southern ships the new Confederate or South Carolina flag. Northern ships left their tall masts bare of colors. The only American flag in the entire harbor waved above Fort Sumter. Along the sandy banks of the harbor Hurlbut saw lines of fortifications with workers busily improving them.[17]

That evening Hurlbut slipped away from his callers and met Lamon outside the Charleston Hotel. The usually boisterous Lamon had managed to keep a low profile; no one yet suspected his business. They went to visit James Petigru, who knew Hurlbut as the son of an old friend. After urging Lamon to see Governor Pickens about visiting the fort, Petigru agreed to meet Hurlbut the next day at 1 p.m. for a more extended conversation. On Monday morning Hurlbut called on every prominent acquaintance he could think of, gleaning the views of each one while concealing his own. That afternoon, while talking with Petigru for two hours, he revealed to him alone the reason for his mission.[18]

What the brooding old lawyer told Hurlbut stunned him. He was the last Unionist left in Charleston; everyone else, even those older heads who in 1832 had staunchly backed Andrew Jackson against the nullifiers, had gone over to the new government. Hurlbut had received the same impression from earlier chats with William H. Trescot; William D. Porter, president of the state senate; A. H. Brown, a member of the secession convention; and several merchants. No one held any allegiance to the Union. The merchants were intoxicated by the belief that the creation of the new republic would bring a golden era when Charleston would become the great commercial emporium for the South that New York had long been for the North.

They believed, Hurlbut realized. All the myths of political economy hammered at so assiduously for years had become axioms to them. That the new constitution blatantly perpetuated the control of the elite did not trouble the majority of people but seemed actually to please them. "In truth," he concluded, "there is not in South Carolina *any people* or any popular thought, or power of popular will." Already a ship with southern papers under a southern flag had sailed for Le Havre, where it hoped to be recognized. Inspectors were being appointed to collect duties on trains that crossed the border. Some said that efforts were under way to annex territory beyond Texas, and to persuade northern Mexico to separate.

Depressed beyond words, Hurlbut bade his sister farewell and caught the Monday night train. There he reunited with Lamon, who told him of his own adventure. Having been graciously received by Pickens, he had presented himself as a confidential agent of the president's to arrange the garrison's transfer to another post. Pickens had sent an aide with him to Sumter, where Lamon conversed privately with Anderson for an hour and a half. Neither man revealed what they discussed, but Anderson confided to Sam Crawford that he would be "amused at the confidential communications" Lamon brought. If nothing else, Lamon had left the officers convinced that the fort would be evacuated.[19]

Back in Charleston, Lamon had asked the governor if a warship could be used to remove the garrison and was told that no such ship would be permitted to enter the harbor. Lamon shrugged. Major Anderson preferred a regular steamer anyway, and Pickens agreed readily to that. Before leaving, Lamon had insinuated that Lincoln truly desired to evacuate the fort and said he would return in a few days. Once back in Washington, he repeated this hope in a letter to Pickens. Of these pledges Lincoln knew nothing. Pickens was pleased but not convinced; he wanted solid evidence of the withdrawal. So did those citizens who heard of Lamon's visit and promise to return. "The people of Charleston," said one woman, "are getting very tired of such *maneuvers.*"[20]

EVERYONE WAS GETTING IMPATIENT, but Seward had no answers for them. Five days had passed since he had assured Judge Campbell that the garrison would be withdrawn within that time. The commissioners checked with General Beauregard, then asked the judge why no official order had been given. On the 21st Campbell went with Judge Nelson to see Seward, who put them off to the next day. They talked at length, Seward assuring them in his buoyant, cheerful manner that all was well and that the evacuation was still on track though he could not explain why the president had not given the order. Lincoln, he said blandly, "was not a man who regarded the same things important that you or I would, and if he did happen to consider a thing important, it would not for that reason be more likely to command his attention."[21]

Campbell asked about Fort Pickens and was told that its status would not be altered. Satisfied, he wrote Martin Crawford that he still had "unabated confidence" that the withdrawal would take place and urged that no new demands be made at present. The cautious Campbell showed the statement to Judge Nelson, who approved it. The next day, the 23rd, Seward was even more expansive in a conversation with the Russian minister, Baron de Stoeckl. There would be no coercion or blockade, he predicted. A peace policy would induce the seceded states to return to the Union; if they did not, they should be allowed to depart in peace. The ultra Republicans were fighting him on this policy, Seward conceded, but he would ultimately prevail.[22]

Stoeckl was even more surprised when Seward expressed a desire to meet the Confederate commissioner A. B. Roman and agreed to invite both of them to tea at the Russian legation two nights later. Roman accepted eagerly, but the next morning Seward sent his regrets, explaining that he could not risk the story's leaking to the papers. A few days later he got support for his convictions from Ward Lamon, who wrote from Charleston after talking with Anderson that "I am satisfied of the policy and propriety of immediately evacuating Fort Sumter." Lamon seemed unconcerned about the propriety of confiding these views to his friend Seward rather than to the president who had sent him there.[23]

On the 25th Seward attended a dinner at the British Embassy and startled Lord Lyons with a saber-rattling speech against foreign aggressors. That same week the Senate ended its prolonged spasm of futility with a last gasp of bickering. Douglas dominated the floor but could not gain support for his resolution, which was finally tabled by a 23–11 vote on the 27th. Two days earlier the Senate had passed a resolution from Lazarus Powell of Kentucky asking Lincoln to show it the dispatches from Major Anderson. Lincoln declined the request, saying it was incompatible with the public interest.[24]

Kentucky's other senator, former Vice President Breckinridge, presented a resolution urging removal of all troops from the South. Clingman of North Carolina followed with a version that also banned any collecting of revenues; both were ignored. Breckinridge struggled with feelings as divided as his state. He resented Douglas for seizing center stage as usual and for cleverly trying to put them in bed together by saying Lincoln had accepted Kentucky's idea of a national convention and constitutional amendment. An irate Breckinridge denied that Kentucky was satisfied, or that he had any kinship with Douglas.[25]

Republican ultras too were restive over the evacuation rumors and went to confront Lincoln at the White House. After what was described as a "contumelious" interview, Lyman Trumbull offered a resolution saying that "the true way to preserve the Union is to enforce the laws of the Union" and urging the president to hold and protect public property in all the states. Clingman and Douglas demanded a roll call to "find out how many men in the Senate are willing to vote to censure the President for withdrawing the troops at Fort Sumter."[26]

"I am not aware," observed Trumbull dryly, "that the troops have been withdrawn from Fort Sumter."

Once again the Senate managed, as it had so often, to duck a vote on a tough question. The body retreated to executive session, then dawdled briefly on patronage matters before adjourning that same day. Like its predecessor, the special session sat longer than intended and achieved less than was hoped. "When war is threatened, when force is paraded," observed newcomer Timothy O. Howe of Wisconsin, "that does not seem to be the happiest time to negotiate." Having failed to resolve the national crisis, the senators journeyed home, unsure of what would await them on their return to Washington.[27]

The uncertainty left the commissioners uneasy at having gone so far out on a limb. In defense they reminded Montgomery that they were buying time for the new government. "We are not wholly prepared with troops and munitions of war for the land service," they noted, "nor have we a navy afloat with which to meet and contest with this Government the issues of war upon the seas." They believed that the peace party in the North was daily growing stronger, and that ultimately the administration would have to deal with them. The hardest step for Lincoln was to order the evacuation in the face of fierce opposition from Republican ultras. "When this first step was taken," they predicted, ". . . the next, and each succeeding one will be less difficult."[28]

ON THE MORNING OF MARCH 25 Mary Chesnut settled herself into a seat on the crowded train for Charleston. John Manning had asked her to save a place for a young lady, and James had obligingly moved to another seat. The young lady turned out to be Manning himself, and he talked about politics. Expect the unexpected in all future elections, he predicted. The state was carved up into cliques that feigned politeness to one another but hungered for office. "The old story," concluded Mary, "the outs want to be in."[29]

She was feeling on the outs herself after a miserable week in Camden. The trip home from Montgomery had been a nightmare in crowded, dusty cars, with James muttering none too softly that he wished they could have separate coaches like the English so as to escape the whiskey-drinking, tobacco-chewing rabble. They had a quarrel, exacerbated by Mary's throbbing impacted tooth. A woman in the car raved loudly about being separated from her daughter. No sooner was she quieted than a soused preacher began spouting Scripture to soothe a distraught widow. To calm her nerves, Mary took some opium and relished the tranquillity it brought.[30]

During the Sunday layover in Augusta, James tried to patch up their spat, but Mary spurned him. "After my stormy youth," she wrote, "I did so hope for peace & tranquil domestic happiness. There is none for me in this world." But at Camden, at least, there were the smiling faces of servants, a hot bath, and soft, white bed linens, and good coffee with fresh cream. Still, she writhed in pain from a backache and neuralgia of the face. James left to avert a duel between a friend who had defended a Negro in a trial and the wretch who had slapped him for doing so. In his absence Mary treated her back with chloroform ointment and blistered herself so badly she could scarcely stand or walk.

The next day she dined with Judge Withers, who was as irascible as ever, abusing everyone that came to mind. She went into Camden to have her tooth pulled and came home in pain to learn that her second cousin Kitty Boykin was to marry a man twice widowed with ten children. The news came from James's sister; they talked much of the night, "raked up & dilated & harrowed up the bitterness of twenty long years," leaving Mary nervous and exhausted. Finding no relief from her misery in the next few days, she escaped gratefully to Charleston. On the trip she enjoyed the company of the charming, outrageously handsome Manning. In the city she drove the Battery with Susan Rutledge and bought something at Russell's Bookshop but felt too sluggish even to try reading it. "Something wrong in the atmosphere here for me," she decided. "It enervates & destroys me." She went shopping for images or "cartes de visite" of the secession celebrities and met Captain Hartstene, who sent her a bouquet and called that evening to chat for an hour.[31]

The Chesnuts had come to town because the secession convention reconvened on the 26th and James had to be there. While he sat through its tedious sessions, Mary basked in a steady stream of callers and admirers. She breakfasted with Manning, walked the Battery with Robert Rutledge, dined with Trescot and others. The attention showered on her displeased James, who ordered her not to walk the Battery with any other men. "Is this not too ridiculous at my time of life," she protested. Still, she delighted at both the attention and the effect it produced on James. The repaying of slights or neglect by kindling fires of jealousy was an old parlor game at which she excelled. Manning seemed especially eager for her company. Despite his duties at the convention, he seemed always on hand or quick with flowers or a note. Once he showed up dressed to have his picture taken. That same day Mary prodded James to dress up and go with her to have their images recorded. It had become the fashion to exchange pictures with friends, but Mary did not like the results. "Mr. Chesnut very good," she said on seeing them, "mine like a washer woman."

Mary was not so dizzied by the social whirl that she could not see behind it the endless jockeying for place. Some, like James Hopkins Adams, were to her eyes shameless in their ambition; others merely looked silly. "This war began a War of Secession," she observed. "It will end a War for the Succession of Places." Even those who already had places were not satisfied.

Milledge Bonham held high rank in the state's militia but was convinced there would be no war and wanted to get into Congress. "As expensive as Washington was," he admitted to William Porcher Miles, "I feel sensibly the absence of $250 per month, out of practice and with a tolerably large family."[32]

While Mary Chesnut basked in the social limelight, Caroline Gilman found pleasure of a very different sort. The military buildup had chased residents from their homes on Sullivans Island, but Caroline secured a permit and took some friends with her for a tour on Friday, the 29th. The wharf was a jumble of soldiers in uniforms of all kinds from drab grays to the brilliant reds of the Zouaves. After passing the guard, they met a lieutenant Caroline knew and drove along the row of summer houses. Nothing about them reminded her of summer. The first battery stood on the lot next to Caroline's house; the second, on Mrs. McDowell's lot. A third was set up in Fort Moultrie, and two more were on the grounds of other friends. She was startled by the youth of the boys manning the cannon. A new battery was going in near her own house, its company quartered at Mr. Hatch's house. The visitors returned to Moultrie, where the men of the Washington Light Infantry were camped in tents, then drove back to the wharf.[33]

The beach glittered with sunlight dancing on calm waters as it had in happier days. In the distance Fort Sumter looked for all the world to her like a noble stag at bay, surrounded by the troops and batteries. Even the much-maligned floating battery was ready to be tested. The men had finished their work and were growing impatient. Beauregard said all was ready. Amid the massed legions of war and their terrible instruments, Caroline still clung doggedly to the hope of peace. As a sign of that belief she brought to the island with her a gardener to arrange her flower beds for the coming spring, when the grounds would no longer be occupied by soldiers and cannon. All the flowers needed was time and room to grow.

But time was running out. On that very day, across the water from where Caroline stood, the last barrel of flour in Fort Sumter was pulled out and opened.[34]

CHAPTER TWENTY

The Great Divide

The impression which I have received is that the course of the President is drifting the country into war, by want of decision. For my part I see nothing but incompetency in the head. The man is not equal to the hour.

—Charles Francis Adams
March 28, 1861[1]

AT SIX ON THE MORNING OF MARCH 27, William H. Russell of the London *Times* awoke to find his train arriving in Washington. He had just passed his first night in the berth of a sleeping car, where the company included some genial prizefighters full of whiskey, song, and laughter on their way to cadge government jobs. One large man with a broken nose and mellow eyes, a showcase of jewelry, rings, chains, and pins, told Russell he was "Going to Washington to get a foreign mission from Bill Seward." The conductor couldn't quiet their boisterous good times, but at last the whiskey took its toll and they lapsed into deep, snoring sleep.[2]

Outside the depot Russell caught his first glimpse of the white marble Capitol with the scaffold and cranes poised above the unfinished cupola. The curb was a clamor of black coachmen seeking riders, but he had the good fortune to meet Henry S. Sanford on the New York ferry and made the trip in his company. Sanford's waiting carriage drove Russell to Willard's down Pennsylvania Avenue with its rows of ailanthus trees in whitewashed sentry boxes. At that hour he saw mostly black faces. Russell marveled at the jumble of buildings between the imposing mass of the Capitol at one end and the Treasury Building at the other.

Willard's looked to be the largest pile of masonry among them. Inside, a crowd of men, their pockets bulging with papers, crowded the halls, hurried up and down the corridors, in and out of doors, seeking the reward of office and determined to have it at whatever cost or inconvenience. The stuffy room given to Russell still bore the litter of testimonial letters left behind by its most recent occupant. Later he managed to get a sitting room with small bedroom attached, giving him more space but no relief from the muggy heat or the vile slime of the hallways, which phalanxes of spittoons failed to keep clean.

The dining hall was a cavern filled with tables and chairs that scraped incessantly on the carpetless floor. Huge numbers of people flocked in to feed and fly away as quickly as possible. Russell heard one man order for breakfast, "Black tea and toast, scrambled eggs, fresh spring shad, wild pigeon, pigs' feet, two robins on toast, oysters," and large quantities of breads and cakes. The waste was as prodigious as the crowd. Russell found no relief anywhere; the smoking room, the bar, the barbershop, the reception room, even the ladies' drawing room, were packed with people.

That evening Russell went gratefully to Henry Sanford's home for dinner. The guests included Senator Henry B. Anthony of Rhode Island, former senator Truman Smith, a journalist, a rail official, and the man he was most eager to meet. Seward's slight, stooped body seemed scarcely able to hold up his large head, with its broad brow, prominent nose, twinkling eyes at once secretive and penetrating, and crown of fine silvery hair. Russell saw at once that Seward was "a subtle, quick man, rejoicing in power, given to perorate and to oracular utterances, fond of badinage, bursting with the importance of state mysteries." After dinner he amused everyone with stories of the pressure put on Lincoln by office seekers and, in his practiced way, talked freely while divulging little.

Russell asked about the rumors in the New York papers that Fort Sumter would be evacuated. "That is a plain lie," Seward retorted. "No such orders have been given. We will give up nothing we have—abandon nothing that has been entrusted to us. If people would only read these statements by the light of the President's inaugural, they would not be deceived." His tone was contemptuous of those who took secession too seriously. "I myself, my brothers, and sisters, have been all secessionists," he said grandly. "We seceded from home when we were young, but we all went back to it sooner or later. These States will all come back in the same way."

Seward took Russell in tow, as he did everyone of importance to him. At the State Department next morning Russell found the old mansion suitably dingy, its appointments and hallways so quiet that "one would see much more bustle in the passages of a Poor Law Board or a parish vestry." Seward sat in his comfortable office ornamented with bookshelves and engravings, smoking a cigar. His son Fred was there: a slight, delicate-looking man with dark eyes, a high forehead, and a modest, amiable manner. They were awaiting the minister of the new kingdom of Italy, who was to have an audience with the president.

The Chevalier Bertinatti soon made his appearance in full court attire of blue and silver lace, white gloves, cocked hat, sword, sash, and riband of the cross of Savoy. Seward took the Chevalier to the White House by carriage while Fred escorted Russell through a private door onto the grounds. The interior of the White House reminded the journalist of a bank with its glass doors and plain heavy chairs until they entered a spacious room that was richly furnished. Seward showed the Chevalier to the center of the room and motioned Fred and Russell to one side, whispering slyly, "You are not supposed to be here."

Russell could scarcely believe the figure that entered the room with a loose, shambling, almost unsteady gait. A wrinkled, ill-fitting black suit gave him the appearance of an undertaker. Wide, projecting ears stood out from a bristling neck of black hair on a long, irregular head with dark, deep-set eyes, a prodigious mouth, a large nose, and a yellow, sinewy neck. He was a remarkable specimen, Russell marveled, with an expression of kindliness and sagacity that belied the absurdity of his appearance. "Although the mouth was made to enjoy a joke," he noted shrewdly, "it could also utter the severest sentence which the head could dictate."

The president smiled at everyone until brought to attention by Seward's staid manner and the grave, formal bows of the Chevalier. Lincoln responded with abrupt, lurching bows, listened attentively as the minister read the royal letter, then read his reply. When the Chevalier retired, Seward introduced the president to Russell. "The London 'Times' is one of the greatest powers in the world,—in fact, I don't know anything which has much more power,—except the Mississippi," Lincoln said affably. "I am glad to know you as its minister."

That evening Russell dined with Seward, his son, and Sanford. They talked politics, Seward insisting again that the government's policy could be found in Lincoln's inaugural. Russell couldn't spot it there, but he enjoyed a rubber of whist, during which Seward extolled the abilities of Jefferson Davis. Back at the hotel, Russell found a card from Lincoln inviting him to dinner at the White House the following day, the 28th. It was to be the first state dinner given by the president, with the cabinet and General Scott in attendance. All day long Russell talked to a steady stream of congressmen, journalists, and prominent visitors and was shocked at the depth of their southern sympathies. Most of them ignored Lincoln except to make him the butt of some joke or gleefully to relate the story of his sneaking into Washington disguised in a Scotch cap and cloak.

At the White House that evening he entered the same reception room as the day before, to find Mary Lincoln seated to receive her guests. Russell saw a plain, plump woman acutely conscious of her new status, wearing a beautiful, brightly colored dress and wielding a fan with great vigor. Everyone was there except Scott; while they waited, Seward introduced Russell to his colleagues and their families. It struck Russell that no one wore lace or ribbon or even epaulets, except one old naval officer who was a veteran of the War of 1812. Some had on evening dress; others, black frock coats. Of the cabinet members he was most impressed by Chase and his beautiful, bright daughter Kate.

But it was Lincoln who fascinated Russell. The gangly president was brilliant in the way he used his famous anecdotes. Where sophisticated men would ease out of an embarrassing position with a shrug or polite remark, Lincoln provoked laughter with a joke and then slipped away. Finally it was announced that Scott had arrived but suffered an attack of his old illness, and the dinner proceeded without him. Russell was seated between Bates and the president's energetic young secretary John Hay. The first formal state dinner offered no brilliance of decor or cuisine. The food, cooked in what Russell called the "Gallo-American" style, was accompanied by French wines and served on a table adorned with vases of flowers.

After dinner they adjourned to the drawing room, where several politicos joined the party. Russell's probes yielded little other than a conviction that Britain, with its strong antislavery sentiments, was duty bound to resist southern attempts to found a nation based on slavery. Except for the diversity of accents, which to his ear sounded like a group of foreigners speaking English, they all seemed so ordinary to him. He returned to Willard's still puzzling over what, if anything, they were doing to address the crisis. More than one editor had already presented an unflattering comparison of Lincoln's policy, or lack of policy, to that of Buchanan. What indeed had Lincoln done any differently?

In the lobby a man introduced himself as the correspondent of a New York paper and asked about the dinner. Russell put him off by saying he was pleased with both the president and the affair. As they chatted, the man claimed that he had created the post of Washington correspondent for the New York papers. "At first I merely wrote news, and no one cared much," he said; "then I spiced it up, squibbed a little, and let off stories of my own. Congressmen contradicted me—issued cards—said they were not facts. The public attention was attracted, and . . . so the Washington correspondence became a feature in all the New York papers by degrees."

Russell nodded and made his way through the swarm of office-seekers still paying court to any congressmen they could find. What a queer spectacle, these men groaning with documents to press upon unwilling victims. Why had so many of them abandoned their callings of a lifetime to come hundreds of miles for the lottery hope of a place that could be theirs for only four years? As advertisements in the hotel attested, cottage industries had grown up to serve their needs for letters, certificates, testimonials, and other blandishments.3

Tomorrow was Good Friday. No one in the city had more crosses to bear than the president who was so facile with a joke. He would need much more than humor, and so far Russell had seen little more. "Everywhere the Southern leaders are forcing on a solution with decision and energy, whilst the Government appears to be helplessly drifting with the current of events. . . . To an outside observer, like myself, it seemed as if they were waiting for events to develop themselves, and rested their policy rather upon acts that had occurred, than upon any definite principle designed to control or direct the future."4

THE CRISIS SEEMED TO IMPLODE on Lincoln that fateful Thursday, the 28th. The *Tribune* excited its readers with the news that two weeks earlier the administration had sent the *Brooklyn* to land reinforcements at Fort Pickens, thereby violating the truce. The Senate adjourned amid calls by Republicans for a special session. On that day too expired the delay granted the commissioners by Montgomery. While Lincoln had been walking through the ritual with the Chevalier and exchanging pleasantries with Russell that afternoon, his mind had churned with information that pulled him toward a decision. He had Hurlbut's report, an oral account from Lamon, and a memo from Fox, with whom he had spoken several times. He had also an interview with Scott that left him deeply disturbed.5

The report from Hurlbut could not have been more unequivocal. "Separate Nationality is a fixed fact . . . an unanimity of sentiment which is to my mind astonishing . . . no attachment to the Union. . . . There is positively nothing to appeal to." Lincoln stared glumly at the words and the supporting argument scrawled across sixteen foolscap pages. Power still remained in the hands of conservatives who hoped for peaceful separation and friendly relations afterward, but there existed an active, restless minority eager to provoke a collision as a means of ending the stalemate and uniting the Confederacy. Neither group, Hurlbut stressed, would be satisfied with anything less than the recognition of absolute independence.6

Hurlbut did not mince words. Any attempt to enforce the law would bring war; no policy could avoid this possibility. If Sumter were surrendered, demands would be made at once for Pickens and the forts in the Florida Keys. Any such course would tarnish the national honor. "I have no doubt," he added, "that a ship known to contain *only provisions* for Sumpter [*sic*] would be stopped & refused admittance. Even the moderate men who desire not to open fire, believe in the safer policy of time and starvation." Lincoln pondered this observation and the one that followed: "At present the garrison can be withdrawn without insult to them or their flag. In a week this may be impossible and probably will."

Lamon told Lincoln much the same thing less cogently. Bates replied to the president's inquiry with an opinion that Lincoln had no right to force collection of duties in the seceded states, and Chase was little more encouraging. Aware that Scott was expected at the state dinner that evening, Lincoln sent a note asking the general to come early. Before leaving for the White House, Scott confided to his aide Erasmus Keyes that the president probably wished to converse about evacuating Forts Sumter and Pickens. Lamon, he added, had told him in confidence of a desire on the part of Governor Pickens to return South Carolina to the Union.[7]

The interview proved a disaster. Scott assumed that Lamon had reported their long discussion about the forts to Lincoln, but he had not. The general presented a memorandum urging the president to abandon *both* Sumter and Pickens. This gesture, he argued, would ensure the loyalty of the border states and, if Governor Pickens was sincere, might bring South Carolina and Florida back into the Union. Lincoln was appalled. Surrendering Pickens had never occurred to him and made no sense at all. Anderson has played us false, he said tersely, and Scott's own inconsistency of views about Fort Pickens bothered him as well. The administration might fall if a more decided policy were not adopted, and he hinted that if Scott could not carry out his views, then Lincoln would find someone who could.[8]

Deeply distressed, Scott lingered awhile but never went into the state dinner. Although he used his dysentery as an excuse, he may simply have been too upset to join the party. The next day he was so troubled that he spent much of the evening and the following day writing a short chronology of Forts Sumter and Pickens to justify his position. Lincoln had also nettled him by saying he had been slow to make the necessary preparations for reinforcing Pickens even though the order had been given on March 5.

Later Lincoln said that the notion of surrendering Pickens gave him a "cold shock." Since taking office, he had pursued a deliberate course, keeping a lid on the crisis while he learned as much as he could as fast as he could. He had tried to make his position clear in the inaugural speech. No troops had been called up, no steps toward mobilization taken, and no overt action launched. He had issued no inflammatory statements or threats that might arouse antagonism in the South, and he had refrained from any attempt to recapture the forts seized by southern states. The "forbearance of this government," he said later, was "extraordinary."[9]

This restraint cost him dearly in some quarters, where prudence was interpreted as vacillation. He expected criticism from ultra Republicans. Hundreds of letters echoed an Ohio Republican who warned Chase that "if Fort Sumter is evacuated, the new administration is done forever, the Republican party is done." Even friendly editors complained of a "do nothing" administration and published editorials with pointed titles like "WANTED—A POLICY!" and "WHAT WILL BE DONE?"[10]

His friends too had grown restless and uneasy. From Gustave Koerner came a pointed admonition that "the strong and enthusiastic Union feeling among the German element, which would have made them draw the sword in a moment for the enforcement of the laws, makes them fret . . . under the present peace policy." Trumbull's resolution in the Senate calling on the president to enforce the laws and hold and protect public property was a shaft aimed not only at Seward's peace (or appeasement) policy but also at Lincoln's inaction. And no one was closer or more loyal to Lincoln than Lyman Trumbull.[11]

In vain did Lincoln remind northerners that it took time to reorganize the government and prepare for action, let alone conduct even ordinary business amid the office-seekers infesting the city. The crisis was in its fifth month, and the thought of more months of suspense and tension was more than people could bear. Lincoln could not help noticing this state of mind among supporters and opponents alike, who taunted him for "backing down" and echoing Buchanan's weak, misguided policy.

For months the prevailing sentiment in the North had seemed to be that time was on the Union's side, that the secession movement would run out of steam, the cotton states would come to their senses, and the border states would see the folly of secession. This belief was what underlay Seward's policy, to which he clung with dogged optimism. But gradually it had eroded, given way to a weary, almost petulant demand for an end to the crisis as well as a more exalted plea to defend the ideals of the Republic that served as a model for the world. Lincoln had not been East long enough to witness this transformation, but since his arrival he had begun to sense its growing strength.

Throughout the ordeal one vociferous camp of Republicans had insisted that compromise or concession spelled doom for the party. But many of the merchants and business interests that had earlier pleaded for peace and conciliation now demanded an end to the uncertainty that paralyzed commerce. Even the wealthy merchant and longtime Buchanan supporter Caleb Cushing conceded that "If civil war comes . . . my legal duty would force me to support." Zachariah Chandler of Michigan welcomed the prospect, observing in a widely publicized letter, "Without a little blood-letting this Union will not, in my estimation, be worth a rush."[12]

By winter the crisis had festered long enough for every element to discover its worse alarms. Westerners feared the possibility of losing control of the lower Mississippi River and with it access to the Gulf. As Douglas proclaimed, "We can never consent to being shut up within the circle of a Chinese wall, erected and controlled by others without our permission." Border states dreaded the cost and complexity of a customs and defense system. Eastern interests worried about the diversion of overseas trade to southern ports as well as the loss of southern markets. A prescient few already sensed the profits to be had in a surge of military contracts.[13]

What would happen to existing contracts and debts? How would southern courts treat northern claims? What about admiralty and maritime jurisdiction? Northern copyright and patent rights? How would the North, which had passed a new high tariff, compete with the duty-free ports promised by the South? Patriots and idealists who pleaded for preservation of the noblest government ever devised grew less willing to endure its destruction as the price of peace. The loss of federal forts and facilities grated hard on a people devoted to the ideal of private property. Those with antislavery sentiments relished a crusade against the "Slavocracy," and even those tepid on the subject welcomed the chance to settle once and for all controversies that had tormented American society for decades rather than pass them along to their children.[14]

Lincoln was not slow to sense the fear and discontent that showed itself in growing demands for action. He knew too how many obstacles stood in the way of formulating a coherent policy. Sumter itself was not the problem; it was the flash point for a host of problems that would not be touched even if it were resolved peacefully. But as a flash point it had to be dealt with, and time was running out.

Like the nation itself, Lincoln was approaching a great divide from which there could be no going back whatever course he chose. The republic(s) that emerged on the other side of that divide would be vastly different from the one they now knew and shared. What the new order would be no one could say, but that it would be another world no one could doubt. What Lincoln felt increasingly was the chilling realization of how much depended on what he did or did not do. The hardest thing was to know what *really* mattered, what counted for most in the shifting scheme of things. Later generations would talk about the inescapable loneliness of the presidency. Never was that loneliness more crushing than in the winter of 1860–61, when the lamest of lame ducks and an untested electee grappled with the largest question ever to face the occupant of an office he had just won or was about to surrender.

During the state dinner that evening Lincoln seemed in good humor, spicing the small talk with his usual stream of anecdotes. But his mind was stewing and simmering over the information received that day. As the guests took their leave, Lincoln called the cabinet members back into the Red Room and told them of Scott's recommendation that Pickens be evacuated along with Sumter. They looked at him in stunned silence until Blair spoke up. Scott, he asserted, "is playing the part of a politician, not a general . . . no one pretends that there is any military necessity for the surrender of Fort Pickens." Although Blair denounced Scott's course, no one doubted that his shafts were aimed directly at Seward, whom he considered the éminence grise behind the general.[15]

All night long Lincoln lay awake, his mind feverish with the forts. He awoke on Good Friday morning locked in depression. The cabinet met at noon with Cameron absent and discussed two options: Scott's recommendation to withdraw and the shipping of provisions and reinforcements with due notice to South Carolina. Someone, probably Lincoln, raised the possibility of sending provisions but not reinforcements and notifying Governor Pickens of this peaceful mission. This approach offered an alternative between the extremes of withdrawal or reinforcement. It had the merit of not provoking an immediate clash and, more important, of shifting the burden of decision for war to the other side.[16]

As they talked, Bates despaired of arriving at a conclusion. At his suggestion Lincoln posed questions to which they all jotted down answers and read them aloud. Bates led off by saying that Pickens and the Keys forts should be reinforced whatever was done with Sumter. As for the latter, the time had come "either to evacuate or relieve it." Blair dismissed Scott's advice as worthless; Sumter could and should be relieved without regard to any other factor. Chase favored holding Pickens and provisioning Sumter. If the attempt to supply Sumter was resisted by force, reinforcements should be sent.[17]

Welles was even more adamant about reinforcing Pickens and Sumter. He favored an attempt to provision Sumter with due notice to the governor. "There is little probability that this will be permitted," he conceded, and perhaps reinforcements should be sent as well. "But armed resistance to a peaceable attempt to send provisions to one of our own forts will justify the government in using all the power at its command, to reinforce the garrison and furnish the necessary supplies." If Lincoln had not already seized on this idea, Welles provided it for him in plain language.

Smith dissented. "Believing that Ft Sumter cannot be . . . defended," he asserted, "I regard its evacuation as a necessity." But even he called for "the most vigorous measures for the defense of the other forts" and for blockading southern ports. That left Seward, who continued to oppose any expedition because it would trigger a shooting war. Sumter was the wrong place to start a fight, he insisted; let Anderson retire, but let the government "at every cost prepare for a war at Pensacola and Texas." Still, Seward could see that sentiment had shifted against him. Bates, Chase, and Welles had joined Blair, and already Seward was modifying his own position.

Lincoln saw in their replies what he already believed: None of them expected peace to endure; the crucial issue was when, where, and how hostilities would begin. Even Chase, who had been so cautious two weeks earlier, argued that if war came, it should "be best begun in consequence of military resistance to the efforts of the administration." The responses also supported Lincoln's reluctance to abandon Sumter regardless of who advised doing so. But he had not waited for their views. On the previous day, he had instructed Gustavus Fox to prepare an order for the ships, men, and supplies needed for his proposed expedition.[18]

Fox did so at once in his brisk way. The next day, the 29th, Lincoln scribbled on the bottom of Fox's memorandums an order for Cameron and Welles to prepare an expedition that could sail as early as April 6. It called for readying the *Pocahontas* at Norfolk, the *Pawnee* at Washington, and the *Harriet Lane* at New York along with three hundred men and supplies for twelve months for one hundred men. Fox went to New York to procure a large commercial steamer and three tugs needed for the troops.[19]

The order had gone forth, yet Lincoln had not yet fully committed himself. He had decided to resupply the fort rather than evacuate it. But he had not ordered the expedition to sea, did not even know whether, if launched, it would be sent to Sumter or Pickens. Although he didn't share Seward's optimism that enough time would see the crisis past, he let linger the hope, however faint, that some way to avoid a shooting war might turn up. What that way out might be, he could scarcely fathom. The strain was clearly affecting him. On Saturday, the 30th, his head pounded with a migraine headache all day until, Mary Lincoln noted, he "keeled over" for the first time in years.[20]

Meanwhile, Seward coped with another kind of headache. Nearly every aspect of his plan had gone awry, forcing him to improvise at every turn. Campbell was at his door on the 30th with a telegram from Governor Pickens asking why nothing had been heard from Lamon about the evacuation. Seward promised a reply on Monday, April 1. At the cabinet meeting he had not only modified his views by urging defense of Fort Pickens but also asked Lincoln to consult Captain Montgomery C. Meigs. An outstanding engineer, Meigs had built the Rock Creek Aqueduct and overseen the new dome and wings of the Capitol. In recent months he had worked on the Keys forts and knew the situation at Pickens.[21]

Meigs had been exiled to the Keys because of a lengthy feud with John B. Floyd. Never one to hide his opinions, Meigs defended the efficiency and integrity of his work with such vehemence that Buchanan saw no choice but to dismiss him. Meigs had no love for Buchanan, saying that he "ought to be impeached & convicted of treasonable weakness." The resignation of Floyd and the shakeup of the cabinet enabled Scott and Holt to reinforce the Keys forts and recall Meigs to Washington in February to take charge again of the aqueduct. His friends reveled in his revenge. "They sent Meigs to gather a thistle," said the elder Frank Blair, "but thank God, he has plucked a laurel."

Seward took Meigs to see Lincoln just after the cabinet meeting. He told him he wanted the president to speak with someone who knew what he was talking about and who could climb aboard a horse in the field, which, Seward said, no one would think of in connection with Scott or Totten. Lincoln talked freely with Meigs about all the forts. Men could be found to relieve Sumter, Meigs said, but officers of high rank thought it unwise. Lincoln asked whether Pickens could be held. Certainly, Meigs replied, if the navy had not lost it already.

"Could you not go down there again and take a general command of these three great fortresses and keep them safe?" asked Lincoln, referring to Pickens and Forts Jefferson and Taylor on the Keys. Meigs said he was only a captain and could not command the majors there. Seward brushed aside the objection, saying Meigs must be promoted. The proper thing to do was to put Meigs in charge, and he would have a plan for them by four the next afternoon. After all, Seward added, when Pitt wished Quebec taken, he did not send a veteran general but a bright young man named Wolfe to do the job. Lincoln said he would consider it and let Meigs know in a day or two.

Meigs walked home with Seward, who said he was gratified at the interview. Scott had put the cabinet in a bind by advising the evacuation of both forts, whereas Seward wished to abandon Sumter as too near the capital and to tempt Jefferson Davis to attack it while making a fight at Pickens and in Texas. This would put the burden of war, "which all men of sense saw must come," on those who had provoked it by rebellion. He promised to contact Meigs soon.[22]

"The bewilderment of the LINCOLN Administration is not a whit lessened to-day," observed the *Mercury's Washington correspondent that busy Saturday the 30th. "The outside pressure both for and against . . . a war policy is*

tremendous. Meantime, it is said that the Southern Commissioners, like other people, are getting heartily sick of SEWARD's do-nothing tactics."[23]

Seward was doing plenty that morning. Walking to Scott's headquarters on Seventeenth Street, he found the general at his desk amid a pile of papers. With a smile on his face, he said gravely, "Lieutenant-General Scott, you have officially advised the President . . . that, in your judgment, it will not be practicable to relieve Fort Sumter and Fort Pickens. I have come to you, from the President, to tell you that he directs that Fort Pickens shall be relieved."[24]

Scott caught the humor and echoed the gravity. Placing his huge hands on the table, he pushed himself up with an immense effort until his enormous body towered over Seward. "Well, Mr. Secretary," he replied, "the great Frederick used to say that 'when the King commands, nothing is impossible.' Sir, the President's orders shall be obeyed!"

Still smarting from his interview with Lincoln, Scott scribbled a detailed account of his actions on both forts. He thought he had taken care of Pickens. In January he had finally persuaded Buchanan to send the *Brooklyn* with a company of artillery under Captain Israel Vogdes. But after the truce had been arranged a week later, Holt and Toucy instructed the commander not to land the company unless the fort was attacked. Scott claimed not to have known of this note until March 25, by which time matters had grown more confused. Lincoln had ordered Scott verbally on March 5 to secure all the forts; when nothing was done, he repeated the order in writing on the 11th. Scott dispatched the *Mohawk* to Pensacola with orders for Vogdes to go ashore at Pickens.[25]

Everyone assumed this had been done, though Erasmus Keyes had briefed Scott on the difficulty of landing ordnance matériel on the beach near Pickens. At breakfast on Easter Sunday, the 31st, Scott prodded his aide for more details. Keyes was puzzled by the expression on his chief's face as he listened silently for half an hour on why it would be futile to land heavy guns and carriages on the sandy beach. When he had finished, Scott took a long roll from a pile of maps and plans and handed it to Keyes. "Take this map to Mr. Seward," he ordered, "and repeat to him exactly what you have just said to me about the difficulty of reinforcing Fort Pickens."[26]

Keyes strolled down Sixth Avenue to Seward's house on F Street. He was in no hurry, had no idea that anyone still thought of reinforcing Pickens. He would drop the plans and brief Seward before going on to church. Seward was alone in his parlor when Keyes appeared and handed him the roll. When he started to recite the problems of reinforcing Pickens, Seward cut him off abruptly. "I don't care about the difficulties," he growled. "Where's Captain Meigs?"

"I suppose he's at his house, sir," stammered Keyes.

"Please find him and bring him here."

"I'll call and bring him on my return from church."

"Never mind church to-day; I wish to see him and you here together without delay."[27]

Although baffled and resentful at being ordered about by a civilian, Keyes returned in ten minutes with Meigs. Seward wasted no words. "I wish you two gentlemen to make a plan to reinforce Fort Pickens, see General Scott, and bring your plan to the Executive Mansion at 3 o'clock this afternoon." They nodded and went to the engineer's office, persuaded a custodian to let them in, found the maps they needed, and worked for nearly four hours. Keyes concentrated on the needs of the artillery, his specialty, while Meigs toiled at the engineering details and compiled partial sailing directions. By the time they finished it was nearly 3 p.m., too late to see Scott before going to the White House. They found Lincoln and Seward waiting for them, the former sitting hands behind head at a table with one leg resting on it and the other draped on the chair. Seward asked if they were ready to report. Keyes said yes, but they had not had time to see Scott, and as the general's secretary he hesitated to act without informing his chief. "I'm not General Scott's military secretary," said Meigs, "and I am ready to report."

"There's no time to lose," said Lincoln. "Let us hear your reports, gentlemen."

As Keyes talked of scarps, terrepleins, barbettes, and other terms, Seward protested that he and Lincoln didn't know what they meant. "That's so," drawled Lincoln, dropping his feet to the floor and clasping his hands between his knees, "but we understand that the *rare* rank goes right behind the front!"

When they finished, Lincoln told them to see Scott and prepare to execute the plans. This was the task Keyes dreaded most. By then it was 6 p.m., the general's dinner hour, and when Keyes walked in, he saw Scott's face wreathed in anger and anxiety. He demanded to know where Keyes had been all day. Keyes told him as succinctly as possible what had happened, including Lincoln's order to read the plan without his seeing Scott first. "Did he tell you that?" asked the general.

"He did, sir!"

Keyes watched Scott wrestle with overpowering emotions. The majesty of his manner, so familiar, melted into gloom and sadness. At the table Keyes ate and drank voraciously, invigorated by his experience, while Scott sat musing in silence on past glories and declining powers. Not even the evening's cuisine could brighten his mood.

"Notwithstanding the belligerent bulletins from Fort Pickens," reported the Tribune's man that Easter Sunday, "no apprehension is entertained in official circles of an attack by Gen. Bragg's force. . . . Jefferson Davis has ordered a large force to Pensacola, but probably with no more expectation of assailing it than Governor Pickens had of attacking Fort Sumter."[28]

The session with Keyes and Meigs was about the only relief for Lincoln that Easter Sunday. His headache was gone, but he remained touchy and out of sorts. Zachariah Chandler wrote complaining that "Michigan has been utterly ignored in the distribution of offices," and a delegation from California called to protest the undue influence of E. H. Baker in appointments for that state. Their prepared statement treated Baker harshly and impugned his motives. Lincoln responded by saying he had known Baker for a quarter century, then tore the document up and tossed the pieces into a fireplace before delivering some choice words on the proprieties of complaint. The delegation left quickly, but the president's uncharacteristic lapse of restraint revealed how edgy he was.[29]

Seward noticed these mood swings, if not their similarity to his own, and wondered if Lincoln was losing his grip on the situation. That Seward's own plan was coming unraveled did not improve his mood or his chagrin that Lincoln had ignored his advice on the forts. The president was gradually coming right, he confided to Charles Francis Adams, but there was "no system, no relative ideas, no conception of his situation—much absorption in the details of office dispensation, but little application to great ideas." These were sentiments to which Adams easily subscribed as well.[30]

How to bring Lincoln around to some broader conception of the crisis and the policies necessary to meet it? Seward thought he had an answer. The day before, it had been reported that Spain had annexed Santo Domingo and that France was preparing to take over Haiti. Earlier he had startled Lord Lyons with his bellicose sentiments on foreign policy and flabbergasted Minister Rudolf Schleiden with his notion of a foreign war to relieve domestic tensions. Was this the opportunity he sought? After consulting with Weed, Seward jotted down a memorandum entitled "Some Thoughts for the President's Consideration." He called Henry J. Raymond of the New York *Times* to his house at midnight and obtained from him a pledge of support if Lincoln accepted the plan.

Frederick made a clean copy of the memorandum and was told to deliver it to Lincoln the next morning, April 1. It was a bold but necessary move, Seward conceded, and he wondered how Lincoln would receive it.

IN NEW YORK, Gustavus Fox could not believe the intransigence he encountered from the very men he expected would be most helpful. He had gone to see the shipping magnate William H. Aspinwall to procure ships and Charles H. Marshall, who could furnish the provisions in desiccated form. Both men had earlier given vigorous support to the relief of Fort Sumter, but Fox was surprised to find that they had changed their views entirely. People were becoming reconciled to a withdrawal and favored a stand at Pickens, they said. Why would the administration want to risk everything at Sumter? Such a move would jeopardize the $8 million loan the government was trying to float.[31]

Fox argued with them until midnight, stressing that "The vital point . . . is a naval force that can destroy their naval preparations. All else is easy." Finally Aspinwall and Marshall agreed to help if Fox delayed action until April 2, when the government loan would be offered. "You have no idea of the fears existing with these gentlemen," Fox told Montgomery Blair. He left the meeting "real heart sick, not discouraged, at the delays, obstacles and brief time allowed for a vital measure that should have had months' careful preparations." The next day he learned that Marshall had decided not to be involved. Fox was furious at this loss, since the desiccated provisions took up half the space of others and could easily be carried in bags. Reluctantly Aspinwall agreed to let Fox have the *Baltic* after the loan bids had been received on Tuesday. She had ten small boats, enough to carry troops and provisions. Coal and the provisions could be stowed in bags; bread could be taken instead of flour. But what kind of men, Fox wondered, placed self-interest above patriotism? "I feel like abandoning my country, moving off somewhere," he wrote Blair. "I am sick down to my heel."

Their motives were more varied than Fox knew. Marshall had spent two weeks in Washington and evidently fallen under Seward's spell. Aspinwall wrote Lincoln that same Easter Sunday to explain his views. "Were it even suspected that you contemplated reinforcing Fort Sumter," he warned, "the bids for the loan on Tuesday . . . would be at rates below which Gov. Chase would hesitate to accept—certainly below 90. . . . Any failure now would react on later requirements of the Treasury." The delay, in Aspinwall's view, would garner another 2 or 3 percent on the loan. At the same time he and Marshall deplored any attempt to reinforce Sumter "against the odds which have been allowed to accumulate since the early part of Feby. . . . The public mind is fully prepared for the evacuation . . . as a military necessity entailed . . . by the late Administration."[32]

But Aspinwall drew the line at Sumter. The relief of Pickens would "strengthen the Administration & give courage to the Union men at the South." An Ohioan put it in stronger language. "The evacuation of Fort Sumter is a bitter pill; it is all we can do to bear up against it," he said. ". . . But the evacuation of Fort Pickens,—my God! . . . It would *utterly demoralize the Government!*"[33]

THE LULL IN PREPARATIONS lasted only a few days. To Foster most of the work had to do with strengthening the channel batteries and defenses against an attack from land or sea rather than from the fort. On the 17th the Confederates removed a buoy in the middle ship channel; three days later it was placed on the opposite side of the channel. From the constant gunnery practice Anderson determined how many guns were arrayed against him at each location, although more kept coming. He counted twenty-three on Morris Island, not including mortars. Another new battery was going in at Sullivans Island, making four between Fort Moultrie and the end of the island. Something was doing behind the large battery at Fort Johnson and at the first battery on Morris Island. The floating battery announced its readiness by firing a practice round on the 14th.[34]

Anderson's own preparations were nearly finished. Plagued by shortages, he ordered some flannel shirts made into cartridge bags. On the 26th the last temporary building was pulled down and burned for fuel. Foster closed the remaining loopholes on the first tier. To his surprise, a boat had arrived on the 23rd to deliver the papers, instruments, and furniture he had left on Sullivans Island. From General Totten came instructions to carry away every possible item of government property if the fort was evacuated. Still, confusion reigned over the withdrawal. After Lamon's visit Beauregard wrote offering to let the garrison retire with all honors and salute of its flag in return for a pledge that guns and other property would not be destroyed. Anderson spurned the offer and assured Washington that "I shall give no pledges whatever." Beauregard hastened to soothe the major's wounded feelings, but uncertainty lingered over fort and town alike. The next day Anderson scolded Beauregard for allowing a parcel, intended as an act of kindness, to reach the fort along with the general's letter. He would accept nothing beyond what he was entitled to by their agreement.[35]

On the morning of the 28th Anderson noticed that the floating battery had been towed out of sight. A small troop of cavalry appeared on Sullivans Island. On the 30th the secession convention visited Fort Moultrie and

Morris Island and was saluted by repeated firing of the guns. The last barrel of flour had been issued on the 29th, leaving only hard bread. With provisions so low, Anderson reluctantly asked Foster to discharge his laborers, keeping only enough for a boat crew. "Government must either make a bold push to relieve us or allow us to be withdrawn," Abner Doubleday wrote his wife. "There seems to be no middle course. It will soon be decided." But when?[36]

IN WILLARD'S BARBERSHOP Russell watched in amusement as handsome mulattoes moved smartly around the shaving chairs. Barbering seemed to be the birthright of the free black in the United States, he decided, and he marveled at the perfect equality by which the same nimble fingers could caress the chin of some ruffian one minute and that of a senator the next. The chairs filled early with men eager to be on the hunt for congressmen who could give them a position. One hopeful spied his quarry while still in the chair and sprang into the corridor with a faceful of lather, shouting, "Senator! Senator! Hallo!"[37]

That afternoon of the 30th Russell visited the Washington Navy Yard with a naval officer. They passed through the high brick walls with salutes from two sentries dressed in dark blue tunics with yellow facings, their white gloves holding well-polished rifles. Inside Russell found some red-brick houses, stores, and magazines with plots of grass bordered by fences of pillars and chains. The workshops, belching noise and steam, lay near the Potomac. They entered the small office of Captain John Dahlgren, the acting superintendent and inventor of the Dahlgren gun, a favorite weapon of the navy's even though the sailors called the Dahlgrens "soda-water bottles" because of their shape.

The captain lectured Russell on the proper design of heavy guns and bemoaned the navy's parsimony in refusing to provide him furnaces to cast the weapons. None was cast at Washington; the foundries could manage only boat guns and brass fieldpieces. He rolled out a twelve-pounder to demonstrate for them and threw accurate shrapnel fire twelve hundred yards, firing so rapidly that he kept three shots in the air at the same time. Nearby Russell saw the *Pawnee* being readied for sea duty. Compared with British yards, the Washington Navy Yard seemed a "mere toy," but he kept this observation to himself.

Back at the hotel he found a gorgeous bouquet of flowers with a card from Mary Lincoln inviting him to a reception at three o'clock. He was surprised at how few people attended and was told that Washington ladies still mourned their absent southern friends and had yet to decide on Mrs. Lincoln. They loved to dote on the superiority of the chivalry over vulgar Yankees, but Russell concluded that "if New York be Yankee, there is nothing in which it does not far surpass this preposterous capitol." He saw a homely woman thrust suddenly from obscurity as the wife of a country lawyer into a place where her every smile or frown drew national attention and every detail of her dress flashed across the wires to newspapers in distant towns. Already she was surrounded by courtiers and intriguers insinuating themselves into her favor. What was it John Selden had said? "Those who wish to set a house on fire begin with the thatch."

On Easter Sunday Russell dined with Lord Lyons and the legation staff, the only outsider present being Charles Sumner, who chaired the Senate Foreign Relations Committee. Little was said of politics, but Russell learned that a Mr. Fox, a former naval officer turned master of a commercial steamer, had gone to Fort Sumter; no one knew the object of his mission. The commissioners threatened to return to Montgomery, and everyone wondered anxiously what Virginia would do. Already the authorities at Richmond had hinted they would not allow the Tredegar Iron Works to furnish guns to seaboard forts.

No concession of autonomy would do, Russell realized. If a state could vote itself in or out of the Union, why couldn't it make war or peace and choose what to accept or refuse from the federal government? Yet, walking home afterward with Sumner, Russell thought he heard the senator express a desire to let the slave states go their way if they wished. Earlier Chase had said much the same thing to him, and these were men thought to be ultra in their sentiments. The whole affair remained a puzzle to Russell. "In fact," he concluded, "the Federal system is radically defective against internal convulsion, however excellent it is or may be for purposes of external polity."

APRIL

Ends Without Means

There is a general discontent pervading all classes of society. Everybody asks: what is the policy of the Administration? And everybody replies: Any distinct line of policy, be it war or a recognition of the Southern Confederacy, would be better than this uncertain state of things. Our defeat at the recent elections has taught us a lesson which can hardly be misunderstood. The Republicans are disheartened, groping in the dark, not knowing whether to support or oppose the Administration. . . . [F]oreign governments seem to take advantage of our difficulties; the Spanish invasion of San Domingo is an indication of what we may expect. . . . [T]here is but one way out of this distressing situation. It is to make short work of the secession movement and then to make front against the world abroad. . . . As soon as one vigorous blow is struck, as soon as, for instance, Fort Sumter is reinforced, public opinion in the free states will at once rally to your support.

—Carl Schurz
April 5, 1861[1]

THE FORMATION OF THE CONFEDERATE GOVERNMENT had in one stroke elevated Montgomery from a small, quaint inland town to the capital of a new nation. Might not it, wondered the most ambitious of its residents, also become the seat of a new empire one day soon? Those who dared to dream such lofty dreams knew that peace was essential to their plans, but how to achieve it? They looked with disdain upon the hawkish ultras, whose vision of grandeur hovered vaguely beyond the ruins of war. But no amount of farsightedness could provide the means for reaching that goal or remove the puny but persistent obstacles that blocked their path: Forts Sumter and Pickens.

For Davis and his cabinet the messages from Washington could not have been more mixed. The commissioners insisted repeatedly that the peace movement was gaining strength. On the 1st Crawford and Roman said that Lincoln lacked the courage to evacuate Sumter and hoped to shift responsibility on to Anderson by allowing him to be starved out. A day later they warned that "The war wing presses on the President; he vibrates to that side. . . . Watch at all points." The same day Secretary of War Walker instructed Beauregard to prevent any reinforcement of Sumter and cease all courtesies and supplies to the fort. "The status which you must at once re-establish and rigidly enforce," he emphasized, "is that of hostile forces in the presence of each other."[2]

The commissioners took their cue from Judge Campbell, who saw Seward again on the 1st and came away more baffled than ever. In response to Pickens's inquiry about Lamon's return, Seward told him that Lamon had had no authority from the president to make any such pledge. Then what about the evacuation of Sumter? Campbell demanded. Seward handed him a note stating that Lincoln might desire to supply Sumter but would not do so without first informing Governor Pickens. Campbell stared at it incredulously. "What does this mean?" he asked. "Does the President design to attempt to supply Sumter?"[3]

"I think not," answered Seward mildly. "It is a very irksome thing to him to evacuate it. His ears are open to everyone, and they fill his head with schemes for its supply. I do not think that he will adopt any of them. There is no design to reinforce it."

Campbell was not satisfied. Charleston regarded the evacuation as no longer debatable, he stressed; even a *desire* to reinforce it would be considered an intention and perhaps lead to an attack. Seward asked the judge to wait while he went to see Lincoln. He returned a few minutes later and wrote another note to send to Pickens: "I am satisfied the Government will not undertake to supply Fort Sumter without giving notice to Govr. Pickens." At the same time he left the impression that the note did not at all change the import of their earlier exchanges. Campbell passed along to the commissioners his belief that the delays did not reflect any change in policy but had more to do with the forthcoming government loan and local elections in Connecticut and Rhode Island.[4]

The commissioners agreed with Campbell that the Lincoln administration "dare not deceive *him*, as they know we do not rely upon them but upon him." But Campbell also warned Davis that "the President is light, inconstant, and variable. His ear is open to every one—and his resolutions are easily bent. . . . His reluctance to abandon the forts is undisguised." He reminded Davis that "I make these assurances on my own responsibility. I have no right to mention any name or to pledge any person."[5]

Davis shared the desire for a peace policy and wanted to believe that Pickens too would be given up eventually, but other reports were conflicting. Sifting through the contradictions, Judah Benjamin was convinced there would be war while Toombs believed that Seward's policy would prevail.

However, as long as Washington made neither gestures of peace nor hostile moves, the Confederate government could continue to organize and consolidate its position. On that basis Toombs instructed the commissioners on the 2nd to preserve the status quo and make no demand for an answer. Two days later Beauregard wired that his batteries were in place but lacked trained gunners and good shells and fuses. On the 5th the commissioners reported that "An important move requiring a formidable military and naval force is certainly on foot." The official word had it bound for Santo Domingo, but suspicions grew that this was a ruse to cover reinforcements for Sumter or Pickens.[6]

Then James E. Harvey, a Charleston-born journalist, a close friend of Judge Magrath's, and the newly appointed minister to Portugal, tried to further the cause of peace on his own and wound up muddling matters more than ever. On the morning of the 6th Harvey warned Charleston that it was "Positively determined not to withdraw Anderson. Supplies go immediately supported by naval force." Later that day he contradicted this by saying, "Order issued for withdrawal of Anderson's command," followed by messages that efforts to reconsider the evacuation would fail. That an appointed official would be so indiscreet, let alone commit what many deemed a traitorous act, was bad enough. Later a howl was raised over Harvey's action; for now his telegrams merely fed the confusion that already engulfed Montgomery.

All along Davis and his advisers had assumed that Seward spoke for Lincoln. If events contradicted what Seward told the commissioners or Campbell, therefore, it must be because Seward had lied to them. And if Seward had lied, he must have done so to further some covert policy crafted by him or Lincoln, all of which proved yet again that the Black Republicans could not be trusted in matters of personal honor or diplomacy. It was all a ruse, a blind to mask the secret mobilizing and movement of a relief force. Hearing rumors on the 6th of a fleet's being assembled to carry supplies and of troops' being withdrawn from frontier posts to reinforce the Florida forts, Davis told Campbell, "This is not the course of good will, and does not tend to preserve the peace."[7]

But Davis was no wounded innocent. Much as he longed for peace, he had no intention of leaving either fort in federal hands. The de facto truces at both places were devices as convenient to the Confederates as to the North; the proposed withdrawal from Sumter was a happy escape from the necessity to attack. On the 3rd Davis wrote his old friend Braxton Bragg, the commander at Pensacola, a candid statement of his policy for Pickens. "You will not have failed to notice," he told Bragg, "that the tone of the Northern press indicates a desire to prove a *military* necessity for the abandonment of both Sumter & Pickens." They might try to reinforce the forts, but Davis thought withdrawal more likely.[8]

Nor was it likely the North would launch an attack so long as hope remained of keeping the border states. "There would be to us an advantage in so placing them that an attack by them would be a necessity," Davis reasoned, "but when we are ready to relieve our territory . . . of the presence of a foreign garrison that advantage is overbalanced by other considerations." Pickens was, in short, a military problem to be solved as soon as Bragg had sufficient forces to move. Davis preferred not to fire the first shot but would if necessary, and he offered detailed suggestions for a plan of attack. If Bragg got his forces ready quickly enough, the moment of truth might come at Pickens instead of Sumter.

THICK FOG MOVED INTO THE HARBOR on April Fool's night and blanketed it the next day. Visibility shrank to a few yards, allowing the garrison to see as little as they knew of what was going on around them. It was the perfect April Fool's joke, but Anderson utterly lacked the sense of humor to appreciate it. The absence of orders clarifying his position had frayed his nerves and sapped his stamina. He wrote Washington irritably that his supplies would barely last a week because he had been obliged to share them with the laborers at the fort. Earlier he had told Fox that he could stretch the provisions to the 10th by placing the men on short allowances, but no orders had come to do so, and he had not.[9]

Since Lamon's departure he had expected an order to evacuate, but none came. Meanwhile, supplies from Charleston dwindled, and the major suspected they were being cut entirely. More ominously, Sam Crawford reported two cases of dysentery and expressed the fear that it might spread. For the men, however, the most enervating disease was uncertainty. "Every one is weary of the confinement here," Doubleday wrote his wife. "It is nothing but walking around the parapet, eating and sleeping. . . . How we can get along without fighting in the midst of all this lawlessness it is impossible for me to see."[10]

The ennui was shattered abruptly on the afternoon of the 3rd by the sound of cannon fire. Racing to the parapet, Anderson saw a schooner flying the American flag trying to enter the harbor. The drummer sounded the long roll, and the men rushed to their guns. Mindful of his orders not to provoke a clash without just cause, the major paused to consult his officers. Five advised firing on the batteries; three counseled delay. By then the ship had turned about and anchored out of range. Outraged, he sent Seymour and

Snyder to demand an explanation. The schooner turned out to be carrying a cargo of ice from Boston to Savannah. In the poor weather the skipper had mistaken the harbor for Savannah and run up his flag to secure a pilot. He lay at anchor until assured that he could leave without harm, then went to sea. Anderson thought the ship lucky to escape undamaged except for a shot through her mainsail, and wondered how long it would be before blood was spilled in some such careless way. "I deeply regret," he wrote the next day, "that I did not feel myself at liberty to resent the insult thus offered to the flag of my beloved country."[11]

That day the major confided to his officers for the first time his earlier instructions to act strictly on the defensive. He decided to send one of them to Washington and chose Talbot because he had been reassigned to a new post anyway. Joined by Snyder and carrying dispatches from Anderson, Talbot crossed under a white flag to give the governor details on the schooner incident. Pickens and Beauregard happened to have been on the piazza of the Moultrie House on Sullivans Island when the incident occurred, and their observations coincided with Snyder's report. Pickens could not let Talbot go, however, because he had orders to allow no one to leave the fort or supplies from Charleston to reach it. He also recounted the dispatch from Martin Crawford that no attempt would be made to provision the fort and that Lincoln would not order the withdrawal but leave Anderson to act for himself.[12]

Anderson became furious when told of Crawford's views. "I cannot think that the Government would abandon, without instructions and without advice, a command which has tried to do all its duty to our country," he wrote the War Department with scarcely controlled rage. ". . . After thirty odd years of service I do not wish it to be said that I have treasonably abandoned a post and turned over to unauthorized persons public property intrusted to my charge. I am entitled to this act of justice at the hands of my Government, and I feel confident that I shall not be disappointed."[13]

No orders had come from Washington since those of February 23 advising restraint. Two "official" visitors had come, one talking of relief for the garrison and the other claiming it would be withdrawn. With his supplies almost gone, Anderson's position had never been weaker and that of the enemy never stronger. Foster was drawing on him for food, his store for the engineers having dwindled to eleven codfish, half a barrel of cornmeal, and a seventh of a barrel of grits. "Unless we receive supplies," Anderson warned his superiors, "I shall be compelled to stay here without food, or to abandon this post very early next week."

Was there ever a more perverse climax to an honorable career? Little incidents fed his brooding as well. A revenue cutter anchored less than two hundred yards from the fort and one day boarded the mail boat from Fort Johnson. A mortar battery threw its practice shots uncomfortably near Sumter. Anderson protested each time, and Beauregard took care of them at once, but nothing eased the major's gloom. "The sooner we are out of this fort the better," he said sullenly. "Our flag runs an hourly risk of being insulted, and my hands are tied by my orders, and if that was not the case, I have not the power to protect it."[14]

THE PRESENCE OF THE FORT did not lessen the gaiety of society in Charleston. If anything, the tension of waiting for the withdrawal drove the chivalry more furiously into its winter ritual of calls and dinners. No one reveled more in the whirl than Mary Chesnut. With unabashed pleasure she savored the parade of visits, outings, teas, breakfasts, and dinners, with their delicious glaze of badinage and flirtation. A stream of visitors reinforced the social ranks. Louis and Charlotte Wigfall arrived on the 1st to a hero's welcome, put up at the Mills House, and joined the Chesnuts' merry circle. Charlotte brought with her the last shards of gossip from Washington and tales about everyone from Governor Pickens to Varina Davis.[15]

On the 3rd Mary dressed in her beautiful gray moiré gown and went to the home of Isaac Hayne for a soiree of amusing company and a delicious supper of pâté, lobster, and biscuit glacé. Pickens was there, adorned in a better wig than usual, with his wife, Lucy. Mary found her affected and full of "silly, fine lady airs," which, she conceded grudgingly, seemed to work for her. Lucy flirted unabashedly, "looking *love* into the eyes of the men at every glance," letting William Porcher Miles make "desperate love" to her until Mary could stand it no longer. "Poor goose," she said with more than a hint of jealousy, "she is in the hands of the Philistines." She got no salve from James, who told her she was as great a flirt as Lucy. He complained that Mary didn't tell him everything, and he still smarted over the attention paid by John Manning, who seemed always on hand, at breakfast or with a bunch of violets or whispering to Mary in company.

That evening Mary learned that the convention had finally approved the Confederate constitution in secret session by a vote of 138–21. She dismissed the dissenters as fools, the more so when uneasiness over the constitution prompted the delegates to demand a convention to consider a spate of amendments. James had opposed the resolution but was buried by a vote of 117–15. After the party Mary also heard of a boat's being fired on in the harbor. "I think it a very silly business," she said. "War or peace, which is it."[16]

The Citadel graduation took place on the 5th at the Hibernian Hall.

Mary declined to attend the Cadet's Ball that evening; she longed to go but had no clothes that suited her, having left much of her wardrobe in Camden. The Pickenses attended along with Beauregard and other dignitaries. Everyone agreed it was a brilliant success. "With very many of the girls it is their *first* ball," noted Emma Holmes, "and what gay visions do those magic words conjure up." Her Carrie looked radiant in a sea green tarletan set off by white japonicas in her hair. But amid the laughter and music, the swirling gowns and handsome uniforms, lay a profound uneasiness that nagged with equal urgency at Mary in her parlor. "To day they say an engagement is *imminent*," she wrote. The *Tribune*'s man agreed that "Unless all signs fail, the siege of Fort Sumter . . . is about to commence."[17]

The clash could not come soon enough for Edmund Ruffin, who had returned once again to be present at the creation. "I wish with all my heart," he wrote, ". . . that Lincoln would send a strong squadron to force the passage & attack the defences of Charleston." But he expected no such thing, and he chafed at Montgomery's waiting game. So did the officers commanding the forces around the city. Captain Hartstene put his flotilla of three steamers on alert to guard the approaches to Sumter from the sea and ordered his men to maintain the utmost vigilance. The game of war, with all its tedious preparations and false alarms, had grown as tiresome as the endless parade of contradictory rumors. Whatever was to be, let it come.[18]

Ruffin welcomed this restlessness. "The troops & the citizens," he observed, "are becoming feverishly impatient for the reduction of Fort Sumter, & for the end of the present necessity of retaining the besieging forces."

"DANGERS AND BREAKERS ARE BEFORE US," Seward wrote his wife on April Fool's Day, and they threatened him as well as the nation. The scene with Campbell underscored that time was running out on his policy of delay. He wondered anxiously how Lincoln had received his "Thoughts." The memo was an unprecedented but necessary act if the crisis was to be contained. Seward spelled out his views in a masterful mix of candor and cunning.[19]

After one month the administration still had no foreign or domestic policy, he asserted, largely for reasons beyond its control: the presence of the Senate and the host of office seekers. This impasse could continue no longer; patronage had to be deferred, and policies devised at once. At home, Seward argued, "we must change the question before the public, from one upon, or about Slavery, for a question upon *Union* or *Disunion*. In other words, from what would be regarded as a party question to one of *Patriotism* or *Union*."

The way to do this was to surrender Sumter, defend all the Gulf forts, prepare the navy for a blockade, and put Key West under martial law.

The key to Seward's approach lay in foreign policy. Like Shakespeare's
King Henry, he wished to busy giddy minds with foreign wars. He would
demand immediate explanations from France and Spain for their recent
actions in the hemisphere, and if their replies were not satisfactory, he would
"convene Congress, and declare war against them." He would demand
explanations from Great Britain and Russia as well and send agents to
Canada, Mexico, and Central America to stir up feelings against European
intervention.

Whatever policy was adopted, Seward emphasized, someone had to
direct it energetically and incessantly. "Either the President must do it himself, and be all the while active in it, or devolve it on some member of his
Cabinet." Seward had a particular candidate in mind. "It is not my special
province," he said, "but I neither seek to evade nor assume responsibility."

In this language could be read motives ranging from sincere patriotic
concern to a bold grab for power. Of this move Charles Francis Adams, Jr.,
later said, "[W]hen, plainly, no reaction in the border States was to be longer
hoped for, and the problem of the Southern forts pressed for an immediate
solution . . . Seward lost his head. He found himself fairly beyond his depth;
and he plunged! The foreign-war panacea took possession of him; and
he yielded to it." His unabashed offer to take charge of affairs could be seen
as a foolish act of hubris or the last act of a desperate man whose plans had
crumbled.[20]

But Seward's thinking was more subtle than Adams or others knew.
Spain was his target; a war with it could be easily won, he thought, and might
yield not only Santo Domingo but Cuba and Puerto Rico as well. The old
fear of Cuba as independent or a new state, coupled with the end of slavery
and the slave trade there, would terrify the Confederacy back into the Union.
No southern nation could bear the loss of Cuba, and with it control of the
Gulf, to northern hands. Ending the slave trade would also cement the
North's ties with Britain and blight southern hopes of recognition from
abroad. Farfetched as the thinking was, it had a ruling logic.[21]

But Seward went beyond giving advice to issue an invitation, saying in
effect that if the ordeal had worn Lincoln down, if it had become too much
for him with his inexperience at this level of government, Seward was willing
to step into the breach. It was a polite, even friendly invitation, embossed
with Seward's usual blend of service, helpfulness, and self-service. That he
considered himself more able to deal with these larger affairs of state he need
not and did not say, though he doubtless thought these things, just as he
thought the presidency should have been his in the first place.

The memorandum surely jolted Lincoln, still recovering from his bout of depression. Here was the first major test of his ability to control his cabinet, the first direct test of wills between himself and the man widely viewed as the ruling spirit of the administration. Later that day he wrote out a reply. Whether he gave the note to Seward or told him its contents in person is not known, but there is no doubt that the secretary of state got the message.[22]

Lincoln reminded Seward that the administration did indeed have a policy, spelled out in the inaugural speech, "to hold, occupy and possess the property and places belonging to the government, and to collect the duties, and imposts." Seward had approved it, and Scott had been ordered to implement it. Nothing deviated from Seward's proposed domestic policy except for abandoning Fort Sumter. Lincoln could not see how reinforcing Sumter constituted a party issue while that of Pickens was a national or patriotic one. As for foreign policy, the Spanish move on Santo Domingo was a new development requiring a response. Aside from that, however, he and Seward had prepared appointments and instruction circulars for ministers without a hint that policy was lacking.

In one brief, polite paragraph he rejected Seward's invitation: "If this must be done, *I* must do it. When a general line of policy is adopted, I apprehend there is no danger of its being changed without good reason, continuing to be a subject of unnecessary debate; still, upon points arising in its progress, I wish, and suppose I am entitled to have the advice of all the Cabinet."

No reply from Seward is known to exist. Much later Frederick Seward described Lincoln's response as "kind and dignified." Apparently no other member of the cabinet knew about the exchange, and no word of it leaked to the public. Seward never again confronted the president. He was wise enough to learn from this exchange that he had underestimated Lincoln's ability and strength. It was not a mistake he would make again. Instead the experience drew him closer to Lincoln as a working partner.[23]

This showdown was far from the only business taking place that busy April Fool's Day. Lincoln had asked Scott to give him a daily report and learned that the situation at Pensacola had worsened. The *Brooklyn* had left her post off Fort Pickens to get water and supplies at Key West. Captain Vogdes's company had been moved to the *Sabine* and still awaited orders to land. Scott had sent them by ship and by messenger, but the ships had not made contact, and the messengers had been intercepted by Confederate authorities. Meanwhile, the forces under Braxton Bragg had fortified and armed Fort McRee on the mainland opposite Pickens with guns commanding the harbor and Fort Pickens.[24]

In a separate memo Scott detailed the reinforcing of the Keys forts.

Pickens remained the danger spot. All that day Keyes and Meigs prepared orders for the relief expedition. Meigs's plan was simple but bold. While a transport ship landed men and supplies at Pickens outside the harbor, a warship would divert attention by steaming brazenly past Fort McRee into the harbor to prevent any crossing of southern troops. To hold her position, the ship had to withstand fire from Forts McRee and Barrancas as well as the navy yard. A talented and daring officer was needed to command her. At his earlier meeting with Seward and Lincoln, Meigs recommended a young naval lieutenant named David D. Porter and Colonel Harvey Brown for the army troops.[25]

Porter was about to leave for California when Seward sent for him. They went over Meigs's plan and agreed that everything depended on secrecy. Meanwhile, Meigs and Keyes took their orders to Scott, who signed them without comment. They included a note from Scott to Seward urging him to have Lincoln dispatch to Pensacola the warship needed to defend Pickens from attack. Meigs noticed in the papers that the *Powhatan* had just gone into the Brooklyn Navy Yard for refitting; she was a logical choice. Meigs and Keyes hurried the papers to Seward, who took them to see Lincoln. In urging the plan, Seward stressed to Lincoln that secrecy was crucial; the orders must bypass even Secretary Welles because the Navy Department had so many southern sympathizers.[26]

Lincoln endorsed the plan and signed all the orders presented to him. One ordered the *Powhatan* fitted out to go to sea as quickly as possible under sealed orders. Another relieved her captain, Samuel Mercer, and put Porter in his place. A third instructed all army and navy officers to give Porter and Brown whatever assistance they required. Two others changed the assignment of some naval officers, including Silas Stringham, who was ordered to Pensacola. Money was needed for the expedition, and Congress had provided no secret service funds for the military. Seward's department alone had such funds. With Lincoln's consent he got $10,000 in coin from State, carried it to his house, and gave it to Meigs for his work.[27]

Lincoln also signed an order instructing all army officers to honor any order or requisition made by Keyes. Porter and Brown left for New York; Keyes and Meigs followed on the 3rd. Meanwhile, Gustavus Fox, still upset over the delays in getting ships for his Sumter expedition, headed back to Washington. Montgomery Blair had summoned him on the 1st, saying that Lincoln wished to shape the final orders. Welles had dutifully ordered the *Pocahontas*, *Pawnee*, and *Harriet Lane* to be ready to sail with a month's rations by April 6. These were all small vessels, and Fox worried that his transport ship could not handle the necessary troops and supplies. A larger ship was needed for the overflow.[28]

Welles knew the *Powhatan* was available but in terrible shape from long service in the West Indies. On March 28 he had ordered her taken out of commission for repairs and her crew discharged. But Lincoln's order the next day to prepare an expedition changed everything. On April 1 Welles revoked his earlier order and telegraphed the commandant at the Brooklyn Navy Yard to "Fit out *Powhatan* to go to sea at earliest possible moment." The officers were to be recalled, and the crew held back from discharge or transfer. That evening, as Welles was enjoying his dinner at Willard's, John G. Nicolay, Lincoln's secretary, walked into the dining room and laid a large package on the table. What Welles saw inside was enough to kill his appetite.[29]

The package contained copies of the orders signed by Lincoln for the Pickens expedition, all of them involving the Navy Department and executed without Welles's knowledge. The documents betrayed a knowledge of naval affairs that Welles knew the president did not possess. That Lincoln had permitted these orders to be drafted behind the secretary's back indicated an utter lack of confidence in him, if not some deeper intrigue. Who had done this? Welles wondered. Who else indeed but Seward?[30]

One document in particular appalled Welles: the order sending Stringham to Pensacola and replacing him at the Bureau of Detail with Captain Samuel Barron. A courtly, suave Virginian known as the "naval diplomat," Barron may have been the most popular naval officer in Washington. That reputation did not impress Welles, who regarded Barron as a courtier with southern sympathies and the last man he wanted for his confidential officer. That the section of the order assigning Barron had been written by Porter, as he soon learned, rankled Welles even more. Porter too had many southern friends and had sought duty in the Pacific—a sign to Welles that he wished to duck the coming conflict.[31]

Welles marched to the White House, where he found Lincoln alone at a table. The president looked up from his writing, saw the dark cloud on Welles's heavily bearded face, and sighed, *"What have I done wrong?"* Welles showed him the papers and pressed for an explanation. Lincoln seemed as surprised as Welles at their contents. Seward had been there earlier with three young men, perfecting a plan he had evolved. The young men had drafted the orders, which Lincoln had signed without reading. When the president identified Meigs and Porter as two of the men, Welles asked sharply what the secretary of state had to do with such officers.

Lincoln looked mystified and took the whole blame for the mixup on himself. After hearing the secretary voice his suspicions about Barron, he urged Welles to pay no attention to any part of the orders he opposed. But he refused to disclose the nature of the mission Seward had concocted, insisting that it had to be kept secret. Welles did not press him, and he saw to it that Barron did not receive the proposed assignment. But he remained in the dark about the Pickens expedition and its demands on the navy. That ignorance was to haunt both him and Lincoln.[32]

CAPTAIN ANDREW H. FOOTE had temporary command of the Brooklyn Navy Yard while his superior was on leave. If he craved action in this quiet post, he got all he wanted within the space of a few days. The order to prepare the *Powhatan* at once kept him scrambling not only to get the battered ship ready but also to track down the officers who had gone on leave. The telegram from Welles to fit the *Powhatan* out for sea duty arrived at six-thirty on the evening of the 1st. Twenty minutes later he received the same order from Lincoln, adding that the ship would sail under sealed orders to be sent the next day by messenger.[33]

The next morning Porter handed Foote the orders signed by Lincoln. Foote read them over and over, bewildered by so flagrant a departure from official procedure. An old classmate of Welles's, he was, like most sea dogs, a stickler for protocol. He examined the watermark, fingered the White House embossing, and eyed Porter warily. "How do I know *you* are not a traitor?" he said at last. "Who ever heard of such orders as these emanating direct from the President? I must telegraph to Mr. Welles before I do anything, and ask further instructions."[34]

"Look at these orders again," Porter replied, "and then telegraph at your peril. Under no circumstances must you inform the Navy Department of this expedition." They argued for three hours before Porter convinced Foote that he was not a traitor. Work on the *Powhatan* went forward since Foote had orders from both Lincoln and Welles to get her ready; the question was: Who would take charge of the ship? Meigs arrived to push along the preparations for the supply ships. Foote wired Welles that he hoped to have the *Powhatan* ready by Friday, the 5th, but the irregularities still bothered him. When Meigs showed him a letter authorizing his preparations, he could bear it no longer and telegraphed Welles plaintively, "as the orders do not come direct, I make this report; but as no time is to be lost, I am preparing what is called for."[35]

Meigs and Keyes had to charter three ships, amass more than 12,000 tons of supplies, and see that they were loaded properly. Unaware of these activities, Gustavus Fox grew increasingly frustrated over the preparations for his mission. "My expedition is ordered to be got ready," he told a friend on the 3rd, "but I doubt if we shall get off. Delay, indecision, obstacles." Fox was

convinced that "War will commence at Pensacola." The attempt to land reinforcements there would provoke a fight before Fox even got started. But the
next day he went to see Lincoln in Washington and was told the expedition
to relieve Sumter would go forward without delay.[36]

EVENTS KEPT PUSHING LINCOLN toward the decision he was loath
to make. To his relief the $8 million loan had gone well, fetching more than
$33 million in bids at prices above Chase's expectations. But the local elec-
tions that week went badly, as Republican candidates lost in Connecticut,
Ohio, Brooklyn, Rhode Island, and St. Louis. "Thirty days more of 'Peace
Policy' at Washington," one Ohioan warned Lincoln, "and not only the
Republican Party, but the Government itself will be gone to destruction."
Similar advice came from Carl Schurz in Wisconsin and others who echoed
the *Tribune*'s cry that "if we are to fight, so be it; if we are to have peace, so
much the better. . . . At all events, let this intolerable suspense and uncer-
tainty cease!"[37]

The mounting pressure to act dismayed Lincoln. He had struggled to
keep the door open for Seward's policy of delay as long as possible. The
Pickens expedition was part of that effort, its secrecy designed to prevent the
Confederates from getting wind of the mission and attacking the fort before
the relief force arrived. To that end the president had dissembled with
Welles, feigning ignorance of the orders in that simple, straightforward
manner he had perfected to an art form. So too did he pursue contacts with
Virginia Unionists, as Seward had advocated, but things had gone badly
there. Lincoln and Seward had hoped the convention would repudiate secession and adjourn; instead it continued to sit for seven weeks while secession
strength grew. To Lincoln it became a loaded gun ready to fire on any coercive move by the federal government. Unionists pressed hard for a vote on
secession but admitted that "The Secession party here are straining every
nerve . . . to disorganize the conservative party." On that April Fool's Day
Seward telegraphed the Unionist George W. Summers in Richmond that the
president wished to see him at once in Washington.[38]

Summers replied cautiously, thinking the telegram might be a secessionist trick because the convention was about to decide whether to submit
secession to a popular vote. Two days later Seward brought to the White
House Allan B. Magruder, a Virginian who practiced law in Washington.
Lincoln asked Magruder to go to Richmond and tell Summers he wished to
see him. There was no time to lose; whatever could be done had to be done
quickly. If Summers could not come, let him send a trusted friend. Magruder

reached Richmond that same evening. Summers was convinced but could not leave; the showdown vote was due the next day. After hasty consultation he and his Unionist friends chose John B. Baldwin to go in his place.

Baldwin and Magruder caught the evening train for Washington and were in Seward's office the next morning, April 4. Seward ushered Baldwin to the White House, where he met secretly with Lincoln in a bedroom behind a locked door. What passed between them has remained a subject of controversy, but there is little doubt about the stakes involved or the outcome. Seward hoped to persuade Lincoln to offer the evacuation of Sumter in return for a pledge by Virginia to adjourn its convention. That would eliminate the Sumter problem, bolster the Virginia Unionists, and redeem Seward's faltering policy all in one stroke. But would Lincoln do it?[39]

Lincoln greeted Baldwin by saying he had come too late and should have been there several days earlier. This comment baffled Baldwin, who had rushed to Washington, but before he could seek an explanation, Lincoln asked why the Virginia convention had not yet adjourned. Thrown on the defensive, Baldwin tried to explain how the Unionists were struggling to keep the secessionists at bay and desperately needed help from Lincoln. An adjournment, he stressed, would only allow secessionists to call another, more radical convention. He implored Lincoln to withdraw the troops from both forts, call a national convention, and support constitutional guarantees to protect southern rights.[40]

Lincoln listened closely but with little sympathy. How could he run the government if the money from import revenues was lost? How would he answer his friends and his party if the forts were surrendered? And what about Sumter? Lincoln indicated that its troops must be fed. Baldwin warned that if a single shot was fired at Sumter by either side, Virginia would be out of the Union in forty-eight hours. Nonsense, protested Lincoln. "Mr. President," retorted Baldwin, "I did not come here to argue with you; I am here as a witness. I know the sentiments of the people of Virginia and you do not."

Later controversy flared over whether Lincoln offered to evacuate Sumter if the convention would adjourn—in effect, trade a fort for a state. It is not clear whether he made any such offer—although the next day he told another Virginian, John Minor Botts, that he did—or whether he decided against it. What is clear is that Baldwin heard no such offer and returned to Richmond puzzled over why Lincoln had summoned him in the first place. In the end, however, the misunderstanding did not matter because neither side had anything to trade. The fatal flaw of Virginia Unionists, and those of other border states, was their inability to see that their key demand of non-coercion was fatal to any perpetuation of the Union and could never be acceptable. No Union based on a government incapable of enforcing its laws everywhere could endure.⁴¹

Peace on these terms was an end without means. That same day in Richmond the convention rejected by 88–45 a motion to submit secession to a popular vote, but secession sentiment continued to grow among the delegates restless for some sign of reconciliation from Washington. Shortly after seeing Baldwin, Lincoln informed Gustavus Fox that his expedition would go forward. Disturbing news had just reached the president in the form of Anderson's letter, written on the 1st, stating that his provisions would last only about another week. After his visit Fox had told Lincoln that Anderson could hold out at least until the 15th. Suddenly the time line had shortened; if the relief expedition was to sail, it had to go at once.⁴²

It would sail. Whatever the outcome, Lincoln saw that it must go. He drafted a reply to Anderson, sent over Cameron's signature, urging him to hold out if possible until the expedition arrived, but authorizing surrender if he deemed it necessary to save his men. Orders were given to Fox that same day to command the ships loaded with troops and supplies. Welles was to instruct the naval commander, once in Charleston Harbor, to force a passage if resistance was met. Scott furnished orders for the troops and supplies needed. All Fox had to do was get everything ready to sail at once. He did not know whether to laugh or cry. All winter long he had tried to persuade the government to send an expedition. Now the decision had finally been made, but he had much less time than he originally thought. He reminded Lincoln that he had only nine days to prepare the expedition and sail 637 miles. Anderson's letter cut that time in half, but Lincoln assured Fox that he would fulfill his duty by making the attempt.⁴³

Fox had the passenger steamer *Baltic*, three tugboats, the warships *Pocahontas* and *Pawnee*, and the revenue cutter *Harriet Lane*. What he needed most, he told Welles, was a naval force powerful enough to silence the enemy preparations. Welles offered to add the *Powhatan* to Fox's flotilla. While Fox hurried back to New York to complete his preparations, Welles dispatched orders to the ships. One instructed Foote to get the *Powhatan* ready; another informed Captain Samuel Mercer that he would command the naval forces supporting Fox's expedition. Mercer was to cooperate with Fox and leave New York with the *Powhatan* in time to reach the bar outside Charleston Harbor by the morning of the 11th. The other ships would rendezvous with him there.⁴⁴

That evening Welles went back to Willard's satisfied that the expedition was in good shape. The telegram from Foote troubled him with its reference to executing orders received through "the Navy officer as well as from the Army officer." What was this? Welles wondered. As a precaution he read

Mercer's orders to Lincoln, who approved them. He also sent Foote an order to delay the *Powhatan* until he received further instructions.[45]

Still, nothing led Welles to suspect that his hard day's work was about to come unraveled. He did not know that the *Powhatan* had already been pledged to Porter; neither did Fox, even though he was in New York. Nor did he suspect that Mercer was befuddled by conflicting orders that first relieved him of command of the *Powhatan* and then placed him in charge of the naval force. Commander Foote still did not know whom to believe about the *Powhatan* or whose order should be obeyed. In this weird season April Fool's was not to be limited to a single day.[46]

April Fools

Yesterday we had a picnic on Lake McBride, the occasion being the presentation of a flag to the Dixie Yoemen [sic]. The ladies of the Bradford neighborhood embroidered the banner and . . . we, every one, did our part in the work. . . . The flag was presented by Miss Bradford and received by Captain Gardner. Both made fine speeches and, when that was over, we served an elegant dinner under the magnificent Live Oaks, which have stood guard over the lovely lake for many centuries. After dinner there was target practice and boat-riding; this does not seem like war. The 1st Florida went to Pensacola today. Oh! this is like war.

—Susan Bradford
April 17, 1861[1]

SUCH A CURIOUS LOT THESE AMERICANS, thought William Russell, so full of contradictions of which they were blithely unaware. Take, for example, their patron saint, George Washington, whom they so worshipped. "To doubt his superiority to any man of woman born, is to insult the American people," Russell discovered, yet they had allowed his homestead to fall into ruin with the same indifference with which they had suffered his monument to lay unfinished. Russell took time to visit "the shrine of St. Washington," as one foreign visitor dubbed it, and was appalled by what he saw.[2]

The boat docked at a small, rotting pier, from which a path led up an incline through a dense tangle of briars and weeds to a two-story oblong wooden house. The exterior was undergoing repairs, and the slave huts had been repainted, but the shrubs were untrimmed, and the grass was unkempt under a smatter of chicken feathers. The first-floor rooms looked shabby with dusty, cobwebbed furniture and a broken harpsichord. Above one door hung the key to the Bastille, a gift from Lafayette. The rooms upstairs were closed off, along with the garden, but through the gate Russell saw another wilderness of neglected trees and shrubs. The plain brick tomb with its pointed arch and iron grating stood beneath some shade trees. Within the little mausoleum thick piles of leaves covered the floor and the sarcophagi, obscuring Washington's own grave. Russell left Mount Vernon wondering how a people could combine so much lip service with so little actual respect for their national hero.

On the return trip he visited Fort Washington on the bank of the Potomac, the city's first outpost of defense. The rotten gun carriages, piles of rusty shot, and ramshackle furnaces impressed him no more than the company of regulars on duty. Despite rumors of impending attacks, the sentries took no precautions against surprise. At least the Long Bridge across the river was guarded, but Russell concluded that twenty men armed with revolvers could seize the fort. When he mentioned this to Scott later, the general told him that a few weeks earlier the garrison had consisted of an elderly Irish pensioner and "might have been taken by a bottle of whiskey."

The next day, April 3, Russell visited the commissioners at their hotel and absorbed an hour of earnest, indignant talk about the perfidy of Yankeedom and about being strung along without recognition as ministers of a foreign power. Rumors filled the city of preparations at the navy yard in New York to relieve Pickens and perhaps Sumter as well. Even at a party of diplomats, where politics was rarely mentioned, Russell heard the conviction that Virginia would soon secede. The next day Seward gave him a long, rambling account of how the Buchanan administration had left the new government in a dreadful fix and caused its temporizing. He feared foreign powers might take advantage of this apparent weakness and impressed Russell with the sincerity of his preference for war against a foreign power than against the secessionists.

But war with what? Earlier that day Russell had seen a company of local volunteers in blue tunics and gray pants goose-step past the War Department with a chorus of cheers. Most of them looked to be pathetic creatures or, worse, "Irish and flat-footed, stumpy Germans." Did Seward seriously expect to make an army of such material, let alone threaten foreign nations with it?

He dined that evening at the home of Stephen A. Douglas with an odd mix of guests, including Salmon Chase, Caleb Smith, Commissioner Forsyth, and several members of Congress. Charmed by the grace and good nature of Adele Douglas, he mused on the huge American appetite for abstract theories. Douglas struck him as a man of superior intellect who spoke with energy and precision. The senator spelled out for Russell a curious Zollverein scheme embracing Canada as well and designed to soothe the sectional controversy. He was, Russell concluded, a cut above his duller, more didactic peers.

Dinner the next evening with the southern commissioners and some local friends proved less enlightening. They all dismissed Lincoln with contempt and regarded Seward as their true foe. Russell was amazed at the ferocity of their hatred of New England and the extremism of their views. "Disbelief of anything a Northern man—that is, a Republican—can say," he observed, "is a fixed principle in their minds." They expounded at length on how white men in the southern states were physically superior to those in the North and how the latter were cowards. As for slavery, which Russell loathed, the southerners praised it as their "summum bonum of morality, physical excellence, and social purity" and would entertain no contrary view.

With relief Russell escaped to Scott's company on the 6th. The general inquired about the Crimean War and the Indian Mutiny while professing to have no fears about the safety of Washington. But Russell knew that he had fewer than eight hundred regulars to protect the city and the navy yard and that the head of the latter was suspected of being a traitor. Back at Willard's, the swarm of office seekers still clogged every passage, their ranks swollen by every arriving train. It was time to go South, Russell concluded, to see things there before any outbreak of hostilities. Seward had sneered at southerners as people who were behind the age in every respect from ideas to fashion, with a way of life rooted in the worst part of the last century. But he had never been South, never seen or experienced that way of life for himself. Russell would not make that mistake.[3]

AT THE BROOKLYN NAVY YARD Captain Foote found himself deep in confusion and contradictions. Welles's order to delay the *Powhatan* seemed to refute what Porter and Meigs had told him. When he showed them the telegram, the high-strung Porter declared bitterly that he would not lift another finger for this government but would go to California and occupy himself with surveying. Meigs calmed him down but was equally baffled. Did Welles know about the Pickens expedition? Had he persuaded Lincoln to abandon it? Only one man had the answer; Meigs sent a telegram to Seward. Meanwhile, he soothed Foote with the idea that the Welles message might be bogus.[4]

Seward swore at the inquiry. The mission had been obstructed by conflicting orders from Welles, whom Seward regarded as a petty politico elevated by chance to high office. How was he meddling in this business? It was past 11 p.m. when he went with his son Fred to rouse Welles at Willard's and demand a retraction. Welles was flabbergasted and asked for an explanation. Evidently the telegram referred to the *Powhatan* and Porter's command, Seward replied. Welles bridled at the remark and at Seward's haughty manner. What Porter command? The *Powhatan* was assigned to the Sumter expedition; Seward knew that.[5]

There was a mistake all right, Seward said, and the more they talked, the hotter Welles grew. Aware that Captain Stringham had quarters at Willard's, Welles got him out of bed to confirm his version. Still, Seward stood his ground until Welles insisted that they call on Lincoln even though it was nearly midnight. Sullenly the four men walked to the White House. On the way Seward tried to mollify Welles. As old as he was, he admitted, he had learned a lesson from the encounter and would thereafter attend to his own department alone. "To this," observed Welles, "I cordially assented."

Lincoln was still up at that late hour and eyed his visitors in surprise. His confusion increased when they informed him of the problem. He looked at Welles and then at Seward, then read Meigs's telegram. Surely there must be some mistake, he said. No, said Welles stonily. He reminded Lincoln that he had read and approved the order to Mercer, a fact Stringham confirmed. Lincoln nodded but could not remember that the *Powhatan* was involved. Welles then fetched the original order from the Navy Department. Seward lounged on a sofa in his careless way while Lincoln read the order again. Yes, he murmured, now he remembered it all. He told Seward to restore the *Powhatan* to Mercer. Nothing must interfere with the Sumter mission or cause it to fail.

Seward hesitated. What about the Pickens expedition? he asked. It was equally as important and might be defeated without the *Powhatan*. Pickens had more time, Lincoln replied, but the Sumter expedition had no hours to lose. It would be difficult to get a dispatch to the navy yard so late, said Seward, trying to hedge, but Lincoln was adamant. Seward left to prepare the telegram. Lincoln held Welles awhile longer to explain that Seward had his heart set on the Pickens expedition and that all the blame for the mixup rested on the president alone. He pleaded carelessness, and Welles accepted this even though Lincoln was not a careless man. Seward did not rush to his reluctant errand; the telegram did not go out until nearly three o'clock on the afternoon of the 6th. Addressed to Porter, it said only, "Give the *Powhatan* up to Captain Mercer." He also signed it "Seward" instead of using the president's name. By the time the message reached Brooklyn, another chapter in the fiasco had unfolded.[6]

All that day Meigs rushed about trying to get everything ready for the expedition he hoped would still proceed. His task grew harder when Mercer received his order from Welles to take command of the Sumter flotilla. Twice Meigs went to the navy yard to persuade Foote that the new message could not overturn Lincoln's direct order for the ship. The one man who could have shed light on their confusion was in New York but never came to the navy yard. Welles had taken care of the naval orders for Fox, who had plenty else to do in a very short time and no reason to worry about the *Powhatan*.[7]

Meigs and Porter managed to convince a reluctant Mercer that the direct order from Lincoln took precedence over all else. Together they persuaded Foote to let the *Powhatan* go under Porter's command. Mercer would sail with the ship in nominal command and go ashore at Staten Island. Porter climbed aboard the *Powhatan* and headed out at 2:30 p.m. Half an hour later, Seward's telegram arrived and sent Foote into another spasm of doubt. He dispatched Lieutenant F. A. Roe to give chase and deliver the order. The diligent Roe hired a fast ship and managed to catch up to the *Powhatan* off Staten Island.[8]

Porter read the dispatch with disdain. The fact that he had asked Seward for clarification the day before did not bother him. Mercer had already left the ship and could not be reached; it had taken an hour to get him ashore in a leaky old boat. With supreme impudence he handed Roe a reply to Seward saying, "I received my orders from the President and shall proceed and execute them." To Foote he explained again that his orders came directly from Lincoln, who had not rescinded them. "This is an unpleasant position to be in," he said, "but I will work out of it." He sent Roe on his way and headed out to sea, running south and then east to elude any other pursuers.[9]

Meigs soon followed in the transport *Atlantic*, and Keyes behind him in the *Illinois*. "Keyes and I have done our duty and have set a ball in motion," Meigs recorded privately. "Porter . . . is on his way into the harbor of Pensacola and into it he will go, God permitting, for man will not be able to prevent him." But he did not stop there. Meigs knew what it meant to go out on a limb with tepid support from the administration. During the Buchanan years he had fought a long losing battle with John B. Floyd and seen much of his good work undone. Mindful of his difficulties, he wrote a letter of appeal to Seward:

> By great exertions within less than six days from the time the subject was broached in the office of the President, a war steamer sails from this port. . . . While the throwing of a few men into Fort Pickens may seem a small matter, the opening of a campaign is a great one. Unless this movement is supported by ample supplies and followed up by the navy, it will be a failure. This is the beginning of a war which every statesman and soldier has foreseen since the passage of the South Carolina ordinance. . . . We go to serve our country, and our country should not neglect us or leave us to be strangled in tape, however red.[10]

It was wrong that his friends and even Cousin Lizzie should intrude on the national crisis, but they did, and Lincoln could not ignore them. Jesse Dubois complained again of being slighted, Gustave Koerner was sore because the Berlin mission had gone to Judd instead of him, who knew the language and the customs, and even Orville Browning wrote privately to ask for the Supreme Court seat left vacant by the death of John McLean. Cousin Lizzie merely wanted the Springfield post office for herself. Lincoln saw no way to appoint her but wondered whether an election might not be set up to win it for her. John Stuart told Lincoln not to trouble himself over it. "No one will complain . . . if you do not give her the appointment while very many doubtless would complain of her appointment . . . because the appointment of a lady would be unusual."[11]

Sorting out the stuff in his head during these hectic days was a herculean task in itself. Nothing came singly or allowed the luxury of reflection even in the late hours when the horde of office-seekers slackened. On the 6th Lincoln rose from his late meeting with Seward and Welles to confront the effects of what he had done and what had happened in spite of him. The two expeditions lurched forward even though the *Powhatan* mixup seemed to mock his efforts at coherent policy. He did not know that Seward had delayed sending the telegram to Porter until that afternoon or that Seward that morning had supplied the conflicting information that James E. Harvey passed along to Charleston.[12]

What Lincoln did know was that the Pickens expedition might remain secret, but the one to Sumter had no chance of going unnoticed. Since telling Fox to go ahead on the 4th, Lincoln had not notified Governor Pickens that it was coming even though he had authorized Seward to tell Judge Campbell that no attempt to provision the fort would be made without notice. His sense that the time had come to do this was reinforced when Captain Talbot appeared at the White House bearing a dispatch, dated April 4, in which Major Anderson talked of expecting "hourly" some definite instructions. His meeting with Lamon had led him to believe those orders would be to evacuate, but he would do nothing until a reply was forthcoming from the War Department.[13]

Lincoln decided to send Talbot back with a copy of the message to Anderson, also dated the 4th, that provisions and reinforcements were coming and that he should hold out if possible until their arrival on the 11th or 12th. Talbot would travel in the company of Robert S. Chew, a State Department clerk who was to carry a note from Lincoln to Pickens. The message was carefully worded:

> I am directed by the President of the United States to notify you to expect an attempt will be made to supply Fort-Sumter [*sic*] with provisions only; and that, if such attempt be not resisted, no effort to

throw in men, arms, or amunition [*sic*], will be made, without further notice, or in case of an attack upon the Fort.

Chew was to deliver the message to Governor Pickens only if the fort had not yet been attacked. The order was signed by Cameron to provide military authority. Chew and Talbot left for Charleston that same evening.[14]

The message was as cunning as it was simple. Lincoln was merely sending food to Anderson, who would otherwise be starved out. This was a humanitarian, not an aggressive or hostile act. If the Confederacy let the supplies land, the crisis would be deferred, and the tensions prolonged. To resist the landing, however, would place the onus of firing the first shot on the South. In this ingenious way Lincoln could maintain his declared policy to "hold, occupy and possess" without resorting to an aggressive move.

Lincoln was far too shrewd to believe that the Davis government would let the supplies land, but his intent was not to provoke a clash. He saw no choice but to send relief, come what may. Withdrawing the garrison was not only repugnant to him personally but also political suicide; nor could he stand by and let hunger force Anderson to surrender. Lincoln ran the risk of war because he saw no other option. At the same time he turned this disadvantage into a brilliant gambit like a chess player escaping a trap by springing one of his own. Forced to pick between evacuation and war, he offered Montgomery the choice between war and perpetuation of the status quo.[15]

Later that afternoon a weary officer strode into the Navy Department after an arduous trip from Pensacola. He took off a body pouch and produced two dispatches for Welles, who, fresh from the *Powhatan* mess, read them in alarm and left at once for the White House. A few blocks away Scott was finishing his daily report to Lincoln when a lieutenant knocked on his door with copies of the same dispatches. He too was shocked by what he read and scribbled at the end of his report, "I have no time to comment on this extraordinary conduct." One dispatch came from the frustrated Captain Vogdes, the other from Captain Henry A. Adams, the senior naval officer off Pensacola. Together they revealed the army and navy butting heads. Scott's order of March 12 to put the company into Pickens had finally reached Vogdes on March 31. But when he showed it to Adams, the captain refused to obey because the order was old and seemed to contradict his own orders to make no provocative move that might imperil the January 29 truce. Obviously troubled, the punctilious Adams asked that the orders be clarified to relieve him from "a painful embarrassment."[16]

To their horror Lincoln and Welles realized that Fort Pickens was not secure, as they had assumed, and might fall before Porter could get there. They agreed that a special messenger should be sent with an order for Adams to land the troops. Late that evening Welles told a young naval lieutenant named John L. Worden to proceed to Pensacola as rapidly as possible with the order, which he was to memorize so that it could be destroyed in case he was stopped en route.[17]

"When Mr. Lincoln came into office he found an empty treasury, a demoralized army, and treasonable defection throughout the civil service. He has had to feel his way into public confidence against a factious opposition, and to ascertain the extent of resources at his command, before proceeding to carry out the principles announced in his Inaugural. . . . The time has come when they are to be vindicated peaceably, if the revolted States will permit, or otherwise if they insist upon provoking a collision, and forcing the Government to an attitude of defense."[18]

The *Tribune*'s man, probably James Pike, got the story on the 7th and it ran the next day. He knew about Talbot's visit and his return to Charleston with a message for Pickens that Sumter would be provisioned but not reinforced unless attacked. He grasped the change in policy with remarkable clarity. "The President is unwilling to strike the national flag," he declared, "and determined not to permit the garrison at Fort Sumter to be starved out, or abandoned to . . . a humiliating surrender." Clearly someone had leaked the story, but who?

The *Mercury*'s man in Washington saw the same excitement but not the source. Denouncing the assertions to evacuate Sumter as a ploy, he got wind of an expedition prepared "with a fair amount of secresy [*sic*], vigor, and despatch." He thought that it was headed for Pickens and that Sumter would not be reinforced. The commissioners agreed, but the rumors about preparations made them uneasy. On the 7th they asked Campbell to prod Seward again on the withdrawal from Sumter. The judge wrote Seward that same day and received an undated, unsigned note: "Faith as to Sumter fully kept. Wait and see."[19]

Campbell puzzled over this enigma. Did the pledge refer to the order to evacuate or to the promise to notify Governor Pickens if supplies were sent? Warily he told the commissioners that he still believed nothing would be sent to Sumter without notice but that he no longer felt free to give any assurance about Pickens. Convinced that some hostile move was under way, the commissioners decided to wait no longer. At 9 p.m. their secretary, John T. Pickett, called at Seward's home only to be told that he was out. Pickett gave Fred Seward notice that the commissioners wished an answer to their note of March 12, and said he would call at the State Department the next day at 2 p.m.[20]

A cold rain beat down all day Sunday and poured that night, filling the city's unpaved streets with water a foot deep in some places. Through it waded the staunch Virginia Unionist John Minor Botts to see Seward that afternoon and Lincoln that evening. Later Botts claimed that Lincoln told him he had made the offer to Baldwin to evacuate Sumter if the Virginia convention would adjourn. When Botts offered to take the proposition home, Lincoln said it was too late; the fleet had already sailed. The men in Sumter had to be provisioned, he insisted, and he wished to do this peacefully. "What do I want with war?" he asked. "I am no war man; I want peace more than any man in this country, and will make greater sacrifices to preserve it than any other man in the nation."[21]

Botts left the White House convinced of Lincoln's sincerity. The next day he warned Lincoln of a plot by Virginia secessionists to seize Washington. No one took the threat lightly; rumors to that effect had circulated for too long. Charles P. Stone informed Seward of Commissioner Forsyth's boast to a State Department clerk that within sixty days the Confederacy would extend through Washington to the New York border, that it would "cut off those damned puritan states, east, and never let them come in." A woman just back from Montgomery said Varina Howell Davis asked her to tell her Washington friends that "I shall be happy to see them *in the White House . . . in June*."[22]

Stone was not alone in believing that Confederate leaders were intent on "possessing this Capital, and forcing a revolution here and in the middle states." A strike at Washington made good sense. If war came, its seizure would give the Confederacy instant credibility and a strong bid for foreign recognition, to say nothing of the humiliation it would inflict on the administration. And the city, surrounded by slave states through which any relief force must pass to reach it, was vulnerable to attack. With both Virginia and Maryland so volatile and filled with secessionists, a strike force could easily be raised and reinforced.

Lincoln sent Botts to see Scott, who had long worried about defense of the capital. Four companies of regulars left Washington to embark on the expedition South, leaving only a small contingent of regulars and recruits along with two hundred marines at the navy yard. No other troops were within reach of the city except for about four hundred men at Fort Monroe, whom Scott considered "the *minimum* force needed there, under existing circumstances." The general was convinced that "machinations against the Government & this Capital, are secretly going on, all around us—in Virginia, in Maryland & here, as well as farther South."[23]

Lacking a secret service or funds to pay detectives to ferret out such activities, Scott urged Lincoln to send agents to Baltimore, Annapolis, Alexandria, Richmond, and Norfolk. He also warned that the time might be near to call out state militia to protect the capital. On the 8th he emphasized that "For the defense of the government more troops are wanted. . . . There is a growing apprehension of danger here." Some troops were coming from New York but might not arrive in time. Scott asked for ten companies of militia to guard the public buildings and the White House and for a small war steamer to patrol the Potomac between the Long Bridge and Alexandria. Lincoln complied and was told that perhaps twice that many companies would be needed.[24]

Calling out the state militia was a major step that would provoke outrage in the border states, as would the offer the president had received from black volunteers to help defend the city. With his options dwindling, Lincoln needed to know which states could be counted on to furnish troops. In recent days he had conferred with several northern governors, including Andrew Curtin of Pennsylvania. On this troubled April 8 he wired Curtin, "I think the necessity of being *ready* increases. Look to it." Outside his window the air had turned unseasonably warm, even clammy, and the rain continued to pour. Chew and Talbot were in Charleston by now; Lincoln wondered what reception they had received.[25]

"The Administration has served fair notice on Jefferson Davis and Gov. Pickens of its intention, and leaves with them the grave responsibility of inaugurating civil war. . . . The simple purpose is to relieve a starving garrison."[26]

Promptly at 2 p.m. on the 8th, John Pickett called at the State Department for Seward's reply and received a copy of the memorandum Seward had put on file on March 15. In formal language it rejected politely but firmly the request for recognition, thereby ending a month of hopeful intrigue in the name of peace. Like their predecessors, the commissioners responded angrily, as did Judge Campbell, who felt badly used and accused Seward of "systematic duplicity." As the commissioners prepared to leave for home, confusion reigned among them. That morning they wired Governor Pickens that Sumter would be evacuated and Fort Pickens provisioned. At 3 p.m. Crawford warned Beauregard: "The war policy prevails in the Cabinet at this hour." An hour later they informed Montgomery of the rebuff and added, "Fort Pickens and Texas are the first points of military demonstration."[27]

The collapse of negotiations left Seward's plan in ruins. Yet he could not let the idea go. Restless and eager for an audience, he sent a note asking William Russell to call at nine that evening. Russell had spent an intriguing day at the Smithsonian Institution examining two pythons and Joseph Henry's giant map of North America, which the professor used to show how the climatic conditions of the West barred it forever from supporting a large population, free or slave. Earlier, in the barbershop at Willard's, Russell had picked up rumors of military activity and of Campbell's work as intermediary for the commissioners. He had written Seward asking for a statement, and the invitation arrived.[28]

Ushered into the drawing room, Russell found Seward with his son Fred and daughter-in-law Anna. They invited him to a game of whist with Seward as his partner. Seward talked as he played, and the score reflected which mattered most to him. He assured Russell that all the preparations meant only that the government was taking steps to protect forts that had been neglected. "But we are determined in doing so to make no aggression," he stressed. "The President's inaugural clearly shadows out our policy. We will not go beyond it . . . nor will we withdraw from it."

These comments would have intrigued Russell more had he known of Seward's April 1 memorandum to Lincoln. After a time Seward put down his cards and sent Fred to fetch some papers. Anna lit the gas drop light and, after Fred had returned, left the room with him. Seward offered Russell a cigar and lit one for himself, then proceeded to read in measured tones a long dispatch that was to be given to Lord John Russell by the American minister, Charles Francis Adams. The tone struck William Russell as hostile, if not menacing, in its outright rejection of secession and warning to foreign powers not to recognize the South. Even war with Great Britain seemed possible as a device to reunite the nation.

There will be a reaction, Seward assured him. "When the Southern States see that we mean them no wrong . . . they will see their mistake, and one after another they will come back into the union." The whole process would be over in three months; he was certain of it. As the clock passed midnight, Seward was still talking and the rain still poured in sheets outside his window.

SINCE APRIL FOOL'S DAY a bleak, overcast sky that matched the grim mood of the city had enveloped Charleston. On the 6th the rain began and showed no sign of letting up. The next morning Mary Chesnut awoke with her first headache since leaving Montgomery. It got no better at breakfast, when Charlotte Wigfall joked that James would have been a splendid match for herself, and John Manning, who had written his wife about flirting with Mary, reported that she had requested a likeness of James as a prelude to opening a flirtation with him. A nagging cold dulled her gaiety along with news she thought "*so* warlike I *quake*." Some Hollands bitters helped the cold, but nothing eased her sense of apprehension, made worse by another scolding from James. "I feel he is my all," she wrote, "& should go mad without him." The rest was merely badinage in good fun, which she had no intention of carrying too far.[29]

With the convention winding down, she began packing for the return to Camden. That evening, while she talked to Robert Gourdin and listened to William Porcher Miles brag about his intimacies with certain ladies in Washington, John Manning swept into the room and seated himself on the sofa next to her. "Madam," he declared in a mock-heroic tone, "your country is invaded."

Everyone perked up. Six ships were reported off the bar, Manning told them. Emissaries had come from Washington to announce war. Pickens and Beauregard were holding a council. Mary rushed to tell James, who confirmed the story. Louis Wigfall came in and took the men away with him. Mary went to her room with Charlotte Wigfall, who wept quietly and talked about the horrors of civil war. At 11 p.m. the sound of cannon shattered the silence, followed by loud shouts and tumult. Mary hurried to see what was happening and met former governor John Means, who rushed out of his room in his dressing gown to say that Pickens had stupidly ordered seven cannon shots fired as the signal for the regiments to assemble. "Of course," said Mary, "no sleep for me."[30]

As the Home Guard of men too old for military duty clattered through the city, rousing the troops, the streets filled with soldiers marching and yelling. Beset by so many conflicting reports, Governor Pickens was still trying to find out what was going on even as Chew and Talbot arrived at 6 p.m. on the 8th. Phantom ships kept turning up outside the harbor, put there by endless rumors. The last advice Pickens had from the commissioners said the relief force was headed for Fort Pickens. Then, to his surprise, Talbot appeared at his door asking him to see Chew.[31]

Pickens agreed. Talbot returned with Chew, who read his message to the governor and handed him a copy. The governor asked that Beauregard be brought in, since he was in charge of military affairs, and read him the message. When Pickens mentioned a reply, Chew said he was not authorized to receive any communication. Having framed his statement carefully, Lincoln gave neither Pickens nor Davis any room to deviate from his scenario or debate its meaning. He had boxed them into his options, left them no opportunity to shift the ground on him as he had on them.[32]

After a brief silence Talbot asked if he might visit Fort Sumter. Pickens bowed to Beauregard, who said that no communication would be allowed with the fort except to convey an order for evacuation. Chew and Talbot returned to Washington on the 11 p.m. train, leaving in their wake a stunned city. Word spread quickly of their mission. "Our visions of peace were rudely destroyed today by the return of Talbot," noted a dejected Emma Holmes. ". . . So at last, war is declared. But with the same treacherous, contemptible policy, they seek to throw the onus of opening civil war on us." Edmund Ruffin was ecstatic. "Of course," he noted, "every resistance will be made by our forces."33

How to respond? The day before, pursuant to orders from Montgomery, Beauregard had formally stopped all food to the fort from the city. Shortly after Chew and Talbot departed, he notified Anderson that no mail would be allowed in or out of the fort. Pickens sent Judge Magrath to inform Postmaster Alfred Huger that the governor had decided to seize the fort's mail. On the morning of the 9th a staff officer fetched a bag of Sumter mail from the post office and laid it on a table before Beauregard, Pickens, and the latter's advisers. The bag included two letters from Anderson and one from Foster to Washington.34

Only official letters were opened; private mail was sent back to the post office for delivery. Pickens shoved the letters toward Magrath, who pushed them away, saying he had too often sentenced people to the penitentiary for such tampering. He suggested that Beauregard open them, but the general deferred to the governor. Pickens fingered a letter nervously, then said, "Well, if you are all so fastidious about it, give them to me." Still, he hesitated until prodded by Magrath, whereupon he nearly ripped the letter apart. His eyes widened with astonishment as he read Anderson's report dated the day before, April 8.

The major had just received Cameron's letter of the 4th saying that a relief expedition was on its way. Surprised to learn this after having been led to believe the contrary, he protested that "A movement made now, when the South has been erroneously informed that none such will be attempted, would produce most disastrous results throughout our country." He feared Fox's plan would end in failure and warned that he had barely enough oil to light the lantern for one night. "Colonel Lamon's remark convinced me that the idea, merely hinted at to me by Captain Fox, would not be carried out," he added. "We shall strive to do our duty, though I frankly say that my heart is not in the war which I see is to be thus commenced."35

These revelations told Pickens more about the state of things than he had learned in weeks. Aware of their import, he sent an aide to carry the letters to Montgomery. "You see that the present scheme for supplying the fort is Mr. Fox's," he told Davis. Clearly Fox had violated his pledge to Hartstene to visit Sumter only for peaceful purposes. No one could doubt now that war loomed. While awaiting orders from Montgomery, Beauregard got his troops and command structure ready. The destiny he had long pined for had come at last. Glory was to be his, and after helping found a new nation, he would retire to a farm near New Orleans and live out his years contentedly among family and friends. Or so he said.[36]

More troops were rushed to Morris Island and placed under the command of the prickly Milledge Bonham, who resented having to serve under Beauregard or anyone else. Ten companies were due on the evening train, and another two regiments the next day, by which time Beauregard hoped to have six thousand men posted around the harbor. A new Blakely rifled cannon arrived from Britain that day and was moved into position. "WAR DECLARED," blared the *Mercury*. ". . . We have partially submitted to the insolent military domination of a handful of men in our bay for over three months . . . The gage is thrown down, and we accept the challenge. We will meet the invader, and the God of Battles must decide the issue between the hirelings of Abolition hate and Northern tyranny, and the people of South Carolina defending their freedom and their homes."[37]

That same Tuesday, the 9th, the secession convention, having transferred jurisdiction over the forts, troops, and arms of the state to the Confederacy, finished some housekeeping duties and adjourned. The Chesnuts had planned to leave Charleston that evening, but events moved too quickly for them. James joined Beauregard's staff, along with Wigfall, Manning, Governor Means, and two other dignitaries. The city was mad with excitement; everyone expected an attack that night. Once again rumor reported a fleet off the bar. Edmund Ruffin, as ecstatic in the coming of his destiny as Beauregard was in his, borrowed a musket and joined the Palmetto Guard as a private. The officers and men made him blush with their cheers.[38]

The floating battery was towed out and anchored in a cove near Sullivans Island, but no fleet appeared and no attack came. On Wednesday The Citadel commencement was canceled because the graduates and their teachers were otherwise engaged. Roger Pryor of Virginia arrived in town, checked into the Charleston Hotel, and treated the natives to a fiery speech that evening. "I thank you especially that you have at last annihilated this accursed Union, reeking with corruption and insolent with excess of tyranny," he cried. "Thank God! it is blasted with the lightning wrath of an outraged and indignant people. Not only has it gone, but it has gone forever." As for his native state, Pryor said, "Give the old lady time. She cannot move with the agility of some of the younger daughters. She is a little rheumatic."[39]

Eager to get into the thick of things, Wigfall stayed close to Beauregard and prodded Jefferson Davis as well. "No one now doubts that Lincoln intends War," he wired. "The delay on his part is only to complete his preparations. All here is ready on our side. Our delay, therefore, is to his advantage, and our disadvantage. Let us take Fort Sumter, before we have to fight the fleet and the Fort." In a separate letter he asked impishly, "Would you like to have a lock of Anderson's hair?" With his usual insouciance Wigfall too had put the ball into Davis's court. All they could do now was wait for word from Montgomery.[40]

TIME AND TIMING WEIGHED HEAVILY on Davis and his cabinet. The hope for peace to which the president had clung vanished on the 8th when the commissioners telegraphed that they were denied recognition. He passed the news along to the governors of the seceded states and asked them for 20,000 more troops. The cabinet met for two hours of discussion, but events moved more quickly than rhetoric. That evening the telegram from Pickens arrived informing them of Chew's visit and the notice from Lincoln. Walker wired Beauregard: "Under no circumstances are you to allow provisions to be sent to Fort Sumter." The general replied that provisions had been stopped the day before and that he was calling up all his troops for duty.[41]

The next day the cabinet renewed the debate. What options, if any, remained short of battle? In January Davis had urged Pickens not to attack the fort because it "pressed on nothing but a point of pride." Was the advice still sound? Could he let supplies land or at least withhold fire until the other side fired first? Davis doubted that the troops at Charleston and the hotheads surrounding him could be restrained from war. The credibility of the new government, desperate for recognition abroad, was at stake in this encounter, and so was his own. He must lead boldly or lose his leadership to those who would.

Davis argued for opening the bombardment. The others agreed except for the reckless, hard-drinking Toombs, who surprised everyone by acting like a secretary of state in urging caution and prudence. "The firing upon that fort will inaugurate a civil war greater than any the world has yet seen, and I do not feel competent to advise you," he declared. As the debate warmed, Toombs paced restlessly back and forth, then wheeled abruptly on Davis and snapped, "Mr. President, at this time, it is suicide, murder, and will lose us every friend at the North. You will wantonly strike a hornet's nest which extends from mountains to ocean, and legions, now quiet, will swarm out and sting us to death. It is unnecessary; it puts us in the wrong; it is fatal."[42]

No one listened. To Davis and the others the issue was one of timing: Should Beauregard be ordered to fire at once rather than wait for the expedition to arrive? The cabinet met again on the 10th, and during its discussion the telegram urging Davis to attack arrived from Wigfall. The president could not resist the momentum pushing him toward immediate action and had little desire to do so even though he realized what horrors civil war would bring. Through Walker he sent Beauregard a careful order. If the general was convinced that Chew was an authorized agent of the administration and that Lincoln's notice was genuine, he was to demand immediate evacuation of the fort. "If this is refused, proceed, in such manner as you may determine, to reduce it."[43]

The decision had been made. For Davis, who seldom saw any other view of a matter than his own, it was the right and only decision. To his surprise, Beauregard wired back that he would make the demand at noon the next day. Walker replied that he should act sooner "unless there are special reasons connected with your condition." Back came the terse response: "The reasons are especial for 12 o'clock." What was this? Davis wondered anxiously. Having crossed the Rubicon, he wanted no delays or hesitation. Beauregard was the last man from whom he expected procrastination in such grave matters.[44]

SLOWLY, INEXORABLY their keyhole on the outside world was covered. With the mail stopped, Anderson worried that his letter of the 8th might be opened and its indiscreet statements used against him. Anxiously he asked for its return only to have Beauregard confirm his worst fears that the official letters had been sent to Montgomery. The major had been depressed since the morning of the 8th, when a house at the tip of Sullivans Island was blown up to reveal a well-fortified battery behind it. From this position the guns could enfilade both flanks of the fort and rake the only spot where a ship could anchor at Sumter. Wearily the engineers went to work trying to counter the threat. Lacking material for sandbags, Foster rigged a large double curb of boards and scantling along with some ladders and runways to enable arriving supplies to be brought inside quickly.[45]

Anderson's spirits continued to sag. Belatedly he put the men on half rations, which at best would stretch the bread supply to the 12th, and ordered them to sleep in the gun casements, which offered better protection. Some rice damaged by glass from a shattered window was picked over carefully to augment the bread. The men remained in good spirits, but the long confinement gnawed at them as it did at him. On Wednesday, the 10th, the soldiers, glad for something to do, cheerfully carried shot and shell to the guns. All surplus blankets and clothes, even sheets from the hospital, were cut up to make cartridge bags, but with only six needles in the fort the work went slowly. Sam Crawford watched the preparations on the parapet, then stepped down to the lower battery, where he saw Anderson pacing slowly back and forth among the guns. Lost in thought, his face dark with despair, he seemed to bear the weight of the world on his frail shoulders. That day another battery was unmasked on Sullivans Island.[46]

It was coming, Anderson realized. The war he would have given his life to prevent hovered before him. The question was no longer if but when, and the inescapable answer was very soon. Where was the relief expedition? "We are looking for the relief promised to us," Crawford confided to his diary, "and men can be seen on the parapet at all hours."[47]

At dawn on the 11th Foster spotted the floating battery at the upper end of Sullivans Island between the end of a jetty and the steamboat wharf at a point where it could sweep the left flank of the fort and prevent any landing there. Shortly before 4 p.m. a small boat approached the fort under a white flag. It bore three of Beauregard's aides, James Chesnut, Captain Stephen D. Lee, a West Pointer who had recently changed sides, and A. R. Chisholm. Jeff Davis went out to receive them and was told they had a written message for Anderson. Davis led them to the guard room, where the major soon joined them.[48]

The mood was polite but restrained. Beauregard's message presented the demand for evacuation as generously as possible. He would arrange to take Anderson and his command to any northern post with all company arms, property, and private property. The flag he had defended "so long and with so much fortitude" could be saluted on lowering. Anderson excused himself to consult with his officers. As they gathered silently, the major revealed to them for the first time his December orders from Floyd, which he had been instructed not to tell them, to defend the fort to the last extremity but not to sacrifice the garrison if in his judgment the fort could not be held.[49]

"Was ever such terms granted to a band of starving men?" Crawford mused, but to a man the officers said no. Anderson informed the aides. Escorting them to the main gate, he asked if Beauregard would attack without further notice. Chesnut looked embarrassed and hesitated. "I think not," he said finally. "No, I can say to you that he will not, without further notice."[50]

"I will await the first shot," Anderson said, "and if you do not batter us to pieces, we shall be starved out in a few days."[51]

Chesnut looked at him in surprise and asked if he could report this to Beauregard. Anderson demurred but said it was true. The remark was cryptic, lacking propriety, but compelling. Convinced that it revealed Anderson's desire to avoid bloodshed, Chesnut hurried to tell Beauregard. The general wired the remark to Montgomery and waited anxiously. He hoped to avoid a fight with his old mentor and friend, and he was short of powder—which was the special reason for not presenting the demand at once that he could not give Walker over the telegraph. A shipment of powder was due that evening from Augusta, so he would be ready for whatever option Anderson chose.[52]

At 9:10 p.m. the answer finally came from Montgomery. "Do not desire needlessly to bombard Fort Sumter," Walker telegraphed. If Anderson would state the time at which he would evacuate and promise not to use his guns against the Confederates unless attacked, Beauregard could refrain from an assault. "If this, or its equivalent, be refused," Walker added, "reduce the fort as your judgment decides to be most practicable."

Could the fort be secured without a fight? Beauregard sent Chesnut, Lee, Chisholm, and Roger Pryor back to Sumter at 11 p.m. with these terms. Not only the general but the entire city waited for the reply. After his first trip Chesnut, dressed in a uniform and sash with a sword borrowed from Governor Means, returned to the hotel and told Mary of his interview with Anderson. "Patience oh my soul," she murmured; "if Anderson will not surrender, tonight the bombardment begins." She clung to hope, if only because she had heard about Anderson's letter saying his heart was not in the war. Surely he would see reason! Dinner that day she called their "last merry meal," and the evening was a torment of waiting, interrupted by the summons for James to go back to Sumter. Reluctantly she went to bed and did nothing but toss and turn restlessly.[53]

Out on Morris Island Major P. F. Stevens, the superintendent of The Citadel, who was in charge of the Iron and Point batteries, witnessed an extraordinary sight. Word had come that Anderson would be asked to surrender, and the men stood ready at their guns awaiting the outcome. Watching the fort from a traverse left of the Iron Battery, Stevens saw the United States flag above Sumter suddenly split almost in two. "I wonder if that is emblematical," he said to the men around him. The flag hung in broken form for a brief time, then was hauled down and replaced by a new one. No matter, said the men; it was an omen, and a good one for the fledgling republic.[54]

The Good Fight

What a commentary does this spectacle afford upon the boasted civilization of the 19th century! It is too sad a proof that with all the progress made in Arts & Sciences . . . *with all the great modern* improvements *in* manufactures, & material prosperity, *mankind are no better now than at any previous time. . . . Nations like individuals become arrogant with power.*

—Henry William Ravenel
May 1, 1861[1]

A BRIGHT SUNNY SKY ushered in Friday, April 12, in New York City. The air had the clean, fresh feel of spring. At City Hall, the *Tribune* building, and some of the hotels large American flags honored the birthday of Henry Clay, the much-mourned Great Compromiser dead these nine years. On Park Row the wires from Charleston were ominously silent, leaving those clustered about the newspaper office uneasy. Not until three that afternoon did a message get through, and it contained the words no one wanted to hear. "This day," prophesied Thurlow Weed, "will be remembered as the darkest in our history."[2]

THE RAIN THAT BEAT DOWN UNRELENTINGLY on Washington turned into a wild thunderstorm on the evening of the 9th. The surging waters washed out some bridges outside the city, delaying the departure of the Confederate commissioners and preventing those newly appointed by the Virginia convention from starting their trip to Washington. Earlier that day a telegram sent to *Star* editor W. W. Wallach reported that a bloody fight had opened in Charleston Harbor with heavy government casualties and four ships sunk. Some frantic hours passed before it was revealed to be a hoax.[3]

On the 10th the District militia was ordered out. Sloshing through the mud, they mustered in armories across the city to take the oath. When a few southern sympathizers refused, they were stripped of their uniforms, arms, and accoutrements in front of the other men. A well-equipped company presented itself even though not called and was accepted for duty. "Every day impresses stronger conviction upon the public mind here," wrote Edwin Stanton to Buchanan, "that armed collision will soon take place." To the *Mercury*'s man, however, "The alarm of the Abolitionists at the bare idea of a demonstration by the Southrons against Washington begins to be perfectly ludicrous."4

That afternoon, as Gideon Welles stood outside the Treasury Building, a carriage clattered down the street and pulled up suddenly. Stephen A. Douglas jumped out and went to Welles. The rebels were bent on war, he declared, and about to attack Sumter. Strong measures should be taken at once; any delay meant a terrible civil war. Douglas might differ with the administration, but he would stand by the Union regardless of party. Welles suggested that they go to the State Department and consult Seward. "The look of mingled astonishment and incredulity which came over him," Welles said, "I can never forget."5

"Then you have faith in Seward?" Douglas responded. "Have you made yourself acquainted with what has been going on here all winter? Seward has an understanding with these men. If he has influence with them, why don't he use it?"

Welles persuaded him that Seward was the proper man to receive the information. Leaving Adele Douglas in the carriage, they walked to the State Department. "Lincoln is honest and means well," Douglas said. "He will do well if counseled right." They found Seward, and Douglas told him of the impending attack on Sumter without revealing his sources. Seward promised to see Lincoln but admitted he knew of no way to prevent an attack if reckless men were bent on making one. After they left, Douglas complained that he got no more than he expected from Seward, who was in his view the wrong man for the times. The only hope, he said bleakly, was if Lincoln could act independently of him.

Talk of an impending attack was no secret. The papers were full of the subject, their excitement fanned by the troops galloping through the streets. That same Wednesday the *Pawnee* and *Pocahontas* finally got out to sea after being delayed by the storm. The few officials who knew about the expedition wondered how they were faring in heavy seas. "The storm . . . must have been of great violence on the Sea-coast," Scott fretted, "& I am afraid that some of our transport steamers have been incommoded—perhaps damaged by the gale."6

THE RAIN THAT DRENCHED WASHINGTON crept up the coast toward New York on the 8th, as the *Harriet Lane* sailed under sealed orders for an unknown destination. A large crowd, puzzled by the ship's sudden departure, waved good-bye, leaving the officers and men to debate their course. One unofficial guest aboard, B. S. Osbon of the New York *World*, had his own ideas about where they were going and looked forward to proving himself right. That same evening the steamer *Baltic* with Gustavus Fox aboard dropped down to Sandy Hook and prepared to head out the next morning. Two of the three tugs Fox had engaged had already left; the third was to follow soon afterward.[7]

The sky was foreboding, and a brisk wind was blowing. One of the tugs sprang a leak and, unknown to Fox, returned to port. Later a second followed; the third never left port. By midnight the wind had turned into a southeast gale with heavy swells that continued all day and night on the 9th. The *Harriet Lane* lowered its foresail and fore-topsail and headed into the wind. At 8 a.m. on the 9th the *Baltic* discharged her pilot and started down the coast. Neither ship could take a reading all day under the leaden skies. By the 10th the *Harriet Lane* had made her way to Cape Hatteras, where the crew spotted wreck debris in the water. There was no time to stop; they were already behind schedule.

That afternoon the seas again grew heavy with winds from the northwest. Although no one except Captain John Faunce knew their destination, most suspected Charleston. After dinner, with the weather improved, the small arms were loaded and tested, and the shot racks filled. As the ship approached the rendezvous site ten miles east of the Charleston lighthouse, Osbon and the pilot scrambled up the main crosstrees to study the harbor through their glasses. When darkness fell at 7:30, not a single light or beacon shone from its usual place in the harbor. In the eerie stillness they wondered where the other ships were and what they were to do.

Shortly before 3 a.m. on the 12th the *Baltic* arrived, and Fox went aboard the *Harriet Lane* to brief Faunce. At 7 a.m. the *Pawnee* joined them. Fox took a launch to her and informed Commander S. C. Rowan of his orders to provision Sumter. He wanted the *Pawnee* to follow him to the bar. Rowan replied that he had orders to stand ten miles east of the light and await the *Powhatan*; he was not about to go in and trigger a civil war. Faunce agreed to move, however, and Fox took the *Baltic* in with the *Harriet Lane* as escort. It was near 10 a.m. as the ships approached the bar. Fox planned to take a launch to the fort to ask if he should bring in the supplies, but something was terribly wrong. From the deck he heard heavy guns and saw columns of smoke rising in the distance.

Quickly, Fox turned about and signaled the *Harriet Lane:* "I am going out for the Pawnee; they are firing into Fort Sumter!"

. . . .

ON THE MORNING OF THE 11TH Lieutenant John Worden reached Pensacola and made his way to the headquarters of General Braxton Bragg. Aware that the January agreement sanctioned such visits, Bragg wrote out a pass allowing Worden to visit Captain Adams on the *Sabine*. Did he have written dispatches for Adams? Bragg asked. Only a verbal message, Worden replied. Not until 4 p.m. did he manage to reach the *Wyandotte*, which was anchored in the harbor and serving as a dispatch boat for the *Sabine*. By then a stiff wind had come up and the sea was too rough to cross the bar. Worden spent a restless night on board and saw that the wind had not abated next morning. To ease his impatience, he went ashore to have a look at Fort Pickens.[8]

At noon Worden finally reached the *Sabine* and handed his message to Captain Adams. Preparations were made to land Vogdes's company that same night. Adams gave Worden a written order to carry back to Washington and told him not to bother seeing Bragg before departing. The lieutenant returned to Pensacola at 5 p.m. and caught a train that would carry him north via Montgomery. By then word of his mission had leaked to the Confederate government. "Lieutenant Worden, of U.S. Navy, has gone to Pensacola with dispatches," Leroy Walker wired Bragg. "Intercept them." But Worden had already left. Confederate authorities removed him from the cars at Montgomery and placed him under arrest.[9]

That night Adams moved Vogdes's company and some marines to the fort. A frustrated Bragg demanded to know why the armistice had been broken. Vogdes replied that he knew of no armistice and had acted under direct orders from the government. On the 16th the *Atlantic* arrived, and Meigs quickly unloaded Harvey Brown's troops in Fort Pickens. The *Powhatan* came in two days later, delayed by winds and balky boilers. As Porter steamed toward the harbor, Meigs used the *Atlantic* to block him from entering until he could explain that Brown needed more time to prepare his defenses. Two days later the *Illinois* arrived, giving Pickens a total of eleven hundred troops with six months' supplies. The fort was safe, and the *Powhatan* was not needed for its daring mission. But John Worden spent seven months in a Confederate prison.[10]

THE RAIN KEPT FALLING ON WASHINGTON. William Russell packed up the things he didn't need for his trip south and sent them to New York. A note came from Scott inviting him to dinner on the 11th. Russell liked the general and accepted his vanity as the natural state of one who sought the highest standard in everything. A scruffy-looking troop of mounted volunteers was parading in the street when Russell arrived. The general greeted him in an undress blue frock coat with brass buttons and velvet collar and cuffs. To his surprise, Seward and Bates were there as well and tendered him a warm welcome. The only other guest was Major George W. Cullum, one of Scott's aides.[11]

The volunteers interrupted with loud cheers for Scott. With great effort the general lumbered to the door to give them a few words about rallying around the flag and dying gloriously. The band struck up "Yankee Doodle," prompting Seward to ask for "Hail Columbia!" and "The Star-Spangled Banner." The players also took a swipe at "God Save the Queen" in Russell's honor. Marveling at how easily the general had been dragooned out of his own parlor, Russell concluded, "There is no privacy for public men in America."

The general's modest lodgings were in the home of a renowned French cook, which ensured a splendid meal served by his English valet and a black servant. The wines were equally fine, and the conversation roamed genially over the Crimea and the general's early career. Scott was telling an amusing story when a telegram arrived. He read it with obvious distress, apologized to Russell, and handed it to Seward. He too looked agitated at the contents and gave it to Bates, who grunted in surprise. Scott took it back and stuffed it in his pocket. "You had better not put it there, General," said Seward. "It will be getting lost, or into some other hands." The general nodded and tossed the note into the fire, taking care not to hit the bottles of claret mellowing on the hearth.

Russell saw that they needed to talk and asked Cullum to join him in the garden for a cigar. In the twilight he saw two figures standing at an enclosure near the wall. Sentries, Cullum explained, placed there to protect the general. They returned to the sitting room and chatted for another hour before Russell left with Seward. He asked the secretary if he feared a bold move on Washington. The city was nearly defenseless, Seward admitted, but the other side was as unprepared as the government for aggressive moves. Russell learned nothing about the telegram, but the next morning he heard that the administration had taken decisive steps to test the Confederacy's resolve.

He decided to leave at once for the South, pausing only to visit Seward, Lord Lyons, and the French and Russian ministers, and to leave cards elsewhere. With Richmond still cut off by floods, he had to travel via Baltimore and Norfolk. At 6 p.m. he went in a driving rain to the station and caught the train for Baltimore. The talk on the crowded cars was not kind to Lincoln and his cabinet. "Well, darn me if I wouldn't draw a bead on Old Abe, Seward—aye or General Scott himself," said one man in a fur coat, ". . . if they due [*sic*] try to use their soldiers and sailors to beat down States' Rights."

Baltimore's streets were deep in water when Russell arrived at 8 p.m. As he registered at the Eutaw House, the landlord asked if he had heard the news. "The President of the Telegraph Company tells me he has received a message from his clerk at Charleston that the batteries have opened fire on Sumter because the Government has sent down a fleet to force in supplies." The news spread through the city, and the next morning the landlord came to Russell's room to verify the rumor. "And now," he said, "there's no saying where it will all end."

Some local gentlemen visited Russell after breakfast and assured him that Maryland would secede. Their contempt for the federal government amazed him, as did their ridicule of Lincoln. At the barbershop, however, it was a different story. The black barber asked meekly whether the story of the bombardment was true. Told that it was, he murmured, "De gen'lmen of Baltimore will be quite glad of it. But maybe it'l come bad after all." Russell was intrigued to learn the barber's conviction that slavery was nearing its end. "And what will take place then, do you think?" he asked.

"Wall, sare," replied the barber, " 'spose coloured men will be good as white men."

ALL THURSDAY AFTERNOON AND EVENING people eager to witness the first shots of the war that many hoped would never come thronged the Battery. Every arriving train brought more troops and curiosity seekers from the country. More than six thousand men manned positions around the harbor. Of the seven regiments under Bonham, three were ordered to the city, one was sent to Columbia, and the rest were held in ready reserve. On Morris Island Edmund Ruffin and his comrades remained at their guns expecting a fight until an order to return to quarters came at 10 p.m. Even then Ruffin took off only his coat and shoes before catching some sleep. Those men not on duty napped with their arms at their side. Some sent servants to their country homes to have the graveyard readied.[12]

"Impending, momentarily expected battle, is the culmination of years of steadily increasing encroachment of the North upon the South—of compromising, sentimental generosity, and weak acquiescence on the part of the South. . . . [T]he North is swollen with pride and drunk with insolence. . . . The North needs proof of the earnestness of our intentions and our manhood. Experience shall be their teacher. Let them learn."[13]

Once again Anderson summoned his officers, this time to discuss the offer. They talked mostly about how long the garrison could hold out. Crawford offered his opinion as surgeon that the men could last five days at most, three of them without food. By then the promised supplies would have arrived, and they would have done their duty. No one talked of reserving fire or of any alternative to rejecting the offer. Anderson wrote a careful reply saying he would evacuate by noon on the 15th unless he received "prior to that time controlling instructions from my Government or additional supplies."[14]

The reply, for which they had waited three hours, dismayed Chesnut, Lee, and Chisholm. No choice remained to them. Quickly they penciled a response with Chesnut dictating, Lee scribbling, and Chisholm making a copy. It was about 3:20 a.m. when they handed the note to Anderson informing him that Beauregard would open fire in one hour. Visibly moved, Anderson shook their hands warmly and said he hoped that if they did not meet again in this world they would in a better one.[15]

With the lights all gone, sea and sky ran seamlessly together like a vast black canopy about the fort. It was done, thought Anderson grimly. The waiting was over at last; the nightmare had come true. He walked quietly through the casements, waking the men and giving them the news, telling them to do nothing until he issued orders. The major decided to keep his guns silent until 7 a.m. With no lights or oil for lamps, his men could do nothing until daylight anyway.[16]

The boat carrying the emissaries reached Fort Johnson at 4 a.m. Chesnut ordered Captain George S. James, the commander there, to fire a signal shot that would send the other batteries into action. Eagerly James roused his men and readied the gun. A great admirer of Roger Pryor's, he offered the Virginian the honor of firing the first shot. But Pryor grew nervous and agitated. For once his glib tongue lost its intensity; he faltered, then admitted, "I could not fire the first gun of the war." James claimed the honor for himself. At 4:30 a.m. he sent a 10-inch mortar shell soaring over the harbor. It burst above the fort and announced to a sleeping nation that war had come.[17]

At Cummings Point the drums beat parade at 4 a.m., and the men rushed to their batteries. The furnaces were heated to produce hot shot; all was ready for action. Earlier Captain George B. Cuthbert of the Palmetto Guard had told Ruffin that the company wished him to fire the first shot. Deeply moved, Ruffin did not hesitate. Once the signal shot burst, he sent a shell from a 64-pound columbiad crashing into the southwest angle of Sumter's parapet. A chorus of guns joined in, firing at intervals to conserve ammunition and adjust ranges.[18]

Beauregard had placed his guns well. From Sullivans Island eleven of the thirty cannon at Fort Moultrie, the four guns of the enfilade battery, a lone Dahlgren gun at the point of Sullivans Island, the four guns of the floating battery, and six mortars added their fire to the lone cannon and four mortars at Fort Johnson. Six more guns, including the new Blakely rifle, and half a dozen mortars joined in from the batteries at Cummings Point. Against this ring of forty-three pieces, Fort Sumter had twenty-seven guns on the parapet and twenty-one in the casement along with five cannon on the parade rigged as mortars, four of them aimed at Cummings Point. But Anderson had only seven hundred cartridges, and the six needles in the fort could not make them fast enough to keep up.[19]

Early that morning a damp east wind blew off the water into the city, carrying with it the reports of cannon and later dense clouds of smoke and acrid fumes. Half an hour after the chimes of St. Michael's had tolled four times, the city's fitful sleep ended with the signal gun's report. People jumped out of bed, threw on clothes, and rushed to their windows or rooftops or to the Battery to watch the fight. Mary Chesnut put on her double gown and a shawl, fell prostrate to pray as she had never prayed before, then went to her sister's house to see the battle from the roof. Somewhere in that dark harbor James was moving about in a boat, and her heart ached with anxiety for him.[20]

"War has begun & the battle is now raging!" observed Henry William Ravenel. ". . . When it will end, God only knows." Emma Holmes found it odd that "Every body seems relieved that what has been so long dreaded has come at last and so confident of victory that they seem not to think of the danger of their friends." Caroline Gilman marveled at how clearly the smoke of each gun could be seen and its report heard, and how the house shook with every concussion. "A strange fascination drew us to the windows," she murmured, "to gaze & tremble." But while she trembled, she thrice counted the number of guns firing and marked them on a sheet of paper, "after I gained the courage to look."[21]

That morning Manning breakfasted at a table near Mary Chesnut, then came over and said that they must be friends and not quarrel because he would be under fire all day. The saddest men were those who had no role to play in the fight. Langdon Cheves, who had to go back to his country home, said he felt like the man who did not die at Thermopylae and afterward hanged himself. At last James came in unharmed and curled up on the floor of Beauregard's room to sleep. "Men & women rush in," wrote Mary amid the clamor. "Prayers, imprecations. What scenes."[22]

The reporters had before them the story of a lifetime and could not get at it. George Salter of the New York *Times*, who had made his presence known from the first, crawled atop a cotton bale on a pier to watch the bombardment. When he returned to the hotel to write his dispatch, however, a group of armed locals took him to the city jail. No one from the Associated Press had yet arrived, and the *Tribune* men kept low profiles, managing only snippets of news amid the excitement. In the harbor B. S. Osbon of the *World* watched the fight in frustration from the crosstrees of the *Harriet Lane*, as helpless to get the story out as the ship was to get supplies in to Fort Sumter.[23]

"Never, in the world's history, has any people entered into combat with a higher spirit or a more satisfied, settled, concentrated purpose of achievement, independence, and respect. . . . We rejoice that our people as one man, with serene spirit, are ready for the solemn reckoning with our enemies at hand."[24]

There was no hurry, Anderson realized. Cartridges were scant, and his guns could do little until daylight. Most of the incoming fire was high and passed over the fort. He ordered the men back to bed until reveille, when they formed for roll call and were sent to a paltry breakfast of salt pork. The officers were treated to a bit of farina found by an exultant Crawford in a remote corner of the hospital. By 7:30, when the drums beat assembly, the marksmanship of the enemy had improved. Anderson divided the command into two reliefs that would take turns working four-hour shifts at the guns.[25]

Abner Doubleday took charge of the first shift. He split the men into three groups. The first, under his command, manned the guns aimed at Cummings Point; the second, under Jeff Davis, took aim at Fort Johnson, and the third, officerless until Crawford volunteered his services, targeted Sullivans Island. Anderson imposed a severe handicap on the defenders. Concerned that the parapet was too exposed to fire from the mortars and the enfilade battery, he ordered the men to use only the casement guns. All the heavier guns that fired shells were on the parapet. Without them and without mortars, the fort could return only solid shot against the shot and shell that rained down on them.

When the major showed no interest in firing the first shot at the rebels, Doubleday claimed the honor. "To me," he said later, "it was simply a contest, politically speaking, as to whether virtue or vice should rule." Virtue let loose a 32-pound shot that bounced off the sloping roof of the Iron Battery. As the firing grew regular, the gunners improved their aim, but the lighter casement guns did little damage to the well-fortified batteries around them compared with what the 65- and 128-pound shells of the parapet columbiads might do.

After ninety minutes of futile firing, Doubleday shifted his target to Fort Moultrie but fared no better. He wondered why even direct hits on the embrasures had no effect, unaware that they had been crammed with cotton bales and the rest of the fort smothered with sandbags. His men grew equally irritated at their failure. The captain noticed a crowd watching the fight from the veranda of the Moultrie House, the fine summer hotel used as barracks for the Carolina troops. With relish he sent two 42-pound shot through the second story and watched the spectators tumble over one another to flee the scene. If nothing else, he reminded them that war was not a spectator sport.[26]

All morning long a relentless fire poured in on the fort. Shot and shell riddled the roofs and gables, swept the parapet, and pocked the scarp and gorge walls while mortar blasts exploded around the parade. The new Blakely gun drove its balls deep into the wall and sent showers of brick at the defenders, wounding some slightly. The haze of smoke rising from the bombardment curled with the wind toward the city. The fort's gunners raged in frustration; their aim was splendid, but the shot bounced like "peas upon a trencher," as Doubleday put it. They longed to use the heavier guns on the parapet.

Finally Private John Carmody could stand it no longer. Aware that the barbette guns were loaded and aimed at least crudely, Carmody stole up to the parapet and ran down the line firing each gun at Fort Moultrie. The shots did little damage but drew a blistering return fire as the Confederates thought the parapet guns were coming into play. It was, said a sergeant, "Carmody against the Confederate States; and Carmody had to back down, not because he was beaten, but because he was unable, single-handed, to reload his guns."

On the Cummings Point side, two veteran sergeants waited until the officers were distracted, then sneaked up to the parapet and fired the big 10-inch gun. The shot went high, just grazing the Iron Battery. Doggedly the sergeants reloaded but could not throw the carriage in gear, a job requiring the strength of six men. With reckless abandon they fired anyway. The shot hit just under the middle embrasure of the Iron Battery, but the sergeants had no time to admire it. The recoil flipped the eight-ton gun over, dismounting another gun, and it rolled to the head of the stairs, narrowly missing one of the men. Later it was thought that enemy fire had disabled the guns, an impression the sergeants did not care to correct.

Nothing seemed to go right for the garrison. Their shots hit the floating battery again and again without effect. The battery had been grounded behind a seawall to protect its waterline, and the roof and front deflected or withstood the balls flung against them. Few shots were wasted on the Dahlgren gun or those at Fort Johnson. Still, the supply of cartridge bags dwindled faster than the fort's six needles could replace them. Reluctantly

Anderson ordered the firing reduced to six guns. But the spirit of the men remained high, and even the workmen, who had cringed from the prospect of battle, carried shot and other material and took a hand at manning one of the guns.

For the workers and soldiers alike Sumter had become its own world, and to a man they took pride in its defense. After four hours Crawford and Doubleday were relieved by Dick Meade and Truman Seymour. "Doubleday," asked Seymour, "what is all this uproar about?"

"There is a trifling difference of opinion between us and our neighbors opposite," replied Doubleday, "and we are trying to settle it."

Early in the afternoon someone spotted ships off the bar, and the order was given to dip the flag to them. The salute was returned, and the garrison waited eagerly for the promised supplies and reinforcements. To their dismay, however, the ships made no effort to enter the harbor. They were still on their own, and the enemy fire was taking its toll. Three times the officers' quarters caught fire, but prompt work at the pump by Peter Hart, the sergeant from Anderson's Mexican War days, kept the flames from spreading, as did water cascading from three iron cisterns above the quarters breached by shells.

At 6 p.m. rain began to pour and continued for several hours with a strong wind that whipped up rough waves. Anderson silenced his guns to save cartridges. The enemy fire also slackened and finally dropped off to some mortar shells lobbed at the fort every fifteen minutes through the night. The stormy sea eased fears about a possible assault, but it also cast doubt on the ability of the relief force to land. Foster went outside to inspect the landing area and was satisfied that the ships could still use it. Near midnight Crawford and Snyder examined the walls. They found deep pocks from solid shot and much damage, but the fort stood intact, ready to fight another day. What it needed most was supplies. Where were they, and when would they come?

GOD DAMN THIS WHOLE BOTCHED, bungled operation! Fox could do little more than swear to himself and to the wind. On his way back to the *Pawnee* he met Rowan coming in, as eager now to join the fray as he had been to avoid it earlier. But he had no pilot, and Fox reminded him that the government needed no martyrs at this hour. The *Harriet Lane* had no boats to carry in supplies; the *Pawnee* had only one. Both anchored near the swash channel while Fox took the *Baltic* to the rendezvous point to look for the *Powhatan* and the *Pocahontas*. Neither ship turned up, but a steamer and some merchant vessels reached the bar and anchored, giving distant observers the impression of a large fleet.[27]

Disappointed, Fox returned to the warships and tried to persuade Rowan and Faunce to try landing a couple of boats with provisions. They refused because of the rough sea and bad weather but promised to run the batteries and protect a landing the next morning. Fox went back to the rendezvous point, where he spent the night signaling to ships that never came. All night the wind blew hard with heavy swells, and toward dawn a thick fog rolled in. As the *Baltic* headed back toward the bar, she ran aground on Rattlesnake Shoal and lost time getting off. The heavy swell forced her to anchor in deep water nearly four miles from the warships.

Everyone was seasick from the pitching, but Lieutenant Robert O. Tyler managed to organize and drill a boat crew for the run at Sumter. At 8 a.m. Fox took the boat and headed for the *Pawnee*. As they drew near the ship, Fox saw a huge cloud of black smoke erupt from Fort Sumter, broken only by the flash of Anderson's guns. Meeting with the other officers, he concluded that fire rafts were being used to smoke out the fort. But what could they do? They had only one boat until the *Pocahontas* and *Powhatan* arrived, and the three tugboats were nowhere to be seen. Rowan commandeered a passing ice schooner, and Fox began fitting her out for a run at the fort.

During this work Rowan mentioned that he had a note from Captain Mercer stating that the *Powhatan* had been detached by "superior authority" for other duty. Fox was aghast. Rowan had received the note on the 7th, the day before Fox left; why had he not been told? The *Powhatan* had everything Fox needed: three hundred sailors, howitzers, and, most of all, the fighting launches. Someone had deliberately sabotaged the expedition, and the first name that came to mind was "that timid traitor W. H. Seward." The sense of betrayal never left him. "I do not think I have deserved this treatment," he wrote later, but for now he had to swallow his outrage until some way could be found to assist Anderson.[28]

At two that afternoon the *Pocahontas* finally turned up, and Commander J. P. Gillis went aboard the *Pawnee* to be briefed on the mission. Everyone wanted to assist Sumter regardless of the batteries, but without pilots, buoys, or marks they dared not make the attempt. Gillis agreed with Fox that an effort to land men and supplies should be made that night. Scarcely had they set to work, however, when they noticed that the flagstaff at Sumter had been shot away. Smoke still poured from the fort, but the firing ceased and did not resume. Was it over? They decided to send a boat in under flag of truce to find out. Once again they could do nothing more than wait.[29]

· · ·

THE STORM OF THE PREVIOUS NIGHT gave way to a lovely day. The wind shifted into the west, blowing smoke away from the city, sweeping the harbor clean, and muffling the sound of the guns. The men rose early, forced down some salt pork and the last of the damaged rice, and went to man their guns. Those aimed at Cummings Point were abandoned, and the firing on Fort Moultrie and the inner channel was limited to one gun every ten minutes to conserve cartridge bags. By 8 a.m. the officers' quarters had already been hit twice by hot shot. The fires were put out, but repeated hits started them anew. As the flames spread to lower floors and nearby barracks, every battery around the fort increased its firing to exploit the weakness.[30]

The officers grabbed axes and hacked frantically at the woodwork, but all of it was going up. As the fire spread, Anderson grew uneasy about the magazine. He had been in it the day before, worrying over its exposure to fire no less than to shelling. Now his worst fears were realized. He gave Foster permission to remove as much powder as possible before the magazine had to be sealed. Foster managed to get fifty of the three hundred barrels into remote corners of the casements before the fire forced them to close the heavy copper door and pack earth around it. Earlier the men had carted out armed shells and grenades in wet blankets to get them away from the flames.

Hot shot kept pouring in, feeding the fire belching through the roof, moving from the west to the east barrack until by noon all the woodwork was consumed. The wind sent smoke and cinders into the casements, igniting boxes, beds, and personal effects. Gagging on the smoke, the men watched in horror as the flames exploded some of the shells and grenades and threatened the powder salvaged so laboriously by Foster. Reluctantly Anderson ordered all but five of the barrels thrown through the embrasures into the sea. He also sent Crawford to the parapet to look for any sign of the fleet. Just as Crawford started up, an explosion leveled the granite stairs at the west gorge angle. The fire had ignited some shells stored in the tower there, forcing Crawford to wait until the debris settled before venturing through it.

From the battered parapet Crawford saw the incoming shot and shell descending into the thick smoke and flames. Masses of masonry and brick crumbled with a roar. The heavy entrance gates and all the planking on the windows at the gorge had been blasted away, leaving the fort open to assault. The flagstaff suffered seven hits during the day. One shell fragment cut the lanyard; at one o'clock it crashed to the ground. Hall rushed to secure it on a temporary staff, but it took time to hoist the flag back into place. Fire from the fort's guns stopped entirely for a time. When Doubleday resumed with a few rounds, the enemy gunners cheered the garrison for not quitting.

Anderson surveyed the ruins about him and wondered what there was left to defend except honor itself. His food was gone, his ammunition nearly gone, his fort ablaze, his flag fallen though raised anew, and the promised relief nowhere in sight. After months of waiting he had in a single day gone from limbo to hell, and now he wished only the redeeming grace of having defended country, flag, and honor. He had fought the good fight and was prepared to continue, but with what means? As he pondered this question, a soldier raced up to tell him that a man bearing a white flag and claiming to be Colonel Wigfall had suddenly appeared outside the fort and wished to see him.

ONLY A FEW DAYS LATER William Russell would meet the man Mary Chesnut called "the *inevitable* Wigfall" and marvel at his muscular neck covered by wild masses of black hair tinged with gray, beetling black brows, square jaw with its coarse, powerful mouth, and thick jaws. And the eyes! They struck Russell with their "wonderful depth and light, such as I never saw before but in the head of a wild beast. If you look some day when the sun is not too bright into the eye of the Bengal tiger, in the Regent's Park, as the keeper is coming round, you will form some notion of the expression I mean. It was flashing, fierce, yet calm—with a well of fire burning behind and spouting through it, an eye pitiless in anger, which now and then sought to conceal its expression beneath half closed lids, and then burst out with an angry glare, as if disdaining concealment."[31]

On this day the tiger stalked Morris Island, impatient for action. When the flag above Sumter fell at 1:10 p.m., General James Simons decided to send Chesnut, Manning, and Chisholm to see if Anderson wished to surrender. While their boat was being readied, Wigfall collared Private Gourdin Young of the Palmetto Guard and two black rowers and set out for Sumter on his own in a small skiff, ignoring the shouts for him to return. With Young as helmsman the terrified oarsmen bent furiously to their work, pulling the skiff to the fort amid the rain of incoming shells. Wigfall jumped out of the boat, tied a white handkerchief to the tip of his sword, and strode to the wall. Grasping the sill of an embrasure, he lifted himself up to peer inside. His eyes met those of a startled gunner.[32]

He was hauled inside and demanded to see Anderson, saying he wanted to stop the firing. Snyder led him along the casements past some other officers. "Your flag is down," Wigfall told them, "you are on fire, and you are not firing your guns. General Beauregard wants to stop this." In fact Wigfall had not talked to Beauregard at all and had no authority, but that did not stop him. Jeff Davis pointed to the flag and suggested that Wigfall get his own men to stop firing first. Wigfall jumped into an embrasure looking toward Fort Moultrie and raised his sword with the white handkerchief. Despite his waving, a steady fire still poured into Sumter. One shot crashed just over his head. He swore loudly and sprang back. "I have been fired upon with that flag two or three times," he said. "I think you might stand it once."

Just then Anderson arrived. Wigfall told the major that Beauregard wished the fighting stopped and would give Anderson almost any terms. The major replied that he had already stated his terms to Beauregard but that he was willing to evacuate at once instead of noon on the 15th. Those were the only conditions he would accept. They went over the original offer: The garrison could take its arms and private and company property, salute its flag on lowering, and have transportation to any northern port. Wigfall agreed and returned to his boat. While he crossed back to Cummings Point, Anderson lowered his flag and replaced it with a white one. The firing everywhere ceased.

Chesnut and the others on Morris Island who had watched Wigfall vanish into the embrasure waited anxiously for his return. With a flourish he announced the surrender of the fort and was greeted with cheers. In Charleston Beauregard knew nothing of these events, but he had seen the flag fall and sent Lee, Miles, and Pryor in a boat to Sumter. While on the water the flag went back up, and they promptly turned the boat around. Before they had gone far, however, the flag came down again and was replaced by a white one. Bewildered, they reversed course again and rowed to the fort. Their mood was not improved by a sentinel who first warned them off and then insisted that they show a white flag. Indignant at their reception, they demanded to know whether Sumter had surrendered or not.

Anderson came out to meet the visitors and was asked if he required assistance. No, replied the major, my compliments to the general, but no help was needed. The fire had settled about the magazine and had not exploded it, so he thought the real danger passed. Told that they had come from Beauregard, he mentioned that Wigfall had already been there on behalf of the general to negotiate an evacuation. They glanced at one another in confusion. Impossible, they said. They were not authorized to offer terms, and Wigfall had not been at the general's headquarters for two days. This was too much for the major. In this most painful of situations, must he be made a fool of as well? By God, he would raise his flag again, he was sorry he had ever lowered it, and he would order his batteries to reopen fire.[33]

The emissaries prevailed upon Anderson not to act until they could present his terms to Beauregard. Before they left, another boat arrived with two members of the general's staff. They heard Anderson's story and said they were authorized to accept all the terms offered by Wigfall except the saluting of the flag. After some negotiations this too was accepted, and an agreement was formalized that evening for the evacuation to take place on Sunday morning, April 14. At Anderson's request Snyder went under escort to the fleet off the bar to arrange transportation. It was over at last.

With the firing stopped, some of the officers wandered outside to inspect the walls, pocked by hundreds of shot but still intact. From the city they could hear the distant chime of bells and the sound of salutes. Although the ordeal was over, the garrison showed little relief. Dead tired and sullen in defeat, the men grew silent and reserved. They shuffled about, preparing for the evacuation next morning. Now and then they glanced across the water at what appeared to be a large fleet beyond the bar, not knowing that several of the ships were commercial steamers detained by the action. Why, they wondered, had they not joined the fight?[34]

An enraged Gustavus Fox knew the answer. The *Powhatan* had never come, leaving him no way to get men and supplies to the fort. In desperation he had improvised a means, but Sumter surrendered before he could act. By his own admission he would have been knocked to pieces, but he never forgave fate for denying him the chance. A naval officer went in under a flag of truce to arrange for the evacuation. Here was the final bitter irony for Fox: The *Baltic*, which had come to bring reinforcements for Anderson, would instead carry the major and his garrison home.[35]

ALL DAY SATURDAY the Battery, wharves, steeples, and rooftops were jammed with people watching the battle. They could no longer hear the guns because the wind had shifted, but the smoke brought loud cheers. Mary Chesnut saw Trescot following the action through his glass, and William Gilmore Simms, sporting a white beard, come from the country to watch the fight. She felt ill, but the men could not contain their excitement. John Manning preened with delight at discovering that he could remain cool under fire. An exuberant Governor Pickens, who some thought was drinking too much, sent a letter to Governor John Letcher of Virginia. "We can sink the fleet if they attempt to enter the channel," he boasted. "If they land elsewhere we can whip them. . . . The war is commenced, and we will triumph or perish."[36]

When news of the surrender arrived, church bells and cannon salutes punctuated waves of cheers. Huge bonfires and fireworks lit the sky late into the night as crowds surged through the streets in a mood of jubilee, fueled by the relief that not a single man had died in action. Women wept and waved handkerchiefs. "Wonderful, miraculous, unheard of in history, a bloodless victory," said Caroline Gilman, but some celebrants could not escape a sense of foreboding. "The first act in the drama is over!" mused Henry William Ravenel. "Will it end thus, or is it only the opening of a bloody tragedy?"[37]

Sunday dawned clear and warm. The harbor filled with steamers, skiffs, and every kind of boat filled with citizens eager for a glimpse of the fort and the ceremonies. At half past twelve Pickens and his wife boarded a boat with Jamison, Magrath, Beauregard, Chesnut, Manning, Miles, Pryor, and others to watch the state troops take possession of Sumter. As the boat neared the fort, it became obvious that the evacuation had been delayed for some reason. To avoid embarrassment, the boat veered off to Sullivans Island, and the dignitaries climbed out to inspect the works there.[38]

Inside Sumter the men rose early to pack their gear for boarding the steamer *Isabel*, which was to take them over the bar to the *Baltic*. Doubleday arranged the details for firing the salute to the flag. The ceremony held great significance for Anderson as the last full measure of his devotion to duty; it would be no brief salute but a full one hundred shots. Dogged efforts were made to fashion enough cartridges. It bothered Doubleday that sparks might still be lingering from the fire and there was no safe place to put the ammunition, but he sensed it was futile to mention the danger to Anderson. The cartridges were placed alongside each gun amid the brick, masonry, and other debris strewn about the parapet from the bombardment.[39]

The men formed on the parade, and the gunners took their places at the cannon. On the rampart the flag snapped proudly in a stiff wind blowing directly into the muzzles of the guns. Forty-six shots were fired without incident. When the next one was discharged, the wind blew part of an ignited cartridge back onto the pile of cartridges, setting off an explosion that sent chunks of loose masonry hurling in every direction. Private Daniel Hough had his right arm blown off and died instantly. Another private, Edward Galloway, suffered fatal wounds and died three days later. Four other men were hurt, one seriously enough to be hospitalized and left behind.

The irony of this tragedy was more than Anderson could bear. Having brought his command through the ordeal without the loss of life, he watched two of them die from a freak accident during a mere ceremony. Exhausted emotionally as well as physically, the major cut the salute short at fifty shots. The accident delayed their departure from Sumter until four o'clock, when Doubleday again formed the men on the parade. The drummers snapped into their beat, and the double file stepped smartly forward while the musicians played "Yankee Doodle" with defiance. Anderson tucked the tattered silk flag under his arm and carried it like precious treasure.

"I felt for poor Anderson," said James Petigru, the last voice of Union in

Charleston, "deeply abandoned as he was to an obscure fate, to serve as a sort of stepping stone to a conflict in which he could reap no honor and left without a friend to stand by him and his few followers while the fleet looked upon his distress with careless eyes."[40]

Just before their departure Captain Sam Ferguson accepted the keys to the fort, and a company of regulars with the Palmetto Guard entered proudly, Ruffin carrying their flag. The Confederate and palmetto flags were run up on temporary staffs in the presence of Governor Pickens and his entourage. When the ceremony was done, the troops were discharged. Ruffin used the opportunity to scrounge for some shell fragments as souvenirs. To his surprise the fire still smoldered in places. He noticed that the cannonballs had nowhere breached the thick walls.[41]

Sumter was theirs at long last, and with it the burden of a civil war. At the cathedral that day a Te Deum was sung in honor of the victory. The Battery was crowded with people, the harbor with boats proudly flying the Confederate flag. At sunset The Citadel cadets held a dress parade. Those in search of omens were thrilled to notice that on the nights of the 12th and 13th the moon had shown a strange silver crescent similar to the one on the state flag. One man claimed that on the morning of the 13th he had seen a gamecock light on the tomb of Calhoun on Church Street, flap its wings, and crow. Surely these omens meant that victory would be theirs.[42]

Pickens thought so. Later that day he gave a fiery speech from the balcony of the Charleston Hotel. "We have met them," he cried, ". . . let it lead to what it might, even if it leads to blood and ruin. . . . We have defeated their twenty millions, we have met them and conquered them. We have humbled the flag of the United States before the Palmetto and Confederate . . . today it has been humbled before the glorious little state of South Carolina."[43]

None of it impressed James Petigru, who saw only sorrow waiting in the wings. "The universal applause that waits on secessionists and secession," he said, "has not the slightest tendency to shake my conviction that we are on the road to ruin."[44]

The Price of Pride

SHORTLY AFTER DAWN on Sunday, the 14th, the steamer *Georgianna* ran alongside the jetty near Fort Monroe in Virginia. William Russell arose from a fitful sleep and dressed. Before he had finished, a tall, well-dressed black woman opened the cabin door and asked for his ticket. She told him without hesitation that she was a slave as well as the ticket collector. On his way to the upper deck Russell noticed the bar already crowded with men. They invited him to share a cocktail or mint julep and laughed at his explanation that he did not partake before breakfast. Soon afterward the steamer came to a dreary wooden quay lined with booths. Beyond it he could see the dingy town of Portsmouth and the navy yard, where the *Merrimack* lay at anchor along with the *Cumberland*, some old warships, and a fleet of oyster boats idled by the Sabbath.[1]

From there a steam ferry took Russell to Norfolk. Even at that early hour his fellow passengers had their quids going, spraying the deck with parabolas of yellow-brown slime. Everything about the town wore an air of decay, not least the dilapidated Atlantic House with its overpowering smells and swarms of flies. He escaped with relief to the street, where most of the men were of a type new to him: tall, dark, and loose-jointed with low, narrow fore-heads, square jaws, prominent noses, and bright, deep-seated eyes.

The bells of churches tolled on all sides, and he stepped into one. The heat was stifling. As the minister read the psalms, a flurry of excitement arose near the door, and men began stealing out of the church. Russell followed and saw them running toward the hotel. Amid cheers and shouts he made his way to a piece of paper on the wall describing the bombardment and sur-render of Fort Sumter. On the street, men talked joyously of the glorious vic-tory; Russell thought it only meant certain war. He roamed some of the side streets, where he saw innumerable blacks, who said not a word about Sumter even when asked about it. Were they simply ignorant, or cunning and subtle?

He came to a small pier filled with oysters and surrounded by boats.

waiting to receive them. At its end a group of men taunted the crew of a small boat from the *Cumberland*. "You better just pull down that cussed old rag of yours, and bring your old ship over to the Southern Confederacy," brayed one onlooker. "Why don't you go, and touch off your guns at Charleston?" yelled another. The sailors bore it in silence, until their coxswain arrived and stepped into the boat with a parcel under his arm. As the boat pushed away from the pier, someone shouted, "Down with the Yankees! Hurrah for the Southern Confederacy!" A few threw oystershells, one of which hit the coxswain in the head.

"Back water!" he yelled. "Back water all. Hard!" When the boat neared the pier, he leaped ashore, glaring at the crowd. "You cowardly damned set. Who threw the shells?" No one responded until a small, wizened man said, "I guess you'll have shells of another kind if you remain here much longer."

"Why, you poor devils," the sailor roared, "I'd whip any half dozen of you, teeth, knives, and all, in five minutes; and my boys there in the boat would clear your whole town. What do you mean by barking at the Stars and Stripes?" He gestured toward the *Cumberland*. "Why the lads aboard of her would knock every darned seceder in your State into a cocked hat in a brace of shakes! And now who's coming on?" He eyed them defiantly; no one moved toward him, and he returned to the boat and rowed away. This time only muttered threats followed him.

Russell returned to his hotel for a dinner that made him wish "the desire for food had never been invented," and endured a night of mosquito attacks before leaving at dawn for Portsmouth. There he caught a train south and got permission to ride in the cab with the engineer and stoker. Once past the ramshackle rows of streets, sheds, and shanties, the train plunged into a dense forest. Suddenly the track rose onto a gossamer trestle above dark waters filled with the stumps of dead trees and thick growth, trees draped with long creepers and Spanish moss, and bits of wood on which lay turtles, tortoises, and enormous frogs.

"There's many allygaitors come up here at times," said the engineer, "but I don't take much account of them."

The place was called the Dismal Swamp, and it suggested to Russell what the world must have been like after the Flood. The railroad super-intendent, a young man named Robinson, who had given Russell leave to ride in the cab, pressed him for news about Washington politics. Surely you read the papers, Russell replied. "Oh, sir, we can't believe a word we read in our papers," Robinson exclaimed. "They tell a story one day, to contradict it the next." The scenery and the silence of the woods soon lost their charm for Russell. The train paused to take on wood for fuel, then finally cleared the swamp. A flag fluttered atop a pine tree: broad bars of red and white with a blue square in the corner containing seven stars. "That's our flag," said the engineer, who had said little. "That's our flag! And long may it wave—o'er the land of the free and the home of the ber-rave!"

The endless pine forest showed streaks of black smoke from clearings where furnaces and factories churned out pitch, tar, resin, and turpentine. Another Confederate flag waved above a log village. The stations grew larger and more frequent until they reached Goldsboro, where Russell witnessed for the first time widespread enthusiasm for secession. The depot, the hotels, the streets all vibrated with men carrying arms and dressed in some pretense of a uniform, their faces excited and flushed with drink as well as patriotism. Russell learned that they were part of a levy called out by the governor of North Carolina to seize two federal forts left undefended.

They stopped at a wayside inn to dine on pig and other delicacies. Several of the passengers were former government clerks sent packing for refusing to take the oath, and now bound for Montgomery in search of jobs. One man offended Russell with crude jokes about Lincoln and "negro wenches." Nightfall found him in Wilmington, where he got off the train for a sleepless night at a dreary inn. The next morning he crossed the Cape Fear River by ferry and saw stacks of shot and shell on a pier. "They're anti-abolition pills," explained a fellow passenger. Confederate flags flew everywhere over the town, and Russell heard that the forts had been seized without difficulty.

Nowhere did he see any hint of the "affection to the Union" that Seward insisted must bring a change in southern sentiments. What he found instead was the peculiar delusion that King Cotton would force Britain to recognize the Confederacy and support its cause. To his surprise many people, especially women, expressed disappointment that more Yankees had not been killed at Sumter. The train crossed the Pee Dee River and crawled into South Carolina. At dusk on Tuesday, April 16, it approached Charleston. In the distance Russell saw Fort Sumter, a dark square rising above the water with smoke still curling from an angle of its walls. The passengers cheered at the sight of the Confederate flag waving over it. Outside the city Russell saw a regiment marching, cavalry pickets in gardens and fields, and tents visible in the byways. What effect would these sights have had on Seward's views?

It was nearly dark when the train reached the station. Russell went to the Mills House, where he encountered an acquaintance who gave him a full account of the bombardment and surrender. The hotel teemed with dignitaries; in short order he was introduced to Chesnut, Manning, Miles, and an aide to Governor Pickens. After dinner he was taken to meet Beauregard at his headquarters. The general was busy writing dispatches but received his guest cordially. His small, compact frame and quick, intelligent eye struck Russell as very French, as did his manner.

Russell was eager to visit the forts and works. Beauregard assigned his engineer, Major W. H. C. Whiting, as guide. "You shall go everywhere and see everything," he said. "We rely on your discretion, and knowledge of what is fair in dealing with what you see. Of course you don't expect to find regular soldiers in our camps, or very scientific works." Like most officers, the general held reporters in disdain, but this was not some rumormonger or Horace Greeley hireling. This was the renowned correspondent of the most important newspaper in the world. Russell knew the Confederates were eager to please because of their urgent need for recognition abroad. A week earlier one of the *Tribune* men had predicted sourly that Russell would be "lionized, petted, fawned upon, and caressed; the ladies are authorized to take him by storm." But the reporter also noted accurately that Russell could not be made a puppet.[2]

The evening was spent in the Charleston Club with John Manning, whose good looks and personal charm captivated Russell, as it did Mary Chesnut and everyone else. James Chesnut and William Porcher Miles joined them, along with some others of the chivalry, to talk politics. As the argument became hot, Russell grew annoyed with the "extravagant broad menace and rhodomontade" of the Carolinians, who vowed never to yield or be conquered and to welcome invaders to bloody graves. In vain did Russell try to explain how they could never prevail against the North's superior numbers and matériel. "The Yankees are cowardly rascals," they insisted. "We have proved it by kicking and cuffing them till we are tired of it; besides we know John Bull very well. He will make a great fuss about non-interference at first, but when he begins to want cotton he'll come off his perch." How they clung to this mad delusion of cotton as king!

About 8:30 the tolling of a bell interrupted their discussion. "It's for all the coloured people to clear out of the streets and go home," they explained. "The guards will arrest any who are found out without passes in half an hour." Outside the club the streets reminded Russell of Paris in the days of the Revolution of 1848. Bands of armed men roamed about singing loudly, their cheeks flushed with pride or drink. The restaurants, bars, clubs, and taverns overflowed with revelers spilling out into the streets or alleys. The magnificent victory at Sumter had roused them to the euphoric belief that they could not be beaten by the inferiors they despised so much. It was, Russell concluded grimly, a "bloodless Waterloo."

The next morning he went down to the wharf with some of Beauregard's staff. On the way they passed the market, where Russell saw the food stalls tended by black women sucking pipes and old "unkies" who chased away the turkey buzzards that devoured much of the offal and garbage. Near the quay Russell noticed a fine white marble building still unfinished, with blocks of marble scattered about it. "It's a custom-house Uncle Sam was building for our benefit," explained an officer, "but I don't think he'll ever raise a cent for his treasury out of it." An old man stopped one of the officers and begged him to "get me something to do for our glorious cause. Old as I am, I can carry a musket—not far, to be true, but I can kill a Yankee if he comes near." After he left, the officer said the man was wealthy and had two sons in camp on Morris Island, but he had a northern wife and so was suspected of Unionist sentiments.

The quay was crowded with stores, fodder, and supplies for Morris Island. Major Whiting despaired at the ordeal of getting volunteers to obey orders and work together, especially the dandies from prominent families. As they boarded the steamer, Whiting saw some soldiers smoking while lying in hay bales above a store of powder. He asked them politely not to smoke. They assured him that they wouldn't burn the hay this time and went on smoking. Russell saw some reporters from local and New York papers on the steamer. Whiting regarded them with disgust. "If I had my way, I would fling them into the water," he said, "but the General has given them orders to come on board. It is these fellows who have brought all this trouble on our country."

As the steamer slipped down the Ashley River into the harbor, Russell admired the skyline of the city with its steeples and domes, warehouses and cotton stores on the wharves, and brightly colored houses behind the Battery. Slowly the boat slid by Sumter and landed at Morris Island. Through the spray of fine white sand flung by the wind, Russell trudged from battery to battery, examining profiles, walking up parapets, peering at guns. This was indeed a far cry from the Crimea. He concluded that if Anderson had opened on these positions when he first saw them going into place, he could have destroyed them and Moultrie as well.

The island teemed with activity. Officers moved about furiously, and commissary carts rolled between the beach and the camps. Sounds of revelry drifted from the tents. Russell was appalled at the sanitary conditions about the camps and mentioned it to the medical officer with him. "I know it all," said the officer. "But we can do nothing. Remember they're all volunteers, and do just as they please." Every tent seemed a hospitality center with cases of champagne, claret, French pâté, and other delicacies piled outside the canvas.

For the rich and the idle, secession had become the fashion. Young ladies sang and old ones prayed for it; young men could not wait to fight for it, old ones to demonstrate on its behalf. All this from the Gospel according to St. Calhoun, whose heresies had in a generation become Scripture. The depth of their hatred for Yankees, their loathing for the Stars and Stripes and the very words *United States* amazed Russell. It seemed clear to him that the Union could never be restored, that it had gone to pieces in a way that no power on earth could restore to its former shape. He would never have believed such hatred, so monstrous a flight from reality, had he not seen it with his own eyes.

They returned to the beach and shoved off for Fort Sumter. As they approached, Russell could see the damage inflicted by the bombardment. Nothing seemed to have hurt the fort seriously except the fire that burned the barracks. As he stood on the dock, a tall, powerful-looking man weaved his way toward him. Dressed in a blue civilian frock coat with a red sash around the waist from which hung a straight sword, he introduced himself as Colonel Wigfall, a title of his own creation. From his wobbly gait and thick speech Russell knew he was drunk, yet he could not help being impressed by both his appearance and the clarity of his head.

Major Whiting tried to steer Russell toward the fort, only to be elbowed aside by Wigfall. "Here is where I got in," he said, and proceeded to lead Russell from point to point with elaborate explanation of his personal experience while Whiting swore privately about volunteer "colonels." Mindful that Wigfall was reputed to have killed half a dozen men in duels, Russell listened to his rambling narrative, amused by the sword dangling between his legs. They came upon some volunteers clearing away debris. Seeing that they were not accustomed to work, Russell asked why they did not use slaves. "The niggers would blow us all up, they're so stupid," one replied, "and the State would have to pay the owners for any of them who were killed and injured."

"In one respect, then, white men are not so valuable as negroes?"

"Yes, sir, that's a fact."

As they finished the tour, Russell pondered how such vast consequences as a civil war could come from so small an affair as the bombardment. Had anyone ever plunged into such depths of peril more recklessly than these Carolinians? Did none of them look reality in the face?

They returned to the boats and were rowed over to the steamer still anchored at Morris Island. It had grown too late to visit Fort Moultrie; instead everyone retired to the cabin, where a generous dinner had been laid out. Wigfall continued to fortify himself with drink and to share his thoughts with Russell in exuberant fashion. He expounded on the beating of Senator Sumner as one manner of dealing with Yankees and expanded this vision to one of dealing with recalcitrants elsewhere in the world. Then, inexplicably, the calumnies heaped on Sumner were transferred to Lord Lyons, whereupon Russell protested this abuse of the British minister and left the cabin.

Within moments Wigfall followed him on deck, his manner calmer, spewing apologies, with Chesnut, Manning, and Whiting behind him. Russell declared himself satisfied, and they returned to Charleston, though Wigfall did not cease his drinking. It was a bizarre scene to Russell. Here were men in the furnace of rebellion, their lives and fortunes on the line, jesting and carousing as if they had not a care in the world. That night Russell dined at a club filled with officers, who plied him with questions. Asked what had impressed him most about Morris Island, he said a letter-copying machine, a case of official stationery, and a box of red tape, all lying on the beach ready to inaugurate the new republic.

Outside a pale figure was shouting from the balcony of the hotel with clenched fists and uplifted arms. "That's Roger Pryor," said one of the officers. "He says that if them Yankee trash don't listen to reason, and stand from under, we'll march to the North and dictate the terms of peace in Faneuil Hall. Yes, sir—and so we will, certa-i-n su-re!"

How often Russell had heard this braggadocio, and how tedious it had become. The naïveté of it astounded him no less than the myth that King Cotton would conquer all. They were fools, but they were genuine fools because they really believed this claptrap. On the 18th he awoke to the sound of servants padding through the halls with cups of iced milk or water for their mistresses. Their soft chatter and laughter entered his room with the Irish waiter who brought hot water for shaving. He remembered the surprise of one acquaintance at finding white servants in the hotel, but nearly all the waiters in the Mills House were Irish except for a German or two.

In the dining hall, men ate with the same rush as in the North, and read a paper or discussed the news with a companion. Nothing was talked about more than the proclamation issued by Lincoln calling on the states for 75,000 troops to put down the insurrection. Already Virginia, Kentucky, Tennessee, North Carolina, and Missouri had refused, and in every border state the fight over secession had boiled up anew. Later that day the city learned that the Virginia convention had on the 17th voted for secession, 88–55. The news prompted the abstemious Edmund Ruffin, free from exile at last, to drink a glass of ale and another of wine in joyous celebration. That morning Russell was besieged with questions about what "Old Abe and Seward" would do.[3]

Russell had no answer, but he wondered privately whether Seward still thought the whole thing would blow over in sixty days. Jefferson Davis had responded with his own proclamation calling for 32,000 troops and issuing letters of marque and reprisal in anticipation of a northern blockade. What could result from these preparations other than war? Russell visited Beauregard's headquarters and found the general engaged in preparing Sumter to defend the harbor against a possible naval attack. That evening he dined with the British consul, Mr. Bunch, who had assembled a small party of guests, including James Petigru and the venerable Alfred Huger.

Some of the guests annoyed Russell by repeating the tiresome credo that no other consideration would move Britain except its need for cotton. "Why, sir," said one, "we have only to shut off your supply of cotton for a few weeks, and we can create a revolution in Great Britain." Russell turned with relief to Petigru, whose views on secession amused him, and to Huger, whose eyes filled with tears at the prospect of a civil war that he thought the natural result of northern slurs and aggression against the South.

They are materialists, Russell concluded, these Carolinians. For all their railing against the vulgar Yankees' worship of the Almighty Dollar, they prayed at the same altar. Perhaps slavery had done this by causing them to look at the world through a lens of cotton bales and rice bags. To hear them talk of preferring reunion with Great Britain to union with New England bewildered him. How many times had he heard one of them wish that the mother country could spare one of its princes to reign over them? As he walked back to the hotel, he heard guns firing to celebrate the secession ordinance of Virginia. Mounted patrols rode through the streets, and sentries marched to their posts in search of blacks on the streets after curfew.

The next day Russell paused at the market to admire the turkey buzzards, then called on Beauregard. The general was leaving for Montgomery to confer with Davis; Whiting was headed to North Carolina to visit the forts just seized there, and to Virginia for a look at Portsmouth. Russell found it incredible that the Washington government had failed to secure these facilities. Had they learned nothing from the secession crisis? Later he went to see Pickens, whom he knew to be the butt of ridicule by his constituents. The governor was courteous but bored him with a lecture on political economy. The next day he called on the editors of the two major papers and thought the elder Rhett a pompous, hard, ambitious man of some ability. He visited the countinghouses of cotton brokers, called on leading bankers and merchants, and found the same story everywhere: The young men had gone off to war, and business was in limbo. That evening he dined at the hotel with William Trescot, whose common sense he admired, and listened sympathetically to his admission that slavery was the source of many evils for which he had no clear remedy.

By the 20th disturbing news was arriving from every direction. Lincoln announced a blockade of all southern ports from South Carolina to Texas. The commander of the federal arsenal at Harpers Ferry burned the place and retreated into Pennsylvania. A bloody riot erupted in Baltimore between a local mob and a regiment of Massachusetts troops on their way to defend Washington. Confederate forces were trying to seize the navy yard at Norfolk. Several companies of South Carolina troops departed for Virginia, and more were about to follow.[4]

Russell left the city with William Porcher Miles to visit some nearby plantations and did not return until the 24th. The next evening, his last in Charleston, he attended a dinner party given by Petigru for a small group that included Beauregard, Governor and Mrs. Pickens, Manning, Miles, and the host's daughters, Caroline Carson and Sue King. Both were bright and accomplished; Sue was possibly the most formidable woman in Charleston, as unique in her way as her father. She was a novelist with a keen wit and a sharp tongue, whose unconventional ways startled even her friends. Mary Chesnut, who had been a classmate of Sue's at Madame Talvande's school and was no shrinking violet herself, said of her friend, "I am afraid of her as death."[5]

Russell was captivated by them and by his host, whose jovial face with its quizzical expression, and odd falsetto voice, made him as distinctive as his views. He talked of English law, for which he had great reverence, and ignored the prejudice of his guests against New England. Russell marveled at how this rare old man, walking the streets oblivious to the world around him, could alone hold staunch Unionist views and, instead of being driven from the city, become to the locals an emblem of their willingness to tolerate heretics. He expressed his surprise at finding a man with views and attainments so at odds with his surroundings.[6]

"When a similar remark was made to my friend Plutarch," laughed Petigru, "he said: 'I live in a small town and I choose to live there lest it should become still smaller.' "

On April 26 Russell said good-bye to Charleston and left to visit Trescot's Sea Island plantation. No blockading vessels were yet on the horizon. He looked forward to his coming tour of the Sea Islands, Savannah, Montgomery (where he would join many of the friends he had just made in Charleston), and New Orleans. Still, his thoughts kept returning to Petigru, that lone iconoclast among devout secessionists who believed that a bright, shining future awaited them at whatever price. It was a pipe dream, Russell concluded, an illusion doomed to be shattered. Nor were the northerners any better, with their devout belief in democracy and the superiority of their way of life. Their contempt for the South and its institutions ran no less deep, their cocky arrogance more crude but no less self-deceiving. They too seemed willing to pay any price for an unbounded future.

He saw little hope of a future for a people that traded so heavily in illusion. To his American friend John Bigelow he wrote a blunt appraisal:

> I fear, my friend, you are going to immortal smash. That little lump of revolutionary leaven has at last set to work in good earnest and the whole mass of social and political life is fermenting unhealthily. . . . The world will only see in it all the failure of republican institutions in time of pressure as demonstrated by all history—that history which America vainly thought she was going to set right and re-establish on new grounds and principles.[7]

Russell could not know how wrong he would be, how dogged those republican institutions would prove in their fight for survival. Nor could he even imagine how ghastly the price would be for their preservation. When an exhausted nation awoke from the nightmare of civil war almost exactly four years later, secession was dead, slavery was dead, the world of the chivalry was dead, the old Federal Republic of Clay, Calhoun, and Webster was dead, Abraham Lincoln was dead, and upward of 620,000 Americans were dead, a number greater than the total of all the men who died in every other war the United States has fought. But the nation and its institutions endured in a new and stronger form, to face the challenges of another day.

Notes

PROLOGUE: SHIP OF FOILS

1 Alan Hankinson, *Man of Wars* (London, 1982), 154. My portrait of Russell draws heavily from this work.

2 Ibid., 153.

3 Ibid., 85.

4 Ibid., 98.

5 Ibid., 144.

6 Ibid., 152.

7 Ibid., 154.

8 William Howard Russell, *My Diary North and South* (Boston, 1863), 1:7–8.

9 Hankinson, *Man of Wars*, 123, 134–35.

10 William Howard Russell, *My Indian Mutiny Diary*, ed. Michael Edwardes (New York, 1970), 284–85. This is an abridged version of the two-volume original.

11 Ibid., 136.

12 Ibid., 136–37.

13 These scenes aboard ship are taken from Russell, *Diary*, 1:3–8. For Garnett, see Ezra Warner, *Generals in Gray* (Baton Rouge, 1959), 100. Garnett became the first general officer to die in combat during the Civil War.

14 Russell, *Diary*, 1:10–11. The scenes in New York are taken from ibid., 1:11–41.

15 Hankinson, *Man of Wars*, 157.

16 Ibid.

PART ONE: THE BATTLE FOR WASHINGTON
CHAPTER ONE: VOX POPULI

1 Details on election night are in New York *Tribune,* Nov. 7, 8, 12, 1860.

2 C. P. McIntire to Lincoln, Nov. 5, 1860, Abraham Lincoln papers, Library of Congress (hereafter cited as AL).

3 William E. Baringer, *A House Dividing* (Springfield, Ill., 1945), 3.

4 Cameron to Lincoln, Nov. 6, 1860, AL; Weed to Lincoln, Nov. 7, 1860, AL; A Citizen to Lincoln, Nov. 8, 1860, AL.

5 Henry Villard, *Lincoln on the Eve of '61* (New York, 1941), 3–4.

6 New York *Tribune,* Nov. 12, 1860.

7 Frederick W. Seward, *Seward at Washington, as Senator and Secretary of State* (New York, 1891), 460. This is the second of three volumes, each with its own title.

8   Quoted in Baringer, *House Dividing*, 60.

9   Joseph Schafer (ed.), *Intimate Letters of Carl Schurz, 1841–1869* (Madison, Wis., 1928), 230–32; Andrew Hilen (ed.), *The Letters of Henry Wadsworth Longfellow* (Cambridge, Mass., 1972), 4:198; "Diary and Correspondence of Salmon P. Chase," *Annual Report of the American Historical Association*, 1902 (Washington, 1903), 2:484.

10   Chase to Lincoln, Nov. 7, 1860, AL; A. W. Bruner to Benjamin F. Wade, Nov. 10, 1860, Benjamin F. Wade papers, Library of Congress (hereafter cited as BFW).

11   Allan Nevins and Milton Halsey Thomas (eds.), *The Diary of George Templeton Strong* (New York, 1952), 3:60 (hereafter cited as Strong, *Diary*).

12   New York *Tribune*, Nov. 9, 1860.

13   R. S. Holt to Joseph Holt, Nov. 9, 1860, Joseph Holt papers, Library of Congress (hereafter cited as JH); J. Harlan to C. Ballance, Nov. 15, 1860, AL.

14   St. Louis *Missouri Republican*, Nov. 11, 1860; Daniel W. Crofts, *Reluctant Confederates: Upper South Unionists in the Secession Crisis* (Chapel Hill, N.C., 1989), 102; Joseph C. Sitterson, *The Secession Movement in North Carolina* (Chapel Hill, N.C., 1939), 177; Donald E. Reynolds, *Editors Make War: Southern Newspapers in the Secession Crisis* (Nashville, Tenn., 1970), 140–41.

15   Quoted in New York *Tribune*, Nov. 14, 1860; Crofts, *Reluctant Confederates*, 119; Henry T. Shanks, *The Secession Movement in Virginia, 1847–1861* (Richmond, 1934), 121; William K. Scarborough (ed.), *The Diary of Edmund Ruffin* (Baton Rouge, 1972), 1:482 (hereafter cited as Ruffin, *Diary*).

16   Ruffin, *Diary*, 1:482–83; quoted in New York *Tribune*, Nov. 10, 1860.

17   A. Hubbard to William Seward, Nov. 13, 1860, AL; Michael P. Johnson, *Toward a Patriarchal Republic: The Secession of Georgia* (Baton Rouge, 1977), 30; New York *Tribune*, Nov. 19, 1860; John McCardell, *The Idea of a Southern Nation* (New York, 1979), 323–24.

18   Marcus A. de Wolfe Howe (ed.), *Home Letters of General Sherman* (New York, 1909), 180; New York *Tribune*, Nov. 17, 1860.

19   J. W. Burn to ?, Oct. 26, 1860, Burn Family papers, South Caroliniana Library, University of South Carolina (hereafter cited as HCB); Manning to N. Mitchell, Nov. 1, 1860, Mitchell-Pringle papers, South Carolina Historical Society, Charleston.

20   Charleston *Mercury*, Nov. 3, 1860; Mary C. Simms Oliphant and T. C. Duncan Eaves (eds.), *The Letters of William Gilmore Simms* (Columbia, S.C., 1955), 4:255–56; Charleston *Mercury*, Nov. 6, 1860.

21   Charleston *Mercury*, Nov. 8, 1860.

22   Charleston *Courier*, Nov. 9, 1860; New York *Tribune*, Nov. 9, 1860.

23   Trescot to Edward McCrady, Oct. 31 and Nov. 6, 1860, McCrady Family papers, South Caroliniana Library (hereafter cited as EM).

24   J. M. Cazneau to Black, Nov. 6, 1860, Jeremiah S. Black papers, Library of Congress (hereafter cited as JSB).

25   Philip S. Klein, *President James Buchanan: A Biography* (University Park, Pa., 1962), 352.

26   Horatio King to Black, Nov. 7, 1860, JSB; Emerson D. Fite, *The Presidential Campaign of 1860* (New York, 1911), 219.

27   James G. Randall, *Lincoln the President* (New York, 1945), 1:178–80.

28   Ibid., 1:181, 189.

29   Robert W. Johannsen, *Stephen A. Douglas* (New York, 1973), 805; Damon

Wells, *Stephen A. Douglas, the Last Years, 1857–1861* (Austin, Tex., 1971), 241, 254; Fite, *Presidential Campaign*, 207; Allen Johnson, *Stephen A. Douglas: A Study in American Politics* (New York, 1908), 431, 437; David M. Potter, *The Impending Crisis, 1848–61*, comp. and ed. Don E. Fehrenbacher (New York, 1976), 231.

30 Potter, *Impending Crisis*, 265; *Historical Statistics of the United States, Colonial Times to 1970* (Washington, D.C., 1975), 2:1074–76.

31 Potter, *Impending Crisis*, 476–77; Crofts, *Reluctant Confederates*, 75–76.

32 Quoted in James S. Pike, *First Blows of the Civil War* (New York, 1879), 484, 496–97.

33 Randall, *Lincoln the President*, 1:201; Potter, *Impending Crisis*, 406, 439.

34 Allan Nevins, *The Emergence of Lincoln* (New York, 1950), 2:312.

35 *Historical Statistics*, 2:1071–72. The figure in 1876 was 81.8 percent.

CHAPTER TWO: SOMETHING OLD

1 Strong, *Diary*, 2:480.

2 See the discussion in Potter, *Impending Crisis*, 1–17.

3 For this religious diversity, see Curtis D. Johnson, *Redeeming America* (Chicago, 1993).

4 Potter, *Impending Crisis*, 479.

5 Ibid., 484.

6 *Historical Statistics*, 1:14, 118.

7 Potter, *Impending Crisis*, 241–42; Arthur C. Cole, *The Irrepressible Conflict* (New York, 1934), 135; Johnson, *Redeeming America*, 160.

8 Roy F. Nichols, *The Disruption of American Democracy* (New York, 1962), 20–21. The months without elections were January, February, June, and July.

9 Ibid., 23. The official party name was American Democracy.

10 Lyon G. Tyler, *The Letters and Times of the Tylers* (Richmond, 1885), 2:572; Cole, *Irrepressible Conflict*, front page.

11 Chester F. Dunham, *The Attitude of the Clergy Toward the South, 1860–1865* (Toledo, 1942), 92; Bates cabinet memorandum, April 15, 1861, AL.

12 Cole, *Irrepressible Conflict*, 21, 101; Maury Klein, *Unfinished Business: The Railroad in American Life* (Hanover, N.H., 1994), 10–12.

13 Charles H. Ambler (ed.), "Correspondence of Robert M. T. Hunter 1826–1876," *Annual Report of the American Historical Association* (Washington, D.C., 1916), 2:337; Charleston *Mercury*, March 25, 1861.

14 William W. Freehling, *The Road to Disunion: Secessionists at Bay, 1776–1854* (New York, 1990), 127; Andrew A. Lipscomb (ed.), *The Writings of Thomas Jefferson* (Washington, D.C., 1903), 15:249; Potter, *Impending Crisis*, 49.

15 Lipscomb, *Writings of Thomas Jefferson*, 15:249.

16 The Constitution has three indirect references to slavery. The most obvious is Article I, Section 2, providing that three-fifths of the slaves would be counted in apportioning taxes and representatives in the House. Article I, Section 9 forbids Congress from interfering with the importation of slaves before 1808, when the abolition of the slave trade was to take effect. Finally Article IV, Section 2 deals with the return of fugitive

slaves but refers to persons "held to Service or Labour." For more detail, see Alfred H. Kelly and Winfred A. Harbison, *The American Constitution* (New York, 1963), 262–63.

17 Article IV, Section 3.

18 Johnson, *Redeeming America,* 139; Louis Filler, *The Crusade Against Slavery 1830–1860* (New York, 1960), 66, 108–136.

19 Ralph H. Orth and Alfred R. Ferguson (eds.), *The Journals and Miscellaneous Notebooks of Ralph Waldo Emerson* (Cambridge, Mass., 1971), 9:430–31.

20 Potter, *Impending Crisis,* 54–59. California would not be included in the extension.

21 Quoted in George Fort Milton, *The Eve of Conflict: Stephen A. Douglas and the Needless War* (New York, 1934), 50, 57–58.

22 Details of the compromise and its making can be found in Holman Hamilton, *Prologue to Conflict: The Crisis and Compromise of 1850* (Lexington, Ky., 1964).

23 Potter, *Impending Crisis,* 114–16.

CHAPTER THREE: SOMETHING NEW

1 Quoted in Steven A. Channing, *Crisis of Fear: Secession in South Carolina* (New York, 1970), 80.

2 Strong, *Diary,* 2:67.

3 Ibid., 2:130–40.

4 Forrest Wilson, *Crusader in Crinoline* (Philadelphia, 1941), 296–97.

5 Ibid., 324–30.

6 Ibid., 298.

7 The history of the Kansas-Nebraska Act is complex and controversial. For its background, see Potter, *Impending Crisis,* 145–76, and Freehling, *Road to Disunion,* 536–65.

8 Potter, *Impending Crisis,* 160.

9 Ibid., 175; Freehling, *Road to Disunion,* 560.

10 Potter, *Impending Crisis,* 225–65. The Know-Nothings got their name from their pledge to keep all information about the party secret and to respond to inquiries with "I know nothing."

11 Nichols, *Disruption,* 18–32.

12 Klein, *Buchanan,* 107, 260.

13 Ibid., 261–62; Joseph Nathan Kane, *Facts About the Presidents* (New York, 1989), 361.

14 Klein, *Buchanan,* 268–69.

15 David Donald, *Charles Sumner and the Coming of the Civil War* (New York, 1960), 289–95. The full quotation is in Harold S. Schultz, *Nationalism and Sectionalism in South Carolina, 1852–1860* (Durham, N.C., 1950), 117.

16 Donald, *Sumner,* 301–02; Schultz, *Nationalism and Sectionalism,* 117–18.

17 Potter, *Impending Crisis,* 199–224.

18 Ibid., 217–24; Cole, *Irrepressible Conflict,* 86–87.

19 Potter, *Impending Crisis,* 267–96. For a fuller account, see Vincent C. Hopkins, *Dred Scott's Case* (New York, 1951).

20 Carl B. Swisher, *Roger B. Taney* (New York, 1936), 518.

21 Three justices held that Scott could not be a citizen; three others argued that he was not freed by his time in free territory and therefore was a slave ineligible to sue; one justice said the question did not arise, and the remaining two, McLean and Curtis, declared that Scott was a citizen. See Potter, *Impending Crisis,* 277n.

22 Ibid., 280–81, 292.

23 Filler, *Crusade Against Slavery,* 200.

24 Klein, *Buchanan,* 279, 291; Potter, *Impending Crisis,* 297–327.

25 Potter, *Impending Crisis,* 316.

26 For details on the English bill, see ibid., 323–24.

27 Schultz, *Nationalism and Sectionalism,* 153.

28 Potter, *Impending Crisis,* 328–55; Nichols, *Disruption,* 215–22, and the relevant chapters in the works on Douglas by Johannsen, Johnson, and Wells.

29 Roy P. Basler (ed.), *The Collected Works of Abraham Lincoln* (New Brunswick, N.J., 1953), 3:312–13, 315.

30 Potter, *Impending Crisis,* 340.

31 Basler, *Lincoln,* 2:281, 3:145–46.

32 Ibid., 3:11, 15.

33 Alexis de Tocqueville, *Democracy in America* (New York, 1945), 1:394.

34 Basler, *Lincoln,* 2:461.

35 Fite, *Presidential Campaign,* 118.

36 Potter, *Impending Crisis,* 387.

37 Lillian Adele Kibler, *Benjamin F. Perry, South Carolina Unionist* (Durham, N.C., 1946), 288; Frederick Law Olmsted, *The Cotton Kingdom* (New York, 1861), 1:7.

38 Potter, *Impending Crisis,* 356–84.

39 Ibid., 366.

40 Ibid., 378–80; Wendell Phillips, *Speeches, Lectures, and Letters* (Boston, 1863), 271–72.

41 Avery O. Craven, *Edmund Ruffin, Southerner: A Study in Secession* (New York, 1932), 178.

42 Klein, *Buchanan,* 337–38.

43 Potter, *Impending Crisis,* 388–89; Nevins, *Emergence of Lincoln,* 2:119–24.

44 Potter, *Impending Crisis,* 382–83; Nevins, *Emergence of Lincoln,* 2:121; *Congressional Globe,* Jan. 24, 1860, Appendix, 92.

45 Francis Fessenden, *Life and Public Service of William Pitt Fessenden* (Boston, 1907), 1:169.

46 Shanks, *Secession Movement,* 90.

47 Nevins, *Emergence of Lincoln,* 2:130.

48 John Bassett Moore (ed.), *The Works of James Buchanan* (Philadelphia, 1908–1911), 10:234; William J. Evitts, *A Matter of Allegiances: Maryland from 1850 to 1861* (Baltimore, 1974), 46.

49 Evitts, *Matter of Allegiances,* 44.

50 Charles Sumner, *The Works of Charles Sumner* (Boston, 1874–83), 5:326; Basler, *Lincoln,* 3:11–12.

51 Mrs. Roger Pryor, *Reminiscences of Peace and War* (New York, 1904), 101.

CHAPTER FOUR: THE SENATORS FROM SOUTH CAROLINA

1   Russell, *Diary*, 1:258–59.

2   Potter, *Impending Crisis*, 457.

3   Rollin G. Osterweis, *Romanticism and Nationalism in the Old South* (New Haven, Conn., 1949), 82–85.

4   Ibid., 41–53.

5   New York *Tribune*, March 15, 1861; Daniel R. Hundley, *Social Relations in Our Southern States* (New York, 1860), 98–99.

6   New York *Tribune*, March 15, 1861; J. Jeffery Auer (ed.), *Antislavery and Disunion, 1858–1861: Studies in the Rhetoric of Compromise and Conflict* (New York, 1963), 23; Osterweis, *Romanticism*, 56.

7   W. J. Cash, *The Mind of the South* (New York, 1941), 48; McCardell, *Southern Nation*, 237.

8   Hundley, *Social Relations*, 27–30, 57, 69–71.

9   William Oliver Stevens, *Charleston, Historic City of Gardens* (New York, 1939), 242; G. L. Strait to ?, Dec. 8, 1860. Gaston-Strait Family papers, South Caroliniana Library, University of South Carolina.

10 New York *Tribune*, March 15, 1861.

11 Ibid.; McCardell, *Southern Nation*, 304; Olmsted, *Cotton Kingdom*, 1:22.

12 Tocqueville, *Democracy in America*, 1:390.

13 This section on the Chesnuts is drawn largely from Elisabeth Muhlenfeld, *Mary Boykin Chesnut: A Biography* (Baton Rouge, 1981), 40–73. See also *Dictionary of American Biography*, 4:57–58 (hereafter cited as *DAB*).

14 Muhlenfeld, *Chesnut*, 40.

15 Ibid., 48–49.

16 Ibid., 44.

17 Carol Bleser (ed.), *Secret and Sacred: The Diaries of James Henry Hammond, a Southern Slaveholder* (New York, 1988), 215–16.

18 Michael O'Brien and David Moltke-Hansen (eds.), *Intellectual Life in Antebellum Charleston* (Knoxville, Tenn., 1986), 317.

19 Potter, *Impending Crisis*, 104–05, 461–62.

20 Muhlenfeld, *Chesnut*, 109.

21 Ibid., 59, 109; C. Vann Woodward and Elisabeth Muhlenfeld (eds.), *The Private Mary Chesnut* (New York, 1984), 42. This volume consists of Mary Chesnut's original Civil War diaries, which differ in many respects from the version published much later under the title *A Diary from Dixie*. Unless otherwise indicated, all future references to the Chesnut diary refer to this original version (hereafter cited as Chesnut, *Diary*).

22 Chesnut, *Diary*, 44–45.

23 Muhlenfeld, *Chesnut*, 69–70.

24 Ibid., 70–71.

25 Bleser, *Secret and Sacred*, 5–7.

26 The portrait of Hammond in this section is drawn chiefly from Drew Gilpin Faust, *James Henry Hammond and the Old South* (Baton Rouge, 1982).

27 Bleser, *Secret and Sacred*, 5; John Caldwell Guilds, *Simms: A Literary Life* (Fayetteville, N.C., 1992), 113; Faust, *Hammond*, 58.

28 Faust, *Hammond*, 73.

29 Ibid., 85.

30 Ibid., 98, 104.

31 Ibid., 225.

32 O'Brien and Moltke-Hansen, *Antebellum Charleston*, 188–93; Bleser, *Secret and Sacred*, 327.

33 Faust, *Hammond*, 229.

34 Bleser, *Secret and Sacred*, 174.

35 The following episode is drawn primarily from ibid., 163–80.

36 Faust, *Hammond*, 288–89.

37 Ibid., 314–15; Bleser, *Secret and Sacred*, 205, 209, 212–13.

38 Bleser, *Secret and Sacred*, 212–13.

39 Faust, *Hammond*, 315–16.

40 Ibid., 295–303; Bleser, *Secret and Sacred*, 197–206.

41 Bleser, *Secret and Sacred*, 317–18; Faust, *Hammond*, 308–11.

42 Ibid. Spann later married a prominent Virginia woman, but the marriage was never happy. One day after the Civil War ended, she boarded a train for home and never returned. Faust, *Hammond*, 324.

43 Bleser, *Secret and Sacred*, 163, 256.

44 Ibid., 256–57, 263; Faust, *Hammond*, 333; Jon L. Wakelyn, "The Changing Loyalties of James Henry Hammond: A Reconsideration," *South Carolina Historical Magazine* (1974), 75:3.

45 Faust, *Hammond*, 316–19.

46 Ibid., 323–29; Bleser, *Secret and Sacred*, 267–68.

47 Faust, *Hammond*, 330.

48 Ibid., 338–39.

49 Ibid., 340–43.

50 Bleser, *Secret and Sacred*, 274–75.

51 Faust, *Hammond*, 351.

52 Ibid., 355–58.

53 Bleser, *Secret and Sacred*, 260.

CHAPTER FIVE: A TALE OF THREE CITIES

1 New York *Tribune*, Nov. 17, 1860.

2 Robert Molloy, *Charleston: A Gracious Heritage* (New York, 1937), 2–4; C. Vann Woodward (ed.), *Mary Chesnut's Civil War* (New Haven, Conn., 1981), xxxiii.

3 Molloy, *Charleston*, 95, 119–30; Stevens, *Charleston*, 242.

4 Walter J. Fraser, Jr., *Charleston! Charleston!* (Columbia, S.C., 1989), 240; O'Brien and Moltke-Hansen, *Antebellum Charleston*, 297–98; Harriette Kershaw Leiding, *Charleston, Historic and Romantic* (Philadelphia, 1931), 202.

5 Louis B. Wright, *South Carolina: A Bicentennial History* (New York, 1976), 49–59, 100.

6 Stevens, *Charleston*, 233–36.

7 Leiding, *Charleston*, 202; Fraser, *Charleston!*, 240–41; O'Brien and Moltke-Hansen, *Antebellum Charleston*, 42.

8   Fraser, *Charleston!*, 229; Stevens, *Charleston*, 240–41.

9   Fraser, *Charleston!*, 224–25; Molloy, *Charleston*, 4–5; Stevens, *Charleston*, 235–36; O'Brien and Moltke-Hansen, *Antebellum Charleston*, 21.

10   Fraser, *Charleston!*, 221, 223, 232.

11   Freehling, *Road to Disunion*, 222; Lacy K. Ford, Jr., *Origins of Southern Radicalism* (New York, 1988), 113, 303; James M. Banner, "The Problem of South Carolina," in *The Hofstadter Aegis*, ed. Stanley Elkins and Eric McKitrick (New York, 1974), 78; Fraser, *Charleston!*, 221.

12   John B. Edmunds, Jr., *Francis W. Pickens and the Politics of Destruction* (Chapel Hill, 1986), 9; Ford, *Southern Radicalism*, 289.

13   Schultz, *Nationalism and Sectionalism*, 6; O'Brien and Moltke-Hansen, *Antebellum Charleston*, 14.

14   Ford, *Southern Radicalism*, 192; Schultz, *Nationalism and Sectionalism*, 12; Bleser, *Sacred and Secret*, 229.

15   Edmunds, *Pickens*, 3; Fraser, *Charleston!*, 235–42; Russell, *Diary*, 1:163.

16   Fraser, *Charleston!*, 206.

17   Stevens, *Charleston*, 250; Molloy, *Charleston*, 127.

18   Gist message, William H. Gist papers, South Caroliniana Library, University of South Carolina.

19   Charles Edward Cauthen, *South Carolina Goes to War* (Chapel Hill, N.C., 1950), 57; Laura A. White, *Robert Barnwell Rhett, Father of Secession* (New York, 1931), 179.

20   Woodward and Muhlenfeld, *Chesnut*, 4; White, *Rhett*, 170; Faust, *Hammond*, 358.

21   Schultz, *Nationalism and Sectionalism*, 205; Charleston *Mercury*, Nov. 6, 1860.

22   Schultz, *Nationalism and Sectionalism*, 227; Hammond to Simms, Nov. 13, 1860, James H. Hammond papers, South Caroliniana Library, University of South Carolina (hereafter cited as JHH).

23   Oliphant and Eaves, *Simms*, 4:260–61; Petigru to Everett, Oct. 28, 1860, Vanderhorst Family papers, South Carolina Historical Society, Charleston (hereafter cited as AVH).

24   Porter to Hammond, Nov. 11, 1860, Hammond papers, Library of Congress (hereafter cited as HLC); Petigru to Susan Petigru King, Nov. 10, 1860, AVH.

25   "Washington City," *Atlantic Monthly* (January 1861), 7:1, 8; Donn Piatt, *Memories of the Men Who Saved the Union* (New York, 1887), 135; Robert Gray Gunderson, *Old Gentlemen's Convention: The Washington Peace Conference of 1861* (Madison, Wis., 1961), 3–4.

26   Alexander K. McClure, *Colonel Alexander K. McClure's Recollections of Half a Century* (Salem, Mass., 1902), 203; Russell, *Diary*, 2:142–43.

27   Seward, *Seward at Washington*, 516, 519; Glyndon G. Van Deusen, *William Henry Seward* (New York, 1967), 273; Swisher, *Taney*, 536.

28   J. Cutler Andrews, *The North Reports the Civil War* (Pittsburgh, 1955), 36–37; Henry Villard, *Memoirs of Henry Villard* (Boston, 1904), 1:154.

29   T. C. DeLeon, *Four Years in Rebel Capitals* (Mobile, Ala., 1890), 11–12; Mrs. D. Giraud Wright, *A Southern Girl in '61* (New York, 1905), 21–24; Russell, *Diary*,

1:146–47; Ben Perley Poore, *Reminiscences of Sixty Years in the National Metropolis* (Philadelphia, 1886), 1:481–82.

30 DeLeon, *Four Years*, 13; McClure, *Recollections*, 205.

31 Poore, *Reminiscences*, 2:48–49; Pryor, *Reminiscences*, 41–43.

32 Pryor, *Reminiscences*, 70–72, 80–84.

33 Klein, *Buchanan*, 272, 275.

34 Ibid., 334.

35 Ibid., 337.

36 Philip G. Auchampaugh, *James Buchanan and His Cabinet on the Eve of Secession* (Lancaster, Pa., 1926), 98, 115, 122; *DAB*, 18:459–60.

37 Klein, *Buchanan*, 278; Samuel W. Crawford, *The Genesis of the Civil War: The Story of Sumter* (New York, 1887), 213–14.

38 Auchampaugh, *Buchanan*, 99; Gaillard Hunt (ed.), "Narrative and Letter of William Henry Trescot, Concerning Negotiations between South Carolina and President Buchanan in December, 1860," *American Historical Review* (1908), 13:548–49; Klein, *Buchanan*, 278.

39 Pryor, *Reminiscences*, 100; Klein, *Buchanan*, 267, 276; Frank B. Woodford, *Lewis Cass: The Last Jeffersonian* (New Brunswick, N.J., 1950), 314, 316, 321; Auchampaugh, *Buchanan*, 85; *DAB*, 18:600–01.

40 Henry S. Foote, *Casket of Reminiscences* (Washington, D.C., 1874), 95, 97; Horatio King, *Turning on the Light: A Dispassionate Survey of President Buchanan's Administration, from 1860 to Its Close* (Philadelphia, 1895), 59; Nichols, *Disruption*, 379; Chesnut, *Diary*, 20; *DAB*, 9:181–82.

41 Klein, *Buchanan*, 276–78; Chesnut, *Diary*, 33.

42 Trescot to Edward McCrady, Oct. 31, 1860, EM; John G. Nicolay and John Hay, *Abraham Lincoln, A History* (New York, 1890), 2:360–61; Klein, *Buchanan*, 358; U.S. War Department, *Official Records of the Union and Confederate Armies* (Washington, D.C., 1880–1901), Series 1, 1:70 (hereafter cited as *OR*). Most accounts place this event on the day after the election, but Porter says he received his orders from Floyd on the 6th.

43 Klein, *Buchanan*, 355. A copy of Scott's "Views" was sent to Lincoln and is in AL.

44 Ibid., 358; Nicolay and Hay, *Lincoln* 2:360–62.

45 Klein, *Buchanan*, 354, *OR*, 1:69, 71.

46 Klein, *Buchanan*, 358; Nicolay and Hay, *Lincoln*, 2:362–63.

47 Villard, *Memoirs*, 1:141; Baringer, *House Dividing*, 9.

48 Ward Lamon, *Recollections of Abraham Lincoln, 1847–1865* (Washington, D.C., 1911), 457.

49 Ibid., 471–72; Villard, *Lincoln on Eve*, 13–14; Baringer, *House Dividing*, 10; William H. Herndon, *Abraham Lincoln: The True Story of a Great Life* (New York, 1909), 219.

50 Lamon, *Recollections*, 457; Thomas J. McCormack (ed.), *Memoirs of Gustave Koerner 1809–1896* (Cedar Rapids, 1909), 2:104 (hereafter cited as Koerner, *Memoirs*).

51 Baringer, *House Dividing*, 28; Villard, *Memoirs*, 1:142.

52 Piatt, *Memories*, 29–30.

53 Auer, *Antislavery and Disunion*, 399; Villard, *Lincoln on Eve*, 4; Lamon, *Recollections*, 468–69.

54   Villard, *Memoirs,* 1:143–44; Baringer, *House Dividing,* 17–18, 149.

55   Z. Wood to Lincoln, Nov. 5, 1860, AL; Dr. E. P. Metcalf to Lincoln, Nov. 9, 1860, AL; AWH to Lincoln, Nov. 10, 1860, AL; R. C. Carter to Lincoln, Nov. 12, 1860, AL; J. Wilson to Lincoln, Nov. 28, 1860, AL.

56   Henry J. Raymond to Lincoln, Nov. 14, 1860, AL; H. Sanford to Lincoln, Nov. 15, 1860, AL.

57   Lincoln to Prentice, Oct. 29, 1860, AL; Lincoln to Smith, Nov. 10, 1860, AL.

58   Baringer, *House Dividing,* 19.

59   Ibid., 79–88; Villard, *Lincoln on Eve,* 21; H. Draper Hunt, *Hannibal Hamlin of Maine* (Syracuse, 1969), 127–29.

60   Baringer, *House Dividing,* 83–84; A. W. Upham to Lincoln, Nov. 26, 1860, AL; 3 Spartanburgers to Lincoln, Nov. 27, 1860, AL; "A Citizen" to Lincoln, Nov. 8, 1860, AL.

61   Lincoln to Raymond, Nov. 28, 1860, AL.

62   Swett to Lincoln, Nov. 30, 1860, AL; Baringer, *House Dividing,* 72.

63   Lamon, *Recollections,* 480–81; Herndon, *Lincoln,* 151; Baringer, *House Dividing,* 29.

CHAPTER SIX: A CHANGE OF COMMAND

1   Trenholm letter, Julian Mitchell papers, South Carolina Historical Society, Charleston (hereafter cited as JM).

2   Charles W. Elliott, *Winfield Scott, The Soldier and the Man* (New York, 1937), 678; E. D. Keyes, *Fifty Years' Observation of Men and Events* (New York, 1884), 370; Scott to Floyd, Oct. 30, 1860, John J. Crittenden papers, Library of Congress (hereafter cited as JJC).

3   T. M. Anderson, *The Political Conspiracies Preceding the Rebellion, or the True Stories of Sumter and Pickens* (New York, 1882), 5, 61; Eba Anderson Lawton, *Major Robert Anderson and Fort Sumter* (New York, 1911), 4–5.

4   George W. Cullum, *Biographical Register of the Officers and Graduates of the U.S. Military Academy* (Boston, 1891), 1:347–50; Frank Moore (ed.), "The Fall of Fort Sumter," in *Fort Sumter Memorial* (New York, 1915). Latter document has no page numbers.

5   *DAB,* 1:274; Leiding, *Charleston,* 209; Anderson, *Conspiracies,* 7; Lawton, *Anderson,* 16; Maurice Matloff (ed.), *American Military History* (Washington, D.C., 1969), 185.

6   Keyes, *Fifty Years,* 367–68.

7   Cullum, *Biographical Register,* 1:350.

8   *OR,* 1:71.

9   Ibid., 1:71–72, 74–75; Crawford, *Genesis,* 61–63; Abner W. Doubleday, *Reminiscences of Forts Sumter and Moultrie in 1860–61* (New York, 1876), 14–15.

10   Doubleday, *Reminiscences,* 34–35.

11   *OR,* 1:70.

12   Ibid., 1:74–75.

13   Ibid., 1:78–79.

14 Klein, *Buchanan,* 273–74; Richard M. Johnston and William H. Browne, *Life of Alexander H. Stephens* (Philadelphia, 1878), 329.

15 Klein, *Buchanan,* 21, 206; Carl Schurz, *The Reminiscences of Carl Schurz* (New York, 1908), 2:210.

16 Klein, *Buchanan,* 6, 34.

17 Ibid., 140, 142; Moore, *Buchanan,* 3:27, 344–45.

18 Klein, *Buchanan,* 142–44, 147, 213–14, 253, 257; Moore, *Buchanan,* 3:10, 17, 21, 10:233–34.

19 George T. Curtis, *Life of James Buchanan* (New York, 1883), 2:502; Klein, *Buchanan,* 210–11, 332.

20 Klein, *Buchanan,* 124, 206–10, 246, 274–75.

21 Ibid., 332–33; Auchampaugh, *Buchanan,* 125–26.

22 Klein, *Buchanan,* 120, 274, 332–33, 350.

23 Ibid., 274–75.

24 Foote, *Casket of Reminiscences,* 113–14.

25 Klein, *Buchanan,* 272.

26 *DAB,* 18:639; Trescot to Edward McCrady, Oct. 31, 1860, EM.

27 Pryor, *Reminiscences,* 102–03.

28 Trescot to Edward McCrady, Nov. 12, 1860, EM.

29 Nicolay and Hay, *Lincoln,* 2:317.

30 Ibid., 2:319–24.

31 Ibid., 2:323.

32 *Official Records of the Union and Confederate Navies in the War of the Rebellion* (Washington, D.C., 1896), Series I, 4:3–4 (hereafter cited as *ORN*).

33 Moore, *Buchanan,* 11:5.

34 Klein, *Buchanan,* 368–69; Hunt, "Trescot," 533–35.

35 Trescot to Edward McCrady, Nov. 27, 1860, EM.

36 Ibid. Trescot's letter to Gist can be found in Crawford, *Genesis,* 30–31.

37 Crawford, *Genesis,* 31–32.

38 Buchanan's questions and Black's responses are reprinted in Curtis, *Buchanan,* 2:319–24.

39 Trescot to Edward McCrady, Nov. 27 and Nov. 30, 1860, EM. Much later Trescot wrote that Buchanan asked him to deliver the synopsis of the message to Gist on Sunday, December 2, but the transaction is described in the November 30 letter cited above. For the later version, see Hunt, "Trescot," 537–38.

40 Lincoln to Scott, Nov. 9, 1860, AL; Scott to Crittenden, Nov. 12, 1860, JJC.

41 Keyes, *Fifty Years,* 103, 318–23; Margaret Leech, *Reveille in Washington* (New York, 1941), 1–4.

42 Keyes, *Fifty Years,* 39–40, 48, 65, 100–01, 116.

43 Ibid., 19, 29; Pryor, *Reminiscences,* 29; Elliott, *Scott,* 212–13, 249, 254, 355, 411–14.

44 Elliott, *Scott,* 415–16.

45 Keyes, *Fifty Years,* 8, 24–25, 45, 318–19.

46 Ibid., 3, 11, 52, 55–56, 139, 157, 325, 425.

47 Elliott, *Scott,* 679.

CHAPTER SEVEN: THE POLITICS OF BEWILDERMENT

1 Haddock to John J. Crittenden, Dec. 18, 1860, JJC.

2 James Vaulx Drake, *Life of General Robert Hatton* (Nashville, Tenn., 1867), 297; Seward, *Seward at Washington,* 478.

3 Charles T. Congdon, *Reminiscences of a Journalist* (Boston, 1880), 286–87; Leech, *Reveille in Washington,* 20–21.

4 Wells, *Douglas,* 261.

5 Albert D. Kirwan, *John J. Crittenden: The Struggle for the Union* (Lexington, Ky., 1962), 338, 347, 353.

6 Ibid., 103, 344, 366.

7 *Congressional Globe,* 36th Cong., 1st Sess. (Washington, D.C., 1861), 1 (hereafter cited as *Globe*).

8 [James Buchanan], *Mr. Buchanan's Administration on the Eve of the Rebellion* (New York, 1866), 114–15. This source does not give the complete text of the message but includes Buchanan's paraphrasing and interpretation. The complete text can be found in Moore, *Buchanan,* 11:7–43.

9 Moore, *Buchanan,* 11:24–25.

10 [Buchanan], *Mr. Buchanan's Administration,* 124–27; Moore, *Buchanan,* 11:10–20.

11 Seward, *Seward at Washington,* 480; James Ford Rhodes, *History of the United States, 1850–1877* (New York, 1910), 3:138; Martin B. Duberman, *Charles Francis Adams, 1807–1886* (Boston, 1961), 227. See also Trumbull to Lincoln, Dec. 4, 1860, AL, and New York *Tribune,* Dec. 4, 1860.

12 C. A. Addison to Milledge L. Bonham, Dec. 6, 1860, Milledge L. Bonham papers, South Caroliniana Library (hereafter cited as MB); James Petigru Carson (ed.), *Life, Letters and Speeches of James Louis Petigru* (Washington, D.C., 1920), 363.

13 Klein, *Buchanan,* 367.

14 John W. Burgess, *The Civil War and the Constitution, 1859–1865* (New York, 1903), 1:106–07; Auchampaugh, *Buchanan,* 18.

15 Evitts, *Matter of Allegiances,* 159; Nicolay and Hay, *Lincoln,* 3:215; Schurz, *Reminiscences,* 2:213–14; John Sherman, *Recollections of Forty Years in the House, Senate and Cabinet* (New York, 1895), 1:225.

16 Schurz, *Reminiscences,* 2:215; Corwin to Lincoln, Dec. 10, 1860, AL.

17 *Globe,* 3–12.

18 Ibid., 24, 28–29, 32; Potter, *Impending Crisis,* 103.

19 Washburne to Lincoln, Dec. 9, 1860, AL; Trumbull to Lincoln, Dec. 4, 1860, AL; Kenneth M. Stampp, *And the War Came* (Baton Rouge, 1960), 65.

20 Harriet A. Weed (ed.), *Autobiography of Thurlow Weed* (Boston, 1883), 1:307–08; Seward, *Seward at Washington,* 480.

21 Weed, *Autobiography,* 1:308–09.

22 *Globe,* 104–11; Worthington C. Ford (ed.), *Letters of Henry Adams, 1858–1891* (Boston, 1930), 1:206–07.

23 Duberman, *Adams,* 224.

24 Johannsen, *Douglas,* 810; William Salter, *Life of James W. Grimes* (New York, 1876), 131–32; Nevins, *Emergence of Lincoln,* 2:387; Drake, *Hatton,* 299.

25   George Winston Smith and Charles Judah, *Life in the North During the Civil War* (Albuquerque, 1966), 26.

26   Bonham to W. H. Gist, Dec. 3, 1860, MB.

27   Nichols, *Disruption,* 400; U. B. Phillips (ed.), *The Correspondence of Robert Toombs, Alexander H. Stephens, and Howell Cobb* (New York, 1970), 516–17; Kenneth M. Stampp, *America in 1857: A Nation on the Brink* (New York, 1990), 186.

28   Curtis, *Buchanan,* 2:353; Auchampaugh, *Buchanan,* 81.

29   Pike, *First Blows,* 526.

30   Hunt, *Hamlin,* 130.

31   Nicolay and Hay, *Lincoln,* 3:123.

32   The following section is taken from *Journal of the Convention of the People of South Carolina Held in 1860–1861* (Charleston, 1861), 358–59, 372–77 (hereafter cited as *Convention Journal*).

33   Klein, *Buchanan,* 371.

34   Gist to Bonham, Dec. 6, 1860, MB.

35   Hunt, "Trescot," 538–39.

36   Klein, *Buchanan,* 371–72; Moore, *Buchanan,* 11:58.

37   Klein, *Buchanan,* 372; New York *Tribune,* Dec. 15, 1860.

38   Nicolay and Hay, *Lincoln,* 2:436; King to Black, Dec. 14, 1860, JSB; King to Holt, Dec. 14, 1860, MB.

39   Klein, *Buchanan,* 371–73; Auchampaugh, *Buchanan,* 66–69.

40   Drake, *Hatton,* 306; Scott memorandum, March 30, 1861, AL; David C. Mearns, *The Lincoln Papers* (Garden City, N.Y.), 2:503–05.

41   Trumbull to Lincoln, Dec. 14, 1860, AL; Washburne to Lincoln, Dec. 17, 1860, AL.

42   Charles E. Hamlin, *Life and Times of Hannibal Hamlin* (Boston, 1899), 379; Trumbull to Lincoln, Dec. 14, 1860, AL; John Niven, *Gideon Welles: Lincoln's Secretary of the Navy* (New York, 1973), 307; New York *Tribune,* Dec. 17 and Dec. 31, 1860; Frank Blair, Sr., to Lincoln, Dec. 18, 1860, AL; A. Williams to Lincoln, Dec. 19, 1860, AL; Donald, *Sumner,* 368.

43   Fogg to Lincoln, Dec. 17, 1860, AL.

44   Basler, *Lincoln,* 4:149–55.

45   Ibid., 4:154, 157, 159.

46   Baringer, *House Dividing,* 104; New York *Tribune,* Dec. 18, 1860.

47   *Globe,* 101–03.

48   Washburne to Lincoln, Dec. 18, 1860, AL; Drake, *Hatton,* 307; Montgomery Blair to Lincoln, Dec. 14, 1860, AL; Swisher, *Taney,* 537.

49   Salter, *Grimes,* 132.

50   Phillips, *Correspondence,* 523–24.

51   Pryor, *Reminiscences,* 110–12.

52   Channing, *Crisis of Fear,* 268; Freehling, *Road to Disunion,* 82; Schultz, *Nationalism and Sectionalism,* 17.

CHAPTER EIGHT: TURNING POINTS

1 Sallie Hampton to ?, [mid-Dec. 1860], Sarah Hampton papers, South Caroliniana Library, University of South Carolina (hereafter cited as SH).

2 *DAB,* 7:298–99; Mary Forrest [Julia Deane Freeman], *Women of the South* (New York, 1888), 48–67.

3 Caroline Howard Gilman to her children, Dec. 24, 1860, Caroline H. Gilman papers, South Carolina Historical Society, Charleston (hereafter cited as CHG).

4 Ibid., Dec. 24 and Dec. 31, 1860, CHG.

5 Edmunds, *Pickens,* 152–53; M. C. Butler to Bonham, Dec. 11, 1860, MB; White, *Rhett,* 185.

6 Edmunds, *Pickens,* 10, 21–22, 153; Bleser, *Secret and Sacred,* 323–24.

7 Edmunds, *Pickens,* 9, 17, 20, 35.

8 Ibid., 20, 79, 94–126, 143.

9 Ibid., 69, 91, 128–34, 139–40.

10 Ibid., 128, 137, 139; Russell, *Diary,* 1:175.

11 Edmunds, *Pickens,* 140–50.

12 Ibid., 150–53.

13 A copy of this letter is in W. A. Harris (comp.), *The Record of Fort Sumter from Its Occupation by Major Anderson to Its Reduction by South Carolina Troops* (Columbia, S.C., 1862), 7–8, and in Crawford, *Genesis,* 81–83.

14 Crawford, *Genesis,* 88–89.

15 *Convention Journal,* 3–10.

16 Ibid., 12–16.

17 New York *Tribune,* Dec. 24, 1860.

18 *Convention Journal,* 17–40; Ruffin, *Diary,* 1:511. I am grateful to Patton Hash of the South Carolina Historical Society for clarifying why the members moved from one hall to the other and back.

19 *Convention Journal,* 41–52; Cauthen, *South Carolina Goes to War,* 70; Rhodes, *History,* 3:198–99.

20 John S. Ryan to A. F. Girard, Dec. 20, 1860, John S. Ryan papers, South Caroliniana Library, University of South Carolina; Carson, *Petigru,* 364.

21 Rhodes, *History,* 3:200; Crawford, *Genesis,* 87–88.

22 Rhodes, *History,* 3:201–02; *Convention Journal,* 46–47, 52–54.

23 Rhodes, *History,* 3:202–03; Charleston *Mercury,* Dec. 22, 1860; Huger to Mrs. Frank Hampton, Dec. 9, 1860, SH.

24 *Convention Journal,* 32.

25 Ibid., 58–65.

26 Nina Gilman to Aunt Annie, Dec. 21, 1860, CHG.

27 Hunt, "Trescot," 540–41; Moore, *Buchanan,* 11:70–72; Crawford, *Genesis,* 81–88.

28 Moore, *Buchanan,* 11:73.

29 *OR,* 1:90–91; Crawford, *Genesis,* 72–74.

30 *OR,* 1:103; Klein, *Buchanan,* 376.

31 Details on the scandal are in [Buchanan], *Mr. Buchanan's Administration,* 185–87, Klein, *Buchanan,* 377, and Nichols, *Disruption,* 418–20.

32 Hunt, "Trescot," 542.

33   Moore, *Buchanan,* 11:69–70; Andrew C. McLaughlin, *Lewis Cass* (Boston, 1899), 339–40.

34   Moore, *Buchanan,* 11:69.

35   R. W. Thompson to Lincoln, Dec. 25, 1860, AL.

36   Moore, *Buchanan,* 11:75; New York *Tribune,* Dec. 25, 1860.

37   Trescot to Edward McCrady, Dec. 25, 1860, EM.

38   Ibid.; Drake, *Hatton,* 312–13.

39   *OR,* 1:81–82.

40   Ibid., 1:82, 85; Crawford, *Genesis,* 68.

41   Crawford, *Genesis,* 72–75.

42   Ibid., 69.

43   Ibid., 75, 100; Charleston *Mercury,* Dec. 13, 1860, *OR,* 1:93.

44   *OR,* 1:83–85, 95–97.

45   Ibid., 1:98–103; Crawford, *Genesis,* 119–21.

46   *OR,* 1:105–06.

47   Ibid., 1:105–07.

48   Doubleday, *Reminiscences,* 58; Crawford, *Genesis,* 102.

49   This account is drawn from *OR,* 1:2–4, 108–09; Crawford, *Genesis,* 102–08; Doubleday, *Reminiscences,* 60–67; Nicolay and Hay, *Lincoln,* 3:47–55.

50   *OR,* 1:2.

CHAPTER NINE: AT THE BRINK

1   *Globe,* 73, 75.

2   Kirwan, *Crittenden,* 377. The text of the proposals is in *Globe,* 114. A summary can be found in Kirwan, *Crittenden,* 375–76.

3   Potter, *Impending Crisis,* 531–32; Patsy S. Ledbetter, "John J. Crittenden and the Compromise Debacle," *Filson Club History Quarterly* (April 1977), 51:2, 129–30.

4   *Globe,* 116, 158; Nichols, *Disruption,* 414–15. The committee, chosen carefully by Vice President Breckinridge, included Toombs and Davis from the Deep South, Crittenden, Powell (Ky.), and Hunter (Va.) from the border states, Douglas, Bigler, (Pa.), and Henry Rice (Minn.) as northern Democrats, Seward and Jacob Collamer (Vt.) as eastern Republicans, and Wade (Ohio), James Doolittle (Wis.), and James Grimes (Iowa) as western Republicans.

5   *Seward at Washington,* 481–83; New York *Tribune,* Dec. 24, 1860; Weed to Lincoln, Dec. 23, 1860, AL.

6   Seward, *Seward at Washington,* 484–85; Nichols, *Disruption,* 415; New York *Tribune,* Dec. 24–28, 1860.

7   Nichols, *Disruption,* 415–16; Seward to Lincoln, Dec. 26, 1860, AL.

8   Crittenden to L. L. Nicholas, undated, JJC.

9   The following section is drawn largely from Duberman, *Adams,* 227–41.

10   *Globe,* 87.

11   Diary of Charles Francis Adams, Dec. 20, 1860, Massachusetts Historical Society, Boston.

12   Davis proposed to admit both Kansas and New Mexico as states, to acquire no

more territory without a two-thirds vote of both houses of Congress, with the status of slavery to be what it was at the time of acquisition. See Duberman, *Adams,* 233.

13   Corwin to Lincoln, Dec. 24, 1860, AL.

14   Adams diary, Dec. 29, 1860.

15   Ford, *Henry Adams,* 1:213; Duberman, *Adams,* 241.

16   New York *Tribune,* Dec. 31, 1860.

17   *Convention Journal,* 54–112.

18   Crawford, *Genesis,* 89–92.

19   Ibid., 108.

20   Ibid., 107–08; Doubleday, *Reminiscences,* 68–70.

21   Crawford, *Genesis,* 109–12.

22   Ibid., 113–17; Doubleday, *Reminiscences,* 70–76, *OR,* 1:108–09.

23   Doubleday, *Reminiscences,* 72, 81.

24   Crawford, *Genesis,* 116, 125, *OR,* 1:109; *Convention Journal,* 129.

25   *Convention Journal,* 114–15.

26   Milton, *Eve of Conflict,* 519; Fish to Fessenden, Dec. 11, 1860, William P. Fessenden papers, Library of Congress (hereafter cited as WPF); Gilman to Trumbull, Dec. 11, 1860, Lyman Trumbull papers, Library of Congress (hereafter cited as LT).

27   Stampp, *And the War Came,* 124–25; Edward L. Pierce (ed.), *Memoir and Letters of Charles Sumner* (Boston, 1893), 4:2; Carl Schurz to Lincoln, Dec. 18, 1860, AL.

28   Details on the individual conventions are in Ralph A. Wooster, *The Secession Conventions of the South* (Princeton, 1962).

29   Alvan F. Sanborn (ed.), *Reminiscences of Richard Lathers* (New York, 1907), 91–111; Kirwan, *Crittenden,* 379.

30   Sanborn, *Lathers,* 100; New York *Tribune,* Dec. 17 and 18, 1860; Strong, *Diary,* 3:77.

31   Nicolay and Hay, *Lincoln,* 2:420; Johannsen, *Douglas,* 855; Rachel S. Thorndike (ed.), *The Sherman Letters: Correspondence Between General and Senator Sherman from 1837 to 1894* (New York, 1894), 102.

32   J. C. Conkling to Trumbull, Dec. 26, 1860, LT; C. B. Haddock to Lincoln, Dec. 18, 1860, AL; Schurz, *Reminiscences,* 1:173–74; Joseph Medill to Lincoln, Dec. 18, 1860, AL.

33   Koerner to Trumbull, Dec. 10, 1860, LT; Trumbull to Lincoln, Dec. 24, 1860, AL.

34   Boston *Courier,* Dec. 28, 1860; Randall, *Lincoln,* 1:242; Lawrence to John J. Crittenden, Dec. 29, 1860, JJC; Charles Eliot Norton (ed.), *Letters of James Russell Lowell* (New York, 1966), 2:56.

35   Schurz to Lincoln, Dec. 28, 1860, AL; A. Jonas to Lincoln, Dec. 30, 1860, AL; White to Trumbull, Dec. 30, 1860, LT.

36   Nichols, *Disruption,* 420–21; Klein, *Buchanan,* 377–78; J. A. Gibson to Black, Dec. 25, 1860, JSB: Drake, *Hatton,* 313; Howard C. Perkins, *Northern Editorials on Secession* (New York, 1942), 1:202.

37   John W. DuBose, *Life and Times of William Lowndes Yancey* (Birmingham, 1892), 2:576–77; Nichols, *Disruption,* 420–21; Klein, *Buchanan,* 378.

38   Hunt, "Trescot," 543–45.

39   Ibid.; *OR,* 1:3.

40 Hunt, "Trescot," 544-45; Klein, *Buchanan,* 378-79.

41 Crawford, *Genesis,* 145-46.

42 Klein, *Buchanan,* 379; Curtis, *Buchanan,* 2:409; [Buchanan], *Mr. Buchanan's Administration,* 188.

43 Trumbull to Lincoln, Dec. 27, 1860, AL; Drake, *Hatton,* 314.

44 Crawford, *Genesis,* 148-49; *Convention Journal,* 354; Klein, *Buchanan,* 380.

45 Scott to Floyd, Dec. 28, 1860, AL; Nicolay and Hay, *Lincoln,* 3:73-74.

46 *OR,* 1:109-10.

47 Crawford, *Genesis,* 150-51.

48 King, *Turning on the Light,* 36; Fessenden, *Life and Public Services,* 1:119.

49 Nevins, *Emergence of Lincoln,* 2:360; Ford, *Henry Adams,* 1:216.

50 Seward, *Seward at Washington,* 487-88; Stampp, *And the War Came,* 73.

51 Chauncy F. Black, *Essays and Speeches of Jeremiah S. Black* (New York, 1886), 13-14. No copy of Buchanan's original draft has been preserved.

52 Holt to Black, Dec. 30, 1860, JSB.

53 Black, *Essays and Speeches,* 14; Auchampaugh, *Buchanan,* 161-62; Hunt, "Trescot," 545.

54 Scott to Buchanan, Dec. 30, 1860, AL; Horace White, *Life of Lyman Trumbull* (New York, 1913), 122.

55 Klein, *Buchanan,* 381; Nichols, *Disruption,* 425-26; Moore, *Buchanan,* 11:84-86; Stampp, *And the War Came,* 75.

56 Klein, *Buchanan,* 381; Crawford, *Genesis,* 153-55; Black, *Essays and Speeches,* 14-17. The last two sources contain the complete text of Black's memorandum.

57 Moore, *Buchanan,* 11:79-84; *OR,* 1:115-18; Hunt, "Trescot," 552.

58 Crawford, *Genesis,* 159.

59 Hunt, "Trescot," 545-46; Scott to Buchanan, Dec. 31, 1860, AL; Buchanan to Scott, Dec. 31, 1860, AL.

60 Trescot to Edward McCrady, Dec. 31, 1860, EM; Scott to Buchanan, Dec. 31, 1860, AL.

61 Lincoln to Duff Green, Dec. 28, 1860, AL; Lincoln to Trumbull, Dec. 28, 1860, AL; Klein, *Buchanan,* 385-86.

62 Buchanan to Scott, Dec. 31, 1860, AL; *OR,* 1:118.

PART TWO: THE BATTLE OVER SECESSION
CHAPTER TEN: WAR BECKONS

1 Corwin to Lincoln, Jan. 16, 1861, AL.

2 Villard, *Memoirs,* 1:146-48; Baringer, *House Dividing,* 250-51.

3 Stampp, *And the War Came,* 90.

4 Baringer, *House Dividing,* 153-54.

5 Ibid., 182; Dubois to Trumbull, Jan. 22, 1861, LT.

6 Baringer, *House Dividing,* 76-78.

7 Lamon, *Recollections,* 468; Charles Francis Adams, Jr., *Charles Francis Adams, 1835-1915, an Autobiography* (Boston, 1916), 75.

8 Basler, *Lincoln,* 4:148-49; Seward to Lincoln, Dec. 13, 1860, AL; Baringer, *House Dividing,* 86; Weed, *Autobiography,* 2:302.

9 Theodore C. Pease and James G. Randall (eds.), *The Diary of Orville Hickman Browning* (Springfield, Ill., 1927), 1:440; Howard K. Beale (ed.), "The Diary of Edward Bates 1859–1865," *Annual Report of the American Historical Association, 1930* (Washington, D.C., 1933), 164–65 (hereafter cited as Bates, "Diary").

10 George G. Fogg to Lincoln, Dec. 13, 1860, AL.

11 Hamlin, *Life of Hamlin*, 369; Baringer, *House Dividing*, 88; Crawford, *Genesis*, 357; William E. Smith, *The Francis Preston Blair Family in Politics* (New York, 1933), 2:2.

12 Weed, *Autobiography*, 1:603–14; Baringer, *House Dividing*, 115–22.

13 Wilmot to Lincoln, Dec. 12, 1860, AL; Hamlin to Lincoln, Dec. 26, 1860, AL; Trumbull to Lincoln, Dec. 31, 1860, AL; Baringer, *House Dividing*, 96, 123–24.

14 Reeder to Lincoln, Dec. 18 and Dec. 22, 1860, AL; Russell, *Diary*, 1:62; Randall, *Lincoln the President*, 1:148.

15 Bates, "Diary," 171–72; New York *Herald*, Jan. 7, 1861; Basler, *Lincoln*, 4:168; Seward to Lincoln, Dec. 28, 1860, AL; Baringer, *House Dividing*, 126–32.

16 Baringer, *House Dividing*, 133–35; Basler, *Lincoln*, 4:166–67; McClure to Lincoln, Jan. 3, 1861, AL.

17 Lincoln to Cameron, Jan. 3, 1861, AL; Basler, *Lincoln*, 4:169–70.

18 Baringer, *House Dividing*, 248.

19 Villard, *Lincoln on Eve*, 47.

20 Black to Charles R. Buckalew, Jan. 25, 1861, JSB.

21 New York *Tribune*, Jan. 3, 1861; Pryor, *Reminiscences*, 115–16.

22 Ford, *Henry Adams*, 1:217; Drake, *Hatton*, 316.

23 Phillips, *Correspondence*, 528.

24 *OR*, 1:124–25; *Convention Journal*, 370; Curtis, *Buchanan*, 2:392; Crawford, *Genesis*, 182; Moore, *Buchanan*, 11:101.

25 Moore, *Buchanan*, 11:101; Nichols, *Disruption*, 428–29; Klein, *Buchanan*, 388.

26 *OR*, 1:119, 128–32; [Buchanan], *Mr. Buchanan's Administration*, 189; Elliott, *Scott*, 684–85; Crawford, *Genesis*, 169, 175–76.

27 *OR*, 1:120; Robert U. Johnson and Clarence C. Buel (eds.), *Battles and Leaders of the Civil War* (New York, 1887), 1:2.

28 Johannsen, *Douglas*, 819; Klein, *Buchanan*, 390.

29 Johnson and Buel, *Battles and Leaders*, 1:9–12.

30 Crawford, *Genesis*, 169; Washburne to Lincoln, Jan. 4, 1861, AL; Cameron to Lincoln, Jan. 3, 1861, AL; Swett to Lincoln, Jan. 5, 1861, AL; New York *Tribune*, Jan. 8, 1861.

31 Seward, *Seward at Washington*, 490–91; Jefferson Davis, *The Rise and Fall of the Confederate Government* (New York, 1881), 1:204.

32 New York *Tribune*, Jan. 7–9, 1861; Drake, *Hatton*, 317–19; Donald, *Sumner*, 376; Ford, *Henry Adams*, 1:218; Keyes, *Fifty Years*, 372–73.

33 Moore, *Buchanan*, 11:94–99. The italics are in the original.

34 Ibid., 11:97; Klein, *Buchanan*, 390–91; [Buchanan], *Mr. Buchanan's Administration*, 159.

35 Drake, *Hatton*, 318–19; *OR*, 1:252; Crawford, *Genesis*, 178–80.

36 Crawford, *Genesis*, 178–82.

37 Ibid., 183–85; Doubleday, *Reminiscences*, 89; New York *Tribune*, Jan. 14, 1861.

38 Doubleday, *Reminiscences*, 94–105.

39 New York *Tribune*, Jan. 16, 1861.

40 Crawford, *Genesis*, 185–86.

CHAPTER ELEVEN: WAR RECEDES

1 Caroline Gilman to "Aunt Lala," Jan. 11, 1861, CHG.

2 *OR*, 1:133.

3 Johnson and Buel, *Battles and Leaders*, 1:61; Crawford, *Genesis*, 187–90.

4 Crawford, *Genesis*, 190; *OR*, 1:135–36.

5 Crawford, *Genesis*, 190–91; Cauthen, *South Carolina Goes to War*, 80–81. The cabinet included Lieutenant Governor W. W. Harllee as postmaster general, A. G. Magrath as secretary of state, D. F. Jamison as secretary of war, C. G. Memminger as secretary of the treasury, and A. C. Garlington as secretary of the interior.

6 Harris, *Record of Fort Sumter*, 15–17.

7 Ibid., 17–19; *Convention Journal*, 386–87; Charleston *Mercury*, Jan. 4, 1861; Bryan to Crittenden, Jan. 5, 1861, JJC.

8 Ervin to John Manning, Jan. 4, 1861, Miller-Chesnut-Manning papers, South Carolina Historical Society (hereafter cited as MCM); Carson, *Petigru*, 365; New York *Tribune*, Jan. 14 and Jan. 31, 1861.

9 Harris, *Record of Fort Sumter*, 19–23.

10 Ibid., 21; Crawford, *Genesis*, 191–94; Doubleday, *Reminiscences*, 107–09; *OR*, 1:137–38.

11 Crawford, *Genesis*, 193–94; Harris, *Record of Fort Sumter*, 28–29.

12 Crawford, *Genesis*, 195–97; Harris, *Record of Fort Sumter*, 29–32.

13 New York *Tribune*, Jan. 18, 1861.

14 Charleston *Mercury*, Jan. 10, 1861.

15 New York *Tribune*, Jan. 15, 1861.

16 Clarence Phillips Denman, *The Secession Movement in Alabama* (Montgomery, 1933), 144.

17 Susan Bradford Eppes, *Through Some Eventful Years* (Macon, Ga., 1928), 139–146.

18 F. K. Bailey to Trumbull, Jan. 16, 1861, LT; Perkins, *Northern Editorials*, 1:210; Stampp, *And the War Came*, 85; Weed to Lincoln, Jan. 10, 1861, AL.

19 Stampp, *And the War Came*, 90; Auer, *Antislavery and Disunion*, 366; Gunderson, *Old Gentlemen's Convention*, 75–76. A copy of Curtin's speech is in AL.

20 Stampp, *And the War Came*, 85–95; Ford, *Henry Adams*, 1:224.

21 Webb to Lincoln, Jan. 12, 1861, AL.

22 Crawford, *Genesis*, 263–65.

23 Johnson and Buel, *Battles and Leaders*, 1:26.

24 Ibid., 1:27–32.

25 *ORN*, 4:7–11, 22, 26, 29, 33.

26 Johnson and Buel, *Battles and Leaders*, 1:27–28.

27   *ORN*, 4:13–55.

28   Johnson and Buel, *Battles and Leaders*, 1:29–30.

29   Ibid., 1:30–31.

30   Strong, *Diary*, 3:89; Edmunds, *Pickens*, 159.

31   Nichols, *Disruption*, 431–32; Moore, *Buchanan*, 11:105–06.

32   *OR*, 1:136–37; [Buchanan], *Mr. Buchanan's Administration*, 196.

33   Nichols, *Disruption*, 441; Harris, *Record of Fort Sumter*, 32–34.

34   Moore, *Buchanan*, 11:109–11.

35   *OR*, 1:140.

36   Ibid., 1:140–42. A copy of the letter is also in JSB.

37   Black to Charles R. Buckalew, Jan. 25, 1861, JSB.

38   *OR*, 1:444–45, 52:2, 9, 13; Nichols, *Disruption*, 442–43.

39   Keyes, *Fifty Years*, 350, 353, 362.

40   Strong, *Diary*, 3:88; New York *Tribune*, Jan. 12, 1861; Ford, *Henry Adams*, 1:222.

41   Keyes, *Fifty Years*, 351; Klein, *Buchanan*, 390; Drake, *Hatton*, 320, 322; Charleston *Mercury*, Jan. 21, 1861.

42   Charleston *Mercury*, Jan. 21, 1861.

43   Phillips, *Correspondence*, 529, 531.

CHAPTER TWELVE: THE PEACE PUZZLE

1   Salter, *Grimes*, 135–36.

2   Louis M. Starr, *Bohemian Brigade* (New York, 1954), 11–13.

3   Richard A. Schwarzlose, *The Nation's Newsbrokers* (Evanston, Ill., 1989), 1:233; Perkins, *Northern Editorials*, 2:1054.

4   Ibid.; Frank Luther Mott, *American Journalism* (New York, 1950), 304–05; Frederic Hudson, *Journalism in the United States from 1690 to 1872* (New York, 1873), 771.

5   Perkins, *Northern Editorials*, 2:1047–48; Starr, *Bohemian Brigade*, 9, 12.

6   Starr, *Bohemian Brigade*, 15–24; Elmer Davis, *History of the New York Times, 1851–1921* (New York, 1969), 13–17; Hudson, *Journalism*, 634.

7   Starr, *Bohemian Brigade*, 3–6, 16, 22.

8   Ibid., 8.

9   Perkins, *Northern Editorials*, 2:1037, 1050–51.

10   Starr, *Bohemian Brigade*, 10–11, 19–20; Albert Deane Richardson, *The Secret Service: The Field, the Dungeon, and the Escape* (Hartford, 1865), 121–22.

11   R. B. Rhett, Jr., to G. W. Bagby, Jan. 11 and Jan. 30, 1861, G. W. Bagby papers, Virginia Historical Society, Richmond.

12   Ibid., Jan. 12 and Jan. 30, 1861; Charleston *Mercury*, Jan. 22, 1861.

13   Perkins, *Northern Editorials*, 2:1035, 1048; Hudson, *Journalism*, 595–96.

14   James Russell Lowell, "E Pluribus Unum," *Political Essays* (New York, 1966), 86. This article appeared originally in the *Atlantic Monthly* during the winter of 1861.

15   For Simmons, see *Globe*, 408–09.

16   Schurz, *Reminiscences*, 2:212.

17 George Harmon Knoles (ed.), *The Crisis of the Union, 1860–1861* (Baton Rouge, 1965), 98.

18 Oliphant and Eaves, *Simms*, 4:280.

19 Baringer, *House Dividing*, 234; Stampp, *And the War Came*, 143.

20 Randall, *Lincoln the President*, 1:207–10.

21 New York *Tribune*, Jan. 9, 1861; Kenneth E. Colton (ed.), "The Irrepressible Conflict of 1861: The Letters of Samuel Ryan Curtis," *Annals of Iowa* (1942–43), 24:17–18; Nichols, *Disruption*, 445–46.

22 New York *Tribune*, Feb. 2, 1861; Crofts, *Reluctant Confederates*, 201, 204.

23 *Globe*, Appendix, 58.

24 Duberman, *Adams*, 245–49.

25 *Globe*, 411, 416–17, 420, 441, 451, 509, Appendix, 54–55, 66; Drake, *Hatton*, 320–21.

26 *Globe*, 498, 531, Appendix, 80–81, 113.

27 Ibid., 581–82, 631.

28 Ibid., 671.

29 Ibid., Appendix, 124–26.

30 Ibid., Appendix, 126–27.

31 Ford, *Henry Adams*, 1:227; Colton, "Curtis," 17–18.

32 *Globe*, 237, 251–52; Potter, *Impending Crisis*, 549; Horace Greeley, *Recollections of a Busy Life* (New York, 1868), 397.

33 *Globe*, 211, 237, Appendix, 39; Kirwan, *Crittenden*, 392; Washburne to Lincoln, Jan. 4, 1861, AL.

34 *Globe*, 250; Strong, *Diary*, 3:86.

35 Henry Adams, *The Education of Henry Adams* (Boston, 1961), 104.

36 Ibid.; Russell, *Diary*, 1:49–50; Adams, *Autobiography*, 79; Van Deusen, *Seward*, 255–57; Ford, *Henry Adams*, 1:204.

37 Van Deusen, *Seward*, 260–61; Piatt, *Memories*, 135.

38 Van Deusen, *Seward*, 255–62; Frederic Bancroft, *The Life of William Seward* (New York, 1900), 2:70–71.

39 Adams, *Autobiography*, 89; Piatt, *Memories*, 149; Poore, *Reminiscences*, 2:54.

40 Bancroft, *Seward*, 2:73, 75; Weed to Lincoln, Jan. 10, 1861, AL; Seward, *Seward at Washington*, 492; Stampp, *And the War Came*, 109.

41 Benjamin P. Thomas and Harold M. Hyman, *Stanton: The Life and Times of Lincoln's Secretary of War* (New York, 1962), 91–100.

42 Seward to Lincoln, Dec. 29, 1860, AL.

43 Seward, *Seward at Washington*, 491; Seward to Lincoln, Jan. 8, 1861, AL.

44 New York *Tribune*, Jan. 13, 1861; Seward, *Seward at Washington*, 493–94; *Globe*, 341–44.

45 Charleston *Mercury*, Jan. 14 and Jan. 16, 1861; Fawn M. Brodie, *Thaddeus Stevens: The Scourge of the South* (New York, 1959), 140; Keyes, *Fifty Years*, 352; Van Deusen, *Seward*, 245; Ralph Haswell Lutz, "Rudolf Schleiden and the Visit to Richmond, April 25, 1861," *Annual Report of the American Historical Association* (1915), 210.

46 Auer, *Antislavery and Disunion*, 314; Seward, *Seward at Washington*, 496–97.

47 Seward, *Seward at Washington*, 496–97.

48 Ibid., 497; Lutz, "Schleiden," 210.

49 John A. Campbell, "Papers of John A. Campbell, 1861–1865," *Southern Historical Society Papers* (1917), 44; Ford, *Henry Adams*, 1:225.

50 *Globe*, 484–89; White, *Trumbull*, 121; Charleston *Mercury*, Jan. 26, 1861.

51 Nichols, *Disruption*, 467; *Globe*, 519.

52 Nichols, *Disruption*, 446–47.

53 *Globe*, 589, 657–70.

54 Potter, *Impending Crisis*, 551; Stampp, *And the War Came*, 166–67; [Buchanan], *Mr. Buchanan's Administration*, 206–07; Tyler, *Tyler*, 2:587–90.

55 Tyler, *Tyler*, 2:590–91; Moore, *Buchanan*, 11:113–14; Gunderson, *Old Gentlemen's Convention*, 9.

56 Charleston *Mercury*, Feb. 2, 1861.

57 *ORN*, 4:74; Charleston *Mercury*, Jan. 30, 1861; Moore, *Buchanan*, 11:123–24.

CHAPTER THIRTEEN: FAREWELLS AND FOREBODINGS

1 *Globe*, Appendix, 250.

2 Douglas Southall Freeman, *R. E. Lee: A Biography* (New York, 1934), 1:411, 420–25.

3 Walter L. Buenger, *Secession and Union in Texas* (Austin, Tex., 1984), 119–50. The quotation is on p. 148.

4 Freeman, *Lee*, 1:424–29.

5 Klein, *Buchanan*, 401.

6 Crawford, *Genesis*, 275–77.

7 *Globe*, 720–21.

8 Russell, *Diary*, 1:252–53; Wright, *Southern Girl*, 30; T. C. DeLeon, *Belles, Beaux and Brains of the 60's* (New York, 1907), 93; Richardson, *Secret Service*, 43; *Globe*, 721–22; Tyler, *Tyler*, 2:598; New York *Tribune*, Jan. 5, 1861.

9 *Globe*, 788–90.

10 Moore, *Buchanan*, 11:132–38.

11 Ibid., 11:139–41.

12 Ibid., 11:141–43.

13 King, *Turning on the Light*, 43; Keyes, *Fifty Years*, 362–63; Washburne to Lincoln, Feb. 3, 1861, AL.

14 New York *Tribune*, Feb. 4, 1861; Morgan Dix (ed.), *Memoirs of John Adams Dix* (New York, 1883), 1:370–73.

15 Sumner, *Works*, 5:463; Pierce, *Sumner*, 4:16; Adams, *Education*, 102–03; Donald, *Sumner*, 372–73; Thomas and Hyman, *Stanton*, 111.

16 Donald, *Sumner*, 370–71.

17 Ibid., 373–79; Pierce, *Sumner*, 4:13; Ford, *Henry Adams*, 1:229.

18 Adams, *Autobiography*, 80–82; Donald, *Sumner*, 380–81.

19 Donald, *Sumner*, 381; Gunderson, *Old Gentlemen's Convention*, 39–40.

20 Morton to Lincoln, Jan. 29, 1861, AL; Ebenezer Peck to Trumbull, Feb. 2, 1861, LT; Weed to Lincoln, Jan. 28, 1861, AL; Gunderson, *Old Gentlemen's Convention*, 36–37.

21 Charleston *Mercury*, Feb. 4, 1861; New York *Tribune*, Feb. 5, 1861; Gunderson, *Old Gentlemen's Convention*, 43.

22 Gunderson, *Old Gentlemen's Convention*, 10–13.

23 Kane, *Facts*, 61–62; Drake, *Hatton*, 324; Tyler, *Tyler*, 2:598.

24 DeLeon, *Four Years*, 23.

25 Charles Robert Lee, Jr., *The Confederate Constitutions* (Chapel Hill, N.C., 1963), 8–20.

26 Ibid.; Nichols, *Disruption*, 464; Russell, *Diary*, 1:242.

27 Russell, *Diary*, 1:242, 244; DeLeon, *Belles, Beaux and Brains*, 47–48.

28 DeLeon, *Belles, Beaux and Brains*, 51; Charleston *Mercury*, Feb. 6, 1861; Thomas R. R. Cobb, "The Correspondence of Thomas Reade Rootes Cobb, 1860–1862," *Publications of the Southern History Association* (May and July 1907), 11:3, 159–60; Nichols, *Disruption*, 456.

29 Chesnut, *Diary*, 4–5, 10, 33.

30 Ibid., 5–7.

31 Lee, *Confederate Constitutions*, 47–50.

32 Cobb, "Correspondence," 161–64; Charleston *Mercury*, Feb. 8, 1861.

33 Nichols, *Disruption*, 457–58; Lee, *Confederate Constitutions*, 54–57.

34 Johnson, *Patriarchal Republic*, 122–23; Cobb, "Correspondence," 167; Lee, *Confederate Constitutions*, 27.

35 Lee, *Confederate Constitutions*, 60–72. The changes included a ban on the foreign slave trade; giving Congress power to forbid the import of slaves from states outside the Confederacy; empowering the president to veto items in appropriation bills; and forbidding Congress to appropriate funds except on a direct request and estimate from the president or head of a department.

36 Nichols, *Disruption*, 457; Phillips, *Correspondence*, 537; Cobb, "Correspondence," 171–72; Charleston *Mercury*, Feb. 8, 1861.

37 Nichols, *Disruption*, 459–61; Cobb, "Correspondence," 167–73.

38 Cobb, "Correspondence," 165, 172–73.

39 *OR*, 1:138–39, 146–47, 155.

40 Ibid., 1:147, 159, 160–61, 163–65, 170.

41 Ibid., 1:163, 174; Crawford, *Genesis*, 210.

42 *OR*, 1:143, 156, 163; Crawford, *Genesis*, 198–200.

43 *OR*, 1:139, 156.

44 Ibid., 1:144.

45 Ibid., 1:144–46, 151; Crawford, *Genesis*, 201–02.

46 *OR*, 1:154, 159–60; Crawford, *Genesis*, 202–03.

47 *OR*, 1:145, 151–52, 159–63; Crawford, *Genesis*, 206–07.

CHAPTER FOURTEEN: TWO JOURNEYS

1 Stanton Ling Davis, *Pennsylvania Politics, 1860–1863* (Cleveland, 1935), 170.

2 William C. Davis, *Jefferson Davis: The Man and His Hour* (New York, 1991), 297; Nicolay and Hay, *Lincoln*, 3:208–09; Faust, *Hammond*, 360; Lucius E. Chittenden, *Recollections of President Lincoln and His Administration* (New York, 1891), 95.

3 Varina Howell Davis, *Jefferson Davis: A Memoir* (New York, 1890), 2:18–19; William Davis, *Jefferson Davis*, 296–301.

4 Varina Davis, *Jefferson Davis*, 2:12.

5   This sketch of Davis is drawn primarily from William Davis, *Jefferson Davis*, 1–297, and Holman Hamilton, *The Three Kentucky Presidents* (Lexington, Ky., 1978), 10–12.

6   William Davis, *Jefferson Davis*, 97.

7   Varina Davis, *Jefferson Davis*, 1:206.

8   Ibid., 1:267.

9   Ishbel Ross, *The First Lady of the South: The Life of Mrs. Jefferson Davis* (New York, 1958), 82–86; Varina Davis, *Jefferson Davis*, 1:571, 575–81.

10   Poore, *Reminiscences*, 1:539–40; Wright, *Southern Girl*, 29; DeLeon, *Four Years*, 25; Russell, *Diary*, 1:249–50; Charleston *Mercury*, Feb. 22, 1861.

11   William Davis, *Jefferson Davis*, 304–10.

12   Cobb, "Correspondence," 177–78, 180–81.

13   Ibid., 182–83; Charleston *Mercury*, Feb. 22, 1861; Katherine M. Jones, *Heroines of Dixie* (Indianapolis, 1955), 13–14; William Davis, *Jefferson Davis*, 307.

14   Chesnut, *Diary*, 12.

15   William Davis, *Jefferson Davis*, 307–10.

16   Varina Davis, *Jefferson Davis*, 2:33.

17   Cobb, "Correspondence," 236–37.

18   Villard, *Lincoln on Eve*, 62; Baringer, *House Dividing*, 250–51.

19   Villard, *Lincoln on Eve*, 57–58; Baringer, *House Dividing*, 248–49.

20   Villard, *Lincoln on Eve*, 55; Baringer, *House Dividing*, 252–54; Carl Sandburg, *Abraham Lincoln: The Prairie Years* (New York, 1926), 2:415–17; Lamon, *Reminiscences*, 462–65.

21   M. Huntington to Lincoln, Jan. 20, 1861, AL; Herndon, *Lincoln*, 188.

22   Baringer, *House Dividing*, 176–85, 254; Judd to Lincoln, Jan. 11, 1861, AL.

23   Baringer, *House Dividing*, 159, 165–76, 188, 254; A. D. Mitchell to Lincoln, Jan. 21, 1861, AL.

24   "Minister" to Lincoln, Jan. 18, 1861, AL; Fessenden to Lincoln, Jan. 20, 1861, AL; Grimes to Lincoln, Jan. 20, 1861, AL; Trumbull to Lincoln, Jan. 20, 1861, AL.

25   J. A. Gurley to Lincoln, Jan. 24, 1861, AL; Seward to Lincoln, Jan. 27, 1861, AL; Baringer, *House Dividing*, 252.

26   Basler, *Lincoln*, 4:183; Baringer, *House Dividing*, 256.

27   Baringer, *House Dividing*, 245; Browning, *Diary*, 1:453.

28   Baringer, *House Dividing*, 257, 259; Villard, *Lincoln on Eve*, 63.

29   Baringer, *House Dividing*, 164, 263; Villard, *Lincoln on Eve*, 64, 67.

30   Baringer, *House Dividing*, 261–63; Herndon, *Lincoln*, 192–94.

31   Lamon, *Recollections*, 476–77.

32   Villard, *Lincoln on Eve*, 70–71.

33   Ibid.; Baringer, *House Dividing*, 264–66.

34   Basler, *Lincoln*, 4:190–91. Basler includes three versions of this farewell speech. I have used the first, which was written in the hands of Lincoln himself and his secretary, John G. Nicolay.

35   Lamon, *Recollections*, 482.

36   Baringer, *House Dividing*, 267–68.

37   Basler, *Lincoln*, 4:191.

38   Villard, *Lincoln on Eve*, 75–76; Villard, *Memoirs*, 1:151; Lamon, *Recollections*, 484–85.

39   Villard, *Lincoln on Eve*, 77–78.

40   Basler, *Lincoln*, 4:195.

41   Villard, *Lincoln on Eve*, 77–79.

42   Charles R. Williams (ed.), *Diary and Letters of Rutherford Birchard Hayes* (Columbus, Ohio, 1922–26), 2:5.

43   Villard, *Lincoln on Eve*, 81–85; New York *Tribune*, Feb. 14 and Feb. 16, 1861.

44   Basler, *Lincoln*, 4:211.

45   Ibid., 4:216–17.

46   Ibid., 4:217–19; Villard, *Lincoln on Eve*, 87–88; New York *Tribune*, Feb. 18, 1861.

47   Basler, *Lincoln*, 4:219–21; Villard, *Lincoln on Eve*, 88–90; New York *Tribune*, Feb. 18, 1861.

48   Willard L. King, *Lincoln's Manager, David Davis* (Cambridge, Mass., 1960), 176.

49   Theodore C. Smith, *Life and Letters of James Abram Garfield* (New Haven, Conn., 1925), 1:155; New York *Tribune*, Feb. 19, 1861; Villard, *Lincoln on Eve*, 96.

50   New York *Tribune*, Feb. 19, 1861; Villard, *Lincoln on Eve*, 91–96.

51   Basler, *Lincoln*, 4:227–30; Baringer, *House Dividing*, 283–85.

52   Baringer, *House Dividing*, 285–87.

53   New York *Herald*, Feb. 21, 1861; New York *Tribune*, Feb. 21, 1861; Basler, *Lincoln*, 4:232–33.

54   Ibid.; Hamlin, *Life of Hamlin*, 387–88; Hunt, *Hamlin*, 143.

55   New York *Tribune*, Feb. 21 and Feb. 22, 1861; Baringer, *House Dividing*, 287–90; Basler, *Lincoln*, 4:233–38.

56   Basler, *Lincoln*, 4:238–39; Norma B. Cuthbert (ed.), *Lincoln and the Baltimore Plot* (San Merino, Cal., 1949), 10.

CHAPTER FIFTEEN: PLUMS AND NUTS

1   Clay to Lincoln, Feb. 6, 1861, AL.

2   Cuthbert, *Baltimore Plot*, 3–5, 23–25, 125–26.

3   Ibid., 25–62, 129; Randall, *Lincoln the President*, 1:288–90.

4   Cuthbert, *Baltimore Plot*, 62–67.

5   Ibid., 77–78, 110, 131–32; Lamon, *Lincoln*, 519–21; Randall, *Lincoln the President*, 1:287.

6   W. G. Snethen to Lincoln, Feb. 15, 1861, AL; A lady to Lincoln, undated, AL; G. W. Hazzard to Lincoln, undated, AL.

7   Basler, *Lincoln*, 4:240–42.

8   Ibid., 4:243–45; Cuthbert, *Baltimore Plot*, 69–85; Lamon, *Lincoln*, 522–27.

9   Cuthbert, *Baltimore Plot*, 81.

10   Ibid., 82, 148–49; Evitts, *Matter of Allegiances*, 174.

11   Evitts, *Matter of Allegiances*, 1–130, 161; George P. Radcliffe, *Governor Thomas H. Hicks of Maryland and the Civil War* (Baltimore, 1901), 11, 15; William C. Wright, *The Secession Movement in the Middle Atlantic States* (Rutherford, N.J., 1973), 27–28.

12   Wright, *Middle Atlantic States*, 21–25.

13   Ibid., 24–35.

14   Ibid., 34, 36; New York *Tribune*, Jan. 16, 1861.

15   Hicks to Crittenden, Jan. 19, 1861, JJC; Wright, *Middle Atlantic States*, 39; Radcliffe, *Hicks*, 21–42, 45–46; H. W. Thomas to Crittenden, Jan. 30, 1861, JJC; Evitts, *Matter of Allegiances*, 163–64; New York *Tribune*, Feb. 16, 1861.

16   New York *Tribune*, Feb. 16, Feb. 18, and Feb. 19, 1861.

17   Cuthbert, *Baltimore Plot*, 133–35; George William Brown, *Baltimore and the Nineteenth of April, 1861* (Baltimore, 1887), 10; New York *Tribune*, Feb. 25, 1861.

18   Cuthbert, *Baltimore Plot*, 133–35; Evitts, *Matter of Allegiances*, 174–75; Lutz, "Schleiden," 210.

19   Cuthbert, *Baltimore Plot*, 82–84; Baringer, *House Dividing*, 295–96.

20   Cuthbert, *Baltimore Plot*, 83–88.

21   Charleston *Mercury*, Feb. 18, 1861; Drake, *Hatton*, 341; Benjamin F. Wade to ?, Feb. 14, 1861, BFW.

22   Nichols, *Disruption*, 474–75; New York *Tribune*, Feb. 13, 1861; Seward, *Seward at Washington*, 505.

23   Nevins, *Emergence of Lincoln*, 2:438.

24   Ibid.; Hamlin, *Life of Hamlin*, 389–90; Baringer, *House Dividing*, 304.

25   Seward, *Seward at Washington*, 511; Baringer, *House Dividing*, 304–05; Klein, *Buchanan*, 401–02.

26   Hamlin, *Life of Hamlin*, 390; Chittenden, *Recollections*, 68–77.

27   Chittenden, *Recollections*, 77.

28   Sherman, *Recollections*, 231; Seward, *Seward at Washington*, 511–12.

29   Seward, *Seward at Washington*, 512–13.

30   Donald, *Sumner*, 383.

31   Charleston *Mercury*, March 1, 1861; New York *Tribune*, Feb. 26, 1861; Seward to Lincoln, Feb. 25, 1861, AL; Baringer, *House Dividing*, 309–10.

32   Baringer, *House Dividing*, 310–12; New York *Tribune*, Feb. 27, 1861.

33   Baringer, *House Dividing*, 313.

34   Ibid., 314–15; Basler, *Lincoln*, 4:246–47.

35   Baringer, *House Dividing*, 319; Johannsen, *Douglas*, 842.

36   Carl Sandburg, *Abraham Lincoln: The War Years* (New York, 1939), 1:94–98; Baringer, *House Dividing*, 315–19; New York *Tribune*, Feb. 28 and March 4, 1861.

37   Sandburg, *War Years*, 1:97; David M. Potter, *Lincoln and His Party in the Secession Crisis* (New Haven, Conn., 1942), 353.

CHAPTER SIXTEEN: THE WAITING GAME

1   Channing, *Crisis of Fear*, 293.

2   Ford, *Henry Adams*, 1:231; Charleston *Mercury*, Feb. 18, 1861; Gunderson, *Old Gentlemen's Convention*, 59.

3   Ford, *Henry Adams*, 1:231; Adams, *Autobiography*, 91; Drake, *Hatton*, 340–43.

4   Nichols, *Disruption*, 449–50, 470–71; Moore, *Buchanan*, 11:125; Klein, *Buchanan*, 399–400; Shanks, *Virginia*, 158.

5   Charleston *Mercury*, Feb. 12, 1861; Klein, *Buchanan*, 397–98.

6   Curtis, *Buchanan*, 2:492–94.

7   Ibid., 2:468–69; King, *Turning on the Light*, 45; *OR*, 1:203.

8   Tyler, *Tyler*, 2:611–12; Robert M. Thompson and Richard Wainwright (eds.), *Confidential Correspondence of Gustavus Vasa Fox* (New York, 1918), 1:3–9; *OR*, 1:169–71.

9   Curtis, *Buchanan*, 2:469–70; Tyler, *Tyler*, 2:613–15; *OR*, 1:177, 179–81, 257; Charleston *Mercury*, Feb. 26, 1861.

10 Keyes, *Fifty Years*, 366; King, *Turning on the Light*, 52–55.

11 Moore, *Buchanan*, 11:150; New York *Tribune*, Feb. 25, 1861.

12 New York *Tribune*, Feb. 23, 1861; Gunderson, *Old Gentlemen's Convention*, 43–51.

13 Gunderson, *Old Gentlemen's Convention*, 51–63.

14 Ibid., 64–80.

15 Ibid., 81–92; Nichols, *Disruption*, 475.

16 Sumner, *Works*, 5:467.

17 *Globe*, 863, Appendix, 135–36.

18 Ibid., 695–96, 939–40, Appendix, 157–58, 270–71.

19 Ibid., Appendix, 169, 172–74.

20 Ibid., 799–800, 836.

21 Nichols, *Disruption*, 466–69.

22 Ibid., 470; *Globe*, 1031–33, 1098, 1230, 1232.

23 *Globe*, 1236; Nichols, *Disruption*, 475–77.

24 Adams, *Autobiography*, 92; *Globe*, 1258–65; Charleston *Mercury*, March 4, 1861.

25 *Globe*, 1281–94.

26 Ibid., 1086, 1088–94, 1243–55, 1267–81, 1295–1300.

27 Colton, "Curtis," 33.

28 Charleston *Mercury*, Feb. 7–12, 1861; Mrs. Thomas Taylor et al., *South Carolina Women in the Confederacy* (Columbia, S.C., 1903), 170; John F. Marszalek (ed.), *The Diary of Miss Emma Holmes 1861–1866* (Baton Rouge, 1979), 8–9 (hereafter cited as Holmes, *Diary*); Edmunds, *Pickens*, 160.

29 New York *Tribune*, Feb. 26, 1861; Carson, *Petigru*, 369–70; Channing, *Crisis of Fear*, 281.

30 New York *Tribune*, March 2, 1861; Richardson, *Secret Service*, 122–24.

31 Starr, *Bohemian Brigade*, 20–21.

32 New York *Tribune*, Feb. 5, 1861.

33 Ibid., Feb. 6, Feb. 8, Feb. 11, and Feb. 12, 1861; Cauthen, *South Carolina Goes to War*, 106.

34 Cauthen, *South Carolina Goes to War*, 107–09; Crawford, *Genesis*, 267; *OR*, 1:254–57.

35 John S. Preston to ?, Feb. 17, 1861, Preston papers, South Caroliniana Library, University of South Carolina.

36 John Echols to ?, Feb. 17, 1861, Echols papers, South Caroliniana Library, University of South Carolina.

37 George H. Reese (ed.), *Proceedings of the Virginia State Convention of 1861* (Richmond, 1965), 1:207–08, 230–31.

38 Shanks, *Virginia*, 158–73; Ruffin, *Diary*, 1:557–58.

39   Charleston *Mercury*, Feb. 19, 1861; Jones, *Heroines of Dixie*, 13–14; Cobb, "Correspondence," 184.

40   Cobb, "Correspondence," 183–84, 234–35; William Davis, *Jefferson Davis*, 311–13.

41   Kelly and Harbison, *American Constitution*, 400–01.

42   William Davis, *Jefferson Davis*, 310–14.

43   Johnston and Browne, *Stephens*, 386–91.

44   Ibid., 386; Chesnut, *Diary*, 10.

45   Chesnut, *Diary*, 8, 10–16.

46   Cobb, "Correspondence," 236–37, 240, 243.

47   *OR*, 1:258.

48   Ibid., 1:258–59.

49   Chesnut, *Diary*, 11.

50   *OR*, 1:169.

51   Crawford, *Genesis*, 204; Johnson and Buel, *Battles and Leaders*, 1:56.

52   Doubleday, *Reminiscences*, 119–23.

53   W. A. Swanberg, *First Blood: The Story of Fort Sumter* (New York, 1957), 207–08.

54   Doubleday, *Reminiscences*, 121; Johnson and Buel, *Battles and Leaders*, 1:54.

55   Doubleday, *Reminiscences*, 122; Johnson and Buel, *Battles and Leaders*, 1:54–60.

56   *OR*, 1:169–85.

57   Ibid., 1:182–83; Crawford, *Genesis*, 273.

58   Anderson to Crittenden, Feb. 19, 1861, JJC; *OR*, 1:187.

59   Anderson to Samuel Cooper, Feb. 28, 1861, AL. The individual estimates prepared by each officer are also in AL.

PART THREE: THE BATTLE OVER FORT SUMTER
CHAPTER SEVENTEEN: LAST GASPS AND FIRST BREATHS

1   Browning to Lincoln, March 26, 1861, AL.

2   *Globe*, 1318–36, 1414–33, Appendix, 301; New York *Tribune*, March 2, March 4, 1861.

3   *Globe*, 1300–18; Nichols, *Disruption*, 477–82; Kirwan, *Crittenden*, 410–21.

4   *Globe*, 1336–61.

5   Ibid., 1361–74.

6   Ibid., 1374–1401; New York *Tribune*, March 5, 1861.

7   *Globe*, 1401–13.

8   Ibid.; Potter, *Impending Crisis*, 551; Stampp, *And the War Came*, 139, 166–67; Knoles, *Crisis of the Union*, 94; New York *Tribune*, March 5, 1861.

9   Piatt, *Memories*, 29–36; Nicolay and Hay, *Lincoln*, 3:373–74; Lamon, *Recollections*, 480–83; Herndon, *Lincoln*, 133, 140–41, 146, 150–55, 189, 219, 231.

10   New York *Tribune*, March 2, 1861; Baringer, *House Dividing*, 320–21.

11   Baringer, *House Dividing*, 327–29; Lamon, *Recollections*, 49–51.

12   Baringer, *House Dividing*, 329–30; Nicolay and Hay, *Lincoln*, 3:370–71; Basler, *Lincoln*, 4:273.

13   Johnson and Buel, *Battles and Leaders*, 1:21, 24-25.

14   Ibid., 1:25; New York *Tribune*, March 4, 1861; Nicolay and Hay, *Lincoln*, 3:324-25.

15   Nicolay and Hay, *Lincoln*, 3:398; Crawford to Robert Toombs, March 3, 1861, Robert Toombs Letterbooks, South Caroliniana Library, University of South Carolina (hereafter cited as RT).

16   Elliott, *Scott*, 695; Keyes, *Fifty Years*, 415; Baringer, *House Dividing*, 331-32.

17   New York *Tribune*, March 5, 1861; Moore, *Buchanan*, 11:156.

18   Sandburg, *War Years*, 1:121.

19   New York *Tribune*, March 5, 1861; Curtis, *Buchanan*, 2:505.

20   Sandburg, *War Years*, 1:122-23; Schurz, *Reminiscences*, 2:219-20.

21   New York *Tribune*, March 5, 1861; Baringer, *House Dividing*, 333-34.

22   Koerner, *Memoirs*, 118; Sandburg, *War Years*, 1:123; Weed, *Autobiography*, 2:337; Elliott, *Scott*, 696.

23   Nicolay and Hay, *Lincoln*, 3:323; Basler, *Lincoln*, 4:271.

24   Sandburg, *War Years*, 1:122; Klein, *Buchanan*, 402.

25   Sandburg, *War Years*, 1:139; Seward, *Seward at Washington*, 517; Keyes, *Fifty Years*, 415.

26   DeLeon, *Belles, Beaux and Brains*, 43-45.

27   Auer, *Antislavery and Disunion*, 409; *OR*, 1:261, 263; Adams, *Autobiography*, 98.

28   Strong, *Diary*, 3:106; New York *Tribune*, March 5, 1861; Davis, *Pennsylvania Politics*, 171-72; Perkins, *Northern Editorials*, 2:623, 645-47.

29   Dwight L. Dumond, *Southern Editorials on Secession* (New York, 1931), 474-75, 478; Sitterson, *Secession Movement in North Carolina*, 232; Reynolds, *Editors Make War*, 191-92; W. C. Wickham to Winfield Scott, March 11, 1861, AL.

30   Auer, *Antislavery and Disunion*, 410; Robert Manson Myers, *Children of Pride* (New Haven, Conn., 1984), 49; Reynolds, *Editors Make War*, 190.

31   Cobb, "Correspondence," 252-53; Chesnut, *Diary*, 23; New York *Tribune*, March 5 and March 12, 1861; Oliphant and Eaves, *Simms*, 4:344; Holmes, *Diary*, 11; Carson, *Petigru*, 373.

32   The entire speech is in Basler, *Lincoln*, 4:262-71.

33   Charleston *Mercury*, March 5, 1861.

34   Seward to Lincoln, March 5, 1861, AL; Chase to Lincoln, March 6, 1861, AL; Seward, *Seward at Washington*, 518; Van Deusen, *Seward*, 253.

35   New York *Tribune*, March 1, 1861; Bates, "Diary," 177.

36   Moore, *Buchanan*, 11:156, 159.

37   Holt to Lincoln, March 5, 1861, AL. The letter can also be found in Moore, *Buchanan*, 11:157-58.

38   Crawford, *Genesis*, 285; Bancroft, *Seward*, 2:125; Curtis, *Buchanan*, 2:529; Basler, *Lincoln*, 4:277.

39   Scott to Seward, March 3, 1861, AL.

40   Seward to Lincoln, March 4, 1861, AL; Scott to Lincoln, March 5, 1861, AL.

41   Howard K. Beale (ed.), *The Diary of Gideon Welles* (New York, 1960), 1:3-5 (hereafter cited as Welles, *Diary*).

CHAPTER EIGHTEEN: UNEASY ARRANGEMENTS

1 Ruffin, *Diary*, 1:567–69.

2 Cobb, "Correspondence," 252–53; Chesnut, *Diary*, 21–23.

3 Chesnut, *Diary*, 20–22.

4 Horace Greeley, *The American Conflict: A History of the Great Rebellion* (Hartford, 1864), 1:417. Italics are in the original.

5 Cobb, "Correspondence," 256–57; William Davis, *Jefferson Davis*, 314–21.

6 Cobb, "Correspondence," 254–55; Allan Nevins, *The War for the Union* (New York, 1959), 1:24.

7 Chesnut, *Diary*, 25; Martin Crawford to Toombs, March 6, 1861, RT; Crawford and Forsyth to Toombs, March 8, 1861, RT; Nicolay and Hay, *Lincoln*, 3:398–400.

8 New York *Herald*, March 10, 1861; *OR*, 1:273; Chesnut, *Diary*, 30–35.

9 Van Deusen, *Seward*, 268–69.

10 Ibid., 30–37, 265–68.

11 Ibid., 259, 269–70; Ford, *Henry Adams*, 1:215; Nevins, *War for the Union*, 1:21.

12 Crofts, *Reluctant Confederates*, 267–69; Crawford to Toombs, March 6, 1861, RT.

13 Bancroft, *Seward*, 2:537.

14 Seward, *Seward at Washington*, 519.

15 Ibid., Seward to Lincoln, March 5 and March 8, 1861, AL; Welles, *Diary*, 1:6–8.

16 Welles, *Diary*, 1:6–7; Bancroft, *Seward*, 2:95.

17 Welles, *Diary*, 1:4–6; Ezra J. Warner, *Generals in Gray* (Baton Rouge, 1959), 62–63; New York *Tribune*, March 3, 1861; Wright, *Middle Atlantic States*, 53–54.

18 Bates, "Diary," 177; Adams, *Autobiography*, 99–100; Nicolay and Hay, *Lincoln*, 3:379–81; Basler, *Lincoln*, 4:279.

19 New York *Tribune*, March 11 and March 12, 1861; Scott to Lincoln, March 11, 1861, AL.

20 *OR*, 1:197; Charleston *Mercury*, March 12, 1861; New York *Tribune*, March 12, 1861.

21 Lincoln to Seward, March 11, 1861, AL; Seward to Lincoln, March 11, 1861, AL; Corwin to Lincoln, March 13, 1861, AL.

22 Bates, "Diary," 176; New York *Tribune*, March 12, 1861; Seward, *Seward at Washington*, 518, 523, 530; Moore, *Buchanan*, 11:164, 169; Hilen, *Longfellow*, 4:220.

23 New York *Tribune*, March 19, 1861; Fessenden, *Life and Public Services*, 1:127; Sandburg, *War Years*, 1:163–65.

24 *Globe*, 1496.

25 Crawford, *Genesis*, 314–25; Crawford and Forsyth to Seward, March 8, 1861, RT; Bancroft, *Seward*, 2:107–13, 542–44.

26 Crawford and Forsyth to Seward, March 8, 1861, RT; "Memorandum A," n.d., RT; Nevins, *War for the Union*, 1:40; Seward to Lincoln, March 9, 1861, AL.

27 Forsyth and Crawford to Seward, March 12, 1861, RT; Forsyth and Crawford to Toombs, March 12, 1861, RT; J. T. Pickett Memorandum, March 14, 1861, RT.

28 Crawford, *Genesis*, 324–25; Seward, *Seward at Washington*, 530–31; Nevins,

War for the Union, 1:40–41; Van Deusen, *Seward*, 278; Forsyth and Crawford to Toombs, March 15, 1861, RT.

29 New York *Tribune*, March 13, 1861; New York *Herald*, March 12 and March 13, 1861; Moore, *Buchanan*, 11:167–69; *OR*, 1:275.

30 *Globe*, 1436–65.

31 Johanssen, *Douglas*, 848–51.

32 Nichols, *Disruption*, 493; *Globe*, 1441–42.

33 Russell, *Diary*, 1:63; Smith, *Blair Family*, 2:2.

34 Welles, *Diary*, 1:8, 12–14; Frank Blair, Sr., to Montgomery Blair, March 12, 1861, AL. Most sources put this scene several days later, after the cabinet debated the question. See for example Smith, *Blair Family*, 2:9–10; Nevins, *War for the Union*, 1:47–48; Crawford, *Genesis*, 364.

35 Crawford, *Genesis*, 347; Nicolay and Hay, *Lincoln*, 3:384–85; Basler, *Lincoln*, 4:284–85.

36 Seward to Lincoln, March 15, 1861, AL. The letter is reproduced in full, with minor differences, in Crawford, *Genesis*, 348–53.

37 Bates to Lincoln, March 15, 1861, AL; Cameron to Lincoln, March 16, 1861, AL; Smith to Lincoln, March 16, 1861, AL; Welles to Lincoln, March 15, 1861, AL.

38 Blair to Lincoln, March 15, 1861, AL; Chase to Lincoln, March 16, 1861, AL.

39 *OR*, 1:198–201.

40 Doubleday, *Reminiscences*, 130; *OR*, 1:208–09; Thompson and Wainwright, *Fox*, 1:9–10.

41 Basler, *Lincoln*, 4:289–90.

42 *OR*, 1:360.

43 Henry G. Connor, *John Archibald Campbell* (Boston, 1920), 122–26. Campbell left the only eyewitness account of this controversial episode. For its limitations, see Potter, *Impending Crisis*, 573.

44 *OR*, 1:273–75; Charleston *Mercury*, March 12, 1861.

45 New York *Tribune*, March 8, 1861; Holmes, *Diary*, 15; Kibler, *Perry*, 348.

46 *OR*, 1:260–61; Ruffin, *Diary*, 1:560; Holmes, *Diary*, 11; DuBose Heyward and Herbert R. Sass, *Fort Sumter* (New York, 1932), 4–5.

47 T. Harry Williams, *P. G. T. Beauregard: Napoleon in Gray* (Baton Rouge, 1955), 34–54.

48 *OR*, 1:264–74.

49 Ibid., 1:25–26, 272; Ruffin, *Diary*, 1:563; New York *Tribune*, March 12, March 15, and March 19, 1861.

50 *OR*, 1:272, 274–75.

51 New York *Tribune*, March 13, 1861.

52 Ibid., March 12, 1861.

CHAPTER NINETEEN: DECISIONS AND DELUSIONS

1 Curtis, *Buchanan*, 2:495–96.

2 *OR*, 1:188–92.

3 Ibid., 1:192–96, 273; New York *Tribune*, March 16, 1861; Doubleday, *Reminiscences*, 129–30.

4 *OR*, 1:195–96; Charleston *Mercury*, March 12, 1861; Charleston *Courier*, March 13, 1861.

5 Crawford, *Genesis*, 290–91. Anderson wrote this letter on April 5.

6 Strong, *Diary*, 3:112.

7 Moore, *Buchanan*, 11:174–75.

8 New York *Tribune*, March 19, 1861; Blair to Lincoln, March 18, 1861, AL; Chase to Lincoln, March 18 and 21, 1861, AL; Seward to Lincoln, March 18, 1861, AL; Bates to Lincoln, March 21, 1861, AL; A. Watson to Lincoln, March 20, 1861, AL; I.N. Arnold to Lincoln, March 21, 1861, AL.

9 New York *Tribune*, March 18 and March 20, 1861; Buenger, *Secession and Union in Texas*, 176; Stampp, *And the War Came*, 275–76.

10 Basler, *Lincoln*, 4:290, 292–93; Nicolay and Hay, *Lincoln*, 3:390–92; Sandburg, *War Years*, 1:190–92.

11 Holmes, *Diary*, 17, 19; Arney R. Childs (ed.), *The Private Journal of Henry William Ravenel* (Columbia, S.C., 1947), 56; Oliphant and Eaves, *Simms*, 4:350.

12 New York *Tribune*, March 22, 1861; Swanberg, *First Blood*, 202, 247.

13 Crawford, *Genesis*, 369–72; Nicolay and Hay, *Lincoln*, 3:389–90; Ari Hoogenboom, "Gustavus Fox and the Relief of Fort Sumter," *Civil War History* (1963), 9:385–87. Hoogenboom argues that neither Pickens nor Beauregard knew who Fox was and did not know he was the author of the plan to relieve Sumter.

14 Crawford, *Genesis*, 372.

15 *OR*, 1:210–11.

16 Ibid., 1:277; Crawford, Roman, and Forsyth to Toombs, March 20, 1861, RT.

17 Hurlbut to Lincoln, March 27, 1861, AL; Nicolay and Hay, *Lincoln*, 3:390–92; Sandburg, *War Years*, 1:190–92. Lamon's own account in his *Recollections*, 69–79, is so inflated in his own favor and contradictory to Hurlbut's contemporary account to Lincoln as to be virtually useless as a source for his mission.

18 New York *Tribune*, March 30, 1861.

19 Crawford, *Genesis*, 373–74; *OR*, 1:221–22, 281–82; New York *Tribune*, March 30, 1861.

20 Nevins, *War for the Union*, 1:54; New York *Tribune*, March 28, 1861; Susan L. Burn to Henry, March 27, 1861, HCB.

21 Commissioners to Toombs, March 20 and March 22, 1861, RT; Campbell, "Papers," 33. Copies of Campbell's statements are also in RT. All other sources begin with Campbell's version, some believing it more than others. See, for example, Bancroft, *Seward*, 2:116–17, Potter, *Impending Crisis*, 573, and Nevins, *War for the Union*, 1:51.

22 Campbell, "Papers," 33–34; Crawford, *Genesis*, 331–32; Bancroft, *Seward*, 2:117.

23 Roman to Toombs, March 25, 1861, RT; Bancroft, *Seward*, 2:107, 117.

24 David M. Potter, *Lincoln and His Party in the Secession Crisis* (New Haven, Conn., 1944), 370; *Globe*, 1498; Basler, *Lincoln*, 4:299.

25 *Globe*, 1501–12; Nichols, *Disruption*, 494–98.

26 *Globe*, 1519–23.

27 Ibid., 1498.

28 Commissioners to Toombs, March 22, 1861, RT.

29 Chesnut, *Diary*, 47.

30 Ibid., 40–47.

31   Ibid., 48–51.

32   Chesnut, *Diary*, 47, 49; Bonham to William Porcher Miles, March 28, 1861, MB.

33   Caroline Gilman to her children, March 31, 1861, CHG.

34   *OR*, 1:228.

CHAPTER TWENTY: THE GREAT DIVIDE

1   Van Deusen, *Seward*, 281.

2   Russell, *Diary*, 1:47–67.

3   Ibid., 1:74–75.

4   Ibid., 1:12, 58.

5   New York *Tribune*, March 28, 1861; Bancroft, *Seward*, 2:123.

6   Hurlbut to Lincoln, March 27, 1861, AL.

7   Keyes, *Fifty Years*, 377–79. No other source mentions that Scott saw Lincoln *before* the state dinner that evening, but the details and sequence of events following support Keyes's version. It explains, among other things, why Scott was at the White House but did not come into dinner later.

8   Nevins, *War for the Union*, 1:54; Marvin R. Cain, *Lincoln's Attorney General: Edward Bates of Missouri* (Columbia, Mo., 1965), 133; Chase to Lincoln, undated, AL; *OR*, 1:200–01; Richard N. Current, *Lincoln and the First Shot* (Philadelphia, 1963), 76.

9   Randall, *Lincoln the President*, 1:330–31; Basler, *Lincoln*, 4:431.

10   Stampp, *And the War Came*, 266–67.

11   Koerner to Lincoln, March 28, 1861, AL; *Globe*, 1519.

12   Stampp, *And the War Came*, 212; Nevins, *War for the Union*, 1:56–57; Kenneth M. Stampp, *The Imperiled Union* (New York, 1980), 180–81; *Globe*, 1247.

13   *Globe*, Appendix, 39–40.

14   Stampp, *And the War Came*, 204–62.

15   Nicolay and Hay, *Lincoln*, 3:394–95; Crawford, *Genesis*, 365.

16   Although no source mentions these specific options, they are clearly reflected in the responses from the cabinet members.

17   Nevins, *War for the Union*, 1:55. The written statements are all in AL. Published versions can be found in Nicolay and Hay, *Lincoln*, 3:430–32.

18   Nicolay and Hay, *Lincoln*, 3:433.

19   *OR*, 1:226–27.

20   Nevins, *War for the Union*, 1:58.

21   Ibid., 1:60; Campbell, "Papers," 34; Seward, *Seward at Washington*, 534, 538–39; M. C. Meigs, "General M. C. Meigs on the Civil War," *American Historical Review* (1920–21), 26:299–300; Nicolay and Hay, *Lincoln*, 3:434–35; Russell F. Weigley, *Quartermaster General of the Union Army: A biography of Montgomery C. Meigs* (New York, 1959), 115–30.

22   Meigs, "Meigs on Civil War," 300; Weigley, *Meigs*, 131–39.

23   Charleston *Mercury*, April 3, 1861.

24   Seward, *Seward at Washington*, 534.

25   Nicolay and Hay, *Lincoln*, 3:394–95; Mearns, *Lincoln Papers*, 508–09; *ORN*, 4:74, 77, 90, 92; Meigs, "Meigs on Civil War," 300.

26   Keyes, *Fifty Years*, 374–84.

27   Ibid., 381–82; Meigs, "Meigs on Civil War," 300; Weigley, *Meigs*, 139–43; Crawford, *Genesis*, 407–10.

28   New York *Tribune*, April 1, 1861.

29   Ibid.; Chandler to Lincoln, March 30, 1861, AL.

30   Van Deusen, *Seward*, 281.

31   Thompson and Wainwright, *Fox*, 1:12–14; Hoogenboom, "Fox and Sumter," 388–89.

32   Aspinwall to Lincoln, March 31, 1861, AL.

33   Potter, *Lincoln and His Party*, 358.

34   *OR*, 1:205–11.

35   *OR*, 1:212–28; Foster to Totten, March 24, 1861, AL.

36   Doubleday to his wife, March 27 and March 29, 1861, AL.

37   Russell, *Diary*, 1:73–80.

CHAPTER TWENTY-ONE: ENDS WITHOUT MEANS

1   Schurz to Lincoln, April 5, 1861, AL.

2   *OR*, 1:283–85; Crawford and Roman to Toombs, April 1 and April 2, 1861, RT; Roman to Toombs, March 29, 1861, RT.

3   Campbell, "Papers," 34–35.

4   Nicolay and Hay, *Lincoln*, 3:411–12, 4:33.

5   Commissioners to Toombs, April 3, 1861, RT; Lynda Lasswell Crist and Mary Seaton Dix (eds.), *The Papers of Jefferson Davis* (Baton Rouge, 1992), 7:88–89.

6   Nicolay and Hay, *Lincoln*, 3:413, 4:32; Commissioners to Toombs, April 3, April 4, and April 5, 1861, RT; Charleston *Mercury*, April 2, April 4, and April 6, 1861; Current, *First Shot*, 129; *OR*, 1:286–88.

7   William Davis, *Jefferson Davis*, 322; Davis, *Rise and Fall*, 1:275; Crist and Dix, *Davis*, 7:92.

8   Grady McWhiney, "The Confederacy's First Shot," *Civil War History* (1968), 14:10–11; Crist and Dix, *Davis*, 7:85–86.

9   *OR*, 1:230–32.

10   Doubleday to his wife, April 2, 1861, AL.

11   *OR*, 1:236–39; Crawford, *Genesis*, 375–77. Crawford, Davis, Doubleday, Foster, and Hall favored firing; Meade, Seymour, and Snyder advised delay.

12   *OR*, 1:236–42; Crawford, *Genesis*, 376–80.

13   *OR*, 1:241.

14   Ibid., 1:245–47, 289–90; Crawford, *Genesis*, 380–81.

15   Chesnut, *Diary*, 51–55; Wright, *Southern Girl*, 35; Charleston *Mercury*, April 4, 1861; New York *Tribune*, April 9, 1861.

16   *Convention Journal*, 243–78.

17   Holmes, *Diary*, 22–23; Chesnut, *Diary*, 55; New York *Tribune*, April 10, 1861.

18   Ruffin, *Diary*, 1:578–79; *ORN*, 4:260.

19   Seward, *Seward at Washington*, 534–35; Seward to Lincoln, April 1, 1861, AL.

20   Adams, *Autobiography*, 88–89.

21 Nevins, *War for the Union*, 1:62–63; Bancroft, *Seward*, 2:134–35. "The attempt to acquire Cuba was a policy of long standing, more or less prominent in the annals of the country from the first administration of George Washington." Fite, *Presidential Campaign*, 141.

22 Basler, *Lincoln*, 4:316–18.

23 Seward, *Seward at Washington*, 535.

24 Scott to Lincoln, April 1, 1861, AL; *ORN*, 4:100–02.

25 Nicolay and Hay, *Lincoln*, 3:437–38; Meigs, "Meigs on Civil War," 300–01; Keyes, *Fifty Years*, 385; Crawford, *Genesis*, 409. Brown was promoted to brevet colonel for this mission.

26 Meigs to Seward, n.d., AL; David D. Porter, *Incidents and Anecdotes of the Civil War* (New York, 1885), 13–16; Crawford, *Genesis*, 408–10; Anderson, *Conspiracies*, 44–48. Porter's account of this affair is greatly embellished in his own favor.

27 *ORN*, 4:108–09; Meigs, "Meigs on Civil War," 301; Crawford, *Genesis*, 411–12; Basler, *Lincoln*, 4:320. Meigs gave receipt for the funds and afterward returned nearly six thousand dollars.

28 *ORN*, 4:227–28; Basler, *Lincoln*, 4:320; Meigs, "Meigs on Civil War," 301; Crawford, *Genesis*, 405, 412; Keyes, *Fifty Years*, 387–88; Thompson and Wainwright, *Fox*, 1:16.

29 *ORN*, 4:227, 229; Welles, *Diary*, 1:16.

30 Niven, *Welles*, 328–29.

31 Welles, *Diary*, 1:16–21; Niven, *Welles*, 331.

32 Niven, *Welles*, 330–31.

33 *ORN*, 4:229–32; Thompson and Wainwright, *Fox*, 1:15–17.

34 Porter, *Incidents and Anecdotes*, 17–20; Crawford, *Genesis*, 412–13; Niven, *Welles*, 332.

35 Meigs, "Meigs on Civil War," 301; *ORN*, 4:232, 234.

36 Keyes, *Fifty Years*, 388–89; Thompson and Wainwright, *Fox*, 1:19; *ORN*, 4:248.

37 Chase to Lincoln, April 2, 1861, AL; J.H. Jordan to Lincoln, April 4, 1861, AL; Carl Schurz to Lincoln, April 5, 1861, AL; New York *Tribune*, April 3, 1861.

38 Potter, *Lincoln and His Party*, 354–58; Crofts, *Reluctant Confederates*, 282, 301–07; Allan B. Magruder, "A Piece of Secret History: President Lincoln and the Virginia Convention of 1861," *Atlantic Monthly* (1875), 35:438–39.

39 For different versions of this tangled episode, see Potter, *Lincoln and His Party*, 354–58; Crofts, *Reluctant Confederates*, 282, 301–07; Current, *First Shot*, 94–97; W. L. Hall, "Lincoln's Interview with John B. Baldwin," *South Atlantic Quarterly* (1914), 13:260–69; Magruder, "Piece of History," 438–45; John Minor Botts, *The Great Rebellion: Its Secret History, Rise, Progress and Disastrous Failure* (New York, 1866), 194–202.

40 Baldwin's version of this meeting is in his pamphlet *Interview Between President Lincoln and Col. John B. Baldwin, April 4th, 1861: Statements and Evidence* (Staunton, Va., 1866), which includes his testimony given in U.S. Congress, Joint Committee on Reconstruction, *Report of the Joint Committee on Reconstruction*, 39th Cong., 1st Sess. (Washington, D.C., 1866), pt. 2, 69–146.

41 Botts apparently saw Lincoln on both April 5 and April 7. See the discussion

in Crofts, *Reluctant Confederates*, 438–39. Virtually every discussion of the disputed points tends to assume that Lincoln always told the truth. Crofts is one of the few historians willing to concede that Lincoln was not above stretching the truth when necessary.

42   Shanks, *Virginia*, 190; *OR*, 1:235.

43   *OR*, 1:235–37; Thompson and Wainwright, *Fox*, 1:20–21; Nicolay and Hay, *Lincoln*, 4:28.

44   Thompson and Wainwright, *Fox*, 1:12; *ORN*, 4:234–36.

45   *ORN*, 4:236–37; Niven, *Welles*, 332–33.

46   Welles, *Diary*, 1:22–23.

CHAPTER TWENTY-TWO: APRIL FOOLS

1   Eppes, *Eventful Years*, 151.

2   Russell, *Diary*, 1:81–91.

3   Ibid., 1:92–97.

4   Meigs, "Meigs on Civil War," 301–02; Niven, *Welles*, 333–34; *ORN*, 4:111–12.

5   Welles, *Diary*, 1:23–25; Niven, *Welles*, 334–35; Nicolay and Hay, *Lincoln*, 4:3–7.

6   *ORN*, 4:112, 237.

7   Meigs, "Meigs on Civil War," 302; Niven, *Welles*, 333.

8   *ORN*, 4:237–40; Porter, *Incidents and Anecdotes*, 21–22.

9   *ORN*, 4:112.

10   Meigs, "Meigs on Civil War," 302; Keyes, *Fifty Years*, 389–93; Weigley, *Meigs*, 78–112.

11   Dubois to Lincoln, April 6, 1861, AL; Koerner to Lincoln, April 5, 1861, AL; Browning to Lincoln, April 9, 1861, AL; Basler, *Lincoln*, 4:303; Stuart to Lincoln, April 3, 1861, AL.

12   Nicolay and Hay, *Lincoln*, 4:31–32; Current, *First Shot*, 107.

13   Nicolay and Hay, *Lincoln*, 4:33–35; *OR*, 1:235–37.

14   Basler, *Lincoln*, 4:323–24.

15   Potter, *Impending Crisis*, 578–79.

16   Welles, *Diary*, 1:29–30; Scott to Lincoln, April 6, 1861, AL; *ORN*, 4:109–10.

17   *ORN*, 4:110–11; Welles, *Diary*, 1:30–31.

18   New York *Tribune*, April 8, 1861. The dispatch is dated April 7.

19   Charleston *Mercury*, April 10, 1861; Crawford, Forsyth, and Roman to Toombs, April 5 and April 6, 1861, RT; Campbell, "Papers," 35, 38–39. The *Mercury* dispatch is dated April 7.

20   Campbell memorandum and statement, April 7, 1861, RT; Crawford, Roman, and Forsyth to Toombs, April 7, 1861, RT; Pickett memorandum, April 7, 1861, RT.

21   Russell, *Diary*, 1:99–100; Botts, *Great Rebellion*, 194–203.

22   Stone to Seward, April 5, 1861, AL.

23   Current, *First Shot*, 113–14; Scott to Lincoln, April 3, 1861, AL.

24   Scott to Lincoln, April 5, April 8, April 9, and April 10, 1861, AL.

25   L. Tilmon to Lincoln, April 8, 1861, AL; Basler, *Lincoln*, 4:324; Russell, *Diary*, 1:100; William B. Hesseltine, *Lincoln and the War Governors* (New York, 1955), 144.

26 New York *Tribune*, April 9, 1861.

27 Forsyth, Roman, and Crawford to Pickens, April 8, 1861, RT; Crawford to Beauregard, April 8, 1861, RT; Forsyth, Roman, and Crawford to Toombs, April 8, 1861, RT; Forsyth, Roman, and Crawford to Seward, April 9, 1861, RT; Campbell, "Papers," 38–41.

28 Russell, *Diary*, 1:100–03.

29 Chesnut, *Diary*, 55–58.

30 Ruffin, *Diary*, 1:582–83.

31 Charleston *Mercury*, April 9, 1861; *ORN*, 4:258; New York *Tribune*, April 10, 1861; *OR*, 1:289, 291.

32 *OR*, 1:251–52; Chew to Lincoln, April 8, 1861, AL.

33 Holmes, *Diary*, 23; Ruffin, *Diary*, 1:582–83.

34 *OR*, 1:248, 250; Crawford, *Genesis*, 383–85.

35 *OR*, 1:294.

36 Ibid., 1:292–93; Crist and Dix, *Davis*, 7:99; Williams, *Beauregard*, 50.

37 *OR*, 1:292–93; Pickens to Bonham, April 8, 1861 (two letters), MB; Charleston *Mercury*, April 9, 1861.

38 *Convention Journal*, 380–81; *OR*, 1:288–89; Chesnut, *Diary*, 57; Holmes, *Diary*, 24; Ruffin, *Diary*, 1:583–84.

39 New York *Tribune*, April 11, 1861; Holmes, *Diary*, 24–25; Charleston *Courier*, April 11, 1861.

40 Wright, *Southern Girl*, 35–36; Crist and Dix, *Davis*, 7:100.

41 *ORN*, 4:259; *OR*, 289–91.

42 William Y. Thompson, *Robert Toombs of Georgia* (Baton Rouge, 1966), 168.

43 Charleston *Mercury*, April 13, 1861; *OR*, 1:297.

44 *OR*, 1:297.

45 Ibid., 1:16–17; Crawford, *Genesis*, 383; Doubleday, *Reminiscences*, 140.

46 Crawford, *Genesis*, 398–99; *OR*, 1:17–18.

47 Diary of Samuel W. Crawford, April 11, 1861, Samuel W. Crawford papers, Library of Congress.

48 *OR*, 1:59, 250.

49 Ibid., 1:13, 30, 59; Crawford, *Genesis*, 423.

50 Charleston *Courier*, April 13, 1861; Crawford, *Genesis*, 424.

51 Johnson and Buel, *Battles and Leaders*, 1:75, 82.

52 Ibid., 1:13–14, 30, 300–01; *OR*, 1:13, 59; Williams, *Beauregard*, 57; Crawford, *Diary*, April 11, 1861.

53 Chesnut, *Diary*, 58–59.

54 *OR*, 1:49.

CHAPTER TWENTY-THREE: THE GOOD FIGHT

1 Childs, *Ravenel*, 67.

2 Starr, *Bohemian Brigade*, 28–29; Weed, *Autobiography*, 2:327.

3 Russell, *Diary*, 1:103; *ORN*, 4:260; Crofts, *Reluctant Confederates*, 310–11; J. N. Martin to Wallach, April 9, 1861, AL; Scott to Lincoln, April 10, 1861, AL; New York *Tribune*, April 11, 1861.

4   Scott to Lincoln, April 10 and April 11, 1861, AL; New York *Tribune*, April 11, 1861; Charleston *Mercury*, April 11, 1861; Curtis, *Buchanan*, 2:539–40.

5   Welles, *Diary*, 1:32–35.

6   *ORN*, 4:243; Scott to Lincoln, April 10, 1861, AL.

7   New York *World*, April 23, 1861; *ORN*, 4:244, 249, 253–54; Starr, *Bohemian Brigade*, 28–29; Thompson and Wainwright, *Fox*, 1:31–32.

8   *ORN*, 4:136–37.

9   Ibid., 4:135–37.

10   Ibid., 4:115–24, 135–38; Nicolay and Hay, *Lincoln*, 4:12–17; Welles, *Diary*, 1:31.

11   Russell, *Diary*, 1:105–15.

12   Holmes, *Diary*, 25; Ruffin, *Diary*, 1:585–86; New York *Tribune*, April 12, 1861; S. R. Gist to Bonham, April 11, 1861, MB; Caroline Gilman to her children, April 11, 1861, CHG; *OR*, 1:44.

13   Charleston *Mercury*, April 11, 1861.

14   Crawford, *Genesis*, 425; *OR*, 1:14, 60.

15   Randall, *Lincoln the President*, 1:341; Johnson and Buel, *Battles and Leaders*, 1:75–76, 82.

16   Crawford, *Genesis*, 426; Doubleday, *Reminiscences*, 142.

17   *OR*, 1:60; Johnson and Buel, *Battles and Leaders*, 1:76.

18   *OR*, 1:18, 39–40, 44, 54; Ruffin, *Diary*, 1:588–89; Crawford, *Genesis*, 427.

19   *OR*, 1:18–19, 39–40.

20   Chesnut, *Diary*, 59.

21   Childs, *Ravenel*, 61; Holmes, *Diary*, 25–26; Gilman to her children, April 16, 1861, CHG. The undated sheet with the gun count is in CHG.

22   Chesnut, *Diary*, 58–59.

23   Starr, *Bohemian Brigade*, 28–29.

24   Charleston *Mercury*, April 12, 1861.

25   Johnson and Buel, *Battles and Leaders*, 1:65–70; *OR*, 1:18–21; Crawford, *Genesis*, 429–33; Doubleday, *Reminiscences*, 143–49.

26   Doubleday, *Reminiscences*, 161–62; Johnson and Buel, *Battles and Leaders*, 1:68.

27   *ORN*, 4:244, 248–50; Thompson and Wainwright, *Fox*, 1:32–33; New York *World*, April 23, 1861.

28   *ORN*, 4:249–50, 254–55; Thompson and Wainwright, *Fox*, 1:33; Hoogenboom, "Fox and Sumter," 394–96.

29   *ORN*, 4:250–54.

30   *OR*, 1:21–25; Crawford, *Genesis*, 430, 434–46; Johnson and Buel, *Battles and Leaders*, 1:71–73; New York *Tribune*, April 13, 1861.

31   Chesnut, *Diary*, 36; Russell, *Diary*, 1:155.

32   *OR*, 1:23–24, 38, 61, 63–65; Johnson and Buel, *Battles and Leaders*, 1:72–73, 78–79, 82–83; Crawford, *Genesis*, 439–42.

33   *OR*, 1:23–24, 29, 32–33, 62–67, 308–09; Johnson and Buel, *Battles and Leaders*, 1:73, 78–79, 82–83; Crawford, *Genesis*, 441–42.

34   Crawford, *Genesis*, 443–46; Holmes, *Diary*, 28–29; Thompson and Wainwright, *Fox*, 1:33–34.

35 Thompson and Wainwright, *Fox*, 1:34; *ORN*, 1:243–44, 252, 254; New York *World*, April 23, 1861.

36 Holmes, *Diary*, 26–27; Chesnut, *Diary*, 60; New York *Tribune*, April 13 and April 15, 1861; Ruffin, *Diary*, 1:604–05; Reese, *Proceedings*, 3:730.

37 New York *World*, April 23, 1861; Gilman to her children, April 16, 1861, CHG; Childs, *Ravenel*, 63.

38 Charleston *Mercury*, April 15, 1861.

39 Crawford, *Genesis*, 446–47; Doubleday, *Reminiscences*, 171–72; *OR*, 1:24; Ruffin, *Diary*, 1:598–99.

40 Carson, *Petigru*, 378.

41 Ruffin, *Diary*, 1:598–601; Charleston *Mercury*, April 15 and April 16, 1861.

42 Chesnut, *Diary*, 60–61; Holmes, *Diary*, 29–30.

43 Charleston *Mercury*, April 16, 1861; Edmunds, *Pickens*, 163.

44 Carson, *Petigru*, 378.

EPILOGUE: THE PRICE OF PRIDE

1 Russell, *Diary*, 1:116–98.

2 New York *Tribune*, April 9, 1861.

3 Basler, *Lincoln*, 4:331–32; Ruffin, *Diary*, 1:607.

4 Holmes, *Diary*, 33, 36–37.

5 Woodward, *Mary Chesnut's Civil War*, 693; O'Brien and Moltke-Hansen, *Ante-bellum Charleston*, 308–09.

6 Paul Hamilton Hayne, "Ante-Bellum Charleston," *Southern Bivouac* (November 1885), 328; Carson, *Petigru*, 379.

7 Hankinson, *Russell*, 160–61.

Selected Bibliography

Adams, Charles Francis Jr., *Charles Francis Adams, 1835–1915, An Autobiography* (Boston, 1916).

Adams, Henry, *The Education of Henry Adams* (Boston, 1961).

——, *Letters of Henry Adams, 1858–1891*, ed. Worthington C. Ford (Boston, 1930), 2 vols.

——, "The Great Secession Winter of 1860–61," *Massachusetts Historical Society Proceedings* (1910), 43:656–87.

Anderson, T. M., *The Political Conspiracies Preceding the Rebellion, or the True Stories of Sumter and Pickens* (New York, 1882).

Andrews, J. Cutler, *The North Reports the Civil War* (Pittsburgh, 1955).

——, *The South Reports the Civil War* (Princeton, N.J., 1970).

Ash, Steven V., *Middle Tennessee Society Transformed, 1860–1870* (Baton Rouge, La., 1988).

Auchampaugh, Philip G., *James Buchanan and His Cabinet on the Eve of Secession* (Lancaster, Pa., 1926).

Auer, J. Jeffery (ed.), *Antislavery and Disunion, 1858–1861: Studies in the Rhetoric of Compromise and Conflict* (New York, 1963).

Bagby, George W., *John M. Daniel's Latch-Key* (Lynchburg, Va., 1868).

Bancroft, Frederic, *The Life of William Seward* (New York, 1900), 2 vols.

Banner, James M. Jr., "The Problem of South Carolina," in Stanley Elkins and Eric McKitrick (eds.), *The Hofstadter Aegis* (New York, 1974), 60–93.

Baringer, William E., *A House Dividing: Lincoln As President Elect* (Springfield, Ill., 1945).

Barnes, Thurlow Weed, *Memoir of Thurlow Weed* (Boston, 1884).

Barney, William L., *The Secessionist Impulse* (Princeton, N.J., 1974).

Bates, Edward, "The Diary of Edward Bates, 1859–1866," ed. Howard K. Beale, *American Historical Association Annual Report*, 1930, IV (Washington, D.C., 1933).

Bates, William M., "The Last Stand for Union in Georgia," *Georgia Review* (1953), 7:455–67.

Black, Chauncey F., *Essays and Speeches of Jeremiah S. Black* (New York, 1886).

Blaine, James G., *Twenty Years in Congress* (Norwich, Conn., 1884), 2 vols.

Boggs, Marion A. (ed.), *The Alexander Letters* (Athens, Ga., 1980).

Bonham, Milledge L. Jr., "New York and the Election of 1860," *New York History* (1934), 32:124–43.

Botts, John Minor, *The Great Rebellion: Its Secret History, Rise, Progress, and Disastrous Failure* (New York, 1866).

Boyd, William K., "North Carolina on the Eve of Secession," *American Historical Association Annual Report for 1910* (Washington, D.C., 1912), 165-78.

Bradley, Erwin Stanley, *Simon Cameron, Lincoln's Secretary of War* (Philadelphia, 1966).

Brantley, William, "Alabama Secedes," *Alabama Review* (1954), 7:165-85.

Brodie, Fawn M., *Thaddeus Stevens: The Scourge of the South* (New York, 1959).

Brooks, Noah, *Washington in Lincoln's Time* (New York, 1895).

Brooks, U. R., *The South Carolina Bench and Bar* (Columbia, S.C., 1908).

Brown, George William, *Baltimore and the Nineteenth of April, 1861* (Baltimore, 1887).

Browning, Orville Hickman, *The Diary of Orville Hickman Browning*, ed. Theodore C. Pease and James G. Randall (Springfield, Ill., 1927-1933), 2 vols.

Brownlow, W. G., *Sketches of the Rise, Progress, and Decline of Secession* (Philadelphia, 1862).

Bryan, Conn, "The Secession of Georgia," *Georgia Historical Quarterly* (1947), 31:89-111.

[Buchanan, James], *Mr. Buchanan's Administration on the Eve of the Rebellion* (New York, 1866).

Buchanan, James, *The Works of James Buchanan*, ed. John Bassett Moore (Philadelphia, 1908-1911), 12 vols.

Buenger, Walter L., *Secession and Union in Texas* (Austin, Tex., 1984).

Burgess, John W., *The Civil War and the Constitution, 1859-1865* (New York, 1903), 2 vols.

Burnham, W. Dean, *Presidential Ballots, 1836-1892* (Baltimore, 1955).

Butler, Benjamin F., *Private and Official Correspondence of Benjamin F. Butler During the Period of the Civil War*, ed. Jessie A. Marshall (Norwood, Mass., 1917), 5 vols.

Cain, Marvin R., *Lincoln's Attorney General: Edward Bates of Missouri* (Columbia, Mo., 1965).

Calhoun, Richard J. (ed.), *Witness to Sorrow: The Antebellum Autobiography of William J. Grayson* (Columbia, S.C., 1990).

Campbell, J. A., "Papers of John A. Campbell, 1861-1865," *Southern Historical Society Papers* (1917), 4:3-81.

Campbell, Mary Emily Robertson, *The Attitude of Tennesseans Toward the Union, 1847-1861* (New York, 1961).

Capers, Gerald A., *Stephen A. Douglas, Defender of the Union* (Boston, 1959).

Cappon, Lester, *Virginia Newspapers, 1821-1935* (New York, 1936).

Carpenter, Jesse T., *The South as a Conscious Minority, 1789-1861* (New York, 1930).

Carroll, Joseph C., *Slave Insurrections in the United States, 1800-1865* (Boston, 1938).

Caskey, Willie Malvin, *Secession and Restoration of Louisiana* (University, La., 1938).

Catton, Bruce, *The Coming Fury*, (Garden City, N.Y., 1961).

Cauthen, Charles Edward, *South Carolina Goes to War* (Chapel Hill, N.C., 1950).

—— (ed.), *Family Letters of Three Wade Hamptons, 1782-1901* (Columbia, S.C., 1953).

Chandler, Peleg W., *Memoir of Governor Andrews, with Personal Reminiscences* (Boston, 1880).

Channing, Steven A., *Crisis of Fear: Secession in South Carolina* (New York, 1970).

Chase, Salmon P., "Diary and Correspondence of Salmon P. Chase," *American Historical Association Annual Report*, 1902, II (Washington, D.C., 1903).

Chesnut, Mary, *Mary Chesnut's Civil War*, ed. C. Vann Woodward (New Haven, Conn., 1981).

———, *The Private Mary Chesnut*, ed. C. Vann Woodward and Elisabeth Muhlenfeld (New York, 1984).

Chittenden, Lucius E., *Personal Reminiscences, 1840–1890* (New York, 1893).

———, *Recollections of President Lincoln and His Administration* (New York, 1891).

———, *A Report of the Debates and Proceedings in the Secret Sessions of the Conference Convention . . . Held at Washington, D.C., in February, A. D. 1861* (New York, 1864).

Clay-Clopton, Virginia, *A Belle of the Fifties* (New York, 1905).

Cobb, Thomas R. R., "The Correspondence of Thomas Reade Rootes Cobb, 1860–1862," *Publications of the Southern History Association* (May 1907 and July 1907) 11:3, 147–85, 11:4, 233–60.

Cole, Arthur C., *The Irrepressible Conflict* (New York, 1934).

Coleman, Mrs. Chapman, *Life of John J. Crittenden, with Selections from His Correspondence and Speeches* (Philadelphia, 1871), 2 vols.

Colton, Kenneth E. (ed.), "The Irrepressible Conflict of 1861: The Letters of Samuel Ryan Curtis," *Annals of Iowa* (1942–43) 24:14–58.

Congdon, Charles T., *Reminiscences of a Journalist* (Boston, 1880).

Conkling, Alfred R., *Life and Letters of Roscoe Conkling* (New York, 1889).

Connor, Henry G., *John Archibald Campbell* (Boston, 1920).

Coulter, E. Merton, *William G. Brownlow: Fighting Parson of the Southern Highlands* (Chapel Hill, N. C., 1937).

Cox, Samuel S., *Eight Years in Congress* (New York, 1865).

Craven, Avery O., *The Coming of the Civil War* (New York, 1942).

———, *Edmund Ruffin, Southerner: A Study in Secession* (New York, 1932).

———, *The Growth of Southern Nationalism, 1848–1861* (Baton Rouge, La., 1953).

Crawford, Samuel W., *The Genesis of the Civil War: The Story of Sumter* (New York, 1887).

Crenshaw, Ollinger, *The Slave States in the Presidential Election of 1860* (Baltimore, 1945).

Croffut, William A., *An American Procession, 1855–1914: A Personal Chronicle of Famous Men* (Boston, 1931).

Crofts, Daniel W., *Reluctant Confederates: Upper South Unionists in the Secession Crisis* (Chapel Hill, N.C., 1989).

Culberson, Charles A., "General Sam Houston and Secession," *Scribner's Magazine* (1906), 39:584–91.

Current, Richard N., *Lincoln and the First Shot* (Philadelphia, 1963).

Curry, Richard O., *A House Divided: A Study of Statehood Politics and the Copperhead Movement in West Virginia* (Pittsburgh, Pa., 1964).

Curtis, Benjamin R. Jr., *Memoir of Benjamin R. Curtis* (Boston, 1879), 2 vols.

Curtis, George T., *Life of James Buchanan* (New York, 1883), 2 vols.

Cuthbert, Norma B. (ed.), *Lincoln and the Baltimore Plot: 1861* (San Marino, Cal., 1949).

Daniel, Frederick S., *The "Richmond Examiner" During the War, or, The Writings of John M. Daniel* (New York, 1868).

Darden, David L., "Alabama Secession Convention," *Alabama Historical Quarterly* (1941), 3:269–451.

Davis, David Brion, *The Problem of Slavery in Western Culture* (Ithaca, N.Y., 1966).

——, *The Slave Power Conspiracy and the Paranoid Style* (Baton Rouge, La., 1969).

Davis, Jefferson, *Jefferson Davis, Constitutionalist: His Letters, Papers, and Speeches*, ed. Dunbar Rowland (Jackson, Miss., 1923), 10 vols.

——, *The Papers of Jefferson Davis*, eds. Lynda Lasswell Crist and Mary Seaton Dix (Baton Rouge, La., 1992), 8 vols.

——, *The Rise and Fall of the Confederate Government* (New York, 1881), 2 vols.

Davis, Stanton L., *Pennsylvania Politics, 1860–1863* (Cleveland, 1935).

Davis, Varina Howell, *Jefferson Davis, A Memoir* (New York, 1890), 2 vols.

Davis, William C., *Jefferson Davis: The Man and His Hour* (New York, 1991).

De Leon, T. C., *Belles, Beaux and Brains of the 60's* (New York, 1907).

——, *Four Years in Rebel Capitals* (Mobile, Ala., 1890).

Denman, Clarence Phillips, *The Secession Movement in Alabama* (Montgomery, Ala., 1933).

Dennett, Tyler (ed.), *Lincoln and the Civil War in the Diaries and Letters of John Hay* (New York, 1939).

Dew, Charles B., "Who Won the Secession Election in Louisiana?," *Journal of Southern History* (1970), 36:18–32.

Dix, John Adams, *Memoirs of John Adams Dix*, ed. Morgan Dix (New York, 1883), 2 vols.

Dodd, Dorothy (ed.), "Edmund Ruffin's Account of the Florida Secession Convention, 1861: A Diary," *Florida Historical Quarterly* (1933), 12:67–76.

Dodd, Dorothy (ed.), "The Secession Movement in Florida, 1850–1861," *Florida Historical Quarterly* (1933), 12:3–24.

Dodd, William E., *The Cotton Kingdom* (New Haven, Conn., 1919).

Donald, David, *Charles Sumner and the Coming of the Civil War* (New York, 1960).

——, *Lincoln Reconsidered* (New York, 1956).

——, *Lincoln's Herndon* (New York, 1948).

Donnelly, William J., "Conspiracy or Popular Movement: The Historiography of Southern Support for Secession," *North Carolina Historical Review* (1965), 42:70–84.

Doubleday, Abner, *Reminiscences of Forts Sumter and Moultrie in 1860–61* (New York, 1876).

Douglas, Stephen A., *The Letters of Stephen A. Douglas*, ed. Robert W. Johannsen (Urbana, Ill., 1961).

Douglass, Frederick, *The Life and Times of Frederick Douglass* (New York, 1962).

Drake, James Vaulx, *The Life of General Robert Hatton* (Nashville, Tenn., 1867).

Duberman, Martin B., *Charles Francis Adams, 1807–1886* (Boston, 1961).

Du Bose, John W., *The Life and Times of William Lowndes Yancey* (Birmingham, Ala., 1892), 2 vols.

Dumond, Dwight L., *The Secession Movement, 1860–1861* (New York, 1931).

——, *Southern Editorials on Secession* (New York, 1931).

Dunham, Chester, F., *The Attitude of the Northern Clergy Toward the South, 1860–1865* (Toledo, Ohio, 1942).

DuPont, Samuel Francis, *Samuel Francis DuPont: A Selection from His Civil War Letters,* ed. John D. Hayes (Ithaca, N.Y., 1969), vol. 1.

Eaton, Clement, L., *The Growth of Southern Civilization, 1790–1860* (New York, 1961).

———, *The Mind of the Old South* (Baton Rouge, La., 1964).

Edmunds, John B. Jr., *Francis W. Pickens and the Politics of Destruction* (Chapel Hill, N. C., 1986).

Elliott, Charles W., *Winfield Scott, The Soldier and the Man* (New York, 1937).

Emerson, Edward W., *Life and Letters of James Russell Lowell* (Port Washington, N.Y., 1971).

Emerson, Ralph Waldo, *The Letters of Ralph Waldo Emerson*, ed. Ralph L. Rusk (New York, 1939), 6 vols.

Emery, Charles Wilson, "The Iowa Germans in the Election of 1860," *Annals of Iowa*, 3rd Series (1940), 22:421–53.

Eppes, Susan Bradford, *Through Some Eventful Years* (Macon, Ga., 1926).

Evitts, William J., *A Matter of Allegiances: Maryland from 1850 to 1861* (Baltimore, 1974).

Faunt, Joan Reynolds, and John Amasa May, *South Carolina Secedes* (Columbia, S.C., 1960).

Faust, Drew Gilpin, *James Henry Hammond and the Old South* (Baton Rouge, La., 1982).

———, *A Sacred Circle: The Dilemma of the Intellectual in the Old South* (Baltimore, 1977).

Fessenden, Francis, *Life and Public Services of William Pitt Fessenden* (Boston, 1907).

Filler, Louis, *The Crusade Against Slavery, 1830–1860* (New York, 1960).

Fite, Emerson D., *The Presidential Campaign of 1860* (New York, 1911).

Flippin, Percy Scott, *Herschel V. Johnson of Georgia, State-Rights Unionist* (Richmond, 1931).

Floan, Howard R., *The South in Northern Eyes, 1831–1861* (Austin, Tex., 1958).

Foner, Eric, *Free Soil, Free Labor, Free Men* (New York, 1970).

Foote, Henry S., *Casket of Reminiscences* (Washington, D.C., 1874).

Ford, Lacy K. Jr., *Origins of Southern Radicalism: The South Carolina Upcountry, 1800–1860* (New York, 1988).

Foulke, William D., *Life of Oliver P. Morton* (Indianapolis, 1899).

Fox, Gustavus Vasa, *Confidential Correspondence of Gustavus Vasa Fox*, ed. Robert M. Thompson and Richard Wainwright (New York, 1918), 2 vols.

Franklin, John Hope, *The Militant South, 1800–1861* (Cambridge, Mass., 1956).

Fraser, Walter J. Jr., *Charleston! Charleston!* (Columbia, S.C., 1989).

Freehling, William W., *The Road to Disunion: Secessionists at Bay, 1776–1854* (New York, 1990).

Freeman, Douglas Southall, *R. E. Lee: A Biography* (New York, 1934), 4 vols.

Fuess, Claude M., *The Life of Caleb Cushing* (New York, 1923), 2 vols.

Ganaway, Loomis Morton, *New Mexico and the Sectional Controversy, 1846–1861* (Albuquerque, 1944).

Gerson, Armand J., "The Inception of the Montgomery Convention," *American Historical Association Annual Report for 1910* (Washington, D.C., 1912), 181–87.

Glover, Gilbert G., *Immediate Pre-Civil War Compromise Efforts* (Nashville, Tenn., 1934).

Gobright, L.A., *Recollections of Men and Things at Washington During the Third of a Century* (Philadelphia, 1869).

Gorham, George C., *Life and Public Services of Edwin M. Stanton* (Boston, 1899), 2 vols.

Graebner, Norman A. (ed.), *Politics and the Crisis of 1860* (Urbana, Ill., 1961).

Gramling, Oliver, *AP, The Story of News* (New York, 1940).

Grayson, William J., *James Louis Petigru* (New York, 1866).

Greeley, Horace, *The American Conflict* (Hartford, Conn., 1864–1866), 2 vols.

———, *Recollections of a Busy Life* (New York, 1868).

Gunderson, Robert Gray, *Old Gentlemen's Convention: The Washington Peace Conference of 1861* (Madison, Wis., 1961).

Hagood, Johnson, *Memoirs of the War of Secession* (Columbia, S.C., 1910).

Hall, W. L., "Lincoln's Interview with John B. Baldwin," *South Atlantic Quarterly* (1914), 13:260–69.

Hamilton, Holman, *The Three Kentucky Presidents* (Lexington, Ky., 1978).

Hamilton, J. G. de Roulhac, "Lincoln's Election an Immediate Menace to Slavery in the States?," *American Historical Review* (1932), 37:700–11.

Hamlin, Charles E., *Life and Times of Hannibal Hamlin* (Boston, 1899).

Hammond, James Henry, *Secret and Sacred: The Diaries of James Henry Hammond, a Southern Slaveholder*, ed. Carol Bleser (New York, 1988).

Hankinson, Alan, *Man of Wars: William Howard Russell of "The Times"* (London, 1982).

Harris, W. A., *The Record of Fort Sumter* (Columbia, S.C., 1862).

Harris, Wilmer C., *The Public Life of Zachariah Chandler, 1851–1875* (Lansing, Mich., 1917).

Hayes, Rutherford Birchard, *Diary and Letters of Rutherford Birchard Hayes*, ed. Charles R. Williams (Columbus, Ohio, 1922–1926), 5 vols.

Hayne, Paul Hamilton, "Ante-bellum Charleston," *Southern Bivouac* (November 1885), 327–36.

Heck, Frank H., "John C. Breckinridge in the Crisis of 1860–1861," *Journal of Southern History* (1955) 21:316–46.

Herndon, William H., *Abraham Lincoln: The True Story of a Great Life* (New York, 1909).

Hesseltine, William B., *Lincoln and the War Governors* (New York, 1955).

Heyward, DuBose, and Herbert R. Sass, *Fort Sumter, 1861–65* (New York, 1932).

Hicks, Jimmie, "Some Letters Concerning the Knights of the Golden Circle in Texas, 1860–1861," *Southwestern Historical Quarterly* (1961), 65:80–86.

Holmes, Emma, *The Diary of Miss Emma Holmes, 1861–1866*, ed. John F. Marszalek (Baton Rouge, La., 1979).

Holt, Michael F., *The Political Crisis of the 1850s* (New York, 1978).

Hoogenboom, Ari, "Gustavus Fox and the Relief of Fort Sumter," *Civil War History* (1963), 9:383–98.

Howe, Julia Ward, *Reminiscences, 1819–1899* (Boston, 1899).

Howe, Samuel G., *Letters and Journals of Samuel G. Howe,* ed. Laura E. Richards (Boston, 1909), 2 vols.

Hubbart, Henry C., *The Older Middle West, 1840–1880* (New York, 1936).

Hudson, Frederick, *Journalism in the United States, from 1690 to 1872* (New York, 1873).

Hughes, Sarah Forbes, *Letters and Recollections of John Murray Forbes* (Boston, 1899), vol. 1.

Hundley, D. R., *Social Relations in Our Southern States* (New York, 1860).

Hunt, H. Draper, *Hannibal Hamlin of Maine* (Syracuse, N.Y., 1969).

Hunter, Robert M. T., "Correspondence of Robert M. T. Hunter," ed. C. H. Ambler, *Annual Report of the American Historical Association* (1916), 2:336–53.

Johannsen, Robert W., *Stephen A. Douglas* (New York, 1973).

Johnson, Allen, *Stephen A. Douglas: A Study in American Politics* (New York, 1908).

Johnson, Andrew, *The Papers of Andrew Johnson,* ed. Leroy P. Graf and Ralph W. Haskins (Knoxville, Tenn., 1976), vol. 4.

Johnson, Gerald W., *The Secession of the Southern States* (New York, 1933).

Johnson, Michael P., *Toward a Patriarchal Republic: The Secession of Georgia* (Baton Rouge, La., 1977).

Johnston, Richard M. and William H. Browne, *Life of Alexander H. Stephens* (Philadelphia, 1878).

Jones, Katherine M., *Heroines of Dixie* (Indianapolis, 1955).

Julian, George W., *Political Recollections, 1840 to 1872* (Chicago, 1892).

———, *Speeches on Political Questions, 1850–1868* (New York, 1872).

Keene, Jesse L., *The Peace Conference of 1861* (Tuscaloosa, Ala., 1961).

Keyes, Erasmus D., *Fifty Years' Observation of Men and Events* (New York, 1884).

Kibler, Lillian Adele, *Benjamin F. Perry, South Carolina Unionist* (Durham, N.C., 1946).

King, Alvy L., *Louis T. Wigfall, Southern Fire-Eater* (Baton Rouge, La., 1970).

King, Horatio, *Turning on the Light: A Dispassionate Survey of President Buchanan's Administration, from 1860 to Its Close* (Philadelphia, 1895).

King, Willard L., *Lincoln's Manager, David Davis* (Cambridge, Mass., 1960).

King, W. L., *The Newspaper Press of Charleston, S.C.* (Charleston, 1872).

Kirkpatrick, Arthur Roy, "Missouri on the Eve of the Civil War," *Missouri Historical Review* (1961), 55:99–108.

Kirwan, Albert D., *John J. Crittenden: The Struggle for the Union* (Lexington, Ky., 1962).

Klein, Philip S., *President James Buchanan* (University Park, Pa., 1962).

Klingberg, Frank W., "James Buchanan and the Crisis of the Union," *Journal of Southern History* (1943), 9:455–74.

Knoles, George Harmon (ed.), *The Crisis of the Union, 1860–1861* (Baton Rouge, La., 1965).

Knox, Clinton E., "The Possibilities of Compromise in the Senate Committee of Thirteen and the Responsibility for Failure," *Journal of Negro History* (1932), 17:437–65.

Koerner, Gustave, *Memoirs of Gustave Koerner,* ed. Thomas J. McCormack (Cedar Rapids, Ia., 1909).

Lamon, Ward H., *The Life of Abraham Lincoln* (Boston, 1872).

——, *Recollections of Abraham Lincoln, 1847–1865* (Washington, D.C., 1911).

Lanier, Sidney, *Sidney Lanier: Letters 1857–1868*, ed. Charles R. Anderson and Aubrey H. Starke (Baltimore, 1945), vol. 7.

Lathers, Richard, *Reminiscences of Richard Lathers*, ed. Alvan F. Sanborn (New York, 1907).

Lawton, Eba Anderson, *Major Robert Anderson and Fort Sumter* (New York, 1911).

Ledbetter, Patsy S., "John J. Crittenden and the Compromise Debacle," *Filson Club History Quarterly* (April 1977), 51:2, 125–42.

Lee, Charles Robert Jr., *The Confederate Constitutions* (Chapel Hill, N.C., 1963).

Leech, Margaret, *Reveille in Washington* (New York, 1941).

Leiding, Harriette Kershaw, *Charleston, Historic and Romantic* (Philadelphia, 1931).

Lincoln, Abraham, *The Collected Works of Abraham Lincoln*, ed. Roy P. Basler (New Brunswick, N.J., 1953), 8 vols.

Long, E. B., *The Civil War Day by Day* (Garden City, N.Y., 1971).

Longfellow, Henry Wadsworth, *The Letters of Henry Wadsworth Longfellow*, ed. Andrew Hilen (Cambridge, Mass., 1972), vol. 4.

Lothrop, Thornton K., *William Henry Seward* (Boston, 1896).

Lowell, James Russell, "The Election of 1860," *Political Essays* (New York, 1966), 23–53.

——, "E Pluribus Unum," *Atlantic Monthly* (1861), 7:235–46; *Political Essays* (New York, 1966), 57–90.

——, "The Pickens-and-Stealin's Rebellion," *Atlantic Monthly* (1861), 7:757–63; *Political Essays* (New York, 1966), 91–112.

——, "The Question of the Hour," *Atlantic Monthly* (1861), 7:117–21.

Lowrey, Lawrence T., *Northern Opinion of Approaching Secession, October 1859–November 1860* (Northampton, Mass., 1918).

Lutz, Ralph Haswell, "Rudolf Schleiden and the Visit to Richmond, April 25, 1861," *Annual Report of the American Historical Association* (Washington, D.C., 1915), 209–16.

Lyon, William H., "Claiborne Fox Jackson and the Secession Crisis in Missouri," *Missouri Historical Review* (1964), 58:422–41.

Magruder, Allan B., "A Piece of Secret History: President Lincoln and the Virginia Convention of 1861," *Atlantic Monthly* (1875), 35:438–45.

Maher, Edward R. Jr., "Sam Houston and Secession," *Southwestern Historical Quarterly* (1952), 55:448–58.

Mathews, Joseph J., *Reporting the Wars* (Minneapolis, 1957).

Matloff, Maurice (gen. ed.), *American Military History* (Washington, D.C., 1969).

McCardell, John, *The Idea of a Southern Nation* (New York, 1979).

McClure, Alexander K., *Colonel Alexander K. McClure's Recollections of Half a Century* (Salem, Mass., 1902).

——, *Old Times Notes of Pennsylvania* (Philadelphia, 1905), 2 vols.

McKinney, William T., "The Defeat of the Secessionists in Kentucky in 1861," *Journal of Negro History* (1916), 1:377–91.

McLaughlin, Andrew C., *Lewis Cass* (Boston, 1899).

McWhiney, Grady, "The Confederacy's First Shot," *Civil War History* (1968), 14:5–14.

Mearns, David C., *The Lincoln Papers* (Garden City, N.Y., 1948), vol. 1.

Meigs, Montgomery C., "General M. C. Meigs on the Civil War," *American Historical Review* (1920–21), 26:285–303.

Meredith, Roy, *Storm over Sumter* (New York, 1957).

Meynard, Virginia G., *The Venturers: The Hampton, Harrison, and Earle Families of Virginia, South Carolina, and Texas* (Easley, S.C., 1981).

Milton, George Fort, *The Eve of Conflict: Stephen A. Douglas and the Needless War* (Boston, 1934).

Molloy, Robert, *Charleston, A Gracious Heritage* (New York, 1937).

———, *Fort Sumter Memorial* (New York, 1915).

———, *The Rebellion Record: A Diary of American Events with Documents, Narratives, Illustrative Incidents, Poetry, etc.* (New York, 1864–1868), 12 vols.

Moore, John Hammond (ed.), *A Plantation Mistress on the Eve of the Civil War* (Columbia, S.C., 1993).

Mott, Frank L., *American Journalism* (New York, 1950).

Muhlenfeld, Elisabeth, *Mary Boykin Chesnut: A Biography* (Baton Rouge, La., 1981).

Myers, Robert Manson, *Children of Pride* (New Haven, Conn., 1984).

Nevins, Allan, *The Emergence of Lincoln* (New York, 1950), 2 vols.

———, *The War for the Union* (New York, 1959), vol. 1.

Nichols, Roy F., *The Disruption of American Democracy* (New York, 1948).

Nicolay, John G., *The Outbreak of Rebellion* (New York, 1881).

———, and John Hay, *Abraham Lincoln, A History* (New York, 1890), 10 vols.

Niven, John, *Gideon Welles: Lincoln's Secretary of the Navy* (New York, 1973).

O'Brien, Michael and David Moltke-Hansen (eds.), *Intellectual Life in Antebellum Charleston* (Knoxville, Tenn., 1986).

O'Connor, Thomas H., *Lords of the Loom: The Cotton Whigs and the Coming of the Civil War* (New York, 1968).

Olmsted, Frederick Law, *The Cotton Kingdom* (New York, 1861), 2 vols.

Osterweis, Rollin G., *Romanticism and Nationalism in the Old South* (New Haven, Conn., 1949).

Owsley, Frank L., "The Fundamental Cause of the Civil War: Egocentric Sectionalism," *Journal of Southern History* (1941), 7:3–18.

Parker, William B., *The Life and Public Service of Justin Smith Morrill* (Boston, 1924).

Parks, Joseph Howard, *John Bell of Tennessee* (Baton Rouge, La., 1950).

Pearson, Henry G., *James S. Wadsworth of Geneseo* (New York, 1913).

———, *Life of John A. Andrew* (Boston, 1904), 2 vols.

Perkins, Howard C., *Northern Editorials on Secession* (New York, 1942), 2 vols.

Perry, Benjamin F., *Reminiscences of Public Men, with Speeches and Addresses* (Greenville, S.C., 1889).

Petigru, James Louis, *Life, Letters and Speeches of James Louis Petigru*, ed. James Petigru Carson (Washington, D.C., 1920).

Phillips, U. B., *The Correspondence of Robert Toombs, Alexander H. Stephens, and Howell Cobb* (New York, 1970).

———, *The Course of the South to Secession* (New York, 1939).

———, *Life of Robert Toombs* (New York, 1913).

Phillips, Wendell, *Speeches, Lectures, and Letters* (Boston, 1863).

Piatt, Donn, *Memories of the Men Who Saved the Union* (New York, 1887).

Pierce, Edward L., *Memoir and Letters of Charles Sumner* (Boston, 1878–1893), 4 vols.

Pike, James S., *First Blows of the Civil War* (New York, 1879).

Poore, Ben Perley, *Reminiscences of Sixty Years in the National Metropolis* (Philadelphia, 1886), 2 vols.

Porter, David D., *Incidents and Anecdotes of the Civil War* (New York, 1885).

Potter, David M., *The Impending Crisis, 1848–1861*, completed and edited by Don E. Fehrenbacher (New York, 1976).

——, *Lincoln and His Party in the Secession Crisis* (New Haven, Conn., 1942).

——, *The South and the Sectional Conflict* (Baton Rouge, La., 1968).

Pryor, Mrs. Roger, *Reminiscences of Peace and War* (New York, 1904).

Rable, George C., *The Confederate Republic: A Revolution Against Politics* (Chapel Hill, N.C., 1994).

Radcliffe, George P., *Governor Thomas H. Hicks of Maryland and the Civil War* (Baltimore, 1901).

Ramsdell, Charles W., "Lincoln and Fort Sumter," *Journal of Southern History* (1937), 3:259–88.

Randall, James G., *Lincoln the Liberal Statesman* (New York, 1947).

——, *Lincoln the President* (New York, 1945), 2 vols.

Ravenel, Beatrice, *Charleston, the Place and the People* (New York, 1906).

Ravenel, Henry William, *The Private Journal of Henry William Ravenel*, ed. Arney R. Childs (Columbia, S.C., 1947).

Reagan, John H., *Memoirs* (New York, 1906).

Reese, George H. (ed.), *Proceedings of the Virginia State Convention of 1861* (Richmond, 1965), 4 vols.

Reiger, John F., "Secession of Florida from the Union: A Minority Decision?" *Florida Historical Quarterly* (1968), 46:358–68.

Reynolds, Donald E., *Editors Make War: Southern Newspapers in the Secession Crisis* (Nashville, Tenn., 1970).

Rhodes, James Ford, *History of the United States, 1850–1877* (New York, 1910), 7 vols.

Richardson, Albert Deane, *The Secret Service: The Field, the Dungeon, and the Escape* (Hartford, Conn., 1865).

Richardson, James D. (comp.), *A Compilation of the Messages and Papers of the Presidents, 1789–1897* (Washington, D.C., 1896–1899), 10 vols.

Riddle, Albert G., *The Life of Benjamin F. Wade* (Cleveland, 1886).

Ross, Ishbel, *First Lady of the South: The Life of Mrs. Jefferson Davis* (New York, 1958).

Ruffin, Edmund, *The Diary of Edmund Ruffin*, ed. William K. Scarborough (Baton Rouge, La., 1972), vol. 1.

Russell, William H., *My Diary North and South* (Boston, 1863), 2 vols.

Salter, William, *Life of James W. Grimes* (New York, 1876).

Sandburg, Carl, *Abraham Lincoln: The Prairie Years* (New York, 1926), 2 vols.

——, *Abraham Lincoln: The War Years* (New York, 1939). 4 vols.

Sass, Herbert R., *Outspoken: 150 Years of the Charleston "News and Courier"* (Columbia, S.C., 1953).

Schlesinger, Arthur M. Jr., "The Causes of the Civil War: A Note on Historical Sentimentalism," *Partisan Review* (1949), 16:969–81.

Schuckers, Jacob W., *Life and Public Services of Salmon Portland Chase* (New York, 1874).

Schultz, Harold S., *Nationalism and Sectionalism in South Carolina, 1852–1860* (Durham, N.C., 1950).

Schurz, Carl, *Intimate Letters of Carl Schurz, 1841–1869*, ed. Joseph Schafer (Madison, Wis., 1928).

———, *The Reminiscences of Carl Schurz* (New York, 1908), 3 vols.

———, *Speeches, Correspondence and Political Papers of Carl Schurz*, ed. Frederic Bancroft (New York, 1913), 6 vols.

Scott, Winfield, *Memoirs of Lieut.-General Scott, LL.D., Written by Himself* (New York, 1864), 2 vols.

Scroggs, Jack B., "Arkansas in the Secession Crisis," *Arkansas Historical Quarterly* (1953) 12:179–224.

Scrugham, Mary, *The Peaceable Americans of 1860–1861* (New York, 1921).

Sears, Louis Martin, *John Slidell* (Durham, N.C., 1925).

Searcher, Victor, *Lincoln's Journey to Greatness* (Philadelphia, 1960).

Seward, Frederick W., *Reminiscences of a War-Time Statesman and Diplomat, 1830–1915* (New York, 1916).

———, *Seward at Washington, as Senator and Secretary of State* (New York, 1891).

Shanks, Henry T., *The Secession Movement in Virginia, 1847–1861* (Richmond, 1934).

Sherman, John, *Recollections of Forty Years in the House, Senate and Cabinet* (New York, 1895), 2 vols.

Sherman, William T., *Home Letters of General Sherman*, ed. M. A. de Wolfe Howe (New York, 1909).

———, *Memoirs of General William T. Sherman* (New York, 1875), 2 vols.

Simkins, Francis B. and James W. Patton, *The Women of the Confederacy* (Richmond, 1936).

Simms, William Gilmore, *The Letters of William Gilmore Simms*, ed. Mary C. Simms Oliphant and T. C. Duncan Eaves (Columbia, S.C., 1955), vol. 4.

Sitterson, Joseph Carlyle, *The Secession Movement in North Carolina* (Chapel Hill, N.C., 1939).

Smith, George Winston and Charles Judah, *Life in the North During the Civil War* (Albuquerque, 1966).

Smith, Theodore C., *Life and Letters of James Abram Garfield* (New Haven, Conn., 1925), 2 vols.

Smith, William E., *The Francis Preston Blair Family in Politics* (New York, 1933), 2 vols.

Snowden, Yates (ed.), *A History of South Carolina* (Chicago, 1920), 5 vols.

Stampp, Kenneth M., *America in 1857: A Nation on the Brink* (New York, 1990).

———, *And the War Came* (Baton Rouge, La., 1950).

———, *The Imperiled Union* (New York, 1980).

Starr, Louis M., *Bohemian Brigade* (New York, 1954).

Stevens, William Oliver, *Charleston, Historic City of Gardens* (New York, 1939).

Strong, George Templeton, Allan Nevins and Milton Halsey Thomas (eds.), *The Diary of George Templeton Strong* (New York, 1952), 4 vols.

Sumner, Charles, *The Works of Charles Sumner* (Boston, 1874–1883), 15 vols.

Swanberg, W. A., *First Blood: The Story of Fort Sumter* (New York, 1957).

Sweet, William W., *The Methodist Episcopal Church and the Civil War* (Cincinnati, 1912).

Swisher, Carl B., *Roger B. Taney* (New York, 1936).

Taylor, John M., *William Henry Seward: Lincoln's Right Hand* (New York, 1991).

Taylor, Mrs. Thomas, et al. (eds.), *South Carolina Women in the Confederacy* (Columbia, S.C., 1903).

Thayer, William R., *Life and Letters of John Hay* (Boston, 1915), 2 vols.

Thomas, Benjamin P., *Abraham Lincoln* (New York, 1952).

——, and Harold M. Hyman, *Stanton: The Life and Times of Lincoln's Secretary of War* (New York, 1962).

Thompson, William Y., *Robert Toombs of Georgia* (Baton Rouge, La., 1966).

Thorndike, Rachel S. (ed.), *The Sherman Letters: Correspondence Between General and Senator Sherman from 1837 to 1894* (New York, 1894).

Tilley, John S., *Lincoln Takes Command* (Chapel Hill, N.C., 1941).

Trescot, William Henry, "Narrative and Letter of William Henry Trescot, concerning Negotiations Between South Carolina and President Buchanan in December, 1860, ed. Gaillard Hunt, *American Historical Review* (1908), 13:528–56.

Tyler, Lyon G., *The Letters and Times of the Tylers* (Richmond, 1885), 2 vols.

United States War Department, *Official Records of the Union and Confederate Navies in the War of the Rebellion* (Washington, D.C., 1894–1917), vol. 4.

——, *War of the Rebellion: A Compilation of the Official Records of the Union and Confederate Armies* (Washington, D.C., 1880–1901) 128 vols. Series 1, vol. 1.

Van Deusen, Glyndon G., *Horace Greeley, Nineteenth Century Crusader* (Philadelphia, 1953).

——, *Thurlow Weed, Wizard of the Lobby* (Boston, 1947).

——, *William Henry Seward* (New York, 1967).

Villard, Henry, *Lincoln on the Eve of '61*, ed. Harold G. Villard and Oswald Garrison Villard (New York, 1941).

——, *Memoirs* (Boston, 1904), 2 vols.

Wakelyn, Jon L., "The Changing Loyalties of James Henry Hammond: A Reconsideration," *South Carolina Historical Magazine* (1974), 75:1–13.

Wallace, David D., *The History of South Carolina* (New York, 1934), 3 vols.

Walther, Eric H., *The Fire Eaters* (Baton Rouge, La., 1992).

"Washington City," *Atlantic Monthly* (January 1861), 7:1–8.

Watterson, Henry, *"Marse Henry": An Autobiography* (New York, 1919), 2 vols.

Weed, Thurlow, *Autobiography of Thurlow Weed*, ed. Harriet A. Weed (Boston, 1883), 2 vols.

Weigley, Russell F., *Quartermaster General of the Union Army: A Biography of Montgomery C. Meigs* (New York, 1959).

Weisberger, Bernard A., *Reporters for the Union* (Boston, 1953).

Weiss, John, *Life and Correspondence of Theodore Parker* (New York, 1864), 2 vols.

Welles, Gideon, *The Diary of Gideon Welles*, ed. Howard K. Beale (New York, 1960), 3 vols.

——, *Diary of Gideon Welles, Secretary of the Navy under Lincoln and Johnson*, ed. John T. Morse, Jr. (Boston, 1911), 3 vols.

——, "Fort Sumter," *Galaxy* (1870), 10:613–37.

Welling, J. C., "The Proposed Evacuation of Fort Sumter," *Nation* (Dec. 4, 1879), 29:383–84.

Wells, Damon, *Stephen Douglas: The Last Years, 1857–1861* (Austin, Tex., 1971).

White, Horace, *Life of Lyman Trumbull* (New York, 1913).

White, Laura A., *Robert Barnwell Rhett, Father of Secession* (New York, 1931).

Williams, T. Harry, *P. G. T. Beauregard, Napoleon in Gray* (Baton Rouge, La., 1955).

Wilson, Forrest, *Crusader in Crinoline: The Life of Harriet Beecher Stowe* (Philadelphia, 1941).

Wilson, Henry, *History of the Rise and Fall of the Slave Power in America* (1872–77), 3 vols.

——, "Jeremiah S. Black and Edwin M. Stanton," *Atlantic Monthly* (1870), 26:463–75.

Wilson, William Bender, *A Few Acts and Actors in the Tragedy of the Civil War* (Philadelphia, 1892).

Wise, Barton H., *The Life of Henry A. Wise of Virginia, 1806–1876* (New York, 1899).

Woodford, Frank B., *Lewis Cass: The Last Jeffersonian* (New Brunswick, N.J., 1950).

Wooster, Ralph A., *The People in Power: Courthouse and Statehouse in the Lower South, 1850–1860* (Knoxville, Tenn., 1969).

——, *Politicians, Planters and Plain Folk: Courthouse and Statehouse in the Upper South, 1850–1860* (Knoxville, Tenn., 1975).

——, *The Secession Conventions of the South* (Princeton, N.J., 1962).

Wright, Mrs. D. Giraud, *A Southern Girl in '61* (New York, 1905).

Wright, William C., *The Secession Movement in the Middle Atlantic States* (Rutherford, N.J., 1973).

Young, John Russell, *Men and Memories* (New York, 1901).

Zorn, Roman J., "Minnesota Public Opinion and the Secession Controversy, December 1860–April 1861," *Mississippi Valley Historical Review* (1949), 36:435–56.

Index

Aberdeen, Lord, 5
abolitionism, 21, 31, 39, 40, 76
Adams, Charles Francis, 125, 129, 160-2, 185-6, 193, 211, 220-3, 228, 237-8, 275, 277, 310, 327, 349, 362, 395
Adams, Charles Francis, Jr., 238, 281, 287, 376
Adams, Henry, 129, 173, 190, 204, 223, 224, 228, 237, 281
Adams, Capt. Henry A., 391-2, 406
Adams, James Hopkins, 147, 347
Adams, John, 112
Adams, John Quincy, 93, 110, 129, 142
Alabama: confederacy convention delegates from, 242; secession of, 166, 203; and seizure of forts, 191, 205-7
Alcott, Louisa May, 58-9
Aldrich, Alfred P., 91
Alexander II, Czar of Russia, 5, 142
Allen, William, 286
American Anti-Slavery Society, 40
American party, 47, 48, 63, 272
Anderson, Eliza, 107, 132-4, 196, 296
Anderson, Larz, 198
Anderson, Maj. Robert, 105-6, 151-2, 165, 198-200, 205, 240, 282-3, 295-9, 337-9, 369, 372-4, 425; assigned to Moultrie, 99, 105; during bombardment, 409-11, 413-16; Buchanan and reinforcements for, 114, 118-19, 131, 132, 134, 175; defense preparations of, 364-5; dispatches to Washington from, 297, 312, 313, 319-20, 326, 345, 372, 390, 397; and emissaries from Washington, 332-3, 341-2, 344, 345; and evacuation of Sumter, 334, 358, 371; expedition for relief of, 236, 283, 391; Henry Adams on, 204; and interception of mail, 246, 296; move from Moultrie to Sumter, 133, 152-7, 163-5, 168, 170-4, 199, 225; orders for defense of forts given to, 148-9, 152, 176, 297-8, 373; prepares for attack, 400-2; Scott and, 105, 116; and shortages of supplies, 247, 296, 323, 327, 372, 383; and *Star of the West*, 191-2, 195-7, 199; strengthening of Sumter by, 245, 297; surrender of, 416-19; during truce, 200-2, 208-10, 230
Andrew, John, 204, 237
Anthony, Henry B., 340, 350
Arkansas, 274; *see also* border states
Armstrong, Comm. James, 205-7
Army, U.S., 7, 96, 105, 322, 335, 383; Corps of Engineers, 282; Irish immigrants in, 8; Lee in, 233
Arnold, Benedict, 225
Aspinwall, William H., 363-4
Associated Press, 213-14, 227, 411
Atlantic (ship), 389, 406

Bagby, G. W., 216
Baker, E. H., 262, 362
Baker, Edward, 306, 308, 313, 314, 340
Baldwin, John B., 382, 383, 393
Baltic (ship), 363, 383, 405, 413-14, 418, 419
Baltimore, 271-2; and plot against Lincoln, 268-71, 273; riot in, 429; Russell in, 408
Baltimore & Ohio Railroad, 271
Baltimore *Sun*, 273
Bancroft, George, 11
Bank of Charleston, 89
Barbour, James, 324
Barksdale, William, 113
Barnum, P. T., 266
Barnwell, Robert W., 144, 147, 172, 293
Barrancas, Fort, 205, 378
Barron, Capt. Samuel, 379-80
Bates, Edward, 26, 185-6, 188, 318, 319, 326, 332, 340, 352, 354, 357, 358
Bayard, James A., 48
Beauregard, Pierre G. T., 334-6, 348, 364, 370, 371, 373, 394, 396-8; assumes command of Confederate forces, 322, 335,

Beauregard, Pierre G. T. (*continued*)
338; and bombardment of Sumter, 409, 410;
and Charleston social life, 375;
commissioners and, 344; and emissaries
from Lincoln, 342, 396, 399–400;
evacuation of Sumter demanded by, 401–2;
relieved of command at West Point, 234–5;
Russell and, 423–4, 428, 429; and surrender
of Sumter, 416–19
Bell, John, 24, 27, 28, 30, 63, 253, 272, 278
Benjamin, Judah P., 48, 130, 235, 293, 370
Bennett, James Gordon, 14, 149, 204, 214
Benning, Henry L., 24
Benton, Thomas Hart, 38
Berret, James E., 239, 278, 315
Bertinatti, Chevalier, 348–9
Bigelow, John, 215, 430
Bigler, William, 159, 170, 223, 229, 277, 306
Bingham, John A., 221, 308
Black Hawk War, 106
Black, Jeremiah S., 26–7, 96–9, 114–16, 130,
135, 149, 169, 171, 174–6, 189, 191, 194,
209–11, 225, 226
blacks, free, 90, 223, 365
Blair, Austin, 204
Blair, Frank, 136, 137, 186, 275, 331, 359
Blair, Montgomery, 184, 186–7, 275, 283, 310,
318, 330–2, 340, 357, 358, 363, 378
Blair, Samuel S., 233
Bonham, Milledge L., 130, 133, 142, 148, 348,
398, 408
border states: and Lincoln's election,
22–3; peace conference delegates from,
279; and secession, 193, 219–20, 222,
355, 427; Unionists in, 325; *see also specific
states*
Boston *Courier*, 166
Botts, John Minor, 187, 382, 393
Bouligny, John E., 138
Boutwell, George S., 239
Boyce, William, 113
Boykin, Kitty, 347
Bradford, Edward, 203
Bradford, Susan, 203, 385
Bragg, Braxton, 322, 371–2, 377, 406
Breckinridge, John C., 23, 27, 30, 63, 124, 169,
220, 253, 272, 277, 309, 314, 339, 345
Brigham, Charles D., 216, 289–90
Bright, Jesse, 48
Britain, 327, 376, 395; antislavery sentiments

in, 352; Confederacy and, 423, 428; India
and, 5–7, 387; war with Russia, 4–5
Brooklyn (ship), 191, 192, 229, 353, 360, 377
Brooklyn Navy Yard, 378–80, 387
Brooks, Preston, 49–50
Brown, Albert G., 24
Brown, Alexander H., 289–90, 343
Brown, George W., 273
Brown, Col. Harvey, 378, 406
Brown, Joe, 290
Brown, John, 50, 58–60, 63, 85, 252
Brown v. Board of Education of Topeka (1954),
51
Browne, William M., 135, 150, 322–3
Browning, Orville H., 186, 259, 305, 390
Brownlow, Parson, 65, 316
Bryan, C. S., 145, 201
Bryant, William Cullen, 22, 184
Buchanan, James, 23, 26–7, 61, 63, 105, 109–12,
218, 226, 272, 294, 340, 404; cabinet of, 23,
96–9, 130, 173–4, 191, 208, 277; and
Charleston forts, 113–15, 118, 132–6, 148–9,
169–72, 174–77, 191–2, 225, 230, 235–7,
282–3, 320, 327, 331, 332; Crittenden
plan supported by, 237; departs from
Washington, 319; and departure of
southern senators, 234–5; Douglas and, 54,
55, 57, 59; and *Dred Scot* case, 51–3, 109;
election of, 28–9; extension of Missouri
Compromise favored by, 41; final days in
office of, 282–4; inauguration of, 48–9, 102,
109; lack of leadership of, 138; Lecompton
Constitution endorsed by, 53–5; and
Lincoln's arrival in Washington, 275, 277; at
Lincoln's inauguration, 311–13, 315;
Lincoln's policies compared with, 352, 355;
Meigs and, 359, 389; message to Congress,
124–6, 131, 175, 194, 229; and peace
conference, 220; Pickens and, 143, 144,
147–8; plot to kidnap, 169; Republicans
and, 168; and secession, 146–7, 150–1, 208;
Seward on, 386; during Sumter truce,
208–10, 360; and *Star of the West* incident,
202–4, 208; and Washington social life, 72,
95, 138–9, 189–90, 211, 234
Buell, Maj. Don Carlos, 148–9, 152, 171, 176
Burnett, Henry, 286–7
Burr, Aaron, 117
Butler, Andrew P., 49, 84
Butler, William, 184

Calhoun, John C., 7, 34, 41, 42, 46, 62, 70, 74-5, 82, 84, 85, 89, 142, 143, 242, 294, 420, 430

California, admission to Union of, 40-2

Call, Gen. Richard K., 203

Cameron, Simon, 20, 184-9, 193, 220, 256, 258, 267, 278, 288, 310, 318-19, 323, 332, 340, 357-8, 383, 391, 397

Campbell, John A., 137-8, 211, 228, 333, 334, 344, 358, 370, 371, 375, 390, 392, 394, 395

Canada, 376; proposed annexation of, 340

Carey, John, 286, 287

Carmody, John, 412

Carson, Caroline, 429

Cass, Lewis, 41, 42, 97-9, 114, 134, 135, 150, 277

Catron, John, 51, 52

Chandler, Zachariah, 307, 355-6, 362

Charleston, 86-92, 198, 203; forts at, 98, 118, 159 (*see also* Moultrie, Fort; Sumter, Fort); port of, collection of duties at, 194; Russell in, 423-9; secession convention in, 144-7; social life in, 289, 335, 347-8, 374-5; *Tribune* correspondent in, 216, 289-90

Charleston *Courier*, 152

Charleston *Mercury*, 25, 37, 152, 163, 201, 202, 211, 214, 216, 226-7, 230, 238, 242, 243, 289, 318, 327, 334, 359-60, 392, 398, 404

Chase, Kate, 352

Chase, Salmon P., 21-2, 42-3, 184, 279, 285, 309, 325, 354, 357, 381; cabinet appointment of, 158, 175, 186, 188, 278, 310, 318; and expedition to relieve Sumter, 332, 358, 363; and office seekers, 328, 340; at peace conference, 238, 239, 276; Russell and, 352, 366, 386

Chase, Col. W. H., 207

Chesnut, James, 67-74, 85, 86, 91, 124, 241, 294, 321, 346-7, 374, 395-6; and fall of Sumter, 401, 402, 409, 410, 416, 417, 419; joins Beauregard's staff, 398; Russell and, 423, 424, 427; at secession convention, 144; in Senate, 25, 67, 72, 73, 92, 113, 124

Chesnut, Mary, 67-73, 91, 97, 241, 294-5, 317, 321-3, 346-8, 374-5, 395-6, 398, 402, 410, 416, 418, 424, 429

Cheves, Langdon, 70, 82, 410

Chew, Robert S., 390-1, 394, 396-7, 399, 400

Chicago *Tribune*, 103

Chisholm, A. R., 401, 402, 409, 416

chivalry, Southern, 64-6, 74, 88, 89, 112, 142, 222, 253, 366, 430

Clay, Cassius M., 268

Clay, Clement, 72, 209, 228, 293

Clay, Mrs. Clement, 314-15

Clay, Henry, 34, 41, 42, 62, 124, 127, 129, 225, 239, 242, 257, 294, 403, 430

Clay, James B., 239

Clay, Virginia, 72

Clemens, Sherrard, 228, 278

Clingman, Thomas L., 127, 329, 345

Cobb, Howell, 25-6, 48, 96, 98, 99, 110, 112-14, 116, 130, 134, 135, 145, 234, 241-4, 255, 291, 294

Cobb, Marion, 244

Cobb, Mary Ann, 97, 131, 138

Cobb, Thomas R. R., 241-4, 254, 256, 292, 293, 295, 317, 322

Cochrane, John, 229

Colcock, W. F., 25, 165

Colfax, Schuyler, 184, 219, 262

Collamer, Jacob, 161

Compromise of 1850, 42-3, 46, 60, 127, 257, 313

Congress, U.S., 26, 58, 61, 93, 94, 112, 115, 116, 118, 142, 151, 190, 204, 208, 238, 282, 327, 348, 386; Buchanan in, 110; Buchanan's message to, 124-6, 175, 194; and call for constitutional convention, 131; Cobb in, 96; compromise attempts in, 127, 134, 158-9, 217-20, 223, 255-9, 284, 285-8; Corwin amendment passed by, 311; Davis in, 250, 251; during final days of Buchanan administration, 305-9, 312; Hammond in, 77, 78; and inauguration, 313; Lincoln in, 292; and military funding, 378; slavery debate in, 38-42, 44, 51-4, 59; and South Carolina commissioners, 148; Sumner attacked in, 50; Toucey in, 97; *see also* House of Representatives, U.S.; Senate, U.S.

Conkling, Roscoe, 222

Connecticut, elections in, 370, 381

Conner, James, 25

Constitution, U.S., 13, 42, 61, 98, 106, 126, 129, 167, 204, 243, 252, 272, 307; Crittenden and, 124, 308; framing of, 32-3, 36; Lincoln and defense of, 276, 317; reverence for, 110; secession and, 12, 116, 287; slavery and, 32,

Constitution, U.S. (*continued*)
36, 39, 158, 159, 161, 213, 221, 322; state
rights and, 7; "three-fifths" compromise in,
38, 40
Constitutional Union party, 27, 63
Cooper, Gen. Samuel, 157, 322, 326, 338
Corwin, Thomas, 127, 161, 162, 183, 220, 221,
284, 287–8, 306–8, 311, 318, 327
Covode Committee, 59
Cowan, Edgar, 189
Cox, Samuel S., 221
Craven, T. A., 114
Crawford, Martin J., 294, 311, 316, 323, 328,
344, 369, 373
Crawford, S. W., 296
Crawford, Samuel, 154–6, 197, 199, 200, 299,
325, 329, 334, 344, 372, 394, 400–1, 409,
411, 413, 415
Crittenden, John J., 117, 124–5, 127, 129,
158–62, 167, 190, 194, 201, 218, 220–4, 226,
228, 237, 272, 279, 281, 284–5, 287–8, 299,
306–8, 319, 329
Cuba, 26–7, 376
Cullum, George W., 106
Cumberland (ship), 421–2
Curry, Jabez, 243
Curtin, Andrew G., 188, 204, 270, 272, 394
Curtis, Benjamin, 51
Curtis, Samuel, 223, 288–9
Cushing, Caleb, 61, 135, 146, 355
Cushman, Charlotte, 281
Custis, Nellie, 67
Cuthbert, Capt. George B., 409

Dahlgren, Capt. John, 365
Dana, Charles A., 14, 128, 214, 290
Davis, David, 104, 184, 187, 188, 265, 270,
279
Davis, Henry Winter, 127, 160–2, 184, 281,
310
Davis, Lt. Jeff, 108, 155, 156, 163, 197, 199, 296,
299, 411, 417
Davis, Jefferson, 66, 106, 148, 204–5, 210,
248–56, 290, 292–5, 351, 359; and attack
on Sumter, 398–401; Beauregard commis-
sioned by, 335; becomes president of Confederacy, 243–4, 248–9, 253–6, 292; cabinet
appointed by, 293; calls for troops, 427–8;
and evacuation vs. reinforcement of Sumter
and Pickens, 334, 369–72; and expedition
to relieve Sumter, 391, 394, 396, 397;
negotiations with Washington attempted
by, 294; and raising of Confederate Army,
322; in Senate, 60, 72, 127, 130, 159, 170,
228
Davis, Joseph, 249–50
Davis, Reuben, 60
Davis, Sarah Knox "Knoxie" Taylor, 249, 253
Davis, Varina Howell, 72, 248–52, 254, 256,
294, 323, 374, 393
Dayton, William L., 188, 267, 310, 327
De Bow, James, 65, 66
Declaration of Independence, 145, 146, 167,
270, 292
Declaration of the Immediate Causes of
Secession, 162
Delane, John Thadeus, 4
Delaware, *see* border states
Democrats, 34–5, 53, 61, 96, 97, 130, 135, 208,
240, 277, 287, 309, 310, 330; Buchanan
nominated by, 48; and compromise
attempts, 159, 160, 167, 220, 221; defection
to Republic party of, 128, 185, 283; in 1860
elections, 20, 25–7, 29, 30, 63; in Illinois
Senate election of 1858, 57; and Kansas-
Nebraska Act, 47; and Lecompton
Constitution, 54, 313–14; and Lincoln's
arrival in Washington, 277; in Maryland,
271, 272; moderates in, 137, 143; newspapers
and, 175; in northern state governments,
204; Russell and, 12, 13; sectional divisions
in, 59, 252–3; in Union party, 324, 325
DeSaussure, Col. W. G., 164–5
Dickens, Charles, 46
Dix, Dorothea, 268
Dix, John A., 208, 236–7, 319, 329, 338
Dixon, James, 128, 228
Dodge, William E., 276
Doniphan, Alexander W., 279, 285
Doolittle, Senator, 277
Doubleday, Capt. Abner, 108, 155–6, 165, 196,
197, 199, 296, 299, 365, 411–13, 416, 419
Doubleday, Mrs. Abner, 332
Douglas, Adele, 124, 138, 190, 281, 386, 404
Douglas, Stephen A., 42, 48, 49, 123–4, 138,
139, 160, 190, 281, 330, 356, 404; Buchanan
and, 54, 55, 57, 59; compromise attempts
by, 159, 220, 223, 306–8, 345; Davis and,
252–3; debates with Lincoln, 62; in Illinois
Senate race of 1858, 55–7; at inauguration,
313–16; and Kansas-Nebraska Act, 46–7;

and Lincoln's arrival in Washington, 275, 277, 278; popular sovereignty advocated by, 41, 52-3; presidential candidacy of, 19, 27-30, 63; Russell and, 386; Seward and, 228, 324, 324

Drayton, Thomas F., 113, 133

Dred Scott v. Sanford (1857), 51-4, 109, 278, 314

Dubois, Jesse, 184, 262, 263, 389

Dutch immigrants, 87

East India Company, 5

Echols, John, 291

Electoral College, 236

Ellsworth, Col. Elmer E., 20, 262

Elmore, Franklin, 82

Emerson, Ralph Waldo, 41, 59

Emigrant Aid Society, 50

English, William H., 221

Ervin, J. S., 201

Etheridge, Emerson, 222

Everett, Edward, 27, 28, 92, 227, 237

Evitts, William J., 62

Ewing, Thomas, 225, 239

Faunce, Capt. John, 405, 414

Felton, Samuel M., 268-71

Ferguson, Capt. Sam, 420

Ferrand, Capt. Ebenezer, 207

Fessenden, William P., 60, 159, 161, 166, 173, 239, 258, 328, 330

Field, David Dudley, 239

Fillmore, Millard, 34, 48, 265

Fillmore, Mrs. Millard, 95

Fish, Hamilton, 166

Fitzpatrick, Aurelia, 255

Fitzpatrick, Benjamin, 209, 228

FitzSimmons, Paul, 74, 75

Florida, 354, 385; admitted to Union, 31; forts in, 114, 333, 353, 357, 359, 371 (*see also* Pickens, Fort); Lincoln hanged in effigy in, 20, 103; secession of, 10, 166, 203, 205; seizure of federal property in, 191, 205-7

Floyd, John B., 96-9, 107, 112-14, 118, 130, 135, 148, 149, 152, 169-74, 176, 193, 225, 359, 389, 401

Fogg, George G., 136

Foote, Capt. Andrew H., 380, 383, 384, 387-9

Foote, Henry S., 111, 250

Forbes, John Murray, 285

Forsyth, John, 294, 323, 328-30, 334, 386, 393

Foster, Capt. John G., 108, 153, 155, 163, 196, 199, 244-6, 299, 319, 338-9, 342, 364, 397, 400, 401, 415

Foster, Lafayette, 329-30

Founding Fathers, 32-4, 36, 62, 193, 217

Fox, Gustavus V., 283, 331-3, 341-2, 358, 363, 366, 372, 378, 380-1, 383-4, 388, 397, 405, 413-14, 418

France, 26, 327, 362, 376

Fraser, Charles, 88

Free Soil party, 41

Frémont, John C., 28-9, 48, 257, 327

Fugitive Slave Act (1850), 42, 45, 46, 221

Gadsden Purchase, 46

Galloway, Edward, 419

Gardner, Col. J. L., 99, 105, 107, 153

Garfield, James A., 265

Garnett, Muscoe, 112

Garnett, Maj. Robert S., 7

Georgia, 112; abolitionism outlawed in, 39; confederacy convention delegates from, 243-4; secession of, 134, 166, 221; seizure of federal property in, 191

Georgianna (ship), 421

German immigrants, 8, 9, 21, 34, 87, 90

Giddings, Joshua, 54

Gillis, Comm. J. P., 414

Gilman, Caroline, 140-1, 147, 198, 348, 410, 419

Gilman, Lt. Jeremiah, 205-7

Gilman, W. S., 166

Gilmer, John A., 187, 222

Gist, William H., 91, 113, 115, 116, 133-5, 141, 144, 164

Gómez, Francisco, 206

Gourdin, Robert N., 144, 152, 165, 396

Government Printing Office, 287

Greeley, Horace, 13, 22, 145, 167, 184, 214, 223, 258, 264, 278, 285, 424

Green, Duff, 173-4, 177

Greenhow, Rose O'Neal, 72

Gregg, Col. Maxcy, 210, 338

Grier, Robert C., 173

Grimes, James W., 60, 130, 213, 217, 258

Grinnell, Moses, 266

Guthrie, James, 279, 284-5
Gwin, William M., 134, 192, 328, 329

Haddock, C. B., 123
Haiti, 362
Hale, John P., 127, 129, 277, 288, 339-40
Hale, Stephen F., 54, 242
Hall, Lt. Norman C., 154, 156, 199, 202, 208, 297, 299, 415
Hamilton, Andrew, 162
Hamilton, D. H., 147
Hamilton, Fort, 106
Hamlin, Hannibal, 103, 131, 136, 186, 187, 216, 266, 267, 275, 276, 278, 279, 309, 313
Hammond, Catherine FitzSimmons, 74-8, 81-4
Hammond, James Henry, 57, 60, 69, 73-85, 89-92, 124, 142, 248, 281
Hampton, Sallie Baxter, 140
Hampton, Wade, 78-80, 84, 89
Hampton, Wade, Jr., 315
Harlan, James, 23
Harper's Weekly, 214
Harriet Lane (ship), 358, 378, 383, 404-5, 411, 413
Harris, Ira, 278
Harrison, J. Morrison, 229
Harrison, William Henry, 48, 49, 102, 239, 257
Hart, Peter, 196, 413
Hartstene, Capt. H. J., 341, 342, 347, 375, 397
Harvey, James E., 371
Hatch, O. M., 262
Hatton, Robert, 123, 130, 137, 151, 171, 190, 211, 221, 240, 274, 281, 286
Hawkins, George, 211
Hay, John, 262, 273, 352
Hayes, Rutherford B., 263
Hayne, Isaac W., 144, 202, 208-10, 230, 235, 236, 257, 290, 374
Hayne, Paul Hamilton, 88
Hazzard, Capt. George W., 262, 269-70
Helper, Hinton R., 57
Hemphill, John, 227
Henry, Alexander, 267
Henry, Joseph, 395
Herndon, William, 20, 100, 183, 259-60, 310
Hicks, Thomas, 229-30, 271-3, 278
higher-law doctrine, 53
Hill, Joshua, 190

Holmes, Edward, 341
Holmes, Emma, 317, 334, 335, 341, 375, 397, 410
Holmes, Robert Little, 201
Holt, Joseph, 23, 97-9, 131, 134-5, 171, 174, 176-7, 191, 208-9, 230, 234-6, 282-4, 297-9, 312, 319-20, 329, 339-40, 359-60
Holt, R. S., 23
Hoover, Herbert, 30
Hough, Daniel, 419
House of Representatives, U.S., 38, 41, 44, 49-50, 59-60, 127, 129, 142, 238, 273; compromise attempts in, 160-2, 220-2, 286-8; during final days of Buchanan administration, 306, 307; Lincoln in, 19; Lincoln welcomed to Washington by, 278; Republican control of, 228
Houston, Sam, 233, 248, 340
Howard, John, 273
Howard, William A., 287, 288
Hudson, Frederic, 214, 216
Huger, Alfred, 89, 146, 290-1, 397, 428
Huger, Maj. Benjamin, 99, 107, 108, 153
Huguenots, 87
Humphrey, James, 286
Hundley, Daniel R., 65, 66
Hunter, Maj. David, 262, 265, 270
Hunter, Robert M. T., 112, 170, 174, 176, 329
Hunter, William, 93
Hurlbert, William, 14
Hurlbut, Stephen A., 341-3

Illinois, 62; and cabinet appointments, 184; elections in, 19, 29, 55; grain production in, 37; peace conference delegates from, 238
Illinois (ship), 389, 406
Illinois *State Journal*, 262, 316
Impending Crisis of the South (Helper), 57
India, British in, 5-7, 387
Indiana: and cabinet appointments, 184; elections in, 20, 29; peace conference delegates from, 238
Interior Department, U.S., 96, 149, 226, 278, 318
Iowa, 188-9
Irish immigrants, 8, 9, 11, 34, 47, 90
Isabel (ship), 419
Ivanhoe (Scott), 65
Iverson, Alfred, 127, 229

Jackson, Andrew, 35, 54, 62, 117, 131, 135, 137, 173, 187, 194, 206, 242, 257, 331, 343

James, Capt. George S., 409

Jamison, D. F., 144–6, 200, 201, 419

Jefferson, Fort, 114, 359

Jefferson, Thomas, 35, 38, 324

Jews, 87

Johnson, Andrew, 137, 277, 306

Johnson, Fort, 107, 154, 165, 200, 245, 246, 296, 297, 364, 374, 409, 410–12

Johnson, Louisa, 76, 81–3

Johnson, Reverdy, 239, 308

Johnson, Sally, 76, 81–3

Johnson, Samuel, 117

Jones, Thomas D., 256

Judd, Norman, 184, 188, 257, 262, 267–70, 390

Julian, George, 189

Kansas: admission to Union of, 228, 270, 287; Bleeding, 50–1, 53, 252, 314

Kansas-Nebraska Act (1854), 35, 46–7, 50, 60, 129, 313

Keitt, Lawrence, 49, 112–13, 132, 133, 139, 144, 243, 293

Kellogg, William, 136, 286

Kemble, Fanny, 87

Kendall, Amos, 97

Kennedy, John Pendleton, 61–2

Kenney, H. F., 271

Kentucky, 282, 345, 427; peace conference delegates from, 239; Union party in, 340; *see also* border states

Keyes, Erasmus D., 106, 211, 227, 236, 283, 312, 315, 354, 360–2, 378, 389

Kilgore, David, 288

Killinger, John W., 286

King, Horatio, 27, 135, 173, 236, 277

King, Preston, 129, 136, 159

King, Sue, 429

Know-Nothings, *see* American party

Knoxville *Whig*, 316

Koerner, Gustave, 168, 188, 314, 355, 389–90

Kollock, Tom, 76

Lamar, Lucius Q. C., 113

Lamon, Ward, 20, 100, 104, 185, 262, 264, 270, 271, 274, 341–5, 354, 358, 364, 370, 372, 390, 397

Lane, Harriet, 72, 95, 110–12, 138, 234, 275

Lane, Joseph, 25–6, 170, 306

Lathers, Richard, 167

Lawrence, Amos, 168, 237

Lay, George W., 341

Lecompton Constitution, 53–5, 59, 221, 313

Lee, Custis, 72, 234

Lee, Mary Custis, 72

Lee, Robert E., 58, 72, 233–4, 281

Lee, Rooney, 72, 281

Lee, Capt. Stephen D., 401, 409, 417

Letcher, John, 418

Lincoln, Abraham, 7, 100–4, 117, 123, 128–30, 132, 168, 193, 234, 238, 239, 256–67, 299, 371, 373, 395, 404; and Anderson's request for reinforcements, 319–20, 327; in Army, 106; arrival in Washington of, 271, 274–80, 284; birth of, 249; blockade of southern ports by, 429; cabinet appointed by, 102–3, 184–9, 224, 256, 258, 267, 278, 310, 318–19; cabinet meetings of, 325–6, 329; calls for troops, 427; and compromise attempts, 136–7, 159, 160, 256, 258–9, 287, 306; and constitutional convention proposal, 173–4, 177; Corwin's correspondence with, 127; Crittenden and, 307; and Davis plan, 161; death of, 430; and defense of Fort Pickens, 358–61, 377–80, 387–92; Douglas's debates with, 62; election of, 11, 19–30, 73, 85, 91, 98, 112, 125, 220, 253; emissary sent to Charleston by, 396–7, 399, 400; and evacuation of Sumter, 331–4, 344–6, 353–8, 369; and expedition to relieve Sumter, 358, 370, 381, 383–4, 388–92; foreign policy of, 362–3, 375–7; Hurlbut sent to Charleston by, 341; in Illinois senate race of 1858, 55–7; inauguration of, 10, 169, 273, 279–80, 292, 311–18, 321, 336, 338; and office seekers, 100 183–4, 256–8, 327–8, 340, 350, 362, 375, 389–90; and peace conference, 276, 279, 285, 292; personal characteristics, 309–10; plots against, 167, 267–71, 273; and plot to seize Washington, 236, 393–4; ridiculed by southerners, 407, 408, 423; Russell and, 351–3; and *Star of the West* incident, 204; South Carolina commissioners' attitude toward, 386; train trip to Washington, 261–7; and Union party, 324, 325, 330; and Virginia Unionists, 382, 383, 393

Lincoln, Mary Todd, 20, 124, 183, 256, 259–61, 263, 273, 275–6, 315, 351, 358, 365–6

Lincoln, Robert, 261, 262

Lincoln, Sally, 256–7

Lincoln, Tad, 340

Lincoln, Willie, 340

Logan, James B., 239

London *Times*, 3–5, 12, 349, 351

Longfellow, Henry Wadsworth, 21

Longstreet, A. B., 194

Louisiana: secession of, 166, 221, 235; seizure of federal property in, 236

Louisiana Purchase, 40, 46

Louis Philippe, King of France, 112

Louisville *Journal*, 102

Lovejoy, Owen, 129

Lowell, James Russell, 168, 217

Lyell, Charles, 87

Lyons, Lord, 315, 345, 366, 407, 427

Magrath, A. G., 25, 91, 92, 144, 201–2, 289, 371, 397, 419

Magruder, Allan B., 381–2

Maine, 62; admission to Union of, 38; peace conference delegates from, 239

Mallory, Stephen, 170, 209, 228, 293, 294, 321

Manifest Destiny, 31

Manigault, Gabriel, 144

Manning, John L., 25, 73, 81, 144, 294, 346, 347, 395, 396, 398, 410, 416, 418, 419, 423, 424, 427, 429

Marion, Francis, 242

Marshall, Charles H., 363

Marshall, John, 52

Maryland, 61, 192, 193, 271–3; and cabinet appointments, 184, 186, 187; elections in, 34; peace conference delegates from, 239; and secession, 229–30, 277, 393, 408; *see also* border states

Mason, Fort, 233

Mason, James M., 49, 326

Mason, John, 220, 229, 277, 306

Massachusetts, 237, 238, 429; peace conference delegates from, 239, 284

Maynard, Horace, 138, 190

McClernand, John A., 130, 167

McClure, Alexander, 188

McCready, Capt. Edward, 296

McGowan, Capt. John, 195

McLean, John, 51, 148, 174, 390

McRee, Fort, 205, 377, 378

Meade, Lt. Dick, 155, 156, 164, 197, 199, 299, 413

Means, Governor, 398, 402

Medill, Joseph, 103, 136

Meigs, Capt. Montgomery C., 114, 358–9, 361, 362, 378–80, 387–9, 406

Memminger, Christopher, 60, 144, 243, 293

Mercer, Capt. Samuel, 378, 383–4, 388–9, 414

Merrimack (ship), 421

Mexico, 327, 343, 376; war with, 7, 40–2, 106, 117, 168, 196, 250, 335, 413

Michigan, 48

Miles, William Porcher, 54, 113, 132, 133, 144, 210, 291, 348, 374, 396, 417, 419, 423, 424, 429

Militia Act (1795), 287

Minnesota, 29

Mississippi: confederacy convention delegates from, 243; secession of, 166, 203

Missouri, 274, 427; admitted to Union, 38, 39, 41; *see also* border states

Missouri Compromise (1820), 40, 41, 44, 46–7, 51, 52, 129, 158, 160, 220, 285

Mitchell, Julian, 7

Mohawk (ship), 333, 360

Monroe, Fort, 191, 393, 421

Montgomery: Confederate government in, 240–4, 249, 253–5, 282, 283, 286, 291, 293–4, 322, 329, 369; social life in, 292

Montgomery, Ben, 254

Moore, A. B., 145

Moore, Andrew, 294

Morehead, Charles S., 279

Morgan, E. D., 266

Morrill, Justin S., 130

Morris, Isaac N., 129, 160

Morris, Mowbray, 12

Morton, Jeremiah, 292

Morton, Oliver P., 238, 262, 263

Moultrie, Fort, 136, 148, 200, 245, 296, 336, 342, 348, 425, 426; Anderson assigned to, 105–8; in battle for Sumter, 410–12, 415, 417; during nullification crisis, 135; practice firing of guns at, 299, 338, 339; secession convention visits, 364; seizure of, 164–5, 168, 171, 172, 174, 176; and *Star of the West* incident, 195, 210; transfer of forces to Sumter from, 133, 140–1, 144, 149, 152–7, 163, 170

Napoleon, Emperor, 117, 294
Nashville Convention (1850), 69, 70, 82
National Intelligencer, 283
National Rifles, 193
Navy, U.S., 105, 365, 383
Navy Department, U.S., 186, 188, 318, 378–80, 388, 391
Nelson, Samuel, 333, 344
Nelson, Thomas A. R., 160–2, 190
Nesmith, James W., 328
Newhall, Fales H., 59
New Jersey, 29, 184
New Mexico, 221, 222, 259, 306
New York, 9–14; and cabinet appointments, 102, 184, 188, 189; elections in, 20, 22, 26; immigrants in, 8, 11, 34; Lincoln in, 266–7; peace conference delegates from, 239; support for South in, 167
New York *Evening Post*, 22, 215, 216
New York *Herald*, 14, 20, 101, 149, 166, 175, 204, 213–15, 274, 329
New York *Times*, 14, 50, 101, 102, 213–14, 273, 325, 340, 362, 410
New York *Tribune*, 13, 14, 22, 50, 128, 145, 162, 167, 193, 201, 202, 213–16, 239, 265, 271–3, 284, 285, 289–91, 316, 317, 327, 329, 336, 337, 341, 353, 375, 381, 392, 403, 411, 424
New York *World*, 405, 411
Nicolay, John G., 100, 256, 262, 310, 379
North Carolina, 427; peace conference delegates from, 239; seizure of federal forts in, 423, 428; *see also* border states
Northwest Ordinance (1787), 38
nullification crisis, 24, 42, 60, 91, 117, 257, 343

O'Conor, Charles, 167
Ohio: and cabinet appointments, 102, 184; elections in, 21–2, 29, 381; peace conference delegates from, 238, 239
Olmsted, Frederick Law, 14, 66–7, 87
O'Neall, John Belton, 89
O'Neill, Tip, 33
Oregon, 29
Orr, James L., 143, 144, 147
Osbon, B. S., 405, 411
Ould, Robert, 319
Ownes, Rev., 203

Palmetto Guard, 409, 416, 420
Pawnee (ship), 336, 358, 365, 378, 383, 404, 405, 413–14
Pearce, James, 313
Peck, Ebenezer, 262, 263
Pennington, William, 59, 160, 287–8
Pennsylvania, 87, 264; and cabinet appointments, 102, 184, 186–8, 258; elections in, 20, 28–9
Pensacola Navy Yard, 205–6, 208
Perry, Benjamin F., 89, 143, 334–5
Perry, Marshall S., 210
Petigru, James L., 67, 92–3, 125, 145–6, 201, 289, 317, 419–20, 428, 429
Pettigrew, Col. Johnston, 163–5
Peyton, Balie, 187
Philadelphia, Wilmington & Baltimore Railroad, 268
Philadelphia *Inquirer*, 214
Phillips, Wendell, 59
Piatt, Donn, 101, 103
Pickens, Fort, 10, 13, 114, 205–8, 210–11, 229, 320, 333, 340, 344, 363, 391–2; Confederate government and, 243, 244, 295, 322, 369–72; evacuation of, proposed, 354, 357; reinforcement of, 353, 357–61, 364, 377–80, 386, 388–90, 394, 396, 406
Pickens, Francis W., 44, 142–3, 198, 283, 297, 316, 373, 394; and Anderson's move to Sumter, 163–4; becomes governor of South Carolina, 135, 142–4; Buchanan and, 113, 143, 147–8; Charleston social life of, 289, 335, 374, 375; Confederate government and, 290–1, 295, 298, 342, 399; Davis and, 204–5; and emissaries from Washington, 341, 343–4, 354, 370, 390–2, 396, 399; forts seized by, 164–5, 168, 171, 172, 174, 176; Russell and, 423, 428, 429; and secession, 146–7, 162–3; and *Star of the West* incident, 195–7, 199; Sumter's mail seized by, 397; supplies sent to Sumter by, 247; and surrender of Sumter, 418–20; during truce, 200–2, 208–10, 230, 290
Pickens, Lucy Petaway Holcombe, 143, 341, 374, 375, 419, 429
Pickett, John T., 392
Pierce, Franklin, 26, 46, 48, 50, 61, 109, 138, 251
Pierce, Mrs. Franklin, 95
Pike, James S., 162, 193, 216, 235, 238–9, 327, 392

Pinckney, Castle, 107, 108, 153, 156, 164, 171, 201, 245, 297

Pinkerton, Allan, 267–71, 274

Pitt, William, 359

Pocahontas (ship), 358, 378, 383, 404, 413–14

Polk, James K., 41, 95, 97, 110, 250

Pope, Capt. John, 262, 270

popular sovereignty, 41, 47, 52–5, 62, 136

Porter, Lt. David D., 378–80, 383, 387–9, 392

Porter, Maj. Fitz-John, 98, 99, 107

Porter, William D., 92, 343

Potomac Light Infantry, 192

Potter, David, 52

Powell, Lazarus W., 127, 277, 288, 345

Powhatan (ship), 378–80, 383–4, 387–91, 405, 406, 413–14, 418

Prentice, George, 102

Preston, John S., 80, 81, 291

Preston, William C., 89

Protestantism, evangelical, 31, 32, 34, 38, 40

Providence *Journal*, 215

Pryor, Roger, 63, 112, 398, 402, 409, 417, 419, 427

Pryor, Sarah, 139

Puerto Rico, 26–7, 376

Pugh, George, 306–8

Pulaski, Fort, 191

Quitman, John A., 65

Randall, Alexander, 204

Ravenel, Henry William, 296, 403, 410, 419

Ravenel, Mrs. St. Julien, 66

Raymond, Henry J., 14, 102, 103, 214, 362

Reagan, John H., 293

Recollections of a Housekeeper (Gilman), 140

Reeder, Andrew, 187

Republicans, 13, 36, 50, 102, 103, 123, 127–30, 134, 137, 138, 283, 314, 330, 331, 369, 371; abolitionists in, 44; Buchanan and, 130–2, 136, 168, 192; cabinet appointments, 184, 185, 187–9, 258, 278; and compromise attempts, 158–62, 167, 219–21, 223, 225–9, 274, 286–8, 308; election victory of, 19–21, 25, 26, 63, 85, 95, 125, 132, 184, 253; evacuation of Sumter opposed by, 327, 333, 342, 344–6, 355; Floyd denounced as traitor by, 169; and Harpers Ferry raid, 59–61; in Illinois Senate race of 1858, 55–7; during Lincoln's journey to Washington, 262, 266, 269; Lincoln welcomed to Washington by, 277, 279; in local elections, 381; National Committee, 136; newspapers and, 214; office seekers, 100, 184; at peace conference, 238, 242; popular sovereignty and, 52–3; Scott and, 193; sectionalist origins of, 28–9, 47; South Carolina commissioners and, 171; state legislatures controlled by, 204; and Union party, 324, 325

Revolution, 32, 67, 87, 91, 105–6, 112

Rhett, Robert Barnwell, 25, 70, 78, 82, 86, 114, 142, 144, 163, 201, 214–16, 240, 243–4, 253, 254, 292–3, 428

Rhett, Robert Barnwell, Jr., 163

Rhode Island, elections in, 184, 370, 381

Rice, Henry M., 124, 159

Richmond *Dispatch*, 216

Richmond *Whig*, 325

Ripley, R. S., 336

Rives, William C., 239, 276, 278, 279, 291

Roe, Lt. F. A., 389

Roman, A. B., 294, 345, 369

Roman Catholic Church, 34, 47, 118

Roosevelt, Franklin D., 29, 30

Rothschild, Baron, 166

Rowan, Comm. S. C., 405, 413–14

Ruffin, Edmund, 23, 59, 78, 145, 203, 239, 292, 321, 375, 397, 398, 408, 409, 420, 427

Ruffin, Thomas, 239

Russell, William Howard, 3–14, 349–53, 365–6, 385–7, 394–5, 406–8, 416, 421–30

Russia, 340, 376; British war with, 4–5; Pickens in, 113, 143

Rust, Albert, 160–1, 190

Rutledge, Robert, 347

Rutledge, Susan, 347

Sabine (ship), 377, 406

Salter, George, 410

Sanderson, John P., 189

Sanford, Henry S., 340, 349–51

Santo Domingo, 26–7, 362, 369, 371, 376, 377

Sargent, Joseph, 168

Saunders, John S., 315

Schleiden, Rudolf, 362

Schurz, Carl, 21, 167, 169, 218, 259, 381

Scots immigrants, 87
Scott, Dred, 51-4
Scott, Maria Mayo, 117, 118
Scott, Virginia, 118
Scott, Walter, 64-5
Scott, Gen. Winfield, 73, 116-19, 135, 137, 172, 193, 210, 211, 218, 220, 239, 262, 273, 282, 284, 359, 377; and Anderson's request for reinforcements, 319, 320, 326; Anderson visits, 105-6, 116; assassination plot discovered by, 269; Buchanan and, 114, 118-19, 136, 174, 176, 230, 234; Davis and, 248, 251; and defense of Fort Pickens, 333, 360, 361, 378, 391; evacuation of Sumter urged by, 329, 330, 340, 341, 354, 357; and expedition to relieve Sumter, 283, 332, 383, 404; Hammond denounced by, 248; Henry Adams on, 228; and inauguration, 284, 311, 312, 314, 315; and Lincoln's arrival in Washington, 274, 275, 278, 279; on right of secession, 98; Russell and, 386, 387, 406-7; and secessionist plot to seize Washington, 393-4; and *Star of the West*, 191-2; at state dinner, 351, 352
secession, 12, 26, 60-1, 63, 96, 129, 130, 136, 143, 168, 193, 208, 240, 275, 284, 286, 305, 425-6, 430; Beauregard and, 335; border states and, 192; Buchanan and, 98, 99, 125, 135, 150; Congress and, 217-23, 226-7; economy and, 102, 166; Hammond's views on, 85; Lincoln on, 137; origins in nullification crisis of, 24, 60; peace plan and, 229; *see also* secession *under specific states*
Seddon, James, 276, 284, 292
Selden, John, 366
Senate, U.S., 44, 58, 127, 142, 185-7, 278, 330, 339, 345, 355, 375; attack on Sumner in, 49-50; balance of free and slave states in, 38, 41; Buchanan and, 54, 229, 306-9; and cabinet appointments, 258, 318, 329; Chesnut in, 72, 73, 92, 113; compromise attempts in, 158-62, 194, 223-4, 279, 288; Davis in, 170, 250, 252; Foreign Relations Committee, 366; Hammond in, 73, 80-2, 84, 92, 143; Lincoln welcomed to Washington by, 277; Naval Affairs Committee, 293; secession denounced in, 137; Southerners resign from, 92, 113, 228, 235, 241

Seward, Anna, 324, 395
Seward, Frances, 227, 269, 275, 318, 323-5
Seward, Frederick, 324, 327, 350-1, 362, 377, 387, 392, 395
Seward, William H., 7, 13, 54, 57, 173, 193, 268, 285, 292, 323-31, 355, 389, 407, 414; and Anderson's request for reinforcements, 319-20; appointed Secretary of State, 185-6, 188, 189, 224, 258, 310; Davis and, 252; and defense of Fort Pickens, 358-62, 378, 379; and evacuation of Sumter, 333-4, 344-5, 350, 357, 358, 392; foreign policy of, 362-3, 375-7; higher-law doctrine invoked by, 53; and impending attack on Sumter, 404; and inauguration, 312, 314, 316, 318; and Lincoln's arrival in Washington, 274-9; marriage of, 323-4; New York Republican party dominated by, 184, 266; and office seekers, 340; and plot to assassinate Lincoln, 269; Russell and, 350-1, 386, 387, 395, 423; in Senate, 60, 84, 123, 125, 159, 161, 224-9, 237, 238, 308; South Carolina commissioners and, 370, 371, 392-3; and Virginia Unionists, 381-2, 393; and Weed's compromise proposal, 128-9; Welles and, 387-8, 390
Seymour, Horatio, 12
Seymour, Capt. Truman, 208, 156, 196, 297, 299, 413
Sherman, John, 24, 59, 167, 276-7
Sherman, William Tecumseh, 24
Sickles, Dan, 225, 228, 284, 287
Simmons, James F., 218
Simms, William E., 287
Simms, William Gilmore, 25, 77-8, 88-90, 92, 219, 317, 341, 418
Simons, Gen. James, 200, 416
Simonton, Charles H., 144
Sinclair, Dan, 196
Skillen, Kate, 165
Skillen, Sgt., 164
slavery, 8, 38-43, 45-8, 62-4, 90, 110, 137-8, 162, 168, 217, 218, 220, 226-7, 286-7, 305, 387, 428, 430; Anderson and, 106; in border states, 22, 279; British opposition to, 352; Buchanan on, 125; Confederate government and, 295; Constitution and, 32, 36, 39, 158, 159, 161, 213, 221, 322; *Dred Scott* case, 51-5; economics of, 57-8; Hammond and, 75-7, 82, 83; John Brown and, 58-60; Lincoln on,

slavery (*continued*)
136, 258–9; and Lincoln's election, 25, 132;
Mary Chesnut on, 70–1, 321–2; northern
support for, 167; Pickens and, 142; racism
and, 55–7; in Washington, 26
Slemmer, Lt. Adam J., 205–7, 230
Slidell, John, 27, 48, 134, 148, 170, 209, 211,
223, 234, 235, 323
Smith, Caleb B., 184, 186, 189, 257, 262, 279,
318, 332, 357, 386
Smith, Edmund Kirby, 61
Smith, Truman, 102, 340, 350
Smithsonian Institution, 93, 224, 288, 395
Snyder, Lt. George, 155, 199, 299, 342, 373,
413, 416, 418
South Carolina, 7, 32, 74, 137, 148, 209, 246,
286, 290, 354; arms purchases by, 113;
blockade of, 429; commissioners sent to
Washington by, 150–1, 154, 162, 169–70,
172, 329; and Confederate government, 242,
243, 291, 293; ethnic diversity in, 87; and
Lincoln's election, 23–6, 91; military forces
of, 200–1, 210, 298; Pickens becomes
governor of, 135, 142–4; secession of, 10,
90–2, 106, 112–16, 130, 133–4, 138, 139, 141,
144–7, 151, 153, 160, 166, 203, 219, 253, 311,
389; seizure of federal property by, 165, 168,
170–3, 175–8, 235; and surrender of Sumter,
420
South Carolina Program, 240
Spain, 26–7, 362, 369, 376, 377
Spaulding, E. G., 279
Springfield, Ill., 99–100
Stanton, Benjamin, 220–1, 287, 306
Stanton, Edwin M., 135, 169, 171, 172, 174–6,
191, 211, 225, 226, 237, 319, 329, 404
Star of the West (ship), 191, 192, 195–7, 199,
201–4, 207, 208, 210, 215–16, 220, 245, 307
State Department, U.S., 93, 135, 185–6, 188,
310, 318, 326, 328, 350, 393, 404
states rights, 7
Stephens, Alexander H., 109, 240–1, 243–4,
254, 294, 317, 322
Stevens, Maj. P. F., 402
Stevens, Thaddeus, 226
Stoeckl, Baron Edouard de, 112, 227, 344–5
Stokes, William B., 285–6
Stone, Col. Charles P., 192–3, 311, 393
Stowe, Harriet Beecher, 45–6
Stringham, Capt. Silas, 326, 332, 378, 379,
388

Strong, George Templeton, 22, 31, 44, 167,
207, 211, 224, 316, 339–40
Stuart, John, 390
Sullivan, John L., 31
Summers, George W., 279, 291, 381–2
Sumner, Charles, 49–50, 62, 136, 168, 211, 222,
223, 227, 237–9, 277, 278, 285, 306, 316,
328, 366, 426–7
Sumner, Col. E. V., 262, 270, 311
Sumter, Fort, 10, 13, 136, 165, 200, 253, 295–9,
318, 335, 343, 348, 369–75, 425; aid from
Moultrie to, 133, 140–1, 149; Anderson
assigned to Moultrie and, 105–8; Anderson
moves from Moultrie to, 152–7, 163, 170,
176, 208, 225, 240; bombardment of,
408–17, 423; Buchanan's policies and, 172,
174, 176, 191, 208–10, 230, 236; Confederate
government and, 243, 244, 295, 322, 325,
326, 328; demand for placement of state
troops in, 144, 148; evacuation of, proposed
323, 327, 329–34, 340–2, 344–6, 350, 353–8,
364, 382, 393; expedition to relieve, 358,
366, 378, 380–1, 383–4, 386, 388, 390–2,
404–5; gun emplacements aimed at, 336,
338–9; impending attack on, 400–2, 404;
peace conference delegates position on, 279;
Pickens's threats against, 289–91;
preparations for defense of, 364–5; relief of,
discussed, 359, 360, 363; rumors about,
193–4; Russell at, 426; Seward calls for
surrender of, 376, 377; and *Star of the West*
incident, 192, 195–7, 199, 204; surrender of,
416–21, 424; troops needed for
reinforcement of, 299, 312, 320; during
truce, 200–2, 244–7; Wigfall urges seizure
of, 398–400
Supply (ship), 206, 207
Supreme Court, U.S., 44, 51–2, 55, 93, 94, 110,
137, 169, 217, 278, 390
Swett, Leonard, 104, 187, 193
Swiss immigrants, 87

Talbot, Lt. Theodore, 108, 200, 208, 299, 373,
390–2, 394, 396–7
Talleyrand-Perigord, Charles Maurice de,
112
Tallmadge, James, 38
Taney, Roger B., 52, 313–15
Taylor, Bayard, 14
Taylor, Fort, 114, 359

Taylor, Miles, 162

Taylor, Zachary, 49, 102, 230, 249–51, 257, 326

Taylor, Mrs. Zachary, 95

Tennessee, 274, 427; *see also* border states

Texas, 42, 358, 359, 394; annexation of, 31, 40; blockade of, 429; forts in, 169; secession of, 166, 221, 233–5, 340

Thackeray, William Makepeace, 5

Thomas, Philip F., 135, 171, 174, 176, 191, 208

Thompson, Jacob, 25–26, 37, 96, 98–9, 112–14, 116, 130, 149, 169, 171–2, 174, 176, 191, 194, 208, 234, 250

Thompson, Kate, 97, 138, 211, 234, 282

Thompson, Waddy, 84

Throckmorton, James, 234

Tilden, Samuel, 12

Tocqueville, Alexis de, 56–7, 67

Toombs, Robert, 60, 159, 190, 207, 211, 241, 243, 244, 290–4, 322, 342, 370–1, 399

Totten, Gen. Joseph G., 244, 320, 326, 331, 332, 359, 364

Toucey, Isaac, 97–9, 114, 171, 174, 191, 230, 283, 360

Treasury Department, U.S., 188, 208, 226, 258, 278, 283, 310, 318, 363

Tredegar Iron Works, 366

Trenholm, William L., 105

Trent, William P., 88

Trescot, William Henry, 26, 98, 99, 112–16, 125, 133–4, 147–9, 151, 153, 169–70, 174, 176, 191, 212, 294, 343, 418, 428

Trumbull, Lyman, 19, 103, 104, 128, 136, 159, 169, 171, 177, 184, 187, 234, 258, 307–8, 345, 355

Tuck, Amos, 188

Twiggs, Gen. David, 234

Tyler, John, 36, 95, 220, 229, 236, 239–40, 276, 281, 283, 284, 290–2

Tyler, Julia, 239–40

Tyler, Lyon G., 36

Tyler, Lt. Robert O., 414

Uncle Tom's Cabin (Stowe), 45–6

Van Wyck, Charles H., 222

Villard, Henry, 20, 94, 101, 104, 189, 258, 259, 262, 263, 265

Virginia, 7, 64–5, 278, 340, 366, 403; and Lincoln's election, 23; peace effort of, 229, 237–9, 282, 291–2; and secession, 61, 192, 193, 277, 279, 287, 291, 292, 382–3, 393, 427, 428; slave trade in, 42; Unionists in, 325, 381, 382; *see also* border states

Vogdes, Capt. Israel, 360, 377, 391, 406

Wade, Ben, 137, 161–2, 184, 235, 274

Walker, Leroy P., 293, 336, 370, 399, 400, 402, 406

Walker, Robert J., 53, 54

Wallace, W. S., 262

Wallach, W. W., 403

Ward, Col. George T., 203

Ward, Comm. James H., 283, 320, 331

War Department, U.S., 113, 151, 170, 174, 176, 188, 191, 246, 251, 284, 297, 299, 310, 318, 319, 326, 342, 373, 386, 390

War of 1812, 117

Wardlaw, D. L., 142

Warne, Kate, 268, 271

Warren, Fitz-Henry, 29, 189

Washburne, Elihu, 104, 128, 136, 137, 193, 220, 223, 236, 264, 271

Washington, D.C., 93–5, 123–4; defense of, 192–3, 282, 386, 403–4, 429; Lincoln's arrival in, 274–9; and Lincoln's election, 25; during Lincoln's inauguration, 311–15; news correspondents in, 216; peace conference in, 239; plot to seize, 167–9, 268, 393–4; Russell in, 349–53, 365–6, 386–7; slavery in, 26, 39, 42, 259; social life in, 72–3, 94–5, 111–12, 138–9, 189–90, 324; weather in, 211–12, 403

Washington, Fort, 193, 386

Washington, George, 67, 106, 112, 117, 242, 297, 383

Washington, L. Q., 316

Washington *Constitution*, 135, 150

Washington Light Infantry, 140, 144, 348

Washington Navy Yard, 365

Washington *Star*, 403

Webb, James Watson, 204

Webster, Daniel, 34, 42, 62, 129, 227, 257, 294, 329, 430

Weed, Thurlow, 128, 136–7, 159, 168, 184, 185, 187, 204, 225, 227–8, 238, 266, 278, 310, 314, 324, 333, 362, 403

Welles, Gideon, 186, 187, 310, 318, 320, 326,

Welles, Gideon (*continued*)
  332, 357, 358, 378–81, 383–4, 387–8, 390–2,
  404
Whig party, 28, 35, 46, 47, 55, 63, 128, 185,
  240, 250, 271, 310, 324, 325
Whiting, Maj. W. H. C., 295, 421, 425–8
Whitman, Walt, 215
Whitney, Henry, 257
Whittier, John Greenleaf, 21
Wickliffe, Charles A., 239
Wide-Awakes, 28, 100, 267, 311
Wigfall, Charlotte, 72, 374, 395
Wigfall, Col. Louis T., 64, 72, 94, 158, 169,
  194, 210, 229, 235, 283, 307, 314, 316, 329,
  334, 340, 374, 398–400, 416–18,
  426–7
Wilmot, David, 187, 239
Wilmot Proviso (1846), 41, 52

Wilson, Henry, 54, 277, 288
Winthrop, Robert, 237
Wisconsin, 48
Wise, Henry A., 58
Withers, Thomas Jefferson, 74, 294, 347
Wolfe, Gen. James, 359
Wood, Fernando, 266
Wood, W. S., 259, 261, 273
Wool, Gen. John E., 239, 251, 314
Worden, Lt. John L., 392, 406
Wright, John C., 239, 274, 284
Wyandotte (ship), 206, 207, 406

Yancey, William, 240–4, 254–5
Yates, Richard, 189, 262
Young, Gourdin, 416
Yulee, David, 170, 228

PHOTOGRAPHIC SOURCES

Abbreviations used in insert captions

LC	Library of Congress, Washington, D.C.
MF	Mulberry Plantation, Camden, South Carolina
NA	National Archives, Washington, D.C.
SCHS	South Carolina Historical Society, Charleston
SCL	South Caroliniana Library, University of South Carolina, Columbia
USAMHI	U.S. Army Military History Institute, Carlisle Barracks, Pennsylvania
VM	Valentine Museum, Richmond, Virginia

*Title page photograph courtesy of the Medford Historical Society,
Medford, Massachusetts*